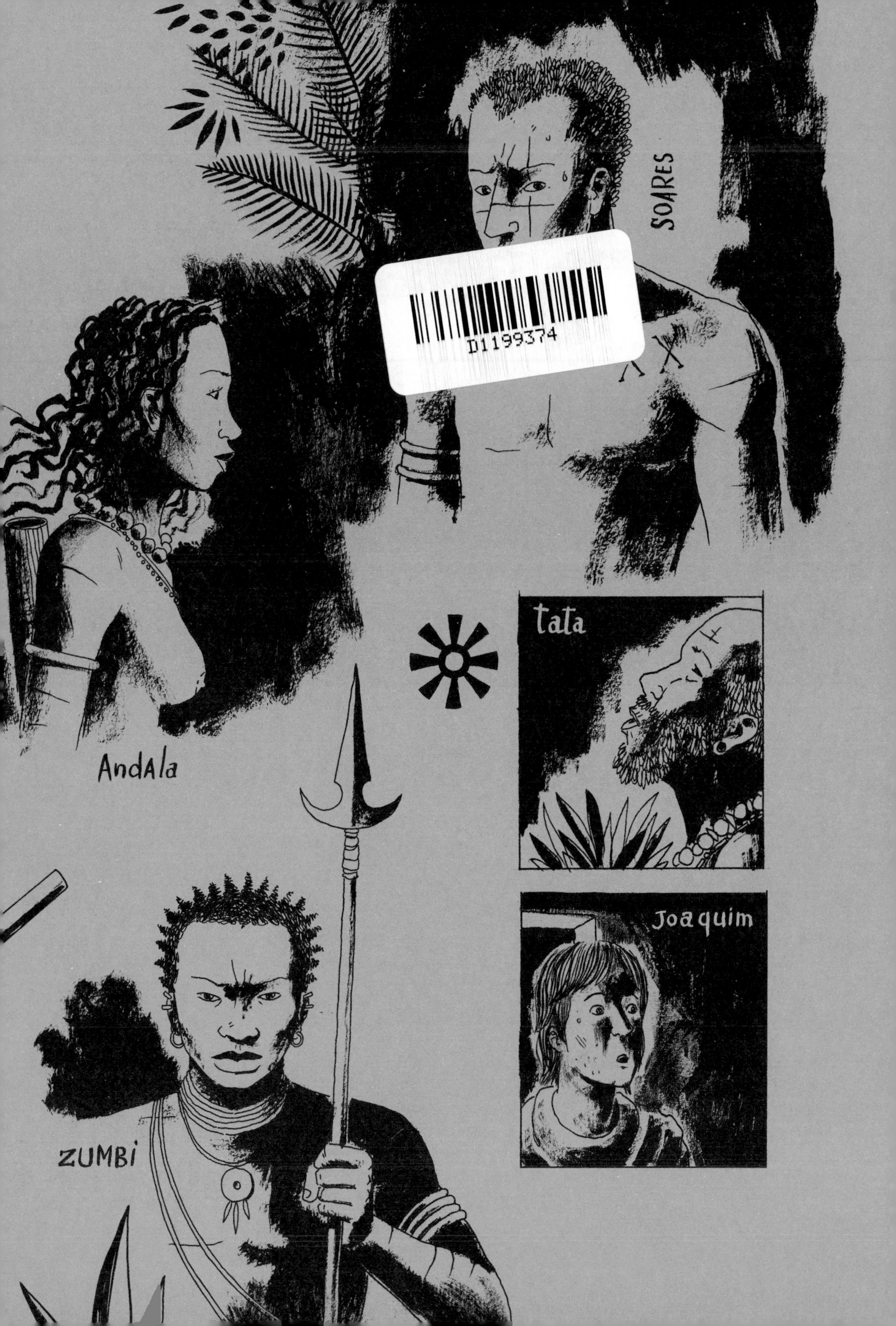
SOARES
Andala
tata
Joaquim
ZUMBi

ANGOLA JANGA

KINGDOM OF RUNAWAY SLAVES

MARCELO D'SALETE

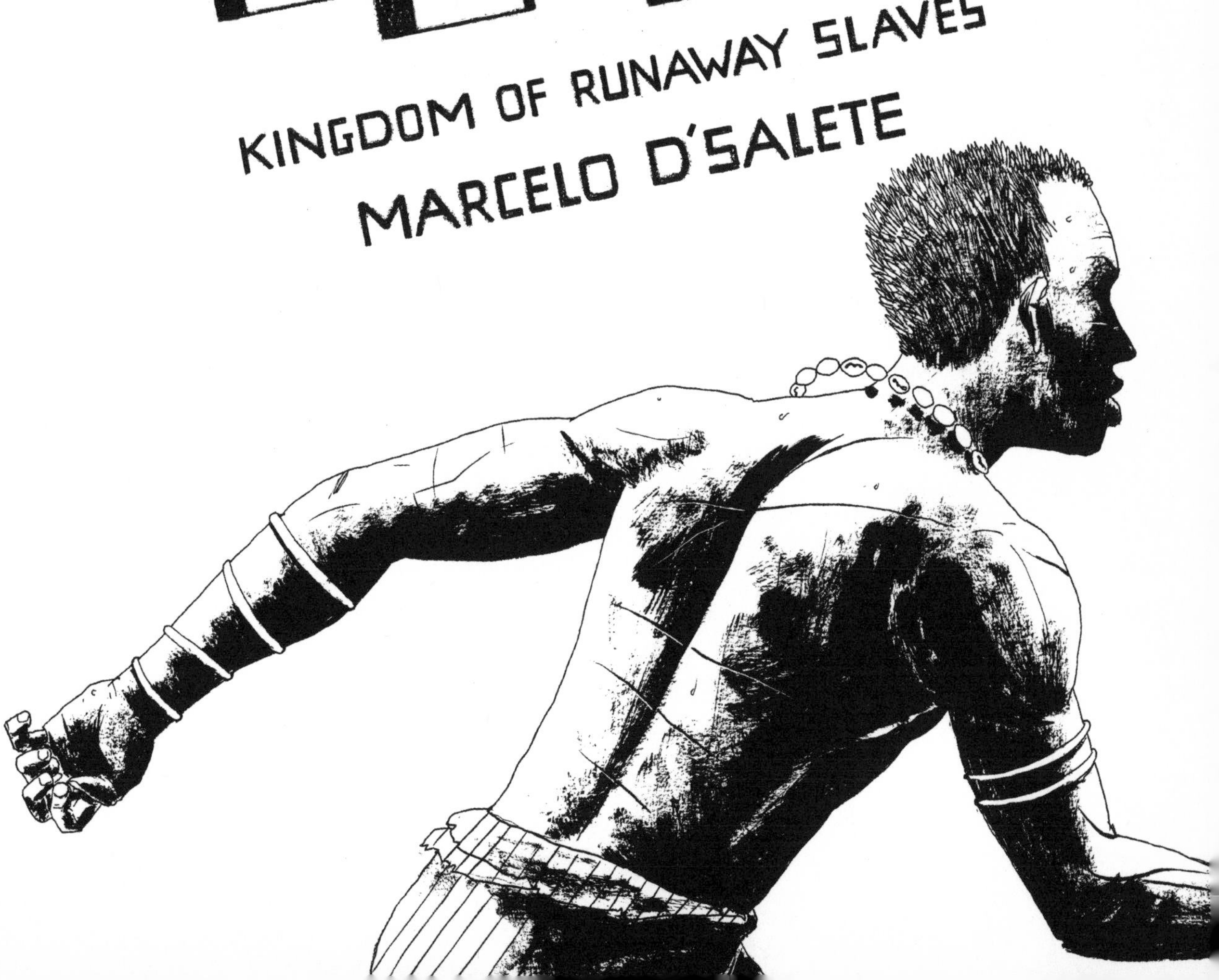

To Lúcia Amani

Translator: Andrea Rosenberg
Editor: Kristy Valenti
Designer: Keeli McCarthy
Supervising Editor: Gary Groth
Production: Paul Baresh
Editorial Assistants: Kassandra Davis, James Ganas, Conrad Groth, Christina Hwang, Emma Levy
Associate Publisher: Eric Reynolds
Publisher: Gary Groth
Publicity and Promotion: Jacq Cohen

 Fantagraphics Books, Inc. 7563 Lake City Way NE, Seattle, WA 98115 (800) 657-1100 www.fantagraphics.com. Follow us on Twitter @fantagraphics and on Facebook.com/Fantagraphics.

Acknowledgments
Lilian Aquino and Guilherme Mazzafera, editors. Brisa Batista, Alaide Souza, Pedro Ricardo, Sheila Souza, Marcos P. Souza, Petrônio Domingues, Allan da Rosa, Rogério de Campos, Mário Medeiros, André Toral, Marcello Quintanilha, Rafael Coutinho, Wagner Willian, Leticia de Castro, Solange Reis, João Pinheiro, Sirlene Barbosa, Serge Ewenczyk, Proac Culturas Negras 2016, and the Museu Afro Brasil.

ISBN: 978-1-68396-191-8
Library of Congress Control Number: 2018949550

First Printing: April 2019
Printed In China

Mocambos and Plantations

In the sixteenth century, the Portuguese occupiers of Brazil began to explore timbering and sugar production. Sugarcane plantations (which included both cultivation fields and mills for processing the cane into sugar) initially depended on the enslavement of indigenous populations and, in the following decades, the forced labor of millions of black men and women.

African slavery expanded at an astonishing pace during the sixteenth and seventeenth centuries. In the Captaincy [administrative region] of Pernambuco, there were twenty-three plantations in 1570. By 1582, the number had grown to sixty-six. Around four thousand Africans a year arrived in Pernambuco on slave ships during the first half of the seventeenth century. In the second half, that number swelled to eight thousand a year. Many captives, brought from the ancient kingdoms of what is now Angola, Congo, and neighboring areas, died during the barbaric, hellish voyage. These enslaved Africans were called *peças* (units), *peças-da-Guiné* (Guinea units), and other dehumanizing terms, and subjected to backbreaking work without rest some twelve to sixteen hours a day. Many died before the age of twenty.

In the late sixteenth century came the first word of runaway slaves who had taken refuge in the Serra da Barriga hills, in an area that today is part of the state of Alagoas but at the time belonged to the General Captaincy of Pernambuco. That was the beginning of Palmares, a fugitive community. The Dutch occupation of Pernambuco between 1630 and 1654 caused chaos on the sugarcane plantations and led to a power vacuum that allowed slaves to escape to Angola Janga (meaning "Little Angola" in Kimbundu, a Bantu language), as Palmares was known.

Angola Janga comprised numerous different *mocambos* (territories inhabited by black people who had escaped). The best known were Macaco, Subupira, Acotirene, Amaro, Tabocas, Dambraganga, Curiva, Andalaquituche, Osenga, and Zumbi. The capital, Macaco, had some six thousand inhabitants (the largest Portuguese town in the region, Recife, had around eight thousand in 1654). In total, there were more than twenty thousand people scattered through the hills. There, the Palmaristas (as the fugitive inhabitants of Palmares were called) grew corn, cassava, beans, sweet potato, and sugarcane, and raised fowl and pigs.

Time and time again, the colonial authorities deployed troops to attack the mocambos in the Serra da Barriga. The Terço dos Henriques, a troop of black soldiers, participated in the fighting against the Dutch and in the assaults on the Palmaristas. Later, the Paulistas joined in the conflict. In addition to direct attacks, there were also attempts to draw up a peace accord. One of these attempts was accepted by the leader Ganga Zumba, but rejected by the group led by Zumbi. These two men were the main leaders of Palmares in the late seventeenth century.

The following story traces some of the twists and turns of the final decades of the largest mocambo in Brazilian history. At the end of the book, appendices include a glossary, maps, and information about the time period.

THE WAY TO ANGOLA JANGA

As from the earliest days of Brazilian settlement a large number of blacks have been coming to and continue to come into the region. Many of them flee to the remote woodland of the *sertão*, where they live in large communities that swell with the addition of children and others who join them or whom they recruit from among our blacks, and then roam at will, doing us great harm ...

—*Governor of Pernambuco Francisco de Brito Freire, 1660s*

In fact, taking advantage of the so-called Batavian occupation (the Dutch occupation of Recife and Olinda between 1630 and 1654), the slaves of Pernambuco and other neighboring captaincies began to escape from captivity because of the "crimes and intractability of their masters," in small, scattered groups at first—almost forty Guinean blacks from the sugarcane estates of Vila do Porto Calvo, according to Rocha Pita—and later in larger groups and in a steady stream, fleeing into the wild lands of Palmares. Taking advantage of the region's impenetrable forests, fertile soils, and abundant timber, game, access to water, and means of defense, a substantial population of fugitives congregated, joining arms in battle and establishing there the largest attempt at black self-governance outside of the African continent.

—*Clóvis Moura*, Rebeliões da Senzala, 1981

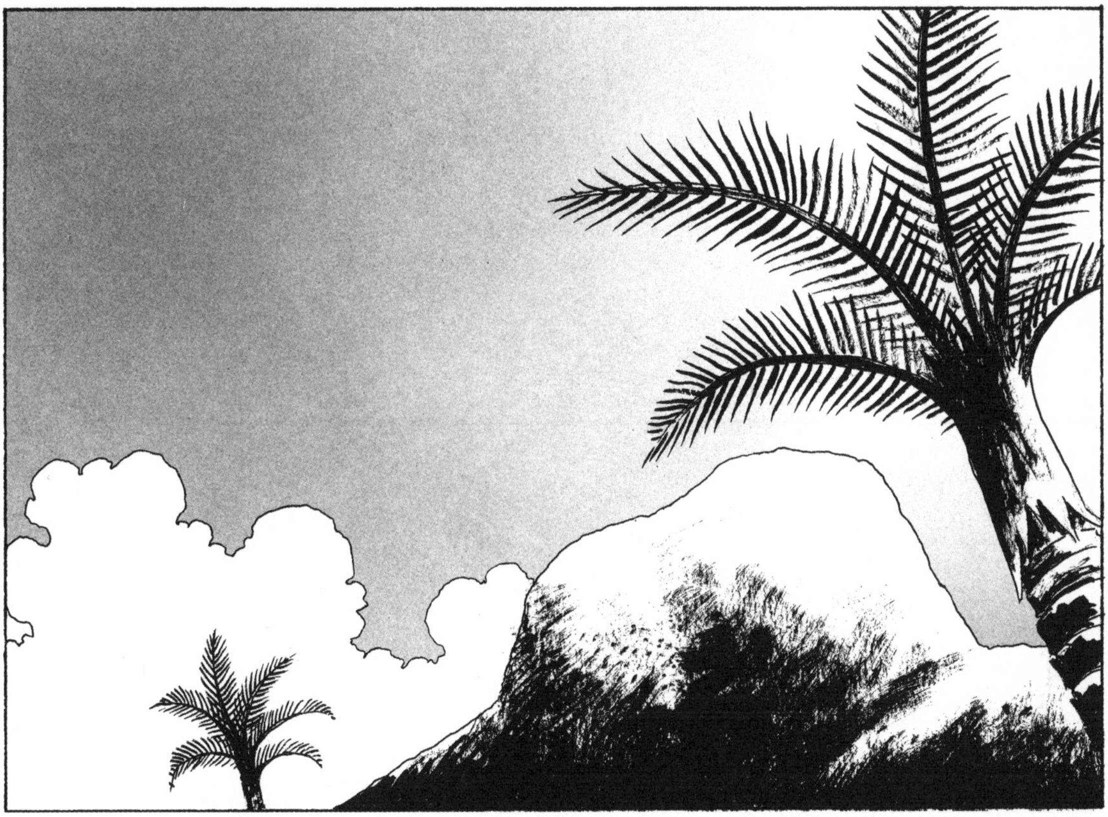

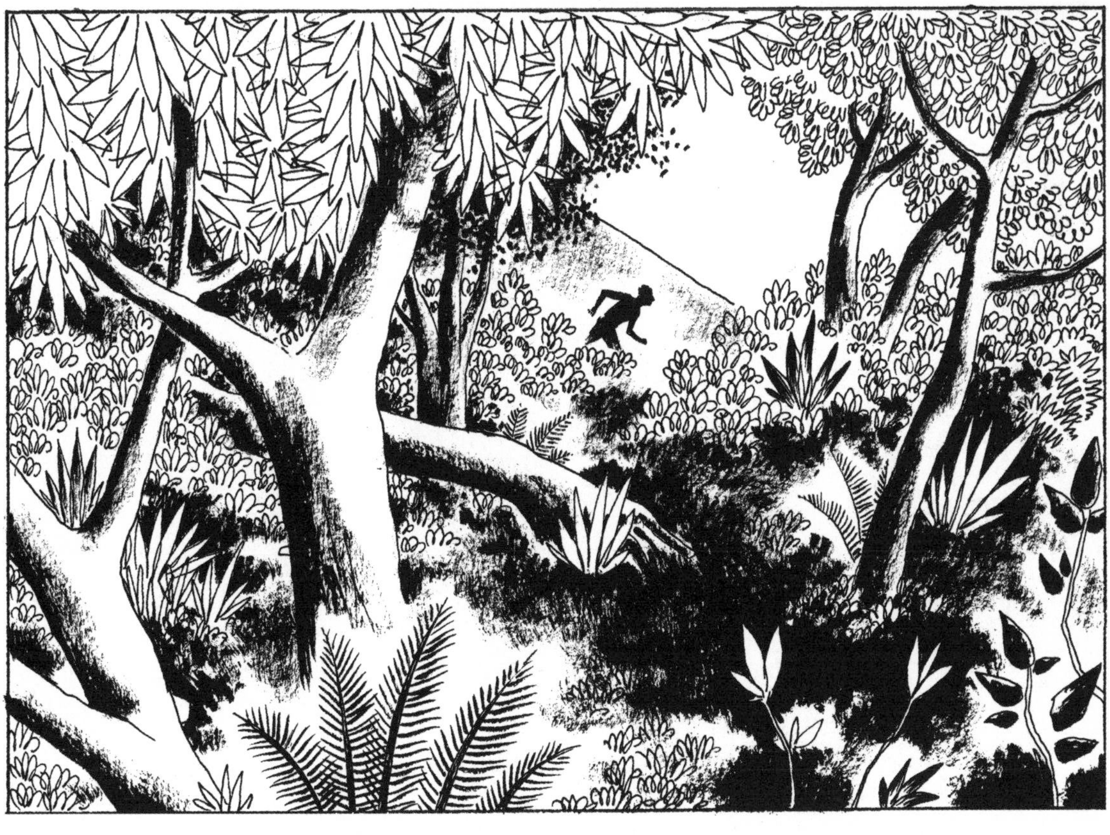

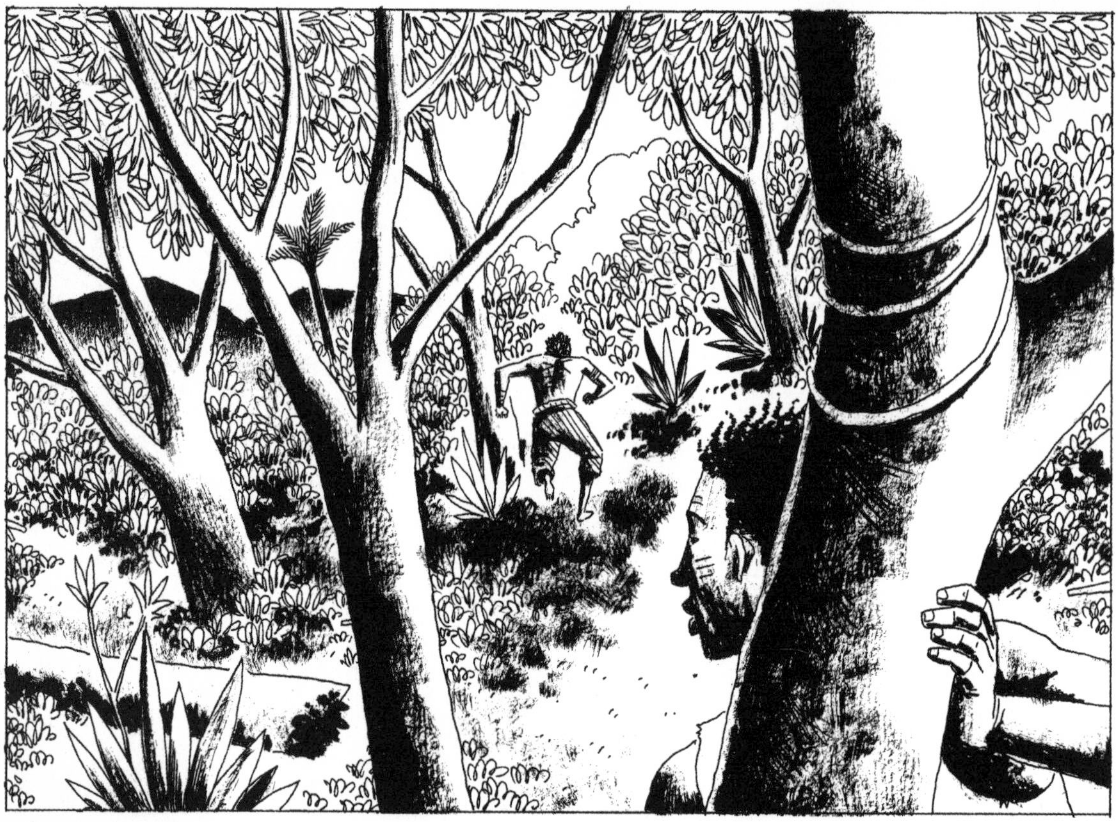

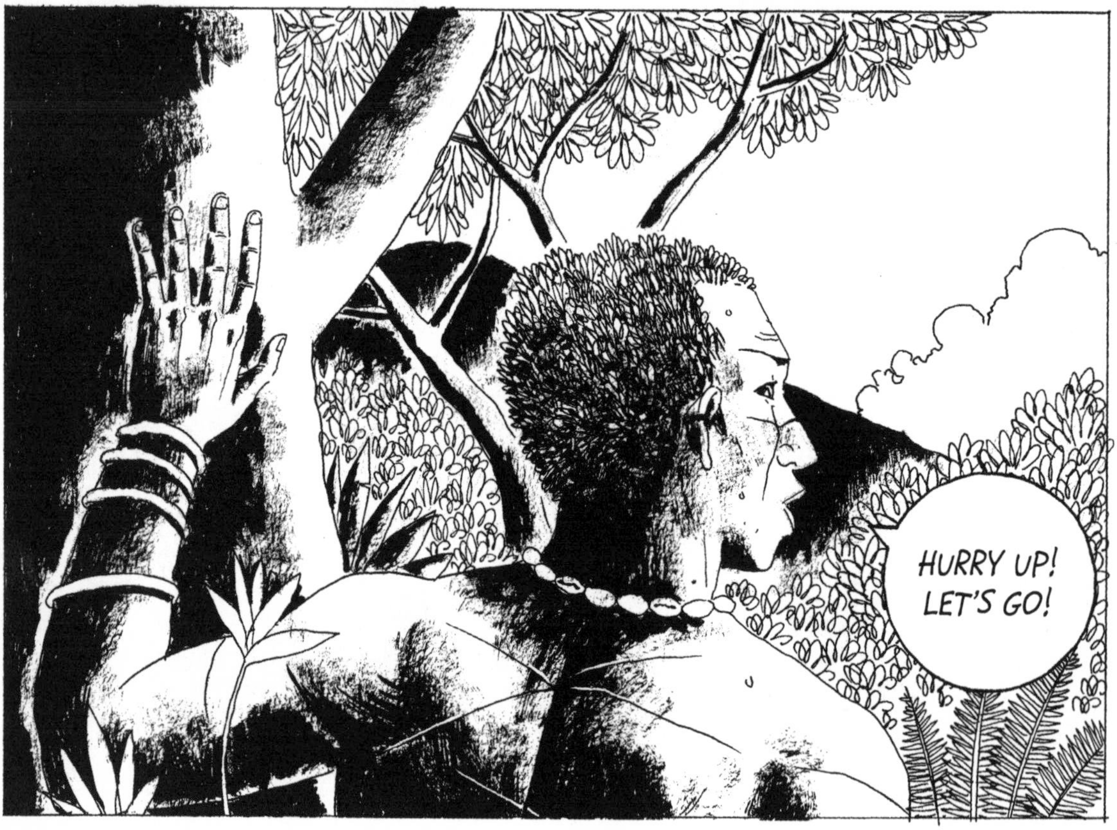
HURRY UP!
LET'S GO!

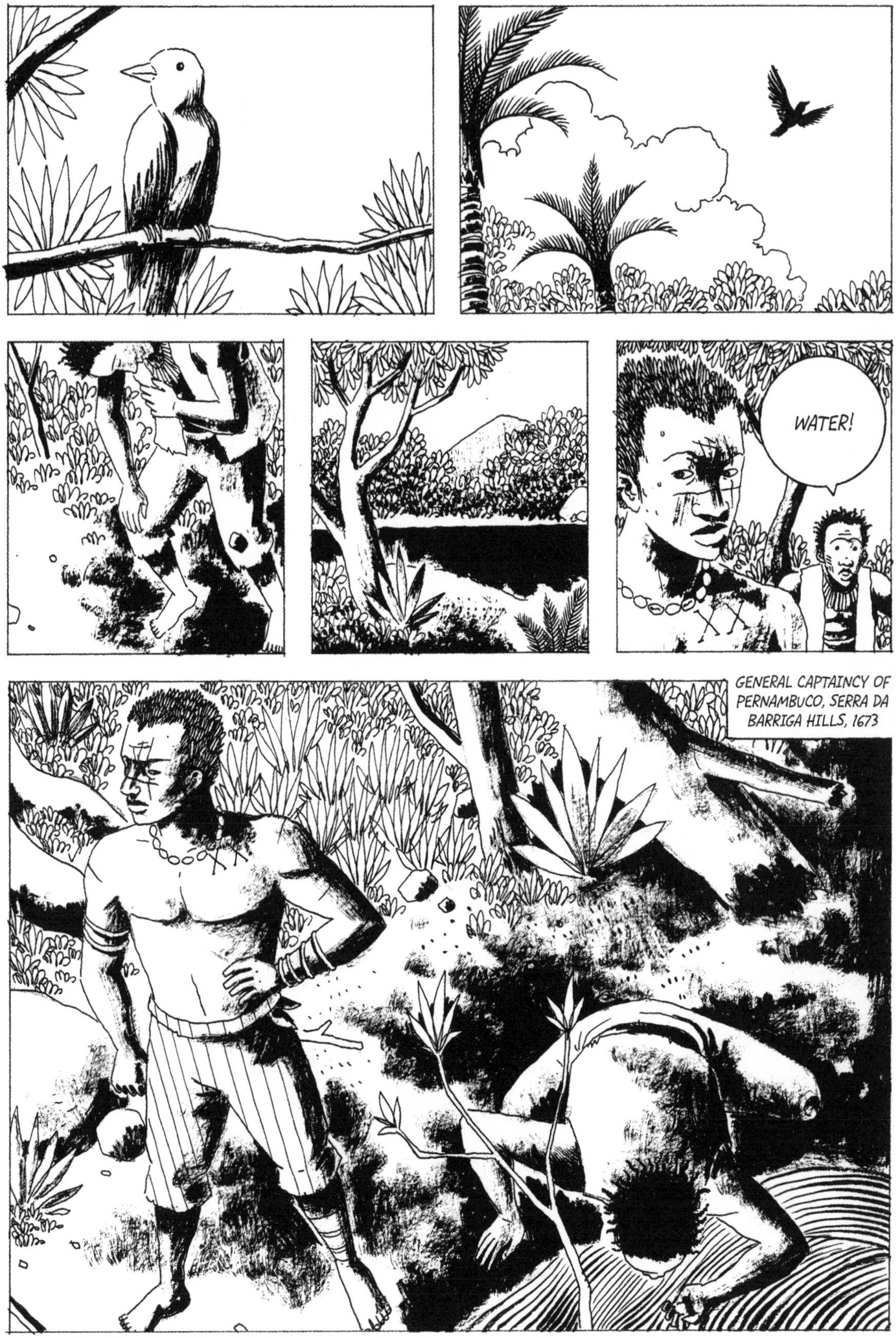
WATER!
GENERAL CAPTAINCY OF PERNAMBUCO, SERRA DA BARRIGA HILLS, 1673

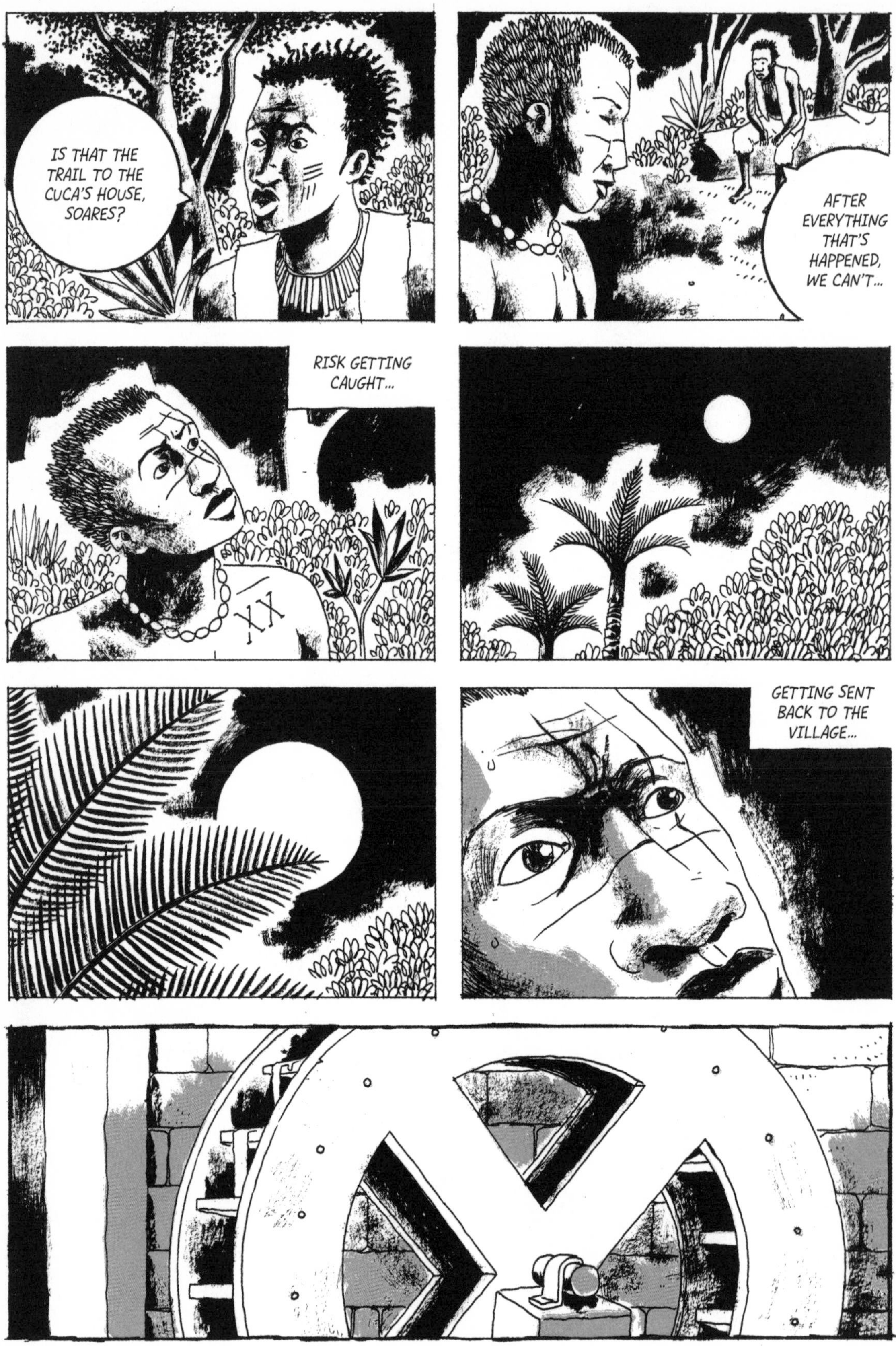
IS THAT THE TRAIL TO THE CUCA'S HOUSE, SOARES?
AFTER EVERYTHING THAT'S HAPPENED, WE CAN'T...
RISK GETTING CAUGHT...
GETTING SENT BACK TO THE VILLAGE...

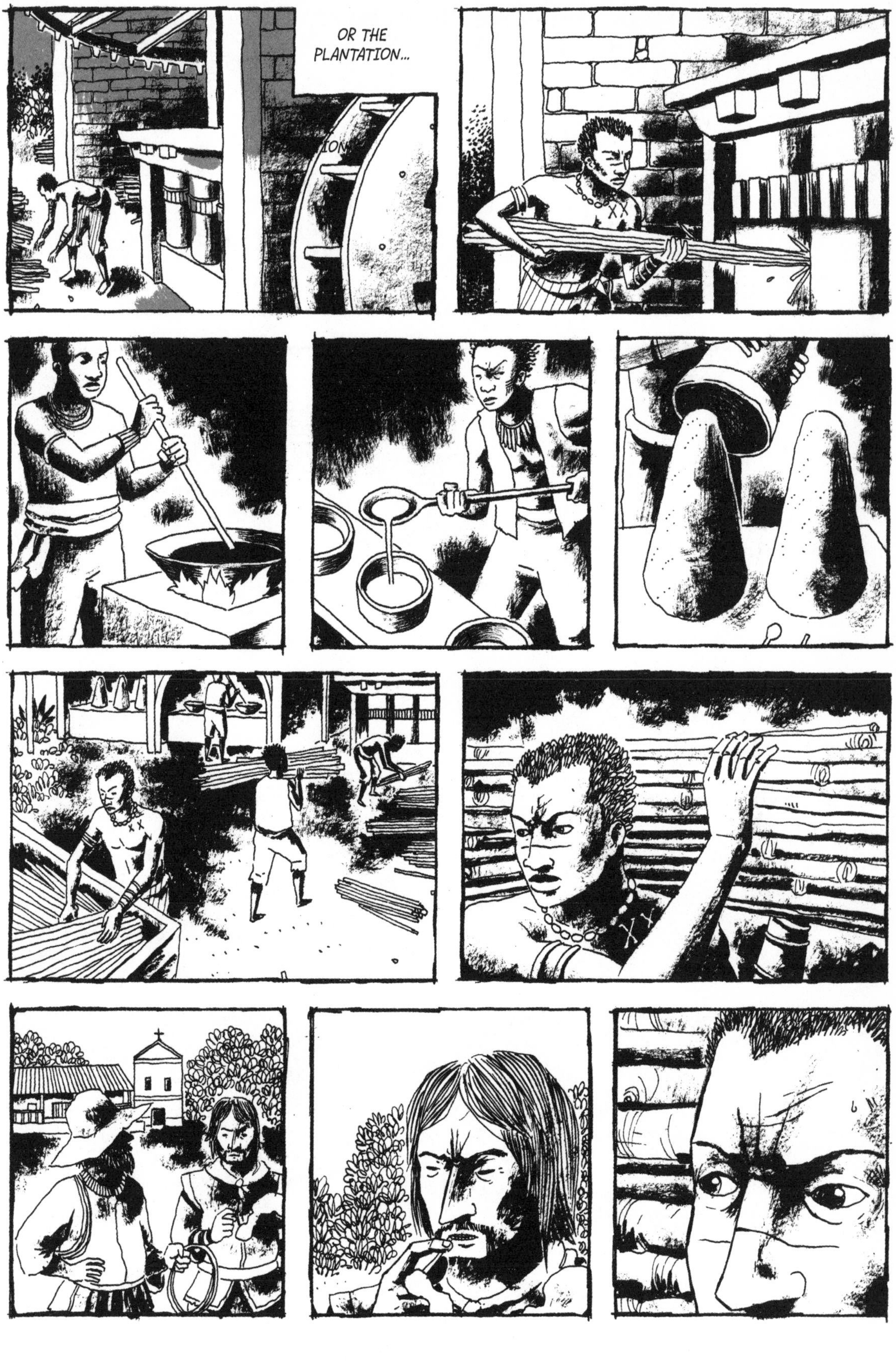
OR THE PLANTATION...

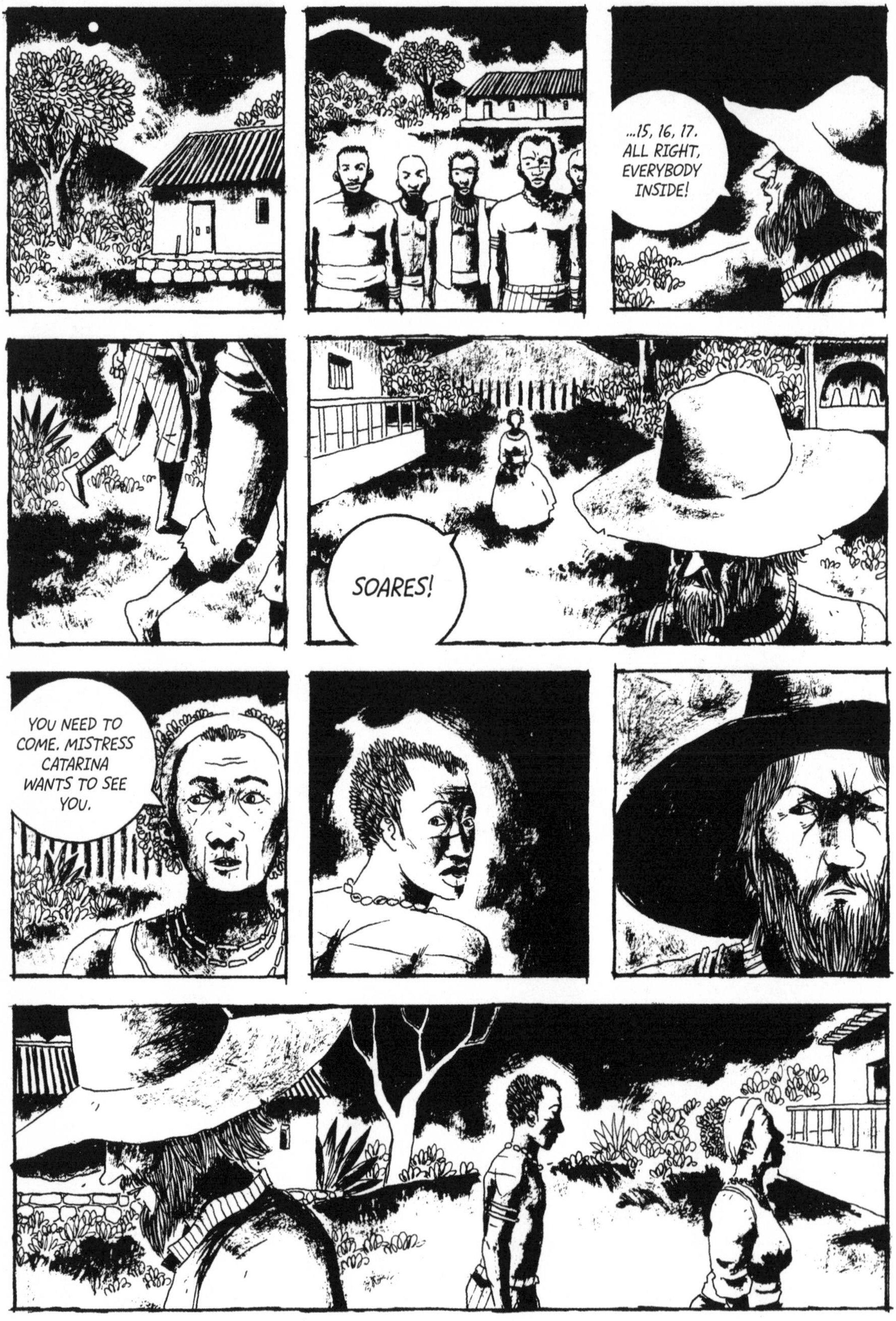
...15, 16, 17. ALL RIGHT, EVERYBODY INSIDE!
SOARES!
YOU NEED TO COME. MISTRESS CATARINA WANTS TO SEE YOU.

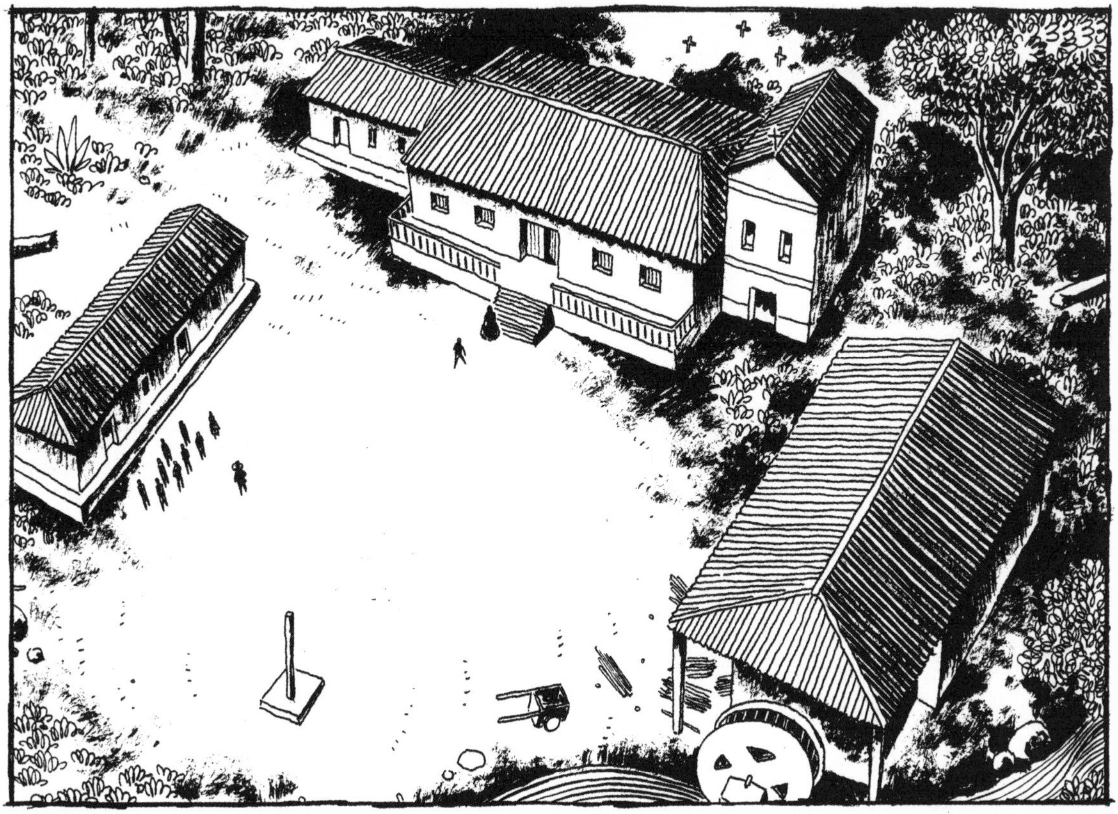

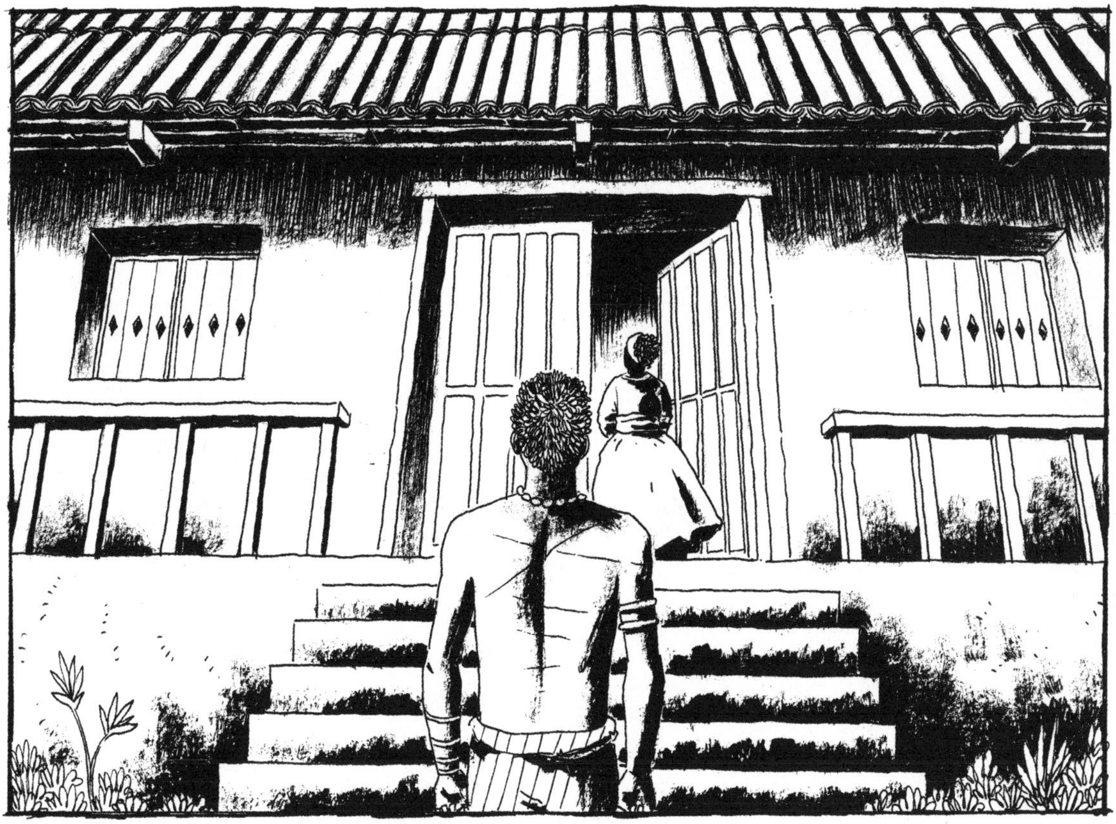

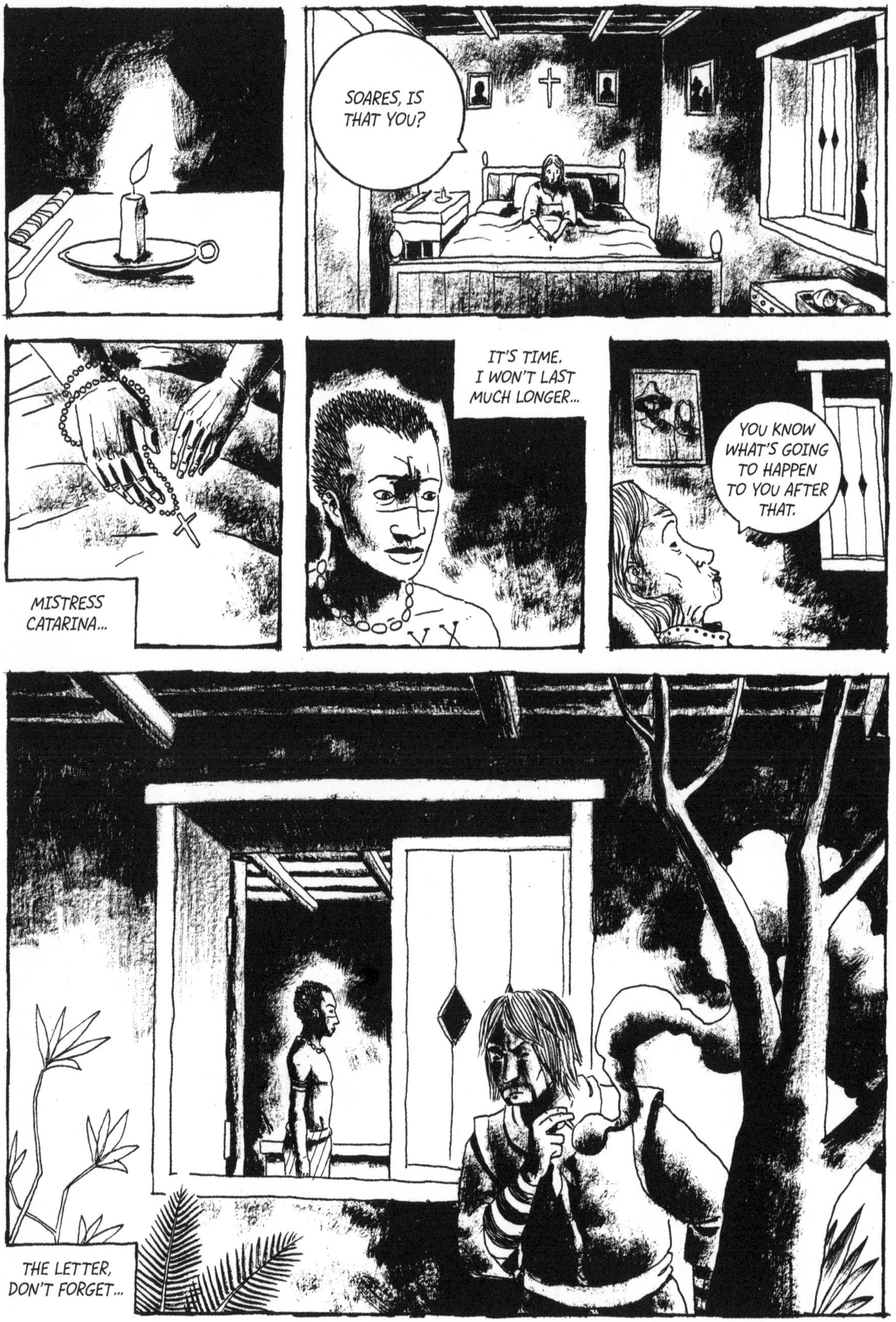
SOARES, IS THAT YOU?
MISTRESS CATARINA...
IT'S TIME. I WON'T LAST MUCH LONGER...
YOU KNOW WHAT'S GOING TO HAPPEN TO YOU AFTER THAT.
THE LETTER, DON'T FORGET...

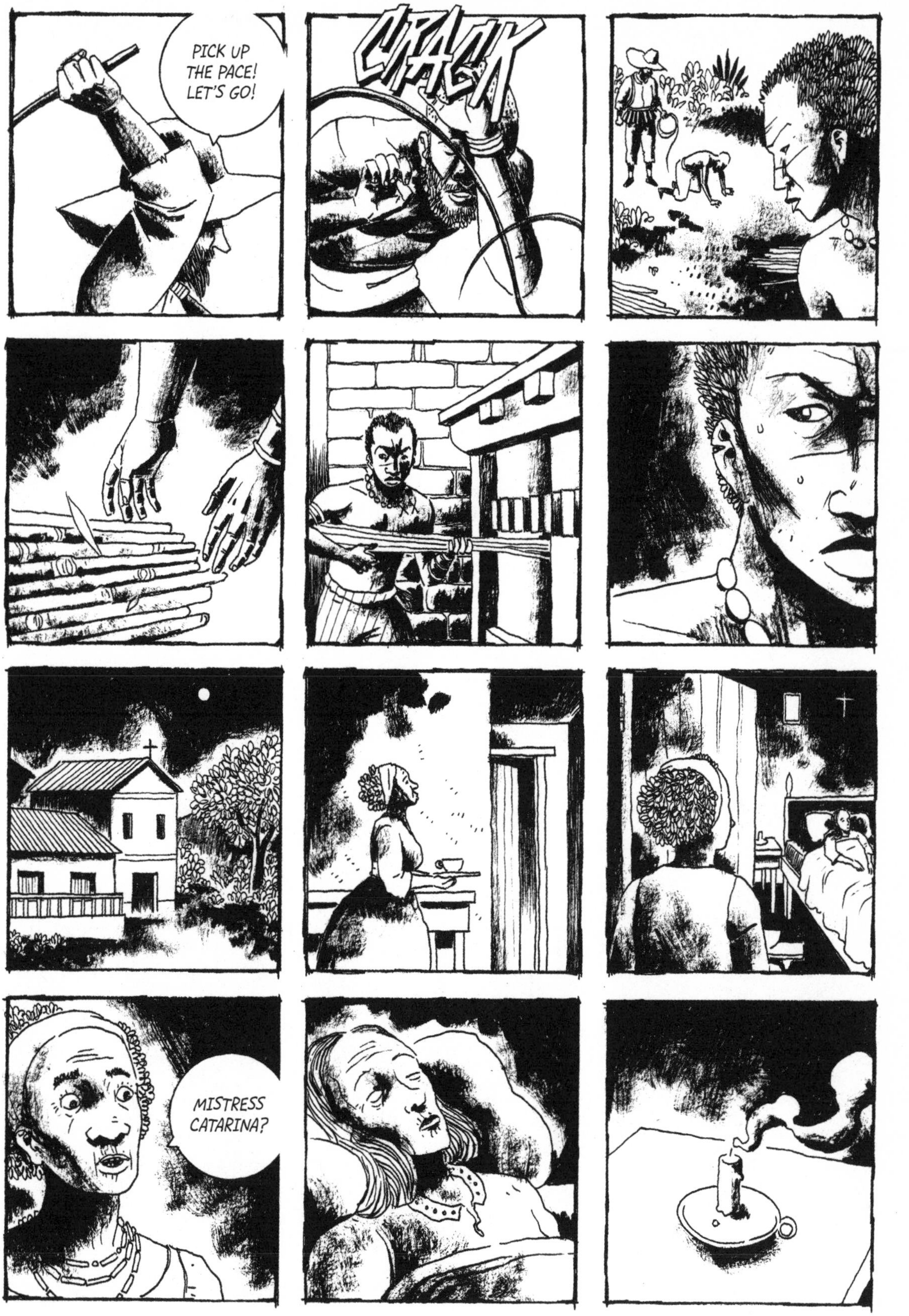
PICK UP THE PACE! LET'S GO!
CRACK
MISTRESS CATARINA?

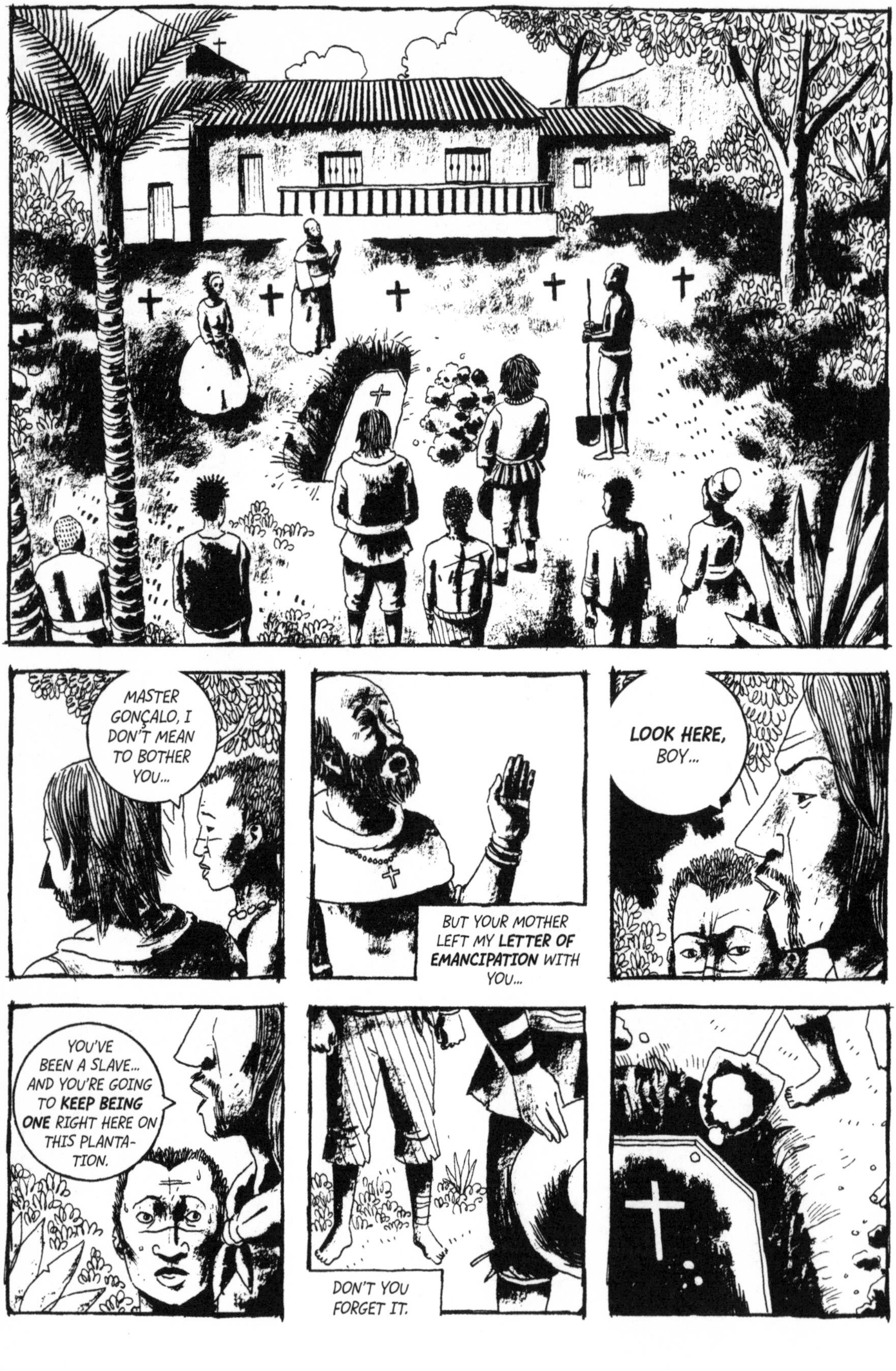
MASTER GONÇALO, I DON'T MEAN TO BOTHER YOU...
BUT YOUR MOTHER LEFT MY **LETTER OF EMANCIPATION** WITH YOU...
LOOK HERE, BOY...
YOU'VE BEEN A SLAVE... AND YOU'RE GOING TO **KEEP BEING ONE** RIGHT HERE ON THIS PLANTA-TION.
DON'T YOU FORGET IT.

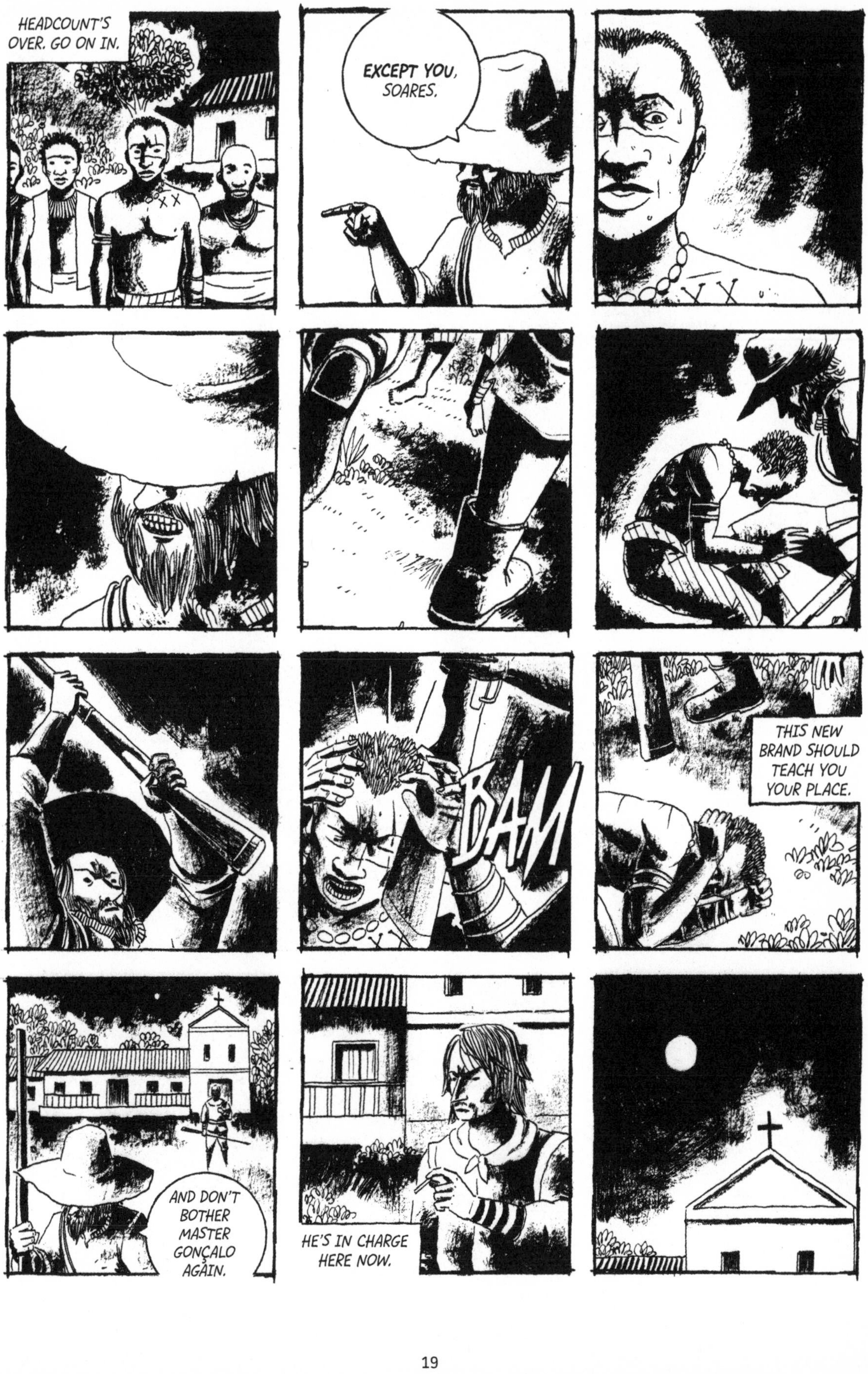
HEADCOUNT'S OVER. GO ON IN.
EXCEPT YOU, SOARES.
BAM
THIS NEW BRAND SHOULD TEACH YOU YOUR PLACE.
AND DON'T BOTHER MASTER GONÇALO AGAIN.
HE'S IN CHARGE HERE NOW.

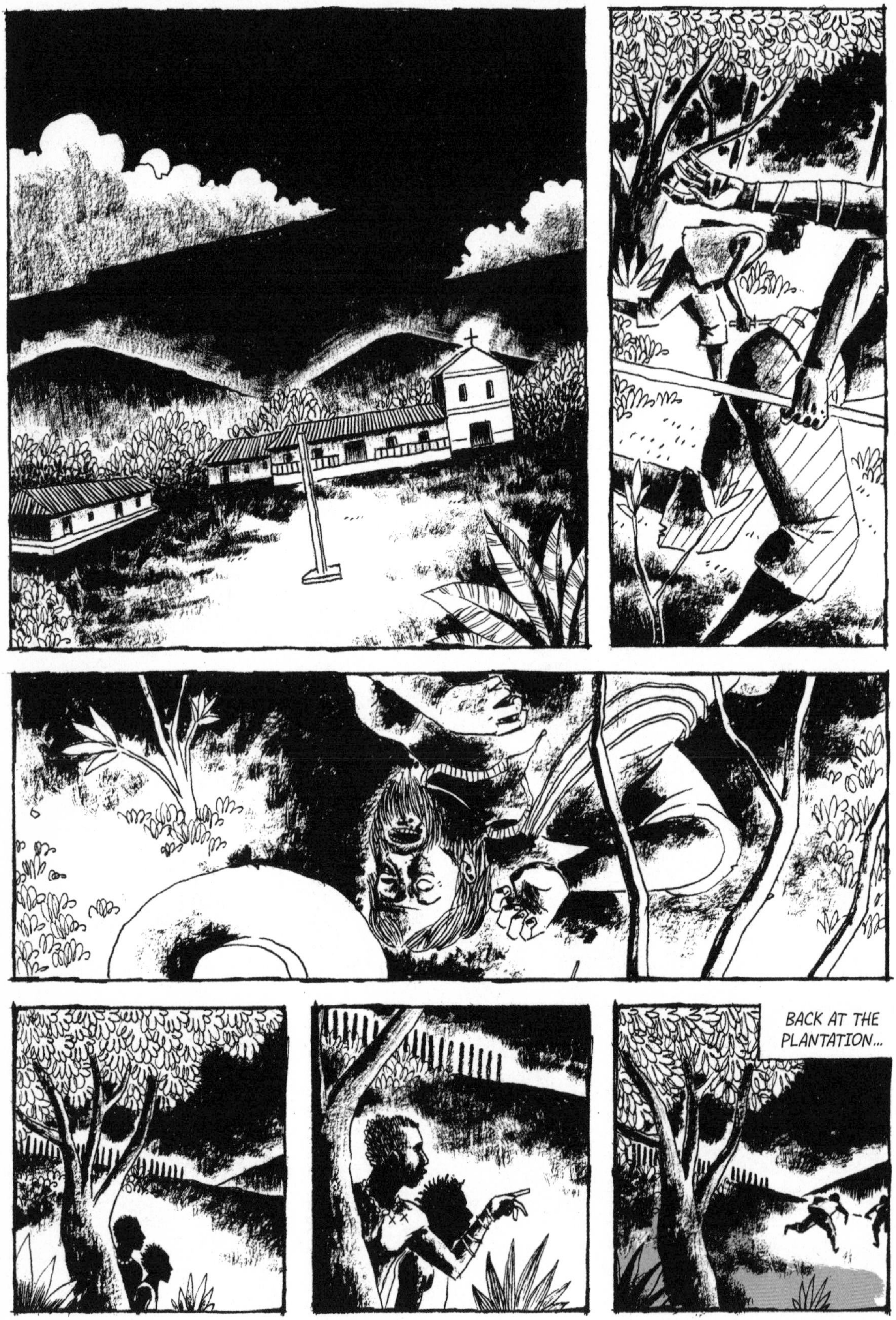
BACK AT THE PLANTATION...

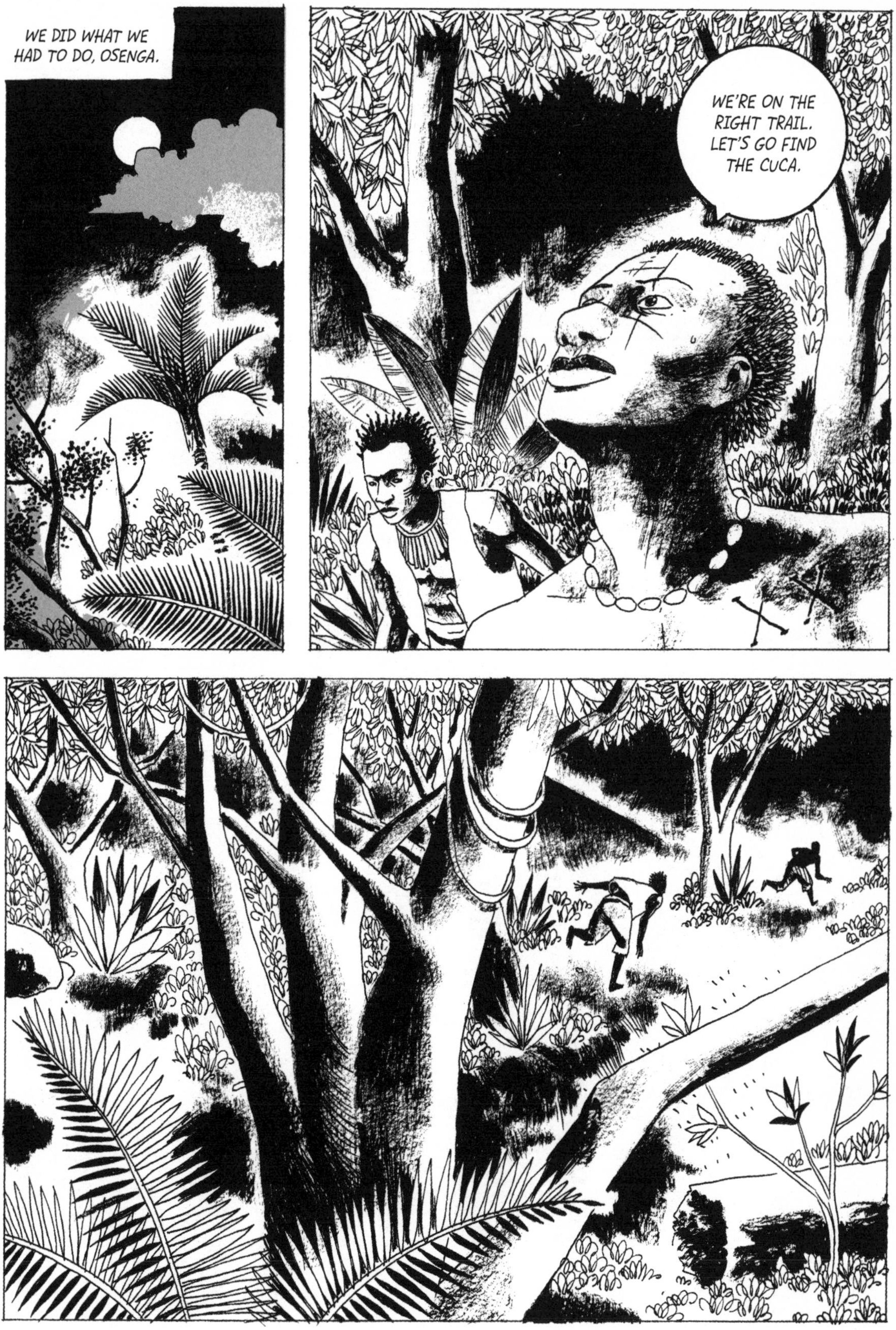
WE DID WHAT WE HAD TO DO, OSENGA.
WE'RE ON THE RIGHT TRAIL. LET'S GO FIND THE CUCA.

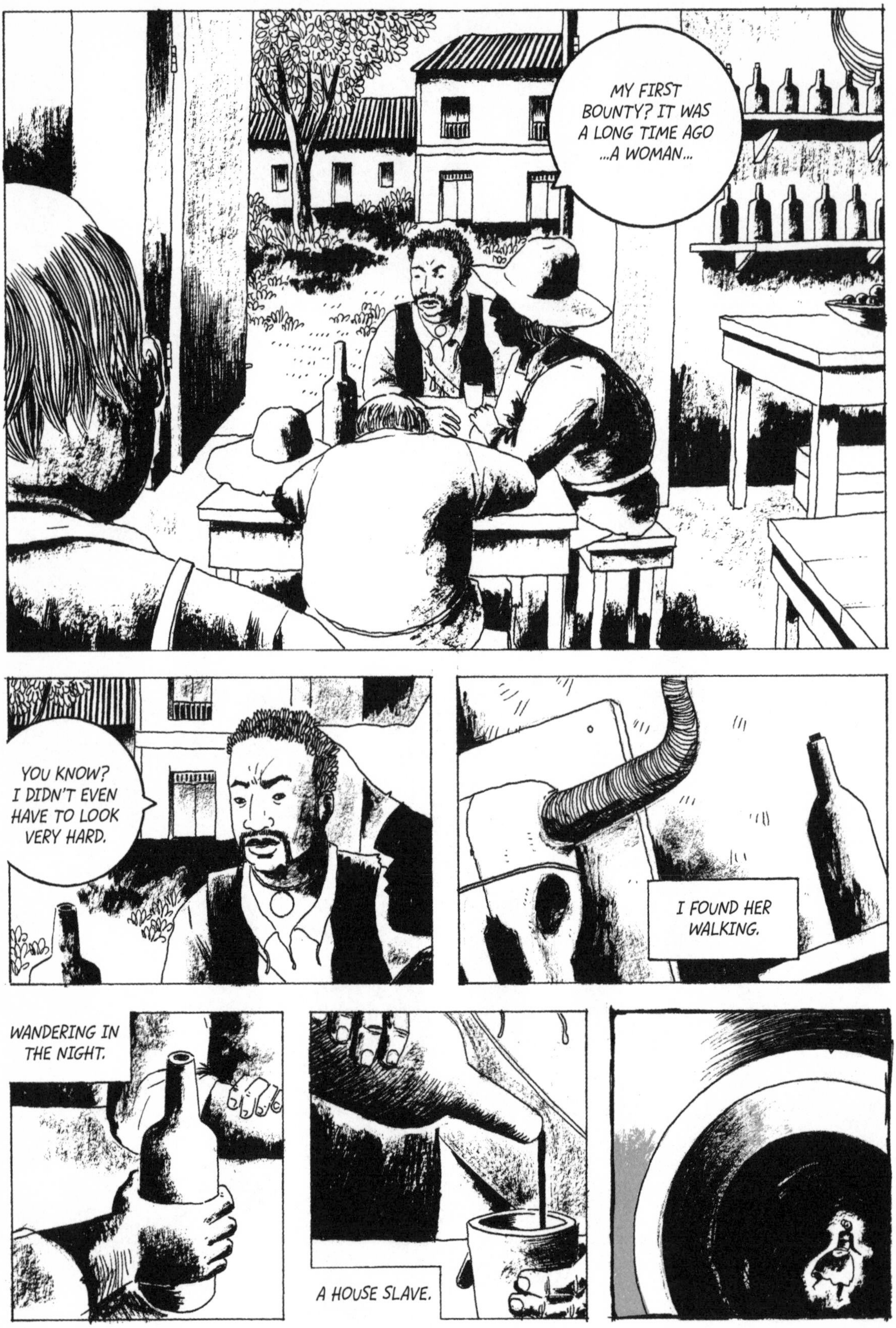
MY FIRST BOUNTY? IT WAS A LONG TIME AGO ...A WOMAN...
YOU KNOW? I DIDN'T EVEN HAVE TO LOOK VERY HARD.
I FOUND HER WALKING.
WANDERING IN THE NIGHT.
A HOUSE SLAVE.

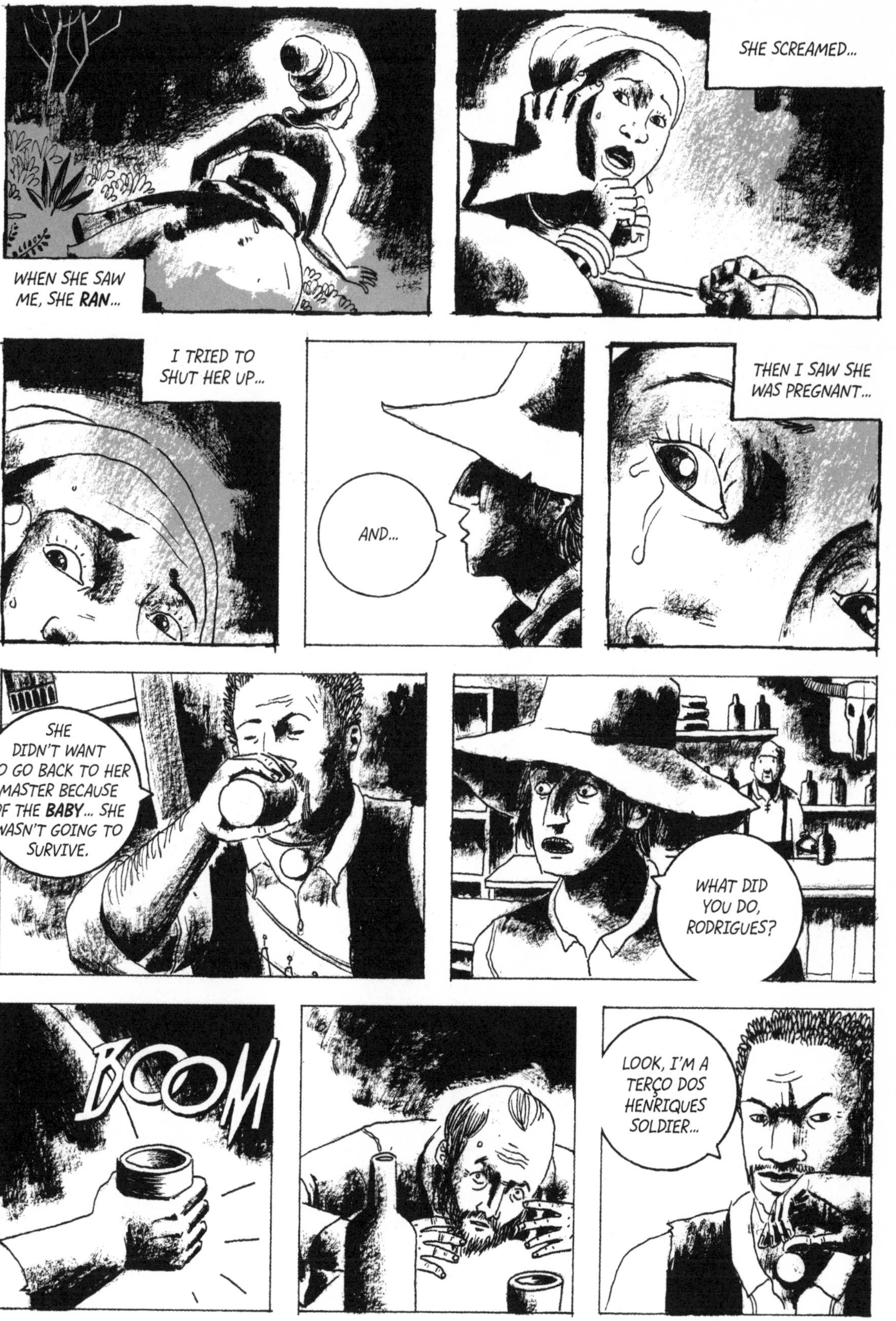
WHEN SHE SAW ME, SHE **RAN**...
SHE SCREAMED...
I TRIED TO SHUT HER UP...
AND...
THEN I SAW SHE WAS PREGNANT...
SHE DIDN'T WANT TO GO BACK TO HER MASTER BECAUSE OF THE **BABY**... SHE WASN'T GOING TO SURVIVE.
WHAT DID YOU DO, RODRIGUES?
BOOM
LOOK, I'M A TERÇO DOS HENRIQUES SOLDIER...

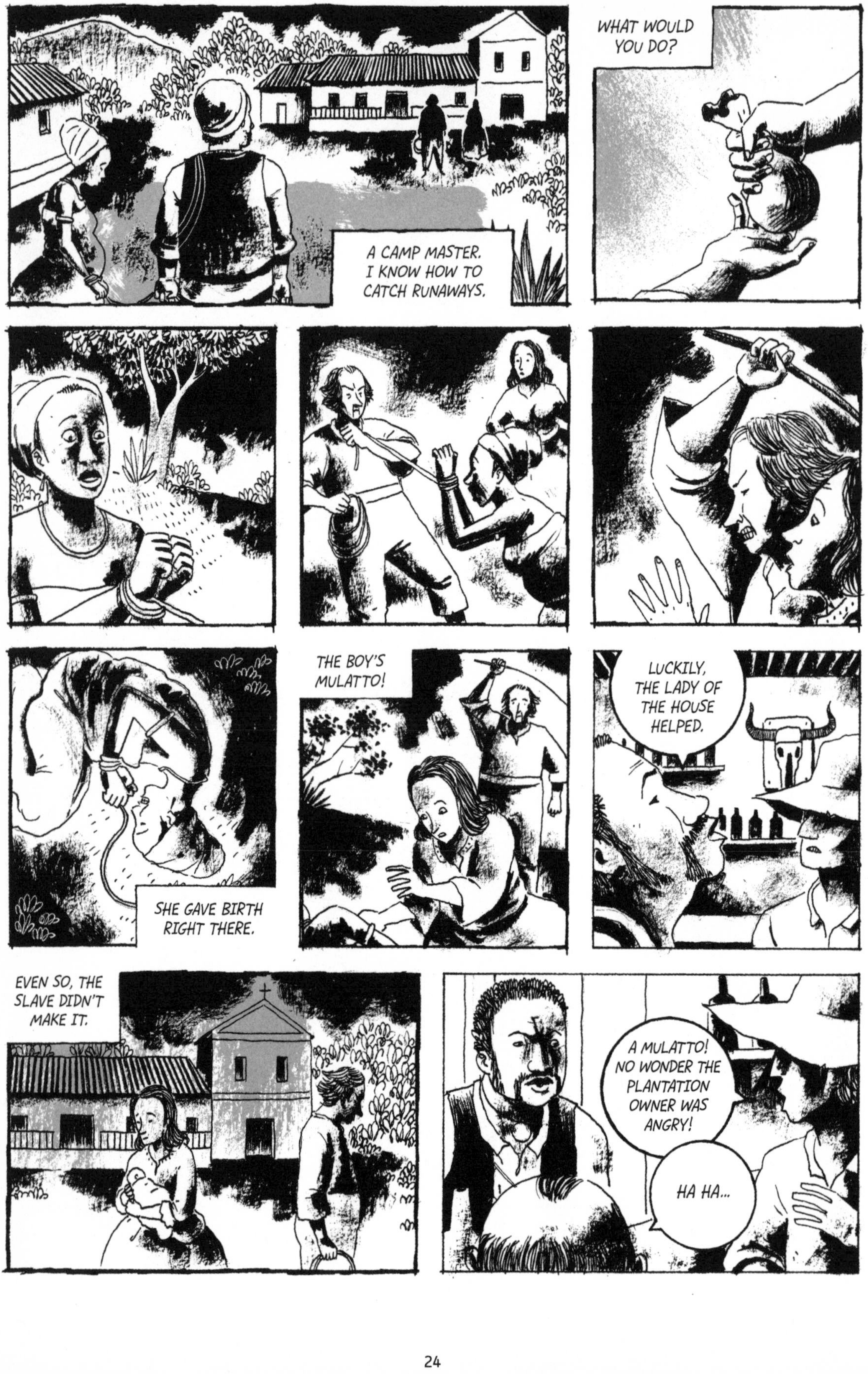
A CAMP MASTER. I KNOW HOW TO CATCH RUNAWAYS.
WHAT WOULD YOU DO?
SHE GAVE BIRTH RIGHT THERE.
THE BOY'S MULATTO!
LUCKILY, THE LADY OF THE HOUSE HELPED.
EVEN SO, THE SLAVE DIDN'T MAKE IT.
A MULATTO! NO WONDER THE PLANTATION OWNER WAS ANGRY!
HA HA...

CATCHING RUNAWAY SLAVES IS EASIER THAN FIGHTING THE DUTCH, HA HA...

THUNK!

YOU'RE KIDDING YOURSELF. THEY KNOW THE LAND BETTER THAN ANY ANIMAL.

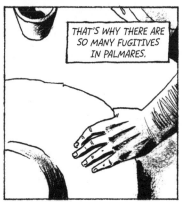

THAT'S WHY THERE ARE SO MANY FUGITIVES IN PALMARES.

DID YOU HEAR, RODRIGUES? TWO UNITS RAN OFF FROM THIS VERY PLANTATION! THEY'RE OUT THERE SOMEWHERE. ONE OF THEM'S A MULATTO...

MAYBE IT'S THAT KID YOU KNOW SO WELL...

EVEN YEARS LATER, I'M STILL WITH THESE BLACKS MARKED BY HARD WORK AND PUNISHMENT...

THERE'S ONLY ONE PLACE THEY CAN GO...

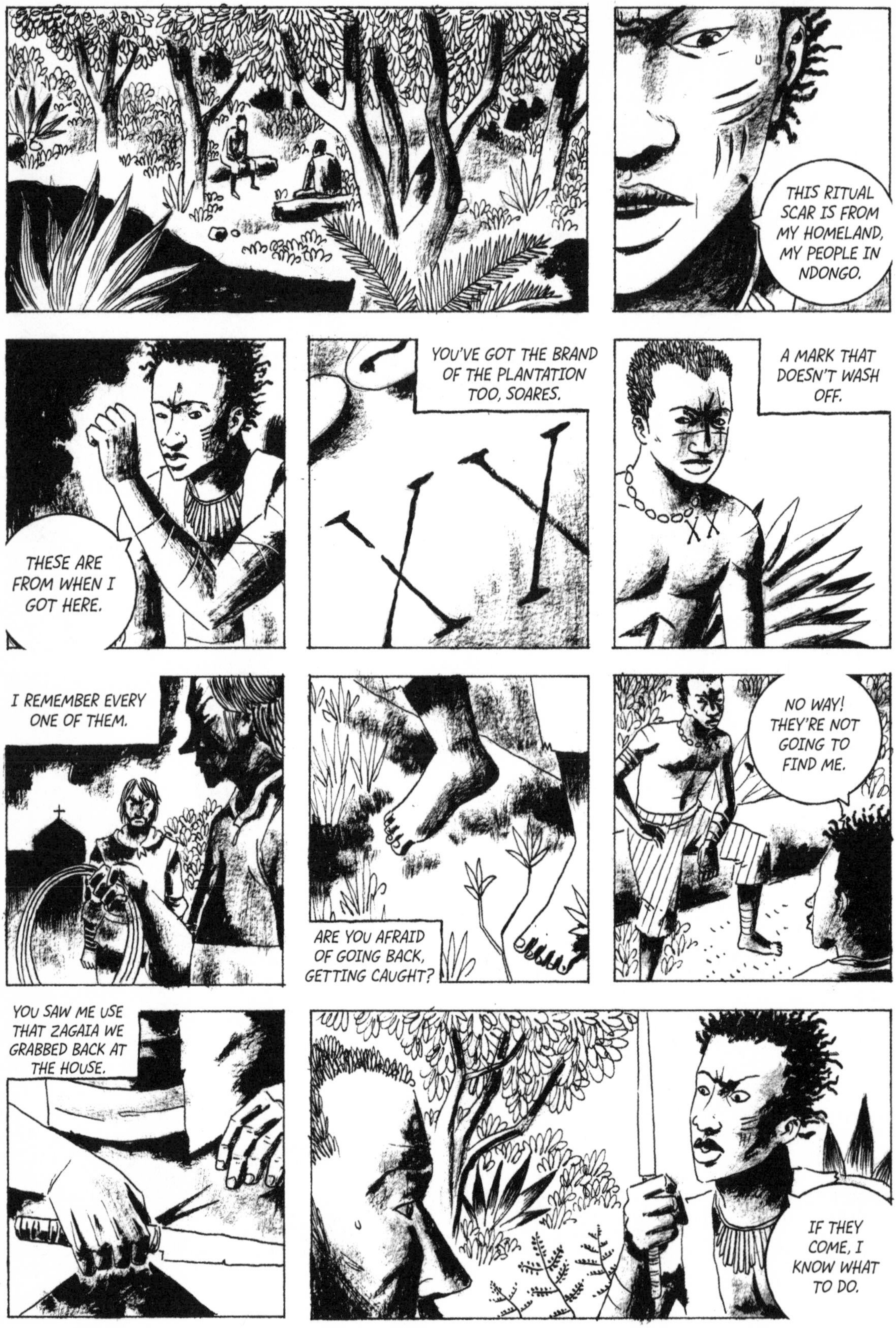
THIS RITUAL SCAR IS FROM MY HOMELAND, MY PEOPLE IN NDONGO.
THESE ARE FROM WHEN I GOT HERE.
YOU'VE GOT THE BRAND OF THE PLANTATION TOO, SOARES.
A MARK THAT DOESN'T WASH OFF.
I REMEMBER EVERY ONE OF THEM.
ARE YOU AFRAID OF GOING BACK, GETTING CAUGHT?
NO WAY! THEY'RE NOT GOING TO FIND ME.
YOU SAW ME USE THAT ZAGAIA WE GRABBED BACK AT THE HOUSE.
IF THEY COME, I KNOW WHAT TO DO.

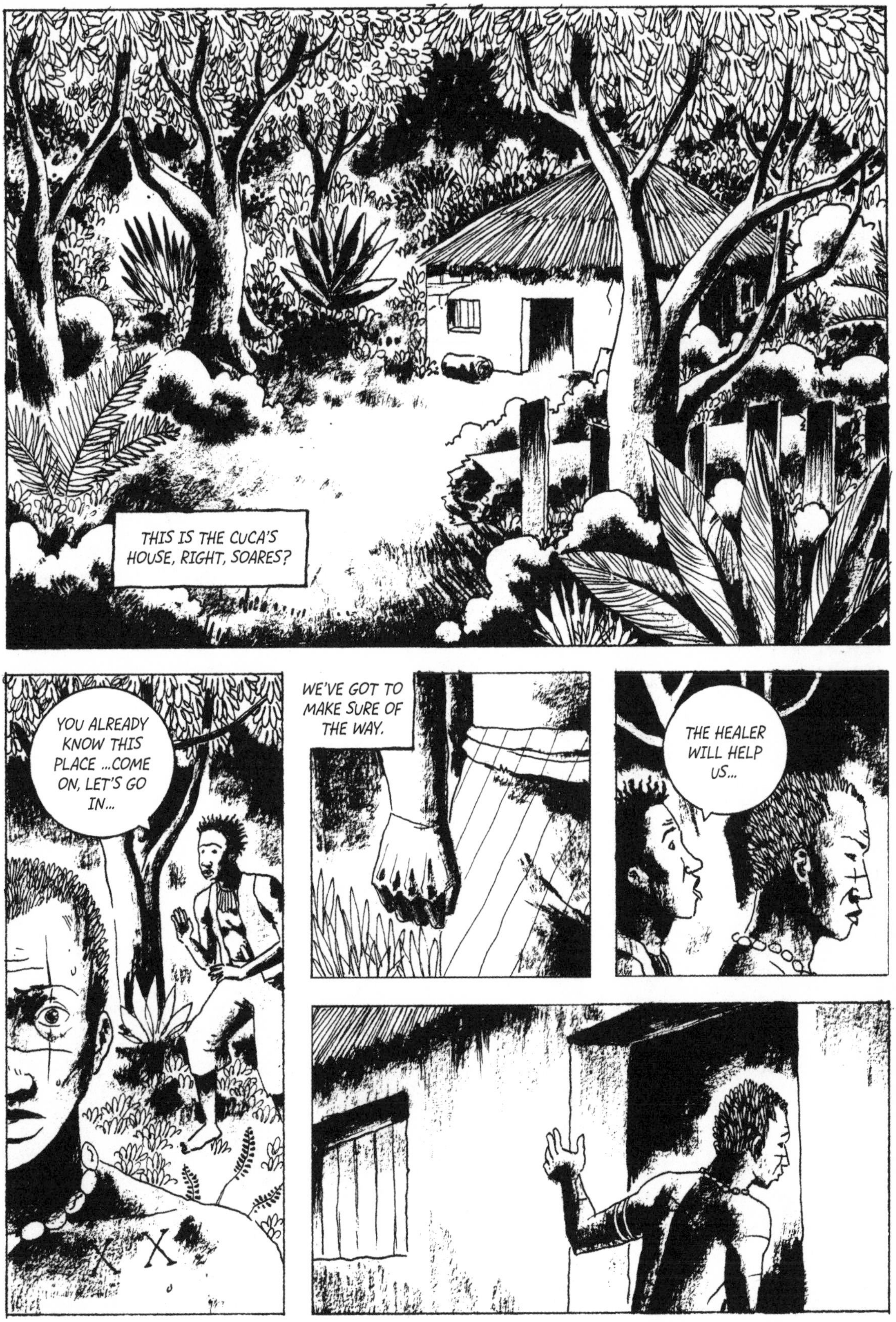
THIS IS THE CUCA'S HOUSE, RIGHT, SOARES?
YOU ALREADY KNOW THIS PLACE ...COME ON, LET'S GO IN...
WE'VE GOT TO MAKE SURE OF THE WAY.
THE HEALER WILL HELP US...

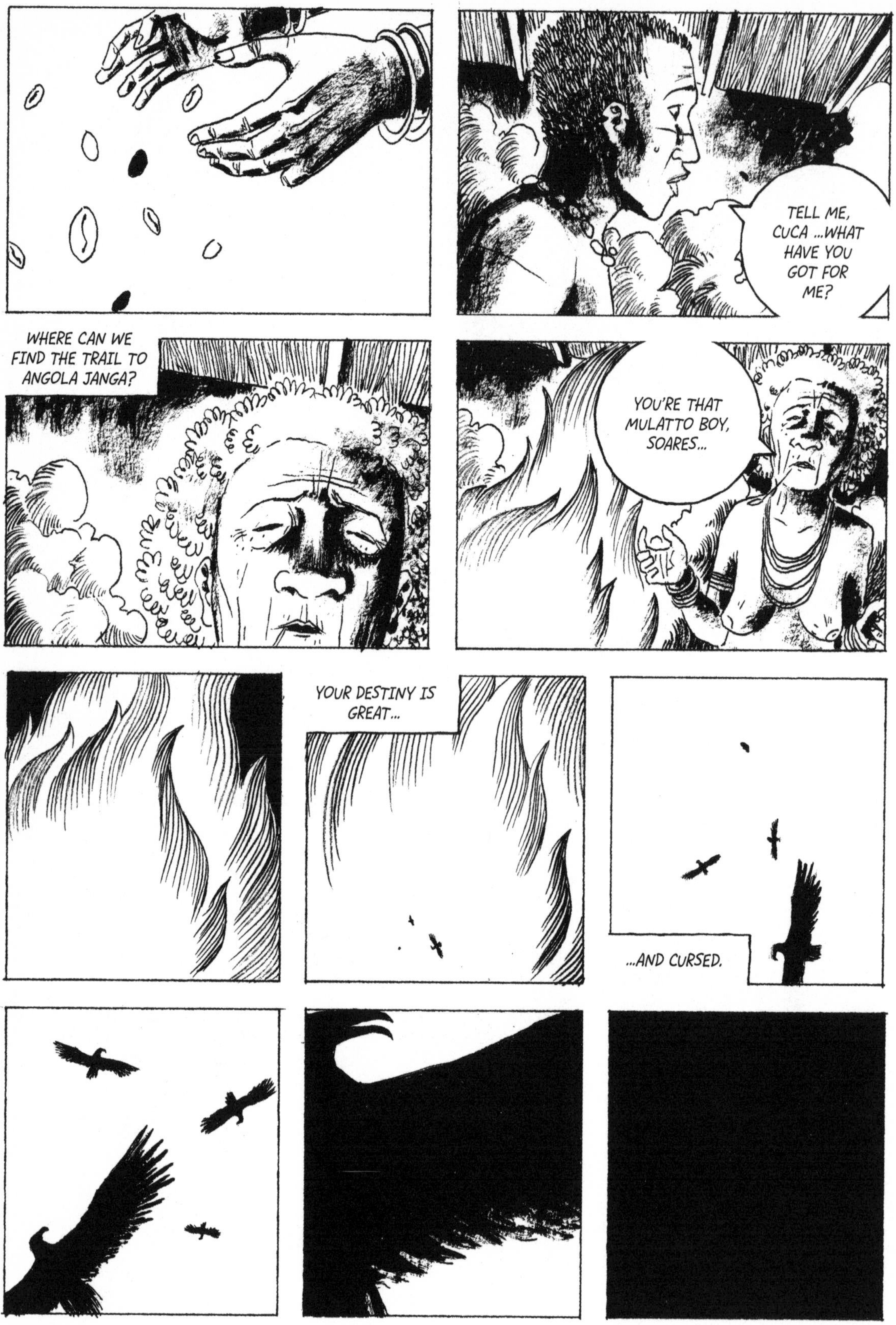
TELL ME, CUCA ...WHAT HAVE YOU GOT FOR ME?
WHERE CAN WE FIND THE TRAIL TO ANGOLA JANGA?
YOU'RE THAT MULATTO BOY, SOARES...
YOUR DESTINY IS GREAT...
...AND CURSED.

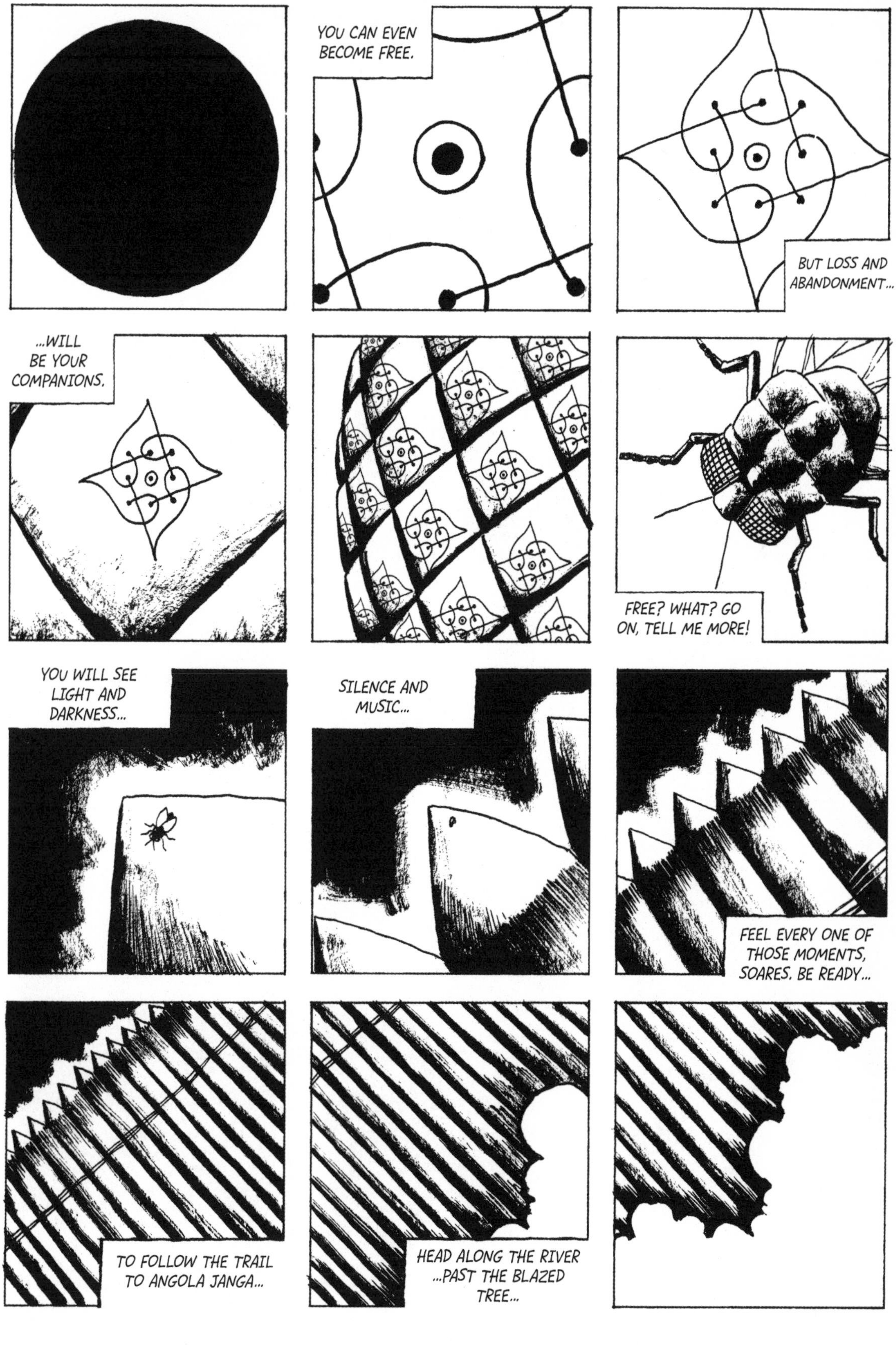
YOU CAN EVEN BECOME FREE.
BUT LOSS AND ABANDONMENT...
...WILL BE YOUR COMPANIONS.
FREE? WHAT? GO ON, TELL ME MORE!
YOU WILL SEE LIGHT AND DARKNESS...
SILENCE AND MUSIC...
FEEL EVERY ONE OF THOSE MOMENTS, SOARES. BE READY...
TO FOLLOW THE TRAIL TO ANGOLA JANGA...
HEAD ALONG THE RIVER ...PAST THE BLAZED TREE...

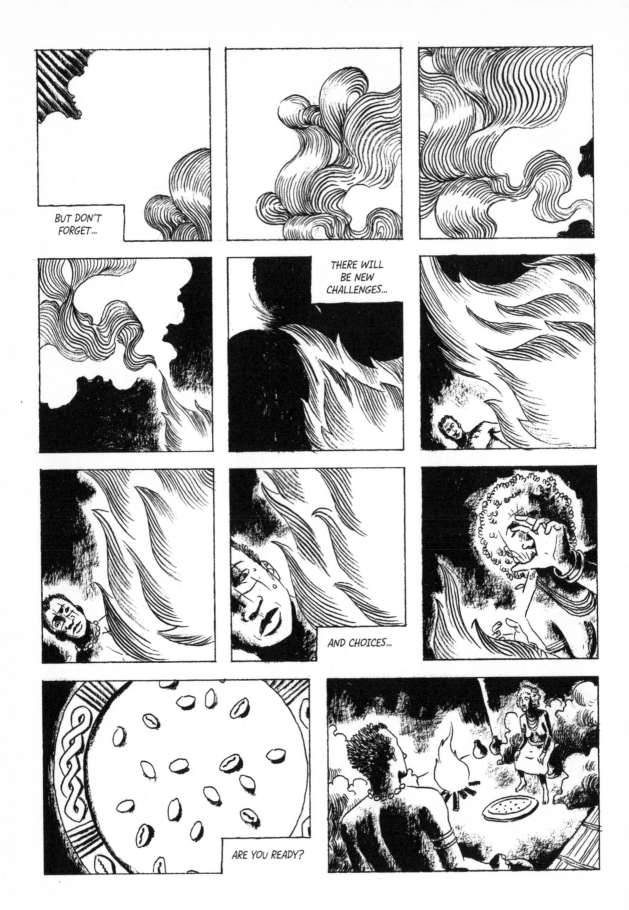

BUT DON'T FORGET...

THERE WILL BE NEW CHALLENGES...

AND CHOICES...

ARE YOU READY?

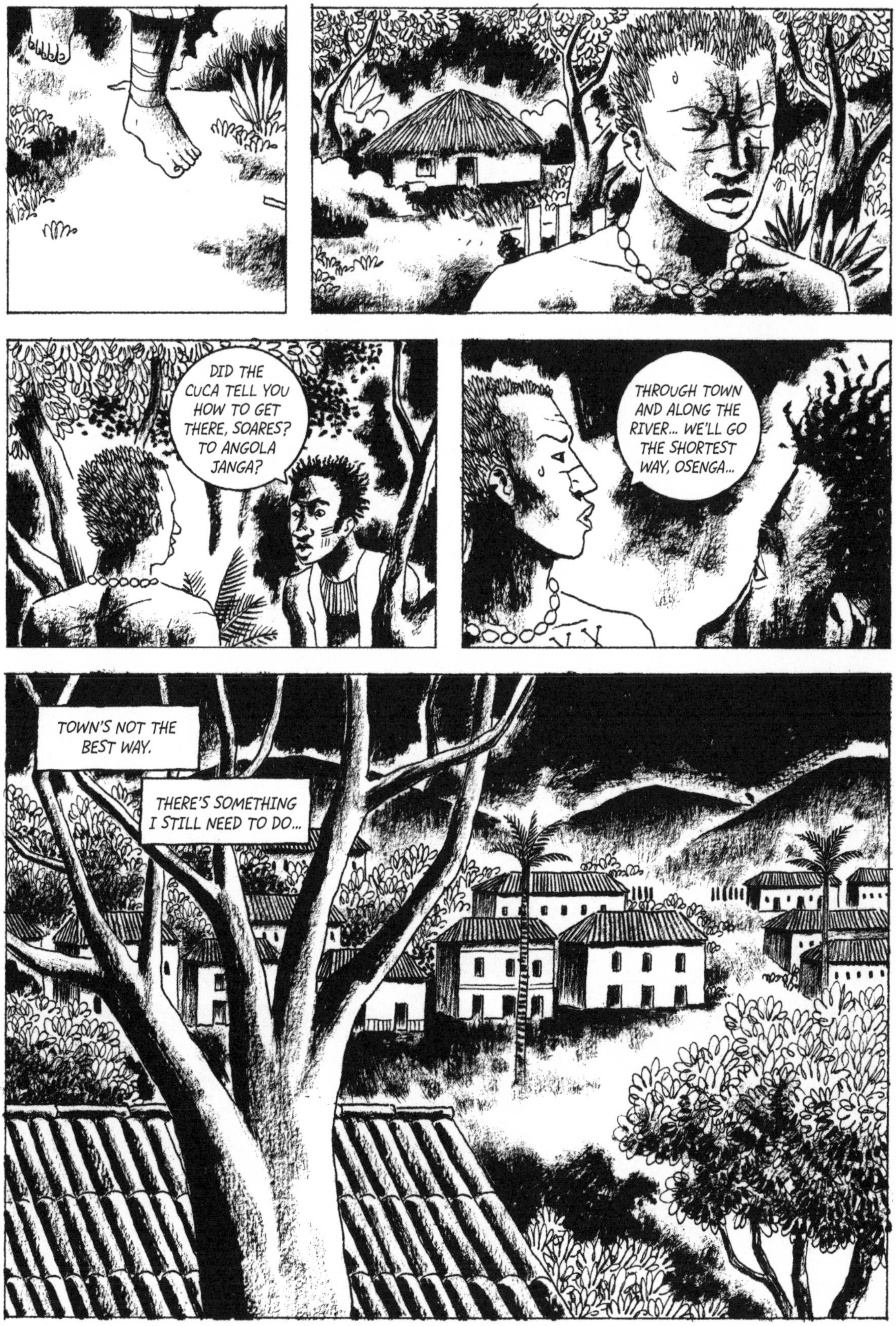
DID THE CUCA TELL YOU HOW TO GET THERE, SOARES? TO ANGOLA JANGA?
THROUGH TOWN AND ALONG THE RIVER... WE'LL GO THE SHORTEST WAY, OSENGA...
TOWN'S NOT THE BEST WAY.
THERE'S SOMETHING I STILL NEED TO DO...

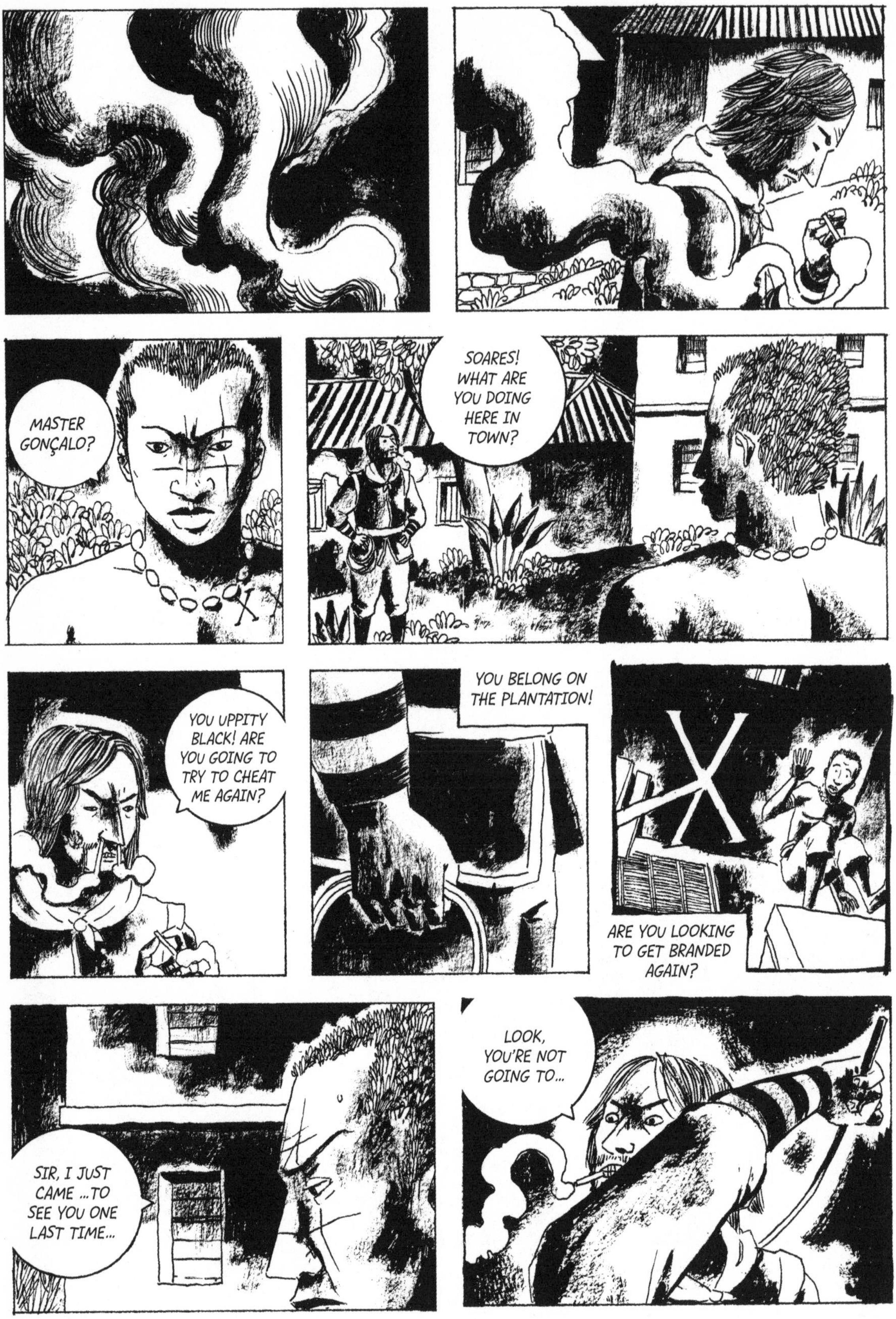
MASTER GONÇALO?
SOARES! WHAT ARE YOU DOING HERE IN TOWN?
YOU UPPITY BLACK! ARE YOU GOING TO TRY TO CHEAT ME AGAIN?
YOU BELONG ON THE PLANTATION!
ARE YOU LOOKING TO GET BRANDED AGAIN?
SIR, I JUST CAME ...TO SEE YOU ONE LAST TIME...
LOOK, YOU'RE NOT GOING TO...

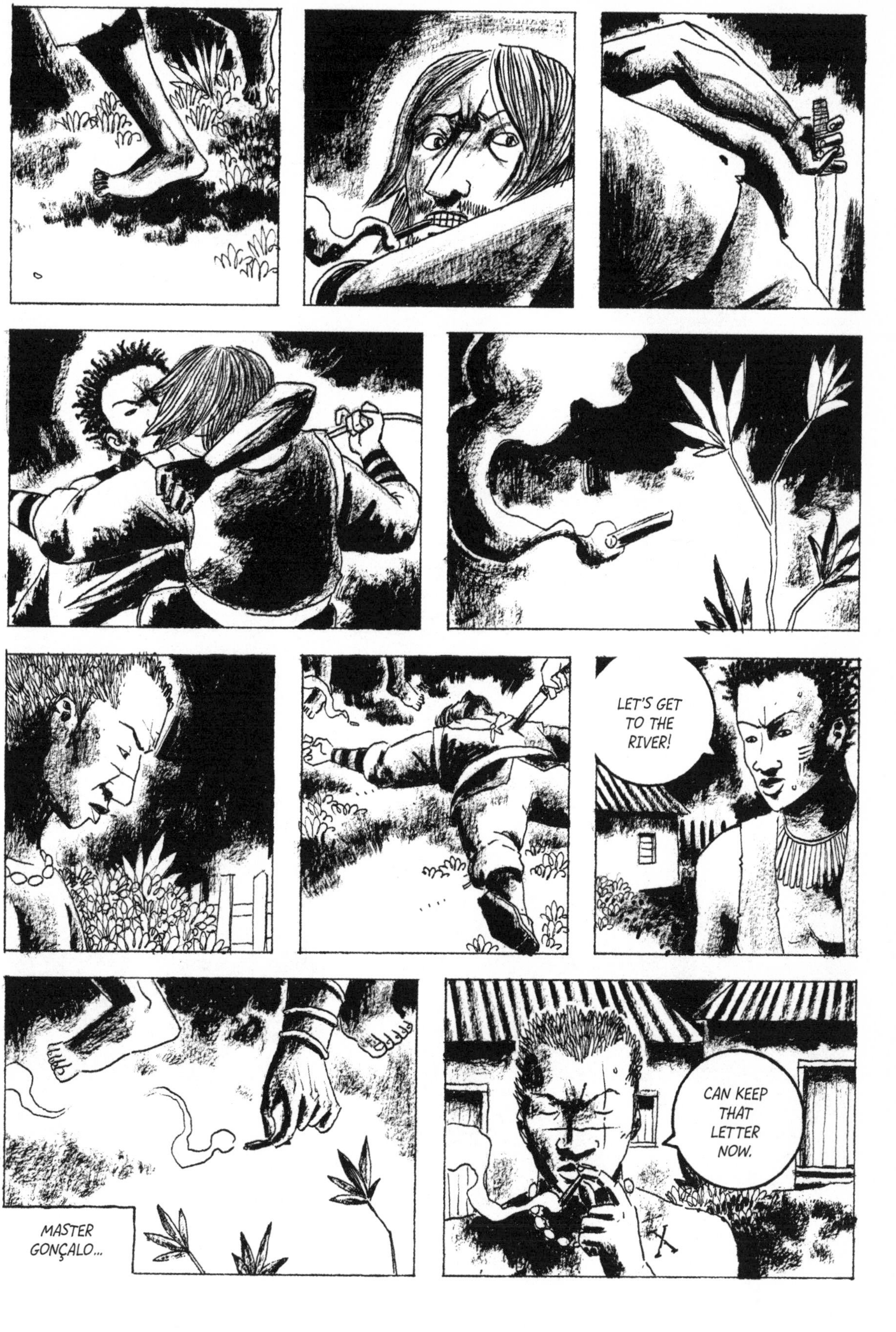
LET'S GET TO THE RIVER!
MASTER GONÇALO...
CAN KEEP THAT LETTER NOW.

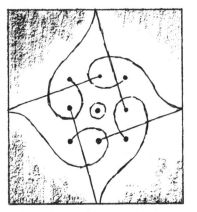

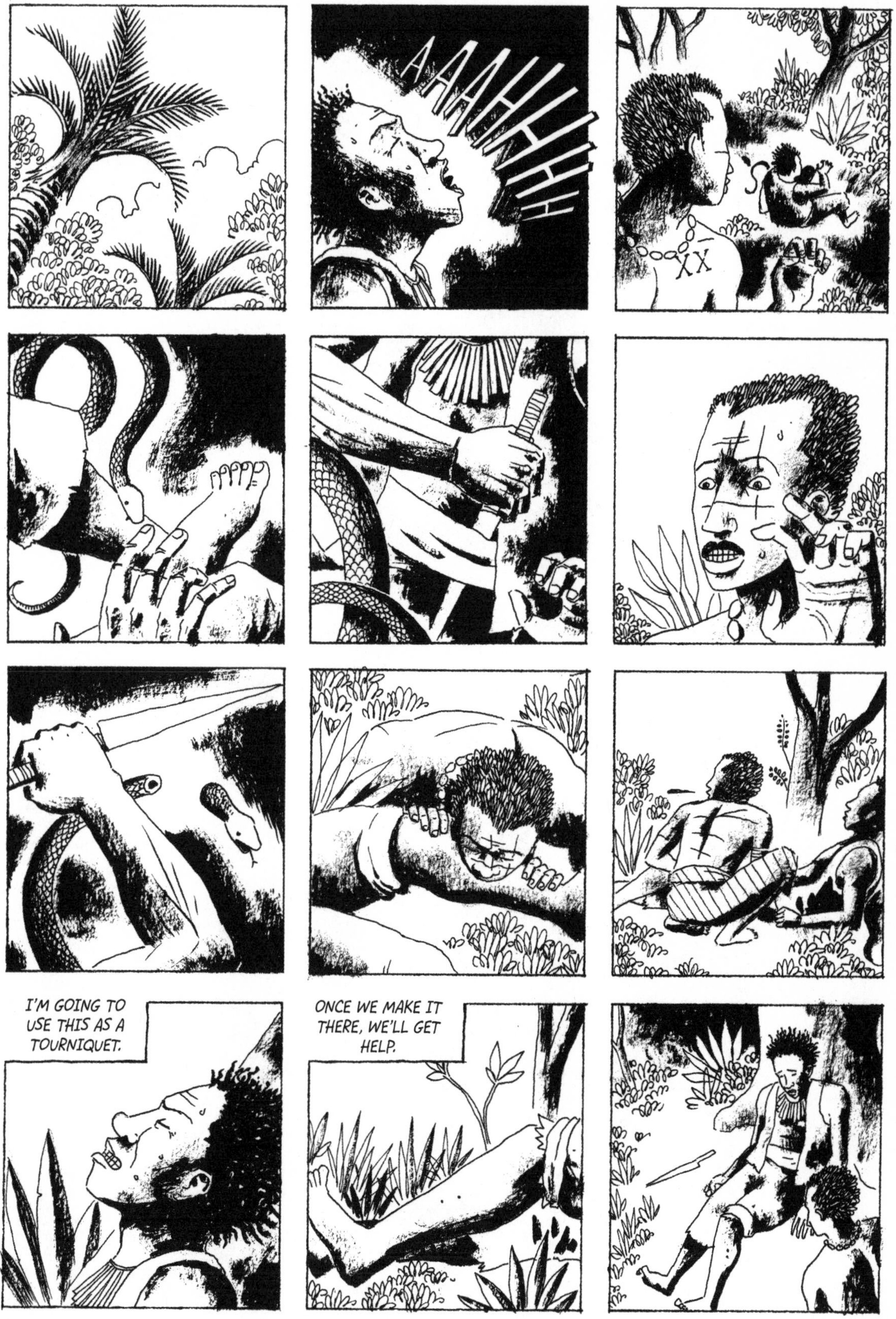
AAAHHHHH
I'M GOING TO USE THIS AS A TOURNIQUET.
ONCE WE MAKE IT THERE, WE'LL GET HELP.

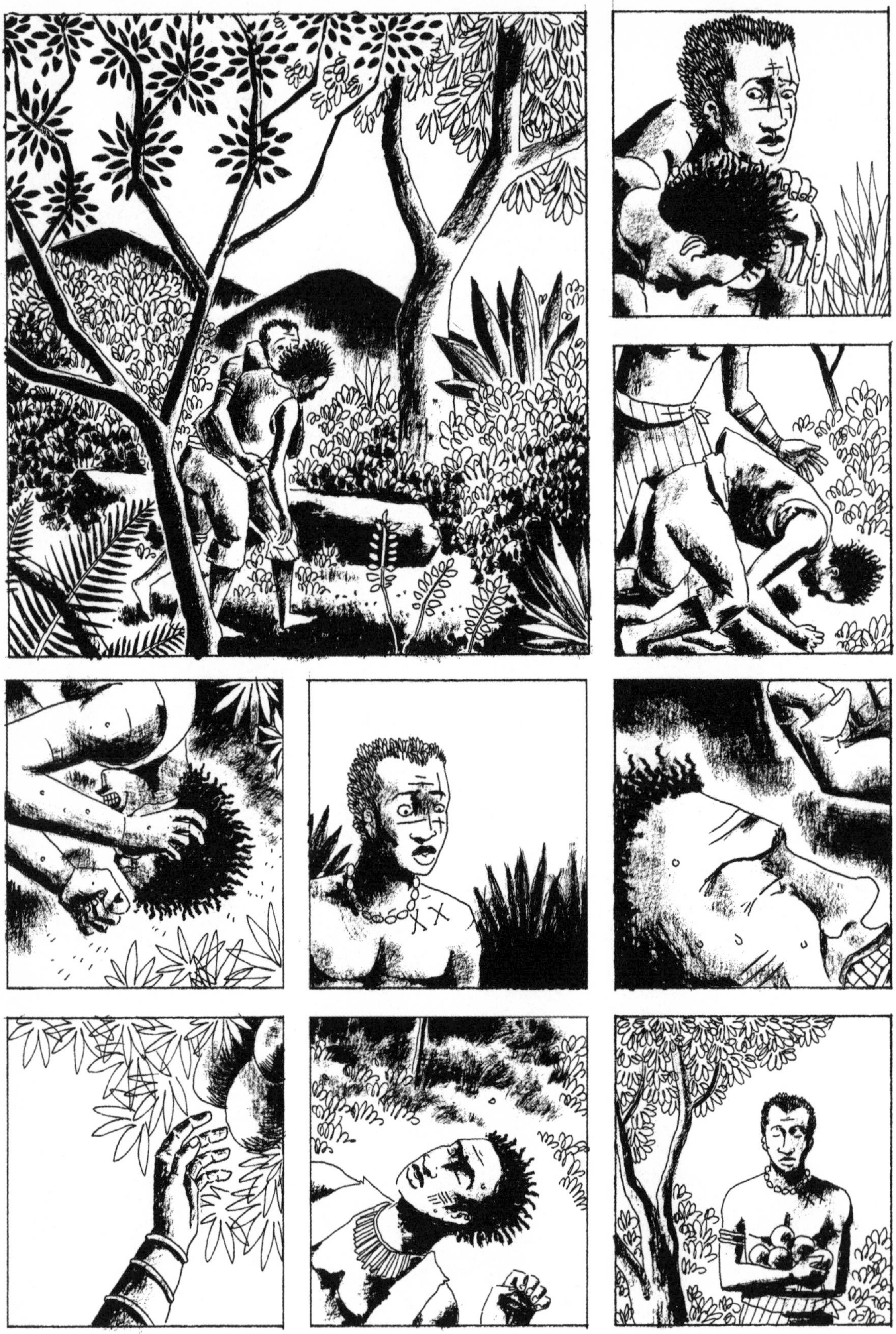

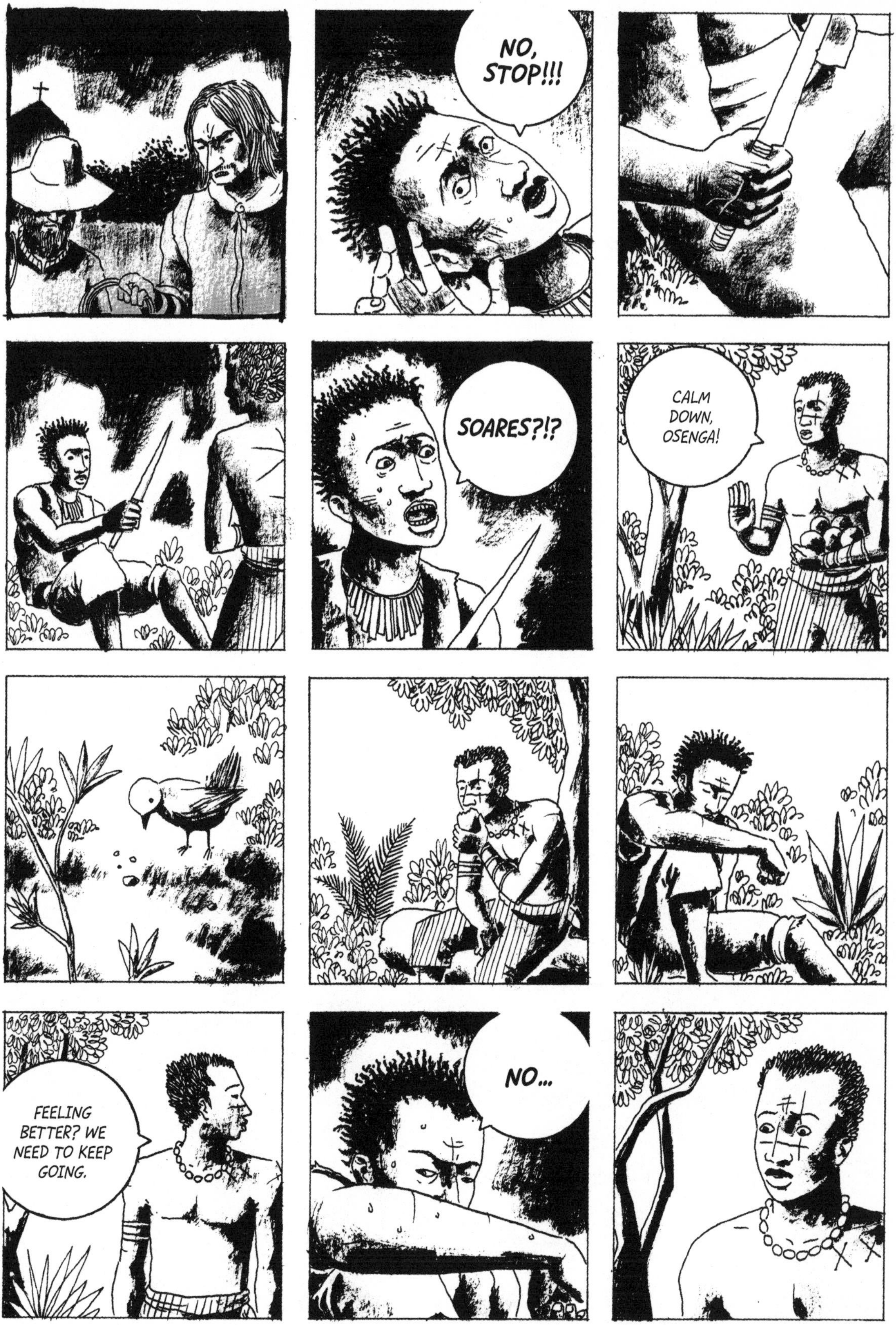
NO, STOP!!!
SOARES?!?
CALM DOWN, OSENGA!
FEELING BETTER? WE NEED TO KEEP GOING.
NO...

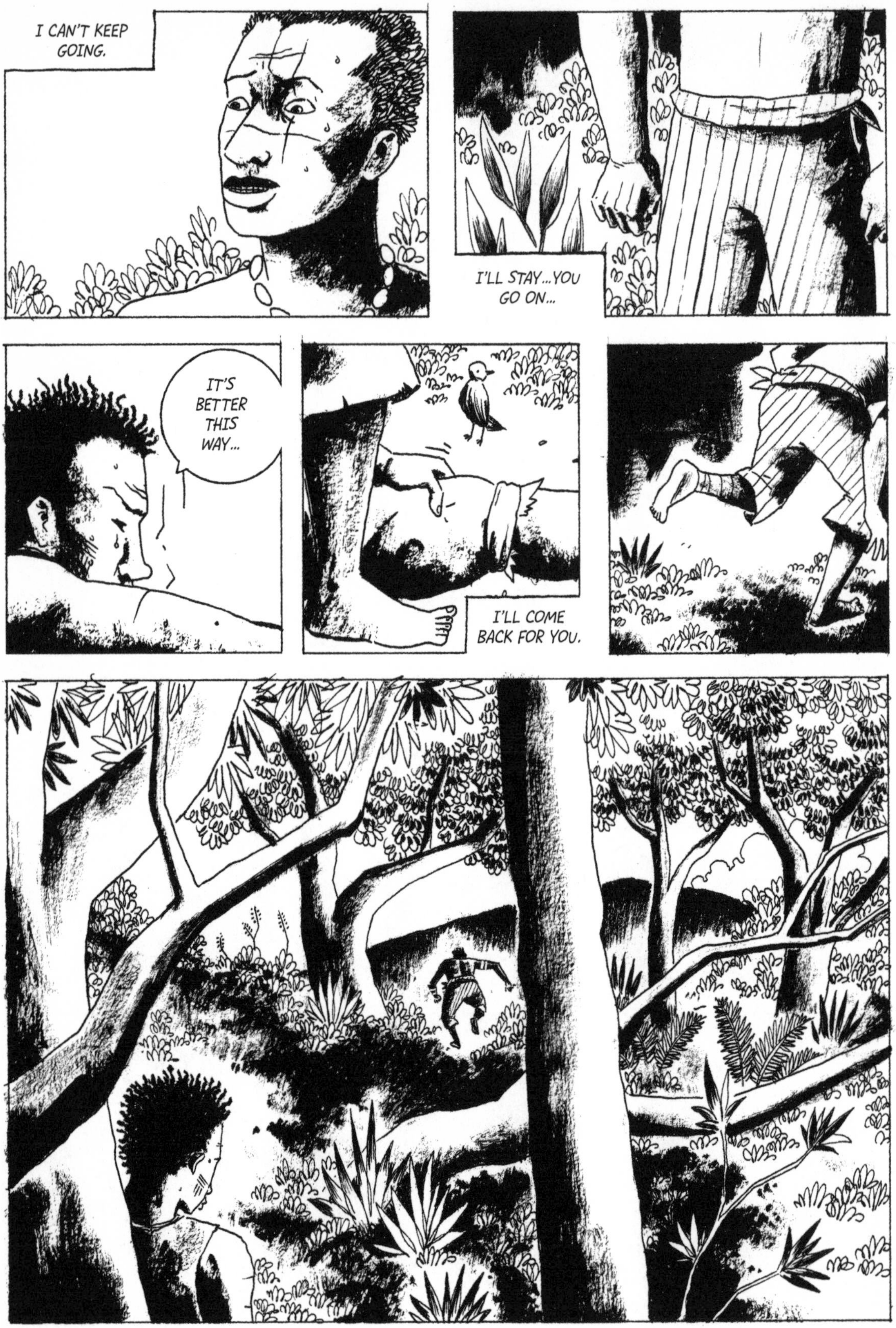
I CAN'T KEEP GOING.
I'LL STAY...YOU GO ON...
IT'S BETTER THIS WAY...
I'LL COME BACK FOR YOU.

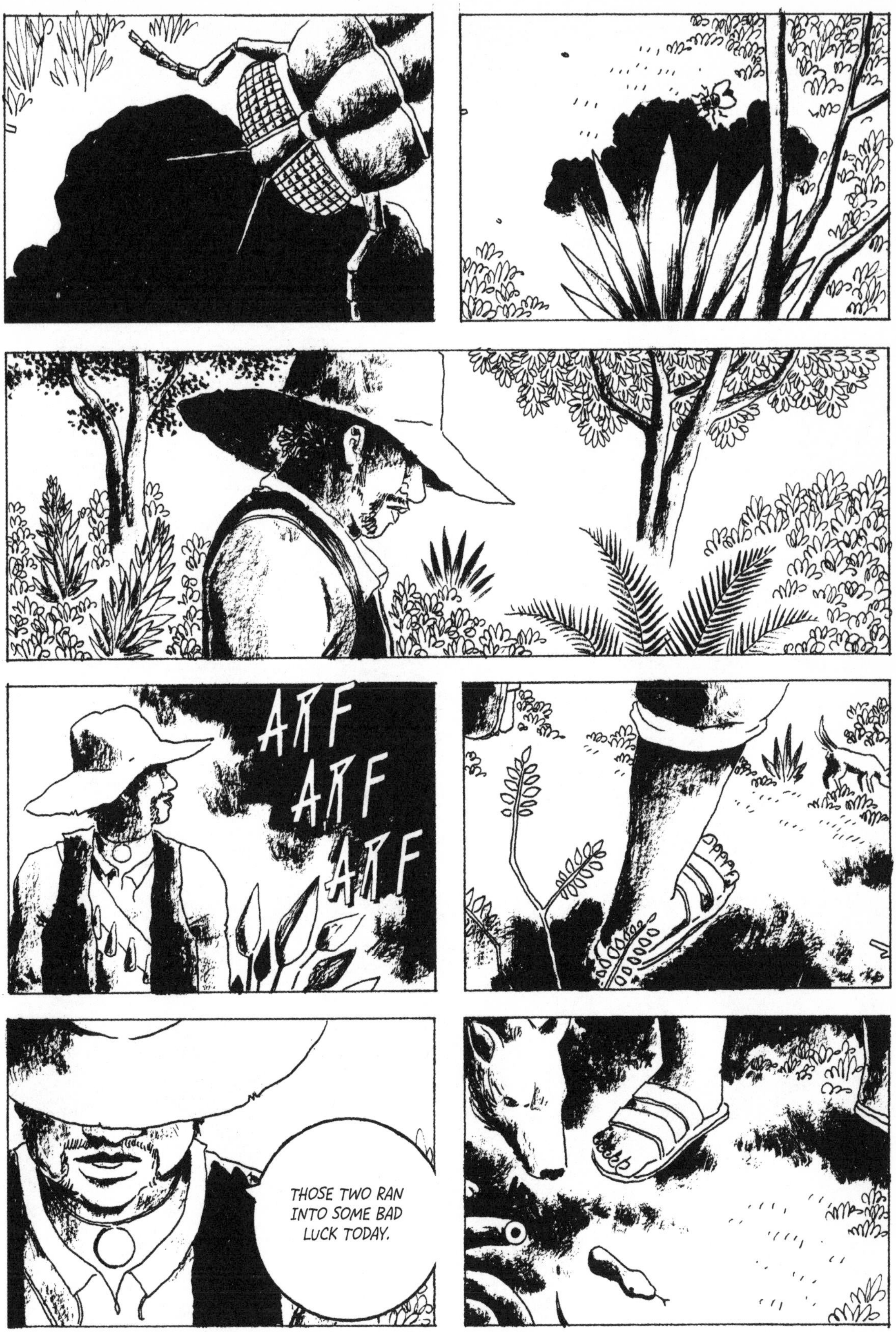
ARF
ARF
ARF
THOSE TWO RAN INTO SOME BAD LUCK TODAY.

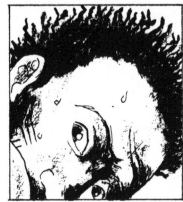

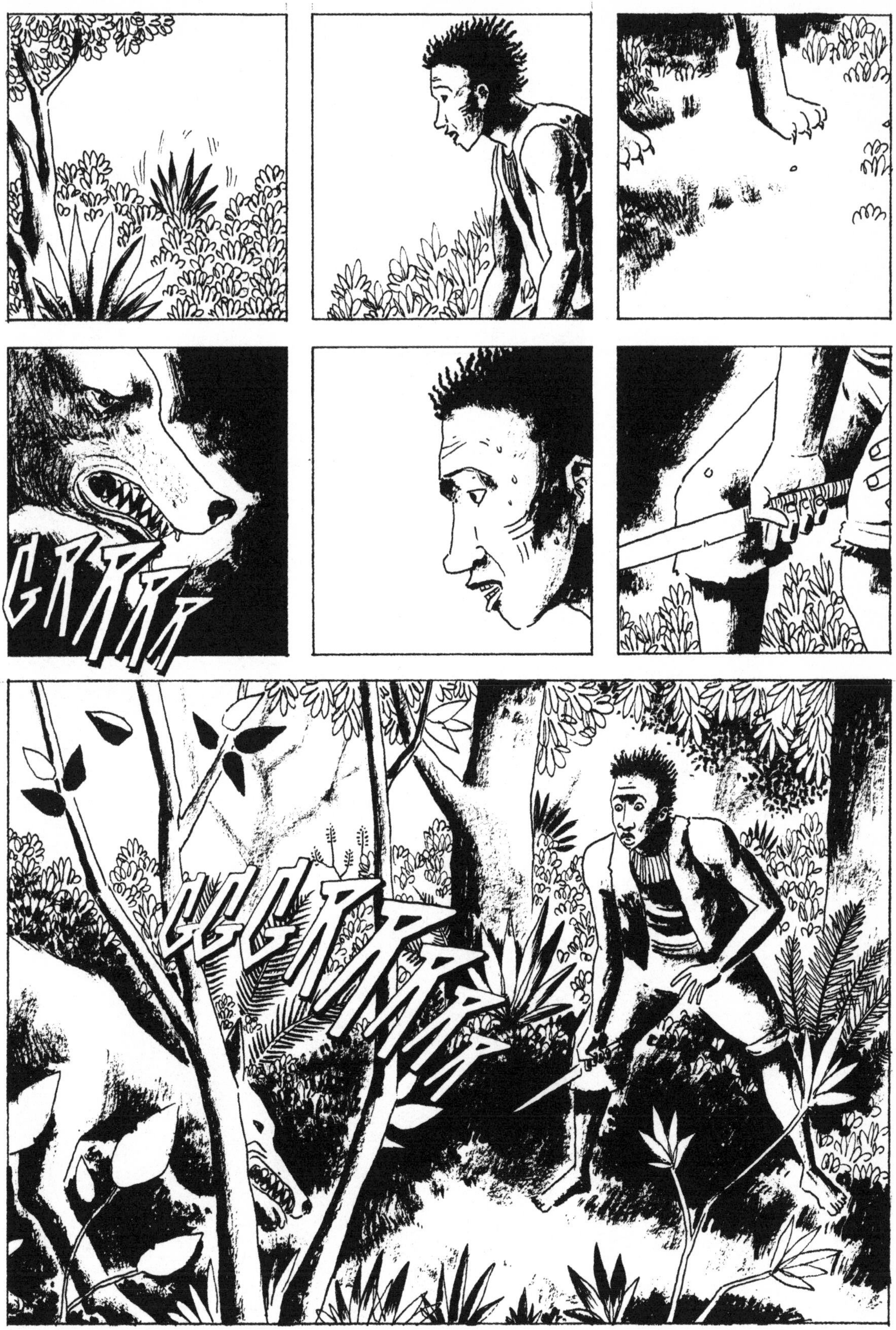
GRRRR
GGGRRRRR

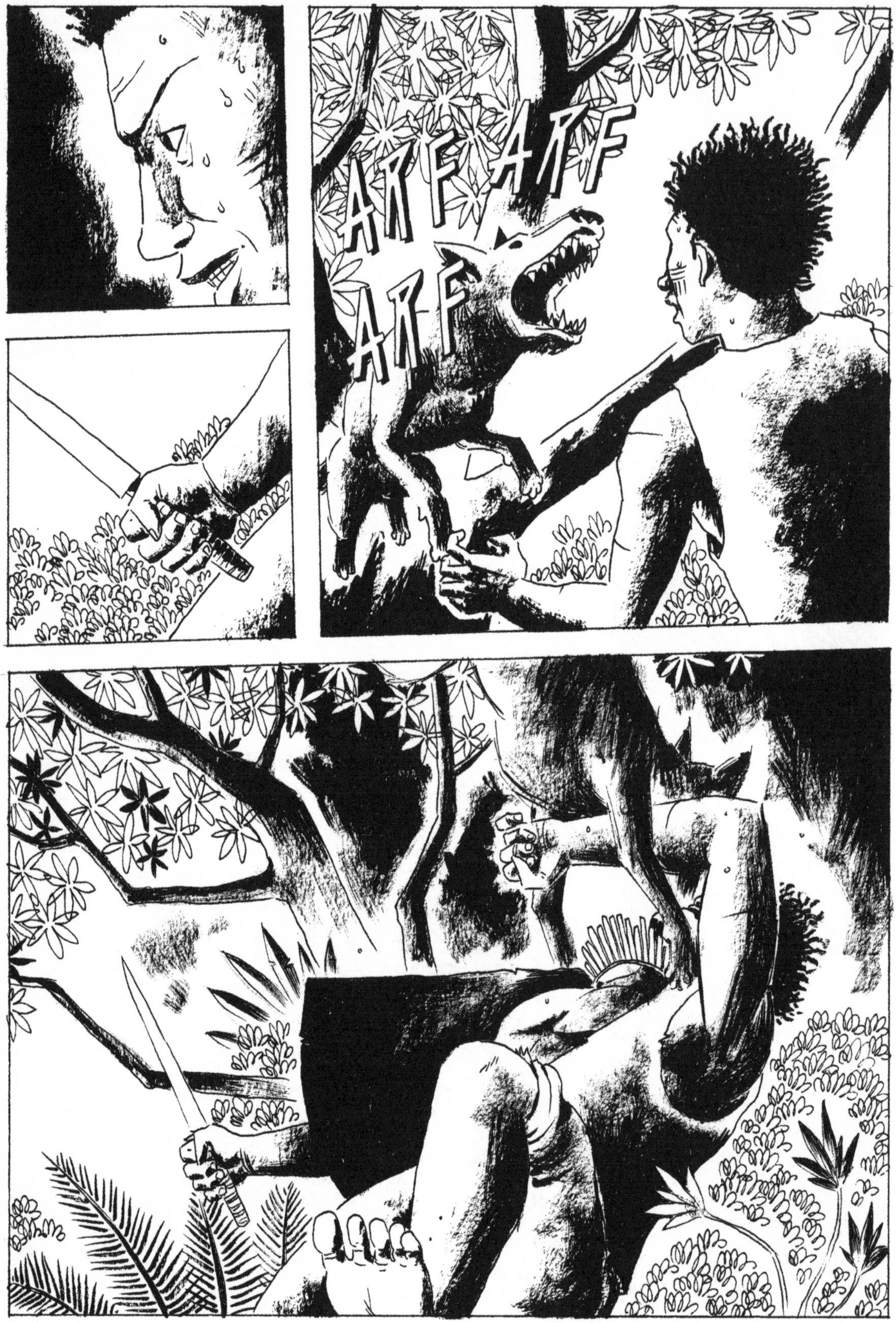
ARF ARF
ARF

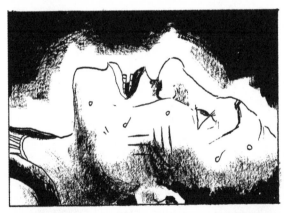

A TRACKING DOG...

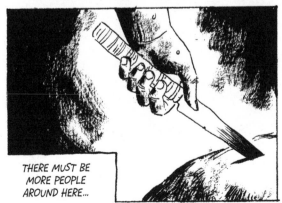

THERE MUST BE MORE PEOPLE AROUND HERE...

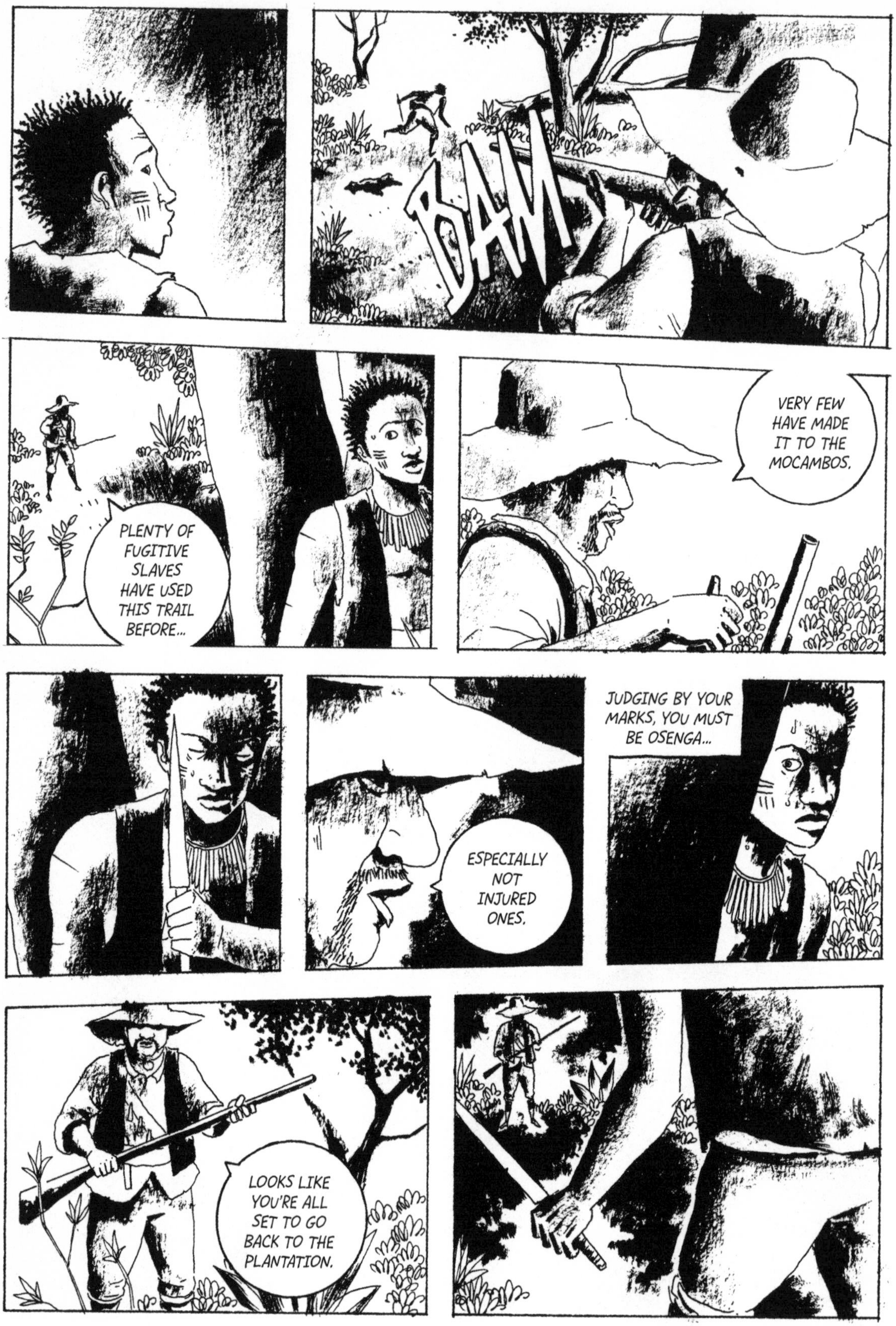
BAM
PLENTY OF FUGITIVE SLAVES HAVE USED THIS TRAIL BEFORE...
VERY FEW HAVE MADE IT TO THE MOCAMBOS.
ESPECIALLY NOT INJURED ONES.
JUDGING BY YOUR MARKS, YOU MUST BE OSENGA...
LOOKS LIKE YOU'RE ALL SET TO GO BACK TO THE PLANTATION.

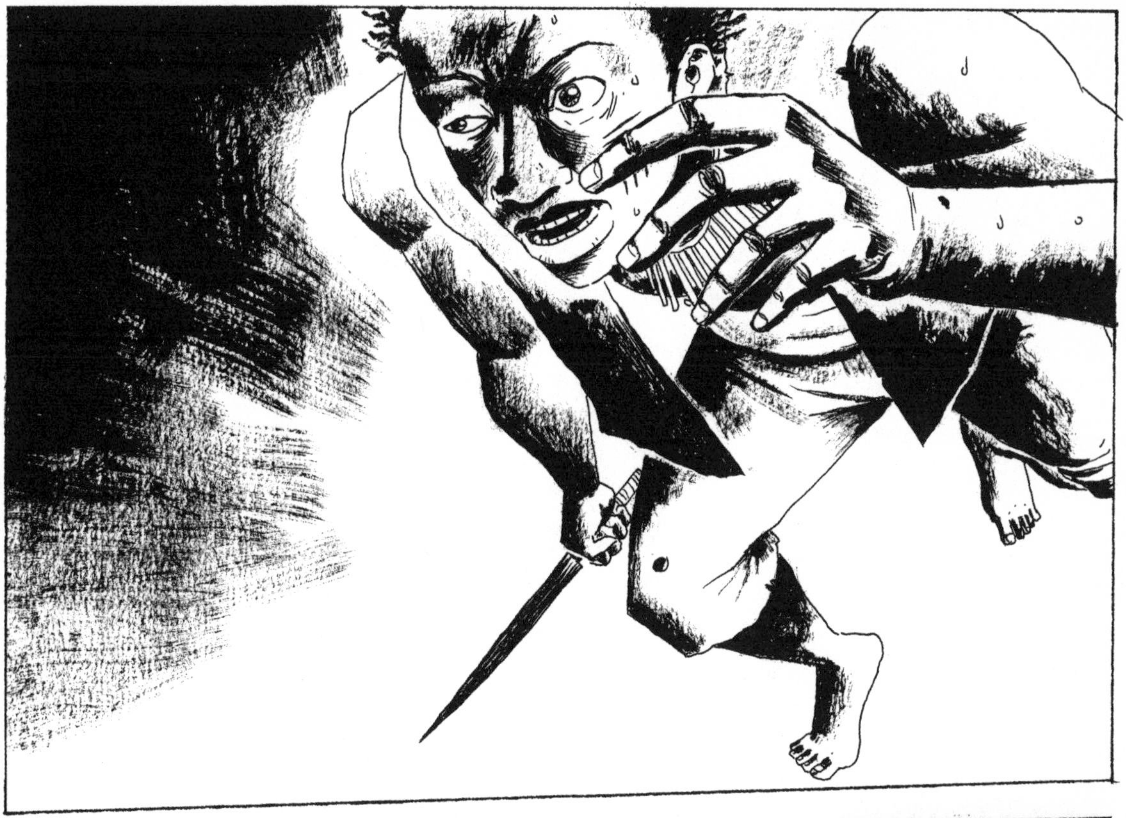

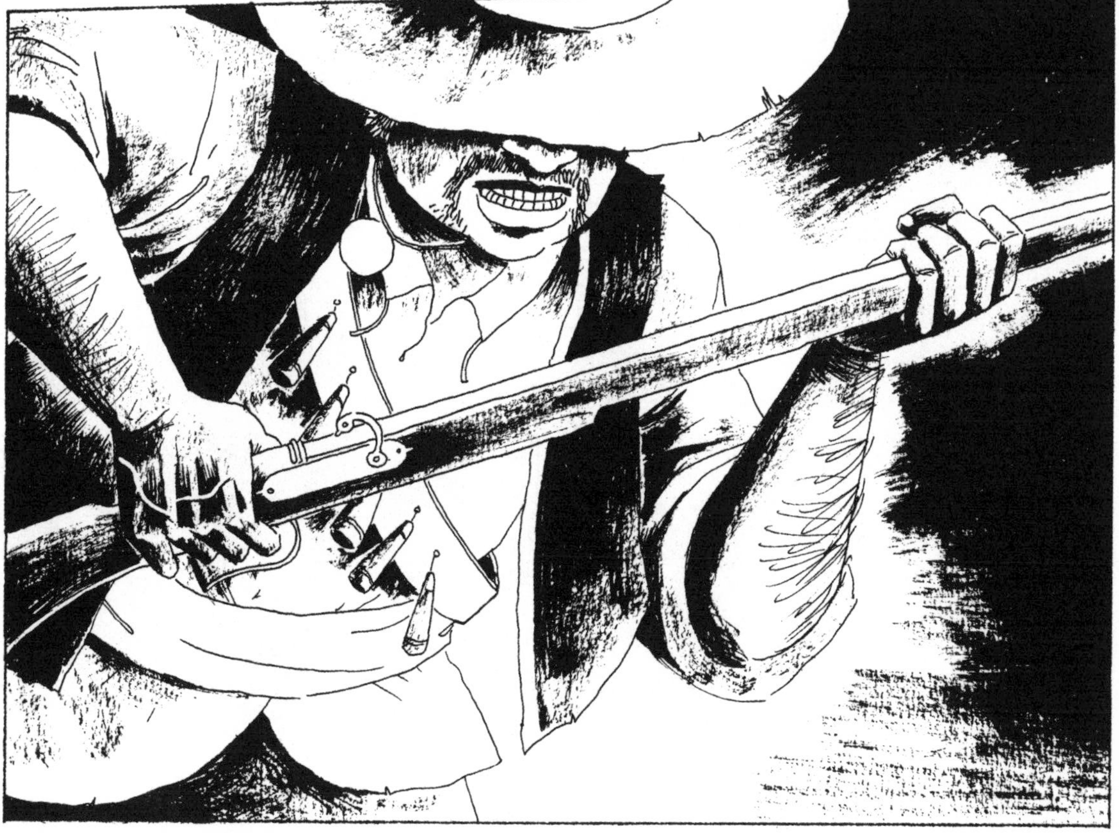

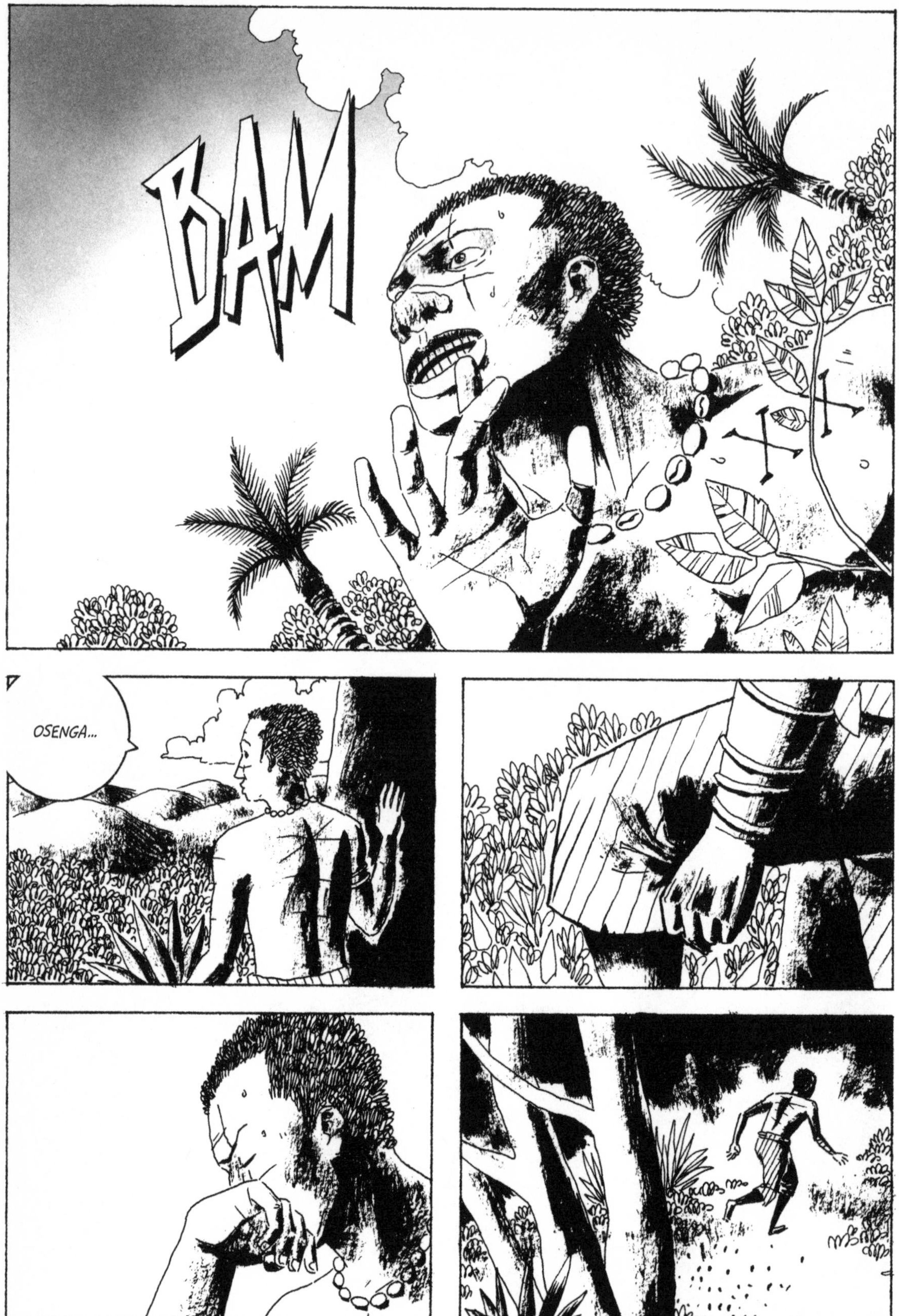
BAM
OSENGA...

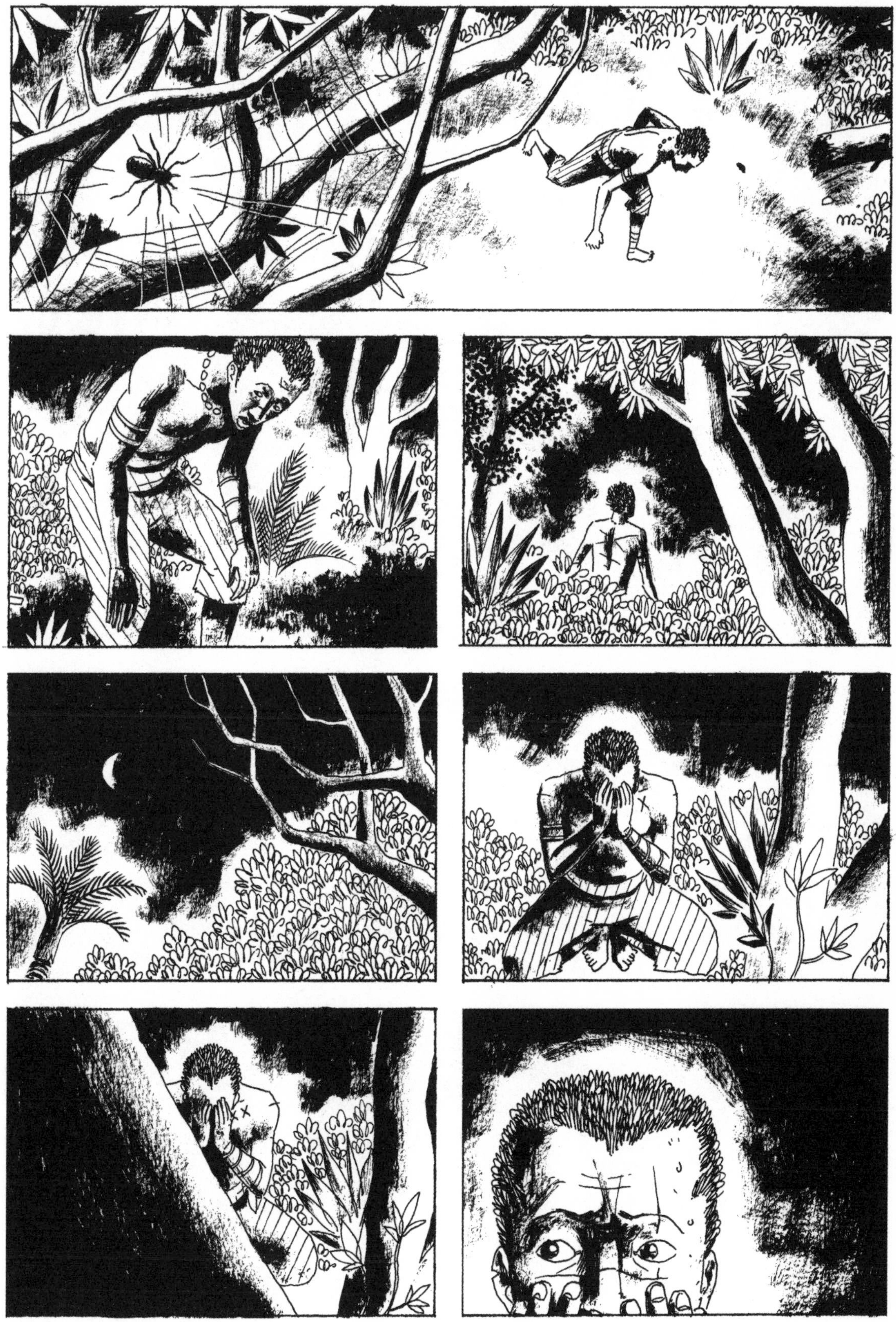

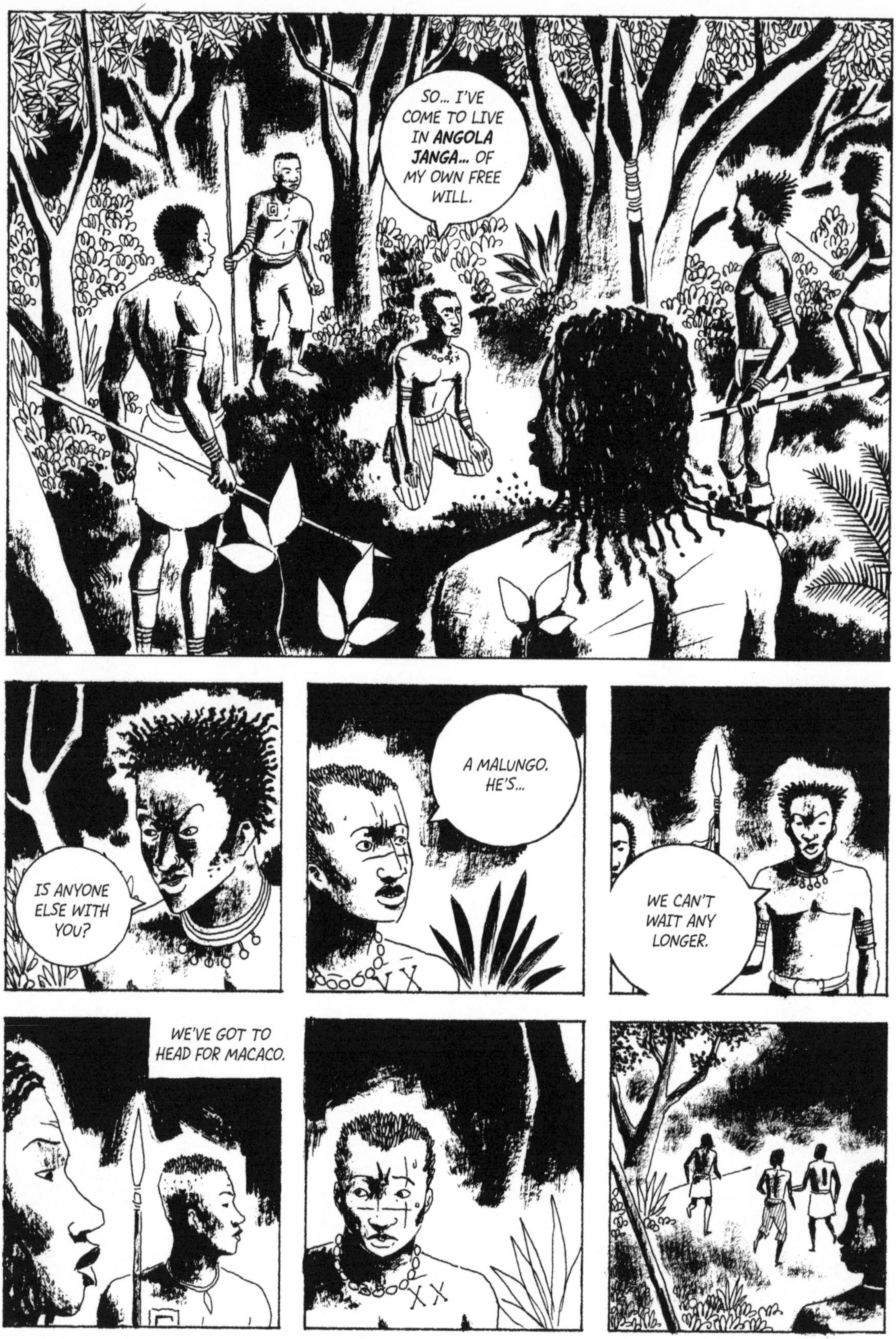
SO... I'VE COME TO LIVE IN ANGOLA JANGA... OF MY OWN FREE WILL.
IS ANYONE ELSE WITH YOU?
A MALUNGO. HE'S...
WE CAN'T WAIT ANY LONGER.
WE'VE GOT TO HEAD FOR MACACO.

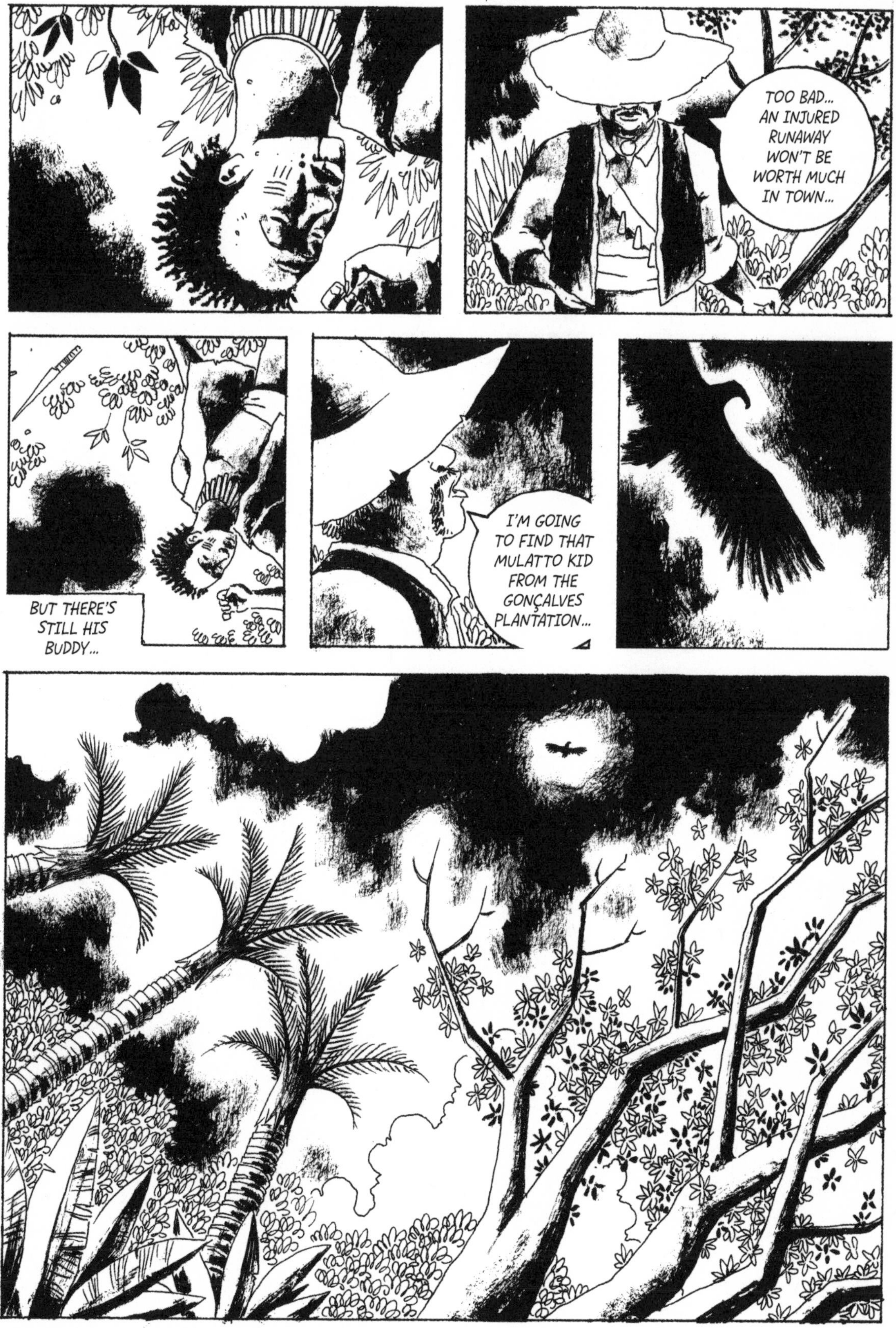
TOO BAD... AN INJURED RUNAWAY WON'T BE WORTH MUCH IN TOWN...
BUT THERE'S STILL HIS BUDDY...
I'M GOING TO FIND THAT MULATTO KID FROM THE GONÇALVES PLANTATION...

BIRTH

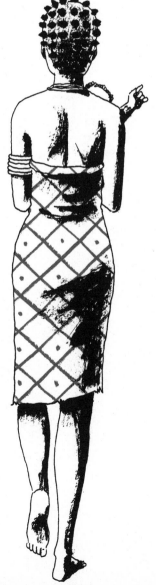

Palmares is flanked by incredibly fertile fields that drink from the São Francisco River, abundant with livestock and crops and full of corrals that have today been emptied by the repeated incursions of blacks who, facing no military opposition, attack, pillage, and lay waste to the entire region, which is the finest in Brazil. Just as they did to the corrals of Francisco Gomes de Abreu, Dona Francisca de Tal, and many other residents of those sertões. . . .

This Palmares where the blacks go has a place, known as Barriga Hill, where at one point fortifications made of stakes and trenches were built to improve the defenses of the large population that there enjoys every convenience and comfort for their sustenance, as the river gives them fish, the forests game, the tree trunks honey, and the palms fronds with which they cover their houses and also use the fibers to make clothing, besides the salt, oil, and wine that human ingenuity has learned to extract from those immensely abundant and fertile trees.

--*Presumed to have been written by João Fernandes Vieira, 1677*

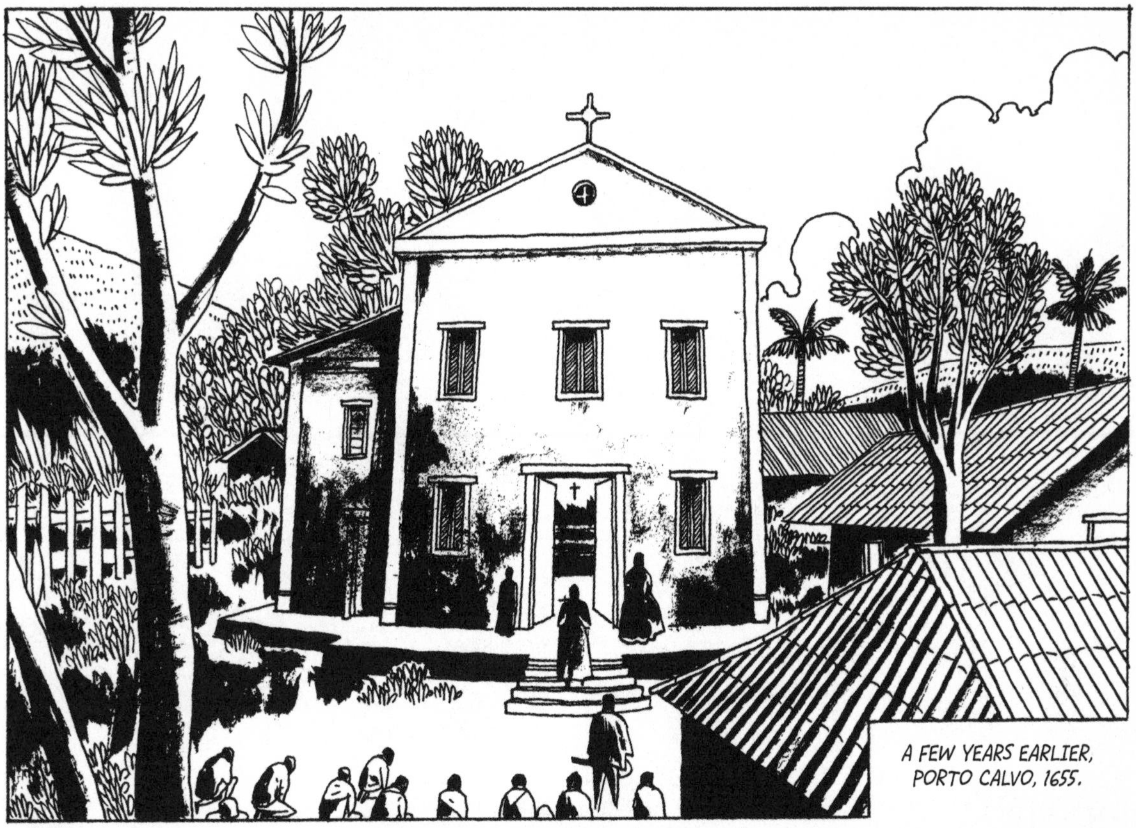
A FEW YEARS EARLIER,
PORTO CALVO, 1655.

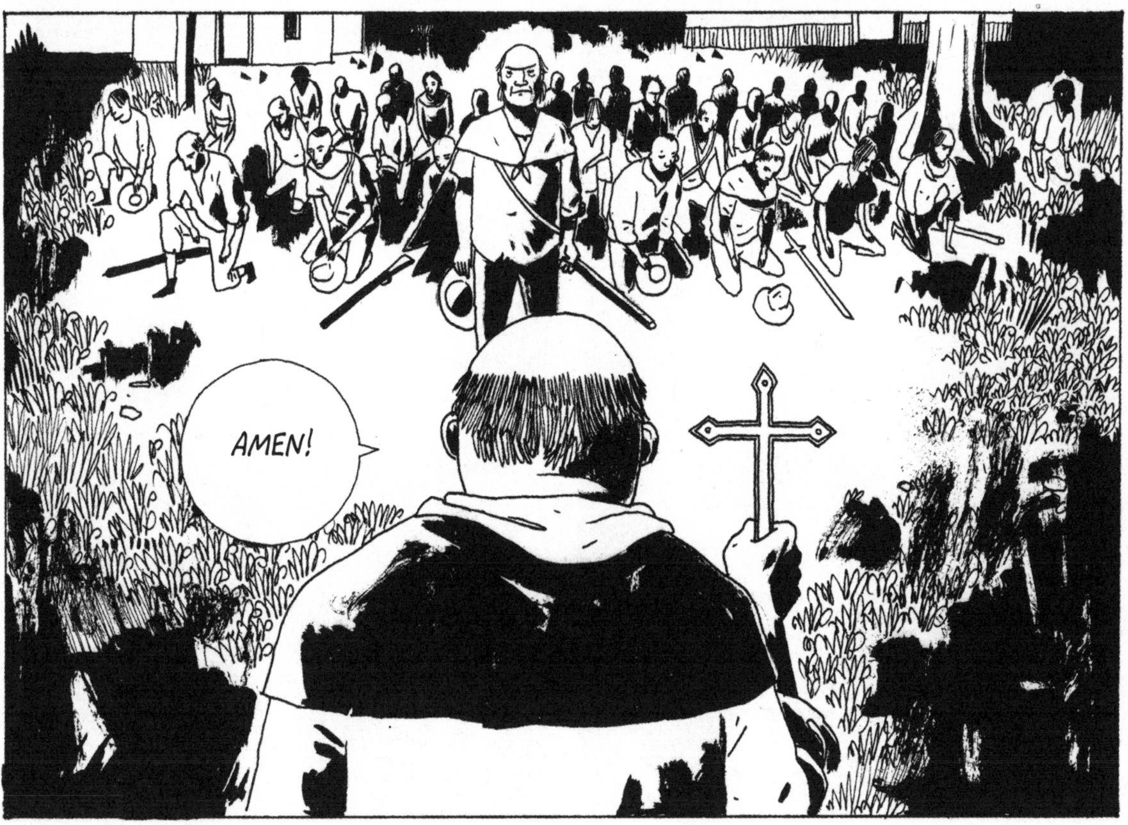
AMEN!

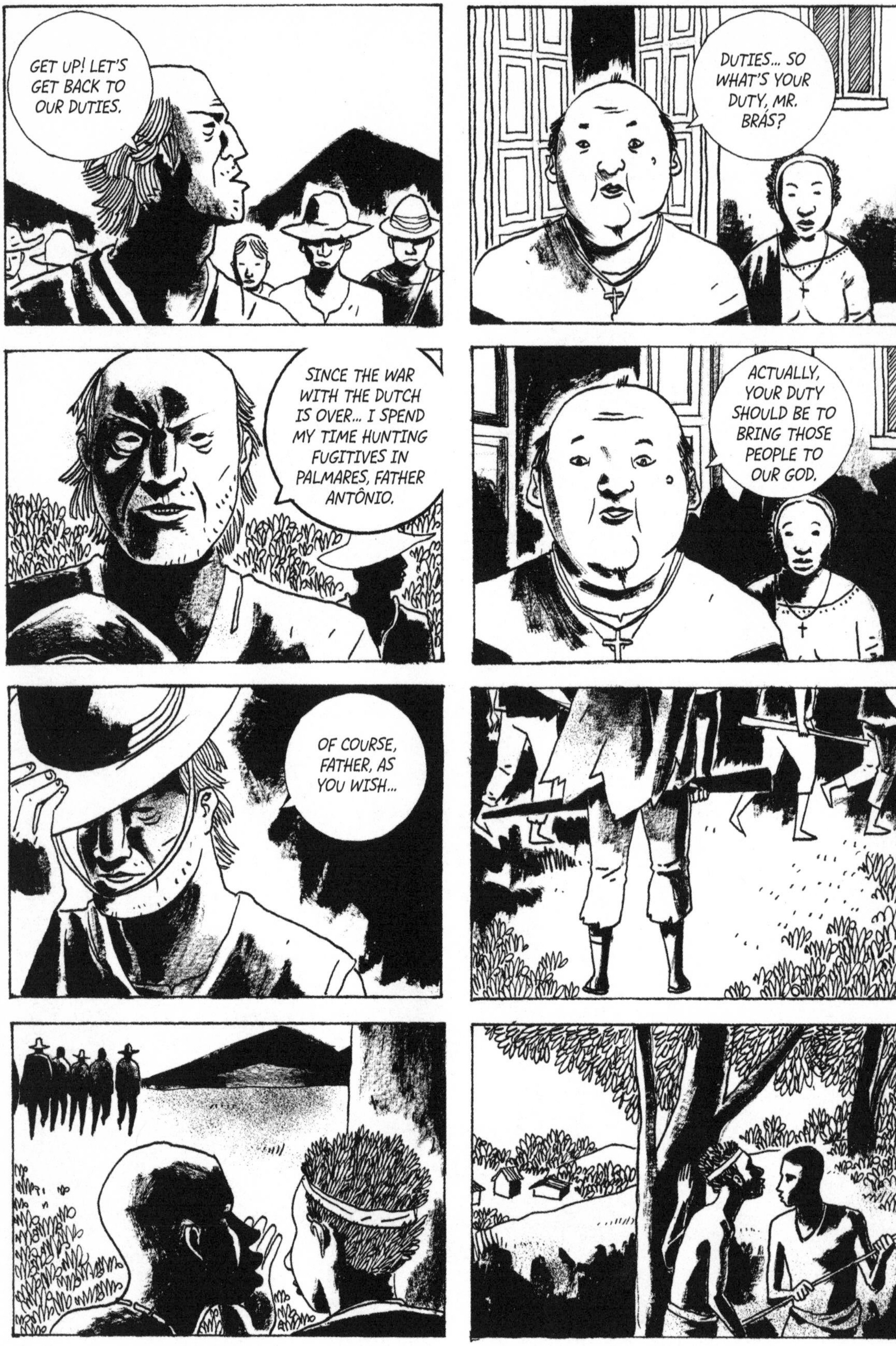
GET UP! LET'S GET BACK TO OUR DUTIES.
DUTIES... SO WHAT'S YOUR DUTY, MR. BRÁS?
SINCE THE WAR WITH THE DUTCH IS OVER... I SPEND MY TIME HUNTING FUGITIVES IN PALMARES, FATHER ANTÔNIO.
ACTUALLY, YOUR DUTY SHOULD BE TO BRING THOSE PEOPLE TO OUR GOD.
OF COURSE, FATHER, AS YOU WISH...

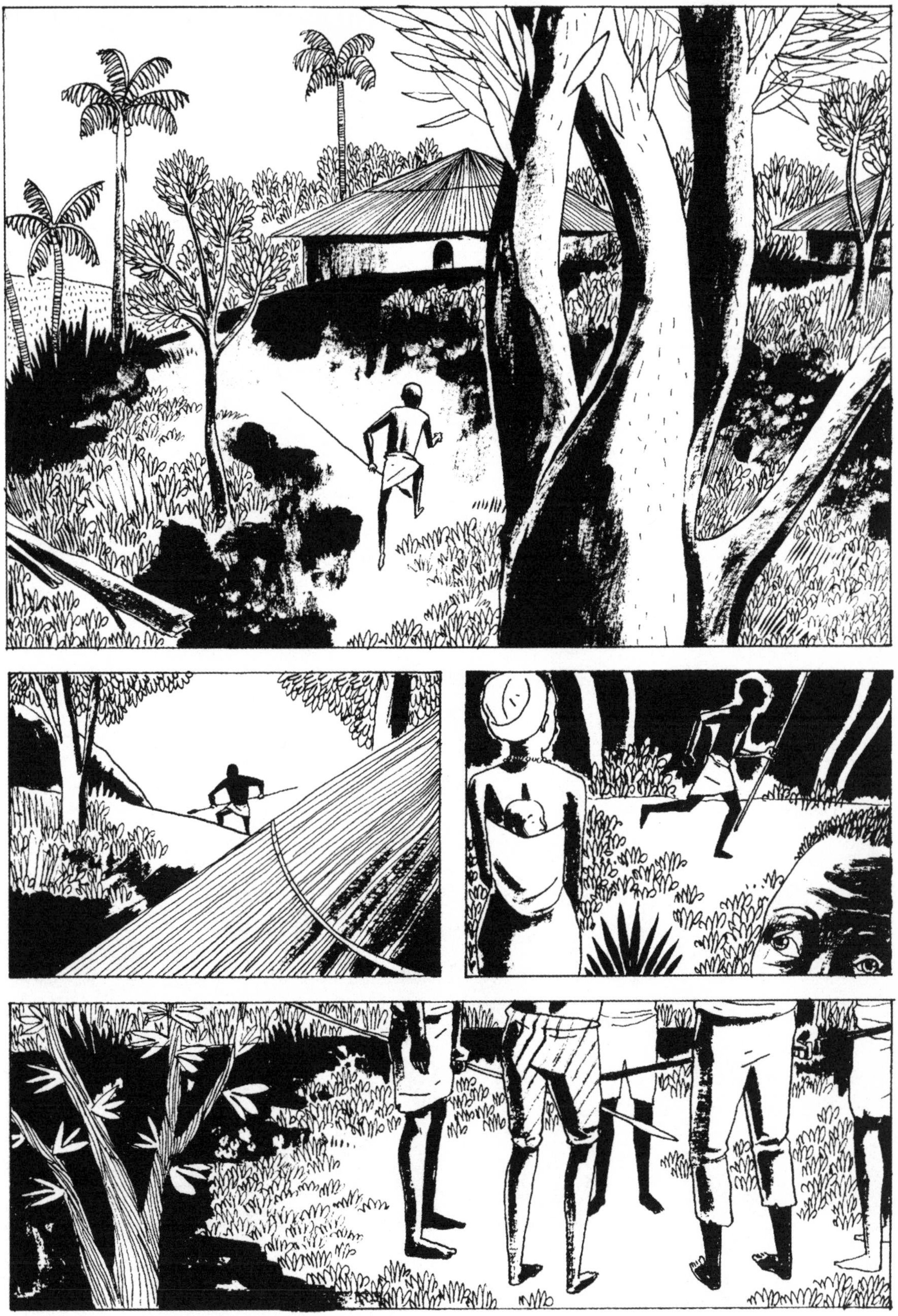

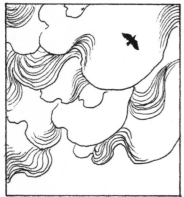

KATANGA, WE'LL WAIT FOR YOU IN MACACO.

TAKE GOOD CARE OF THEM, TATA.

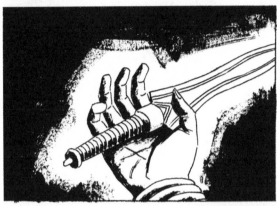

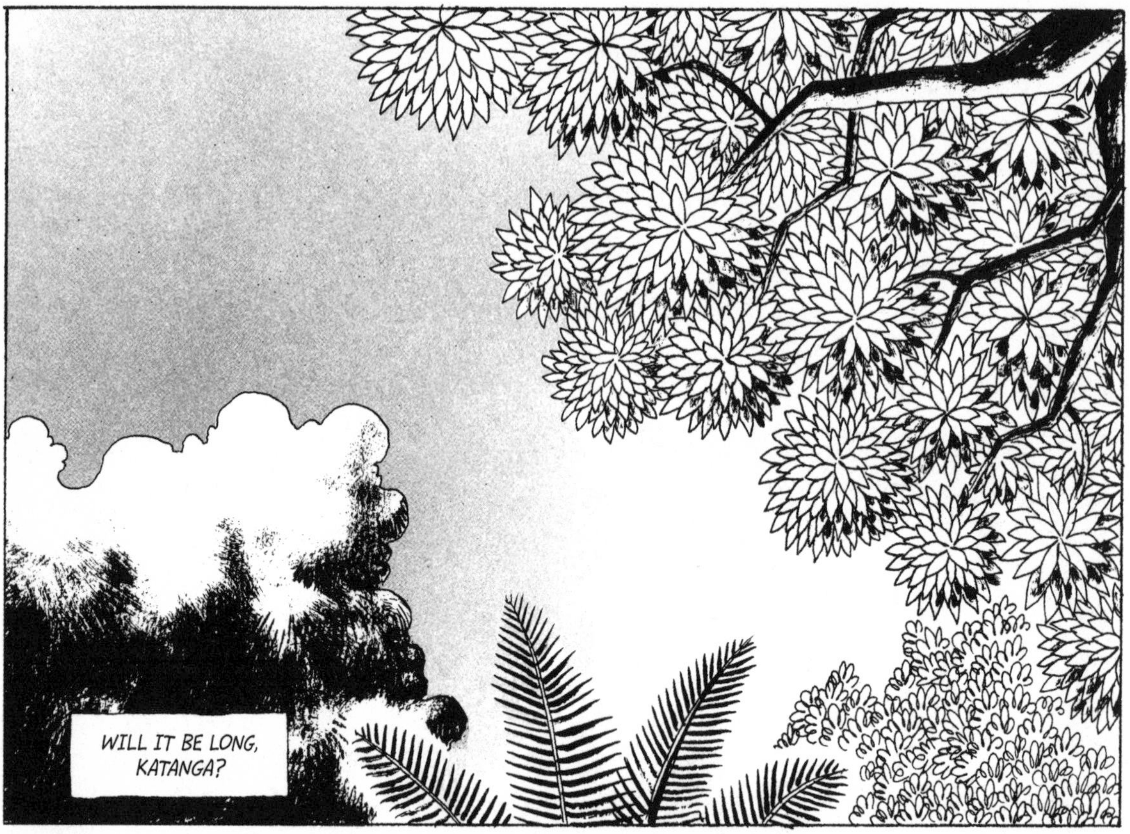
WILL IT BE LONG, KATANGA?

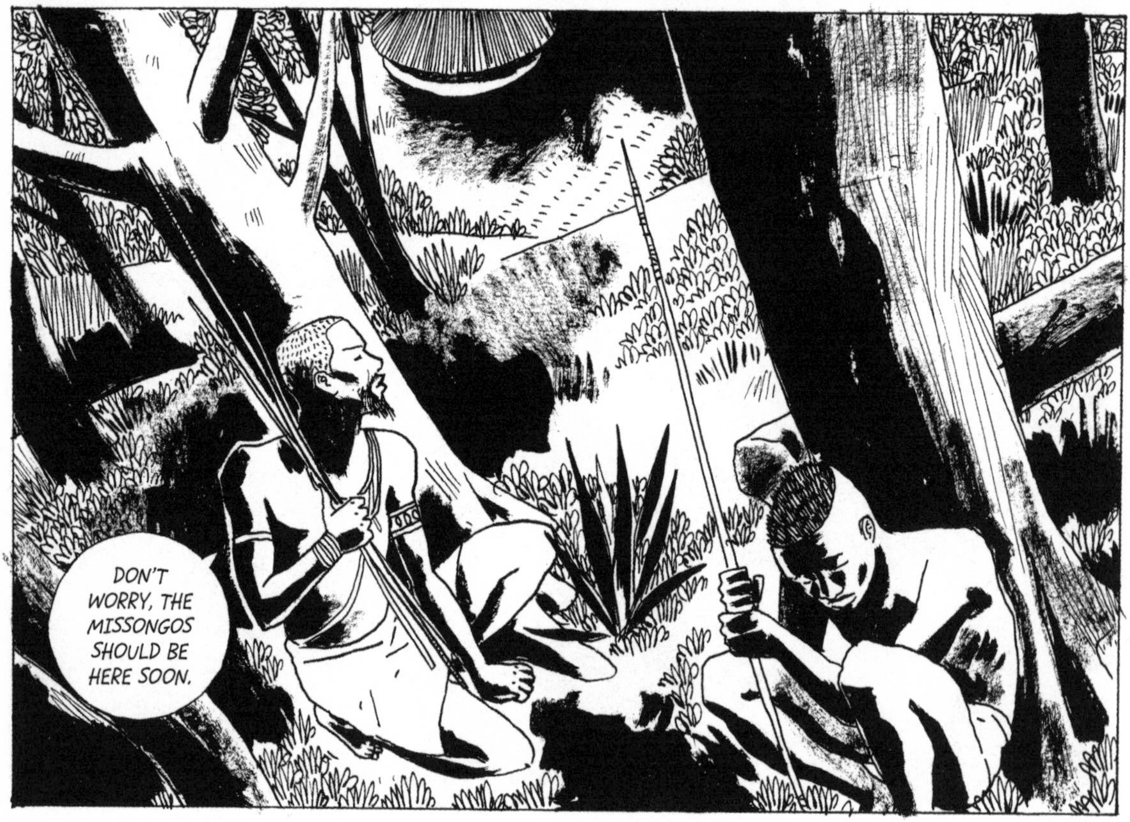
DON'T WORRY, THE MISSONGOS SHOULD BE HERE SOON.

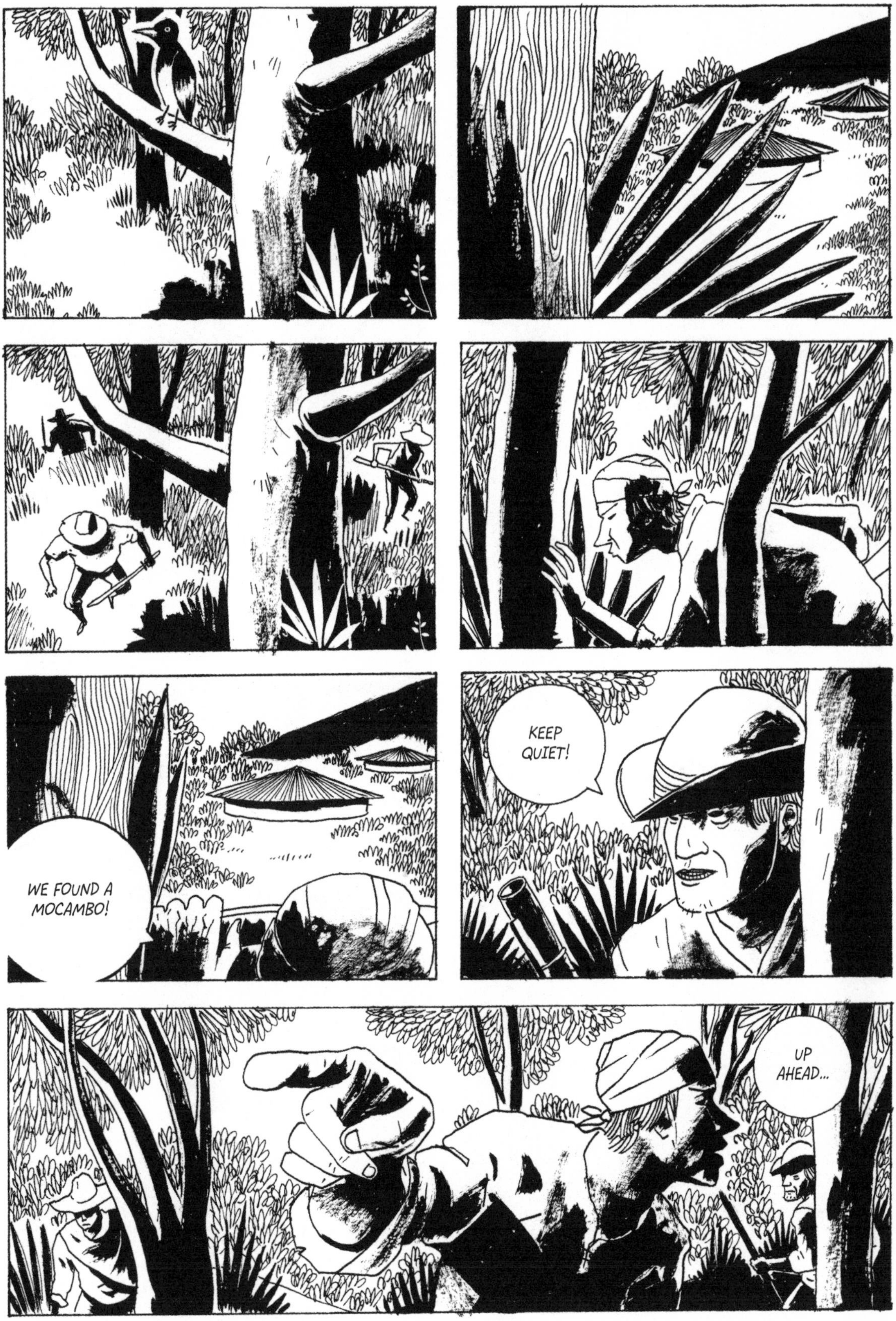
WE FOUND A MOCAMBO!
KEEP QUIET!
UP AHEAD...

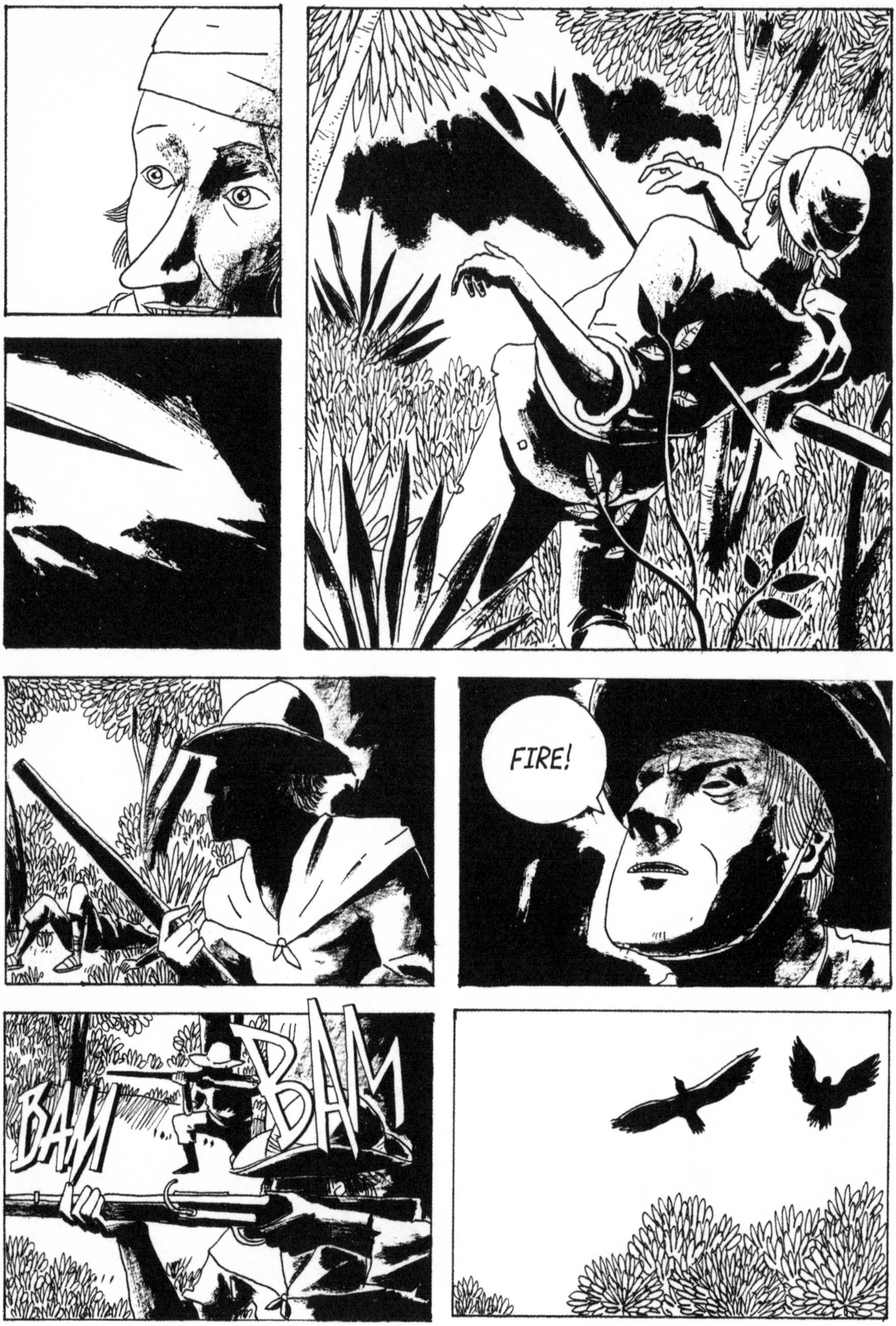
FIRE!
BAM
BAM

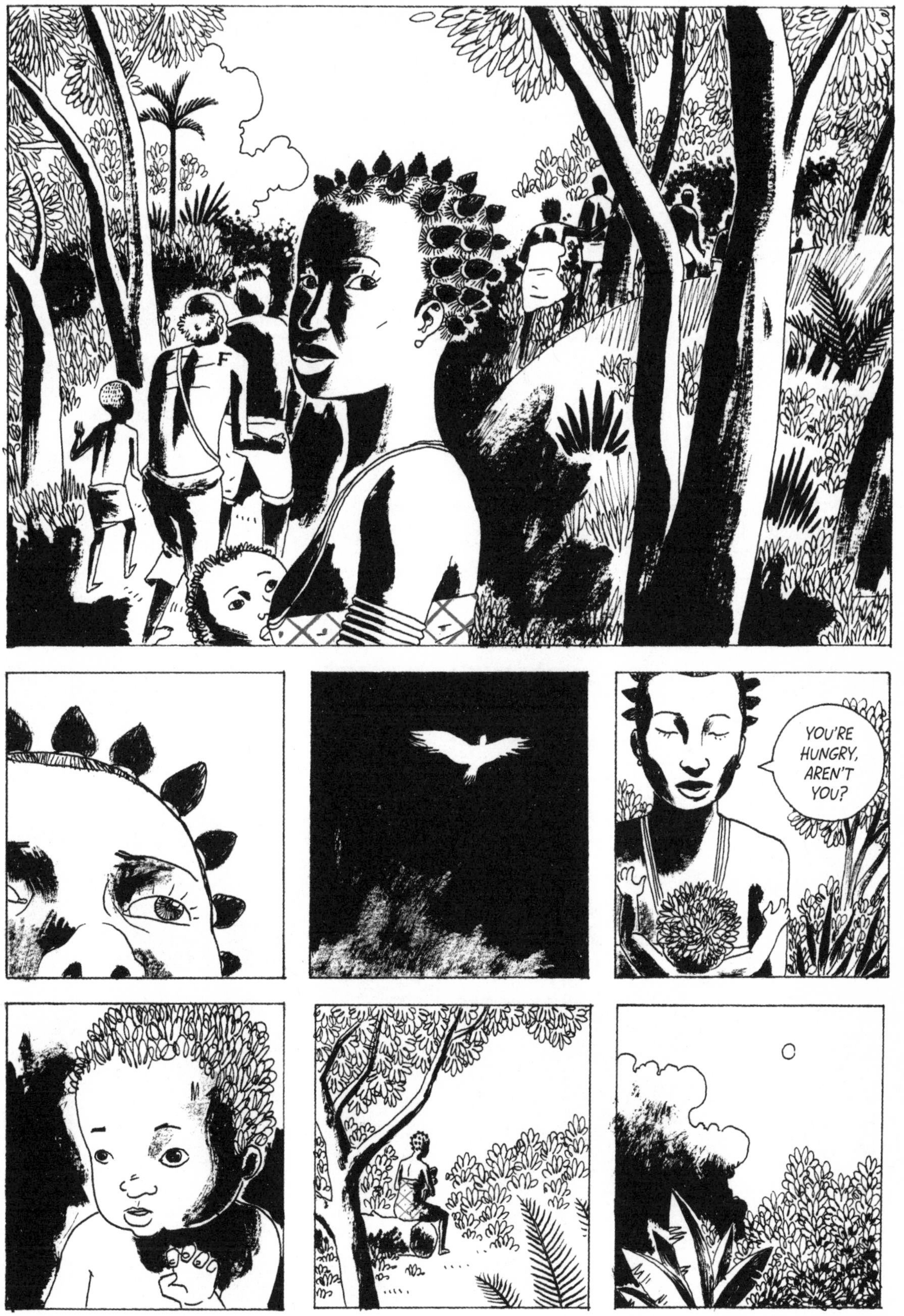
YOU'RE HUNGRY, AREN'T YOU?

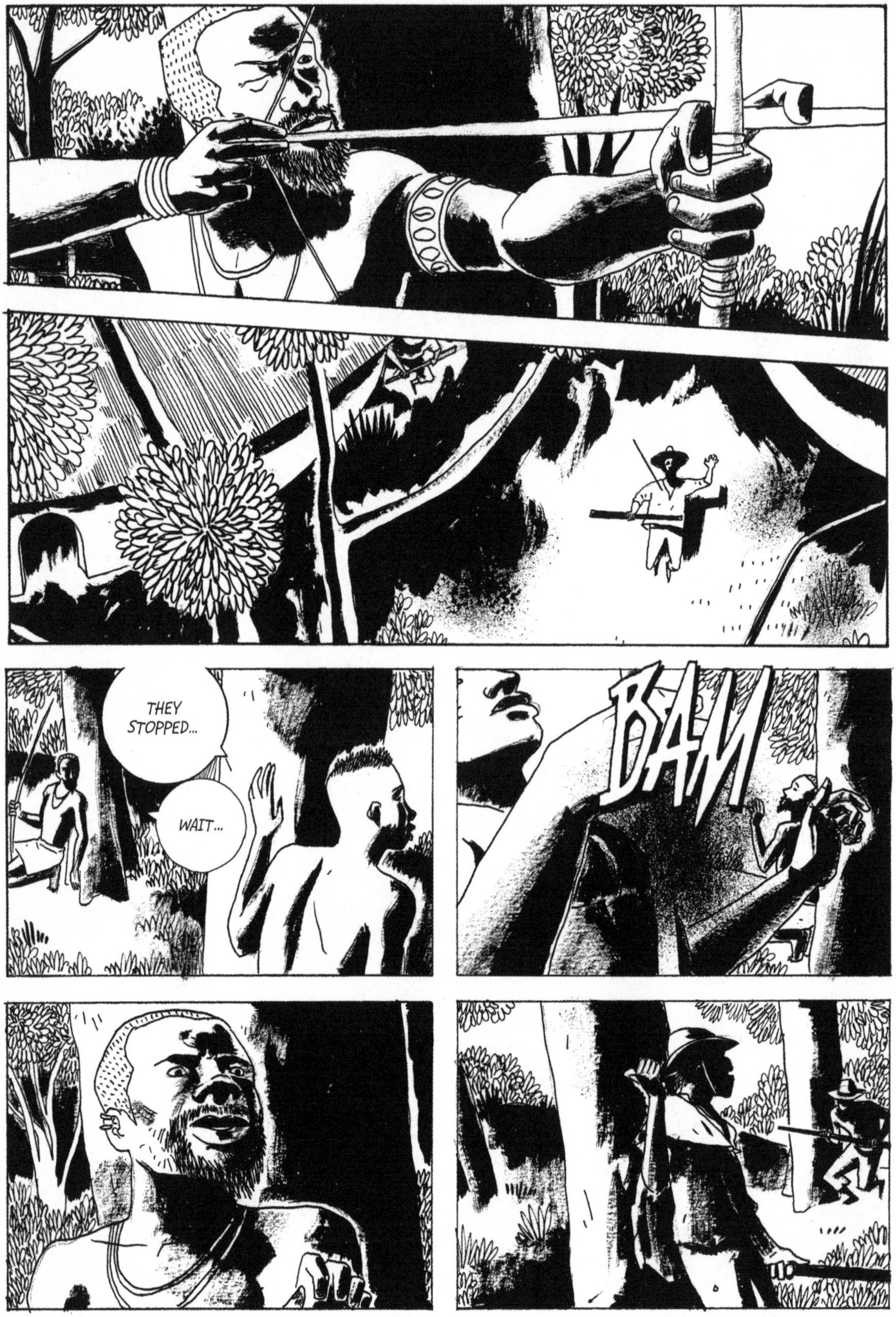
THEY STOPPED...
WAIT...
BAM

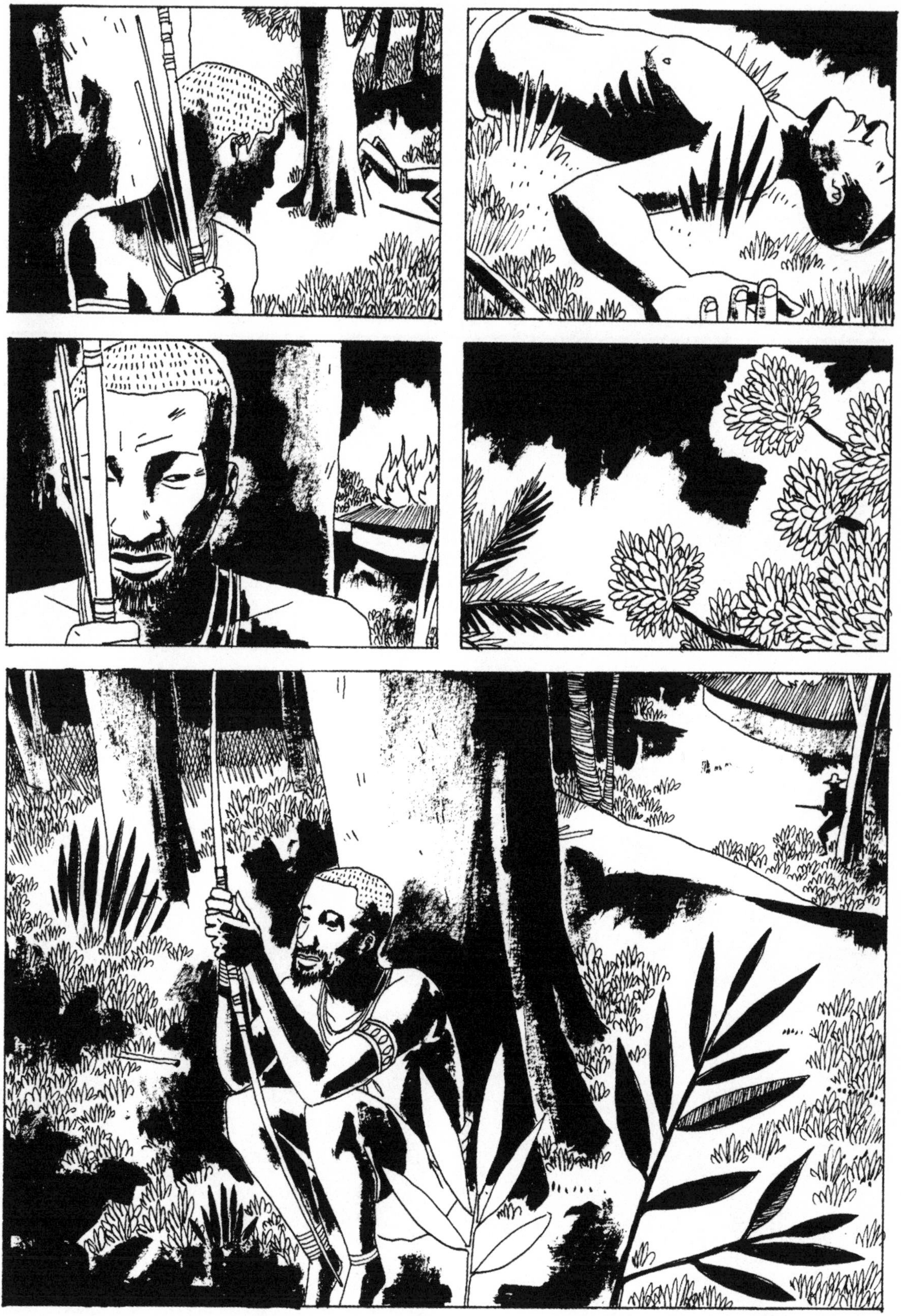

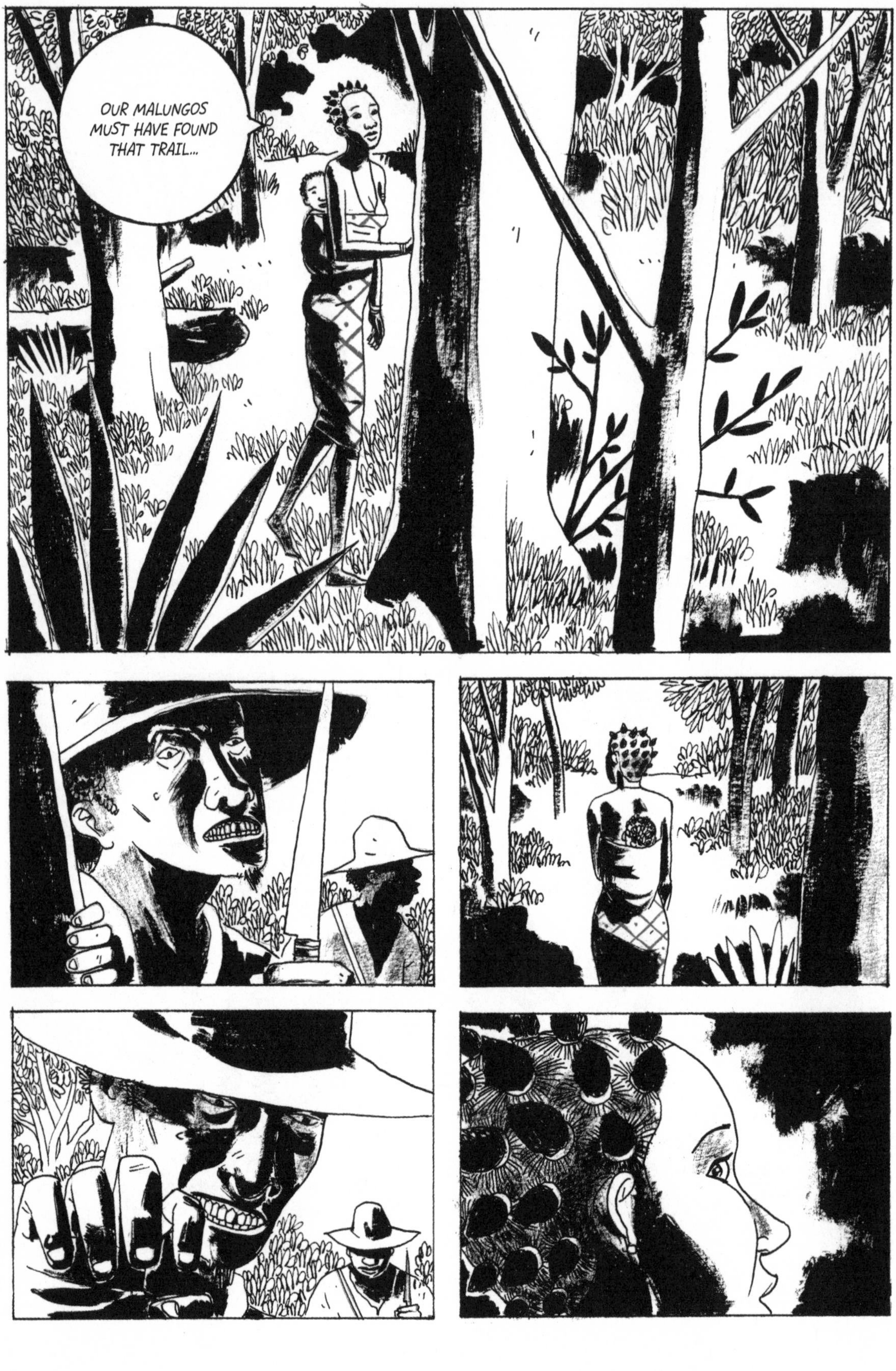
OUR MALUNGOS MUST HAVE FOUND THAT TRAIL...

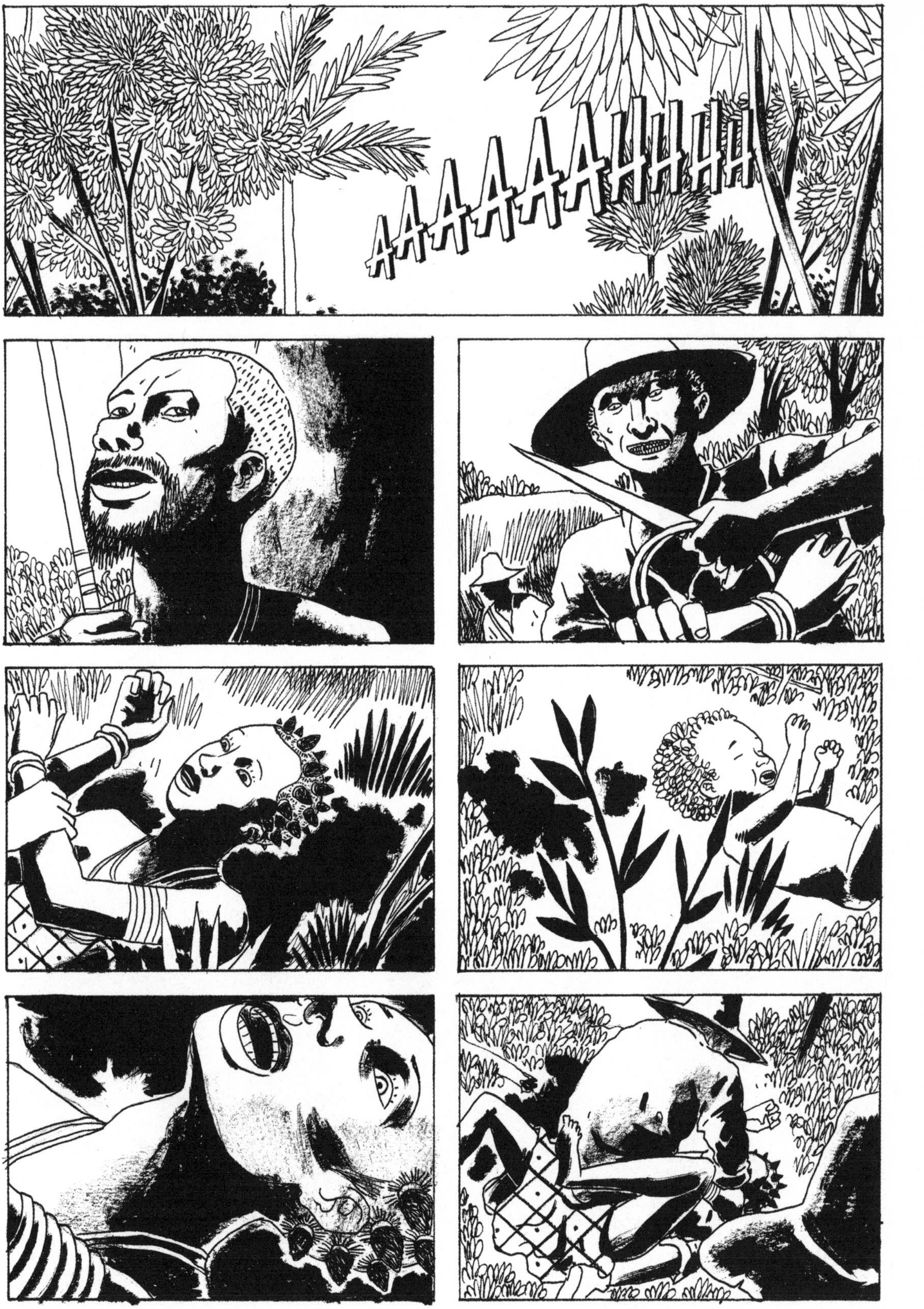
AAAAAAAHHHH

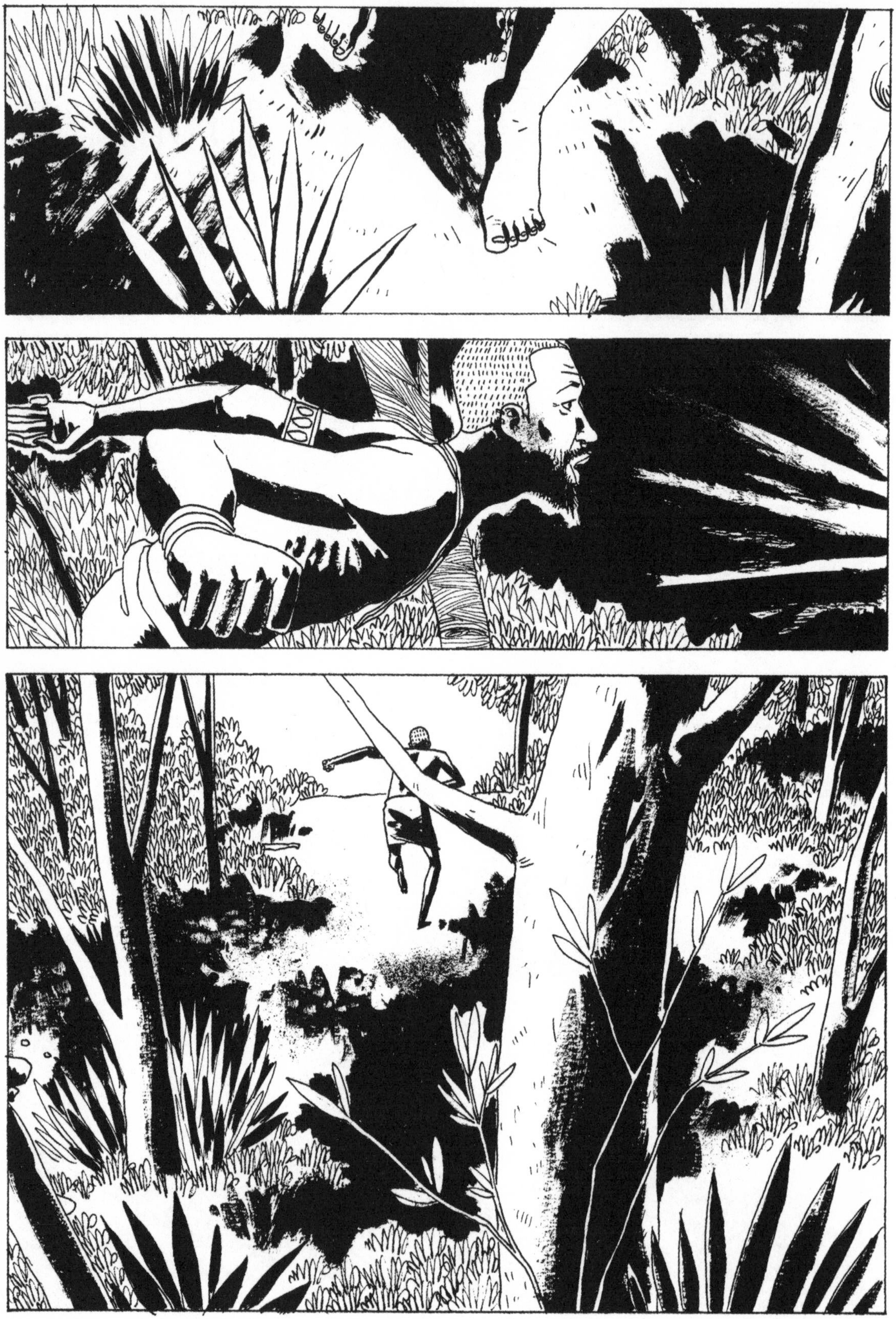

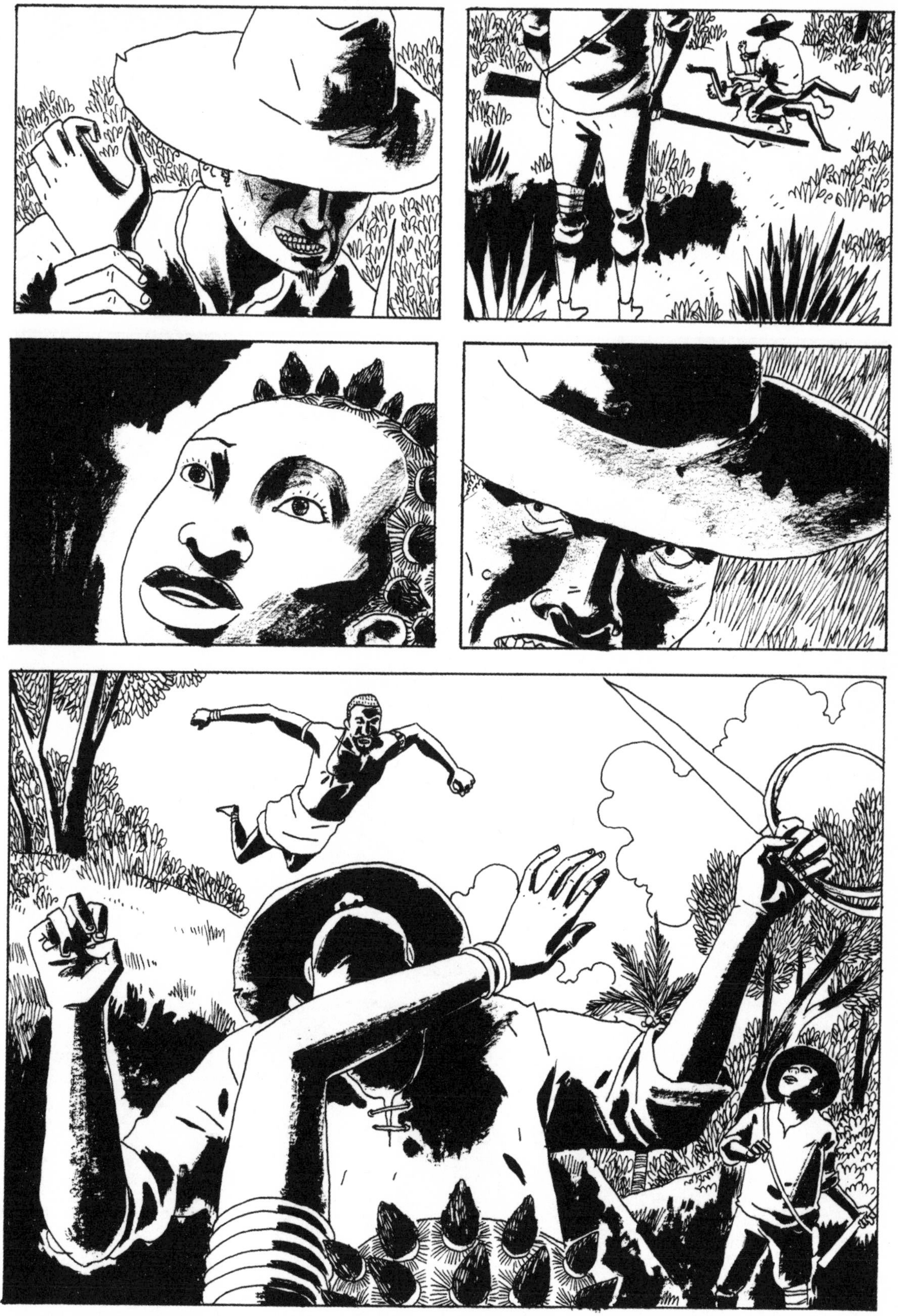

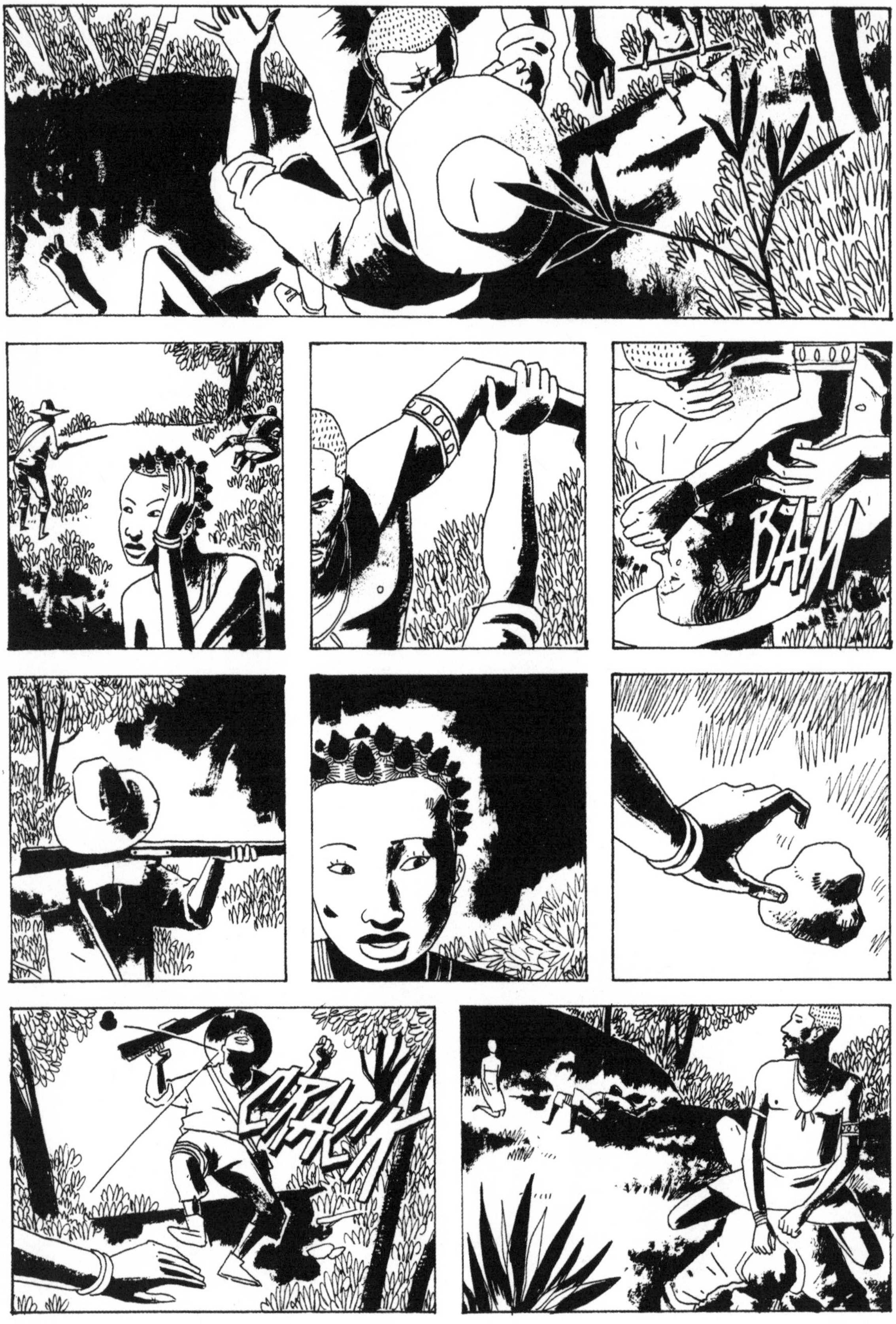
BAM
CRACK

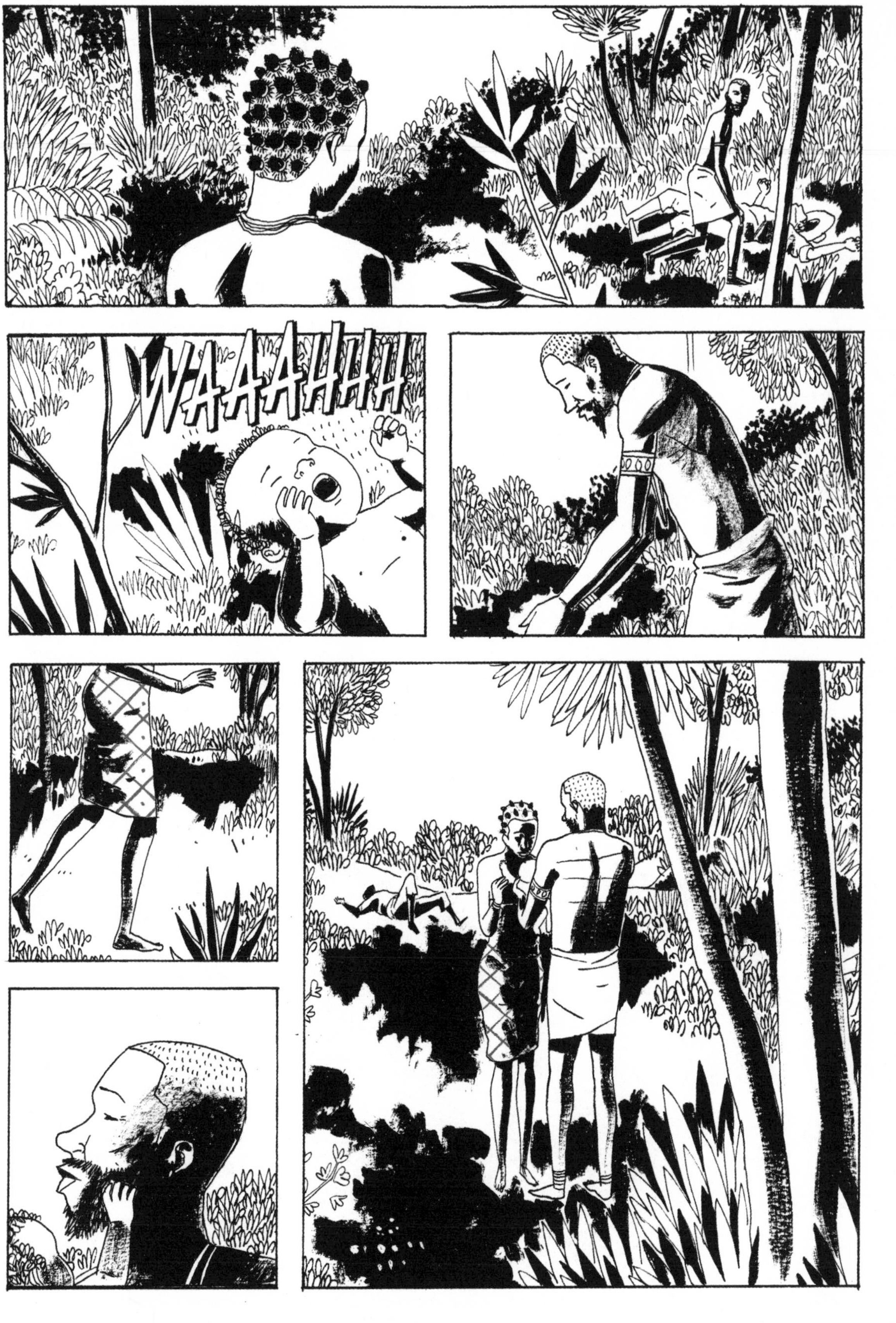
WAAAHHH

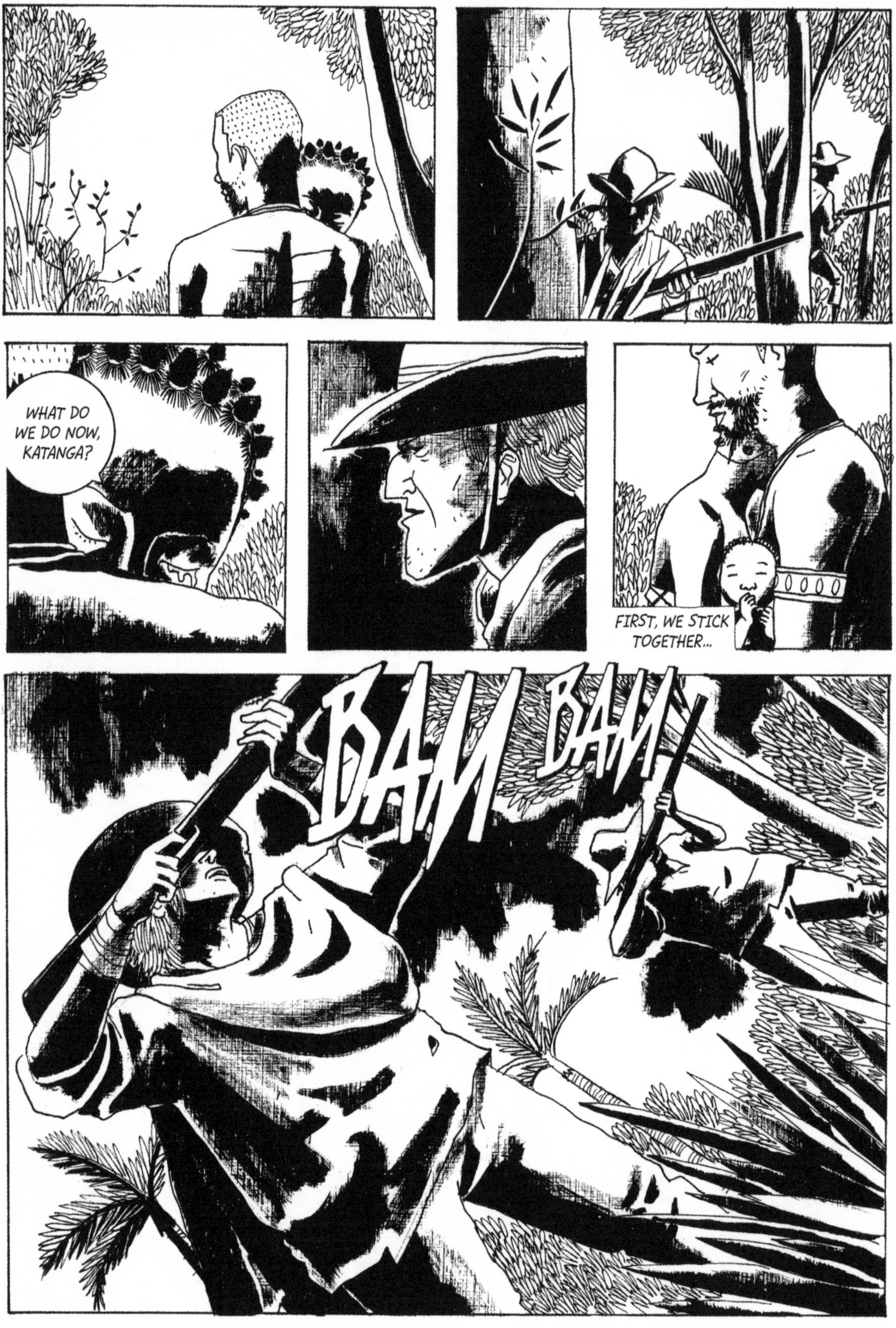
WHAT DO WE DO NOW, KATANGA?
FIRST, WE STICK TOGETHER...
BAM BAM

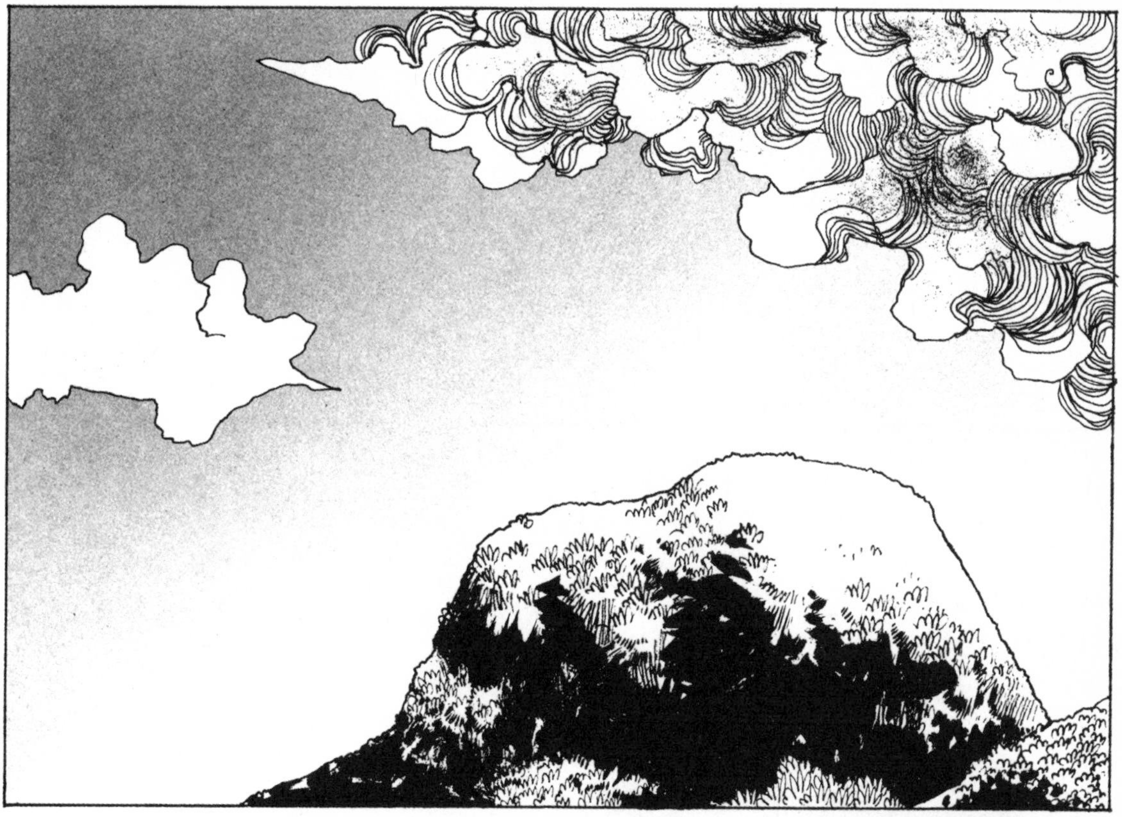

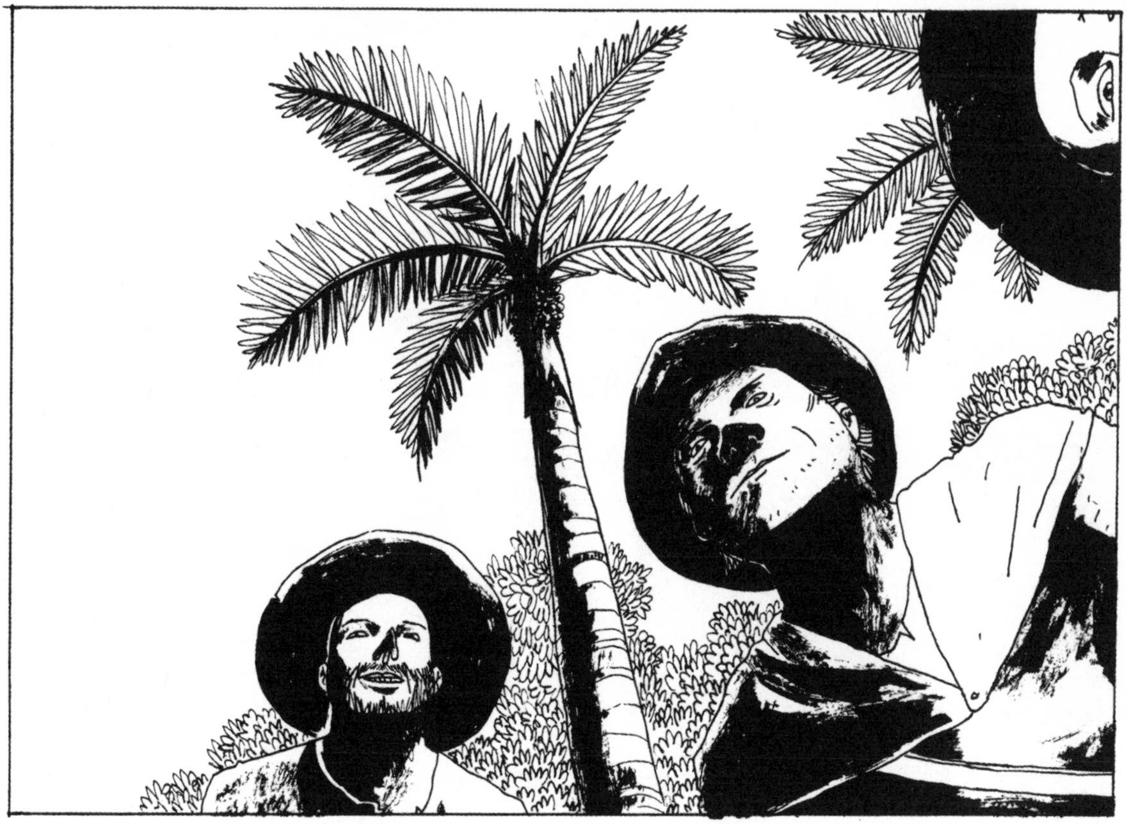

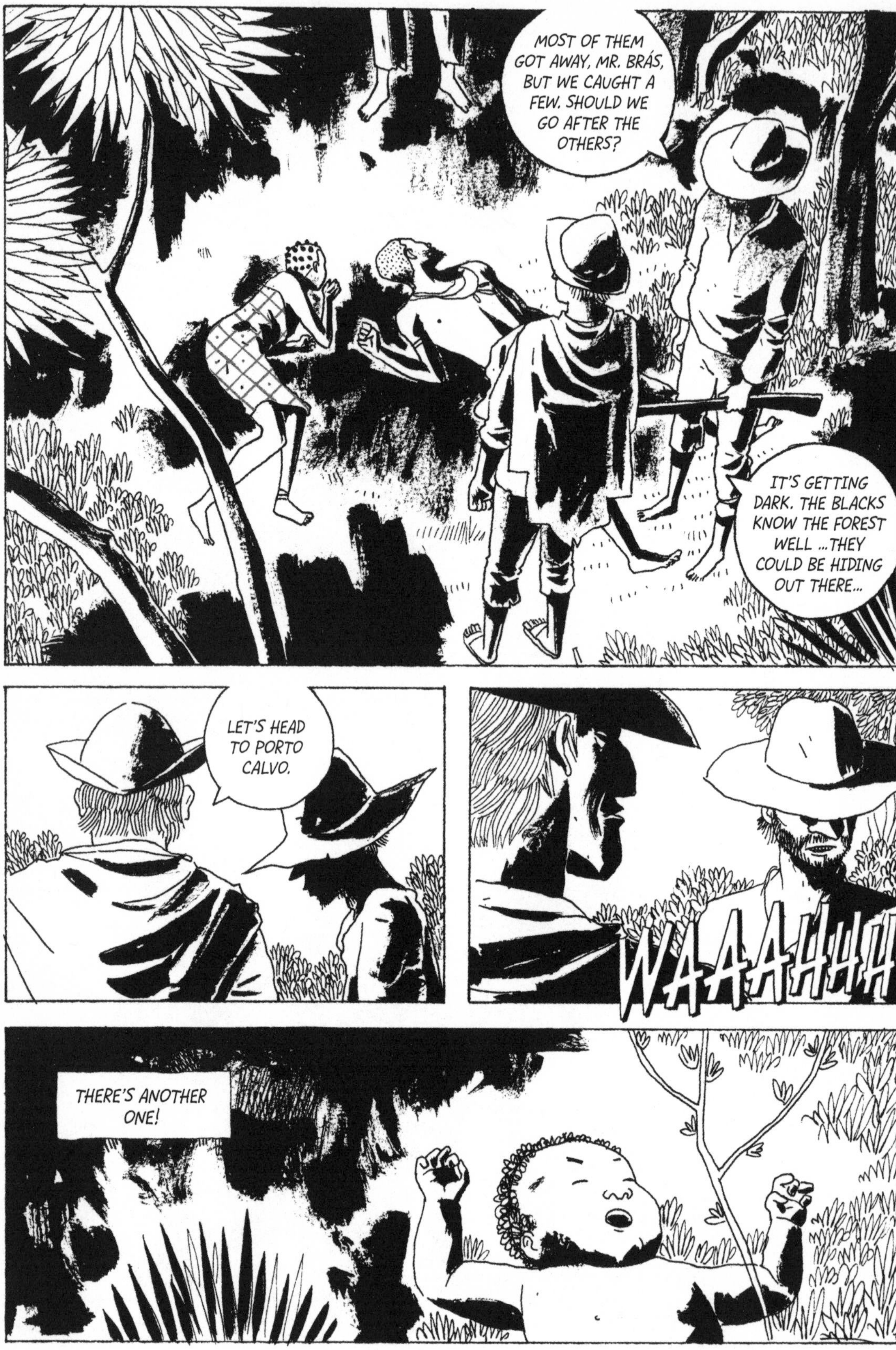
MOST OF THEM GOT AWAY, MR. BRÁS, BUT WE CAUGHT A FEW. SHOULD WE GO AFTER THE OTHERS?
IT'S GETTING DARK. THE BLACKS KNOW THE FOREST WELL ...THEY COULD BE HIDING OUT THERE...
LET'S HEAD TO PORTO CALVO.
WAAAHHH
THERE'S ANOTHER ONE!

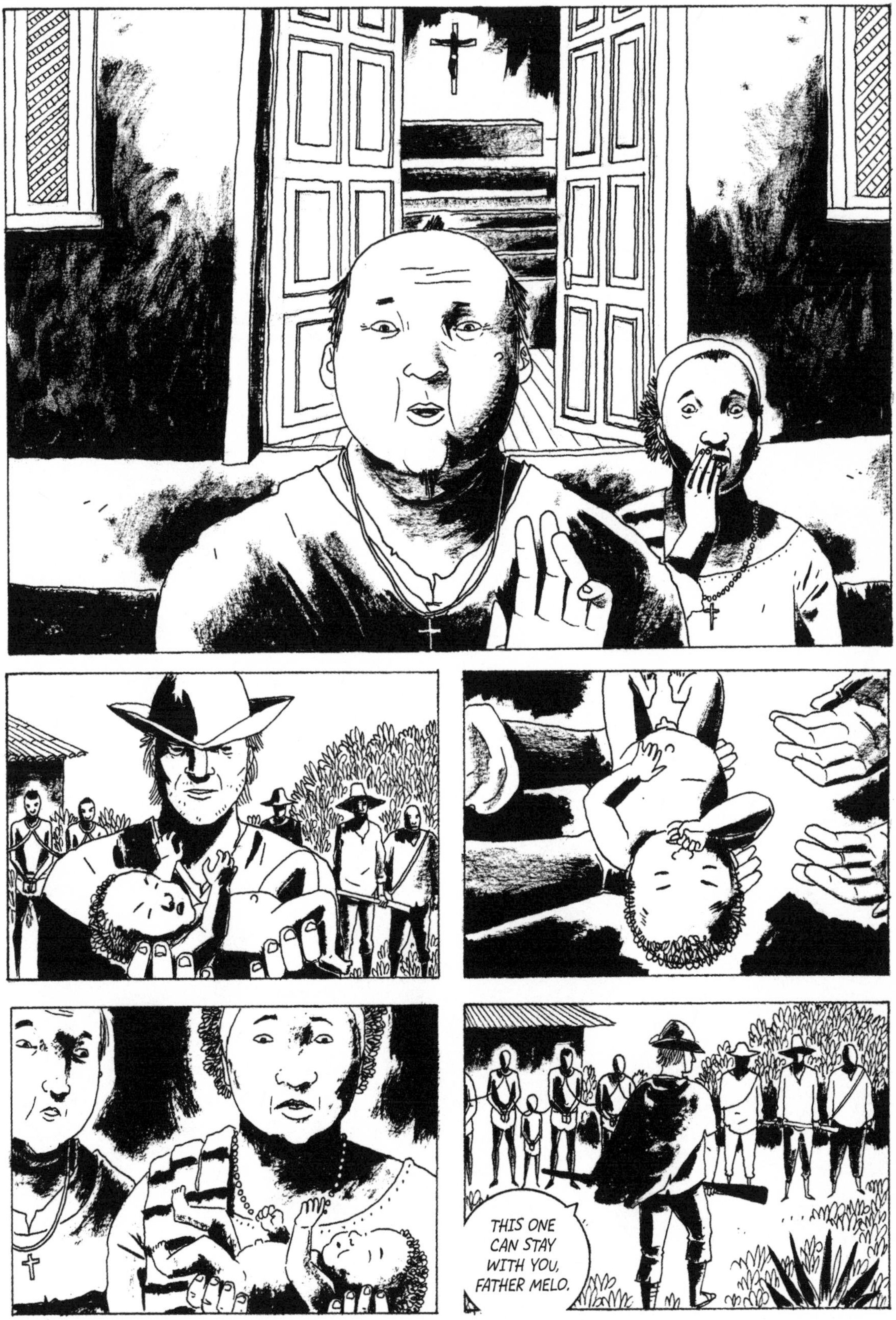
THIS ONE CAN STAY WITH YOU, FATHER MELO.

WE LOST THE MOTHER AND THE BABY, TATA...

LOOK AROUND...

YOU'VE HELPED GET MOST OF THEM HERE SAFE.

...SOON WE'LL REACH GANGA ZUMBA'S MOCAMBO, MACACO...

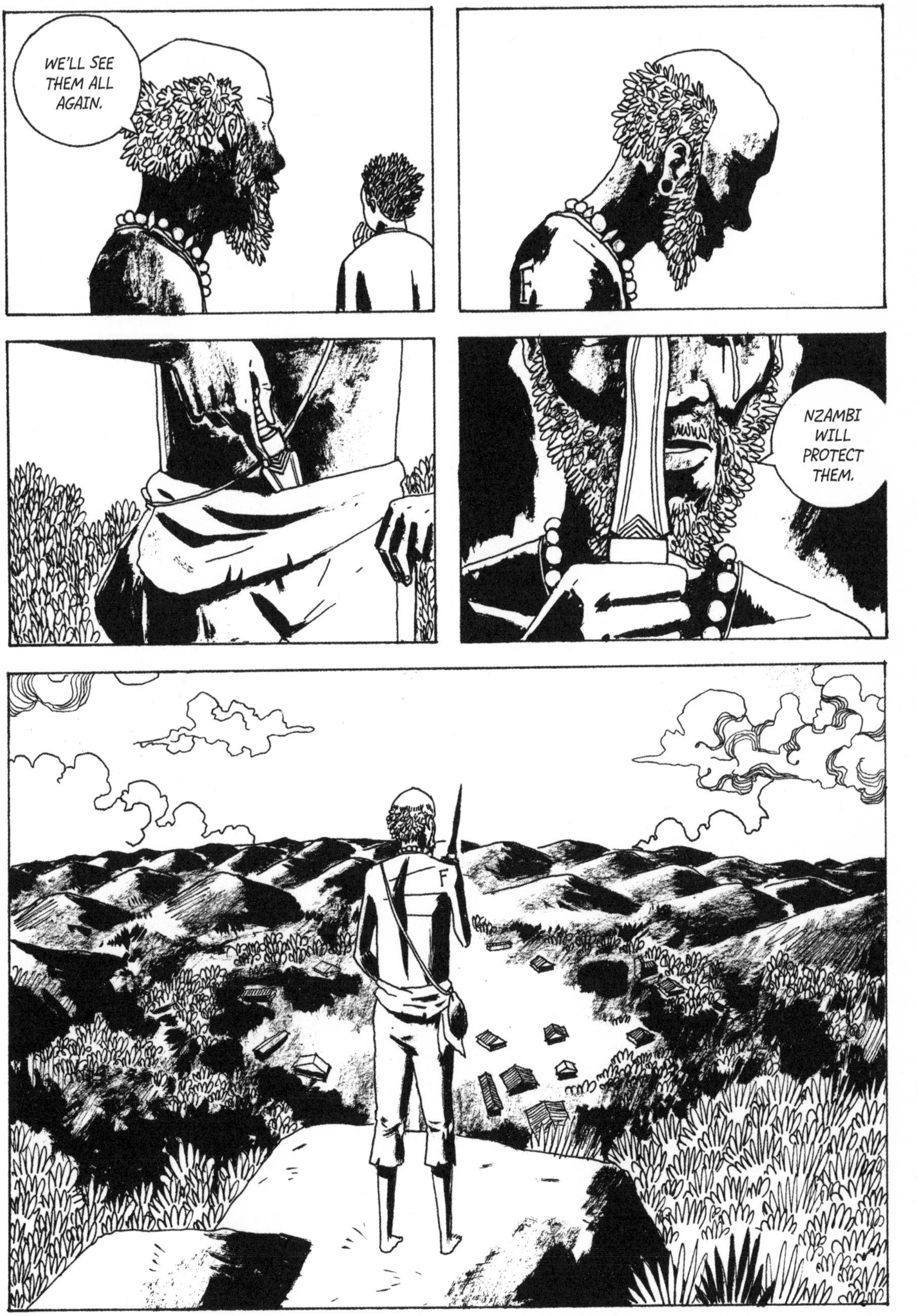
WE'LL SEE THEM ALL AGAIN.
NZAMBI WILL PROTECT THEM.

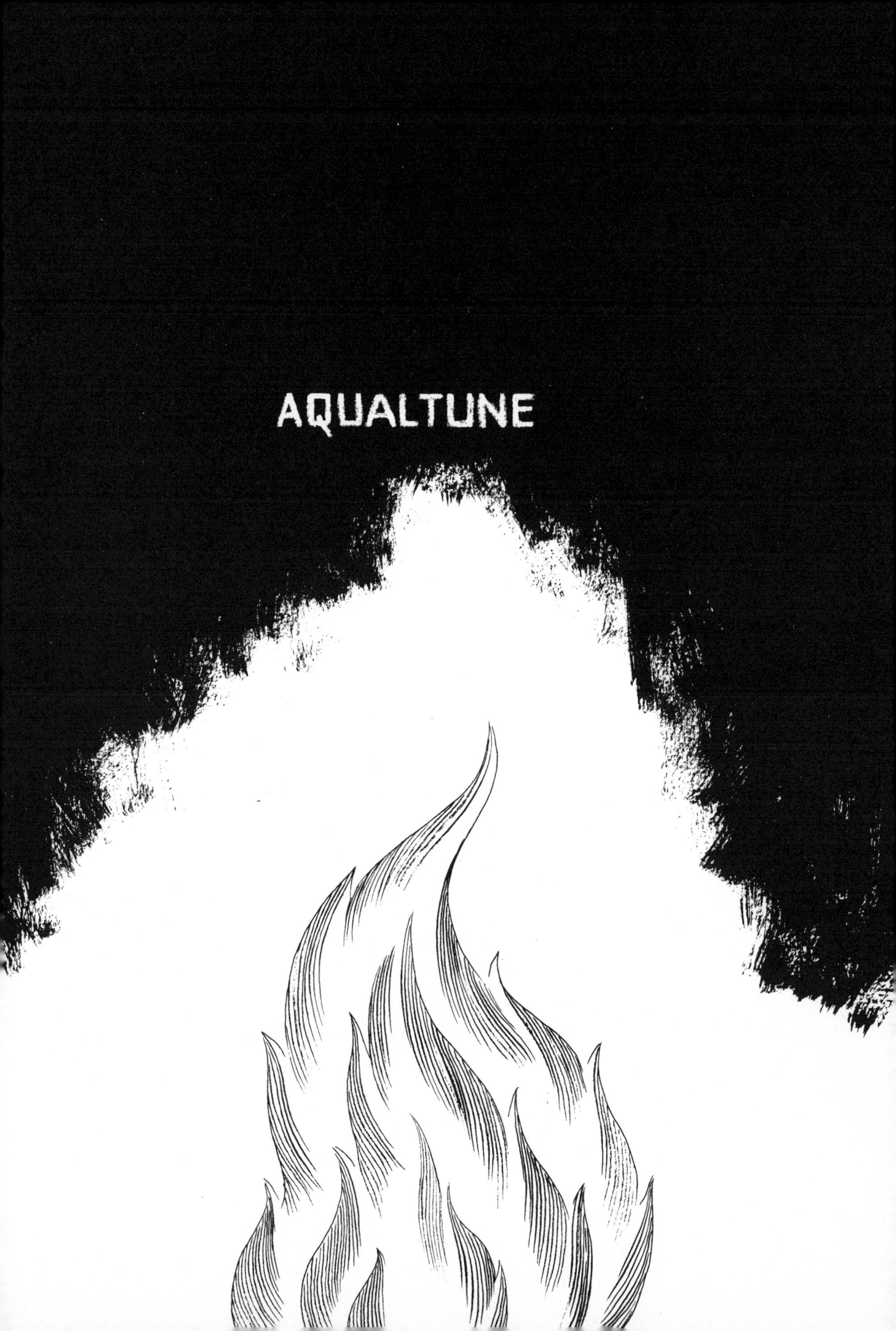
AQUALTUNE

Tremendous was the uproar caused by the sight of those barbarians. For they came in with their bows and arrows and a firearm, their natural parts covered with cloth, others with skins, some with their beards braided, others with beards grown full, others clean-shaven, strong and valiant to a man. . . . They all prostrated themselves at the feet of Dom Pedro de Almeida, and they clapped their hands as a sign of subservience and in celebration of his victory. Then they asked for peace with the whites. . . . [T]hey all prostrated themselves at his feet, saying that they wanted no more war, that the King had sent them to petition for peace, that they'd come to submit to his desires; that they wished to have commerce with the settlers, and trade, and that they wanted to serve His Highness in whatever he commanded them, that they asked only for freedom for those born in Palmares, that they would hand over those who had escaped from our towns, that they would leave Palmares, that we should assign them a place where they could live at his command.

—*chronicle dated June 18, 1678*

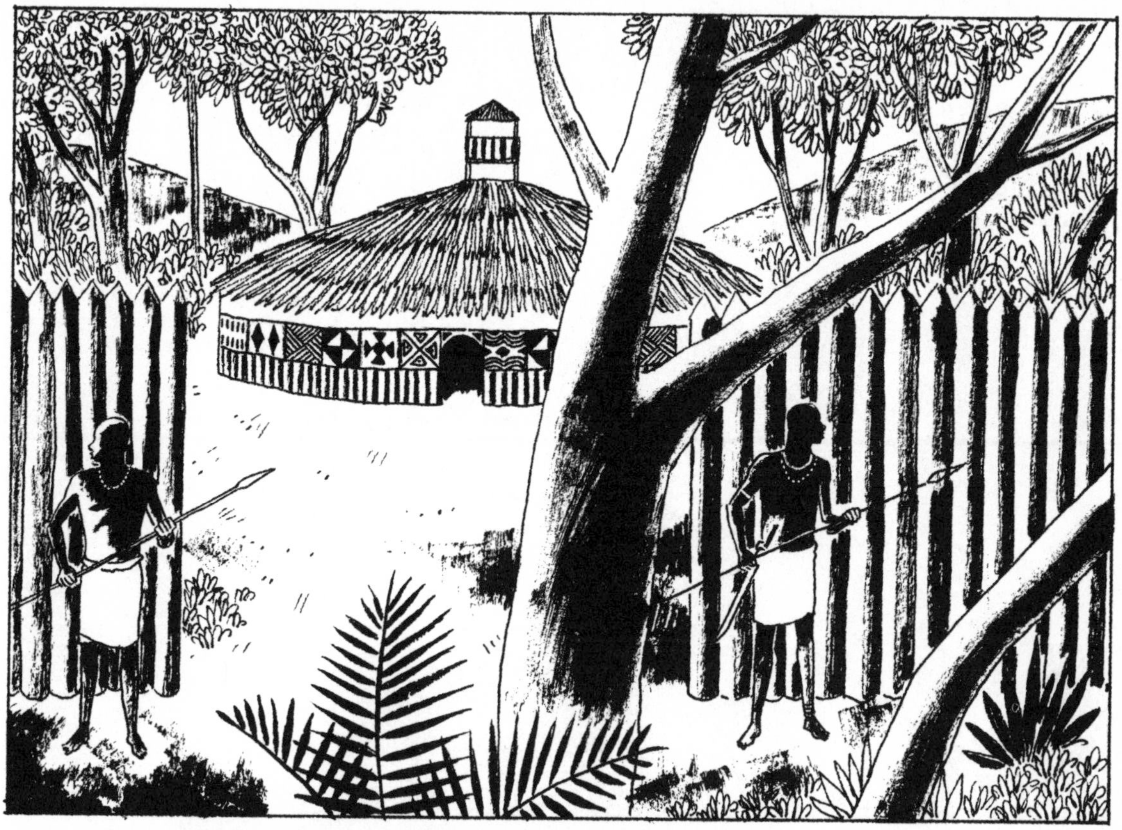

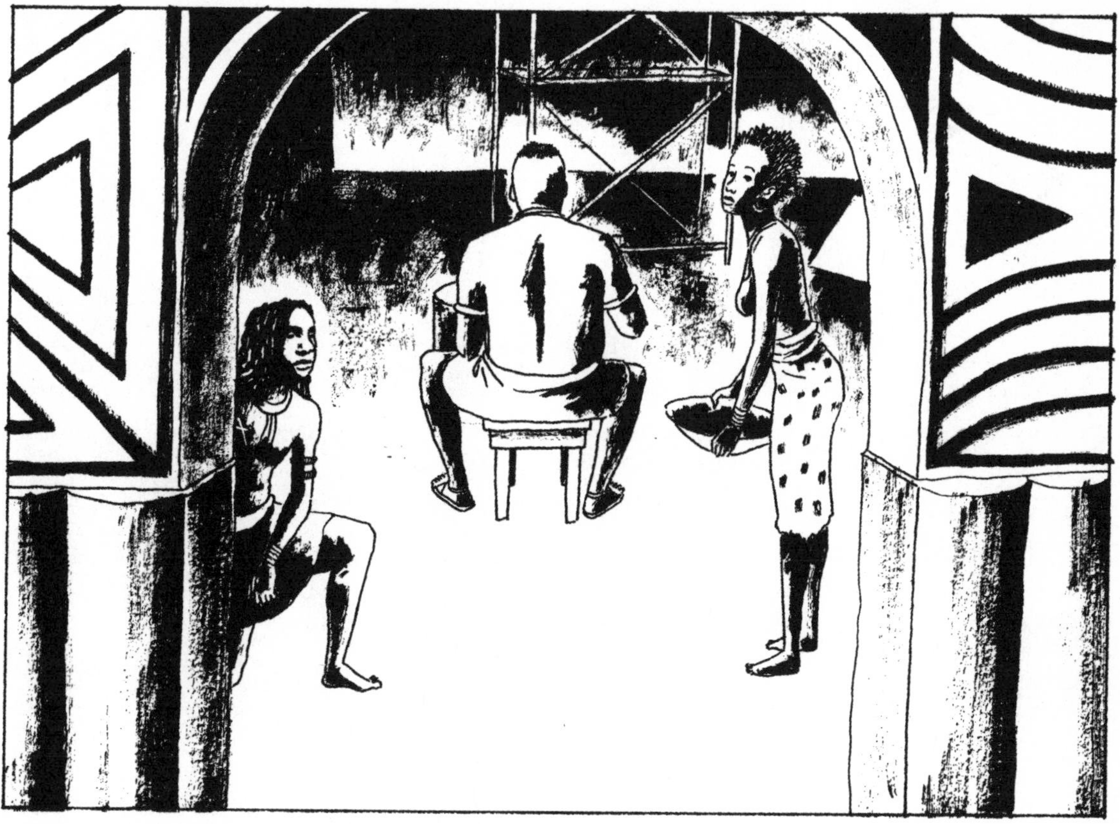

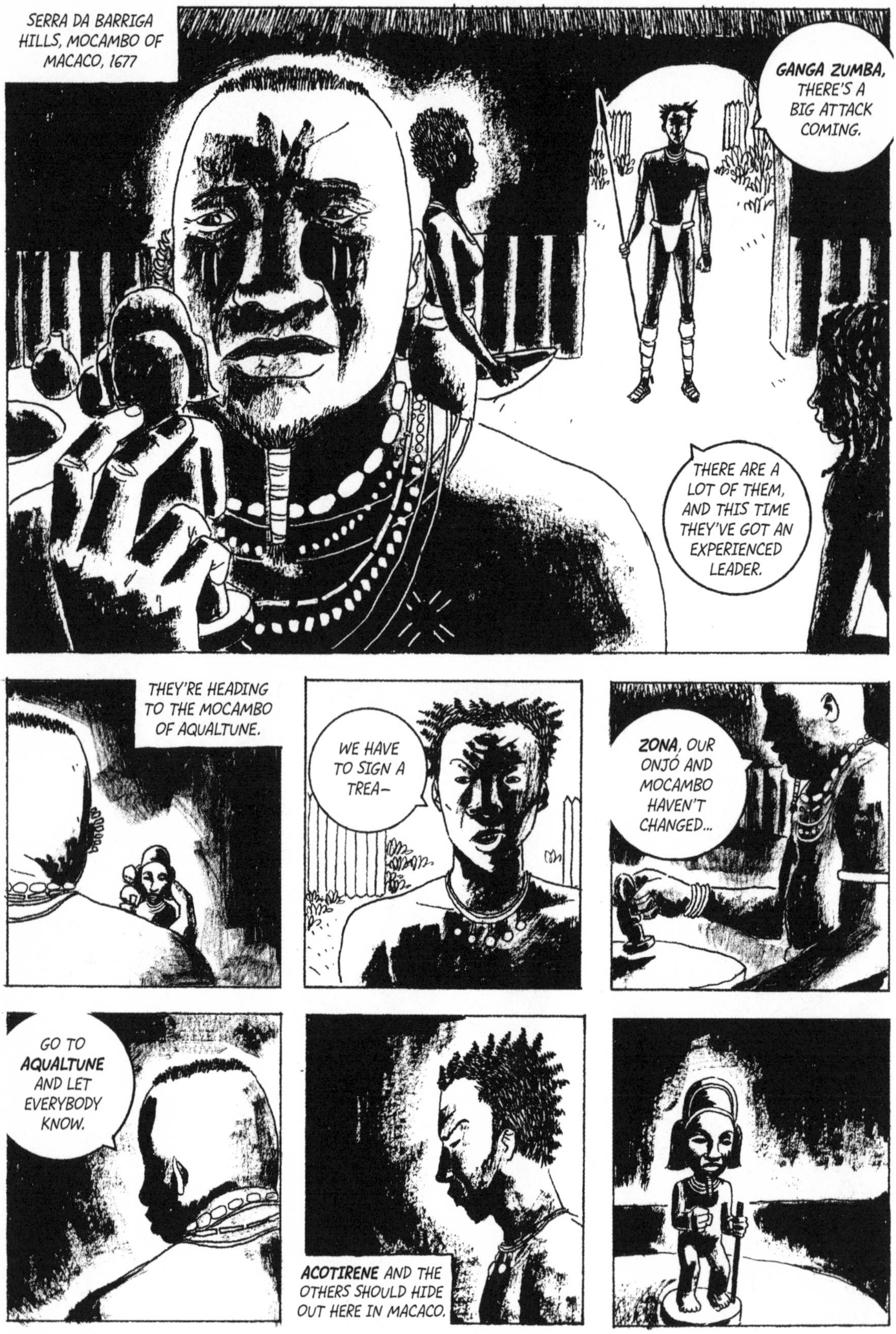
SERRA DA BARRIGA HILLS, MOCAMBO OF MACACO, 1677
GANGA ZUMBA, THERE'S A BIG ATTACK COMING.
THERE ARE A LOT OF THEM, AND THIS TIME THEY'VE GOT AN EXPERIENCED LEADER.
THEY'RE HEADING TO THE MOCAMBO OF AQUALTUNE.
WE HAVE TO SIGN A TREA–
ZONA, OUR ONJÓ AND MOCAMBO HAVEN'T CHANGED...
GO TO AQUALTUNE AND LET EVERYBODY KNOW.
ACOTIRENE AND THE OTHERS SHOULD HIDE OUT HERE IN MACACO.

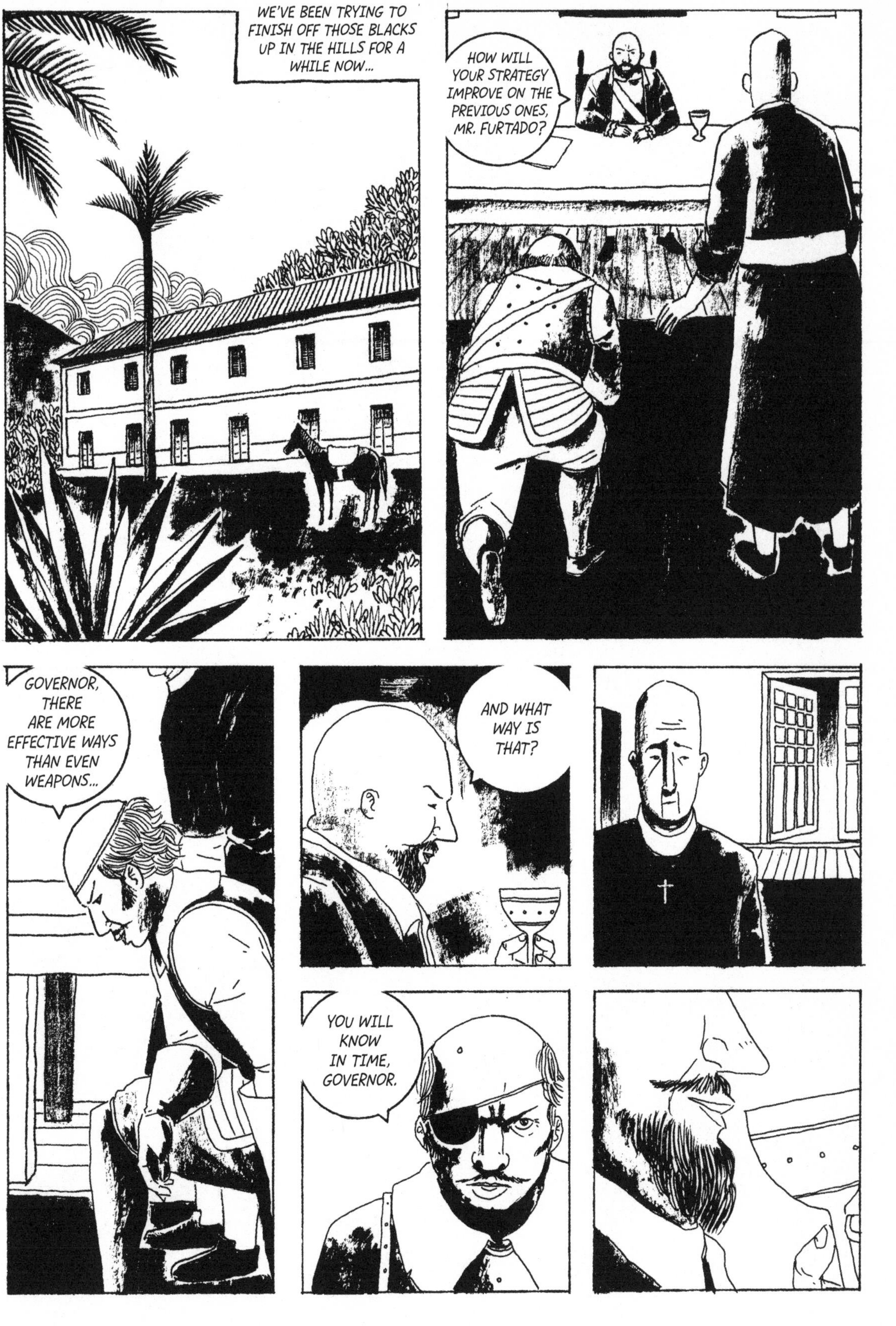
WE'VE BEEN TRYING TO FINISH OFF THOSE BLACKS UP IN THE HILLS FOR A WHILE NOW...
HOW WILL YOUR STRATEGY IMPROVE ON THE PREVIOUS ONES, MR. FURTADO?
GOVERNOR, THERE ARE MORE EFFECTIVE WAYS THAN EVEN WEAPONS...
AND WHAT WAY IS THAT?
YOU WILL KNOW IN TIME, GOVERNOR.

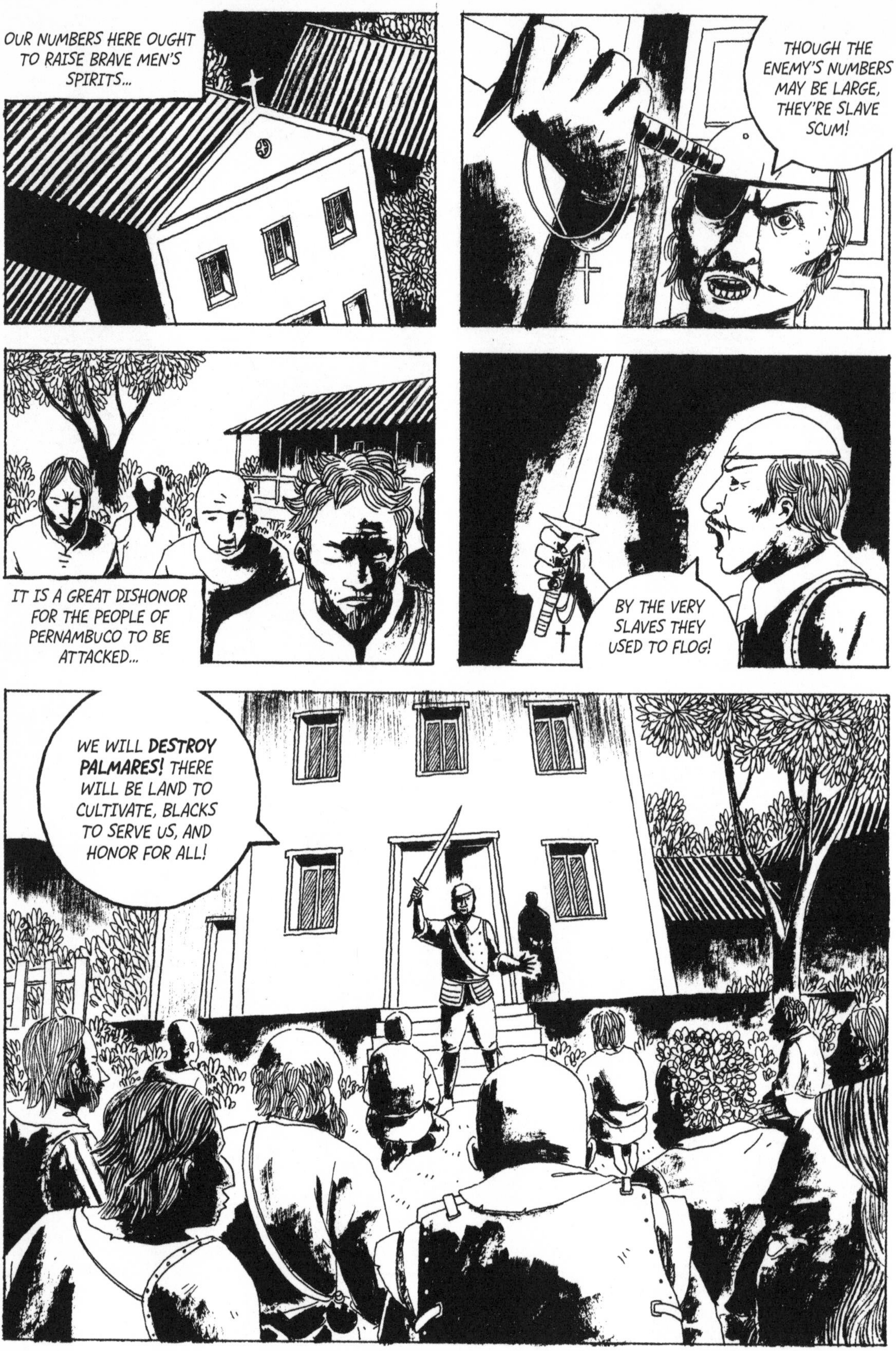
OUR NUMBERS HERE OUGHT TO RAISE BRAVE MEN'S SPIRITS...
THOUGH THE ENEMY'S NUMBERS MAY BE LARGE, THEY'RE SLAVE SCUM!
IT IS A GREAT DISHONOR FOR THE PEOPLE OF PERNAMBUCO TO BE ATTACKED...
BY THE VERY SLAVES THEY USED TO FLOG!
WE WILL **DESTROY PALMARES!** THERE WILL BE LAND TO CULTIVATE, BLACKS TO SERVE US, AND HONOR FOR ALL!

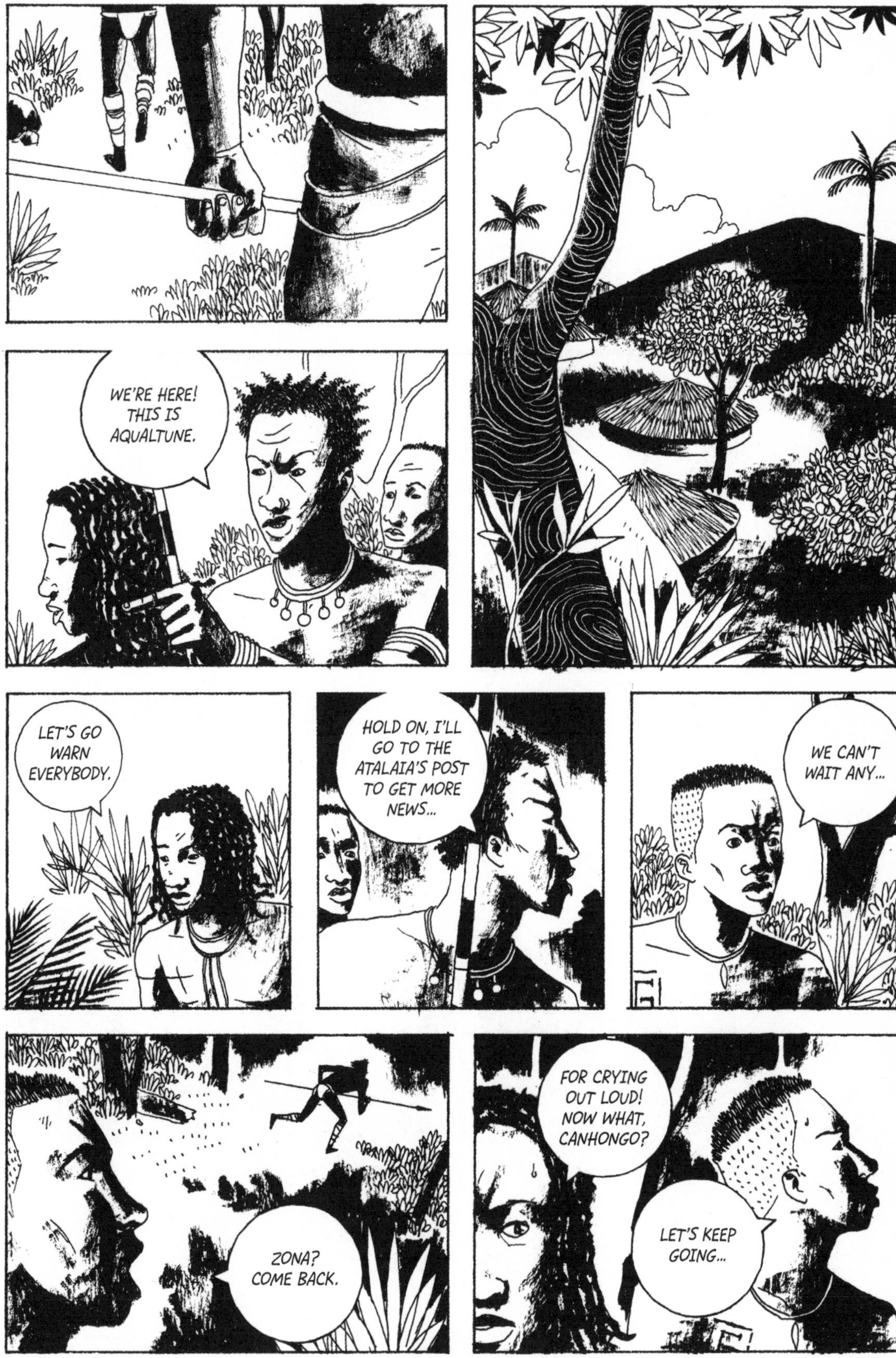
WE'RE HERE! THIS IS AQUALTUNE.
LET'S GO WARN EVERYBODY.
HOLD ON, I'LL GO TO THE ATALAIA'S POST TO GET MORE NEWS...
WE CAN'T WAIT ANY...
ZONA? COME BACK.
FOR CRYING OUT LOUD! NOW WHAT, CANHONGO?
LET'S KEEP GOING...

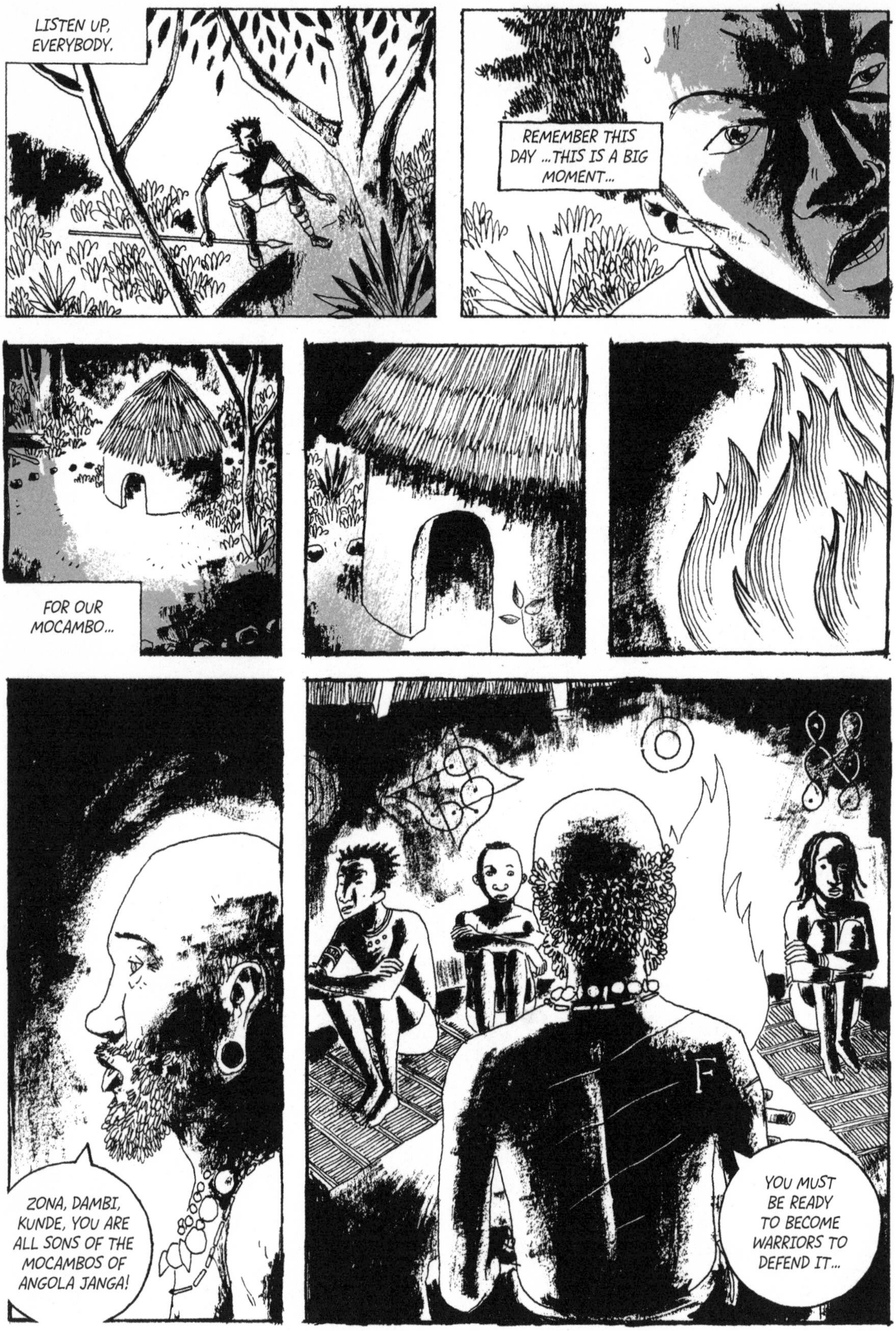
LISTEN UP, EVERYBODY.
REMEMBER THIS DAY ...THIS IS A BIG MOMENT...
FOR OUR MOCAMBO...
ZONA, DAMBI, KUNDE, YOU ARE ALL SONS OF THE MOCAMBOS OF ANGOLA JANGA!
YOU MUST BE READY TO BECOME WARRIORS TO DEFEND IT...

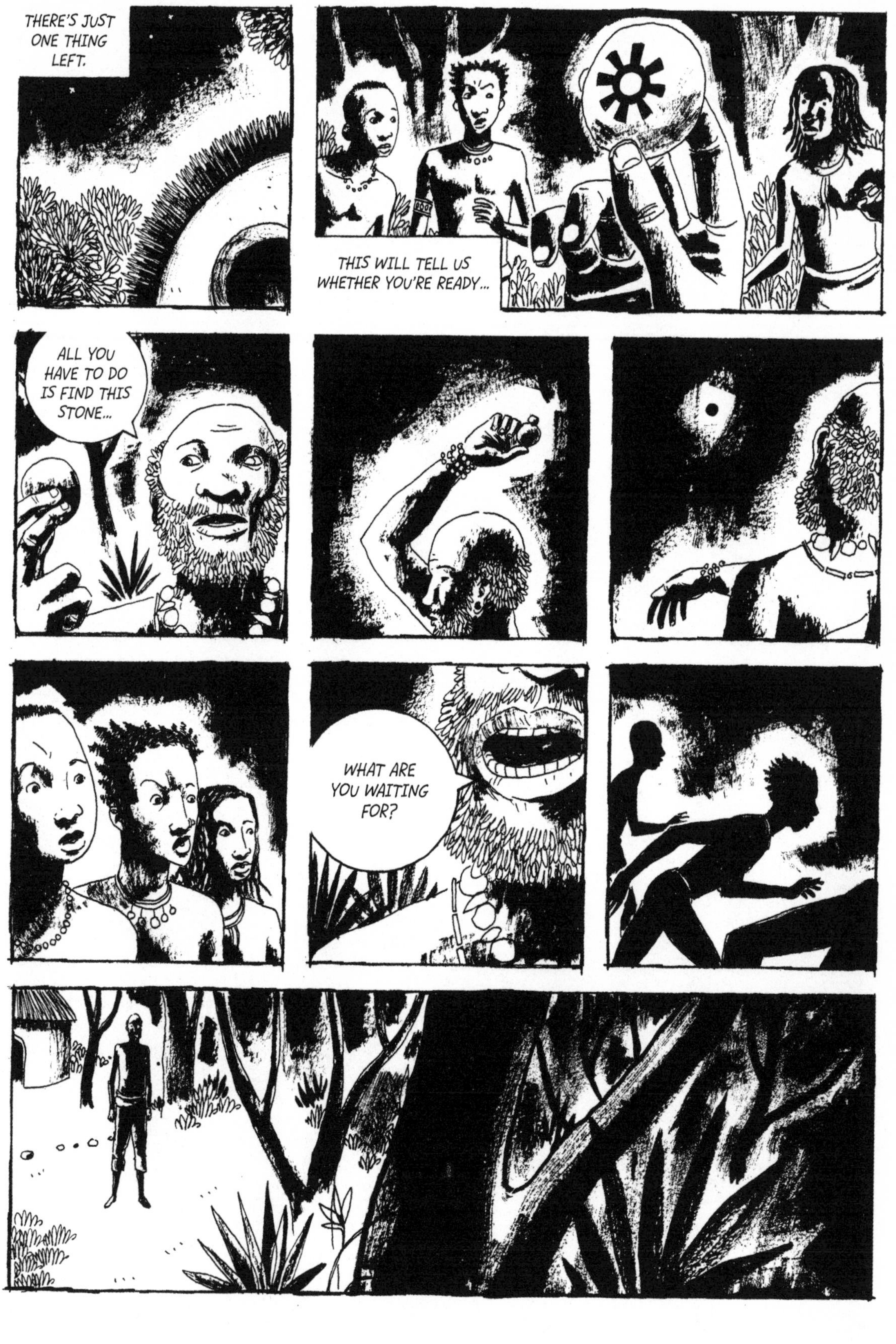
THERE'S JUST ONE THING LEFT.
THIS WILL TELL US WHETHER YOU'RE READY...
ALL YOU HAVE TO DO IS FIND THIS STONE...
WHAT ARE YOU WAITING FOR?

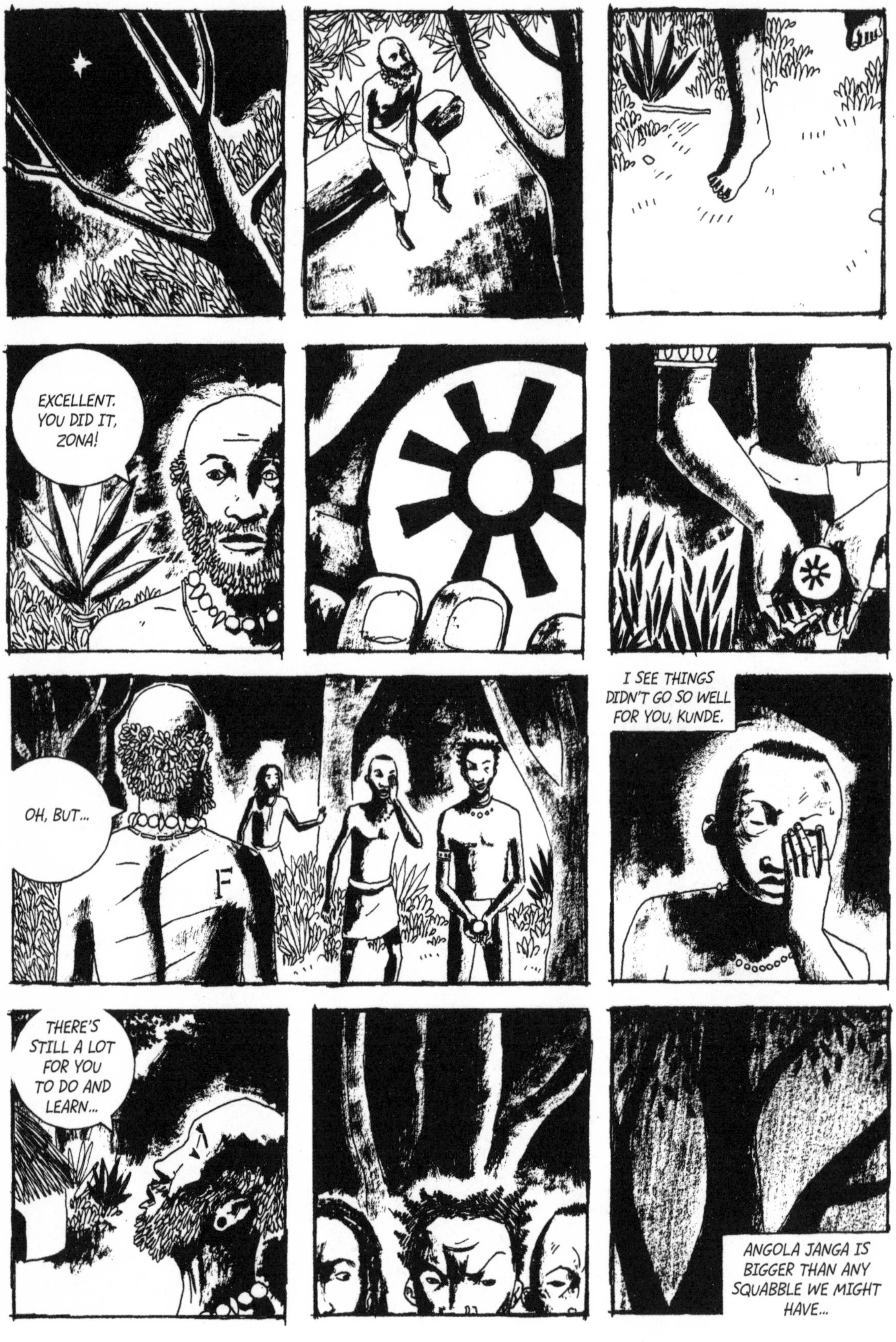
EXCELLENT. YOU DID IT, ZONA!
OH, BUT...
I SEE THINGS DIDN'T GO SO WELL FOR YOU, KUNDE.
THERE'S STILL A LOT FOR YOU TO DO AND LEARN...
ANGOLA JANGA IS BIGGER THAN ANY SQUABBLE WE MIGHT HAVE...

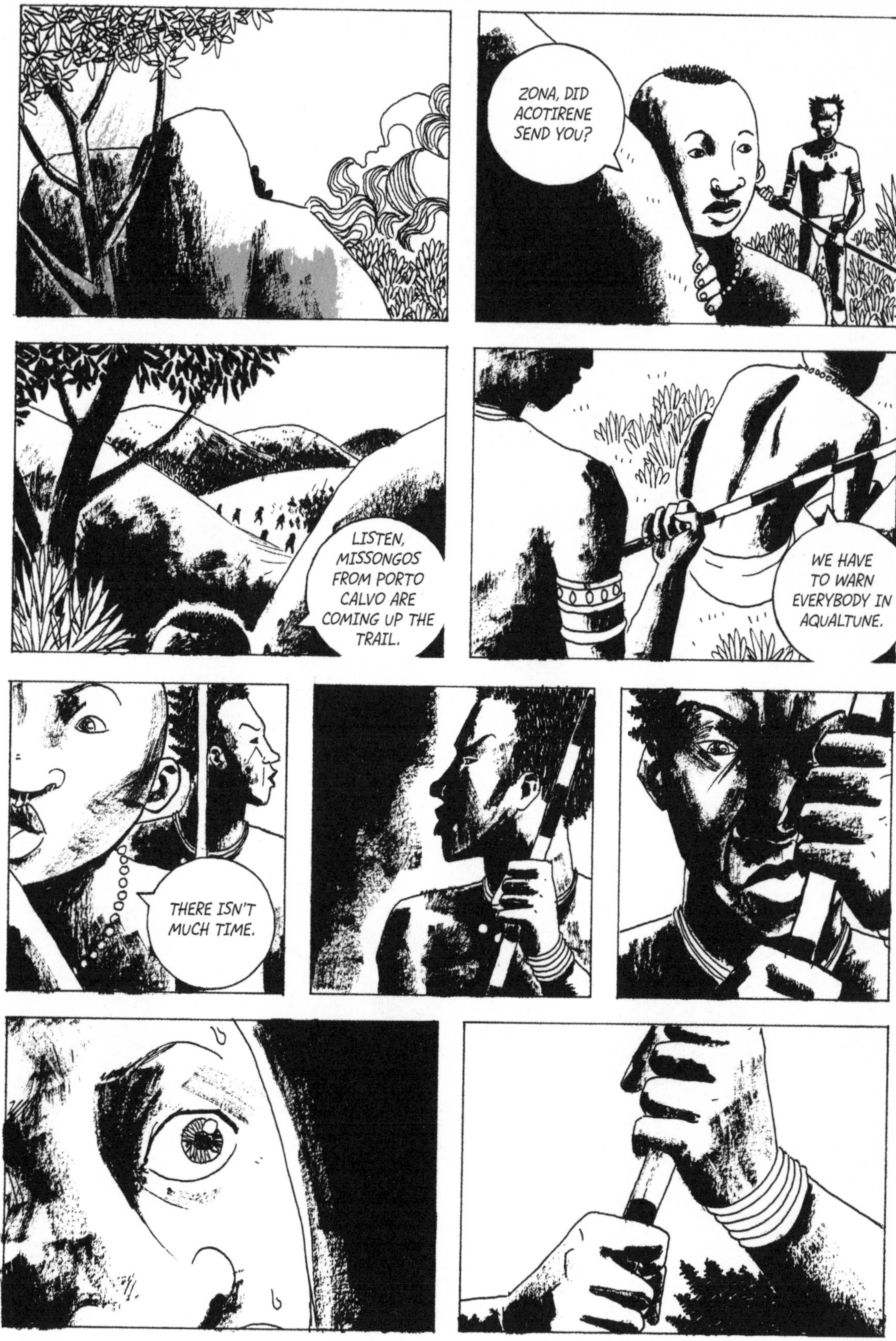
ZONA, DID ACOTIRENE SEND YOU?
LISTEN, MISSONGOS FROM PORTO CALVO ARE COMING UP THE TRAIL.
WE HAVE TO WARN EVERYBODY IN AQUALTUNE.
THERE ISN'T MUCH TIME.

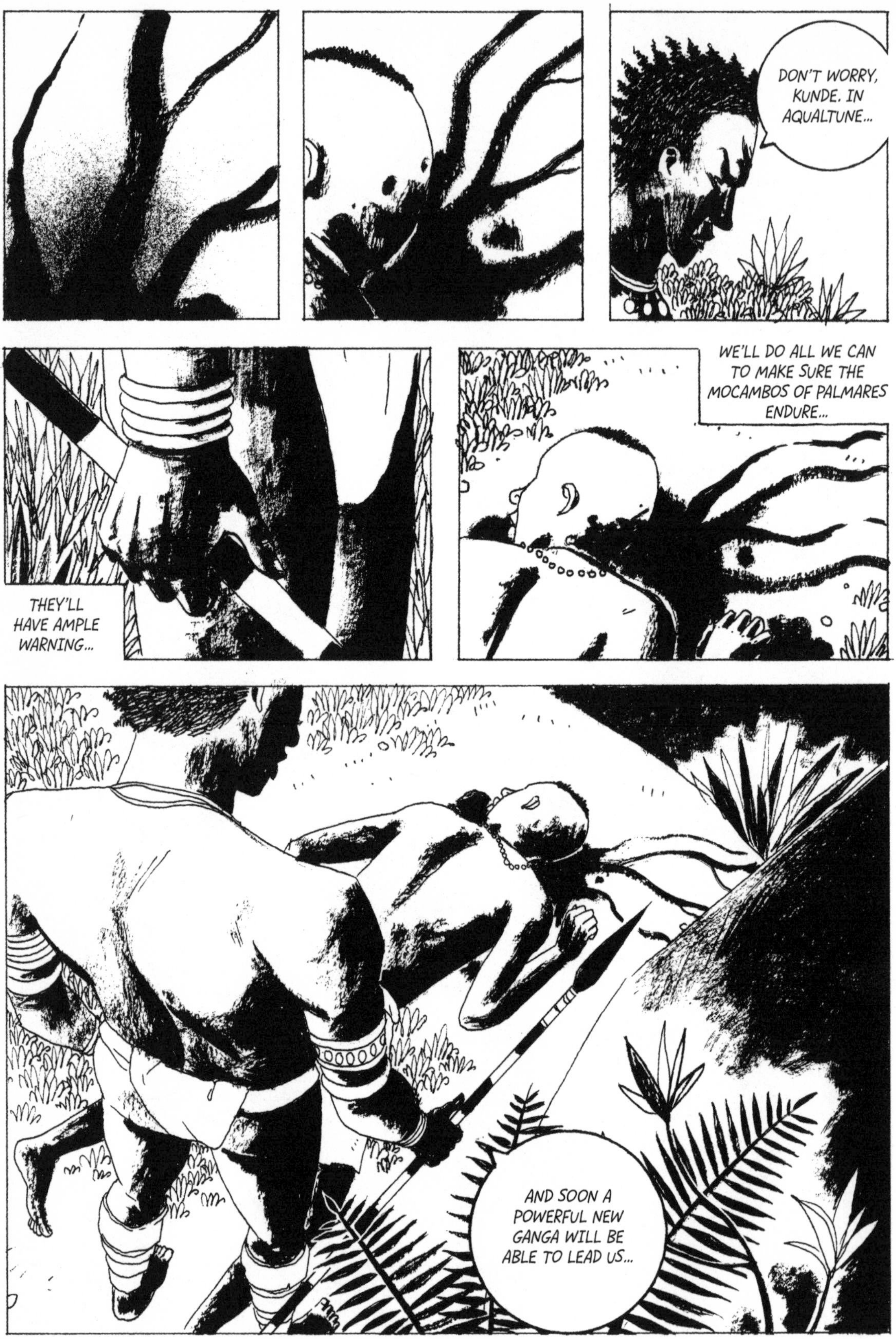
DON'T WORRY, KUNDE. IN AQUALTUNE...
WE'LL DO ALL WE CAN TO MAKE SURE THE MOCAMBOS OF PALMARES ENDURE...
THEY'LL HAVE AMPLE WARNING...
AND SOON A POWERFUL NEW GANGA WILL BE ABLE TO LEAD US...

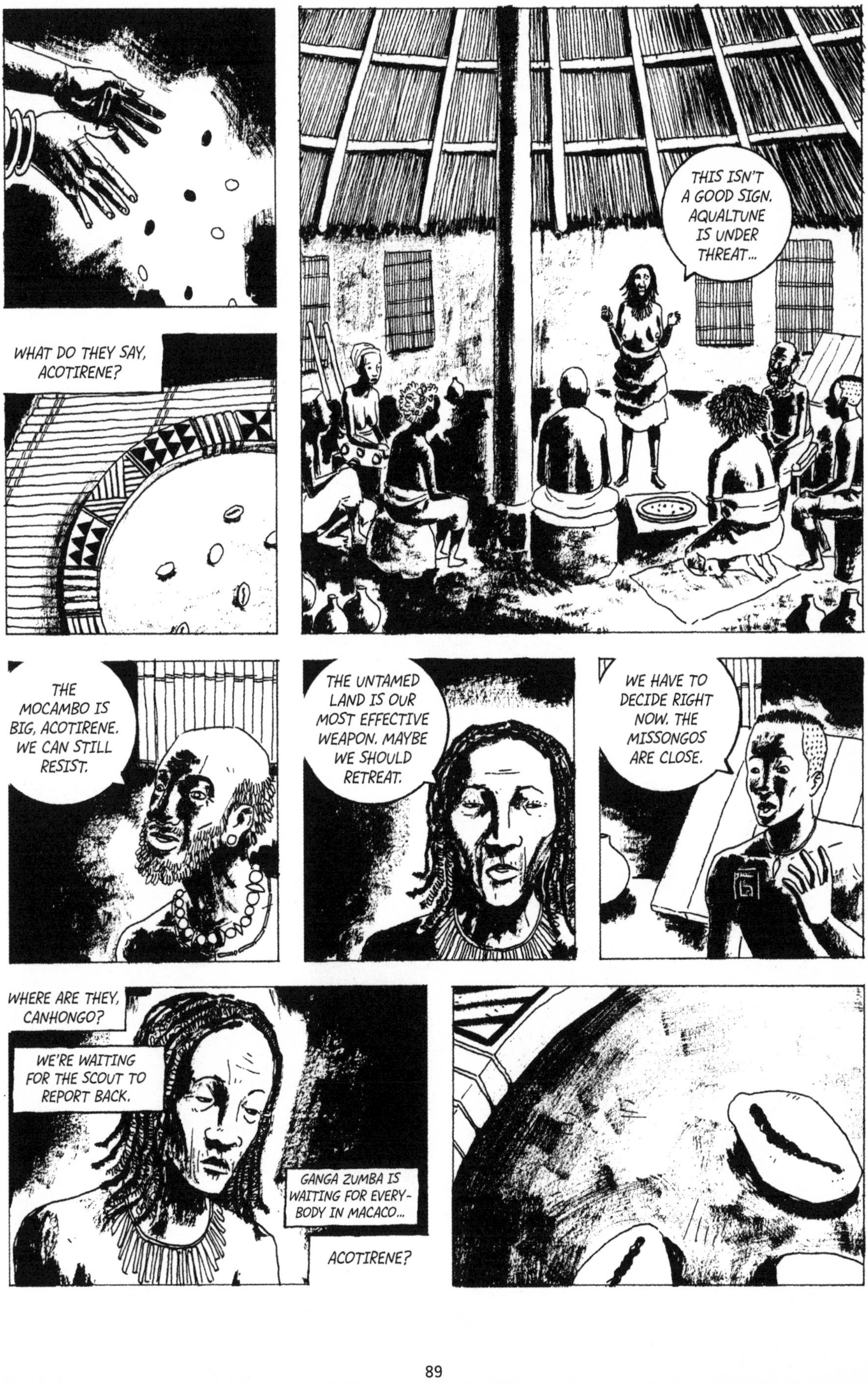
WHAT DO THEY SAY, ACOTIRENE?
THIS ISN'T A GOOD SIGN. AQUALTUNE IS UNDER THREAT...
THE MOCAMBO IS BIG, ACOTIRENE. WE CAN STILL RESIST.
THE UNTAMED LAND IS OUR MOST EFFECTIVE WEAPON. MAYBE WE SHOULD RETREAT.
WE HAVE TO DECIDE RIGHT NOW. THE MISSONGOS ARE CLOSE.
WHERE ARE THEY, CANHONGO?
WE'RE WAITING FOR THE SCOUT TO REPORT BACK.
GANGA ZUMBA IS WAITING FOR EVERY-BODY IN MACACO...
ACOTIRENE?

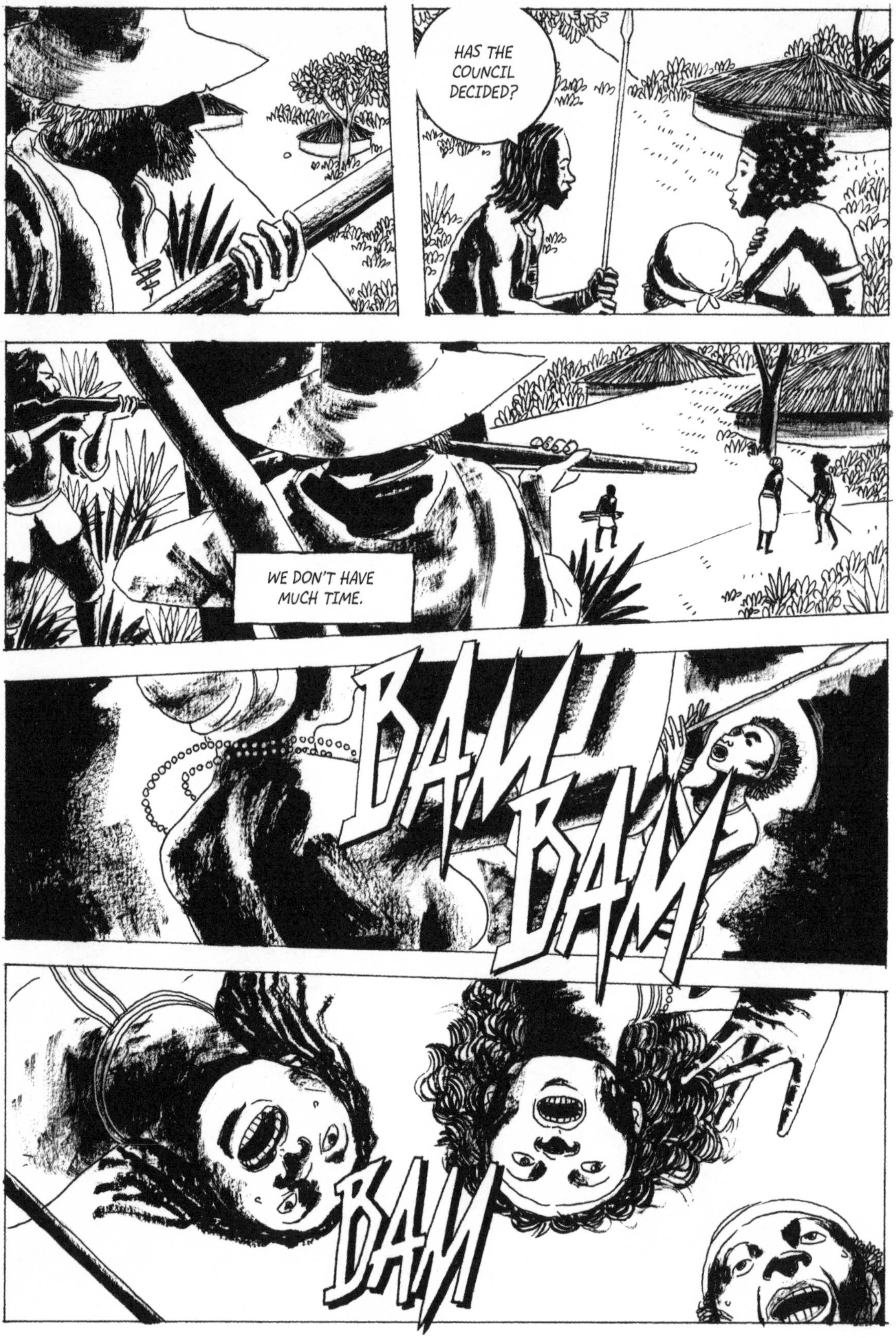
HAS THE COUNCIL DECIDED?
WE DON'T HAVE MUCH TIME.
BAM
BAM
BAM

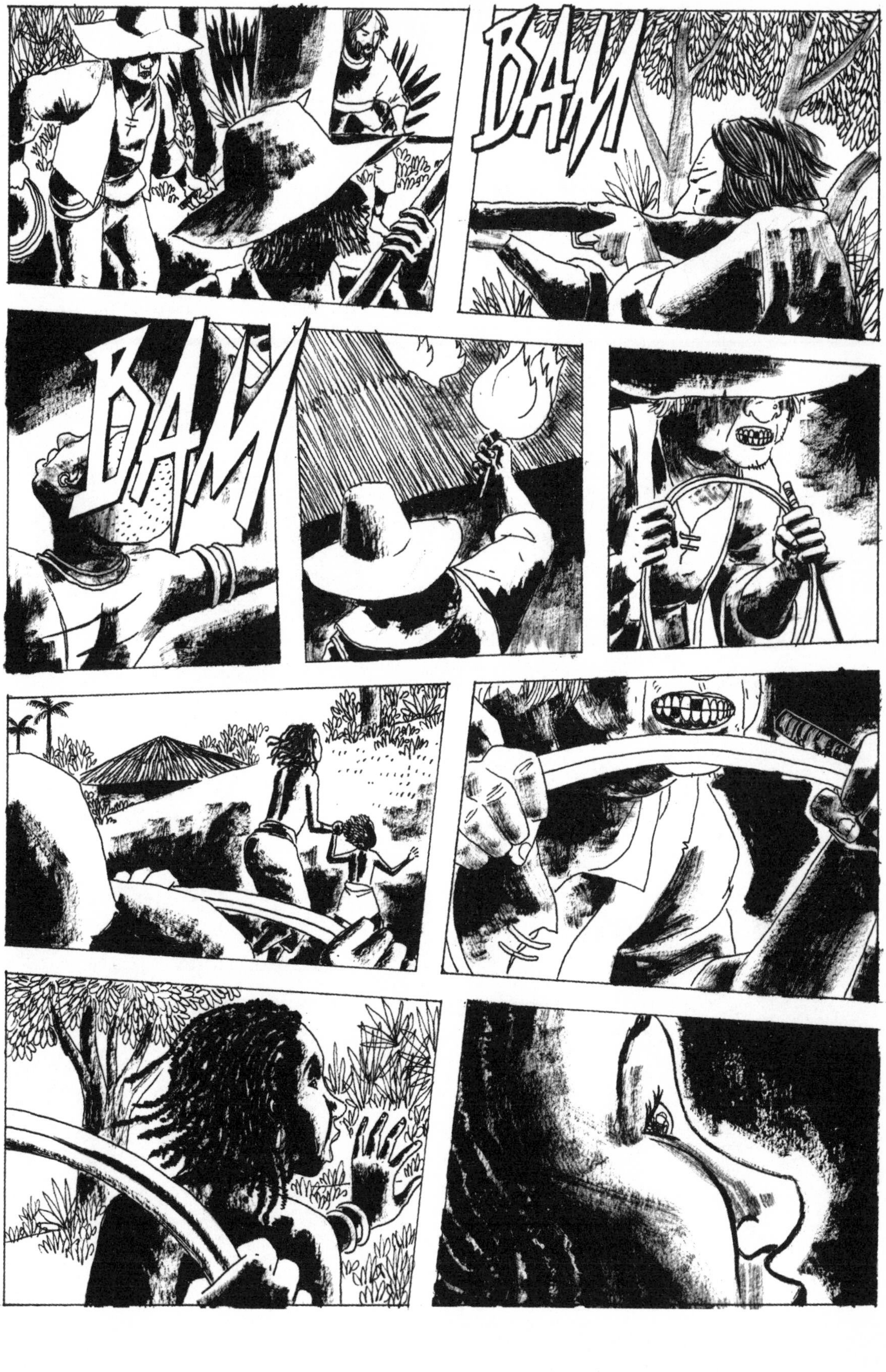
BAM
BAM

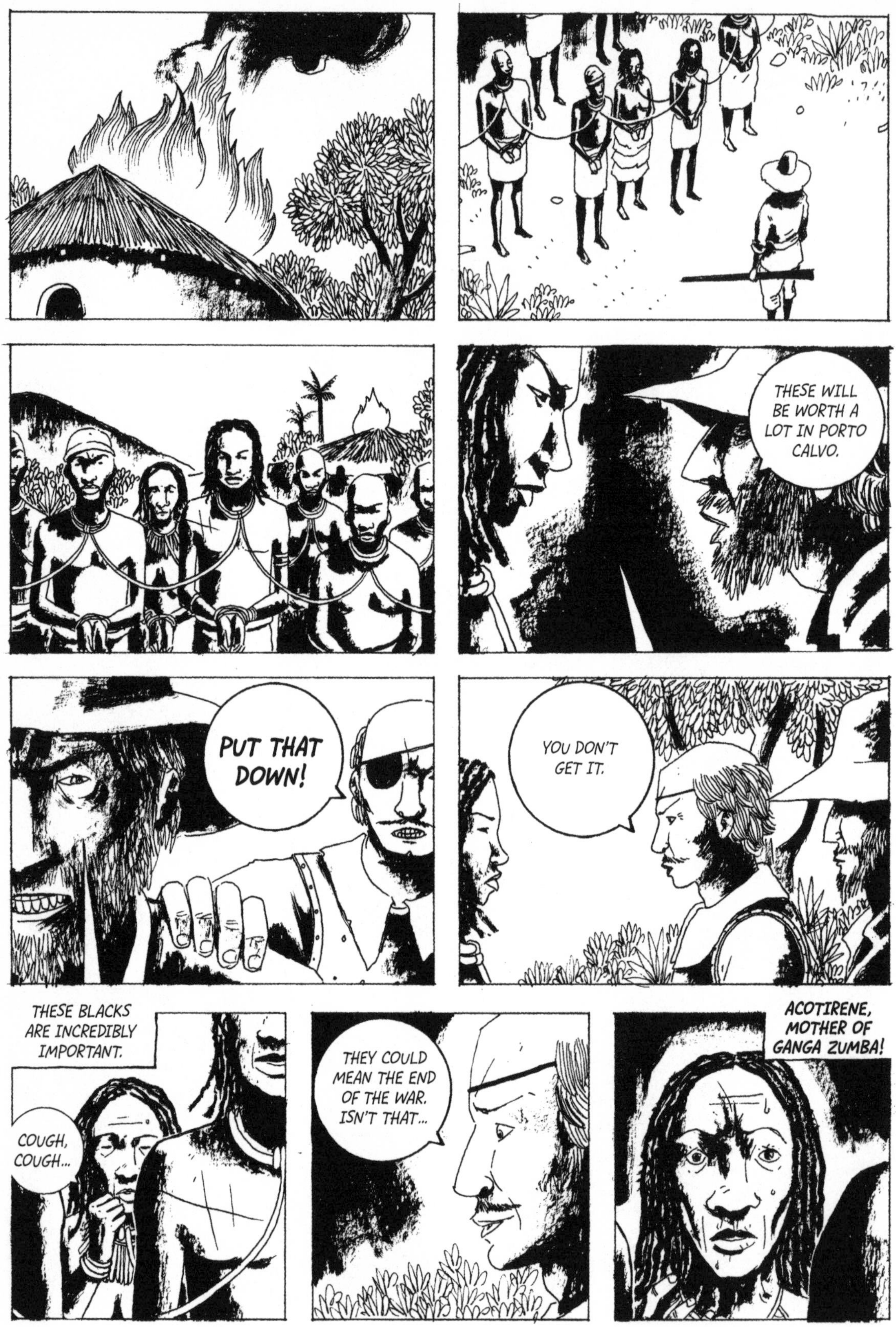
THESE WILL BE WORTH A LOT IN PORTO CALVO.
PUT THAT DOWN!
YOU DON'T GET IT.
THESE BLACKS ARE INCREDIBLY IMPORTANT.
COUGH, COUGH...
THEY COULD MEAN THE END OF THE WAR. ISN'T THAT...
ACOTIRENE, MOTHER OF GANGA ZUMBA!

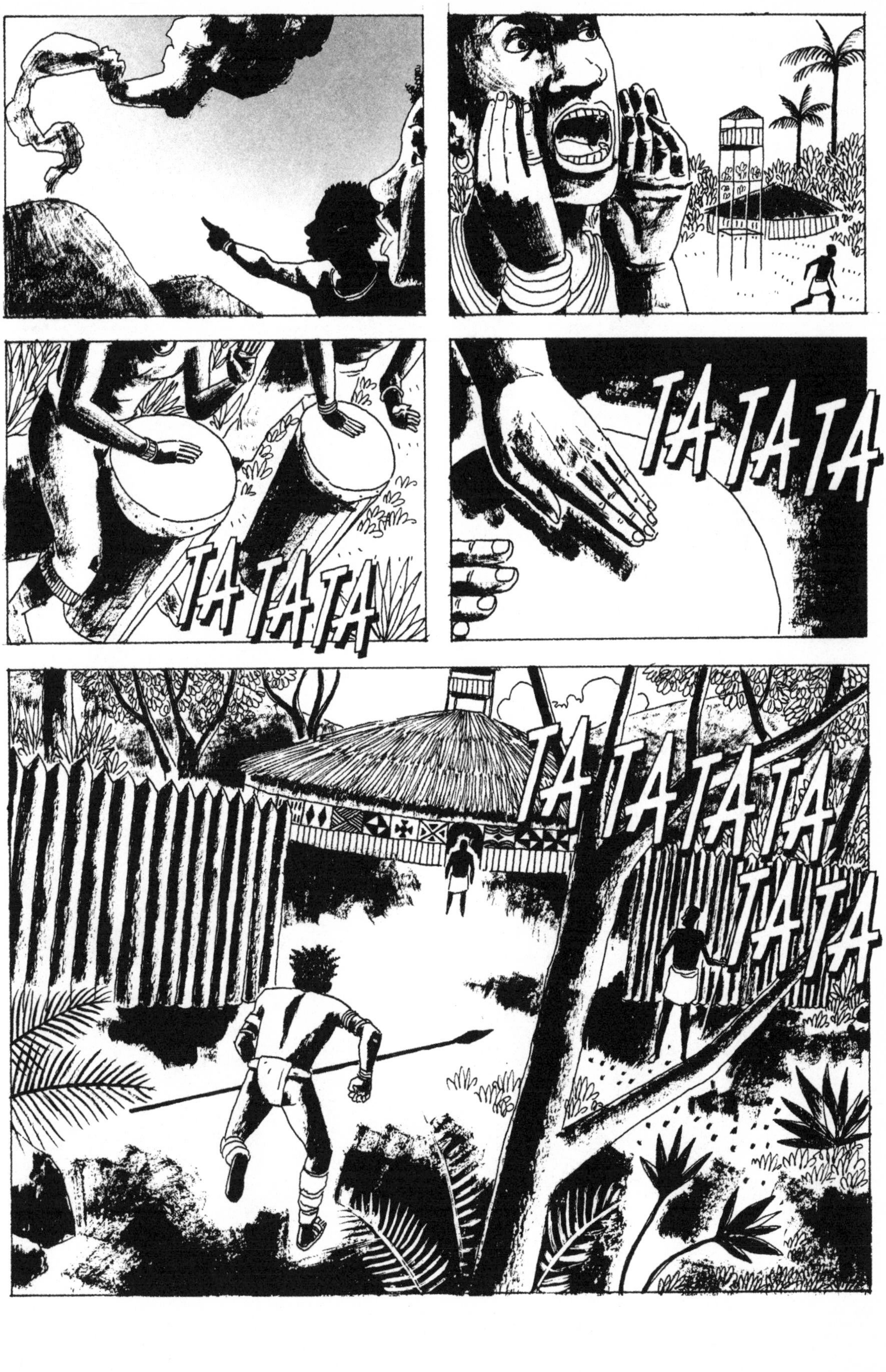
TA TA TA
TA TA TA
TA TA TA TA
TA TA

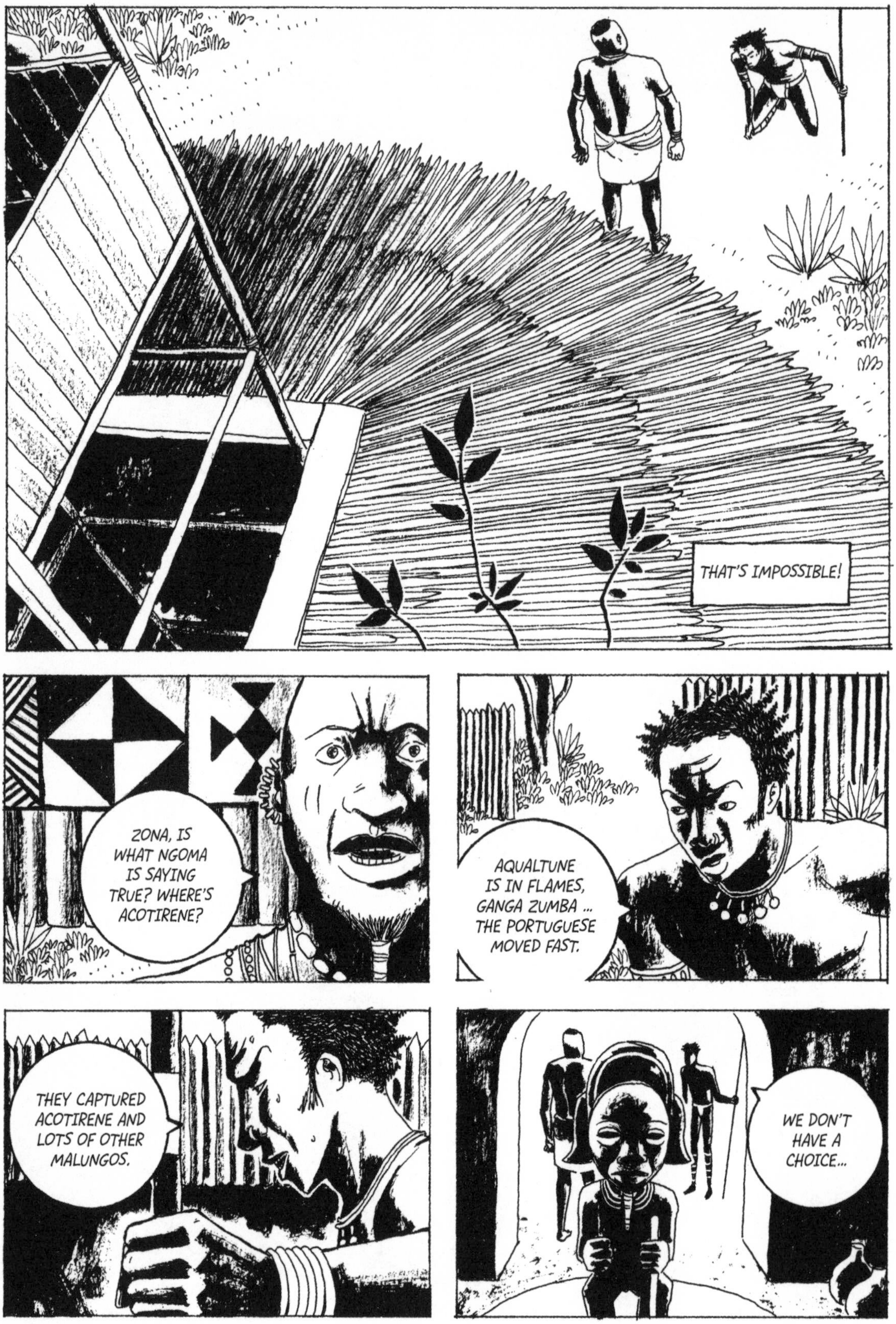
THAT'S IMPOSSIBLE!
ZONA, IS WHAT NGOMA IS SAYING TRUE? WHERE'S ACOTIRENE?
AQUALTUNE IS IN FLAMES, GANGA ZUMBA ... THE PORTUGUESE MOVED FAST.
THEY CAPTURED ACOTIRENE AND LOTS OF OTHER MALUNGOS.
WE DON'T HAVE A CHOICE...

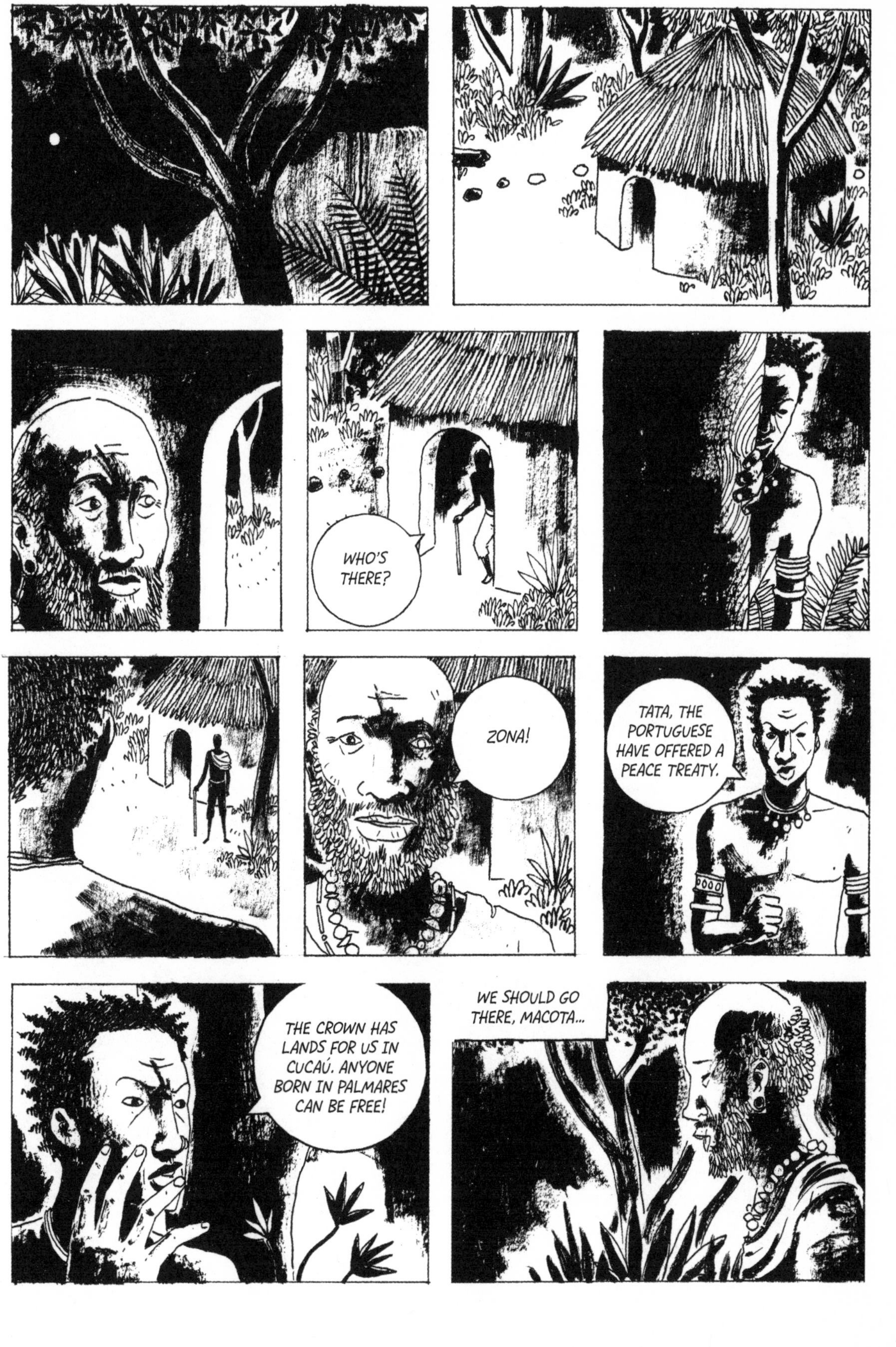
WHO'S THERE?
ZONA!
TATA, THE PORTUGUESE HAVE OFFERED A PEACE TREATY.
THE CROWN HAS LANDS FOR US IN CUCAÚ. ANYONE BORN IN PALMARES CAN BE FREE!
WE SHOULD GO THERE, MACOTA...

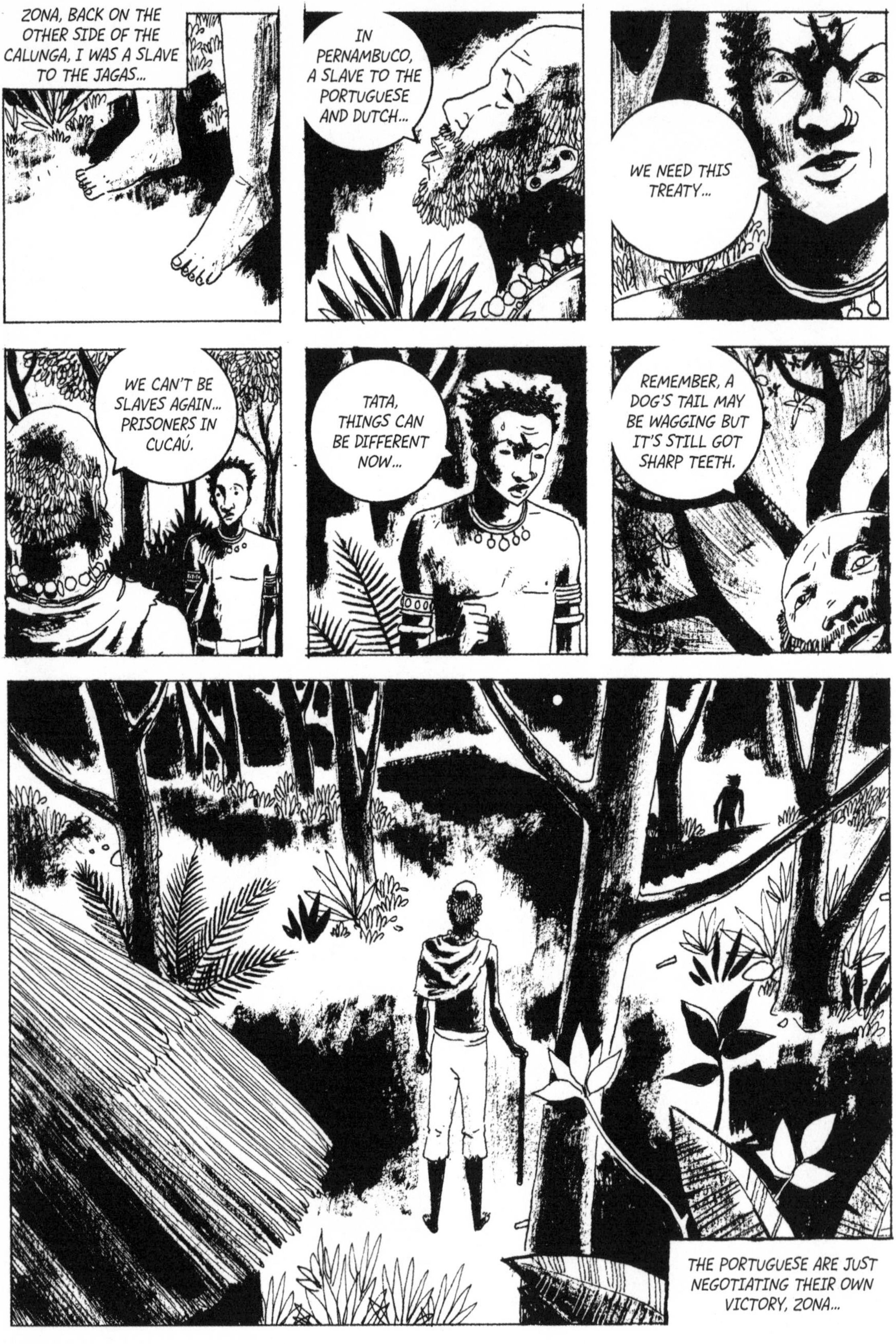
ZONA, BACK ON THE OTHER SIDE OF THE CALUNGA, I WAS A SLAVE TO THE JAGAS...
IN PERNAMBUCO, A SLAVE TO THE PORTUGUESE AND DUTCH...
WE NEED THIS TREATY...
WE CAN'T BE SLAVES AGAIN... PRISONERS IN CUCAÚ.
TATA, THINGS CAN BE DIFFERENT NOW...
REMEMBER, A DOG'S TAIL MAY BE WAGGING BUT IT'S STILL GOT SHARP TEETH.
THE PORTUGUESE ARE JUST NEGOTIATING THEIR OWN VICTORY, ZONA...

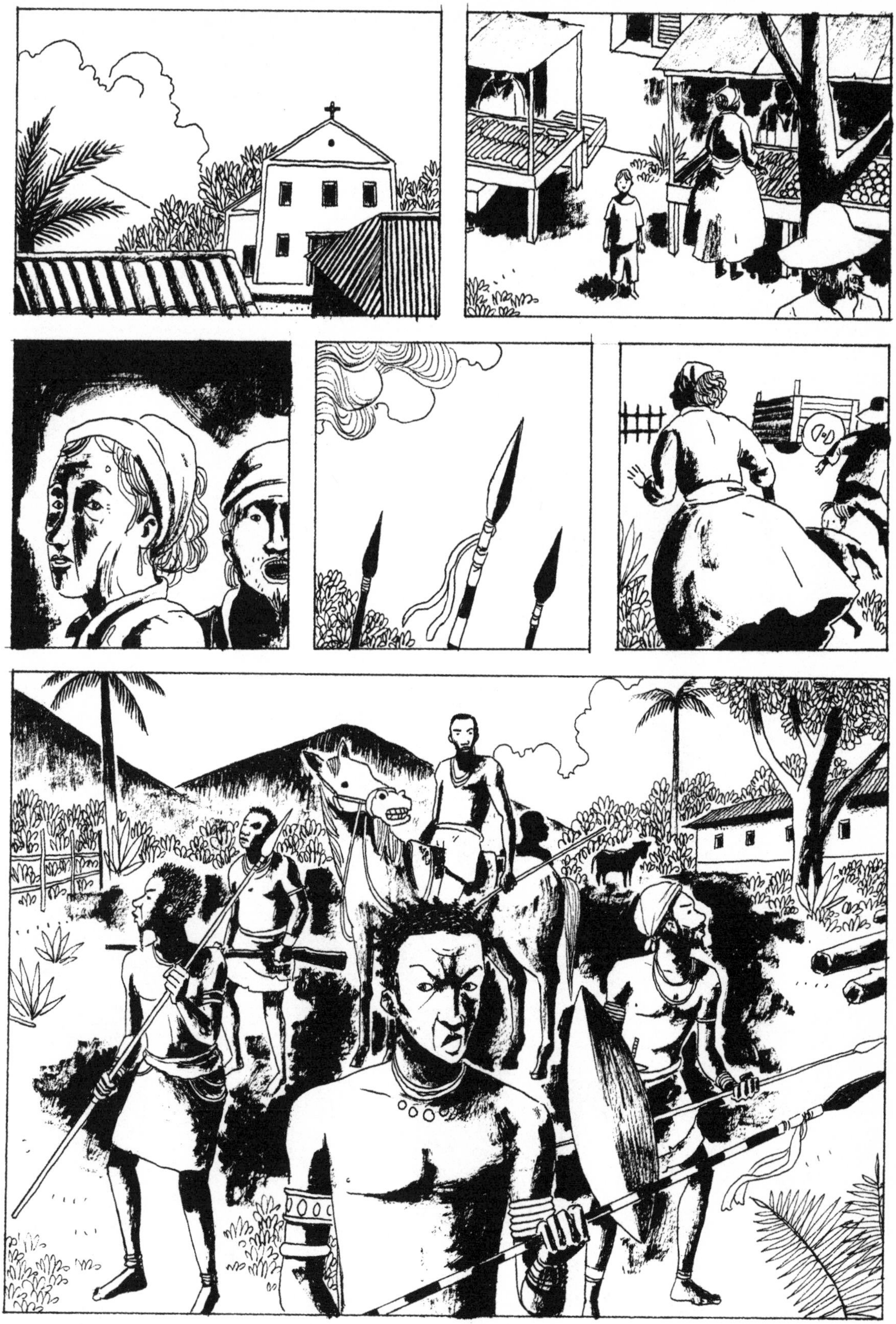

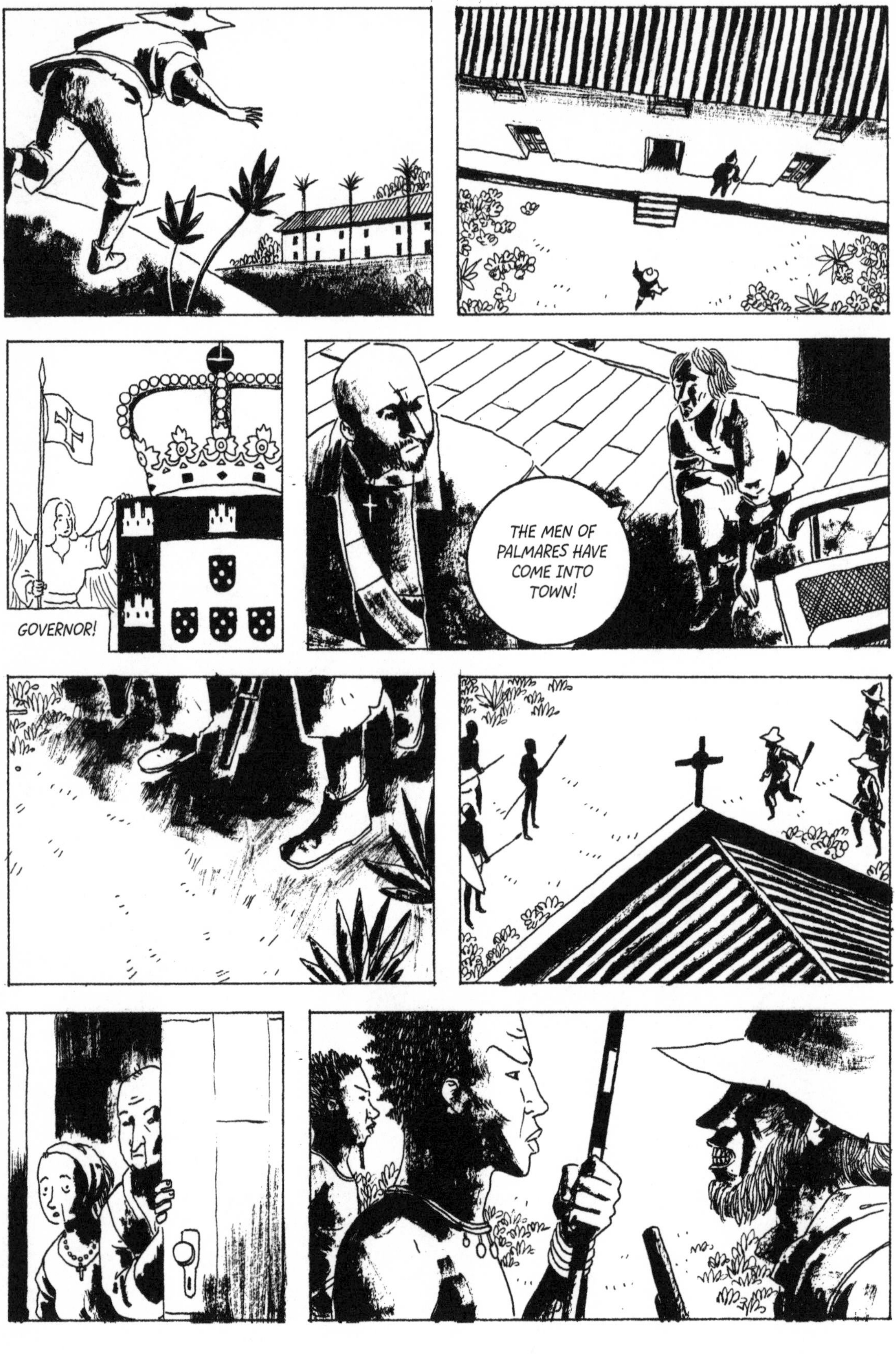
GOVERNOR!
THE MEN OF PALMARES HAVE COME INTO TOWN!

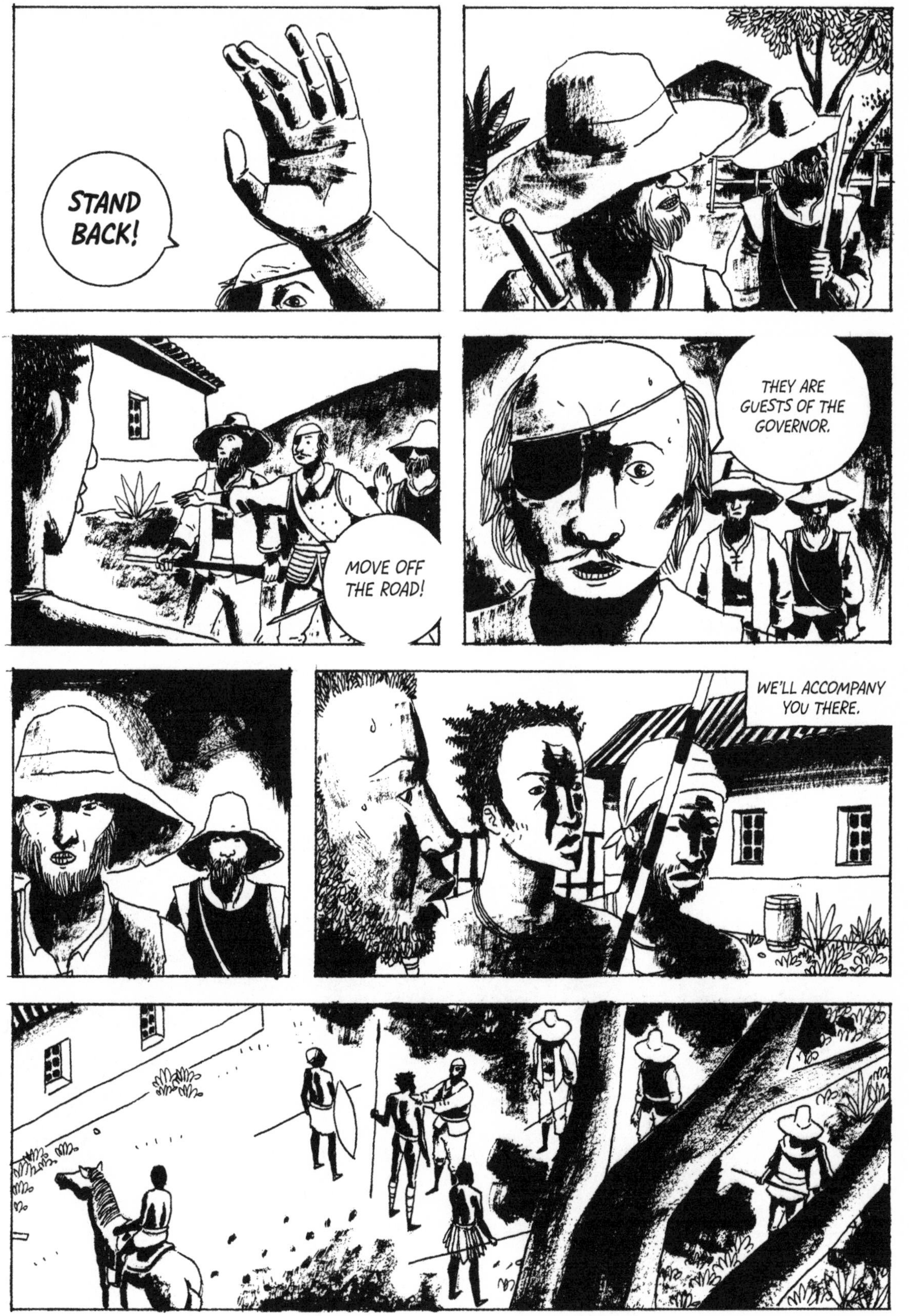
STAND BACK!
MOVE OFF THE ROAD!
THEY ARE GUESTS OF THE GOVERNOR.
WE'LL ACCOMPANY YOU THERE.

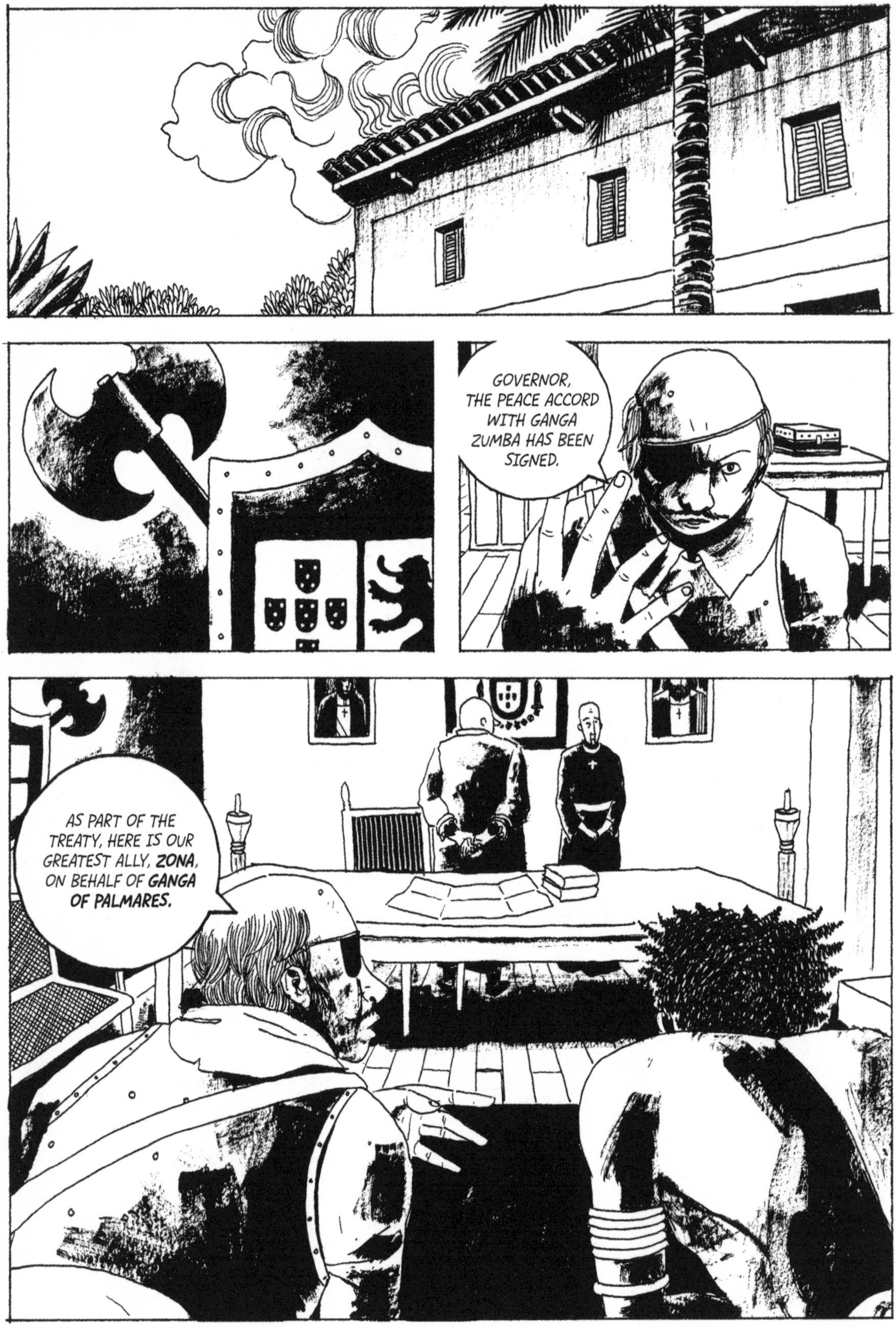
GOVERNOR, THE PEACE ACCORD WITH GANGA ZUMBA HAS BEEN SIGNED.
AS PART OF THE TREATY, HERE IS OUR GREATEST ALLY, **ZONA**, ON BEHALF OF **GANGA OF PALMARES.**

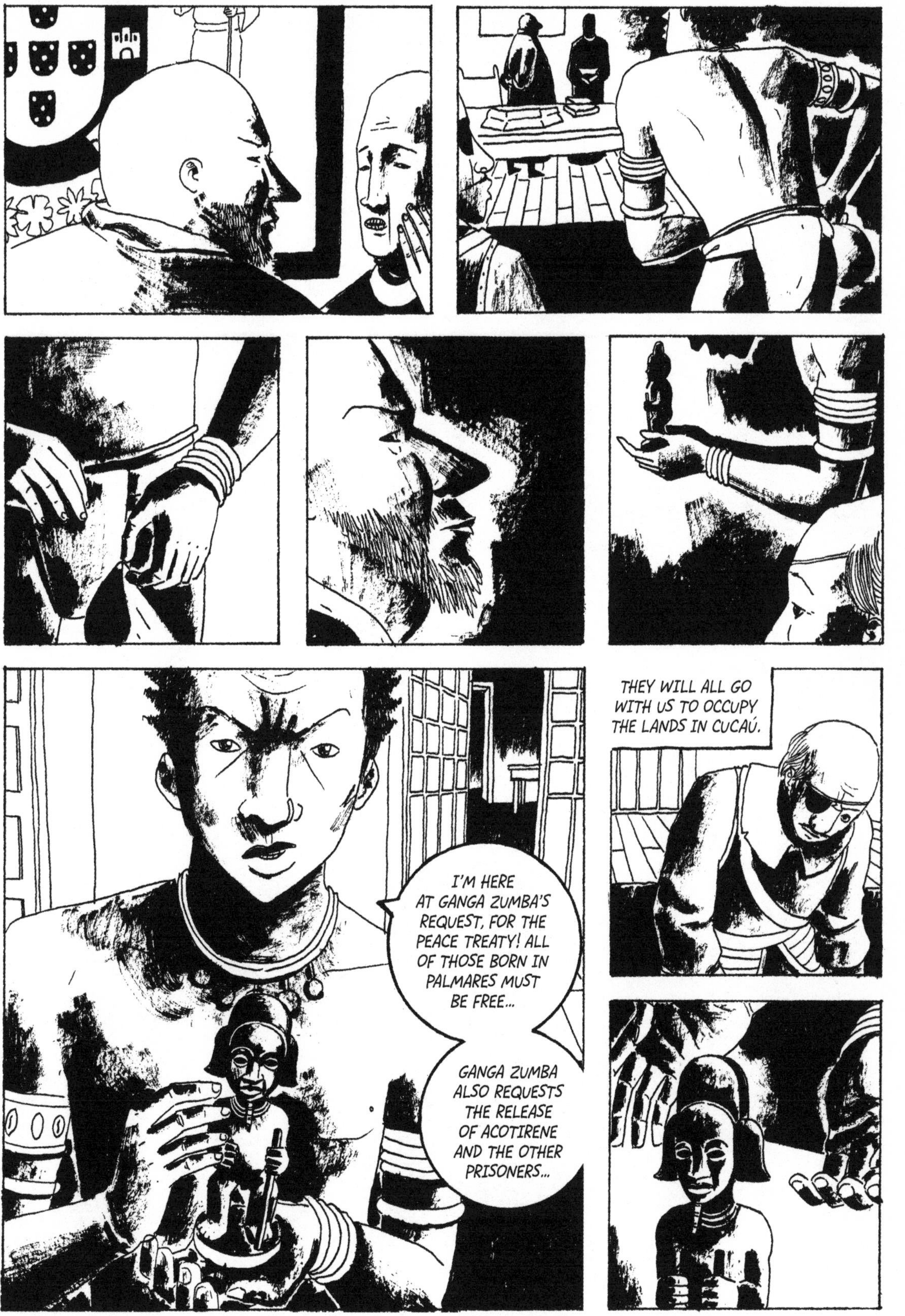
I'M HERE AT GANGA ZUMBA'S REQUEST, FOR THE PEACE TREATY! ALL OF THOSE BORN IN PALMARES MUST BE FREE...
GANGA ZUMBA ALSO REQUESTS THE RELEASE OF ACOTIRENE AND THE OTHER PRISONERS...
THEY WILL ALL GO WITH US TO OCCUPY THE LANDS IN CUCAÚ.

I SEE YOUR METHODS WERE EFFECTIVE, MR. FURTADO...

WE HAVE BEFORE US A GREAT LEADER FOR CUCAÚ!

THE CROWN WILL BE PROUD OF THIS ACHIEVEMENT.

GOVERNOR, AS I MENTIONED, WE HAVE MANY WEAPONS.

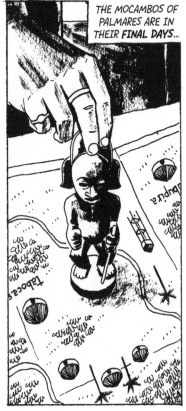

THE MOCAMBOS OF PALMARES ARE IN THEIR **FINAL DAYS**...

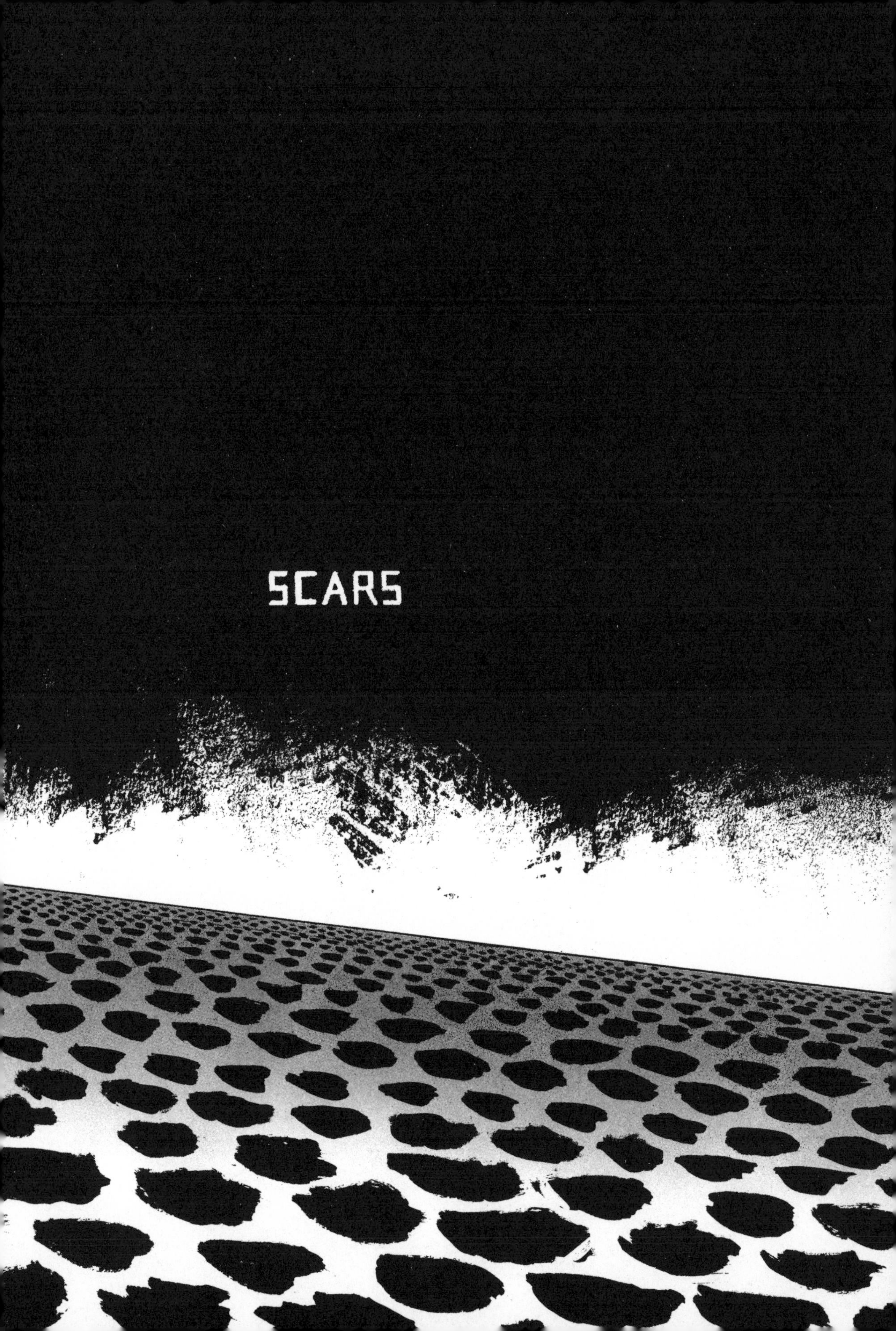
SCARS

A black man of singular courage, great spirit, and unusual stead-
fastness, he watches over his companions, his industry, prudence,
and fortitude putting our people to shame and serving his as an
example.

—*Observation about Zumbi in "Relação das guerras feitas aos Pal-*
mares de Pernambuco no tempo do Governador D. Pedro de Almeida"
[Account of the wars waged against Palmares in Pernambuco under
Governor D. Pedro de Almeida], *from 1675 to 1678.*

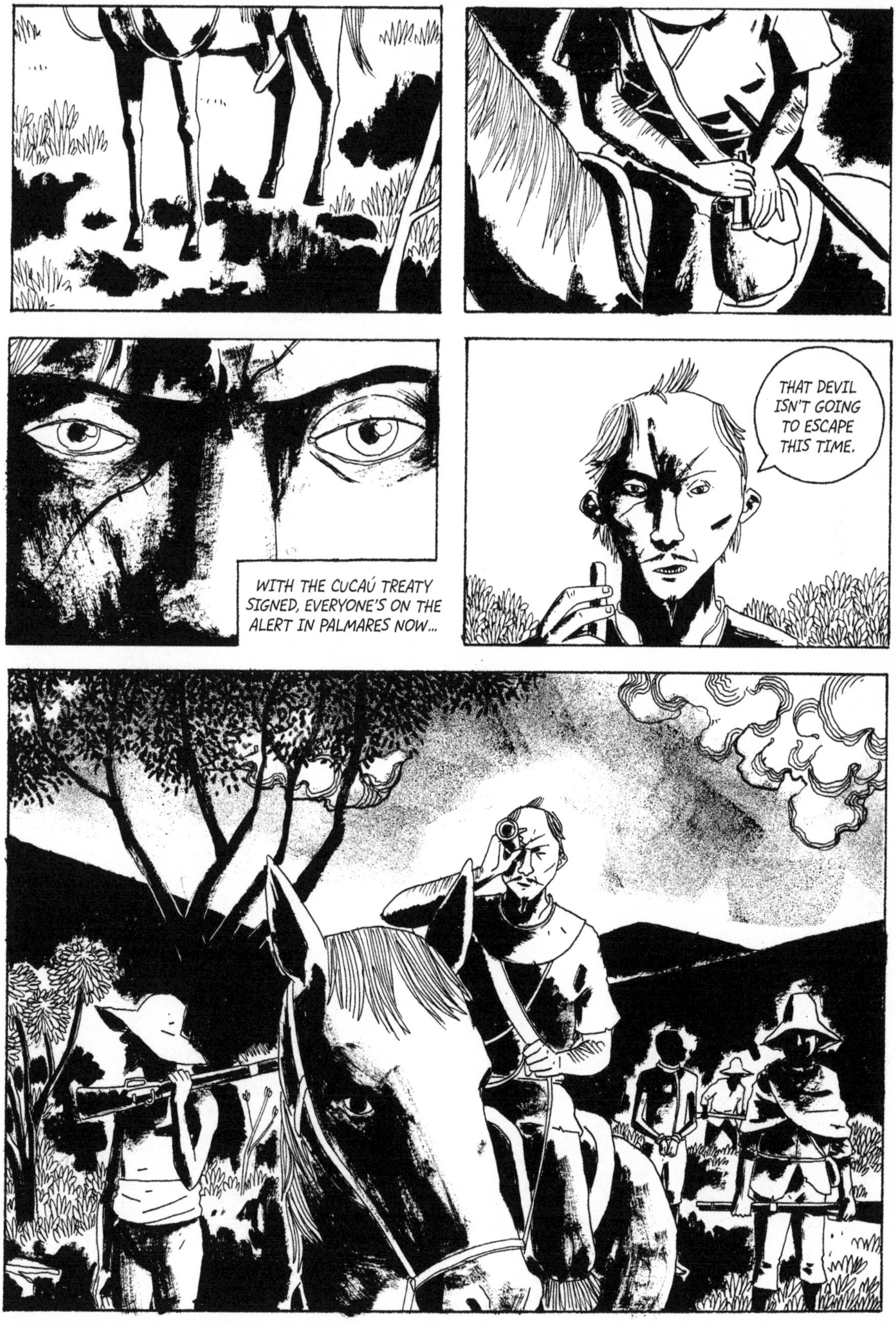
WITH THE CUCAÚ TREATY SIGNED, EVERYONE'S ON THE ALERT IN PALMARES NOW...
THAT DEVIL ISN'T GOING TO ESCAPE THIS TIME.

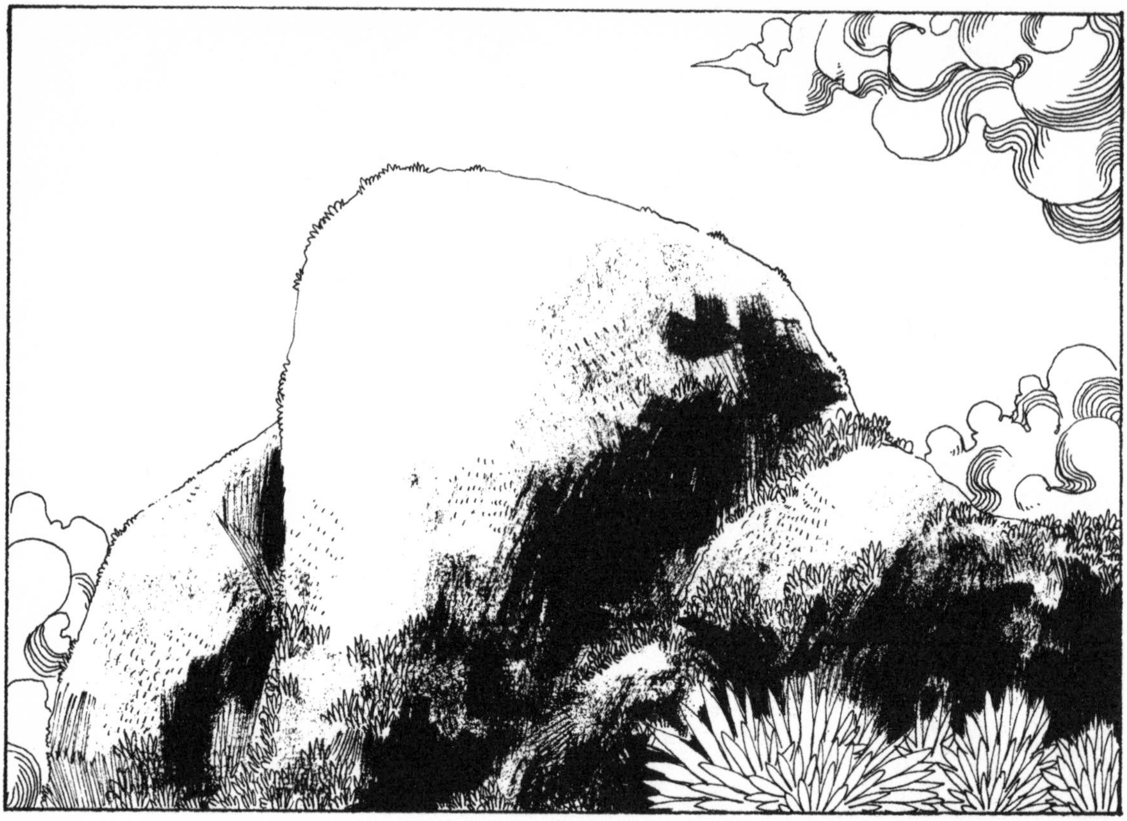

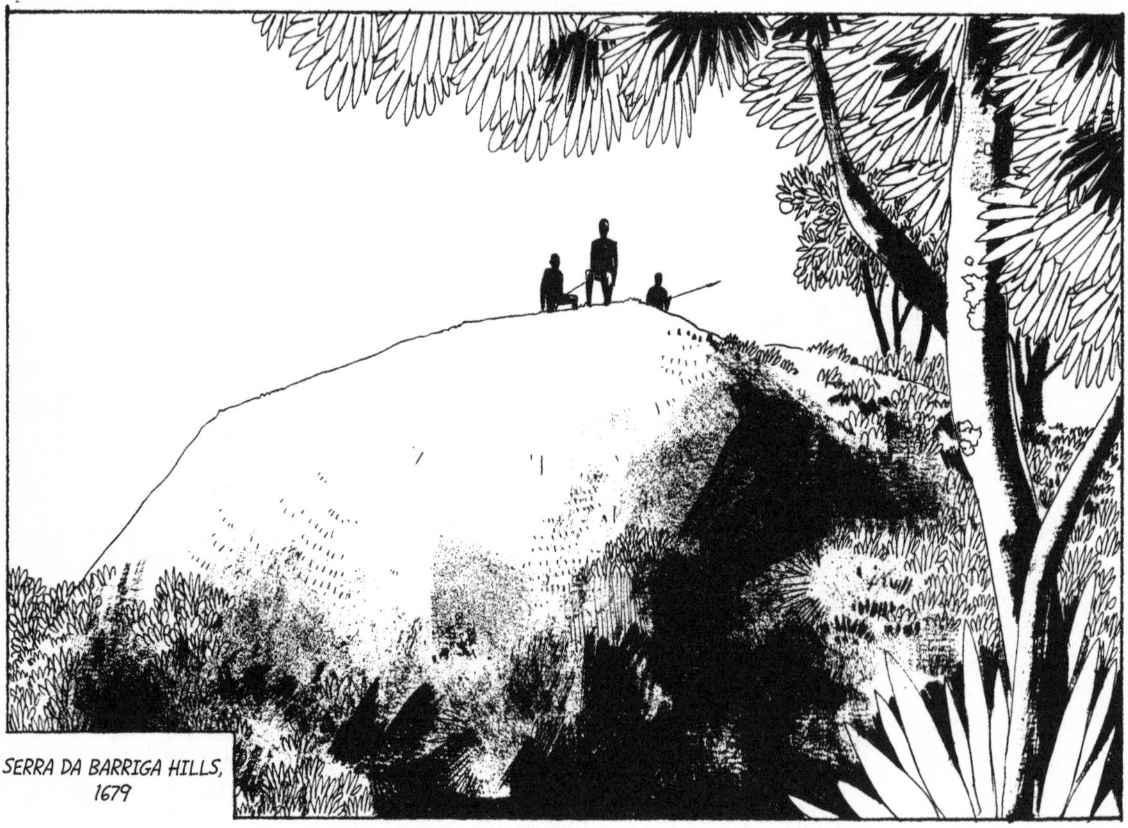
SERRA DA BARRIGA HILLS, 1679

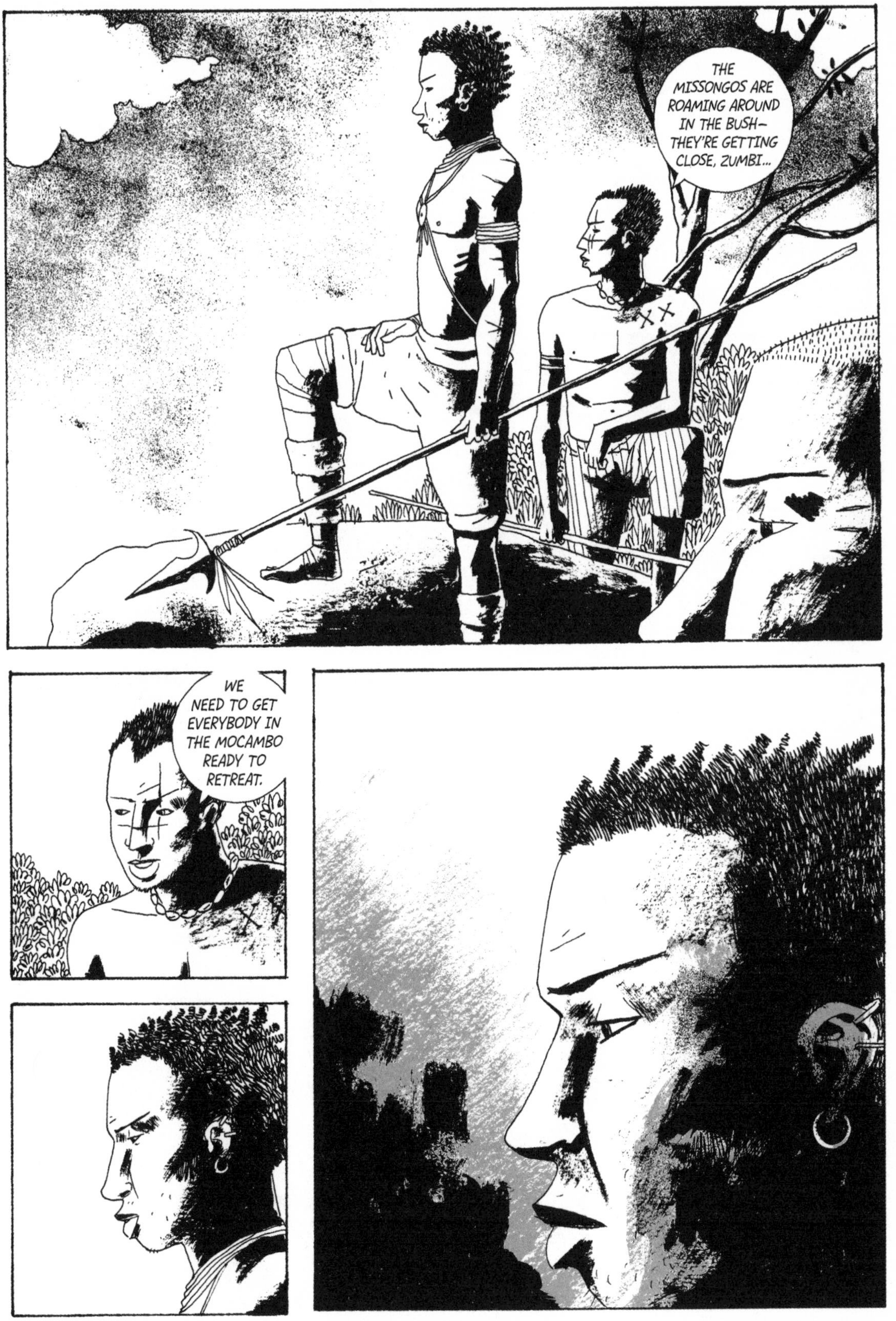
THE MISSONGOS ARE ROAMING AROUND IN THE BUSH— THEY'RE GETTING CLOSE, ZUMBI...
WE NEED TO GET EVERYBODY IN THE MOCAMBO READY TO RETREAT.

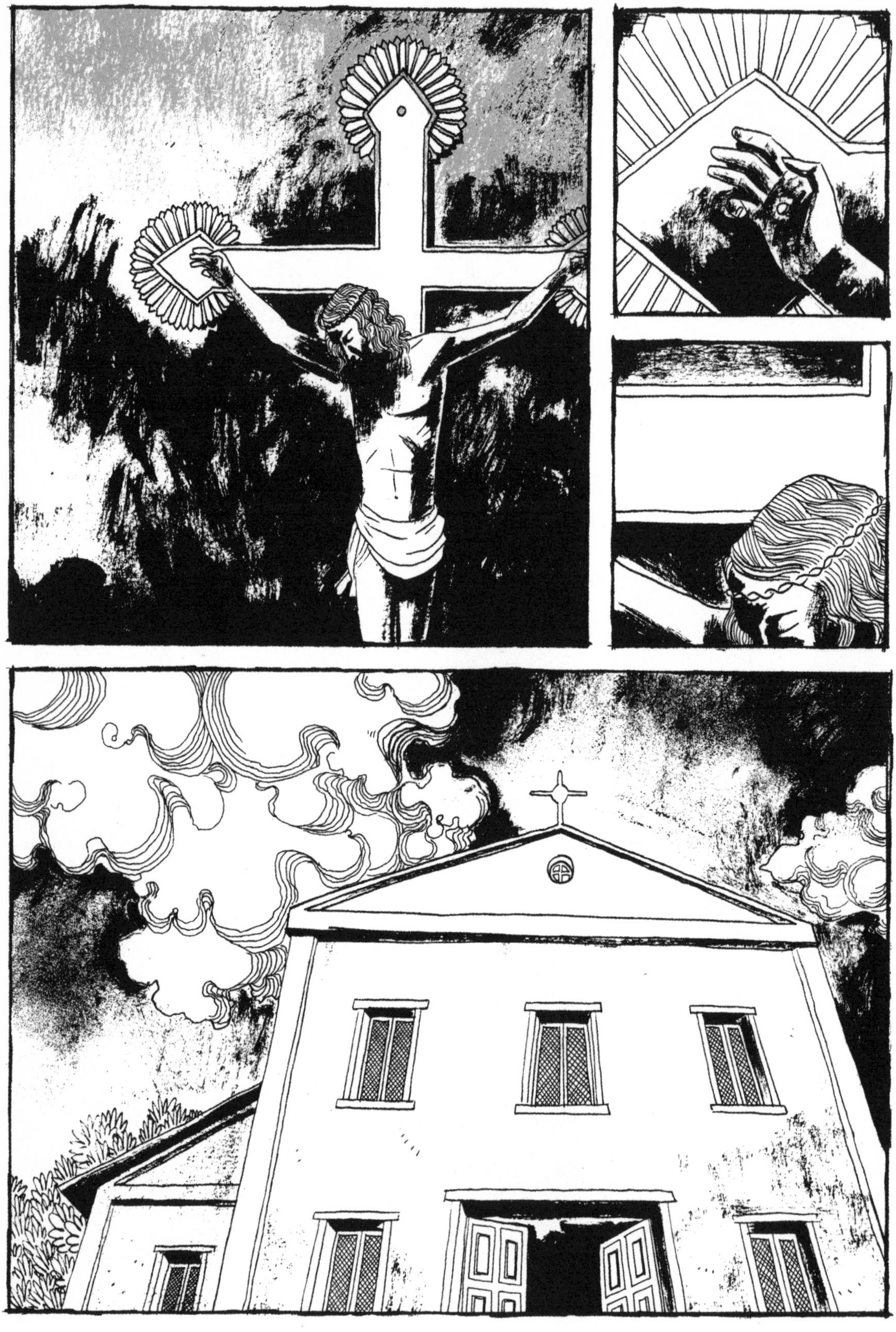

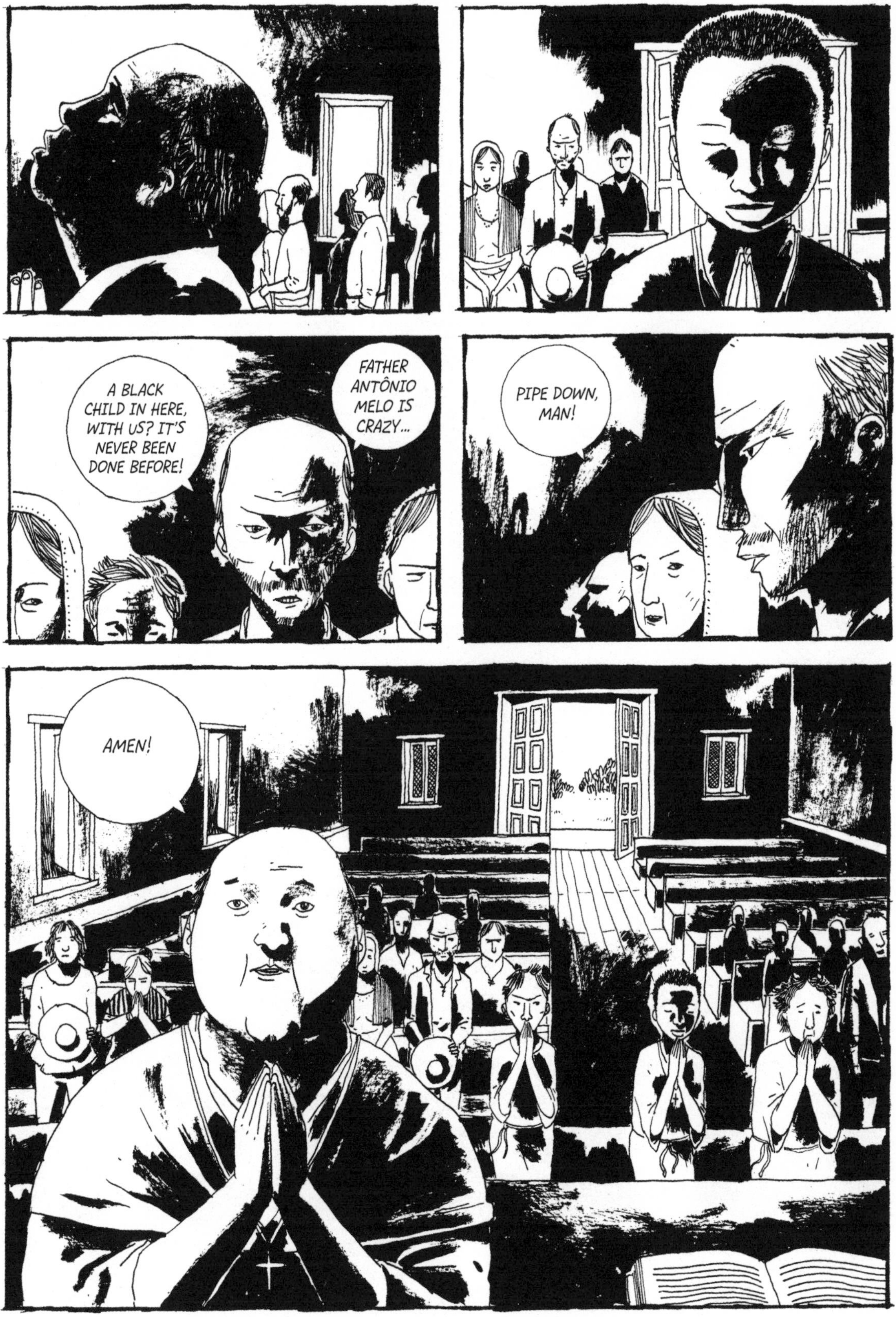
A BLACK CHILD IN HERE, WITH US? IT'S NEVER BEEN DONE BEFORE!
FATHER ANTÔNIO MELO IS CRAZY...
PIPE DOWN, MAN!
AMEN!

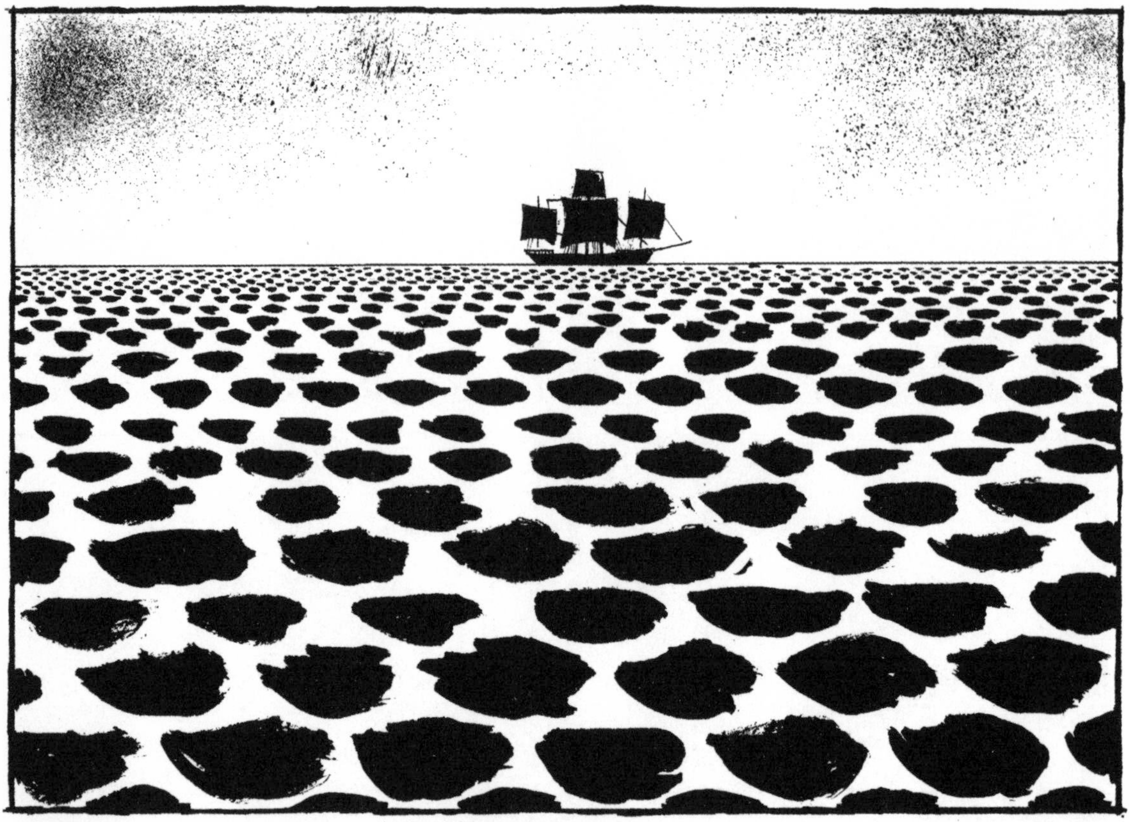

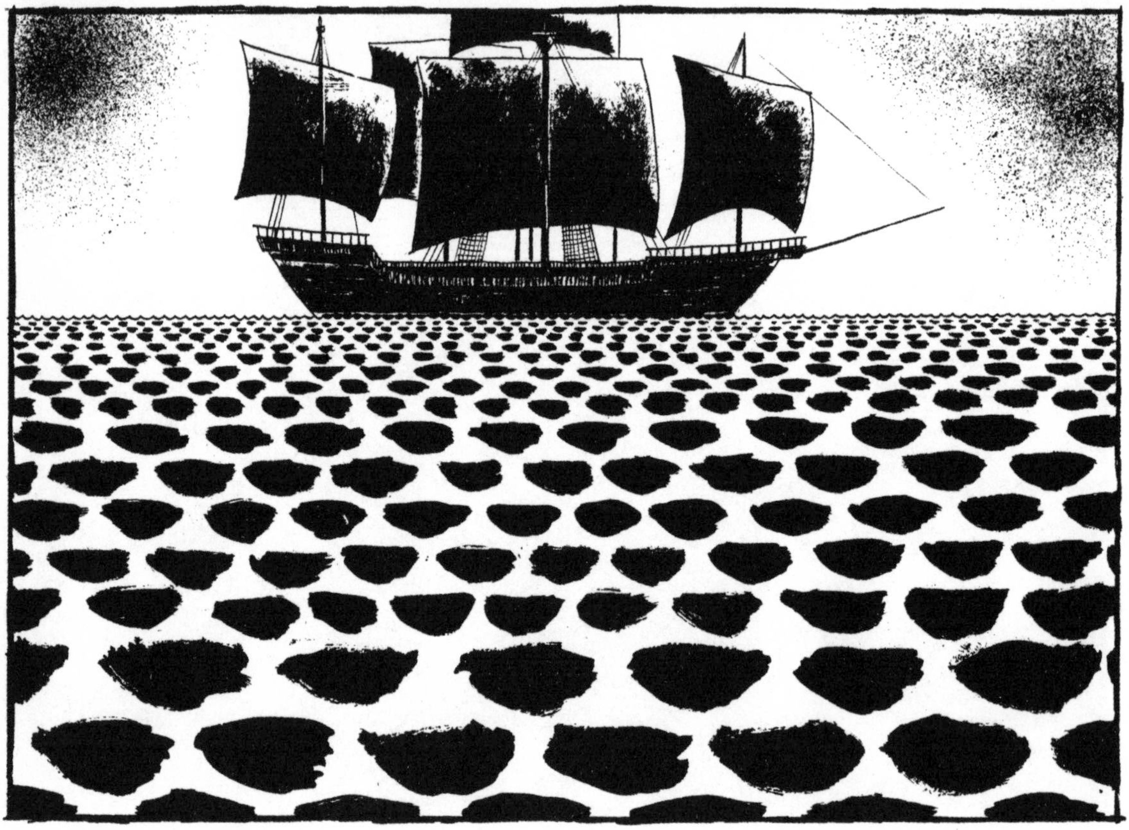

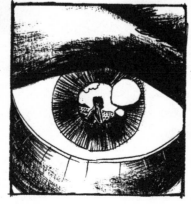

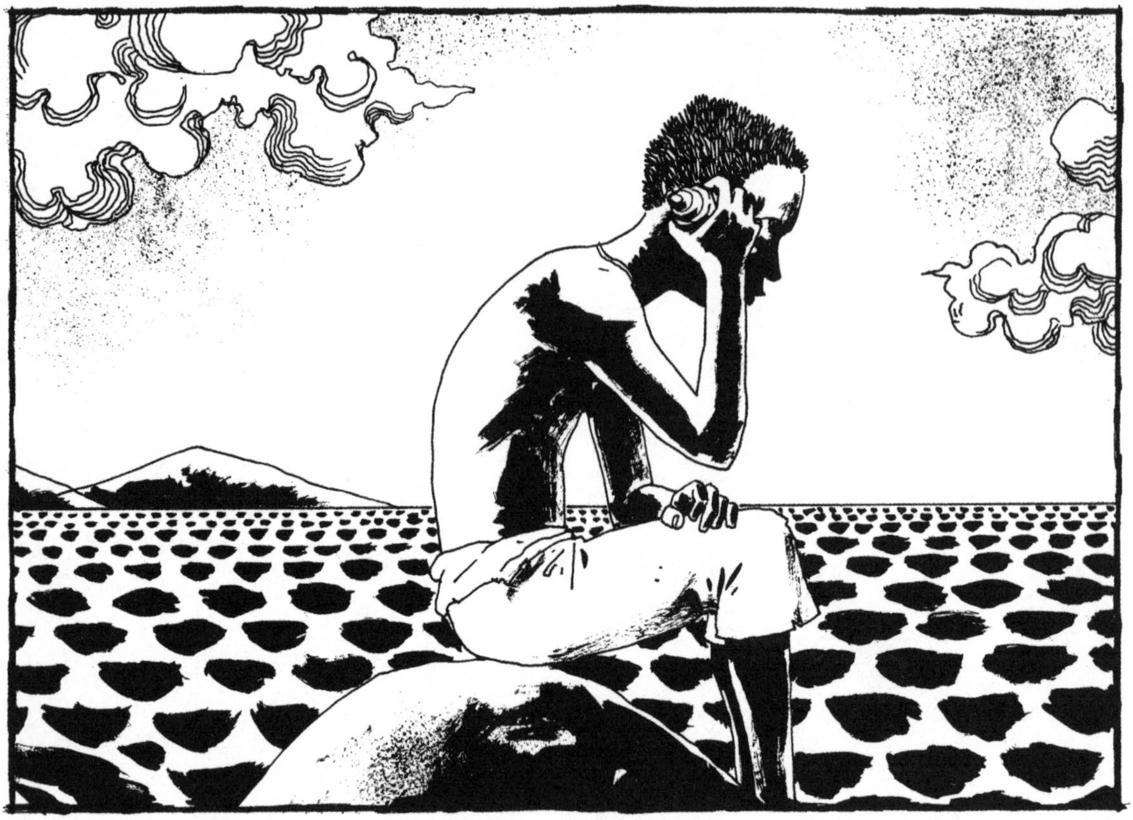

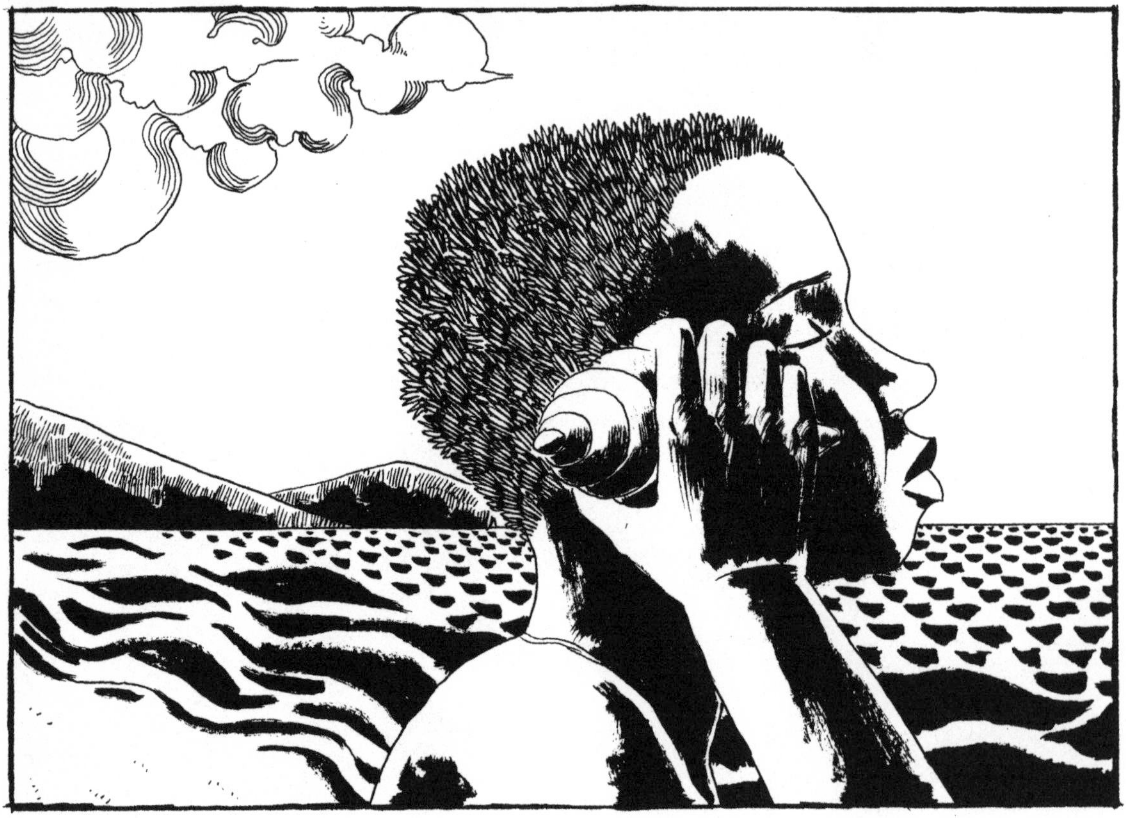

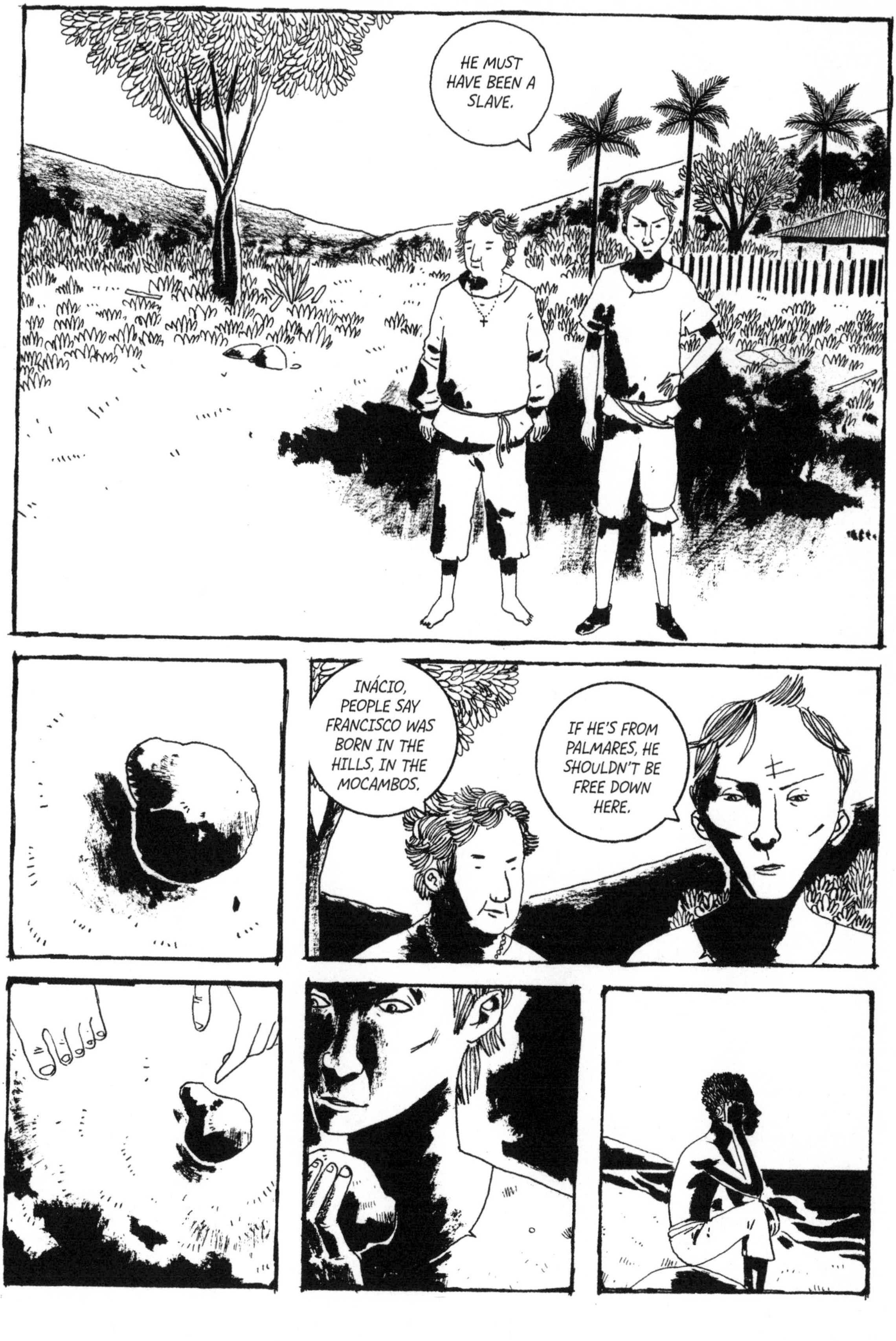
HE MUST HAVE BEEN A SLAVE.
INÁCIO, PEOPLE SAY FRANCISCO WAS BORN IN THE HILLS, IN THE MOCAMBOS.
IF HE'S FROM PALMARES, HE SHOULDN'T BE FREE DOWN HERE.

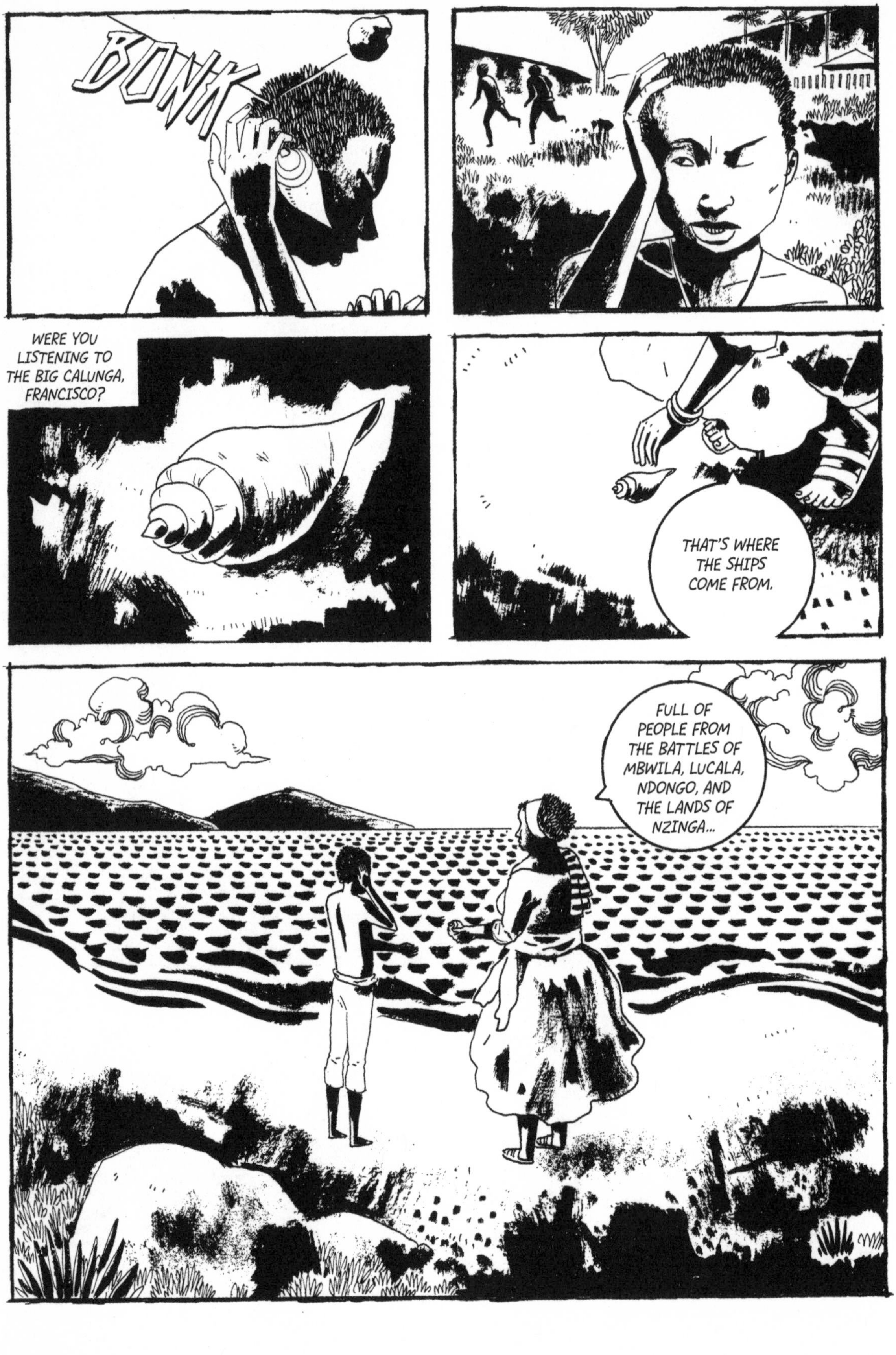
BONK
WERE YOU LISTENING TO THE BIG CALUNGA, FRANCISCO?
THAT'S WHERE THE SHIPS COME FROM.
FULL OF PEOPLE FROM THE BATTLES OF MBWILA, LUCALA, NDONGO, AND THE LANDS OF NZINGA...

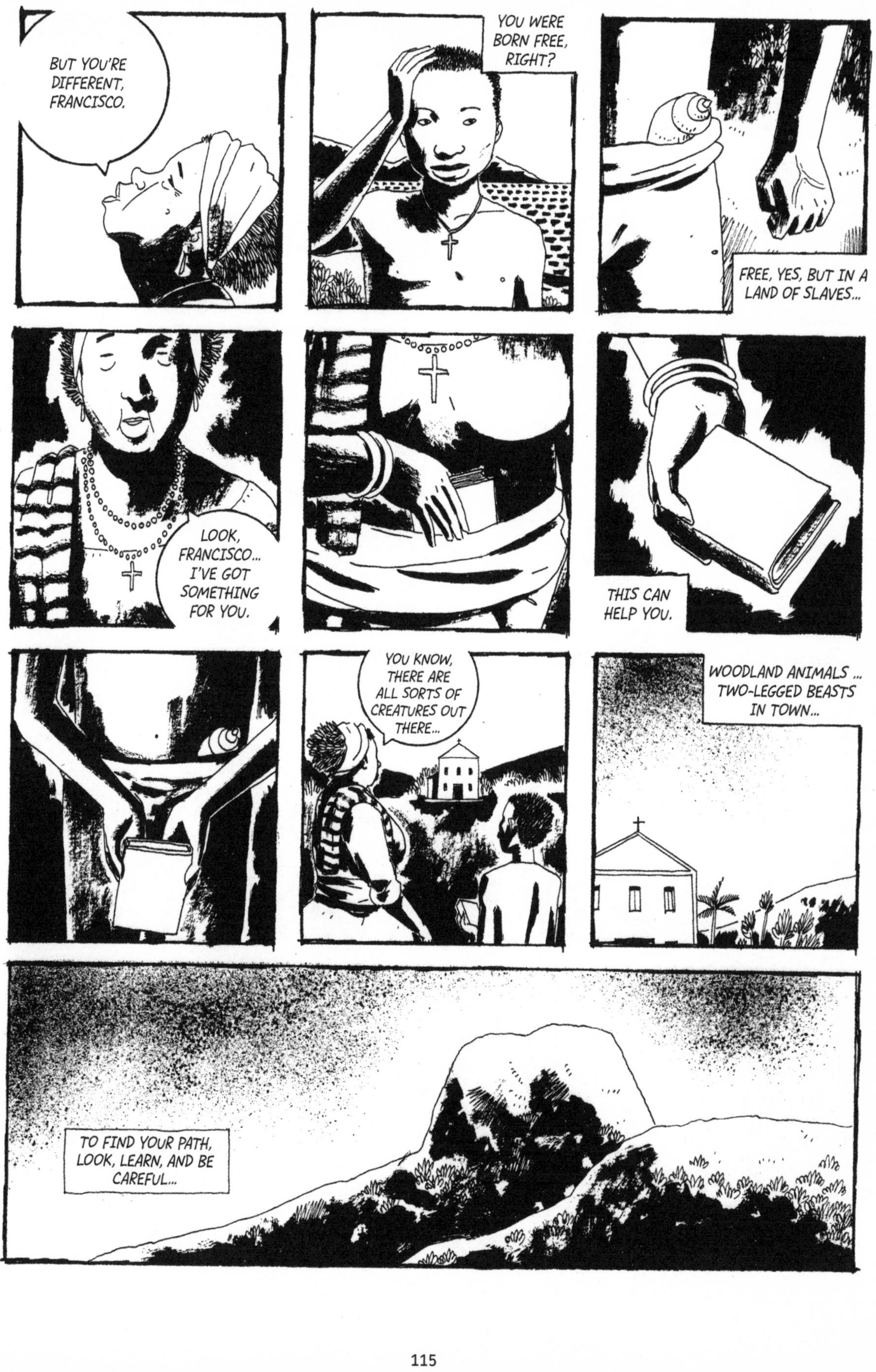
BUT YOU'RE DIFFERENT, FRANCISCO.
YOU WERE BORN FREE, RIGHT?
FREE, YES, BUT IN A LAND OF SLAVES...
LOOK, FRANCISCO... I'VE GOT SOMETHING FOR YOU.
THIS CAN HELP YOU.
YOU KNOW, THERE ARE ALL SORTS OF CREATURES OUT THERE...
WOODLAND ANIMALS ... TWO-LEGGED BEASTS IN TOWN...
TO FIND YOUR PATH, LOOK, LEARN, AND BE CAREFUL...

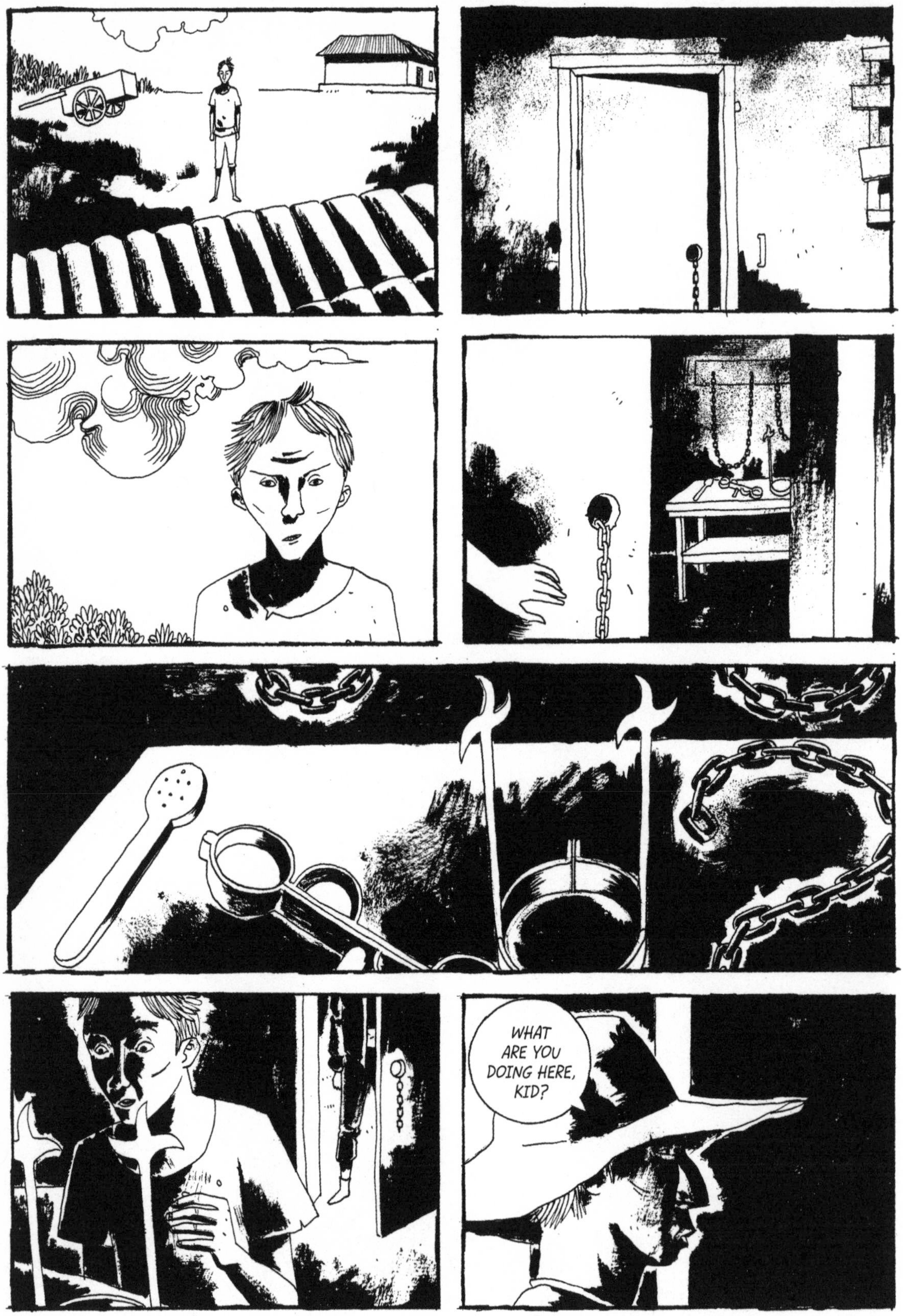
WHAT ARE YOU DOING HERE, KID?

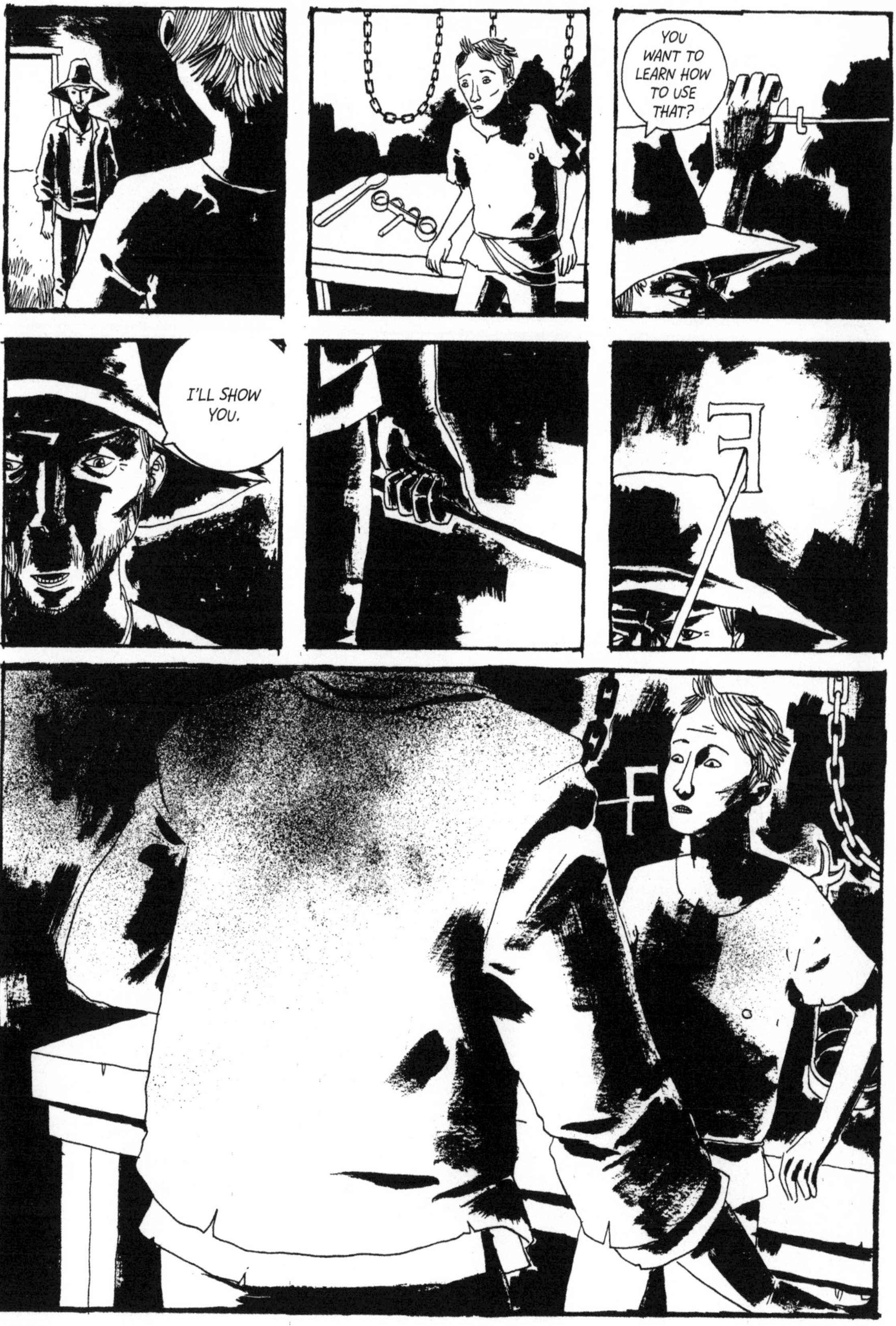
YOU WANT TO LEARN HOW TO USE THAT?
I'LL SHOW YOU.

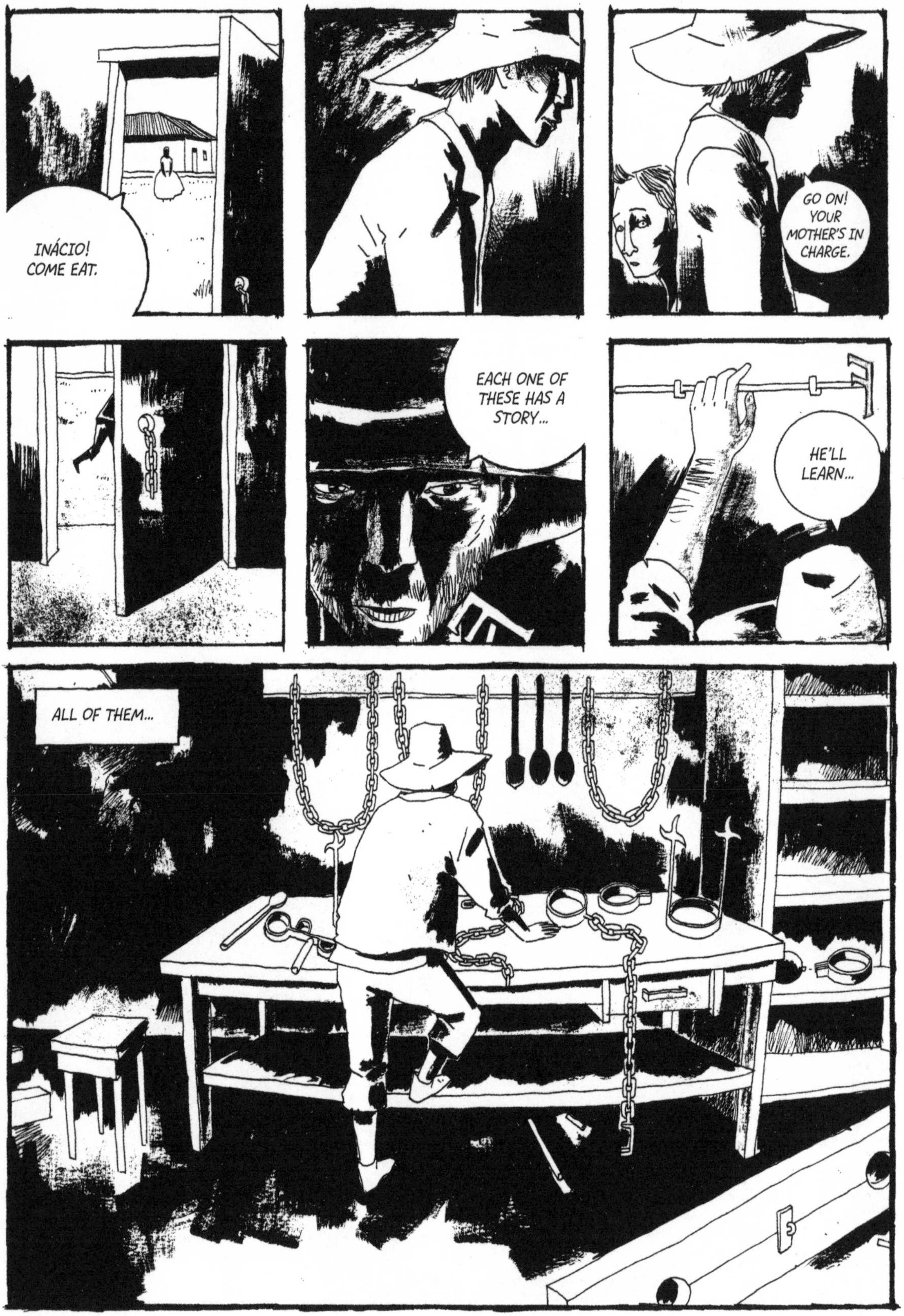
INÁCIO! COME EAT.
GO ON! YOUR MOTHER'S IN CHARGE.
EACH ONE OF THESE HAS A STORY...
HE'LL LEARN...
ALL OF THEM...

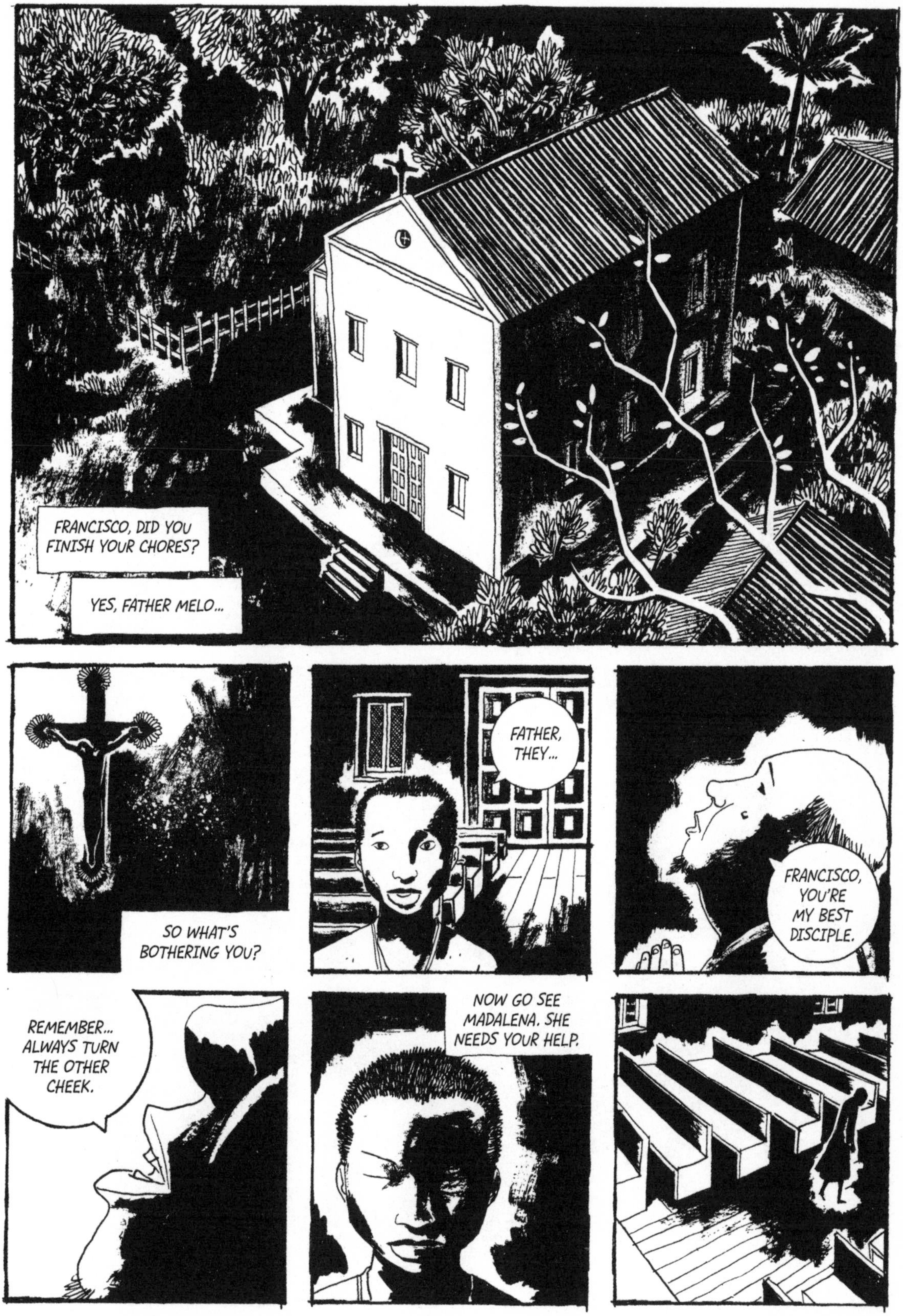
FRANCISCO, DID YOU FINISH YOUR CHORES?
YES, FATHER MELO...
SO WHAT'S BOTHERING YOU?
FATHER, THEY...
FRANCISCO, YOU'RE MY BEST DISCIPLE.
REMEMBER... ALWAYS TURN THE OTHER CHEEK.
NOW GO SEE MADALENA. SHE NEEDS YOUR HELP.

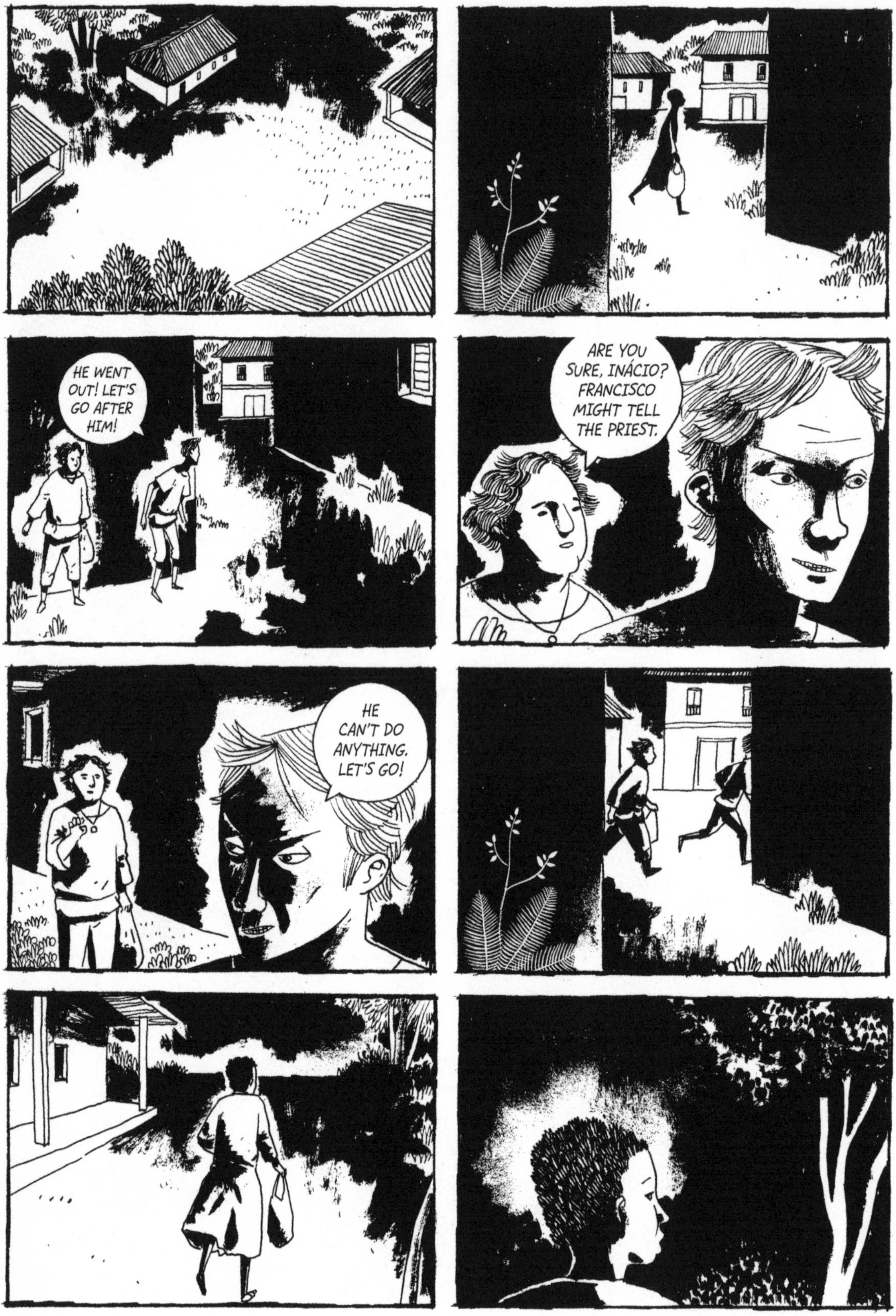
HE WENT OUT! LET'S GO AFTER HIM!
ARE YOU SURE, INÁCIO? FRANCISCO MIGHT TELL THE PRIEST.
HE CAN'T DO ANYTHING. LET'S GO!

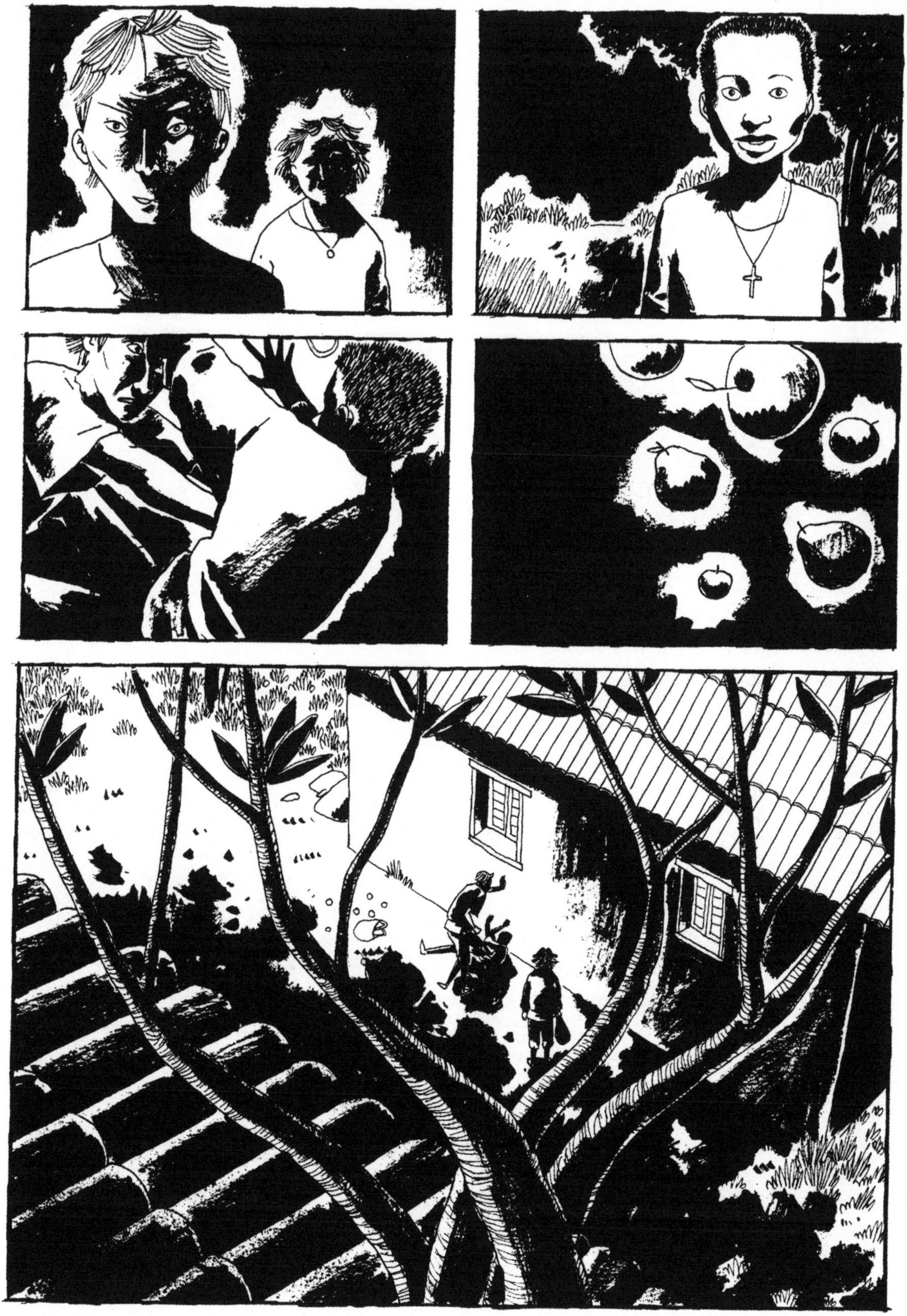

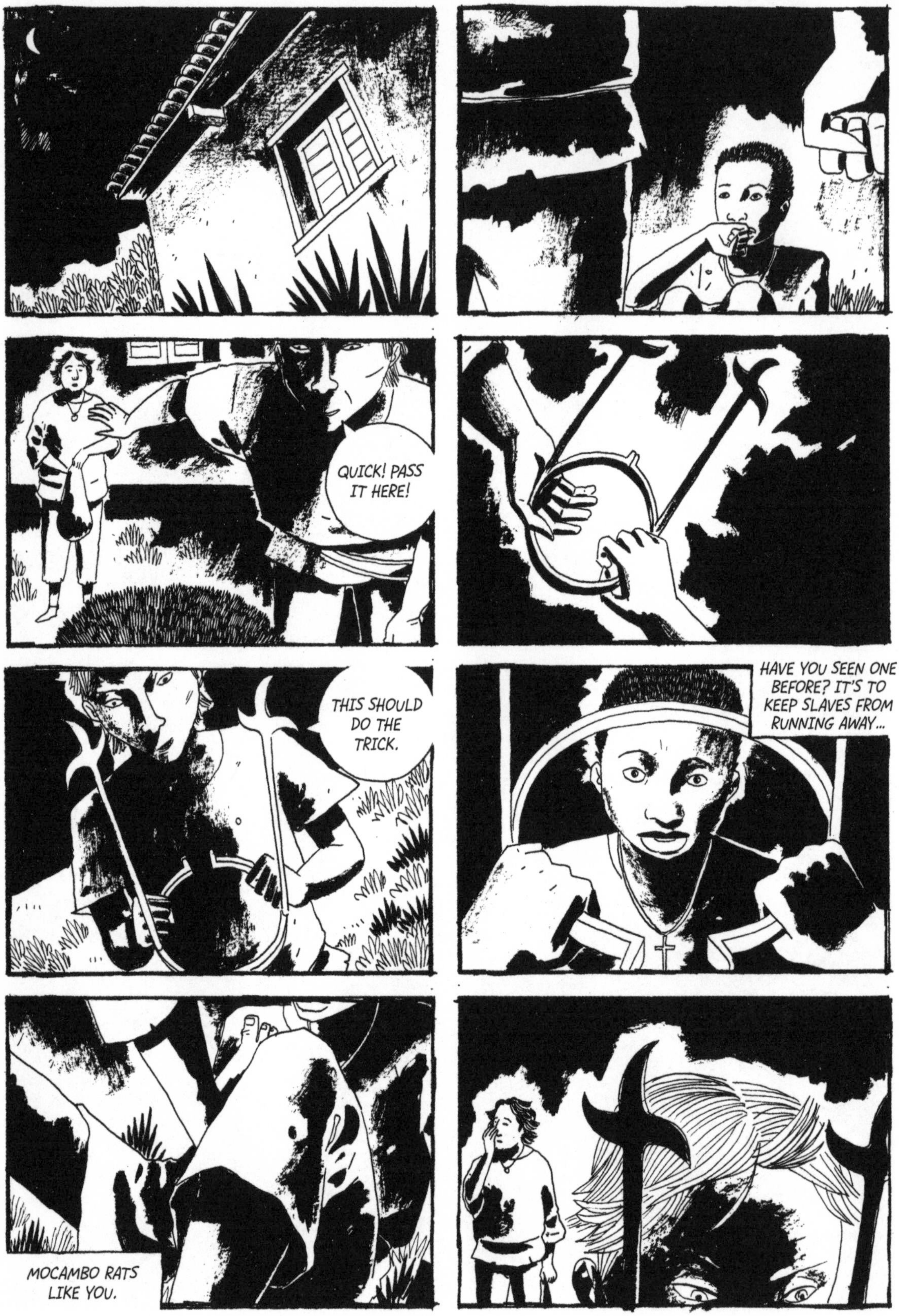
QUICK! PASS IT HERE!
THIS SHOULD DO THE TRICK.
HAVE YOU SEEN ONE BEFORE? IT'S TO KEEP SLAVES FROM RUNNING AWAY...
MOCAMBO RATS LIKE YOU.

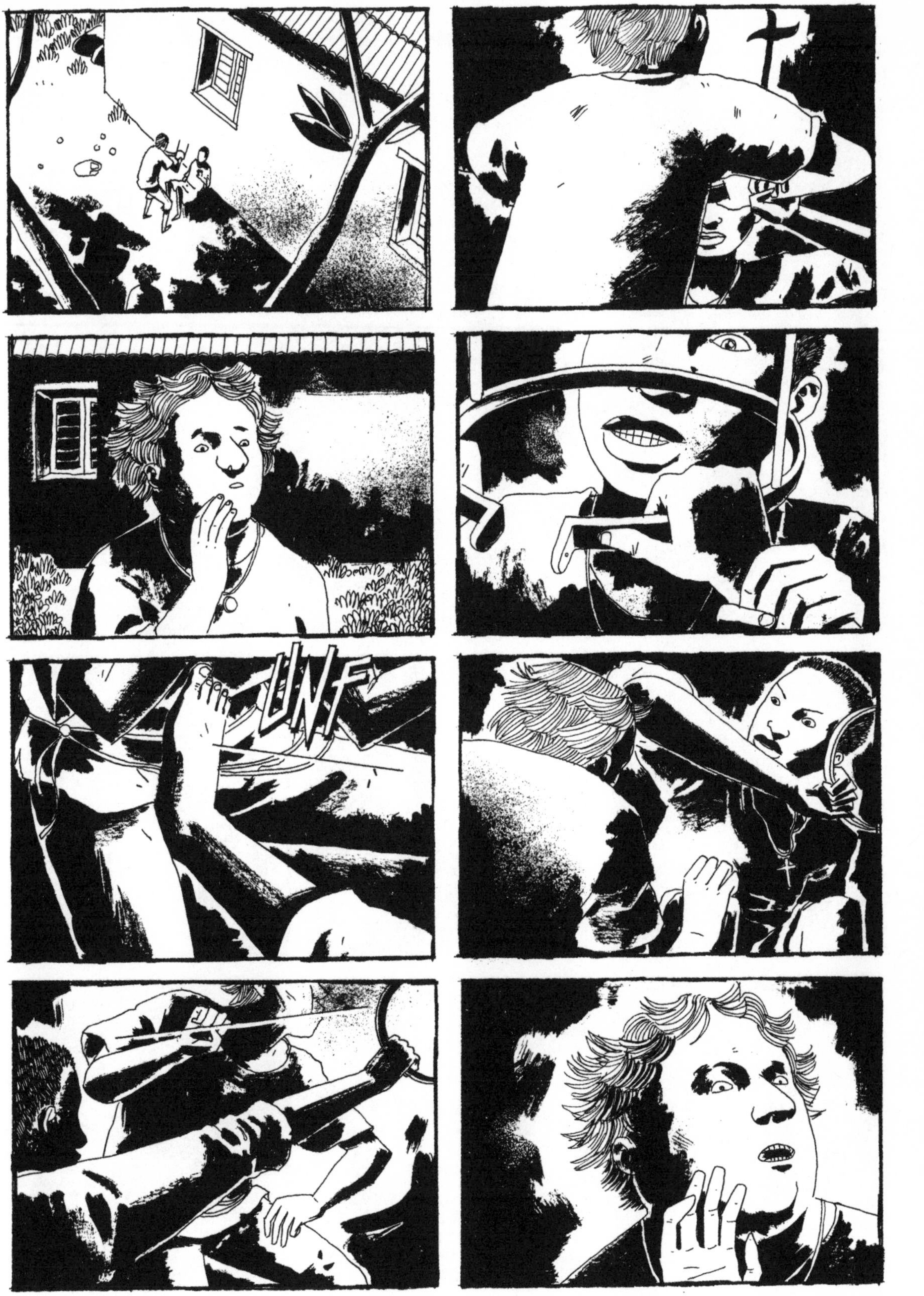
UNF

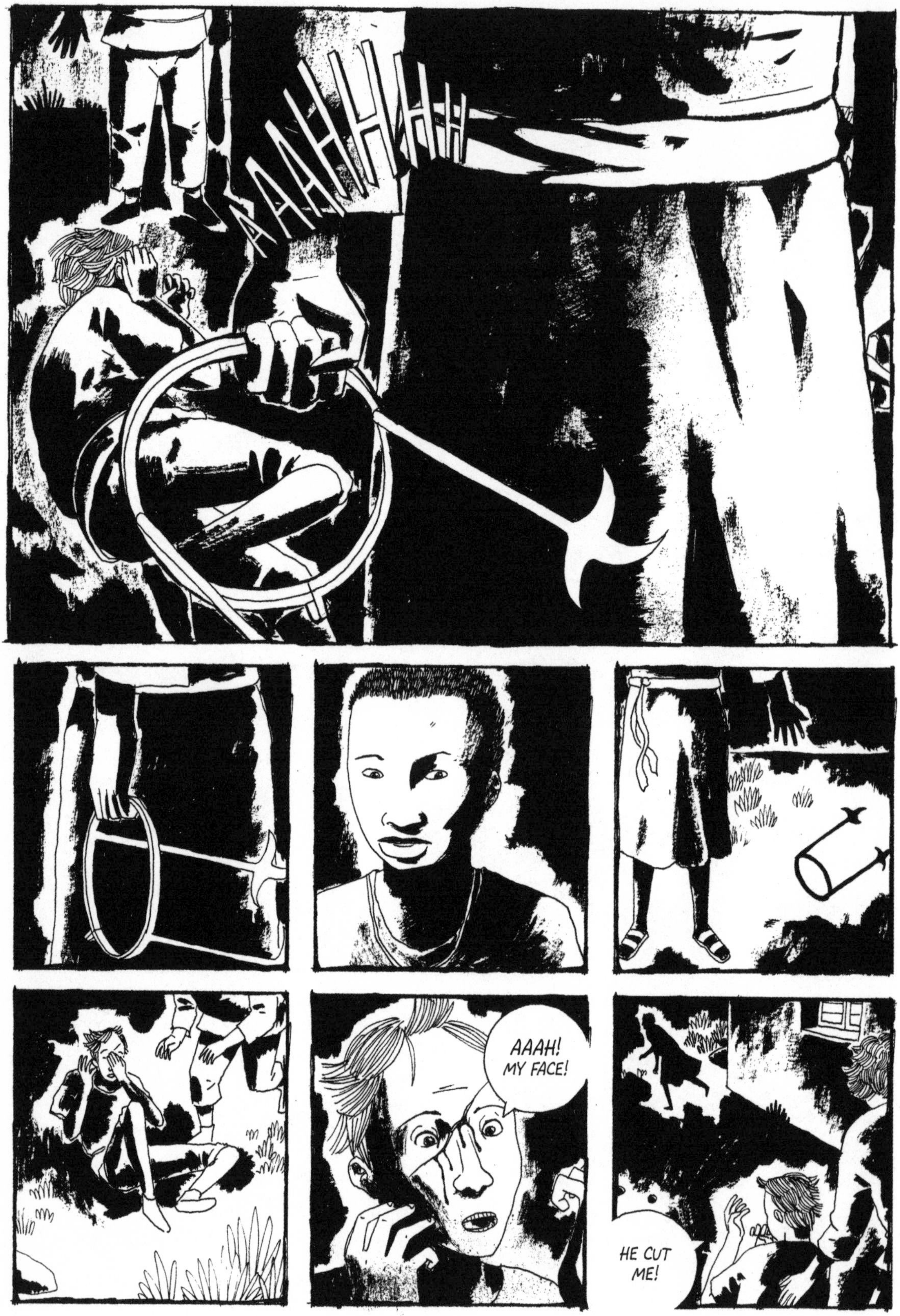
AAAHHHHHH
AAAH! MY FACE!
HE CUT ME!

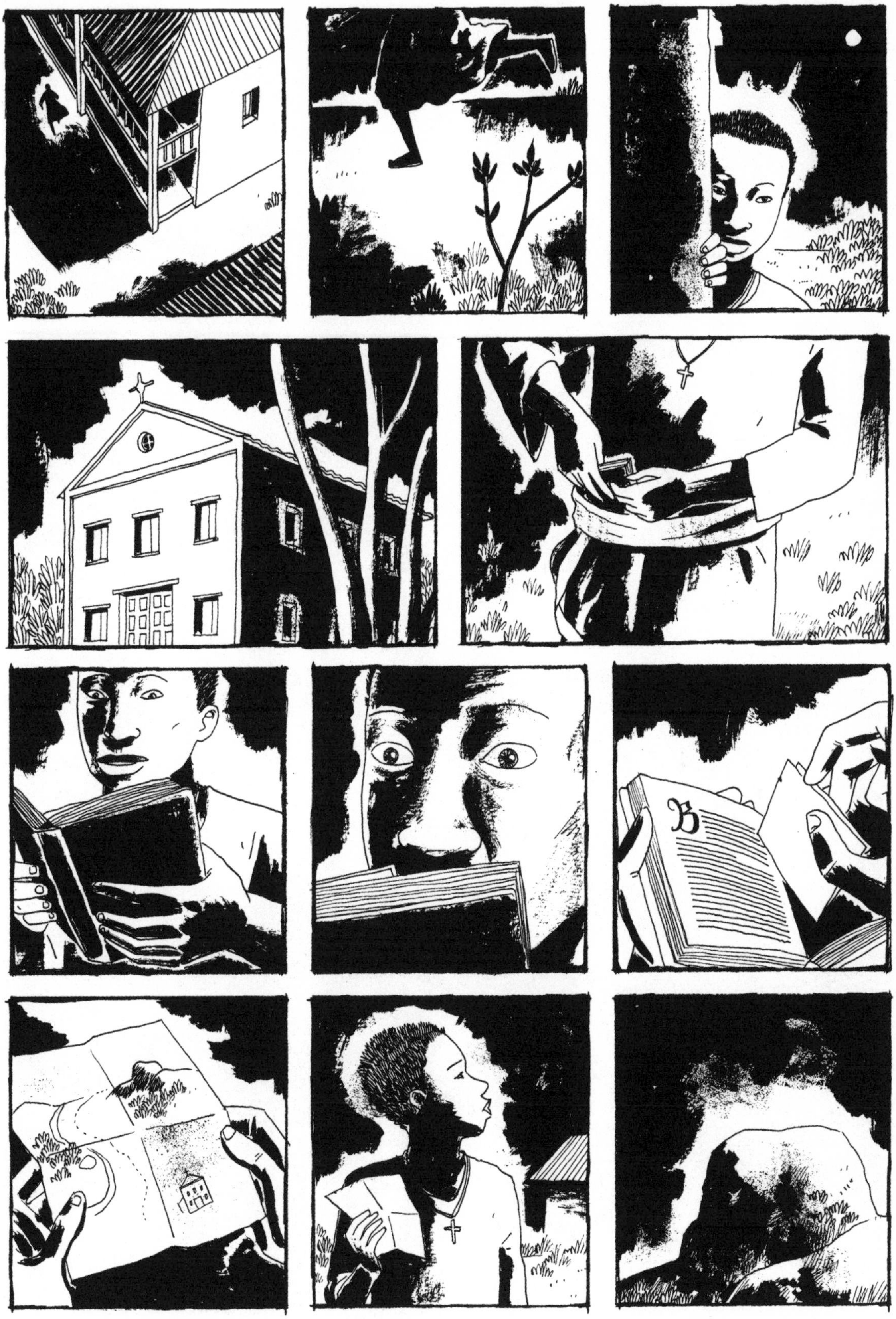

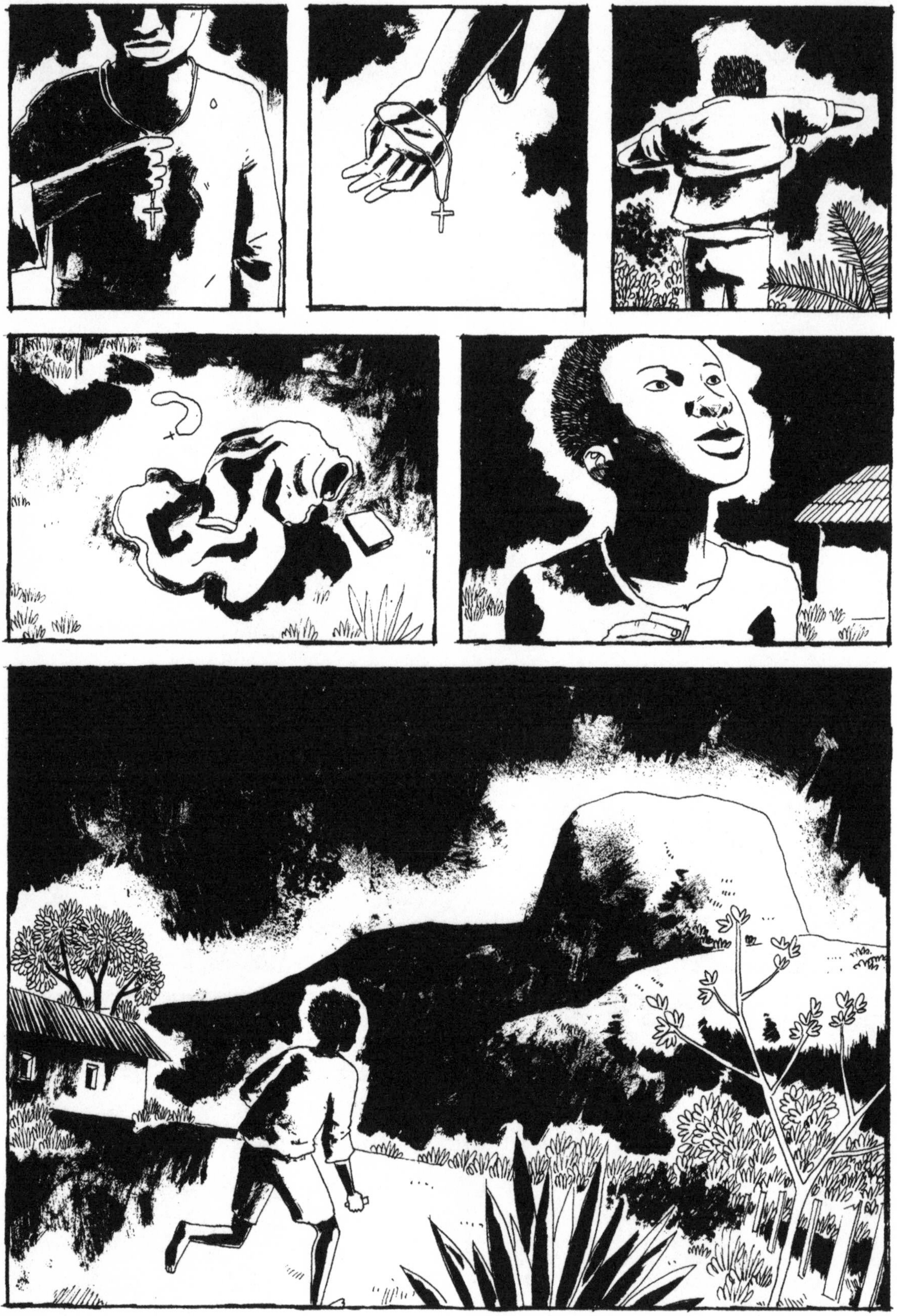

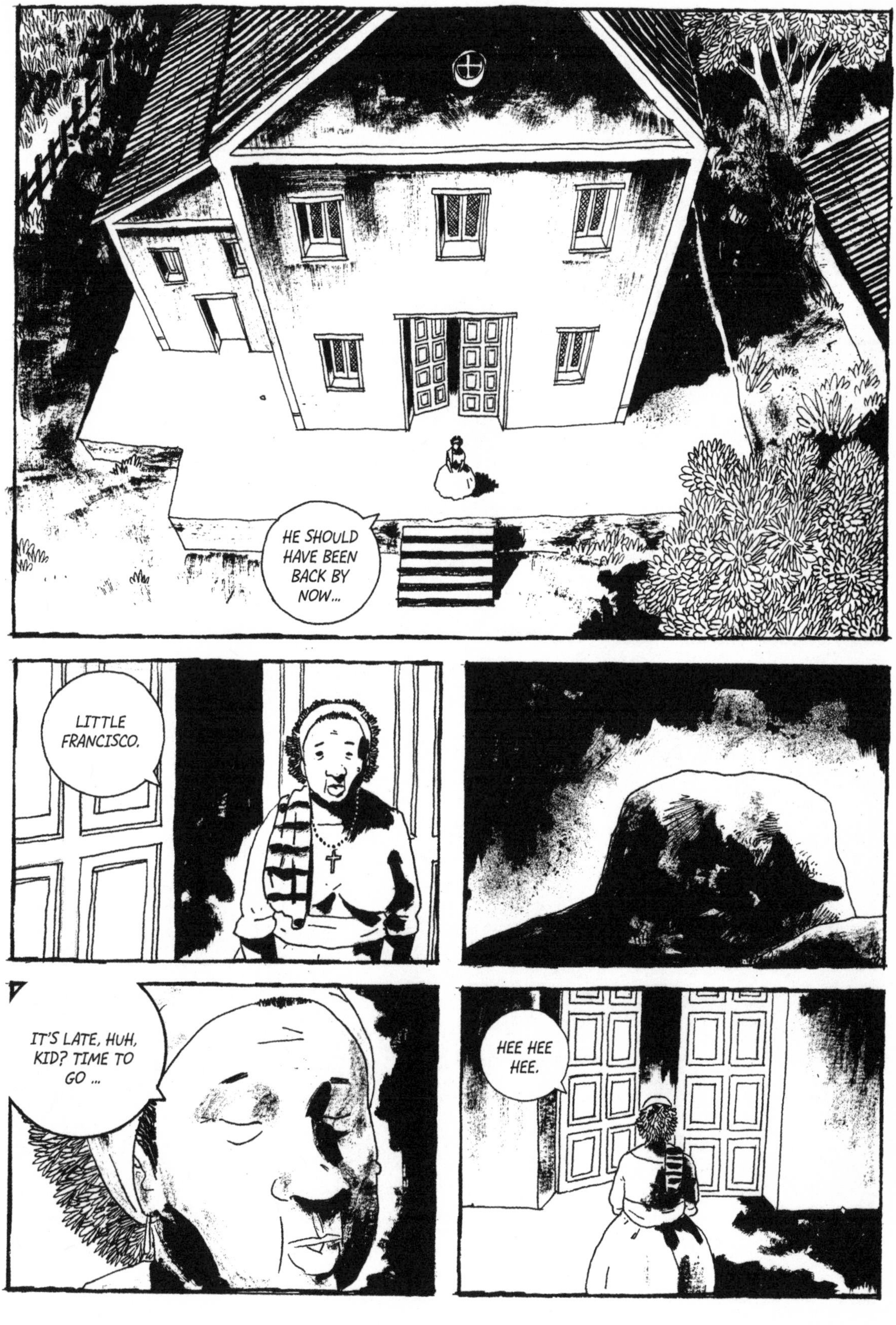
HE SHOULD HAVE BEEN BACK BY NOW...
LITTLE FRANCISCO.
IT'S LATE, HUH, KID? TIME TO GO ...
HEE HEE HEE.

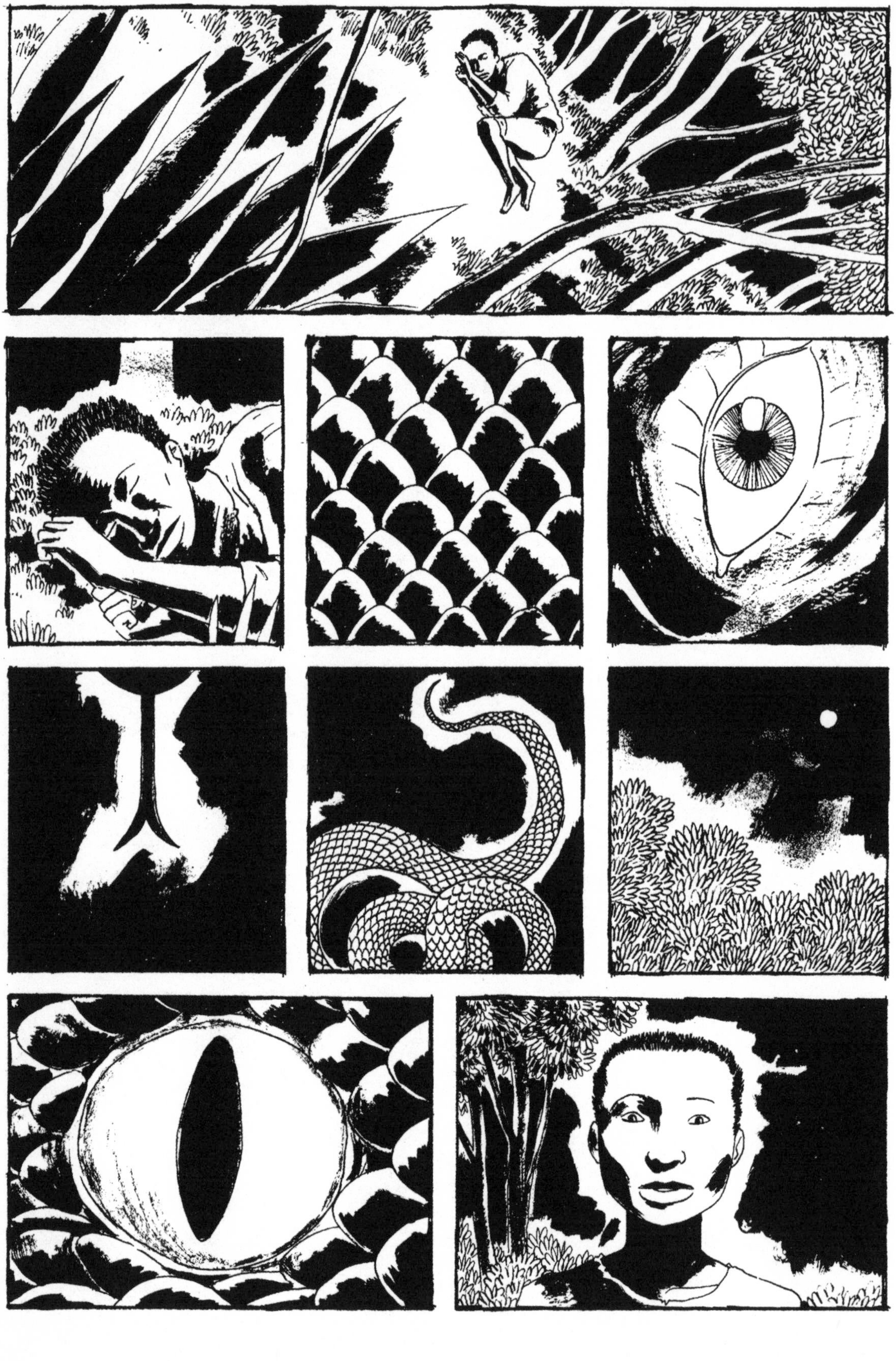

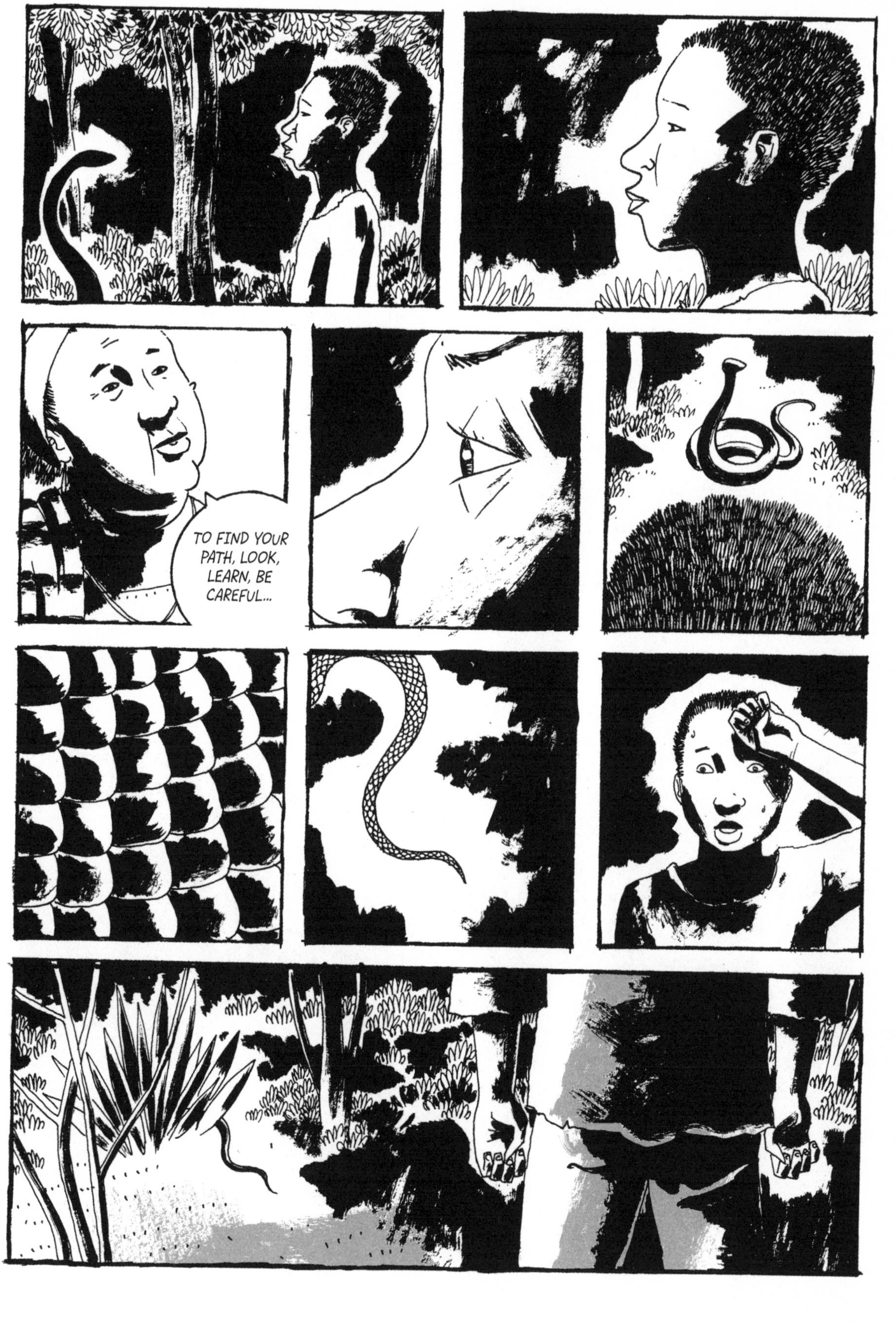
TO FIND YOUR PATH, LOOK, LEARN, BE CAREFUL...

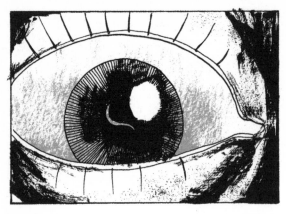

ZUMBI...

THE SOLDIERS ARE ARRIVING. WE'RE WAITING FOR YOUR SIGNAL TO ACT.

SHALL WE RETREAT?

WAIT, SOARES...

WE NEED JUST THE RIGHT MOMENT...

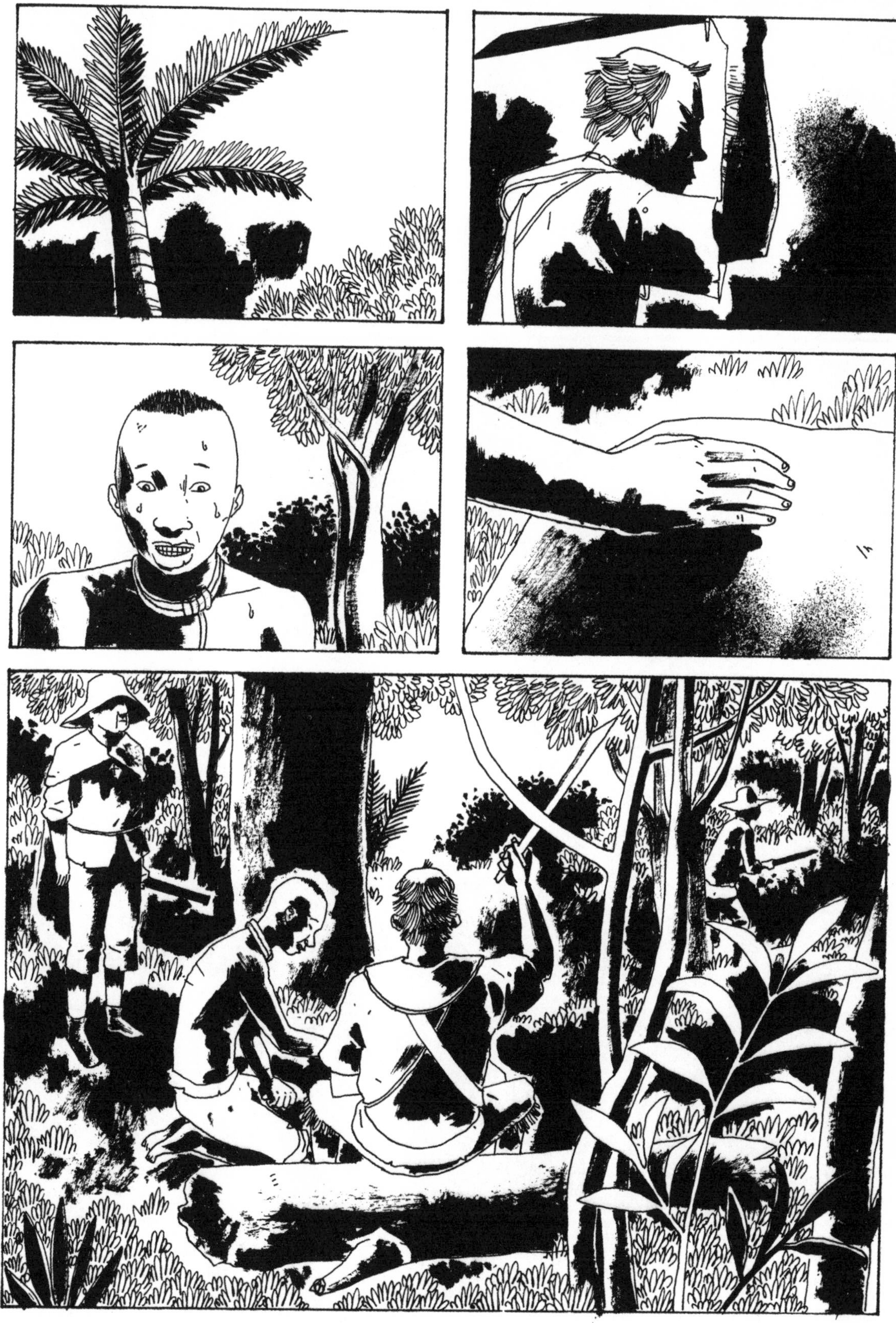

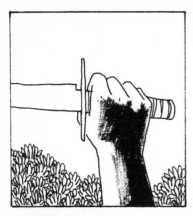

I COUL—

HUH?

AAAAAAHHHH

HE TOOK TOO LONG.

A SLAVE MISSING A FEW FINGERS IS WORTH MORE...

THAN A DEAD ONE.

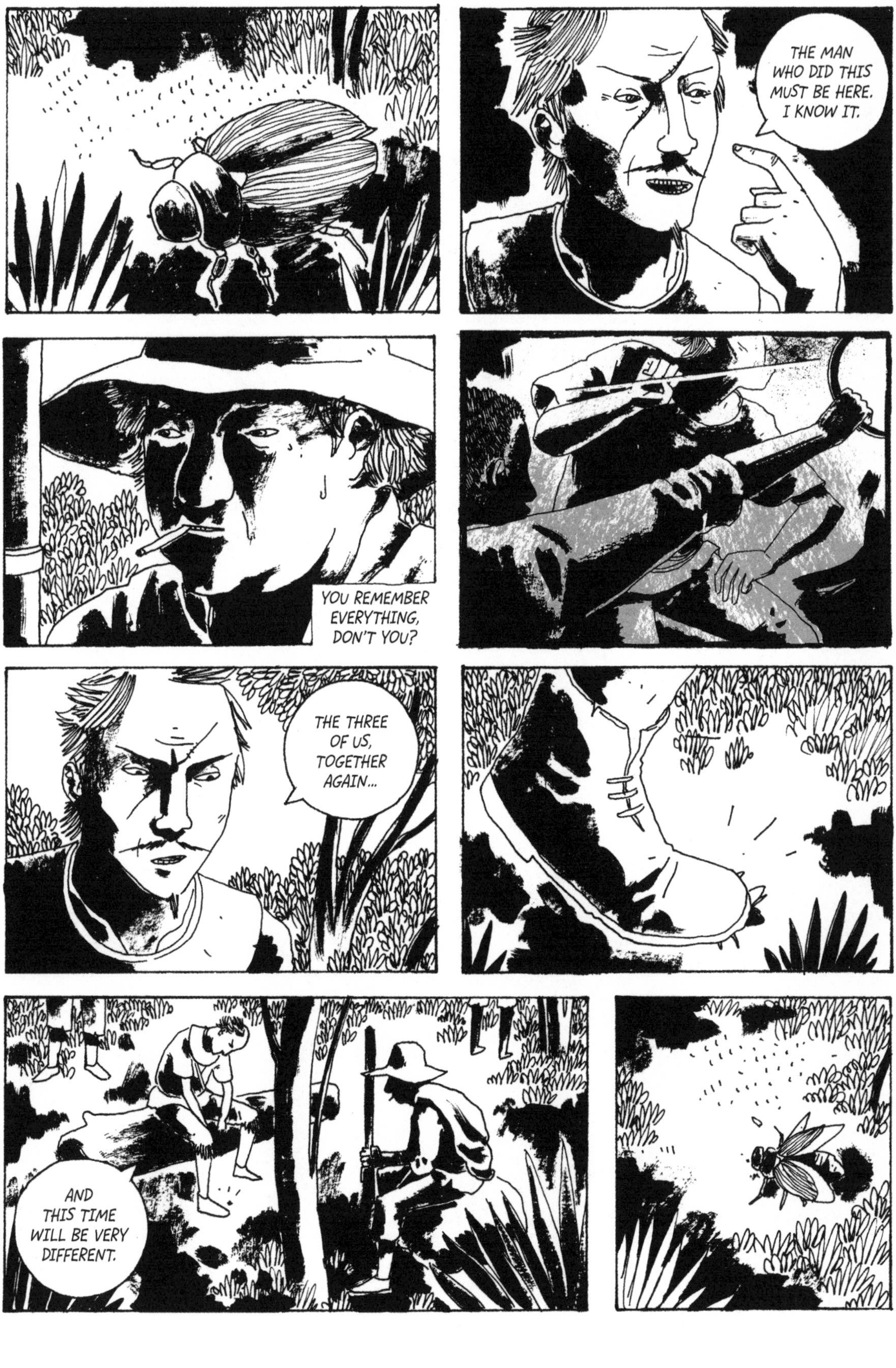
THE MAN WHO DID THIS MUST BE HERE. I KNOW IT.
YOU REMEMBER EVERYTHING, DON'T YOU?
THE THREE OF US, TOGETHER AGAIN...
AND THIS TIME WILL BE VERY DIFFERENT.

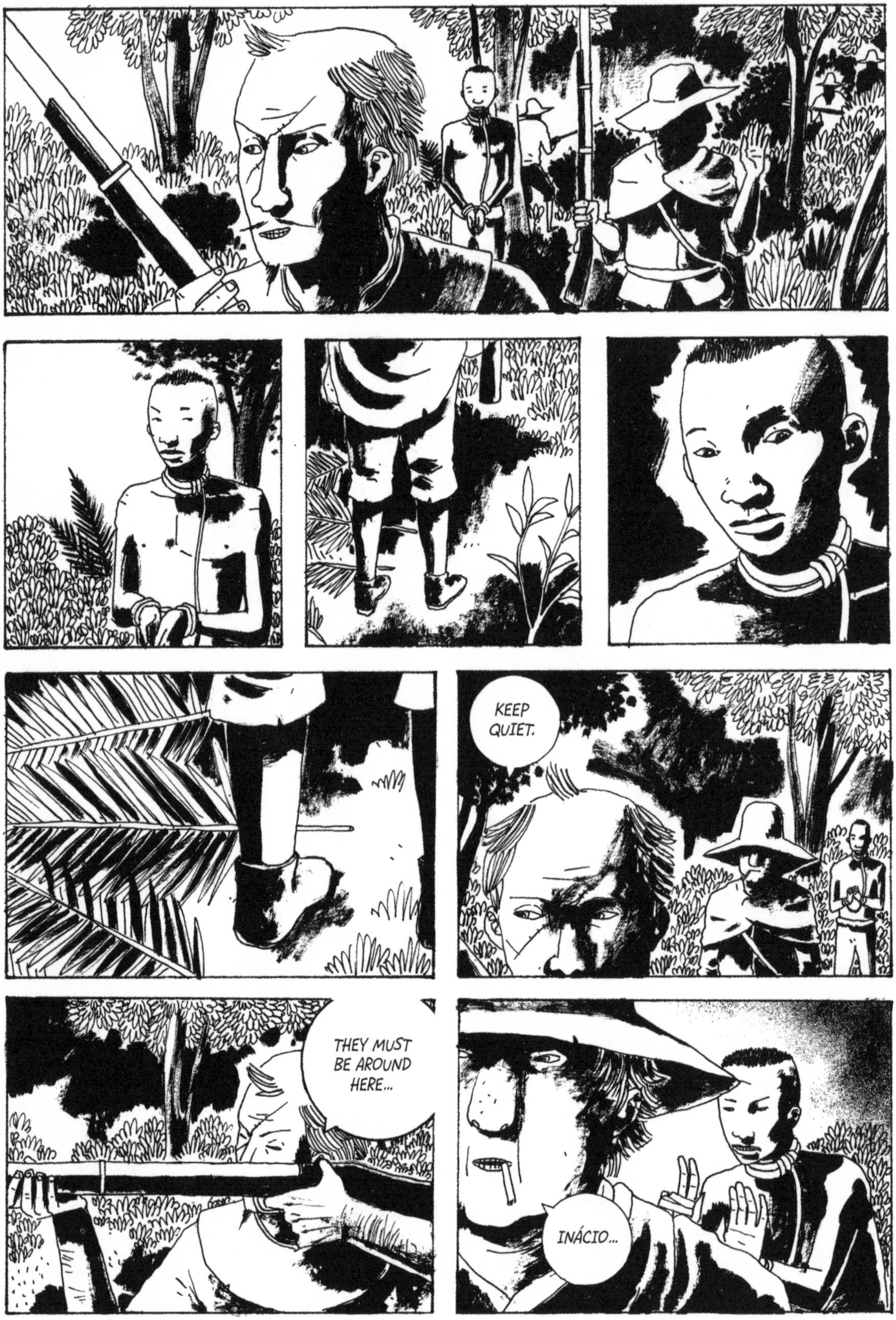
KEEP QUIET.
THEY MUST BE AROUND HERE...
INÁCIO...

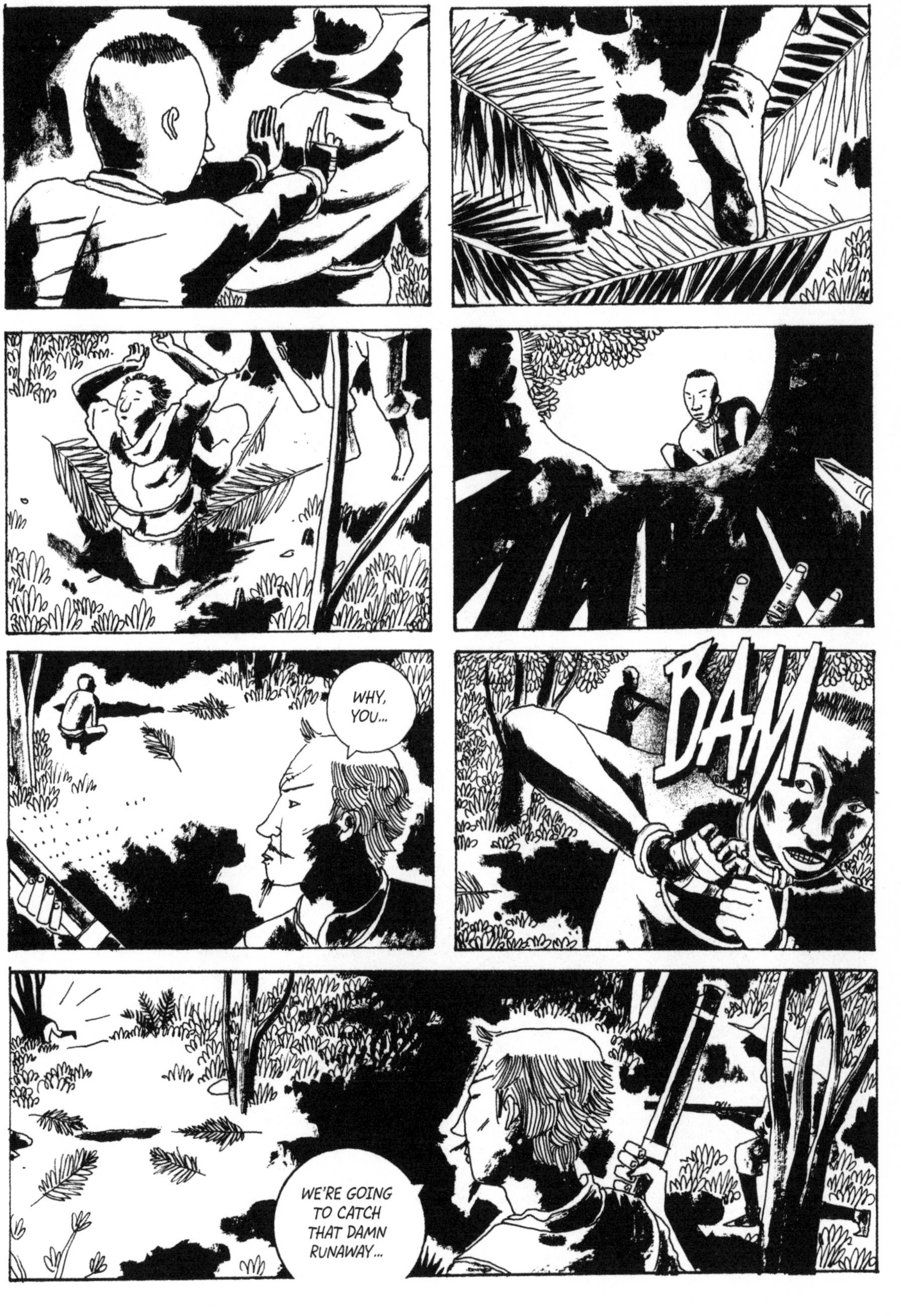
WHY, YOU...
BAM
WE'RE GOING TO CATCH THAT DAMN RUNAWAY...

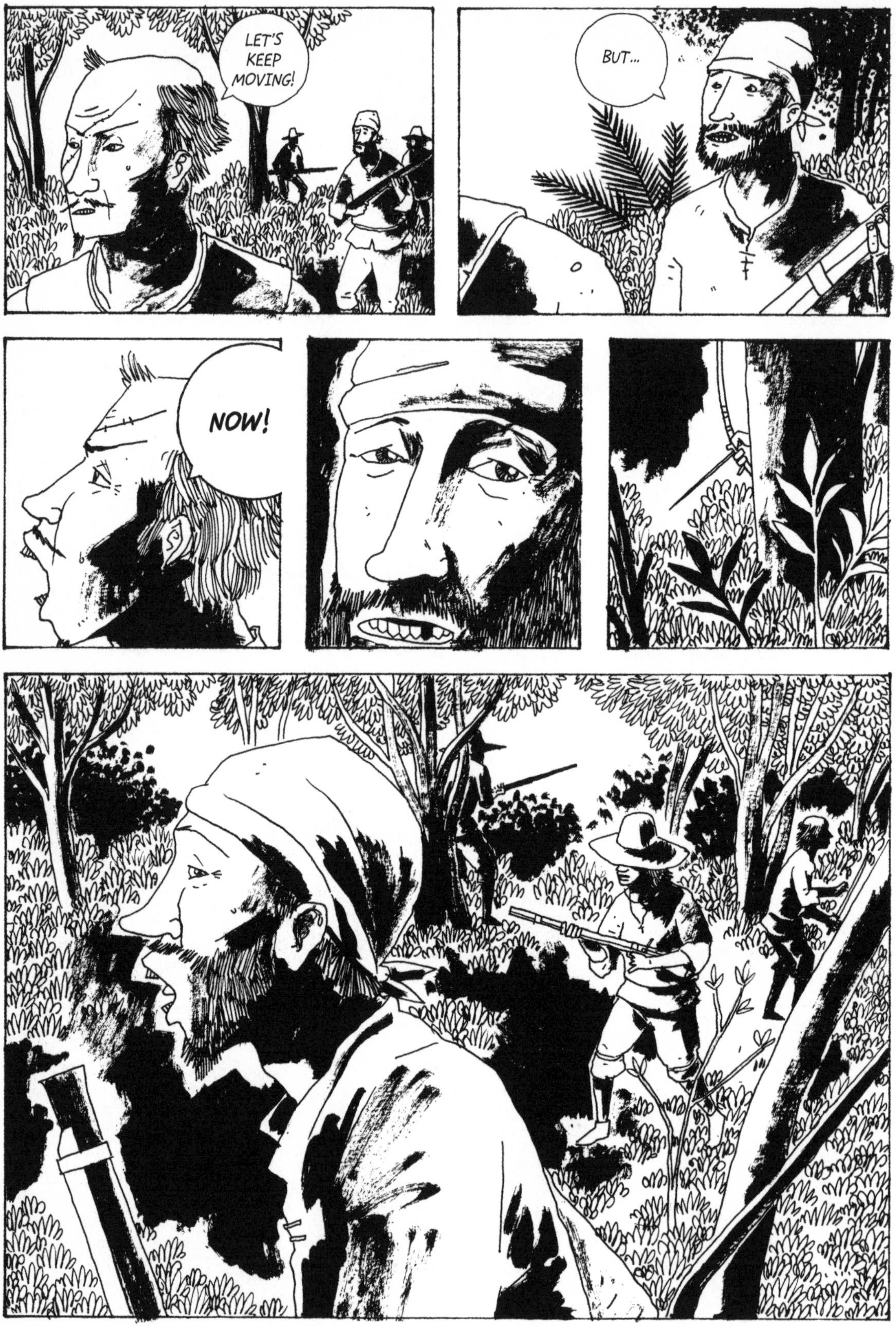
LET'S KEEP MOVING!
BUT...
NOW!

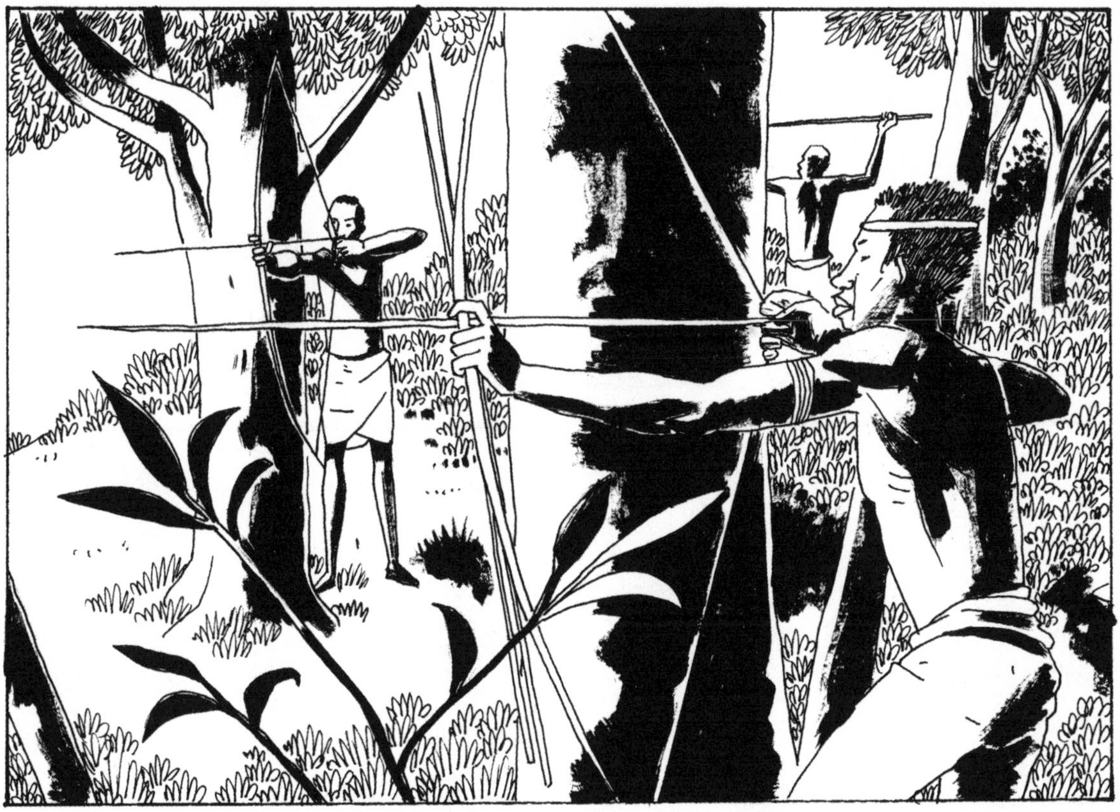

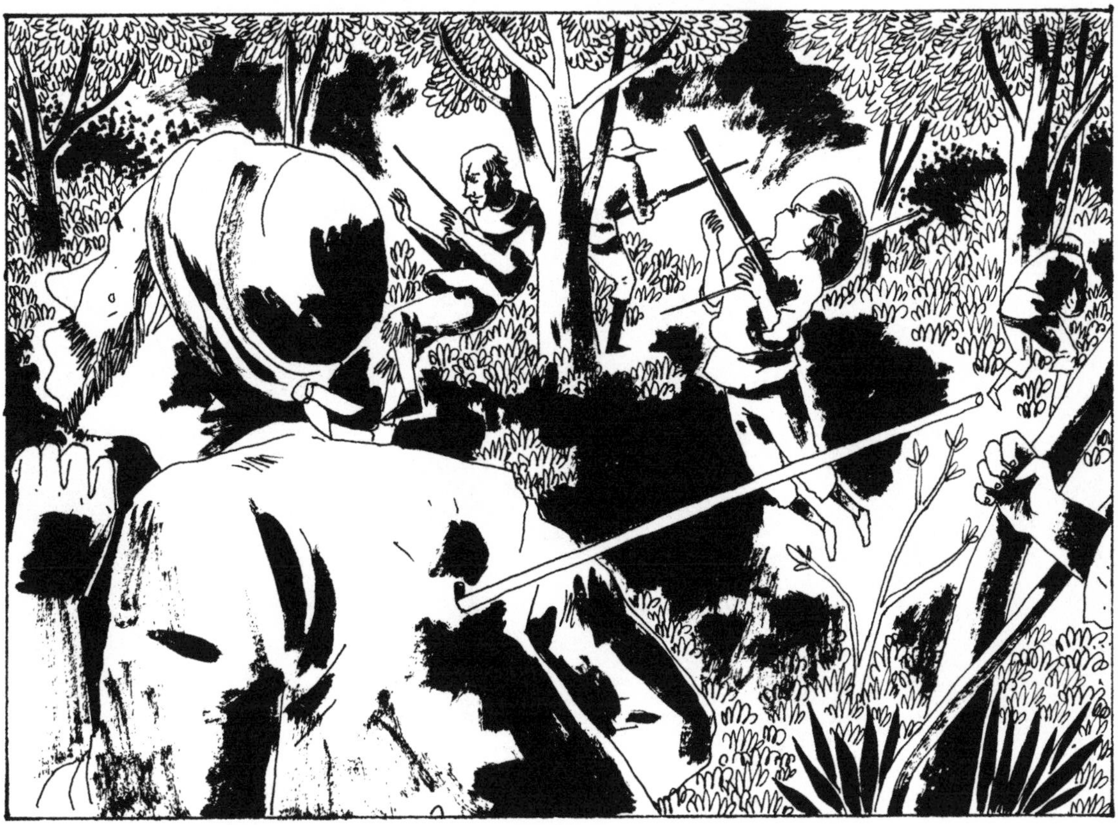

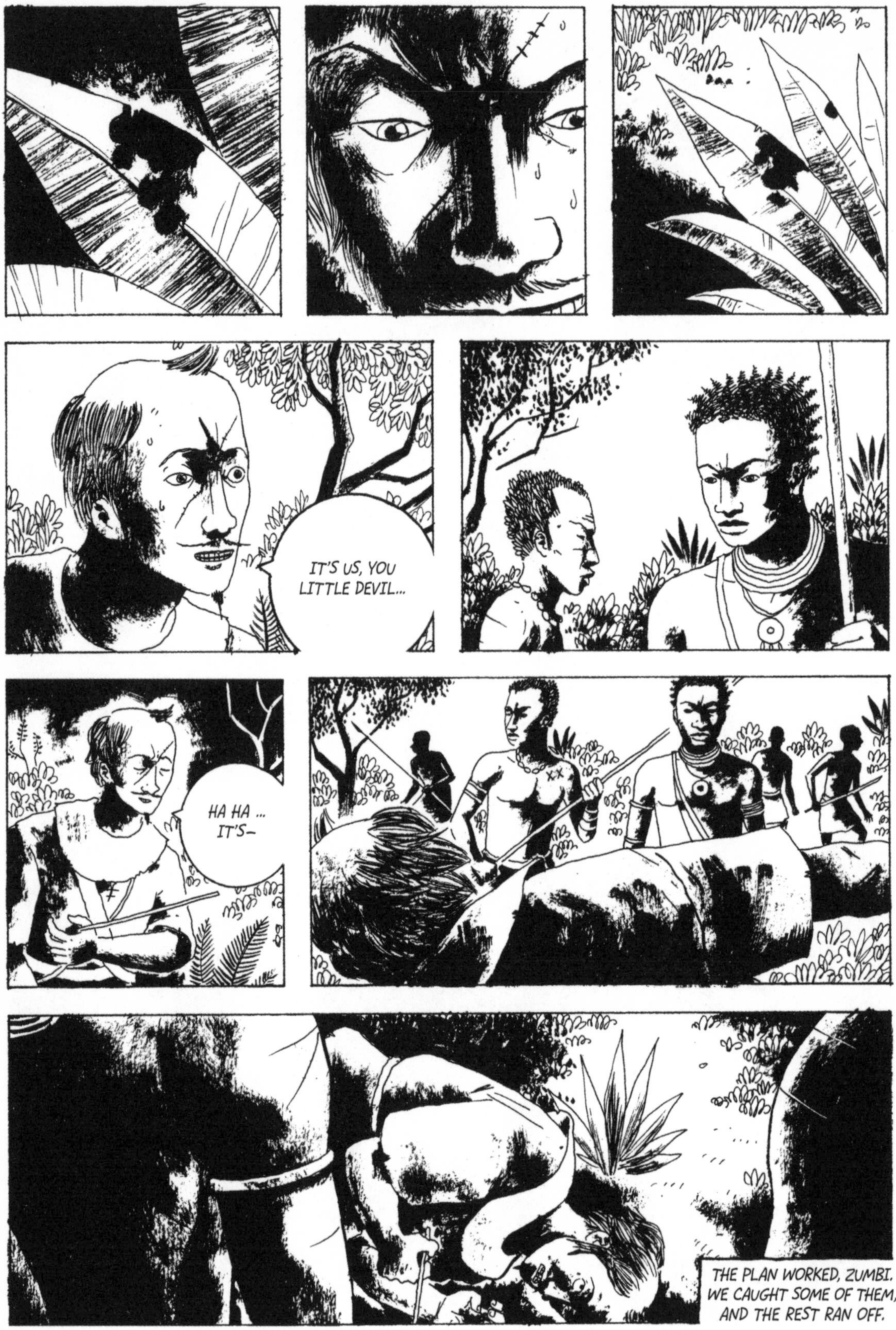
IT'S US, YOU LITTLE DEVIL...
HA HA ... IT'S—
THE PLAN WORKED, ZUMBI. WE CAUGHT SOME OF THEM, AND THE REST RAN OFF.

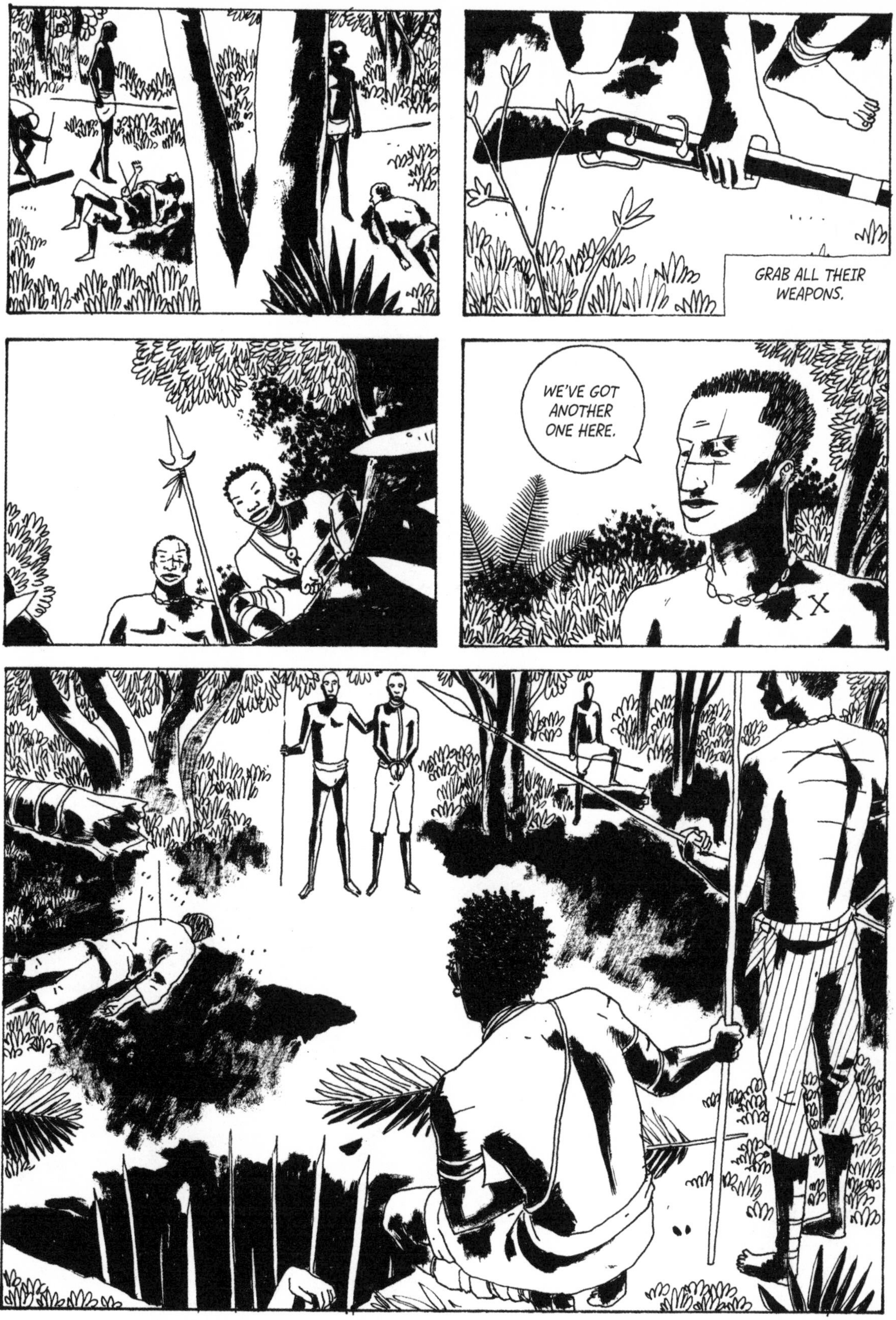
GRAB ALL THEIR WEAPONS.
WE'VE GOT ANOTHER ONE HERE.

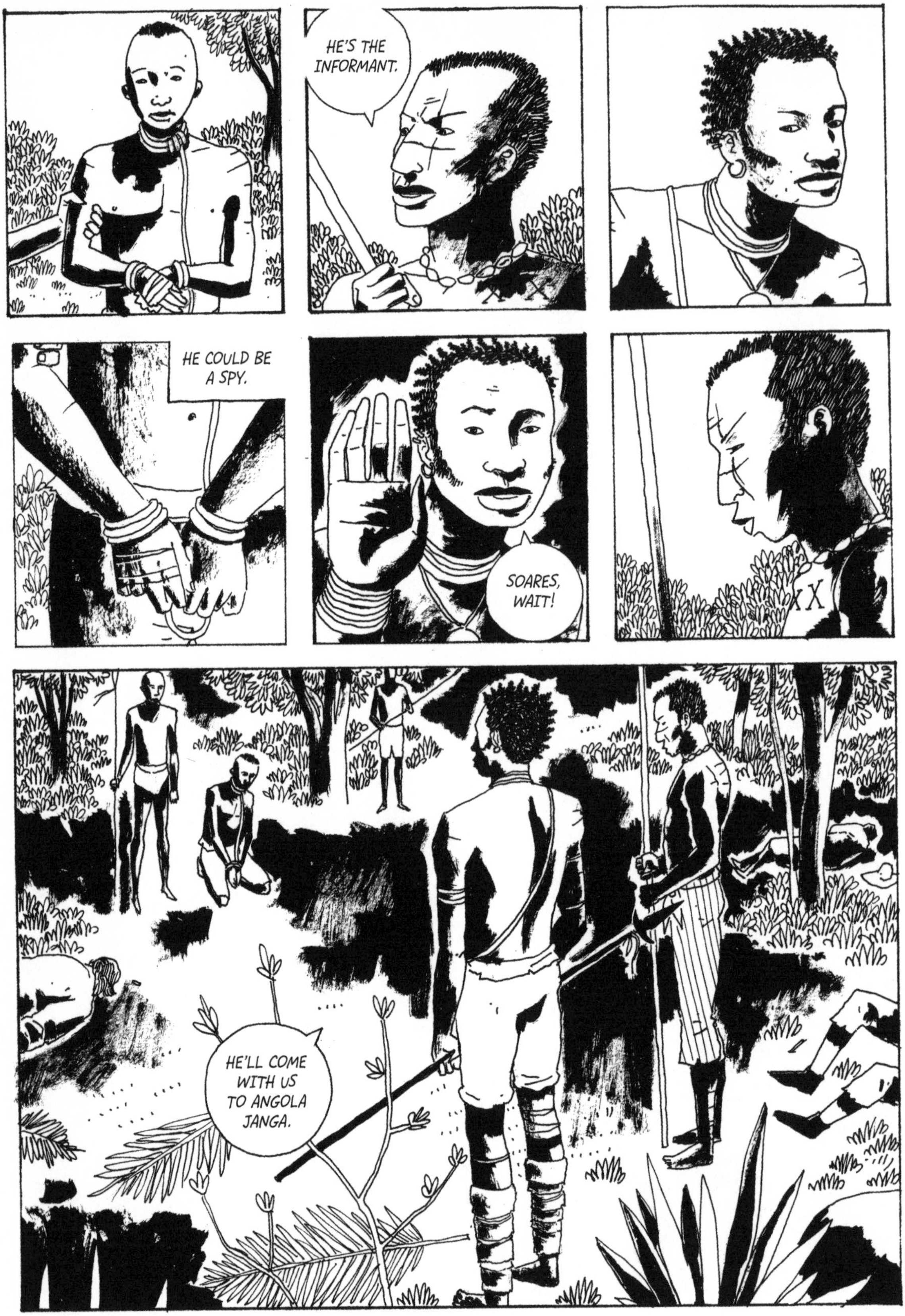
HE'S THE INFORMANT.
HE COULD BE A SPY.
SOARES, WAIT!
HE'LL COME WITH US TO ANGOLA JANGA.

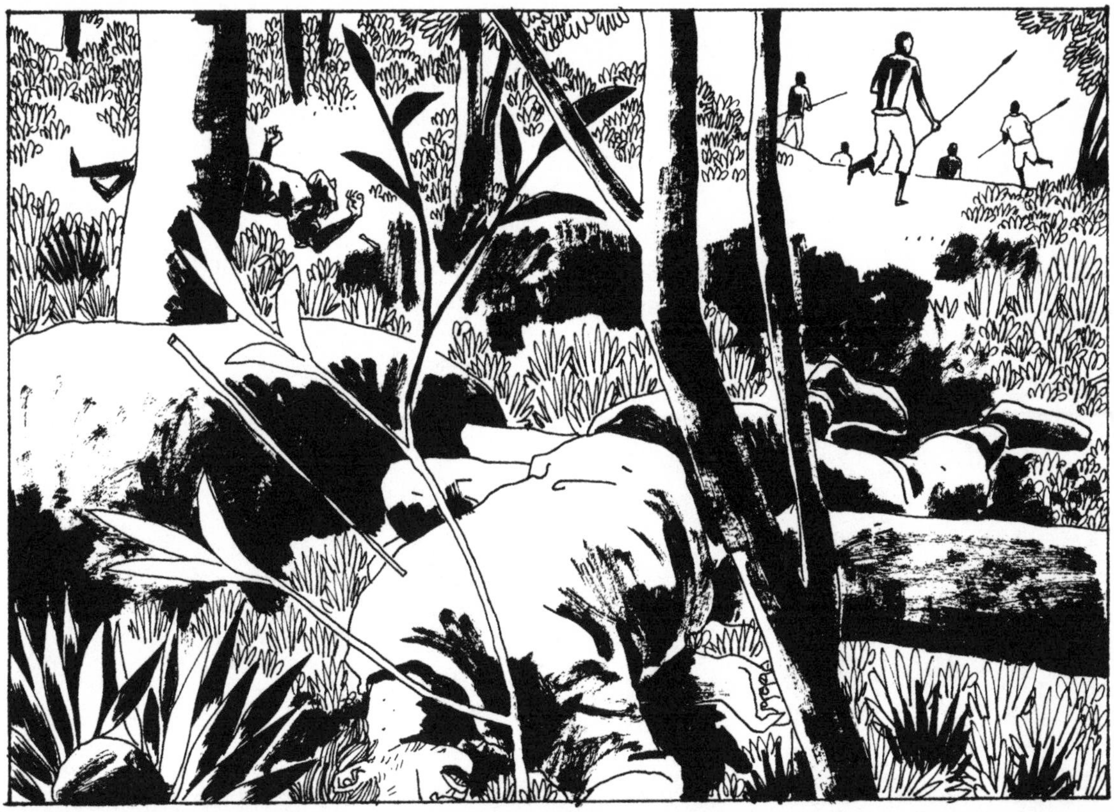

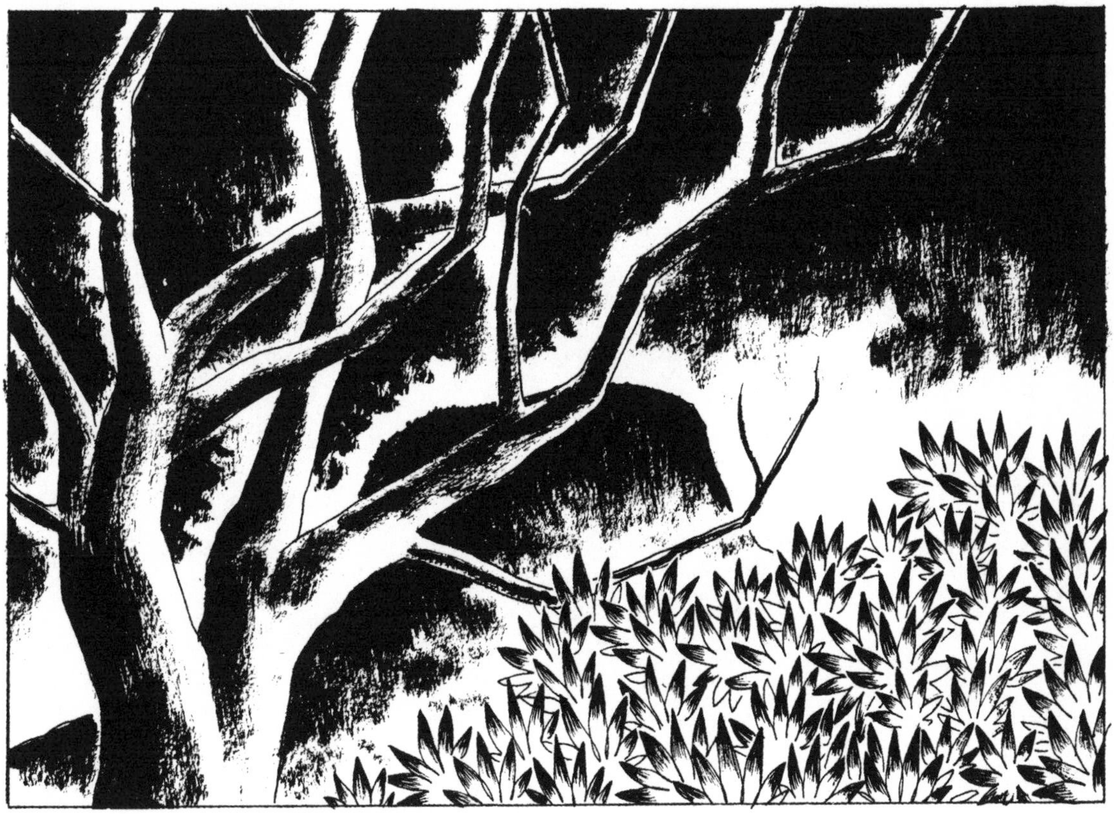

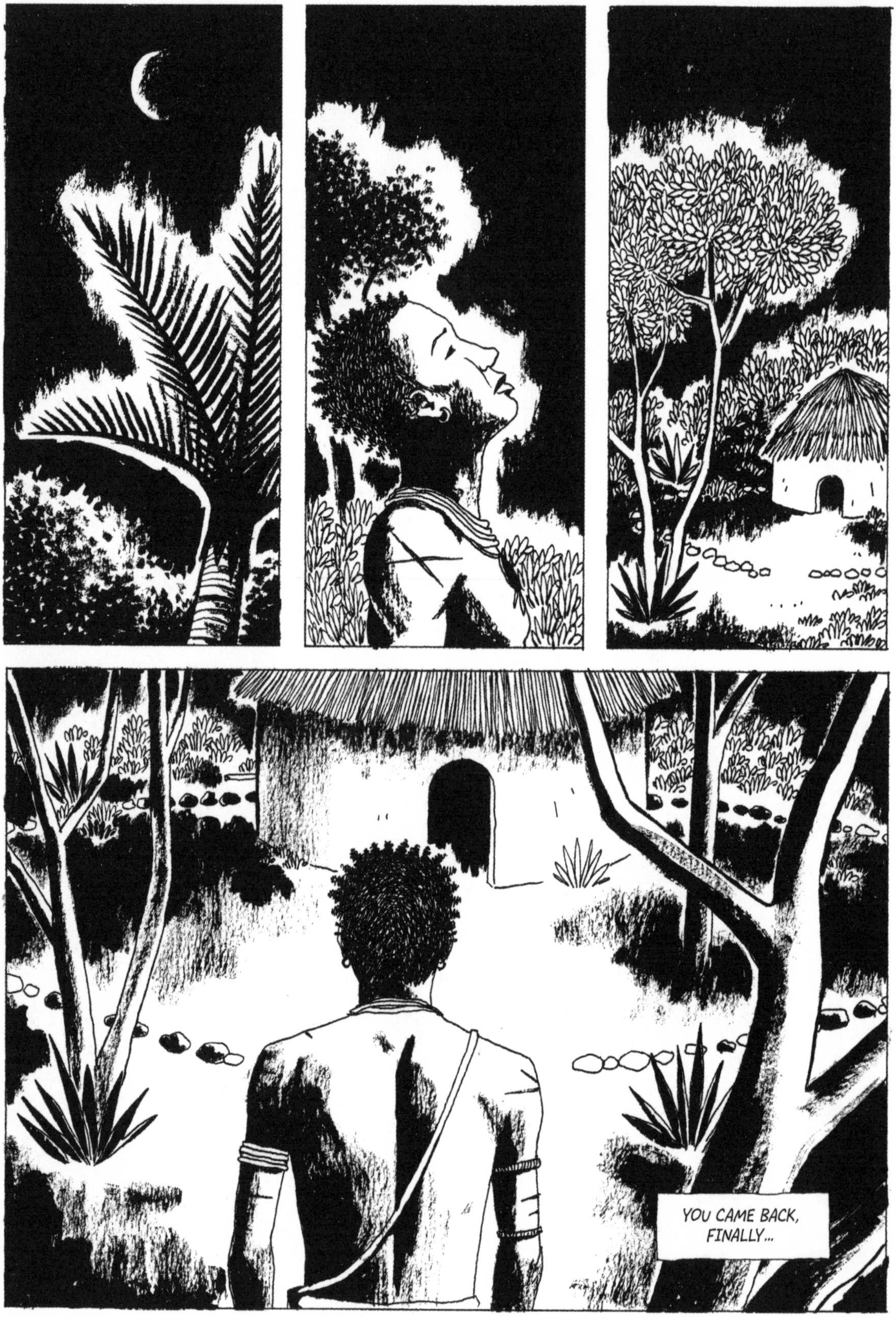
YOU CAME BACK, FINALLY...

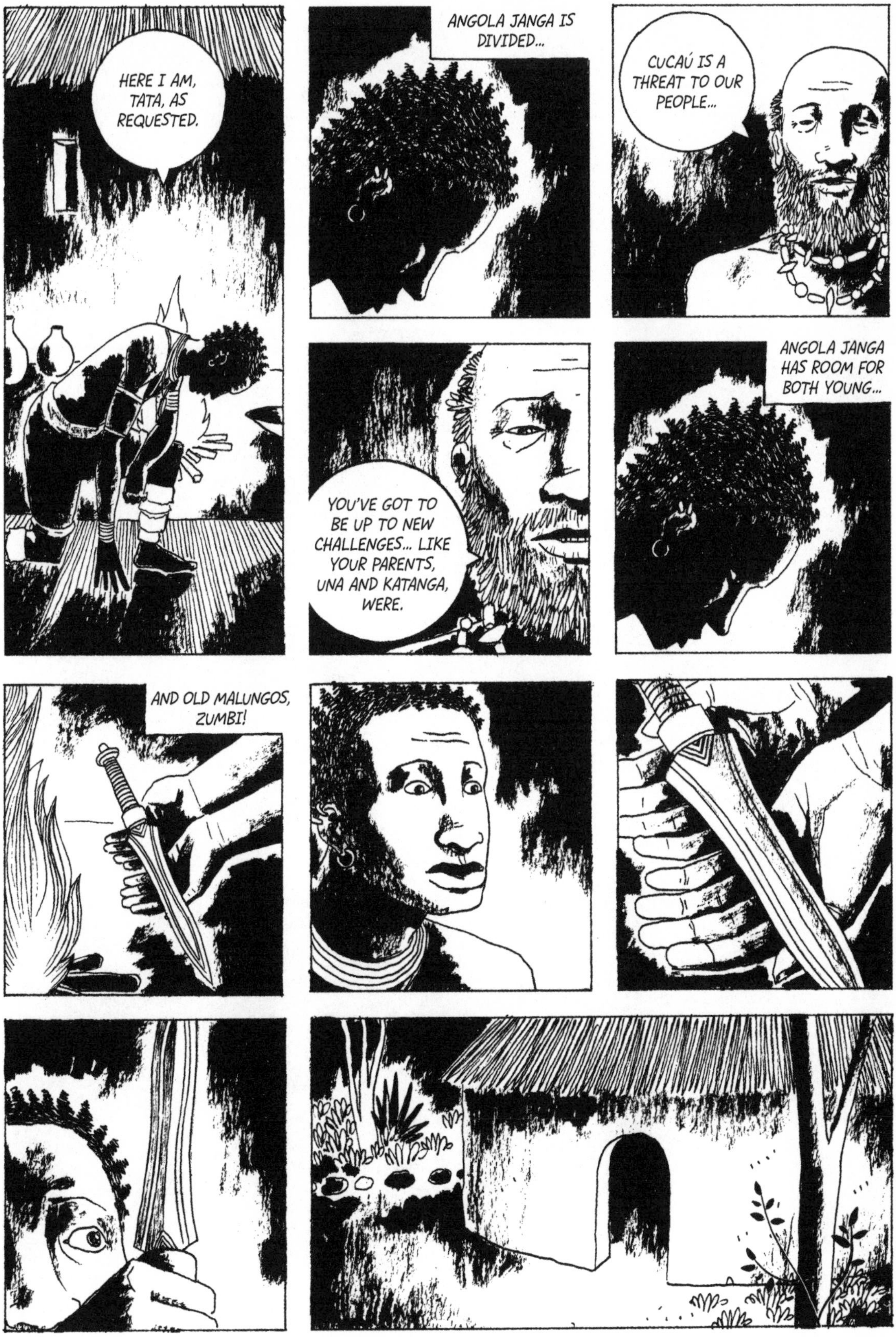
HERE I AM, TATA, AS REQUESTED.
ANGOLA JANGA IS DIVIDED...
CUCAÚ IS A THREAT TO OUR PEOPLE...
YOU'VE GOT TO BE UP TO NEW CHALLENGES... LIKE YOUR PARENTS, UNA AND KATANGA, WERE.
ANGOLA JANGA HAS ROOM FOR BOTH YOUNG...
AND OLD MALUNGOS, ZUMBI!

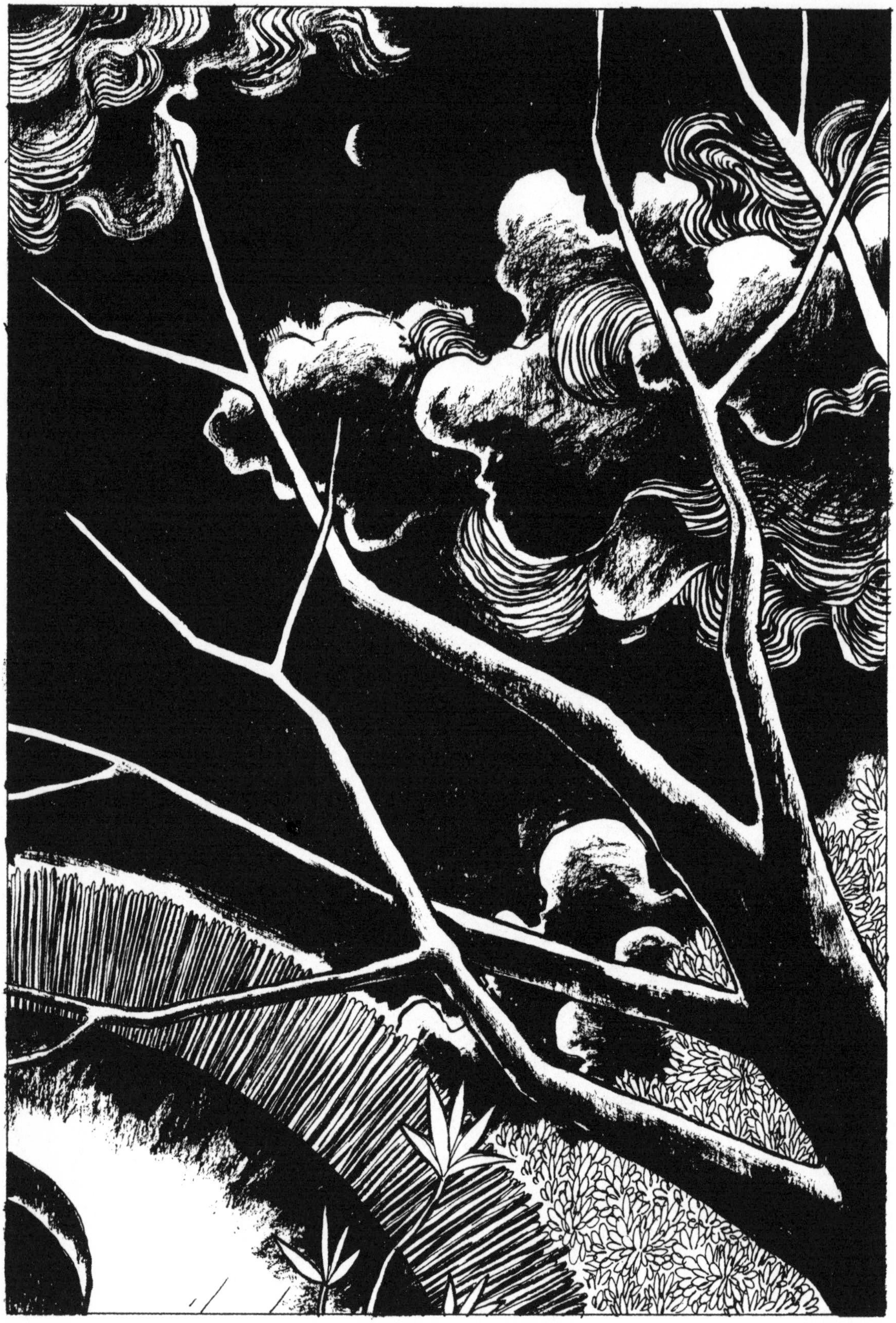

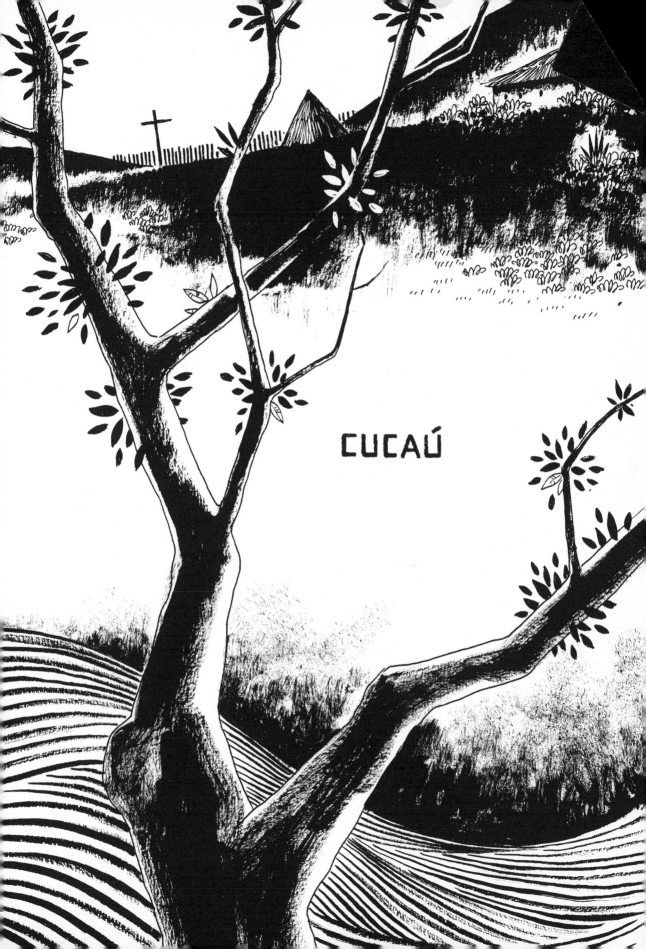

CUCAÚ

[T]hat they should give them as a dwelling place the territory of their choosing and peace for their habitation, and plants; that peace should reign; and that the king should withdraw from inhabiting the appointed place; that those born in Palmares should be free; that they should have commerce and trade with the inhabitants; and that they should obtain favor as His Majesty's vassals; and, looking alertly at the Council, the son responded that if the king Ganga Zumba were given the power to lead a few corsairs, who lived far from the Portuguese cities, the king would lead everybody to our domains, and when any rebel refused him and us obedience, he would overcome him and guide our weapons in defeating him.

—Petition from the King of Palmares, Ganga Zumba, in which he requested peace, liberty, territory, and the return of captured women, 1678

In the month of November 1678, before a group of 140 people, Ganga Zumba went to Recife with the aim of formalizing the peace treaty. He was named an officer of the Portuguese army and two of his sons were adopted by the governor. The authorities immediately put into practice one of the treaty's clauses, which gave the people of Palmares the right to have a territory. And so, Ganga Zumba and his comrades went to live in Cucaú, a region located thirty-two kilometers from Serinhaém.

—Ivan Alves Filho, Memorial dos Palmares [Commemoration of Palmares], 2008

Simple logic suggests that the [Cucaú] treaty would lead to multiple stubborn uprisings, primarily owing to the cruel clause that sacrificed all those born outside of Palmares to captivity. The small number who followed Ganga Zumba indicates that even the beneficiaries of the treaty instinctively mistrusted the intentions of the colonial authorities and the slave masters. In an effort to attract a larger number of residents of Palmares to Cucaú, the Recife authorities even considered granting emancipation to the slaves, but ran up against the opposition of the sugar barons.

—Décio Freitas, Palmares—A guerra dos escravos [Palmares: The Slave War], 1982

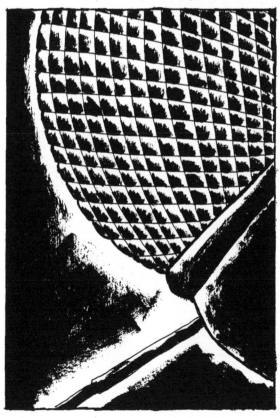

SOARES, YOUR MISSION WILL BE GREAT...

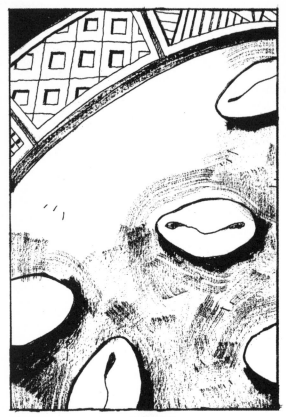

CUCA...
WHAT SHOULD
I DO? WHAT'S
IN STORE
FOR ME?

YOUR DESTINY
WILL BE THAT OF
MANY...

BUT IT PRESENTS
A CHOICE THAT'S
YOURS ALONE...

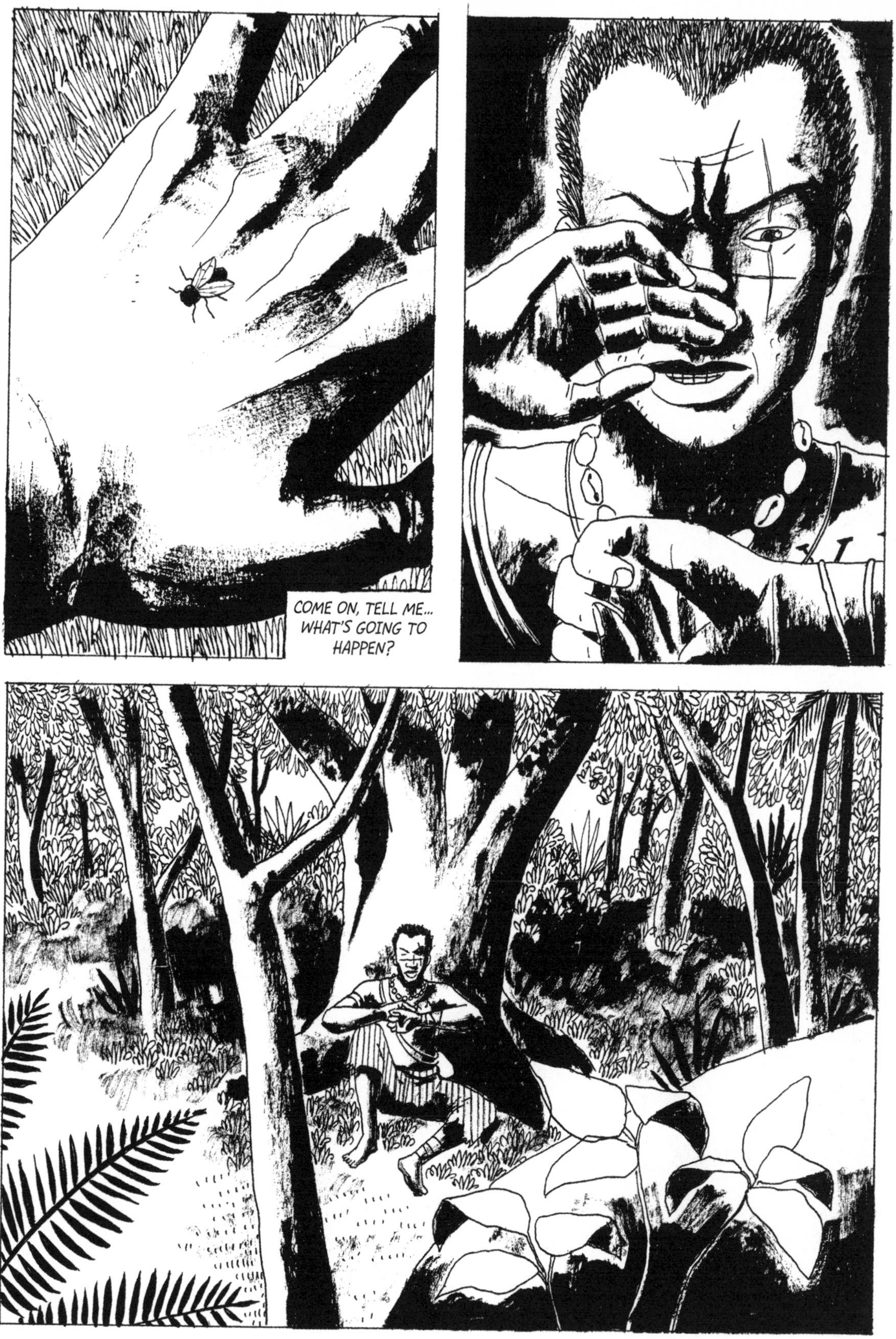
COME ON, TELL ME... WHAT'S GOING TO HAPPEN?

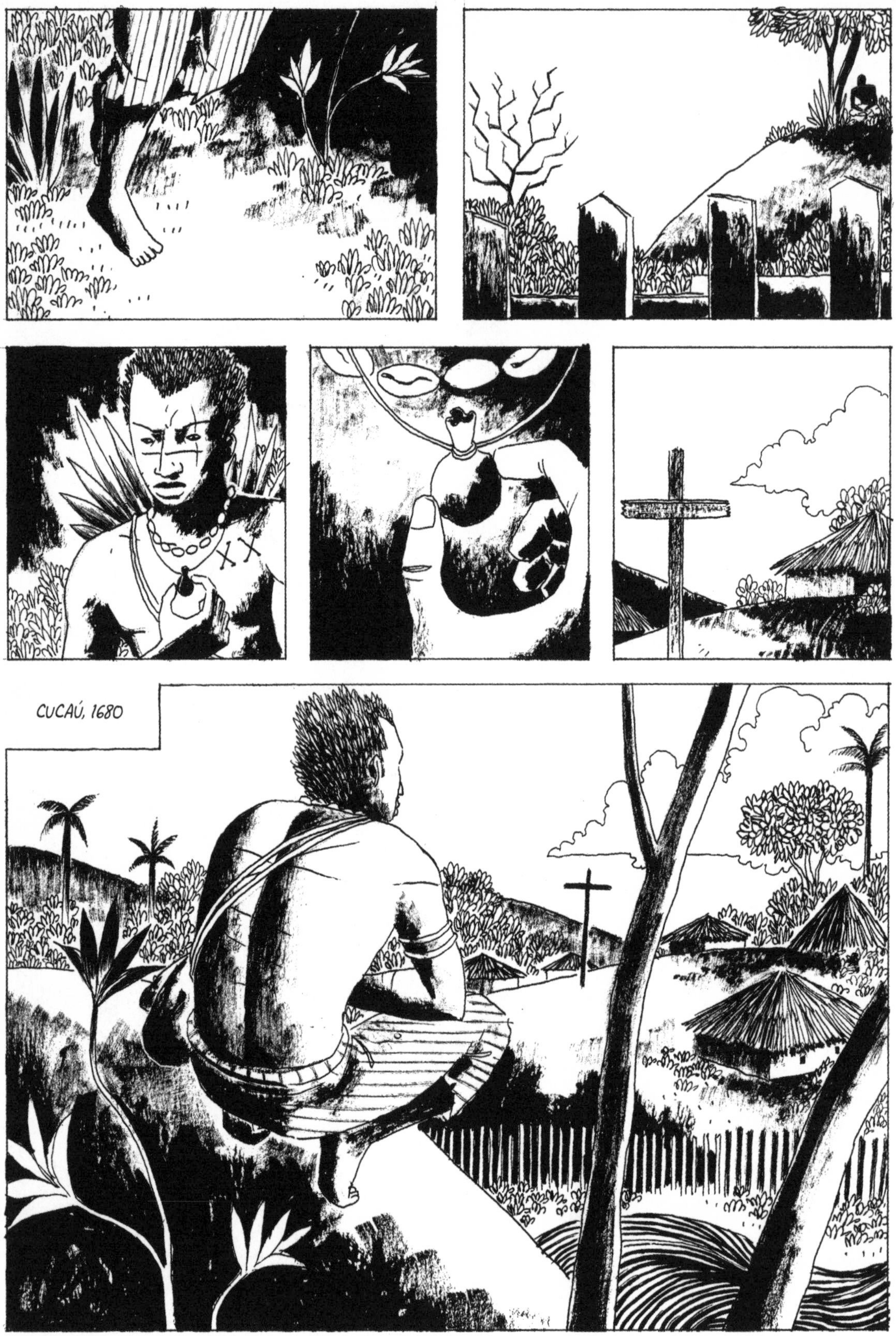
CUCAÚ, 1680

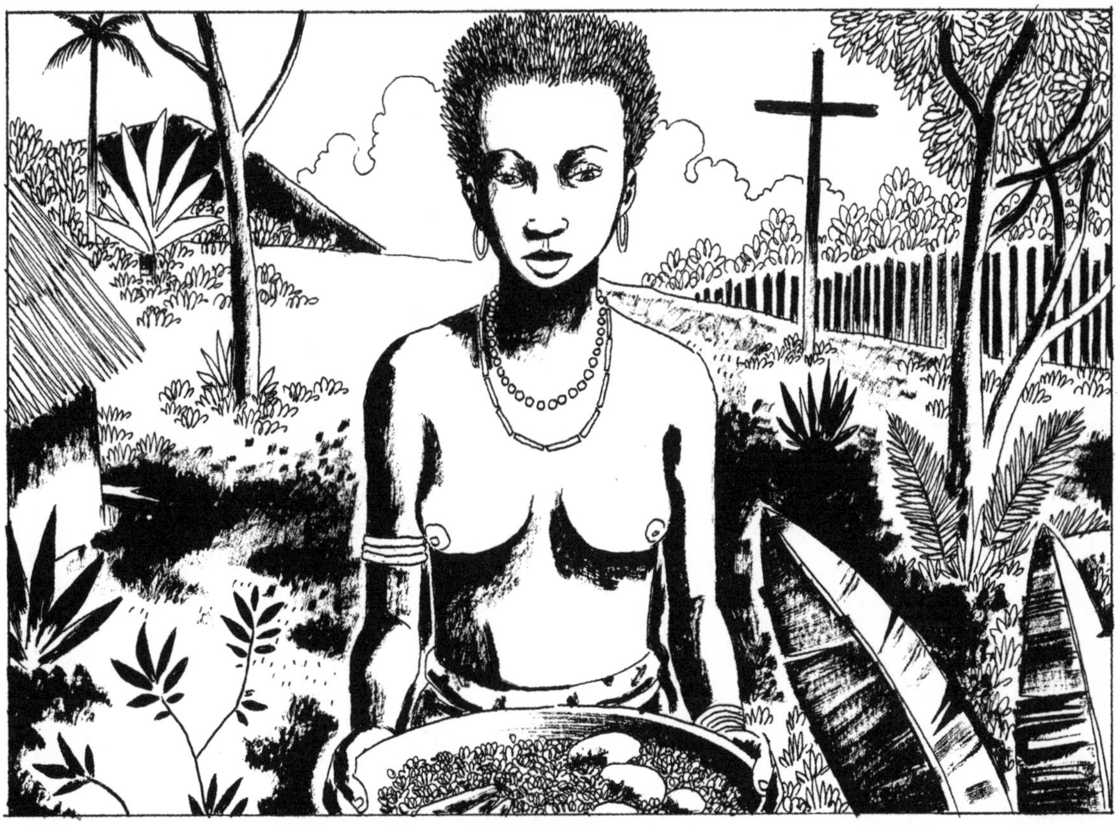

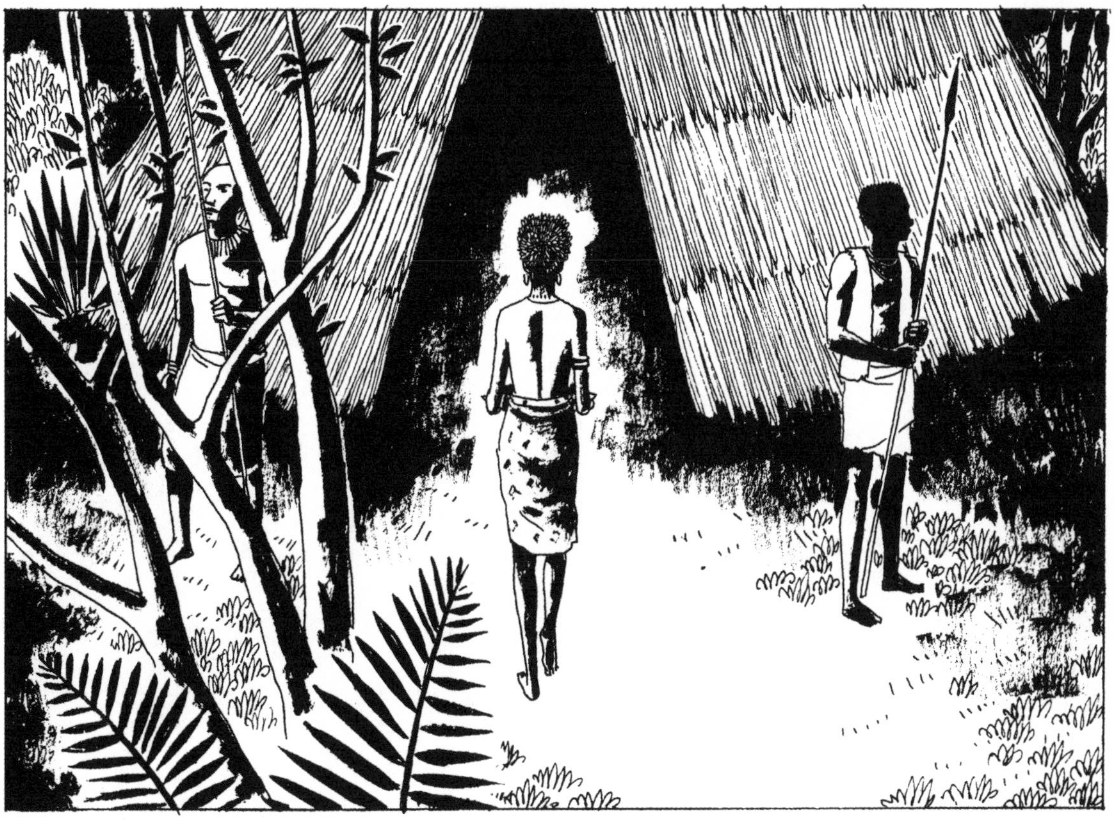

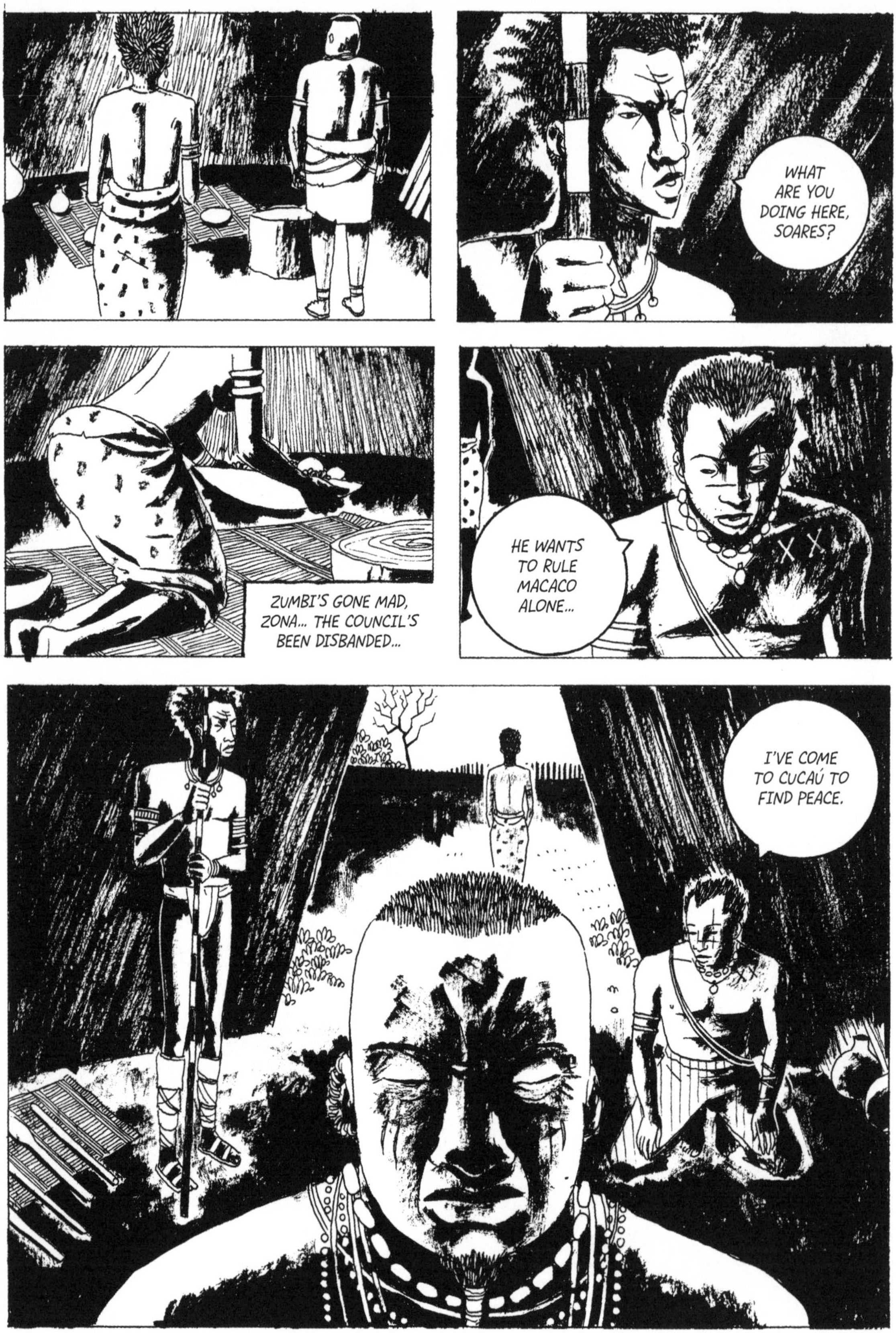
WHAT ARE YOU DOING HERE, SOARES?
ZUMBI'S GONE MAD, ZONA... THE COUNCIL'S BEEN DISBANDED...
HE WANTS TO RULE MACACO ALONE...
I'VE COME TO CUCAÚ TO FIND PEACE.

I'M WITH YOU...

SOARES...

THE MOCAMBOS OF PALMARES WILL BE DESTROYED.

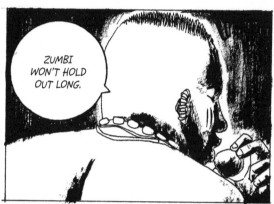

ZUMBI WON'T HOLD OUT LONG.

YOU CAN STAY.

WELL...

ZONA, WE'VE GOT A LOT TO DO TODAY. ACOTIRENE CAN'T HELP ANYMORE...

KEEP AN EYE ON OUR GUEST...

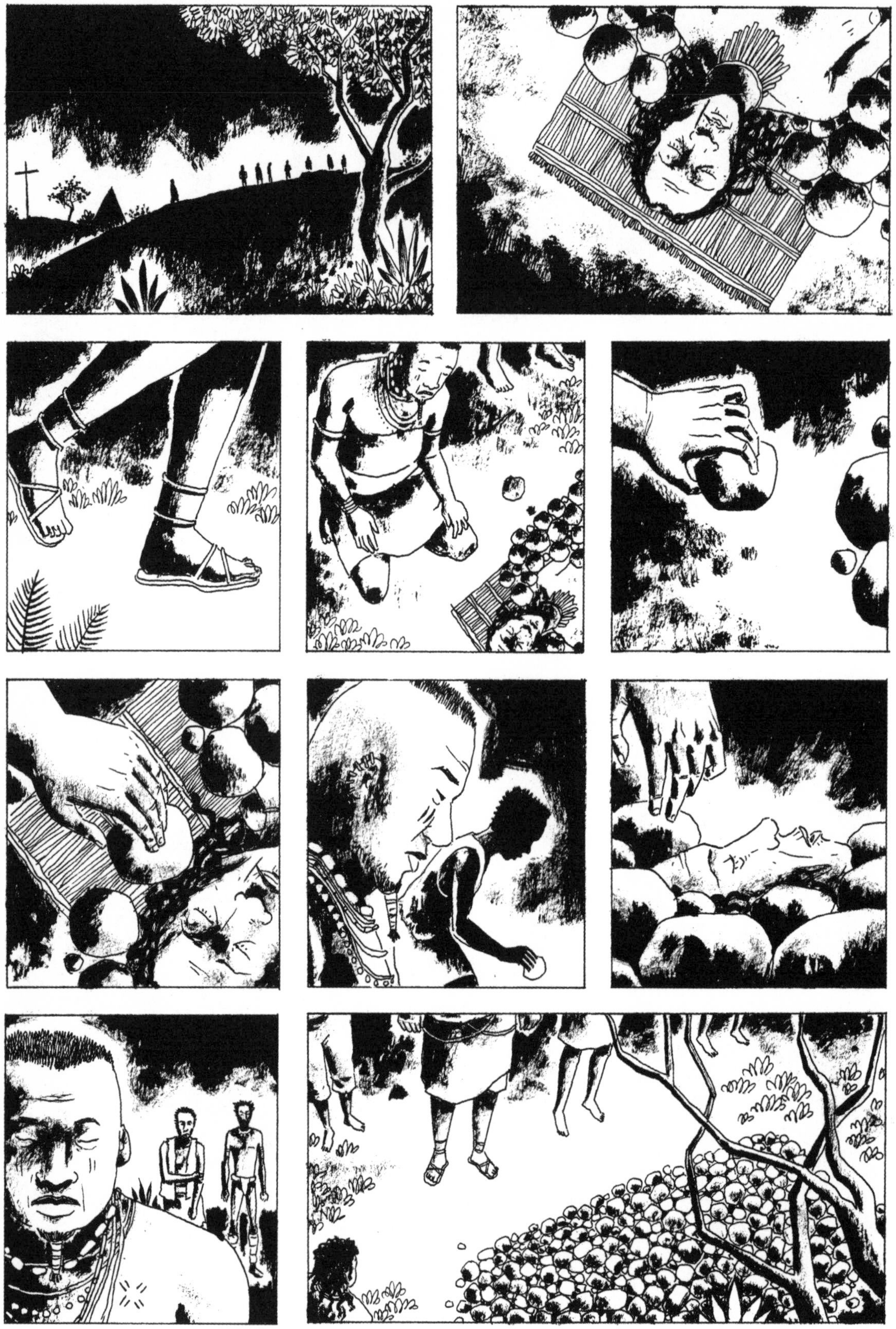

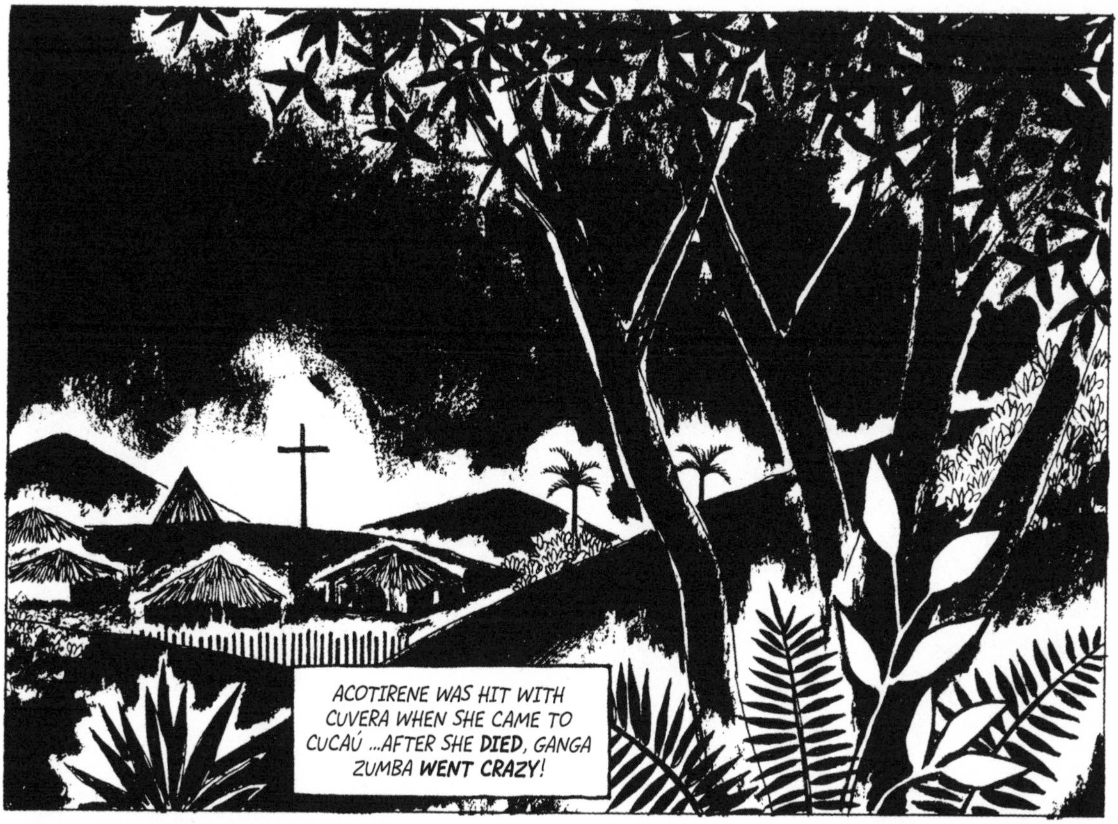
ACOTIRENE WAS HIT WITH CUVERA WHEN SHE CAME TO CUCAÚ ...AFTER SHE **DIED**, GANGA ZUMBA **WENT CRAZY**!

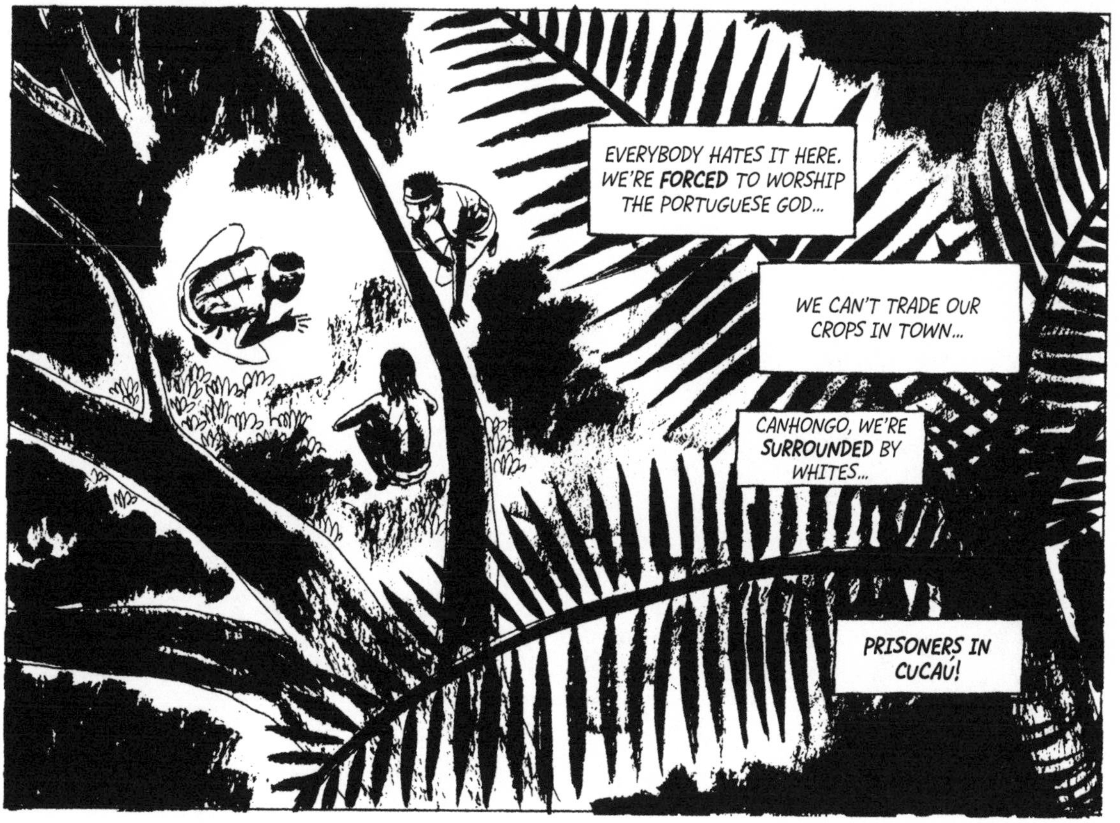
EVERYBODY HATES IT HERE. WE'RE **FORCED** TO WORSHIP THE PORTUGUESE GOD...
WE CAN'T TRADE OUR CROPS IN TOWN...
CANHONGO, WE'RE **SURROUNDED** BY WHITES...
PRISONERS IN CUCAÚ!

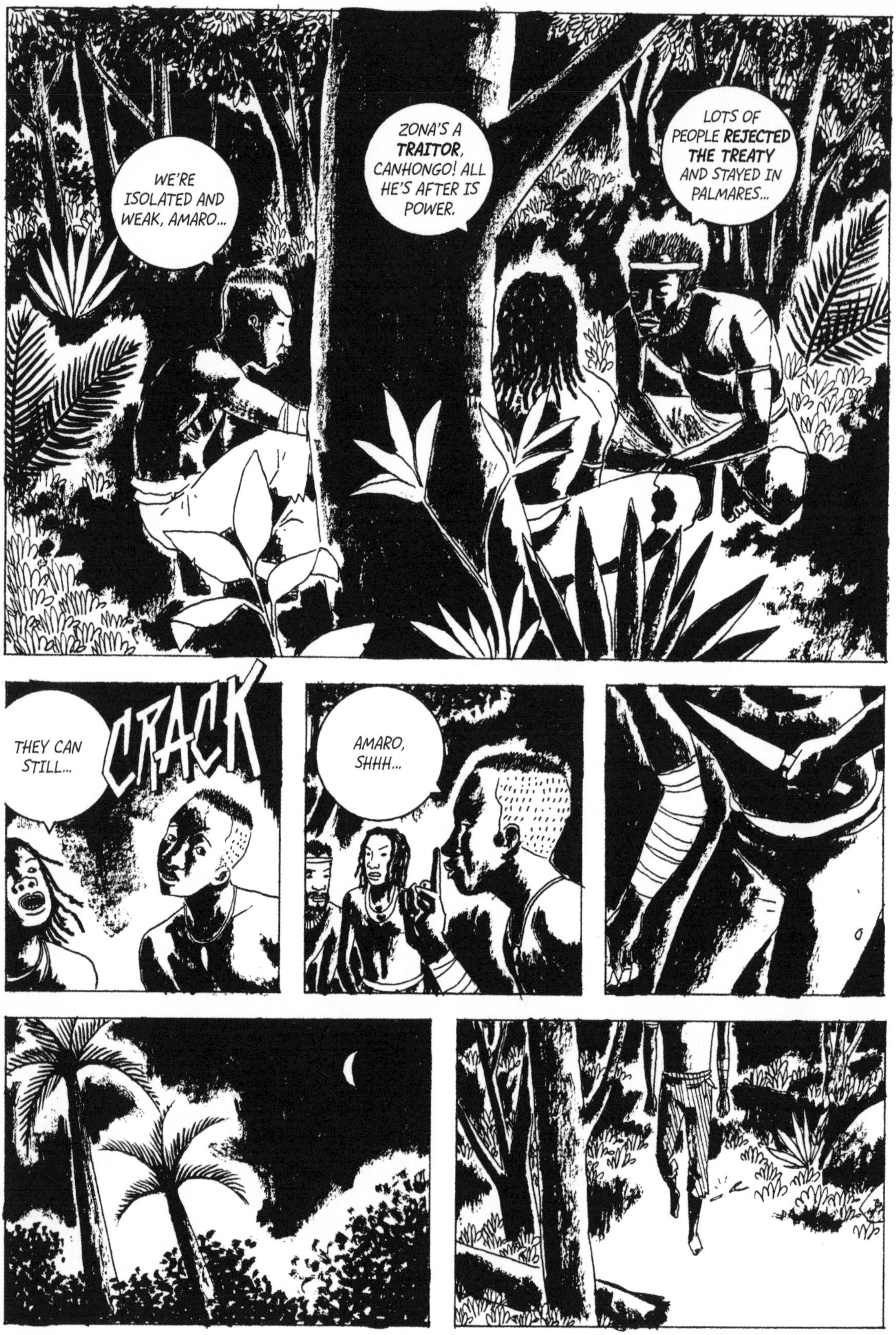
WE'RE ISOLATED AND WEAK, AMARO...
ZONA'S A **TRAITOR**, CANHONGO! ALL HE'S AFTER IS POWER.
LOTS OF PEOPLE **REJECTED THE TREATY** AND STAYED IN PALMARES...
THEY CAN STILL...
CRACK
AMARO, SHHH...

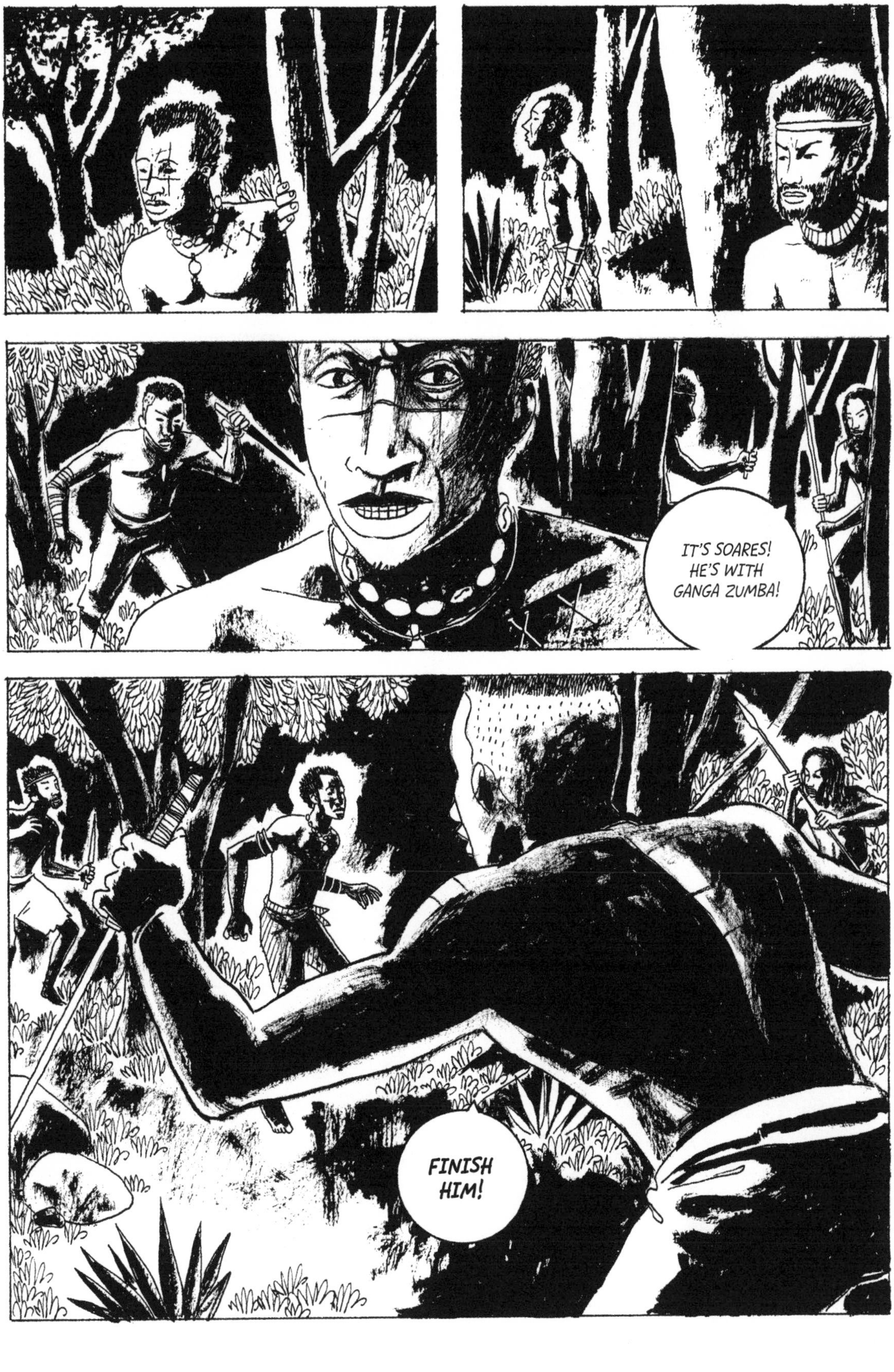
IT'S SOARES! HE'S WITH GANGA ZUMBA!
FINISH HIM!

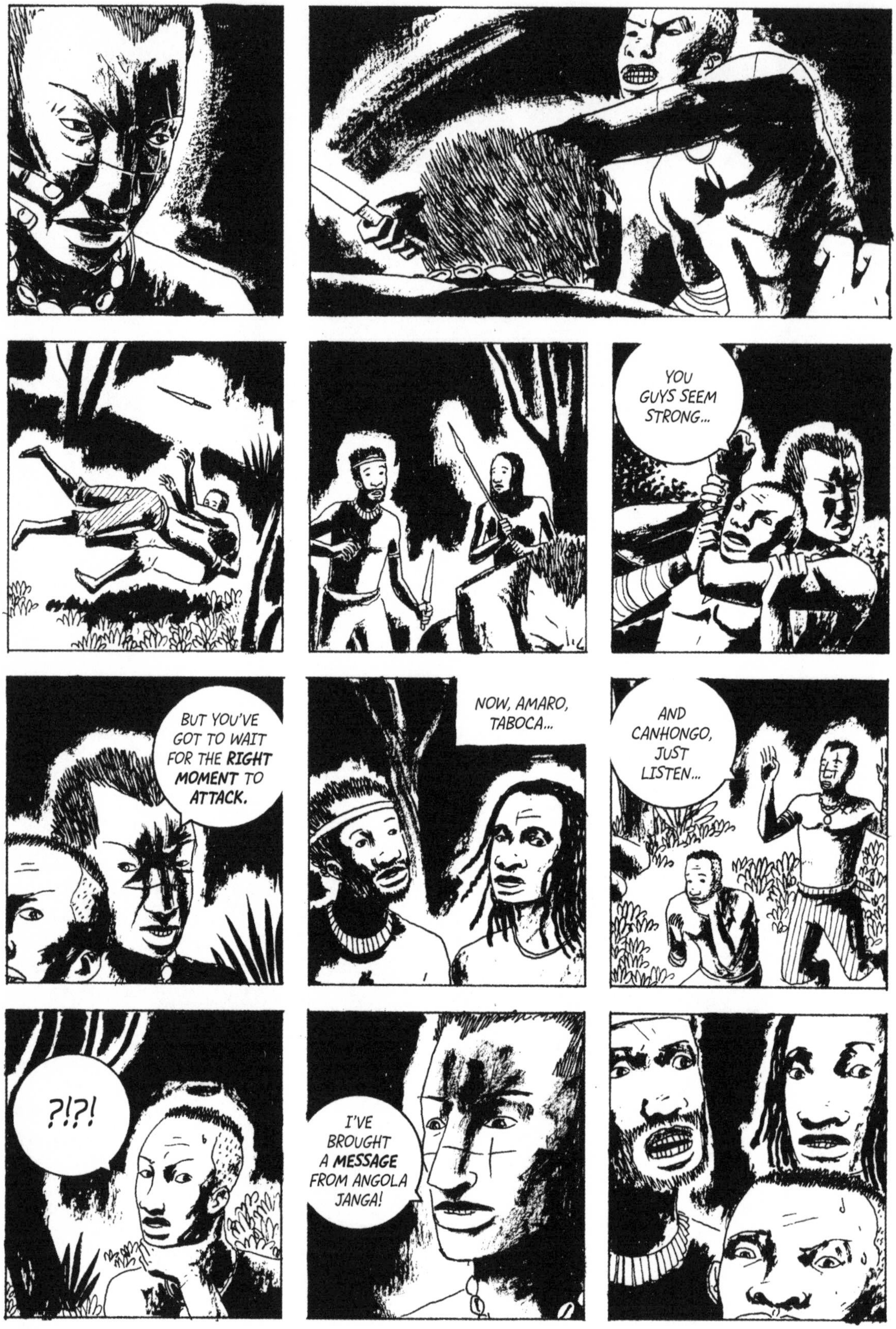
YOU GUYS SEEM STRONG...
BUT YOU'VE GOT TO WAIT FOR THE **RIGHT MOMENT** TO **ATTACK.**
NOW, AMARO, TABOCA...
AND CANHONGO, JUST LISTEN...
?!?!
I'VE BROUGHT A **MESSAGE** FROM ANGOLA JANGA!

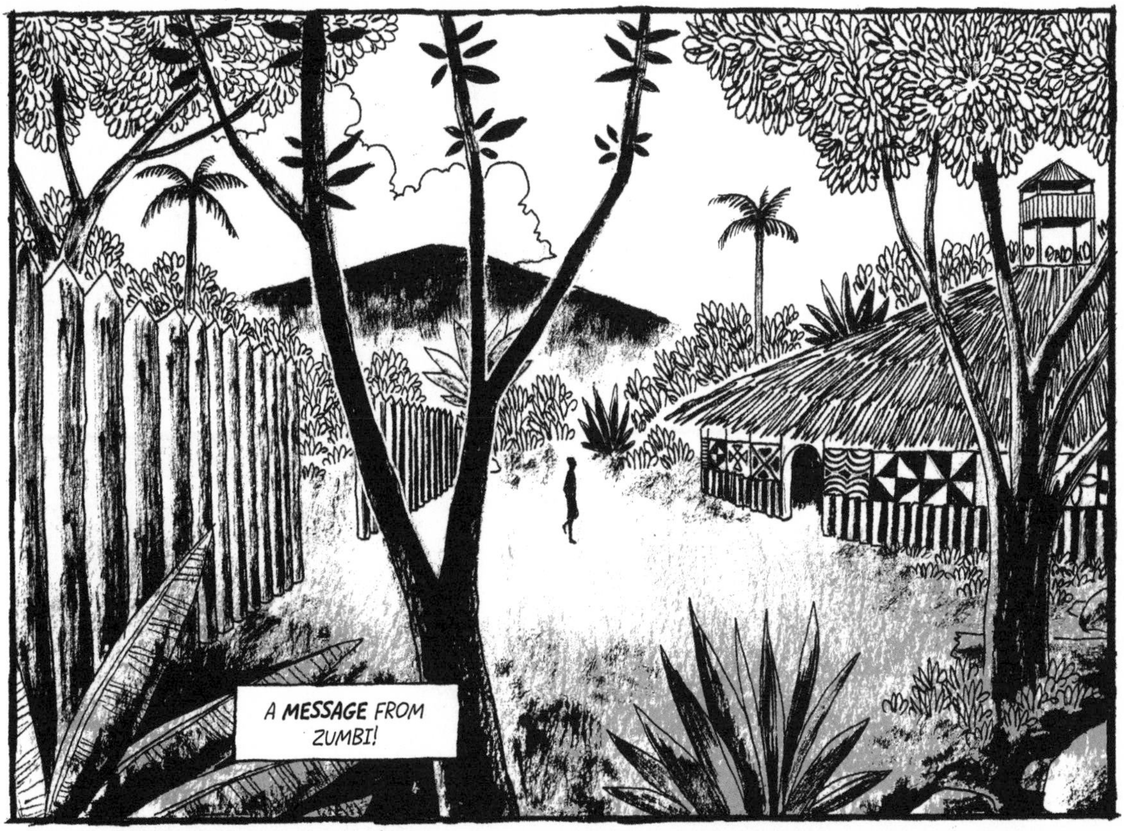
A **MESSAGE** FROM ZUMBI!

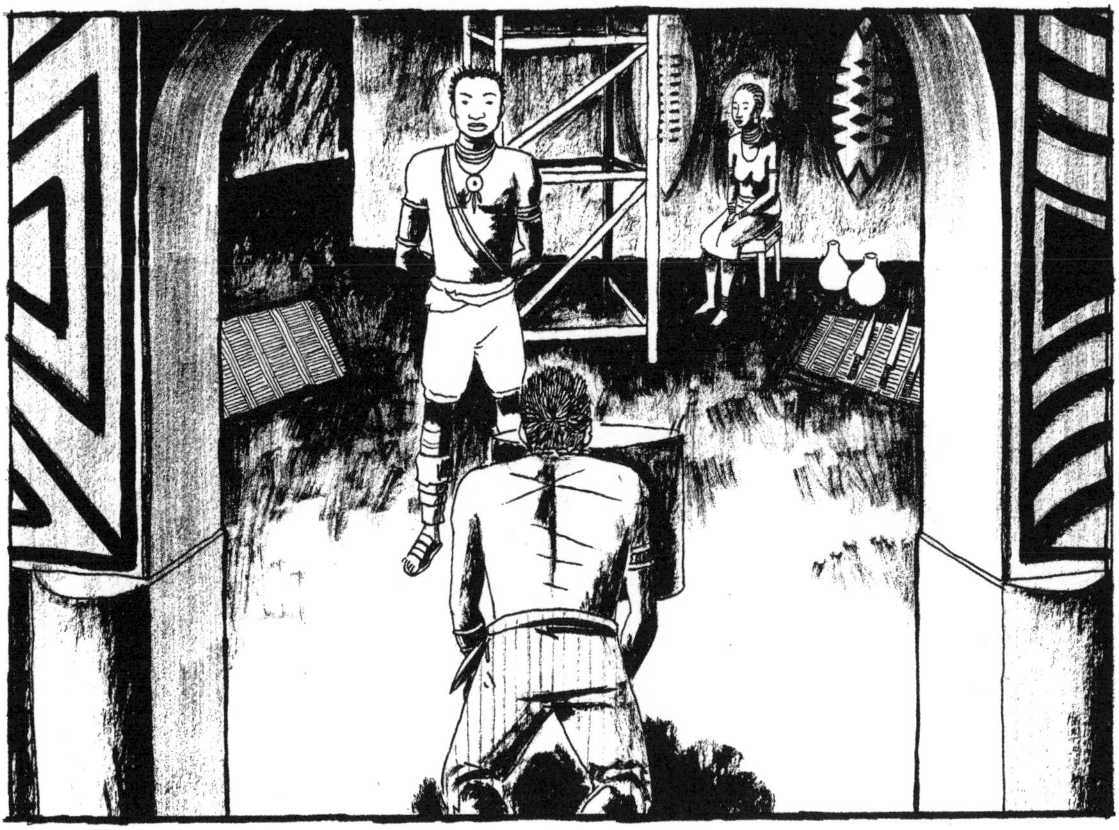

SOARES, THE TRAITORS IN CUCAÚ KNOW OUR LANDS, OUR FORESTS, OUR TRAILS, OUR SECRETS...

THEY KNOW ALL OUR DEFENSES.

IF THE PORTUGUESE FIGURE THAT OUT...

ANGOLA JANGA WILL BE LOST.

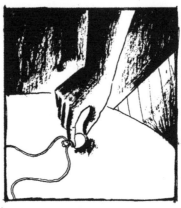

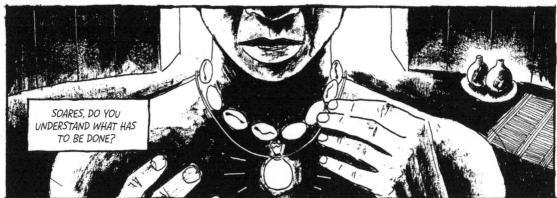

SOARES, DO YOU UNDERSTAND WHAT HAS TO BE DONE?

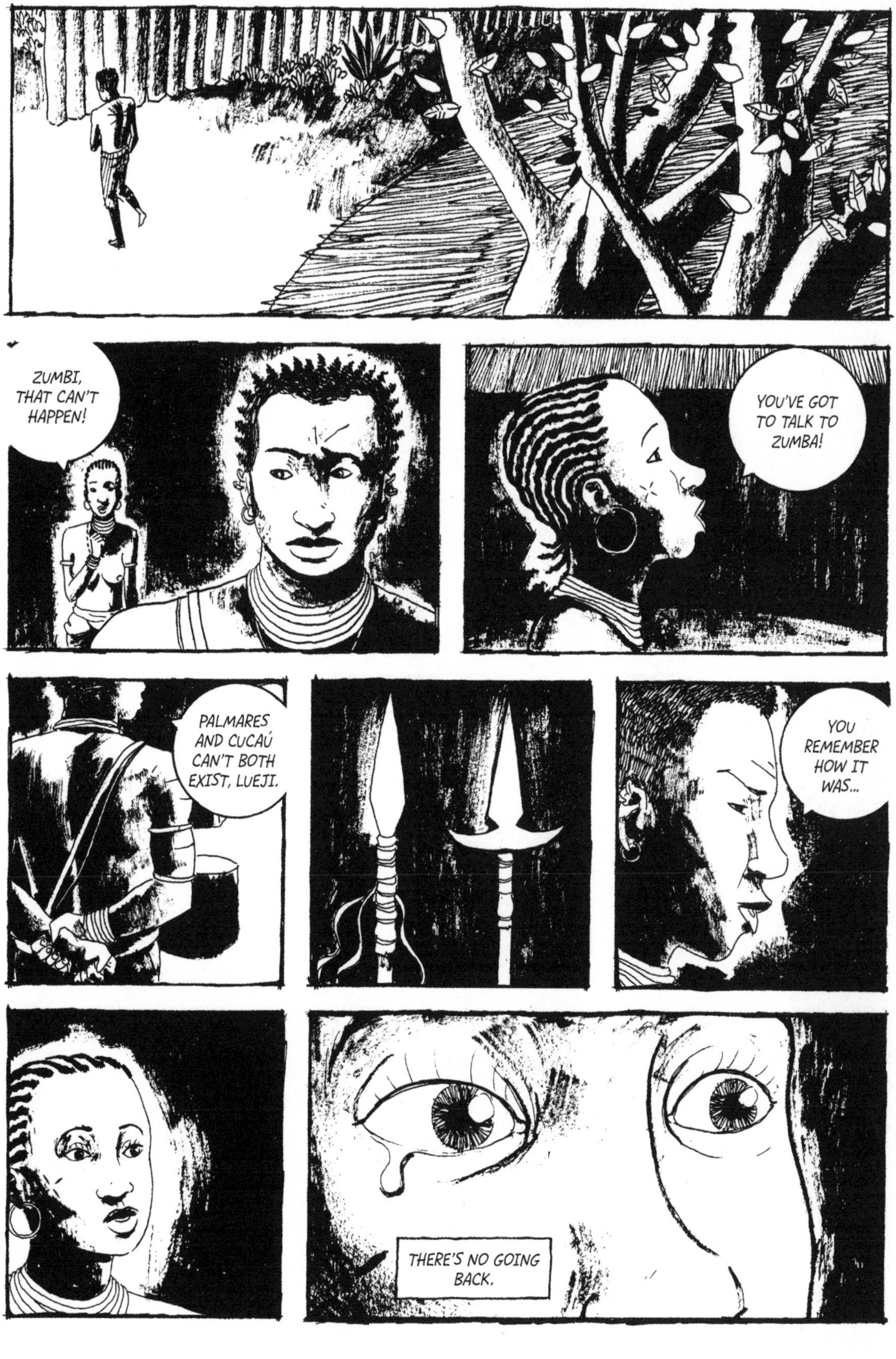
ZUMBI, THAT CAN'T HAPPEN!
YOU'VE GOT TO TALK TO ZUMBA!
PALMARES AND CUCAÚ CAN'T BOTH EXIST, LUEJI.
YOU REMEMBER HOW IT WAS...
THERE'S NO GOING BACK.

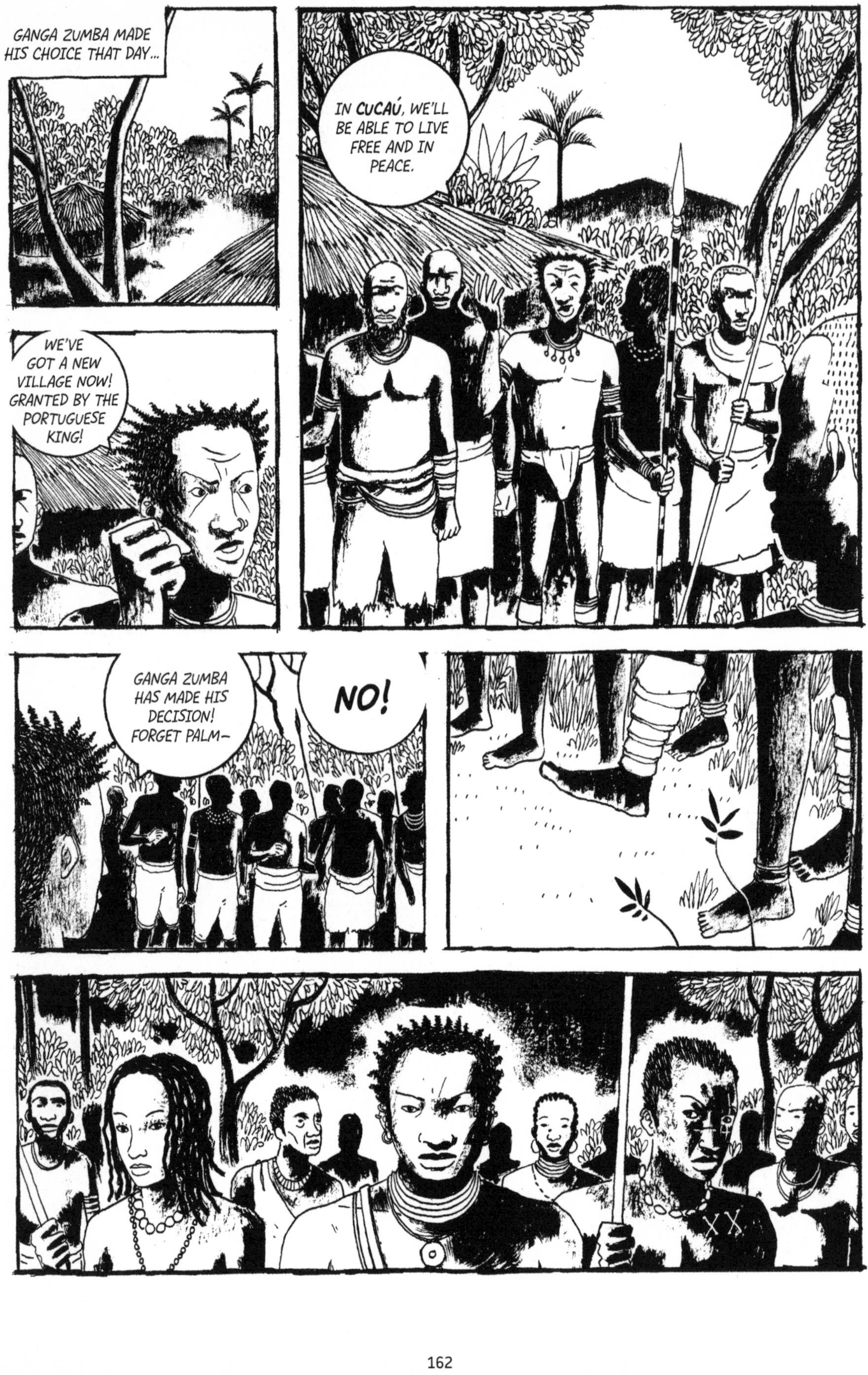
GANGA ZUMBA MADE HIS CHOICE THAT DAY...
IN CUCAÚ, WE'LL BE ABLE TO LIVE FREE AND IN PEACE.
WE'VE GOT A NEW VILLAGE NOW! GRANTED BY THE PORTUGUESE KING!
GANGA ZUMBA HAS MADE HIS DECISION! FORGET PALM—
NO!

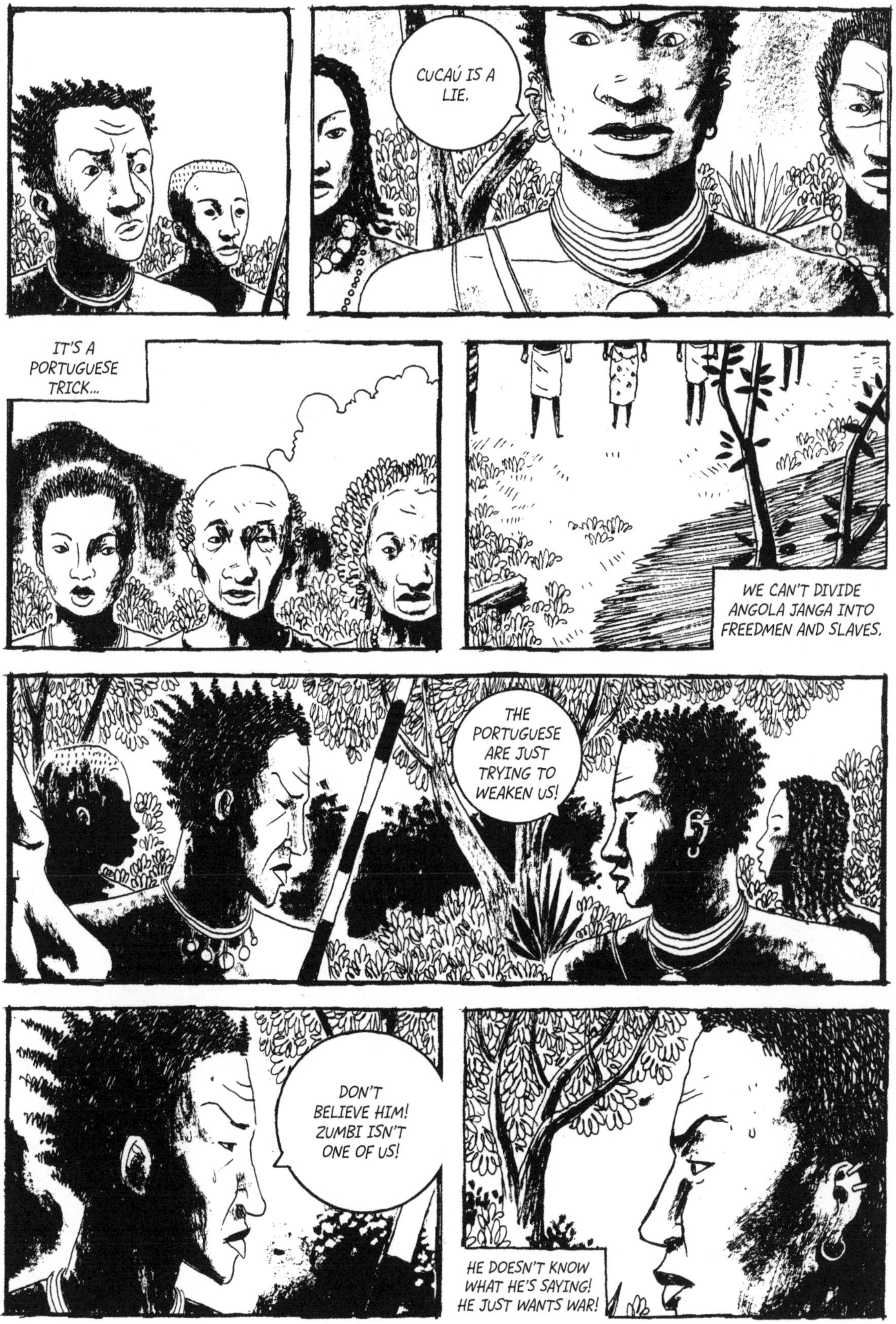

CUCAÚ IS A LIE.
IT'S A PORTUGUESE TRICK...
WE CAN'T DIVIDE ANGOLA JANGA INTO FREEDMEN AND SLAVES.
THE PORTUGUESE ARE JUST TRYING TO WEAKEN US!
DON'T BELIEVE HIM! ZUMBI ISN'T ONE OF US!
HE DOESN'T KNOW WHAT HE'S SAYING! HE JUST WANTS WAR!

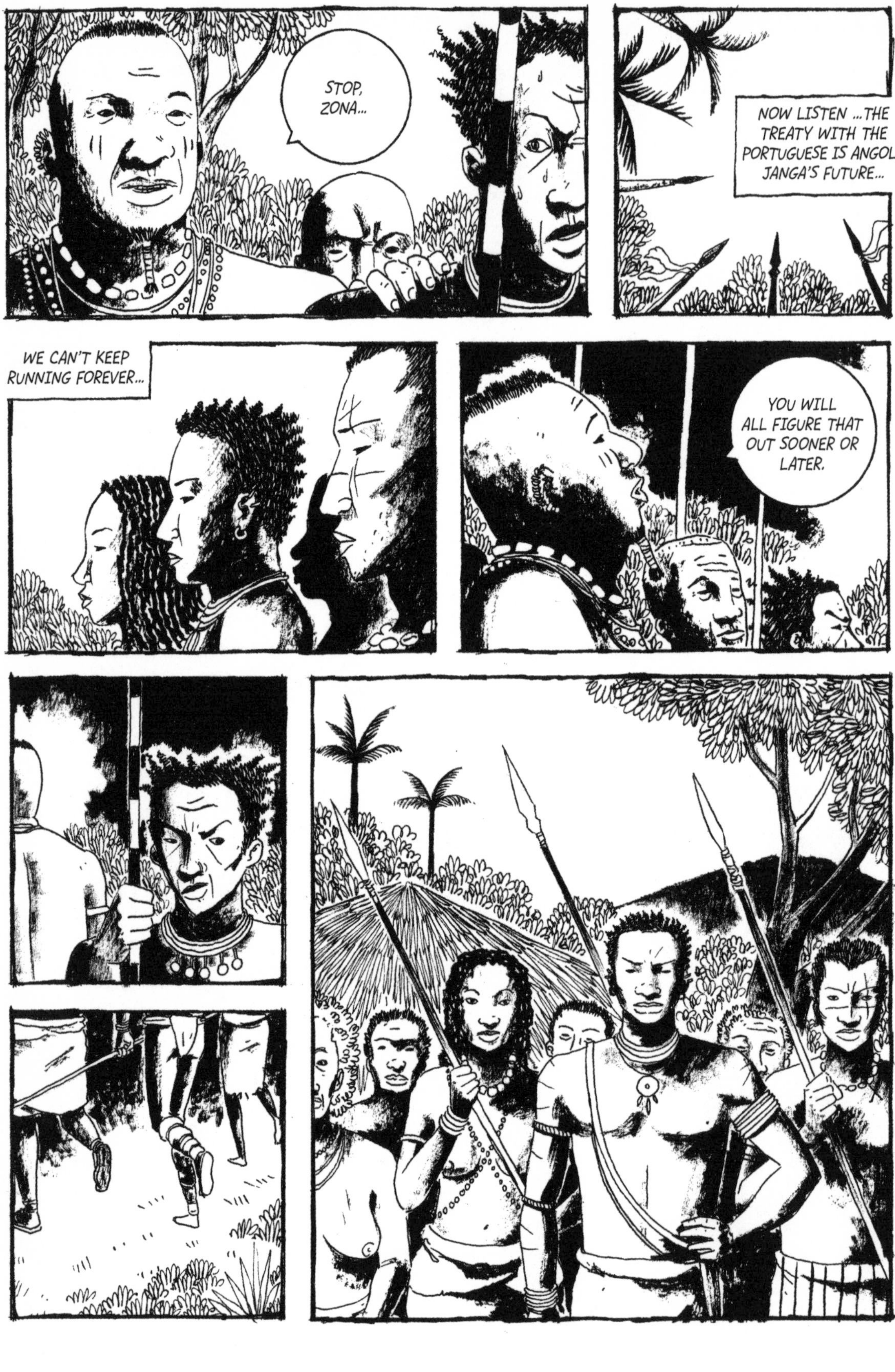
STOP, ZONA...
NOW LISTEN ...THE TREATY WITH THE PORTUGUESE IS ANGOLA JANGA'S FUTURE...
WE CAN'T KEEP RUNNING FOREVER...
YOU WILL ALL FIGURE THAT OUT SOONER OR LATER.

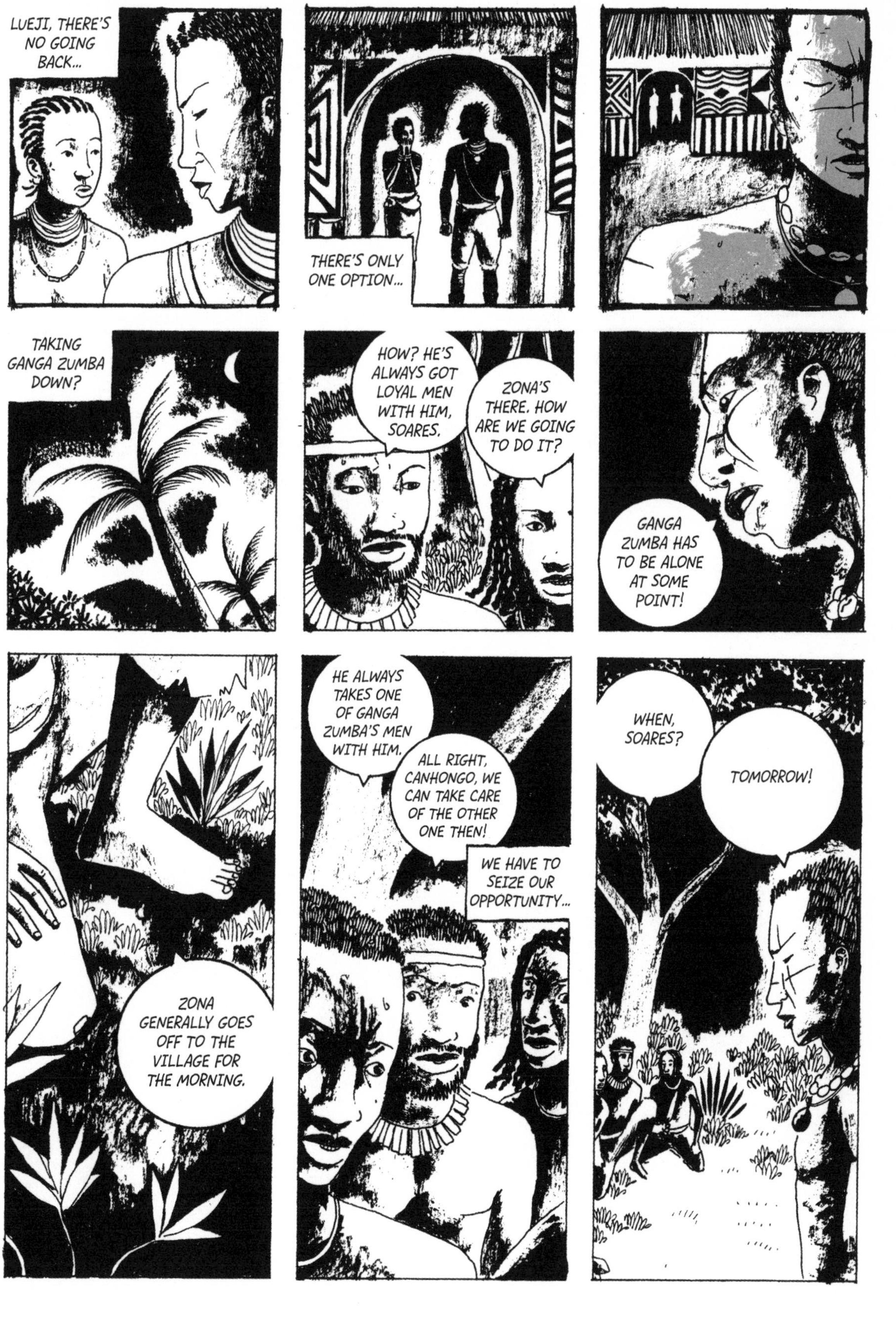

LUEJI, THERE'S NO GOING BACK...
THERE'S ONLY ONE OPTION...
TAKING GANGA ZUMBA DOWN?
HOW? HE'S ALWAYS GOT LOYAL MEN WITH HIM, SOARES.
ZONA'S THERE. HOW ARE WE GOING TO DO IT?
GANGA ZUMBA HAS TO BE ALONE AT SOME POINT!
ZONA GENERALLY GOES OFF TO THE VILLAGE FOR THE MORNING.
HE ALWAYS TAKES ONE OF GANGA ZUMBA'S MEN WITH HIM.
ALL RIGHT, CANHONGO, WE CAN TAKE CARE OF THE OTHER ONE THEN!
WE HAVE TO SEIZE OUR OPPORTUNITY...
WHEN, SOARES?
TOMORROW!

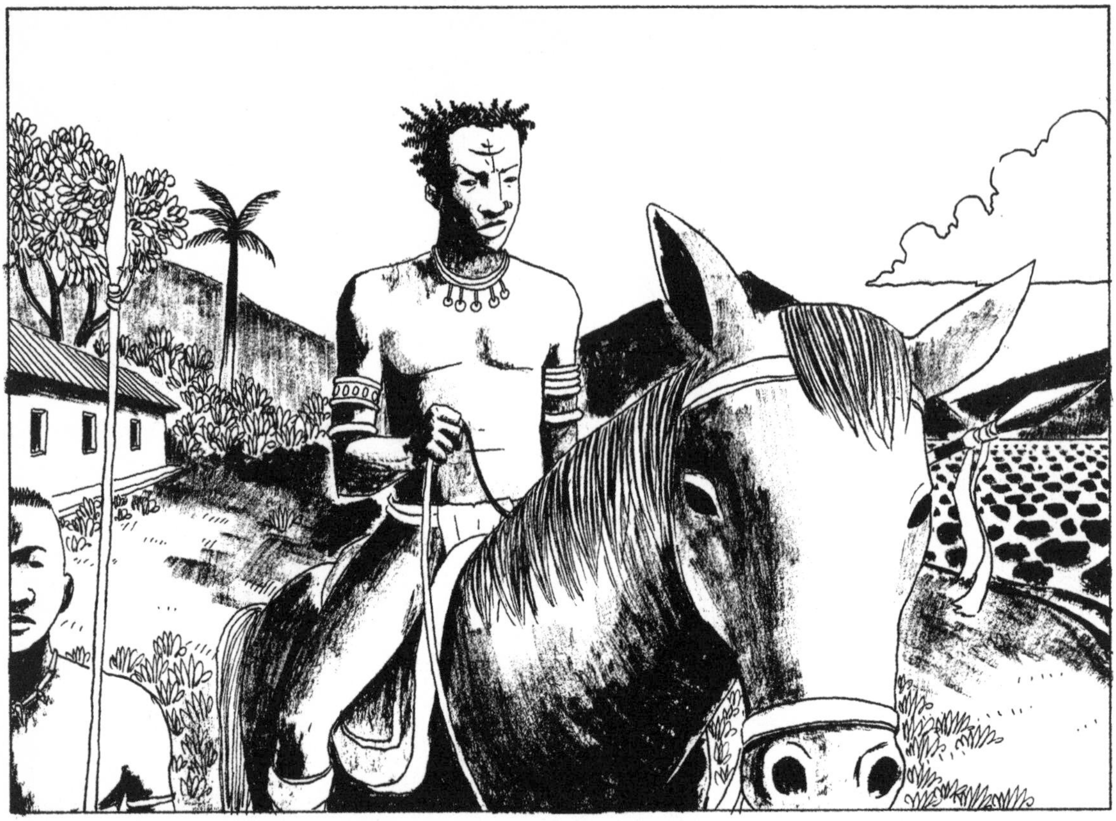

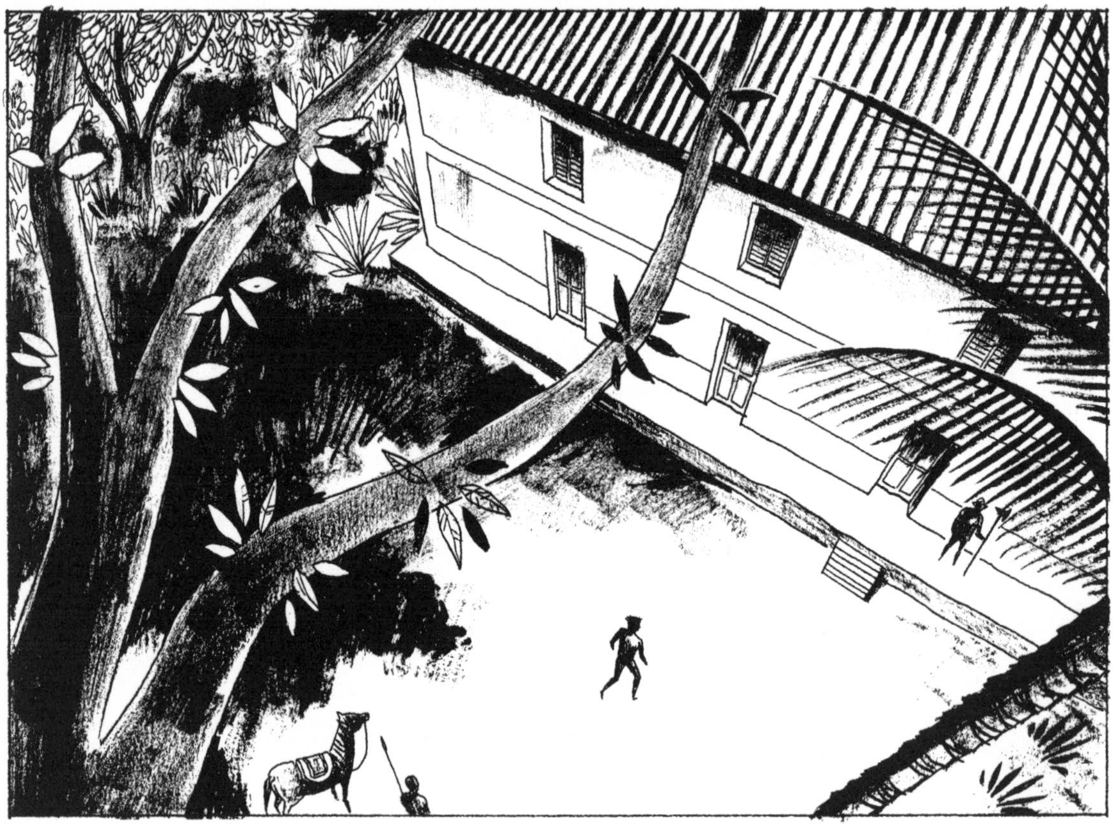

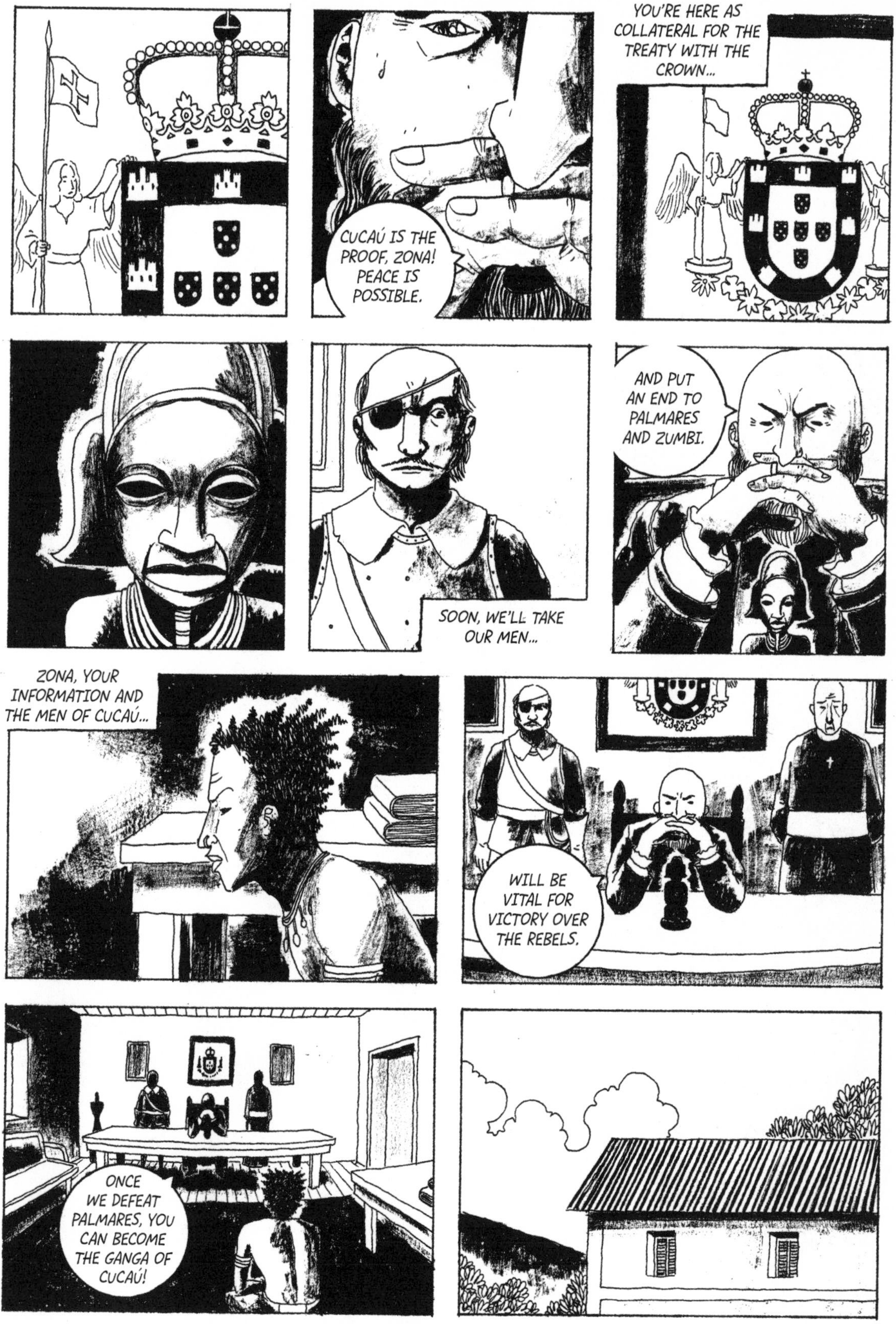
CUCAÚ IS THE PROOF, ZONA! PEACE IS POSSIBLE.
YOU'RE HERE AS COLLATERAL FOR THE TREATY WITH THE CROWN...
SOON, WE'LL TAKE OUR MEN...
AND PUT AN END TO PALMARES AND ZUMBI.
ZONA, YOUR INFORMATION AND THE MEN OF CUCAÚ...
WILL BE VITAL FOR VICTORY OVER THE REBELS.
ONCE WE DEFEAT PALMARES, YOU CAN BECOME THE GANGA OF CUCAÚ!

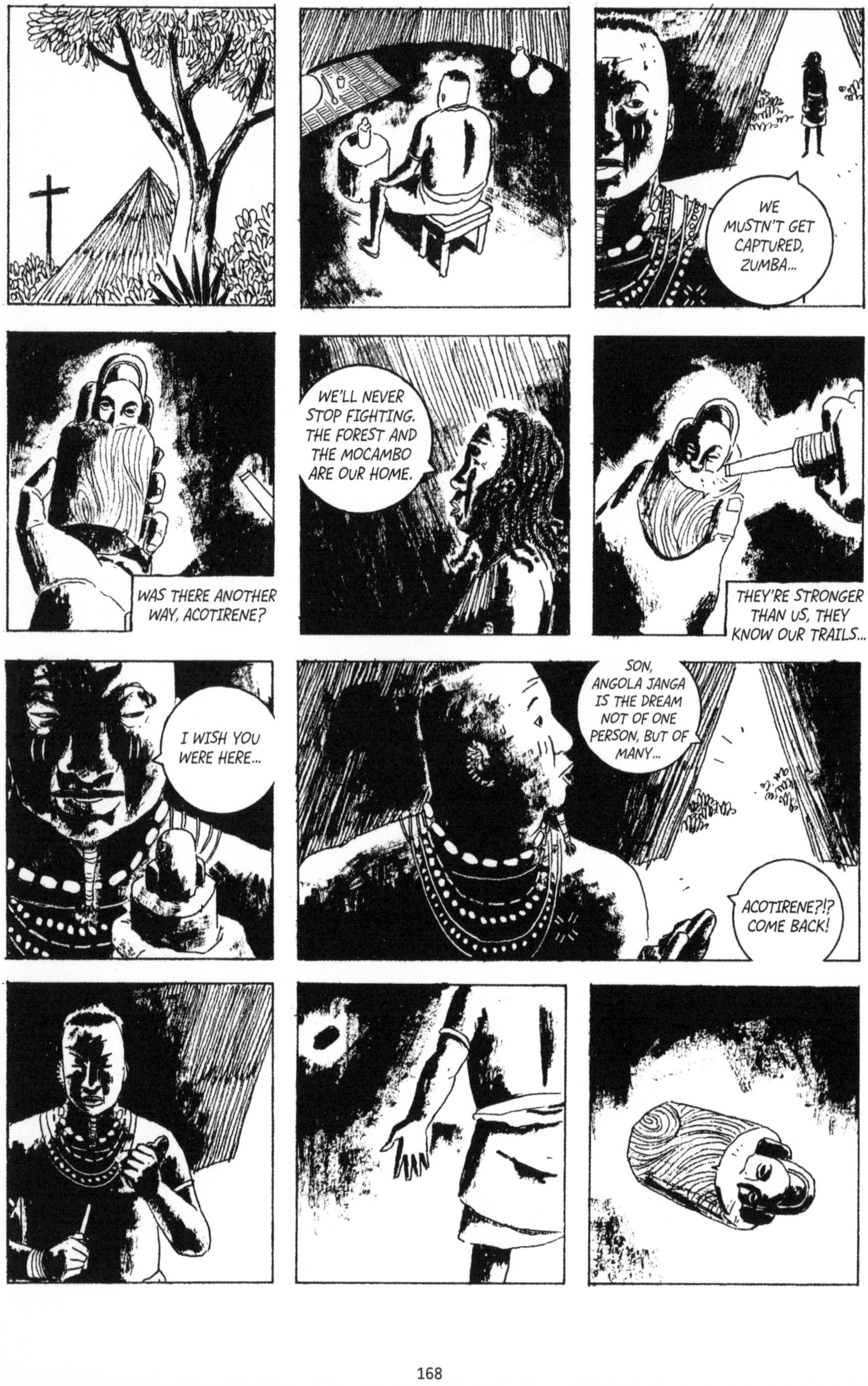
WE MUSTN'T GET CAPTURED, ZUMBA...
WAS THERE ANOTHER WAY, ACOTIRENE?
WE'LL NEVER STOP FIGHTING. THE FOREST AND THE MOCAMBO ARE OUR HOME.
THEY'RE STRONGER THAN US, THEY KNOW OUR TRAILS...
I WISH YOU WERE HERE...
SON, ANGOLA JANGA IS THE DREAM NOT OF ONE PERSON, BUT OF MANY...
ACOTIRENE?!? COME BACK!

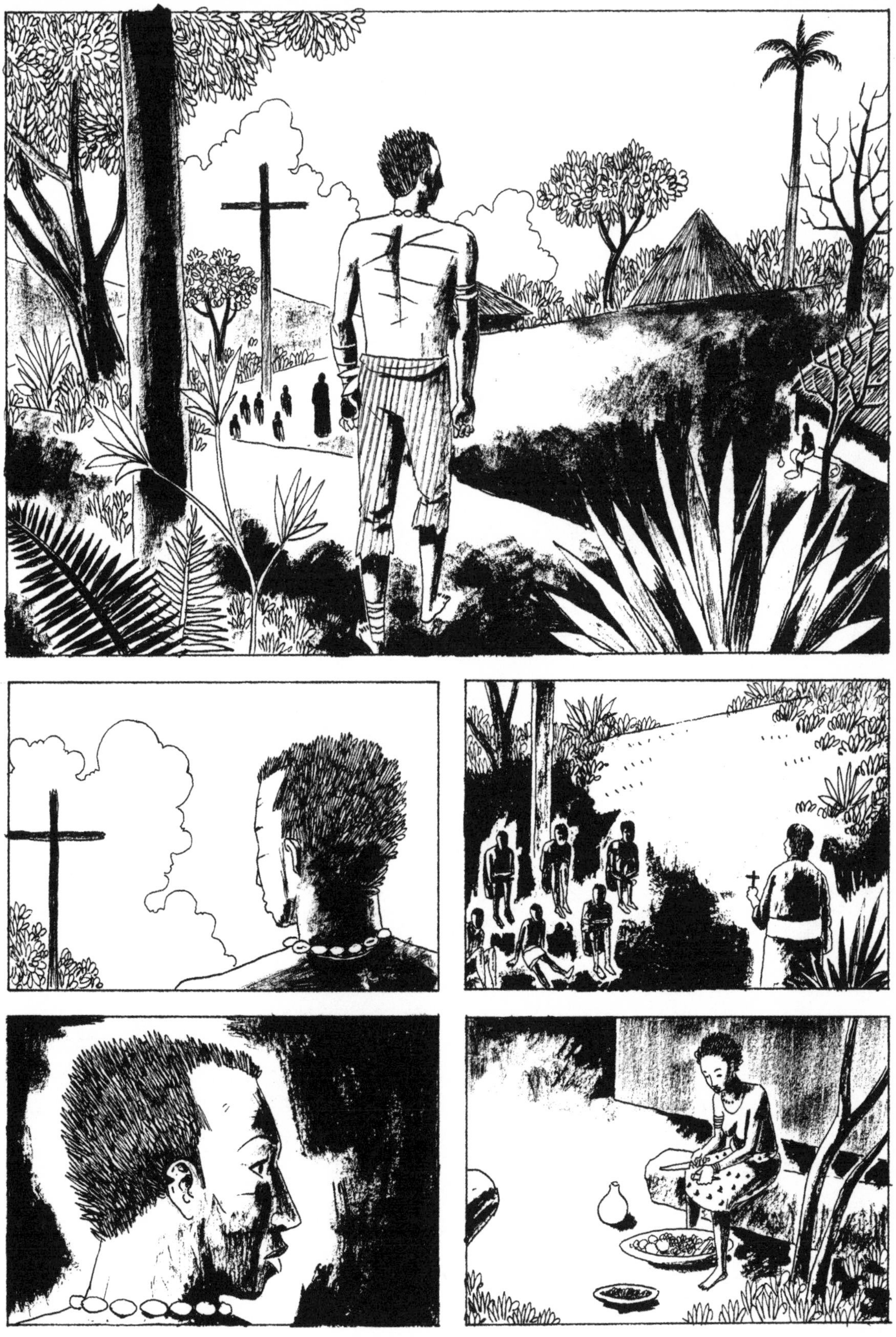

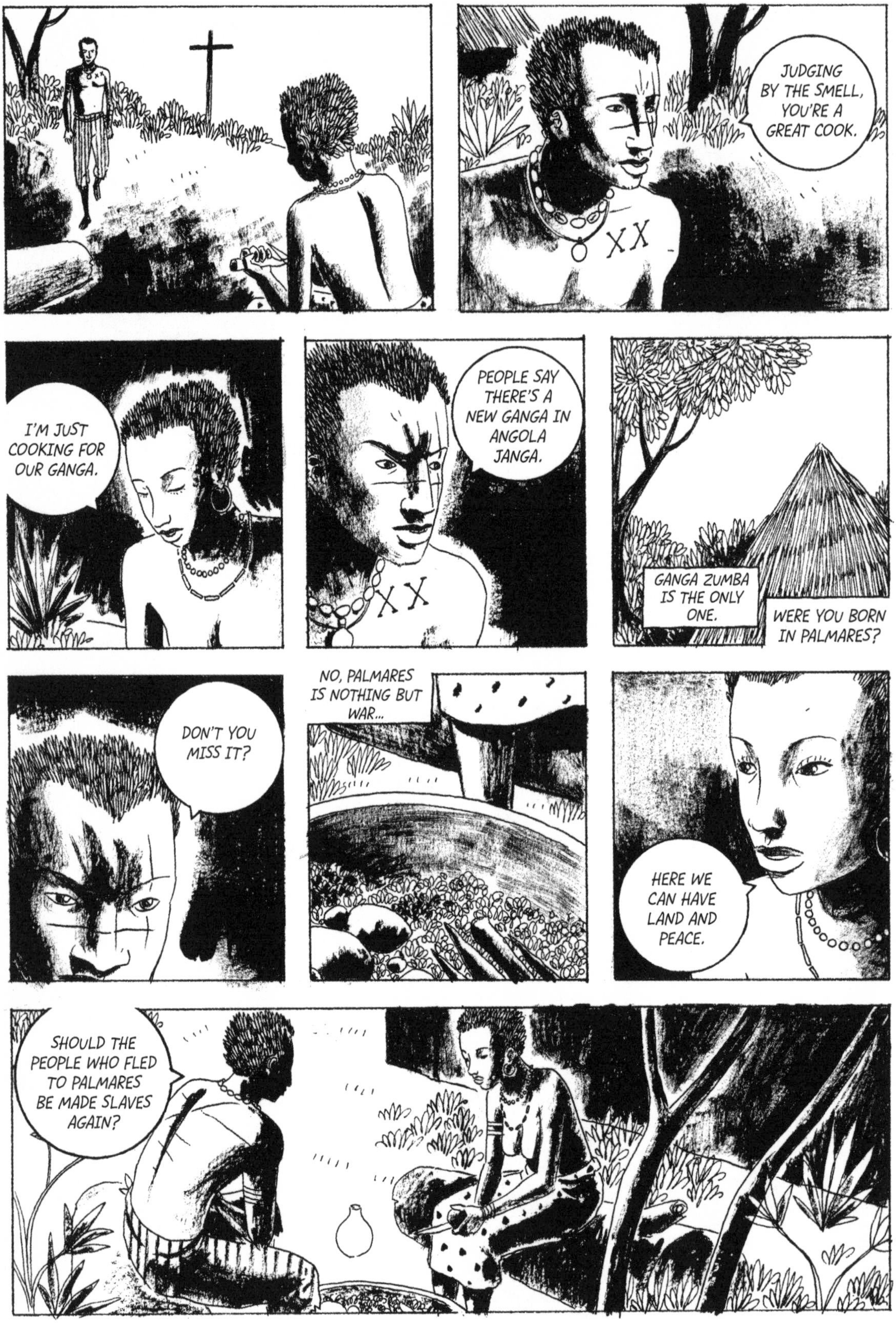
JUDGING BY THE SMELL, YOU'RE A GREAT COOK.
I'M JUST COOKING FOR OUR GANGA.
PEOPLE SAY THERE'S A NEW GANGA IN ANGOLA JANGA.
GANGA ZUMBA IS THE ONLY ONE.
WERE YOU BORN IN PALMARES?
DON'T YOU MISS IT?
NO, PALMARES IS NOTHING BUT WAR...
HERE WE CAN HAVE LAND AND PEACE.
SHOULD THE PEOPLE WHO FLED TO PALMARES BE MADE SLAVES AGAIN?

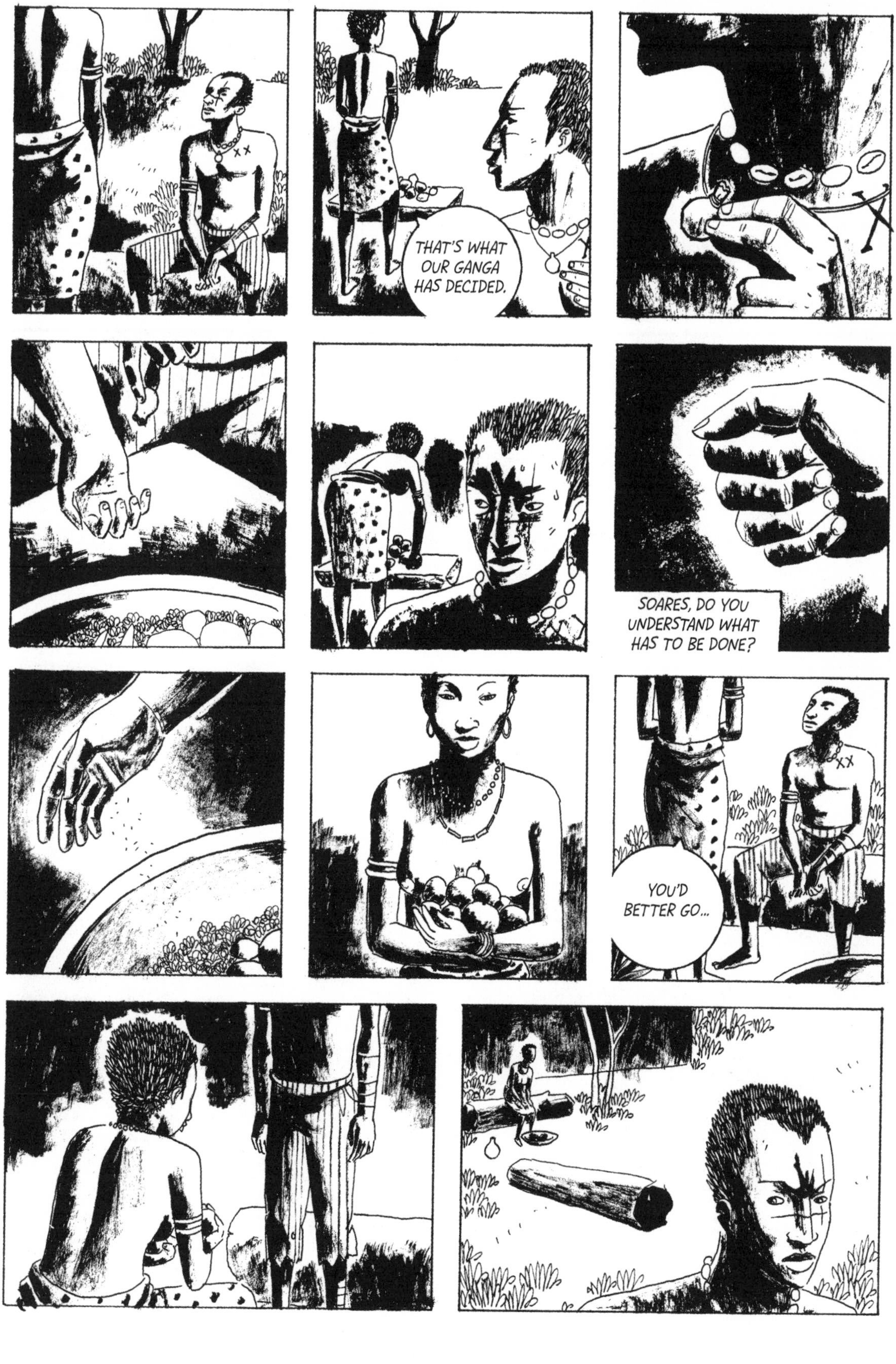
THAT'S WHAT OUR GANGA HAS DECIDED.
SOARES, DO YOU UNDERSTAND WHAT HAS TO BE DONE?
YOU'D BETTER GO...

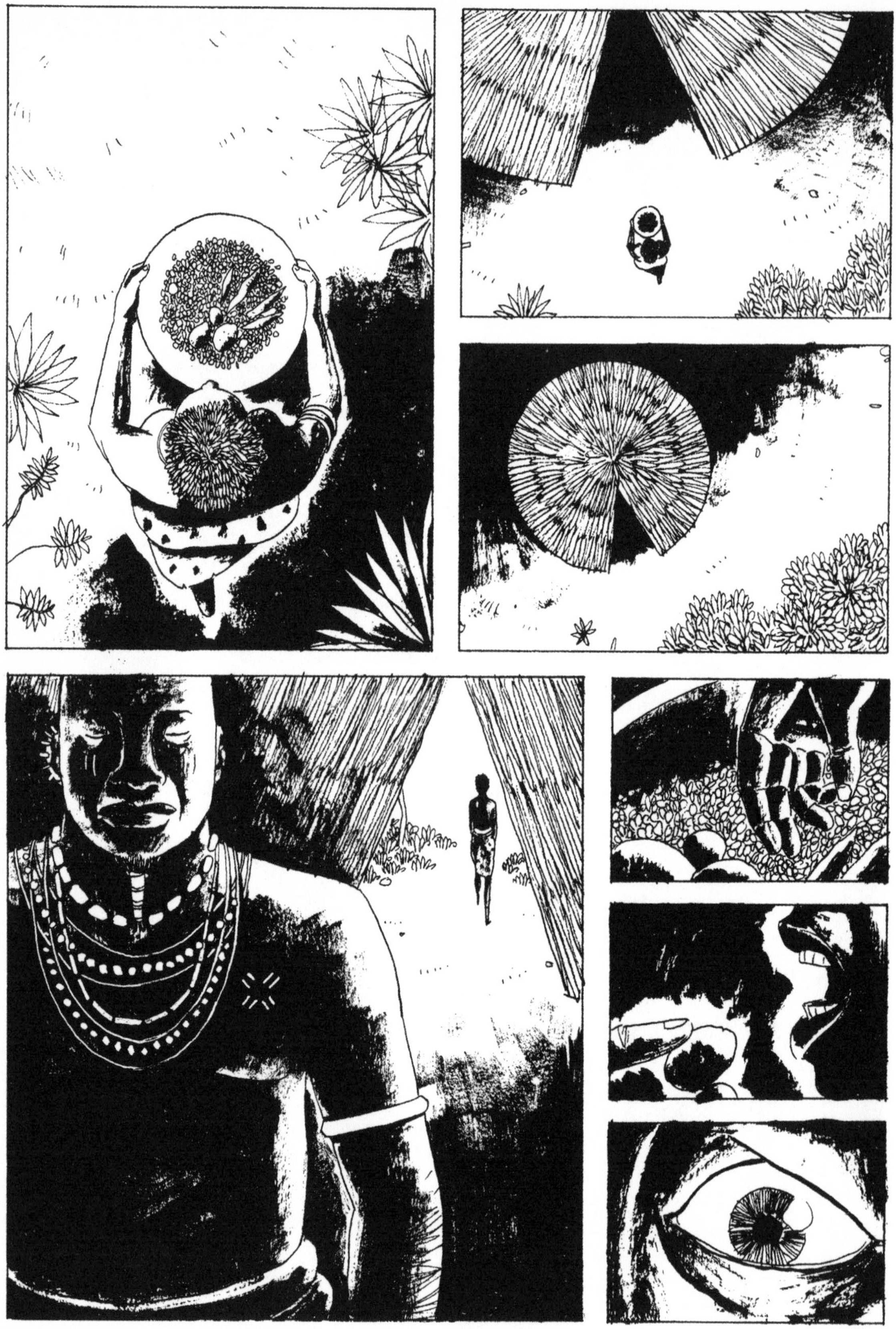

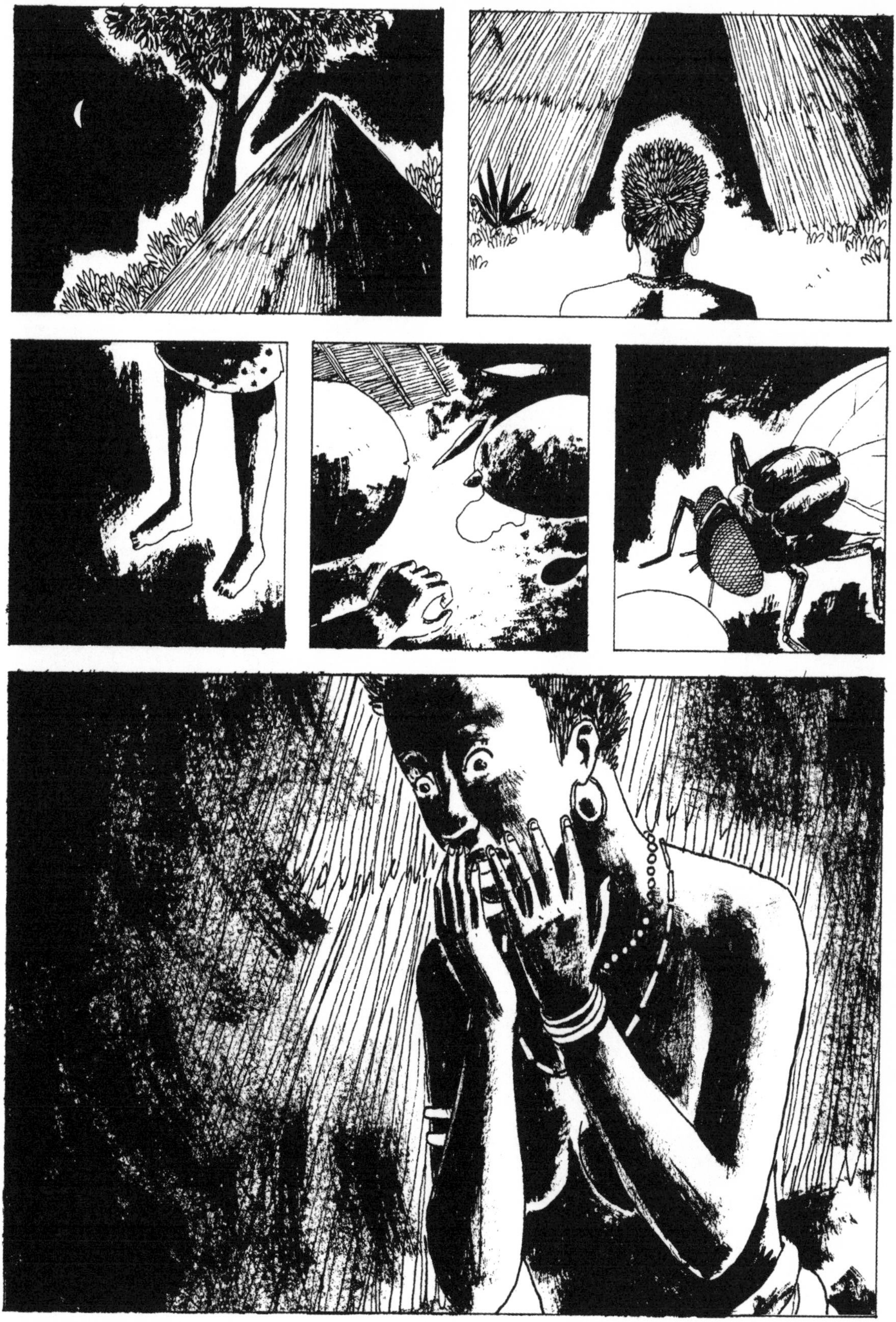

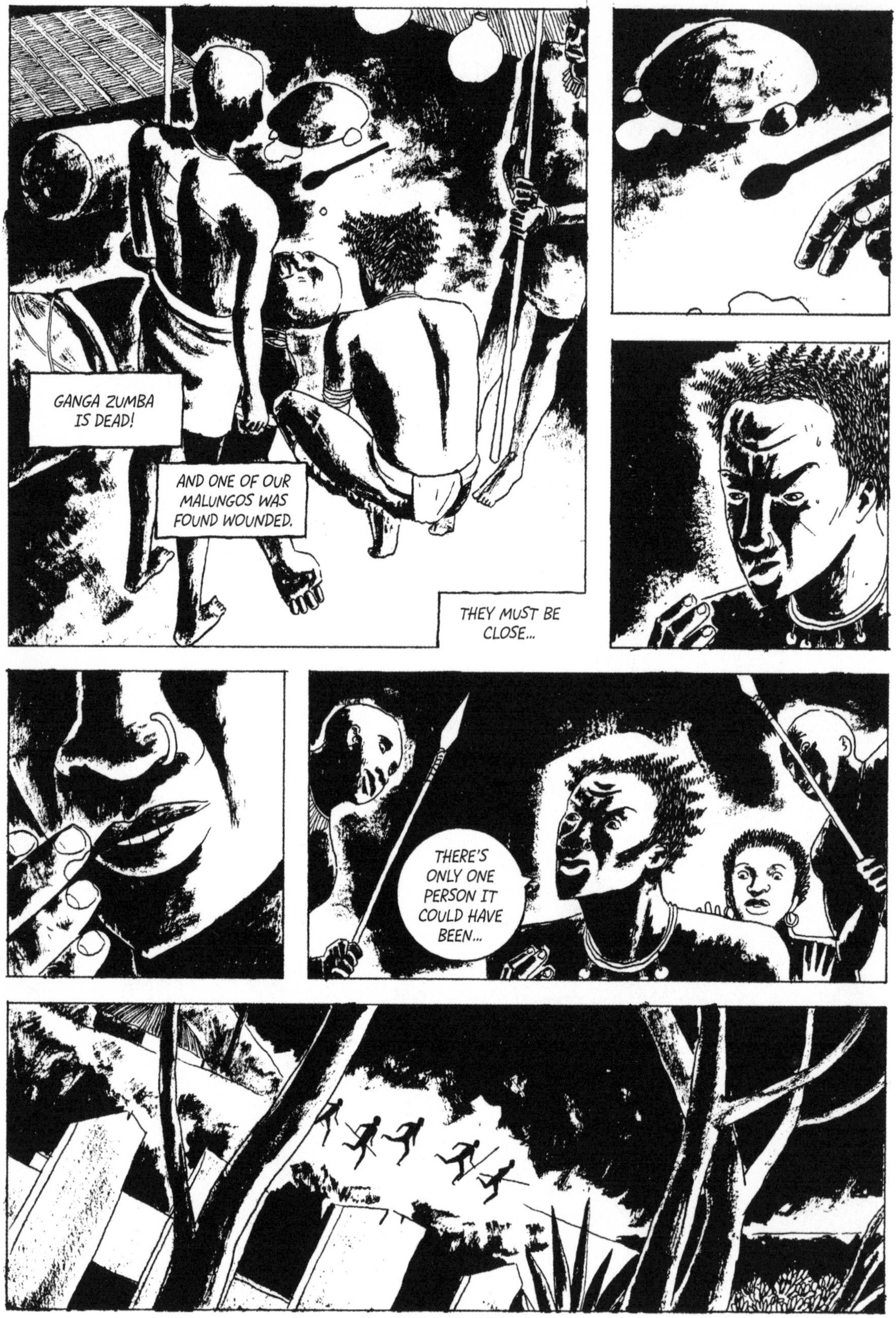
GANGA ZUMBA IS DEAD!
AND ONE OF OUR MALUNGOS WAS FOUND WOUNDED.
THEY MUST BE CLOSE...
THERE'S ONLY ONE PERSON IT COULD HAVE BEEN...

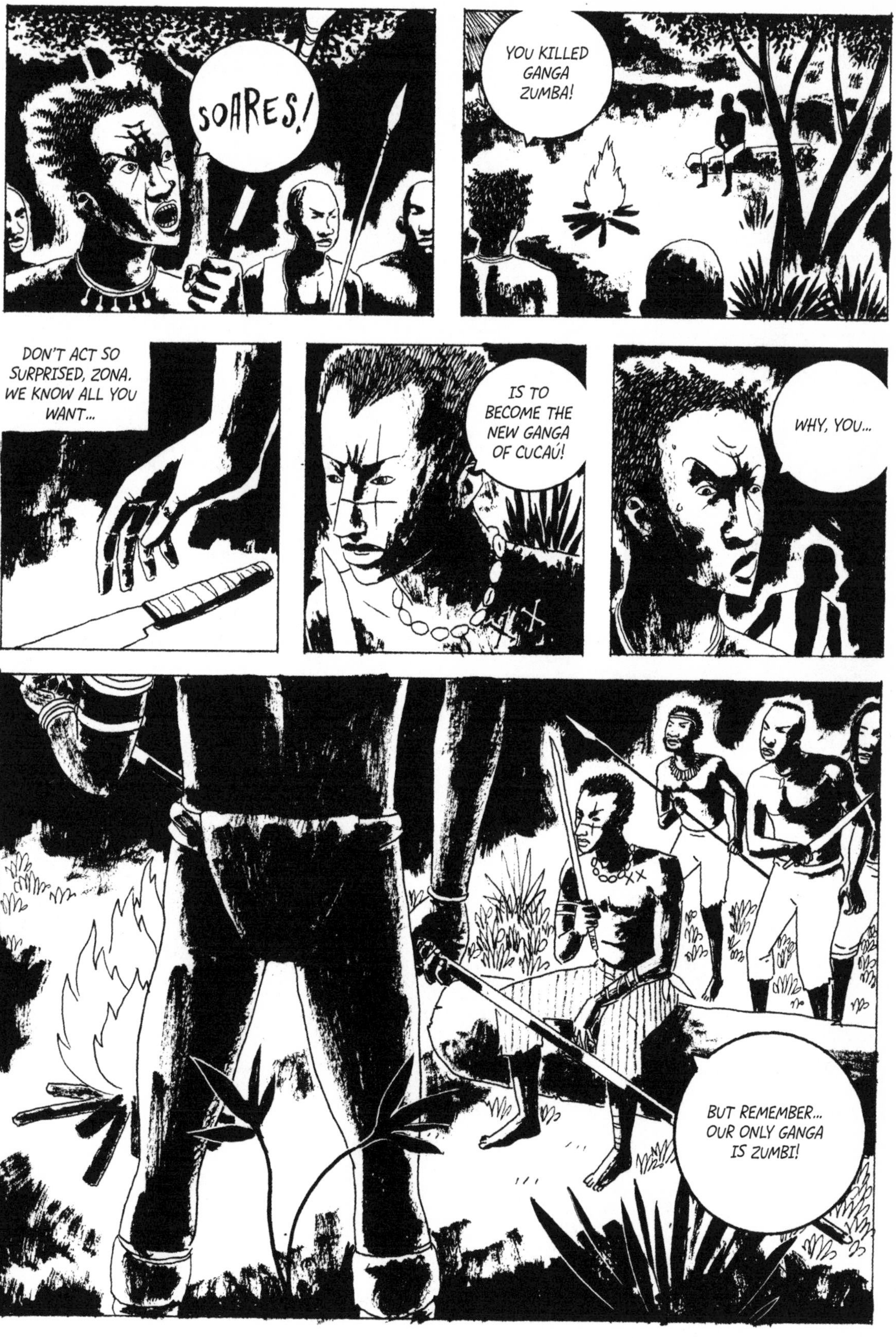

SOARES!
YOU KILLED GANGA ZUMBA!
DON'T ACT SO SURPRISED, ZONA. WE KNOW ALL YOU WANT...
IS TO BECOME THE NEW GANGA OF CUCAÚ!
WHY, YOU...
BUT REMEMBER... OUR ONLY GANGA IS ZUMBI!

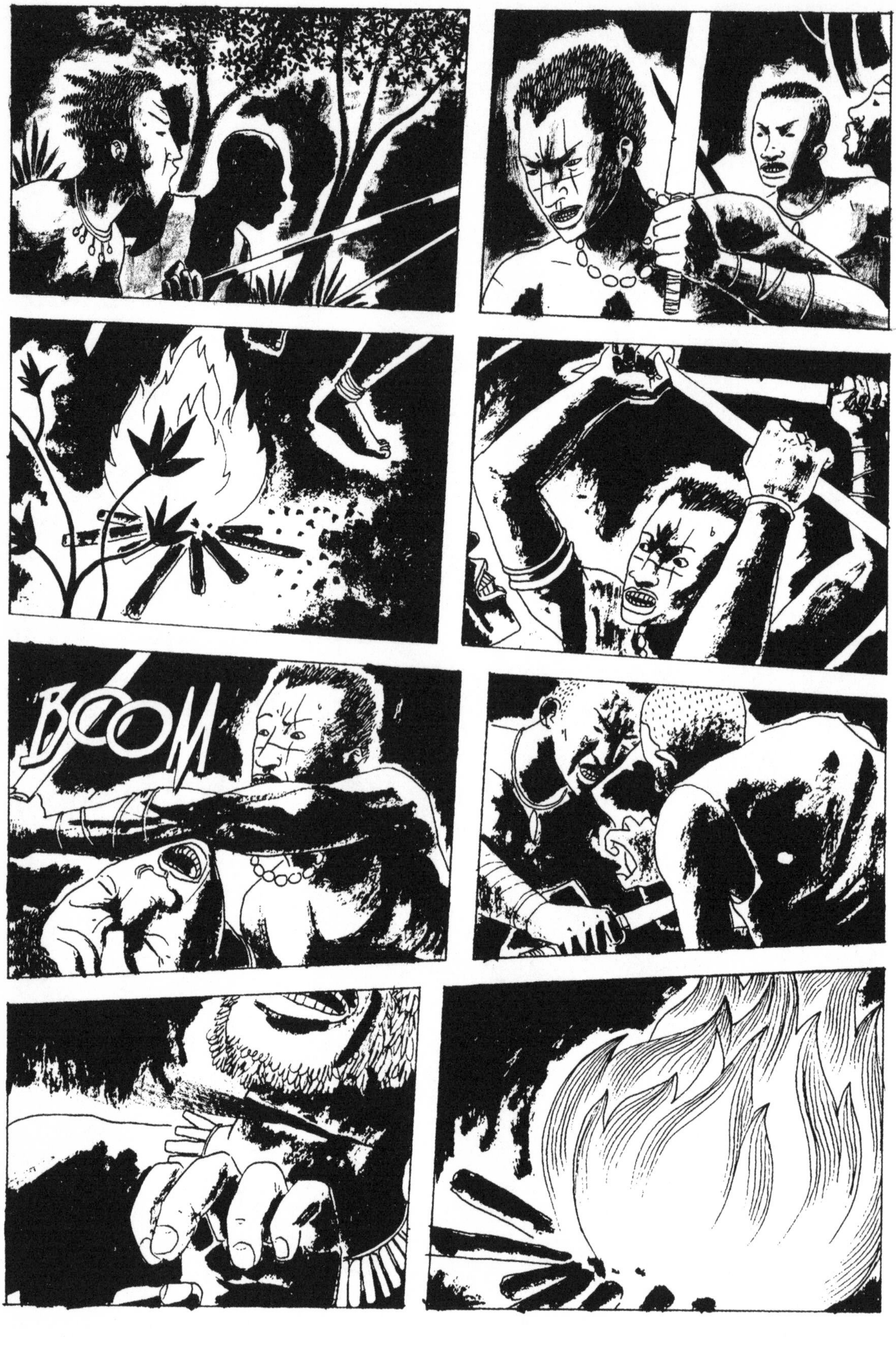
BOOM

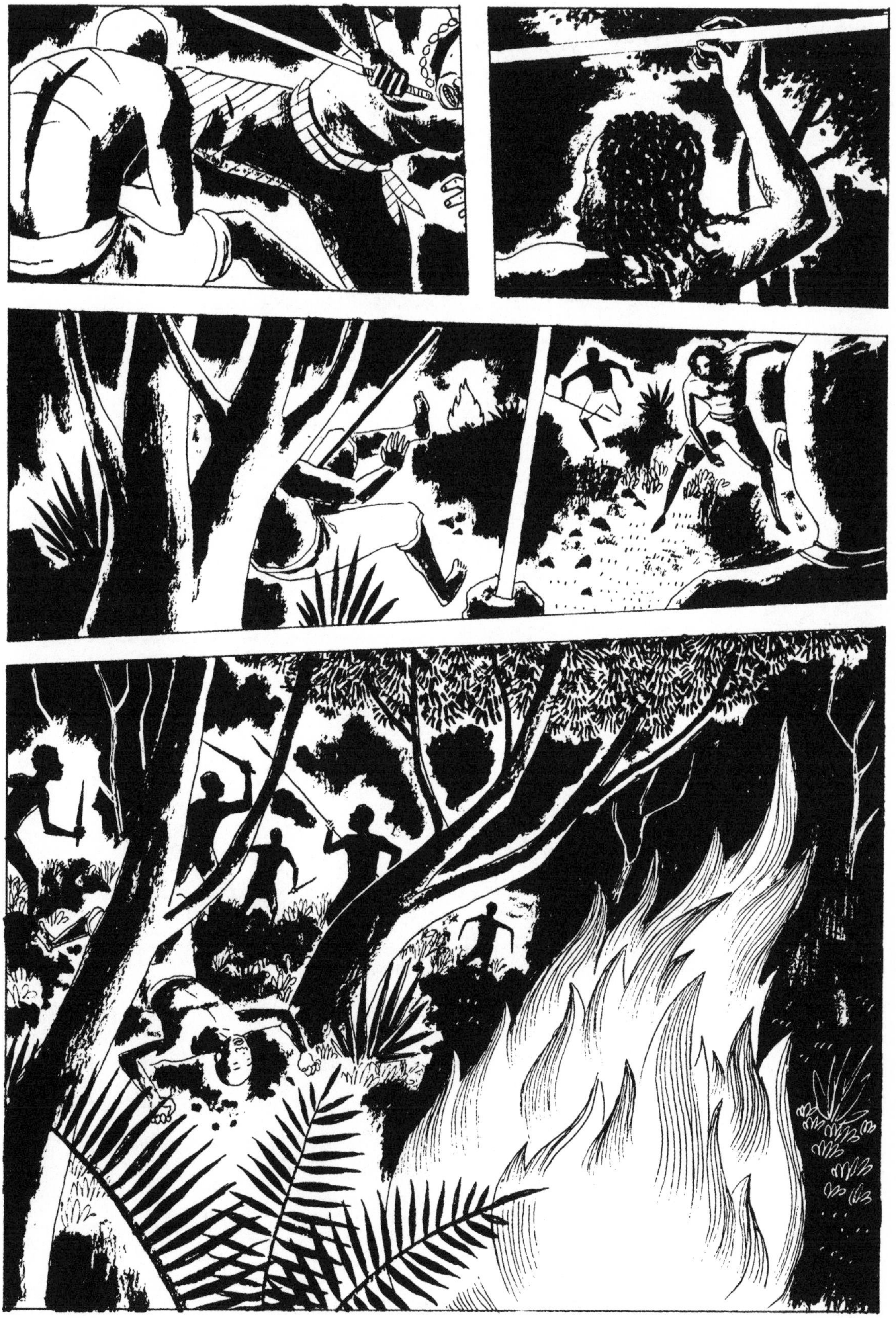

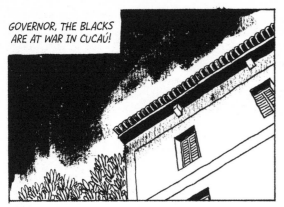

GOVERNOR, THE BLACKS ARE AT WAR IN CUCAÚ!

APPARENTLY, GANGA ZUMBA WAS POISONED!

DAMN IT!

THAT'S GOING TO COMPLICATE NEGOTIATIONS WITH PALMARES!

ON THE OTHER HAND, SIR, WE DID CAPTURE MORE FUGITIVES FOR THE CROWN.

VERY GOOD, FURTADO, GO CRUSH...

ALL THE RESISTANCE IN CUCAÚ!

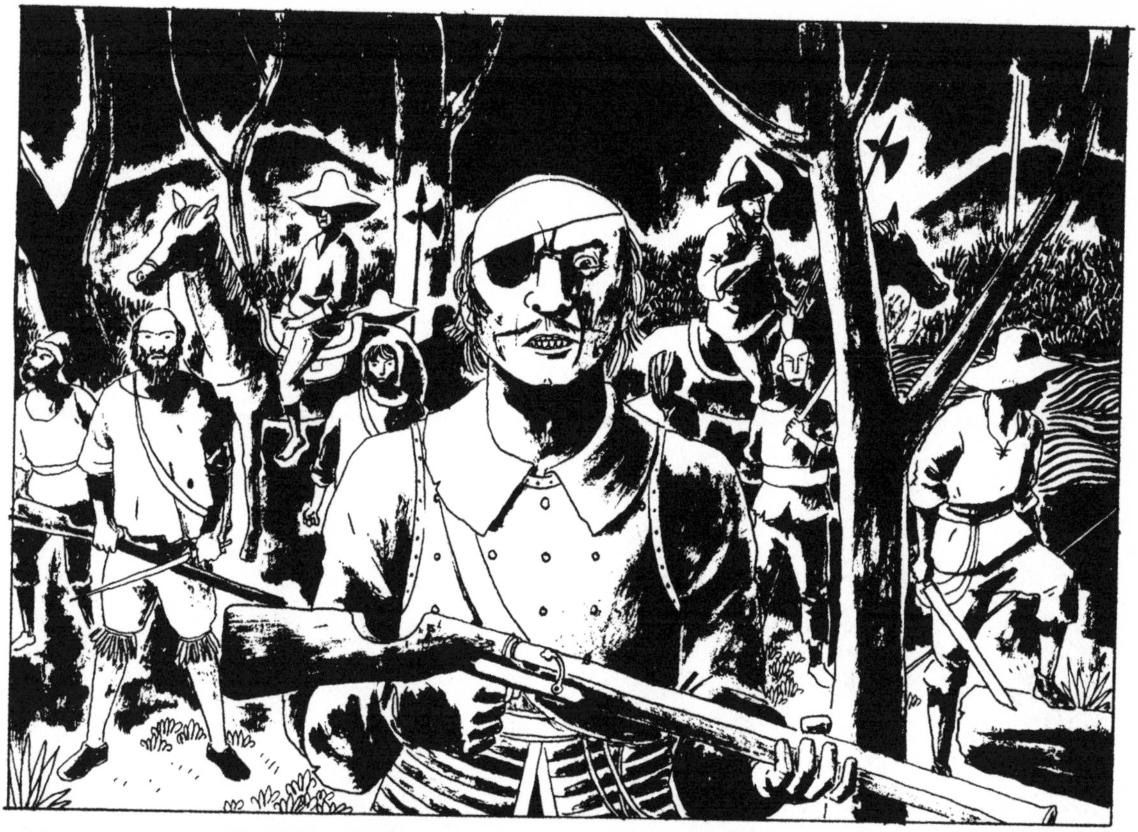

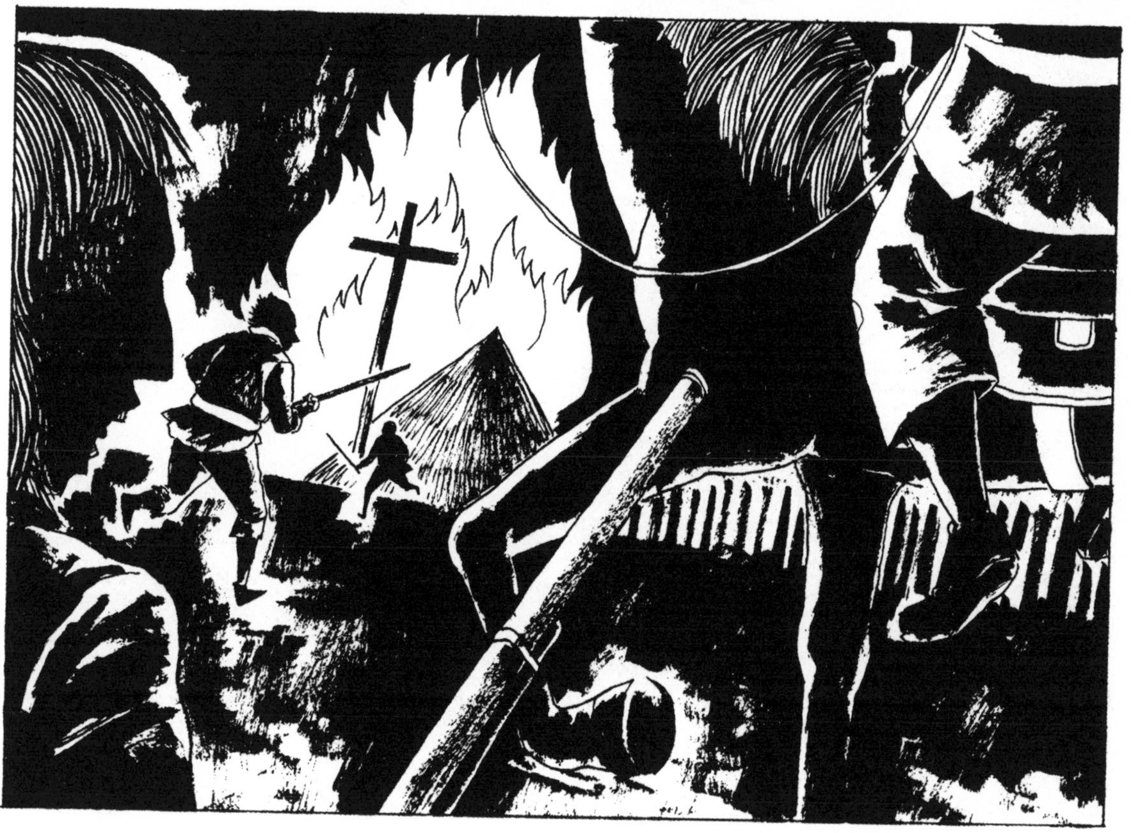

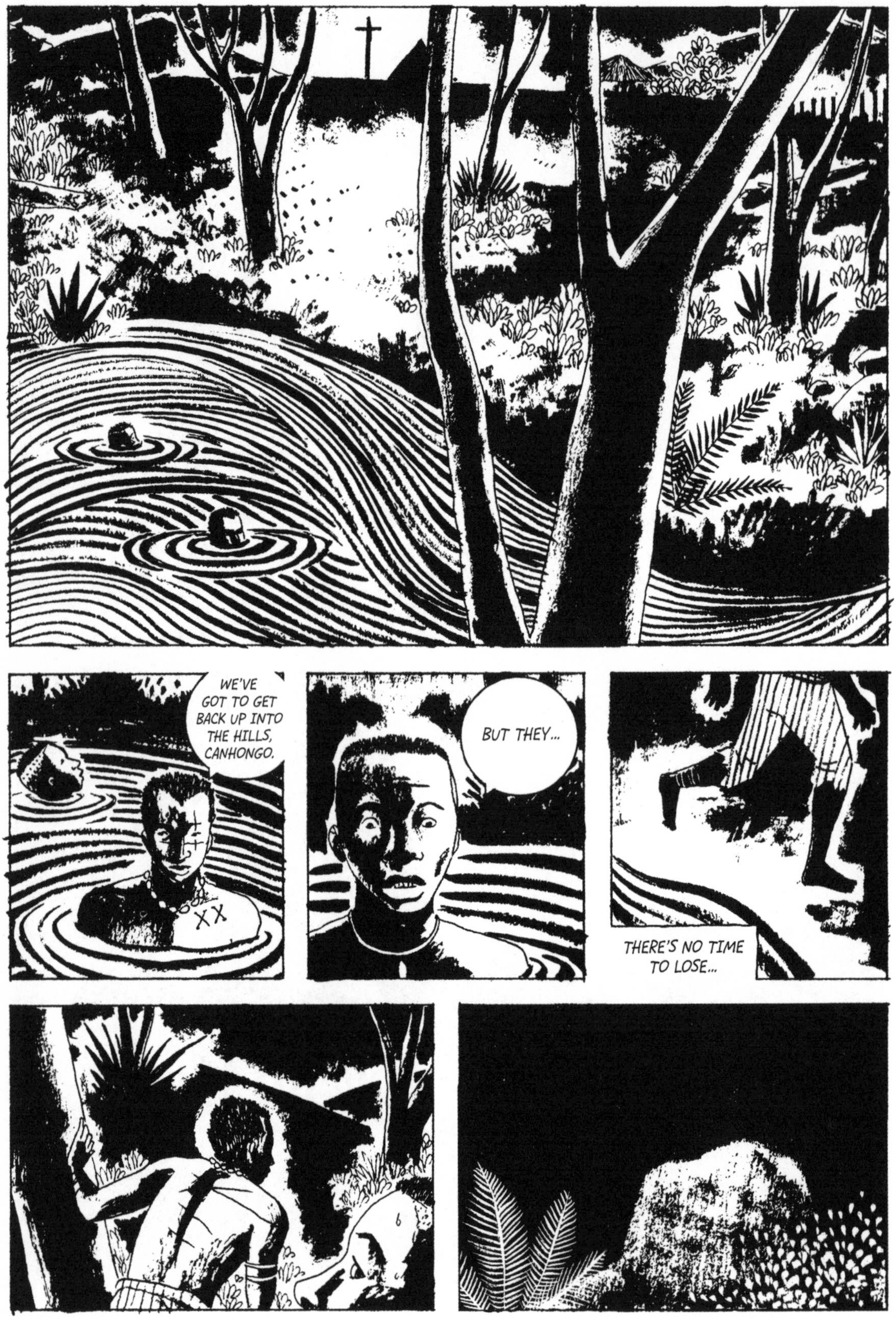
WE'VE GOT TO GET BACK UP INTO THE HILLS, CANHONGO.
BUT THEY...
THERE'S NO TIME TO LOSE...

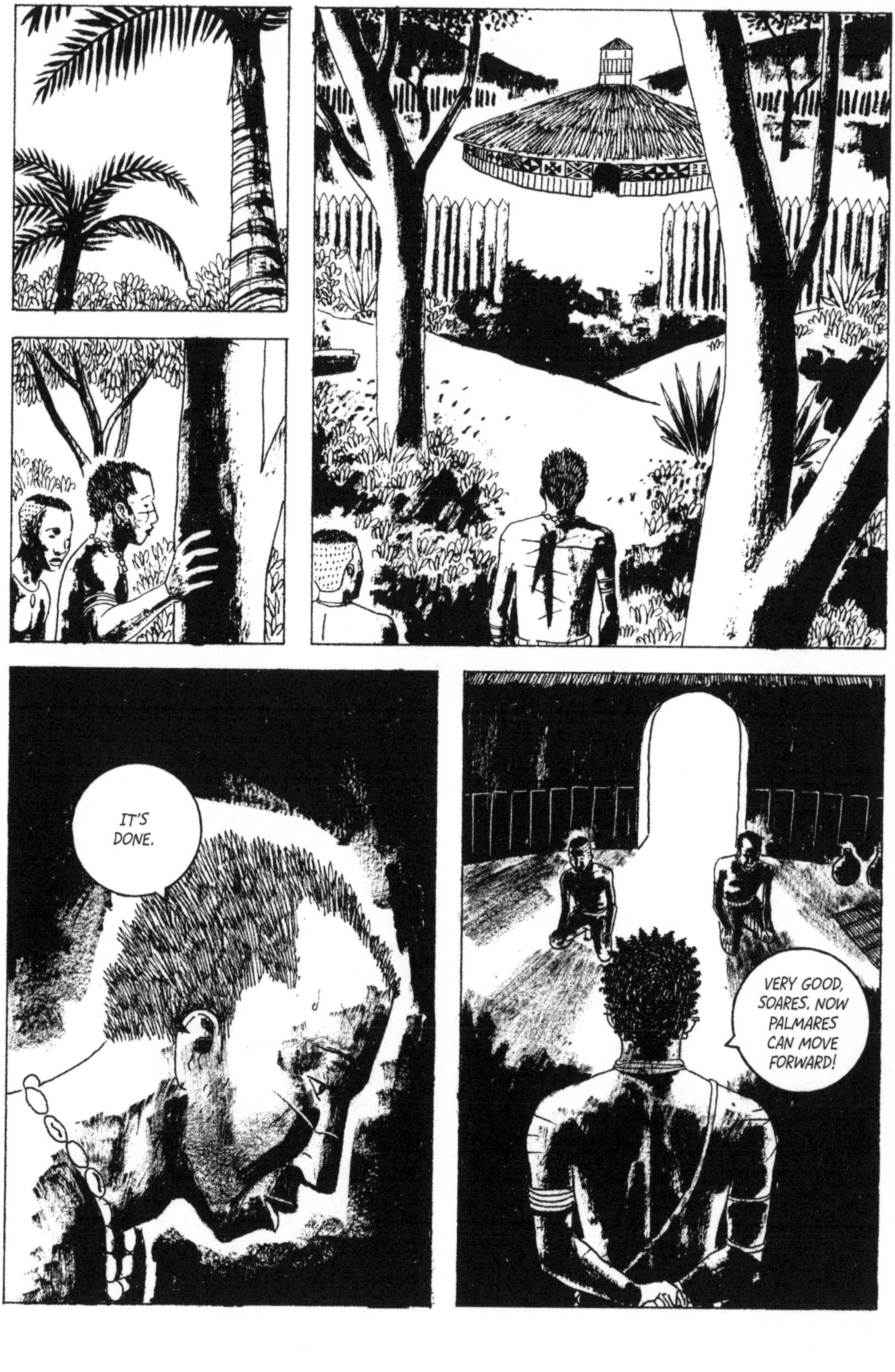
IT'S DONE.
VERY GOOD, SOARES. NOW PALMARES CAN MOVE FORWARD!

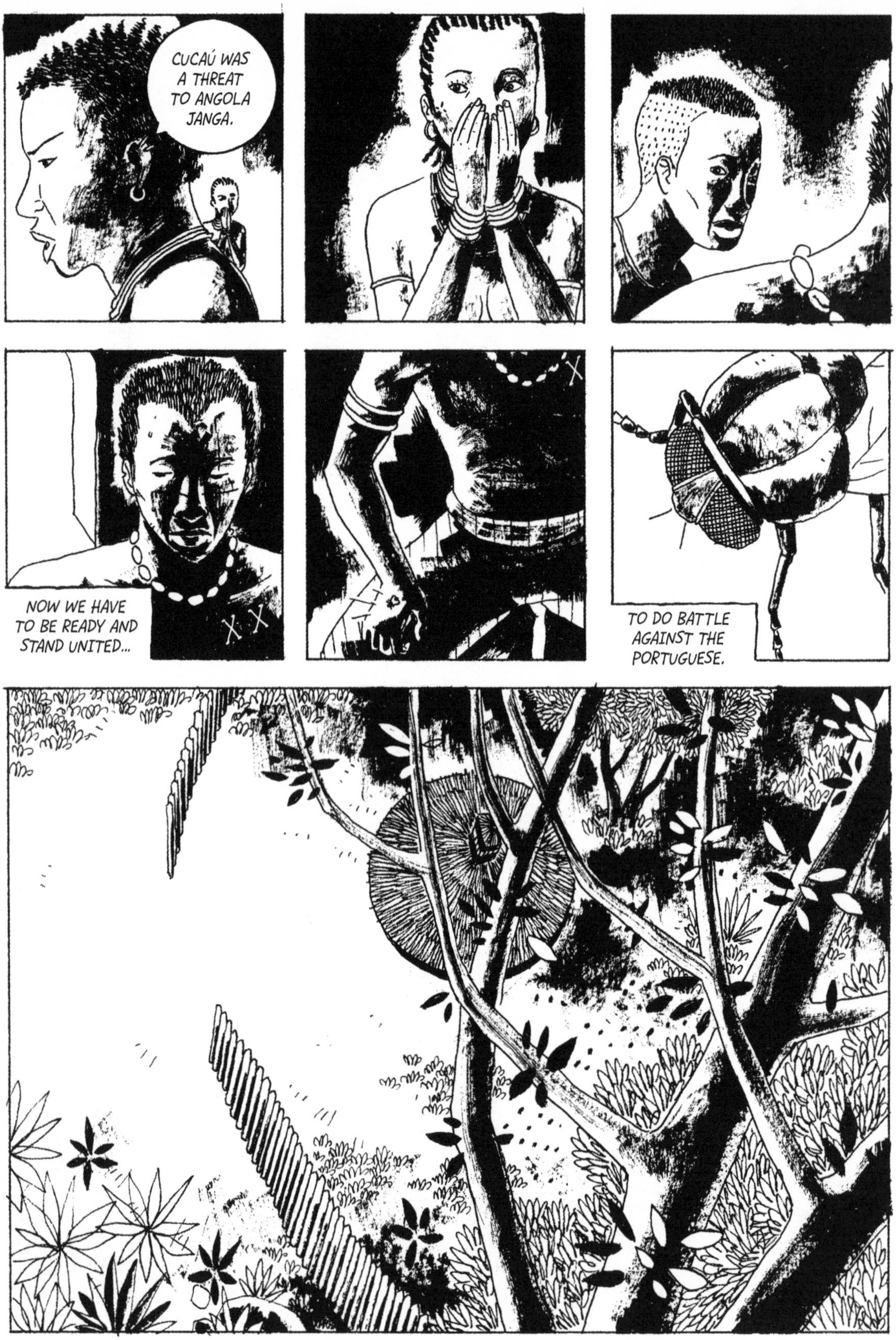

CUCAÚ WAS A THREAT TO ANGOLA JANGA.
NOW WE HAVE TO BE READY AND STAND UNITED...
TO DO BATTLE AGAINST THE PORTUGUESE.

ENCOUNTERS

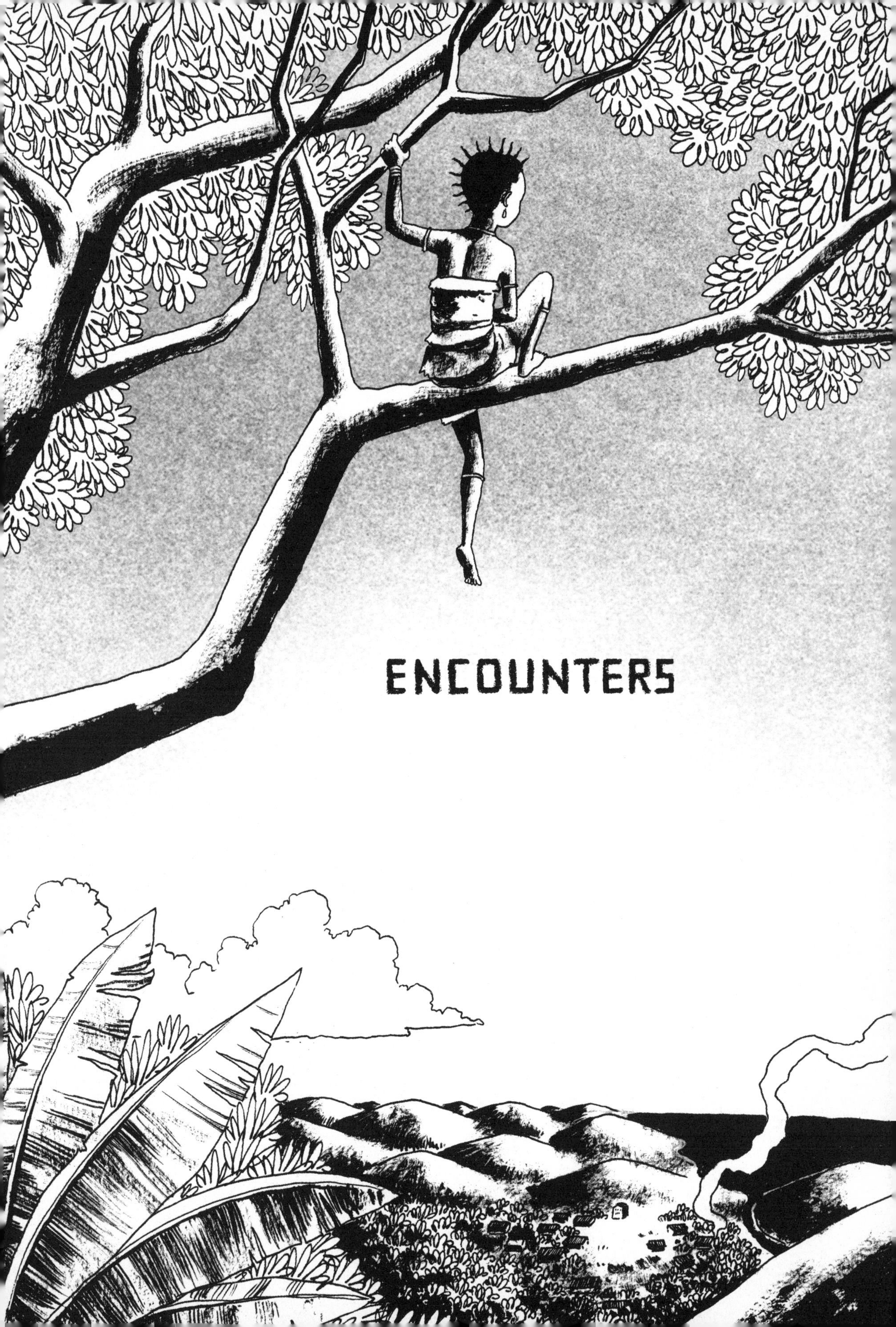

I, the King, make it known to you, Captain Zumbi of Palmares, that I hereby forgive you all the excesses that you have carried out against my Royal Treasury and against the people of Pernambuco, and that I do so in the understanding that your rebellion was right given the evils practiced by some bad masters in disobedience to my royal commands. I invite you to reside in whatever place you wish, with your wife and children, and all your captains, free from any captivity or bondage, as my loyal and faithful subjects, under my royal protection, of which my governor responsible for the administration of this captaincy is aware.

—*Salvaterra, Dom Pedro II, King of Portugal. Letter addressed to Zumbi. It is not known whether the document ever reached its intended recipient. February 26, 1685.*

It is not advisable to make peace with these blacks, for experience has shown that they are always somewhat deceptive in this practice, and as we have a reputation to protect, they remain in captivity and as fugitives...

—*Overseas Council to the King, circa 1690.*

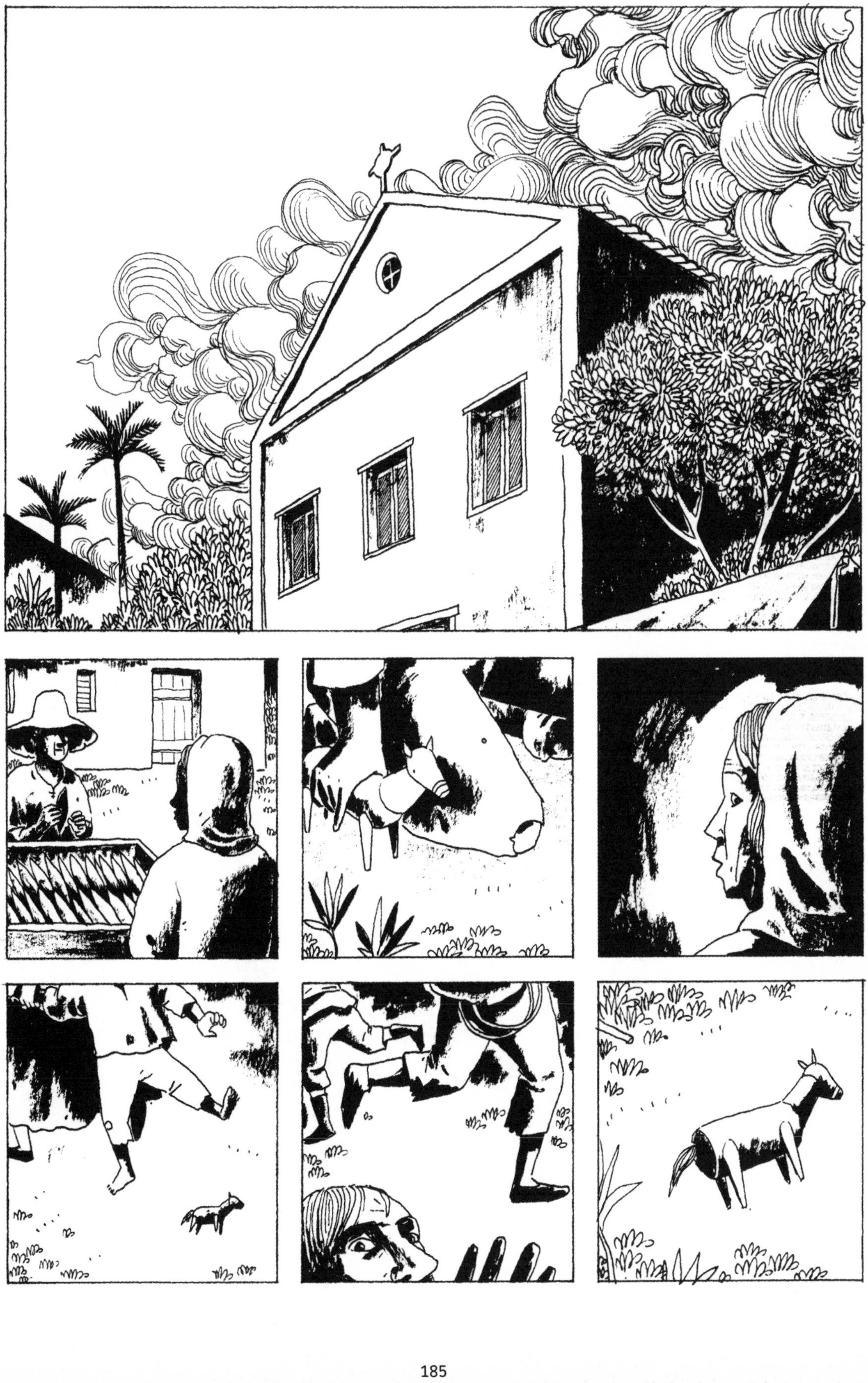

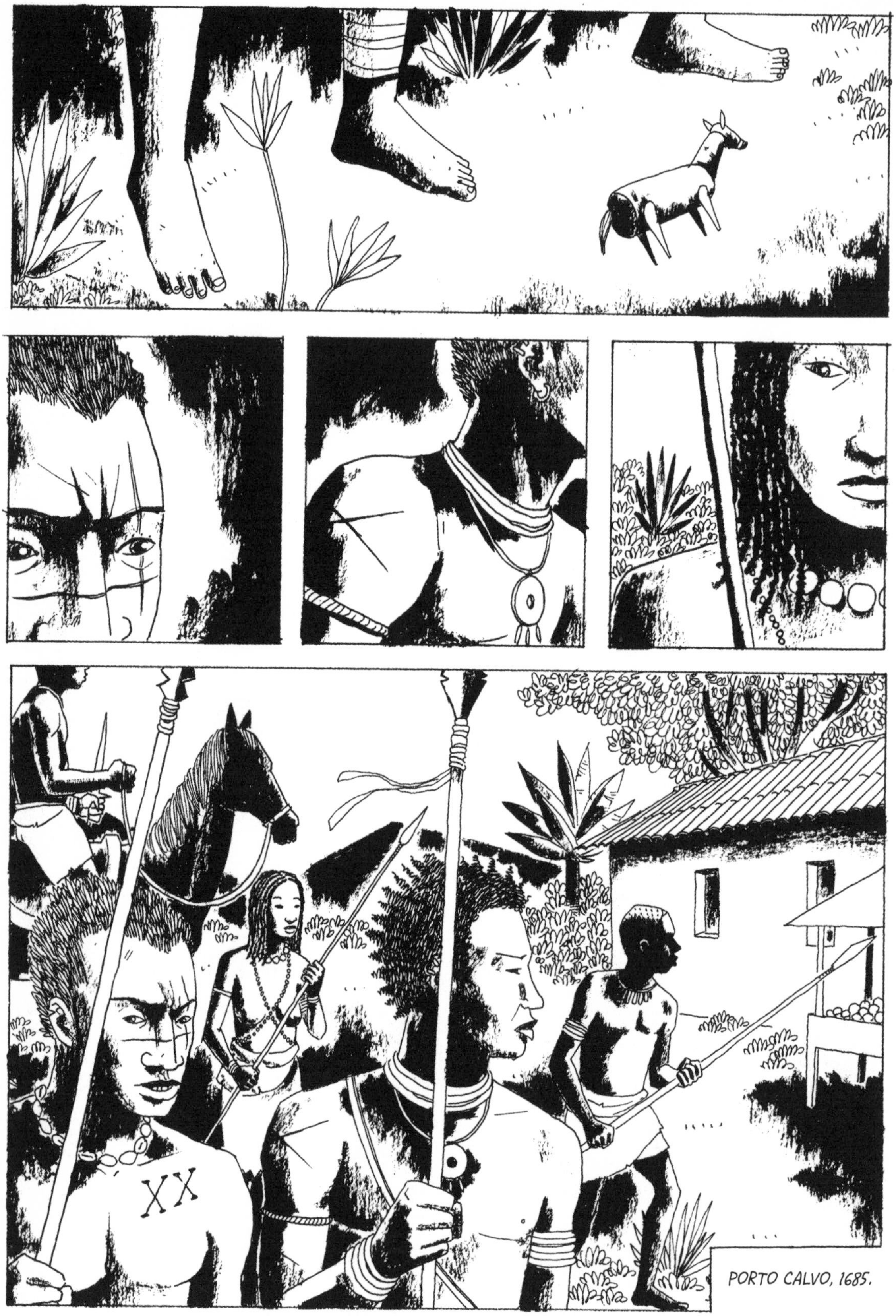
PORTO CALVO, 1685.
XX

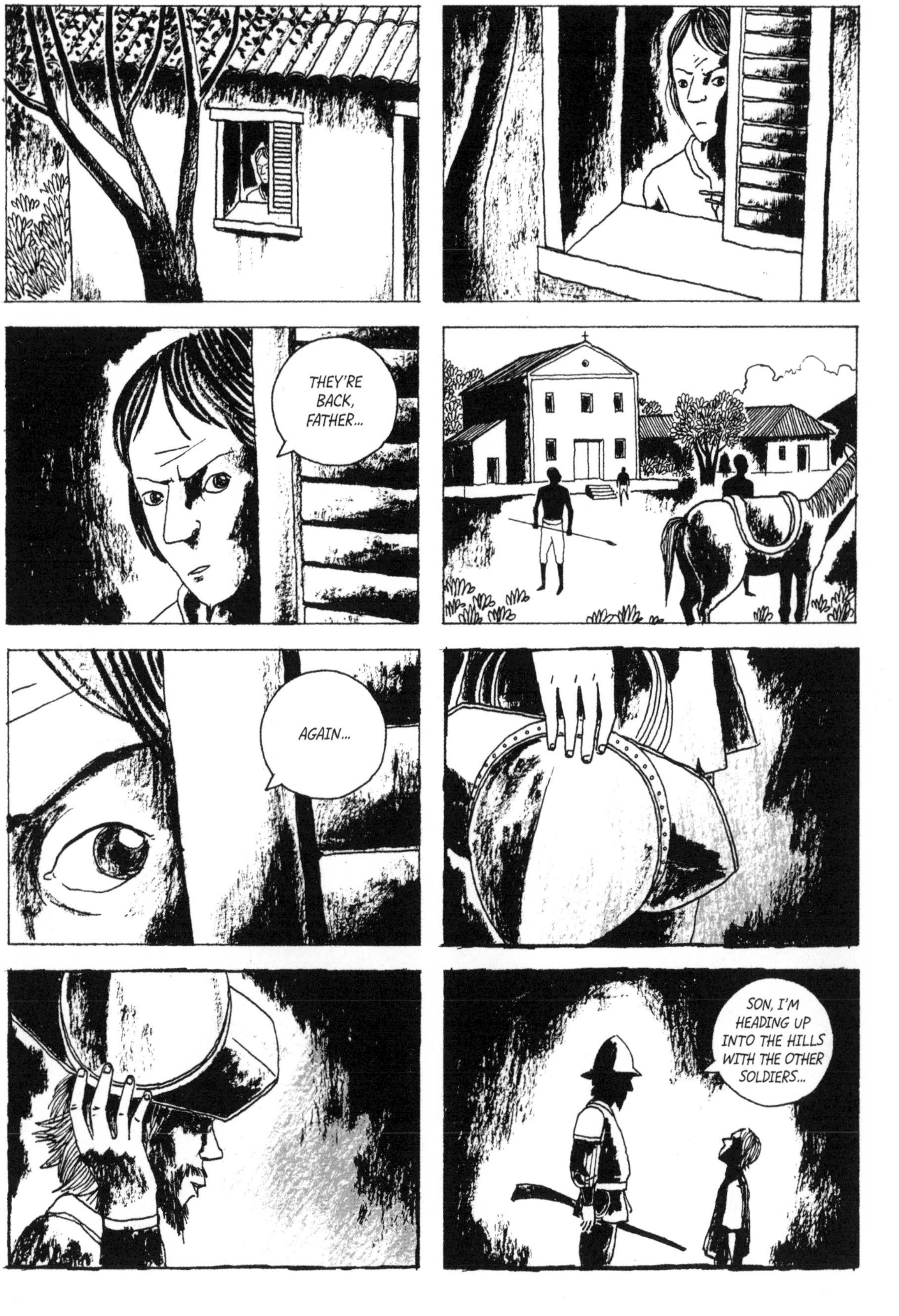
THEY'RE BACK, FATHER...
AGAIN...
SON, I'M HEADING UP INTO THE HILLS WITH THE OTHER SOLDIERS...

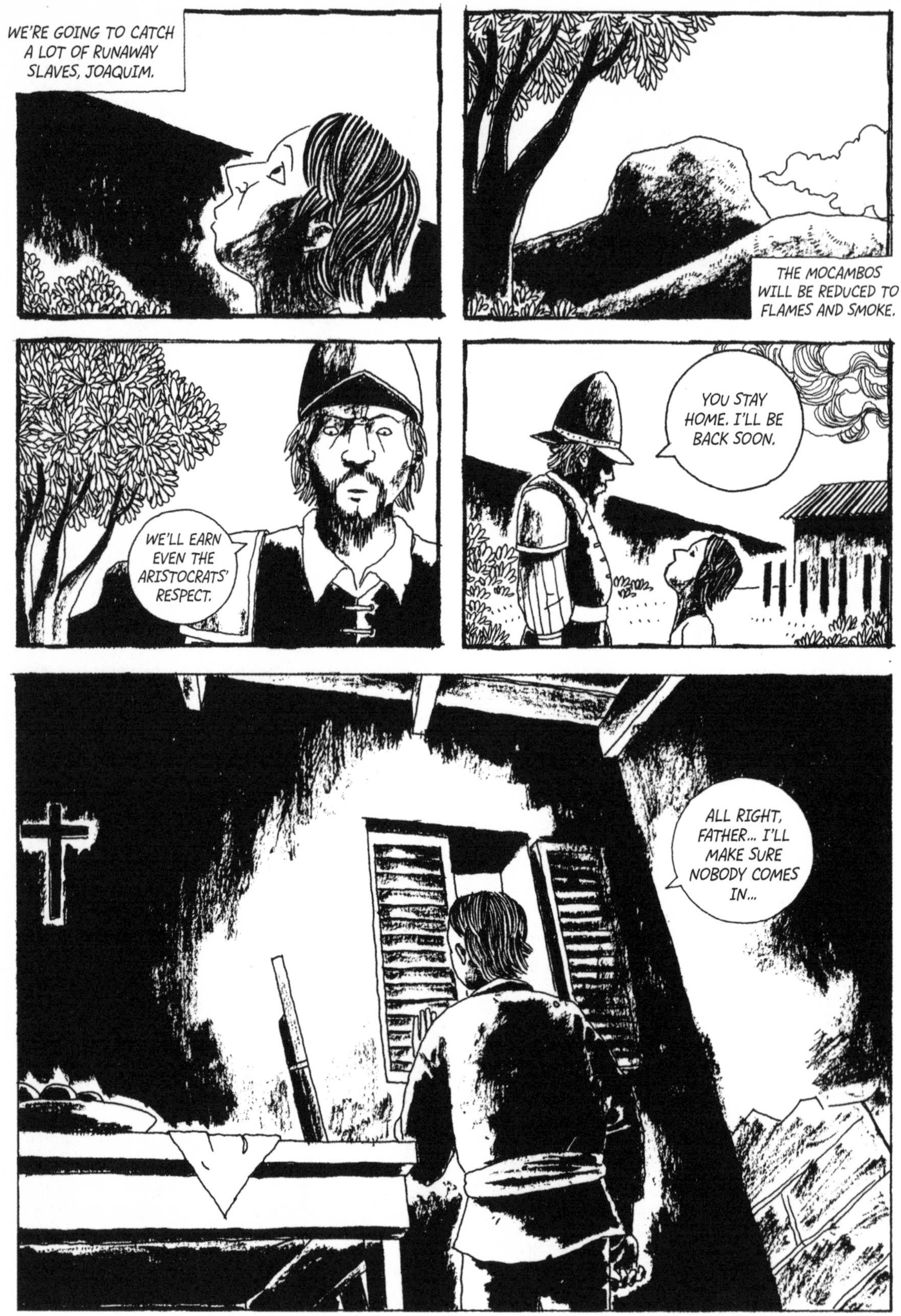
WE'RE GOING TO CATCH A LOT OF RUNAWAY SLAVES, JOAQUIM.
THE MOCAMBOS WILL BE REDUCED TO FLAMES AND SMOKE.
WE'LL EARN EVEN THE ARISTOCRATS' RESPECT.
YOU STAY HOME. I'LL BE BACK SOON.
ALL RIGHT, FATHER... I'LL MAKE SURE NOBODY COMES IN...

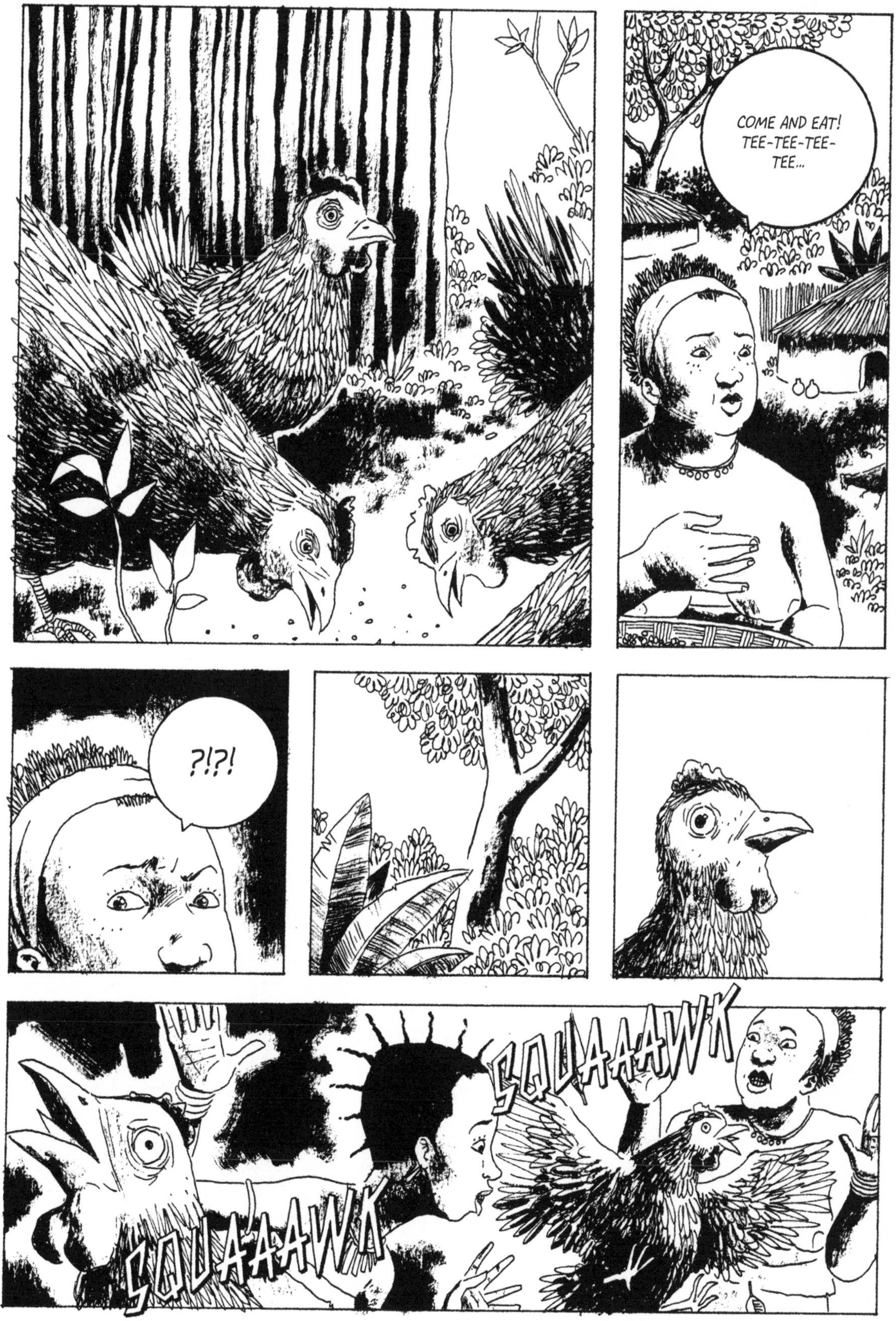
COME AND EAT! TEE-TEE-TEE-TEE...
?!?!
SQUAAAWK
SQUAAAWK

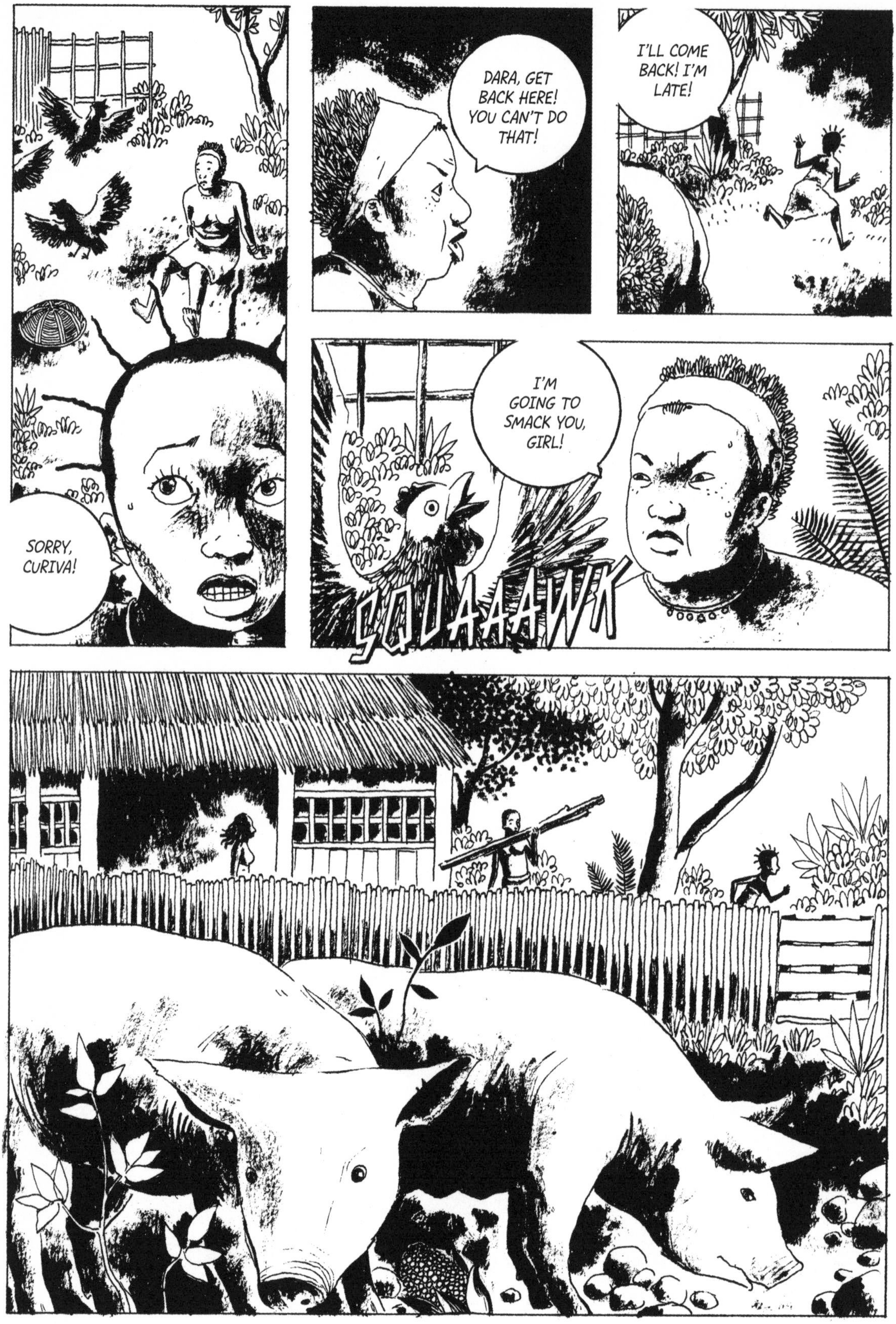
SORRY, CURIVA!
DARA, GET BACK HERE! YOU CAN'T DO THAT!
I'LL COME BACK! I'M LATE!
I'M GOING TO SMACK YOU, GIRL!
SQUAAAAWK

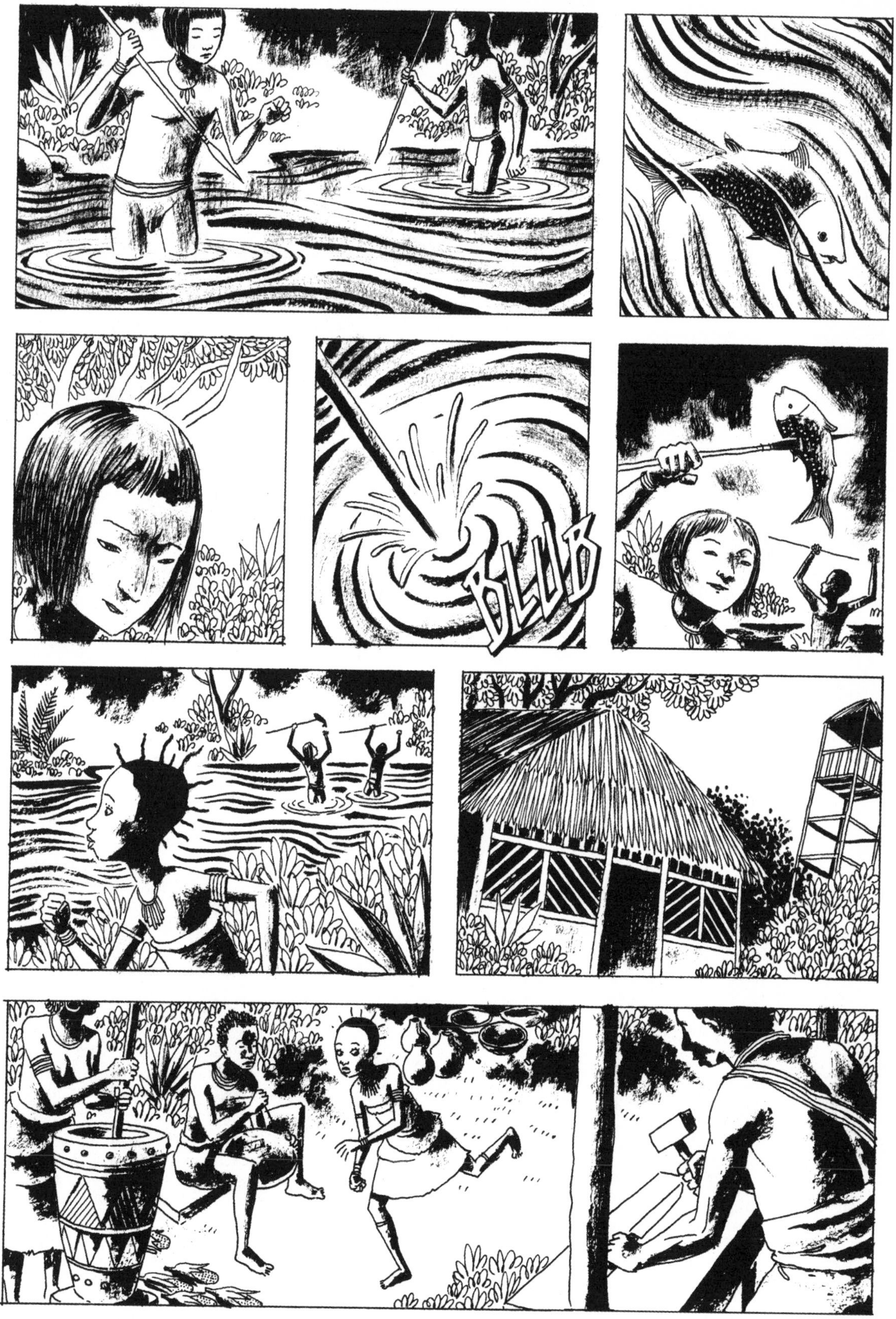
BLUB

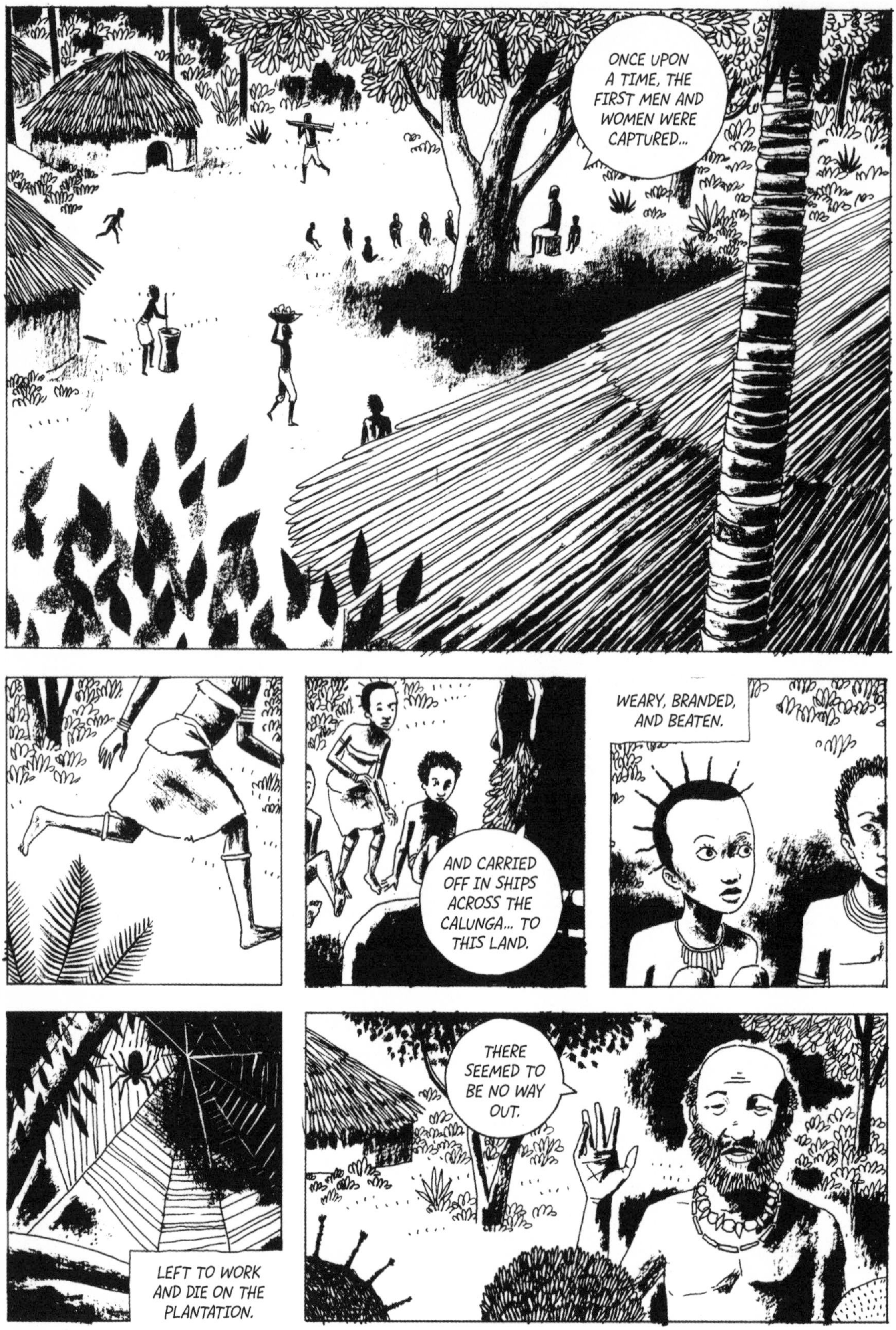
ONCE UPON A TIME, THE FIRST MEN AND WOMEN WERE CAPTURED...
AND CARRIED OFF IN SHIPS ACROSS THE CALUNGA... TO THIS LAND.
WEARY, BRANDED, AND BEATEN.
LEFT TO WORK AND DIE ON THE PLANTATION.
THERE SEEMED TO BE NO WAY OUT.

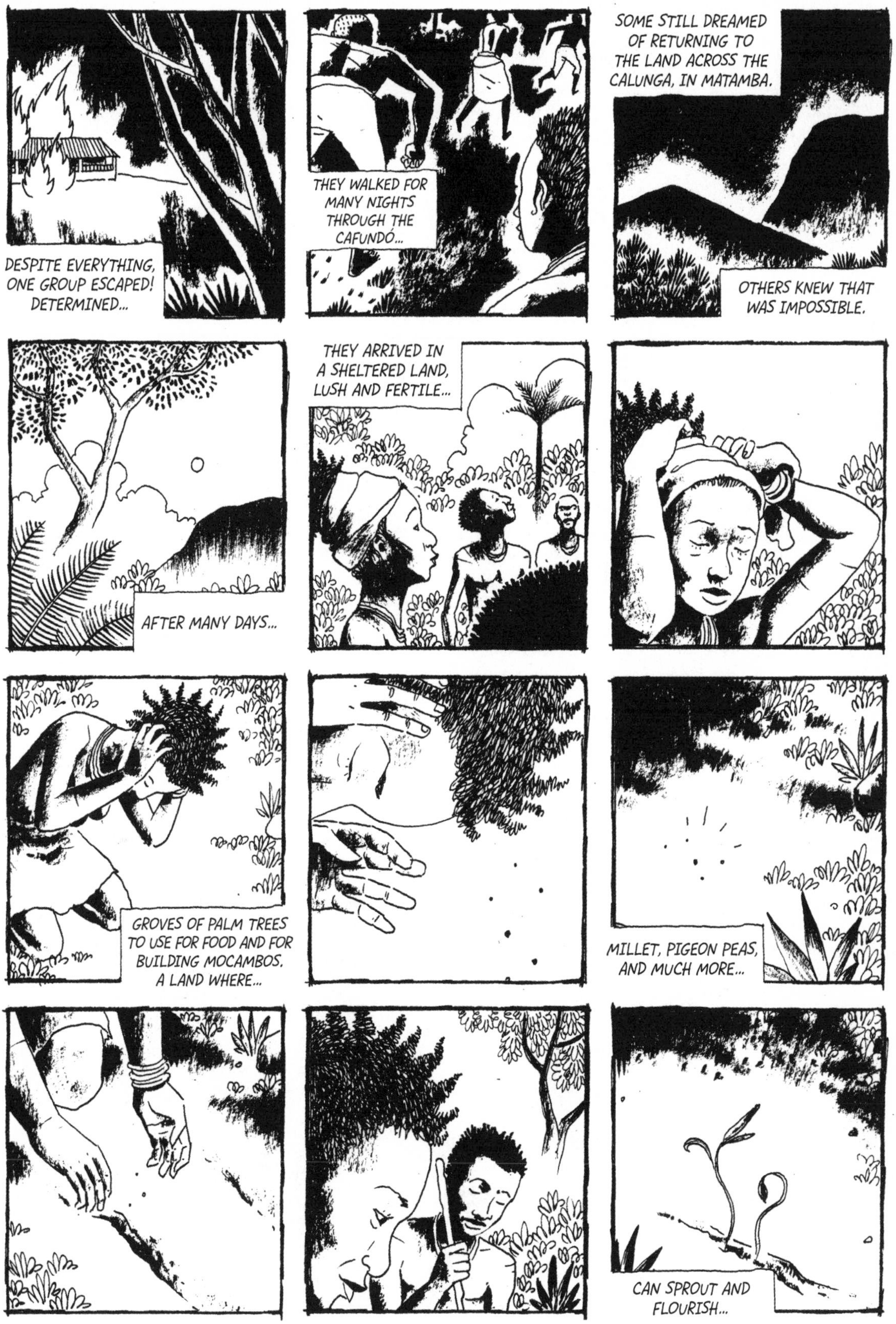
DESPITE EVERYTHING, ONE GROUP ESCAPED! DETERMINED...
THEY WALKED FOR MANY NIGHTS THROUGH THE CAFUNDÓ...
SOME STILL DREAMED OF RETURNING TO THE LAND ACROSS THE CALUNGA, IN MATAMBA.
OTHERS KNEW THAT WAS IMPOSSIBLE.
AFTER MANY DAYS...
THEY ARRIVED IN A SHELTERED LAND, LUSH AND FERTILE...
GROVES OF PALM TREES TO USE FOR FOOD AND FOR BUILDING MOCAMBOS. A LAND WHERE...
MILLET, PIGEON PEAS, AND MUCH MORE...
CAN SPROUT AND FLOURISH...

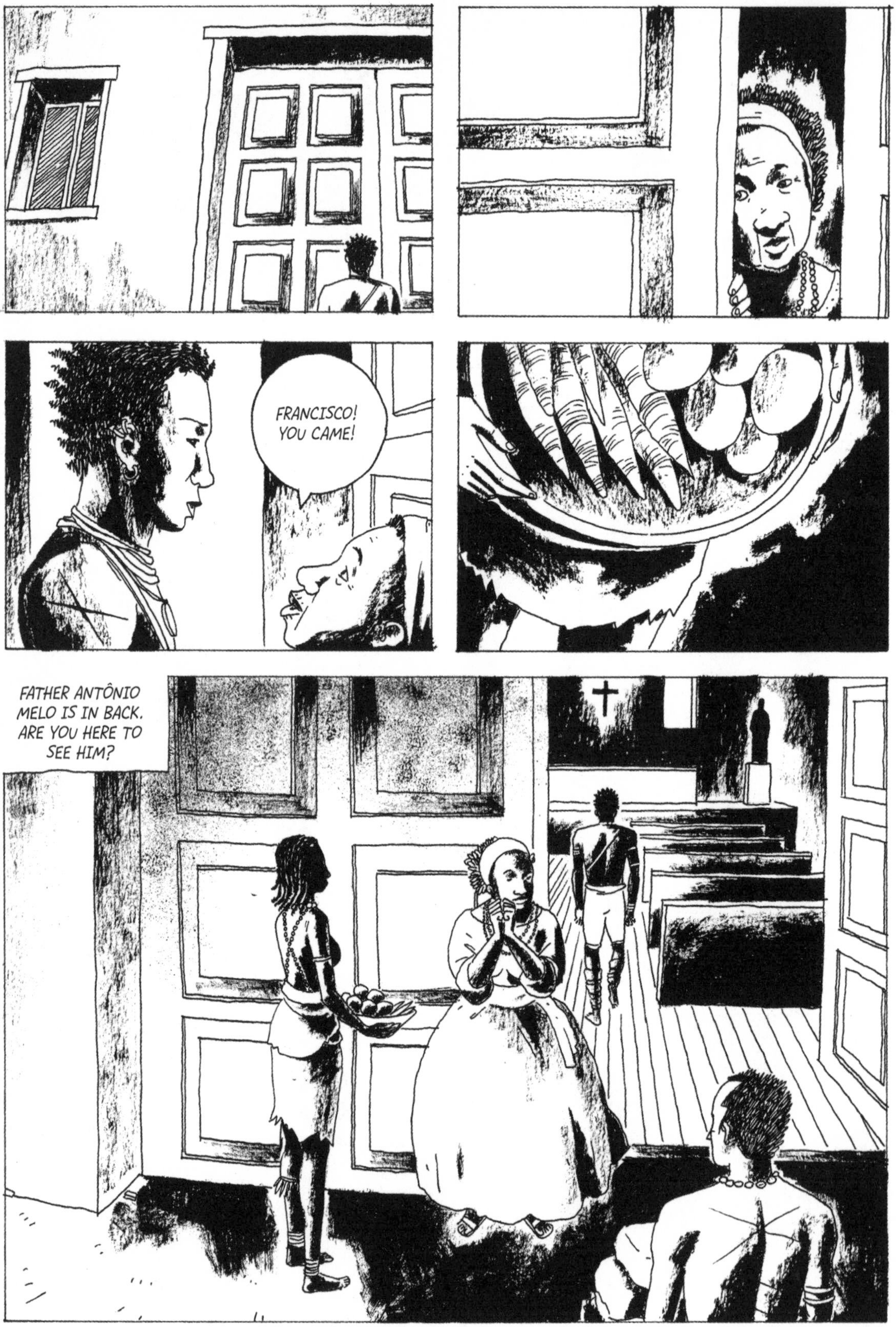
FRANCISCO! YOU CAME!
FATHER ANTÔNIO MELO IS IN BACK. ARE YOU HERE TO SEE HIM?

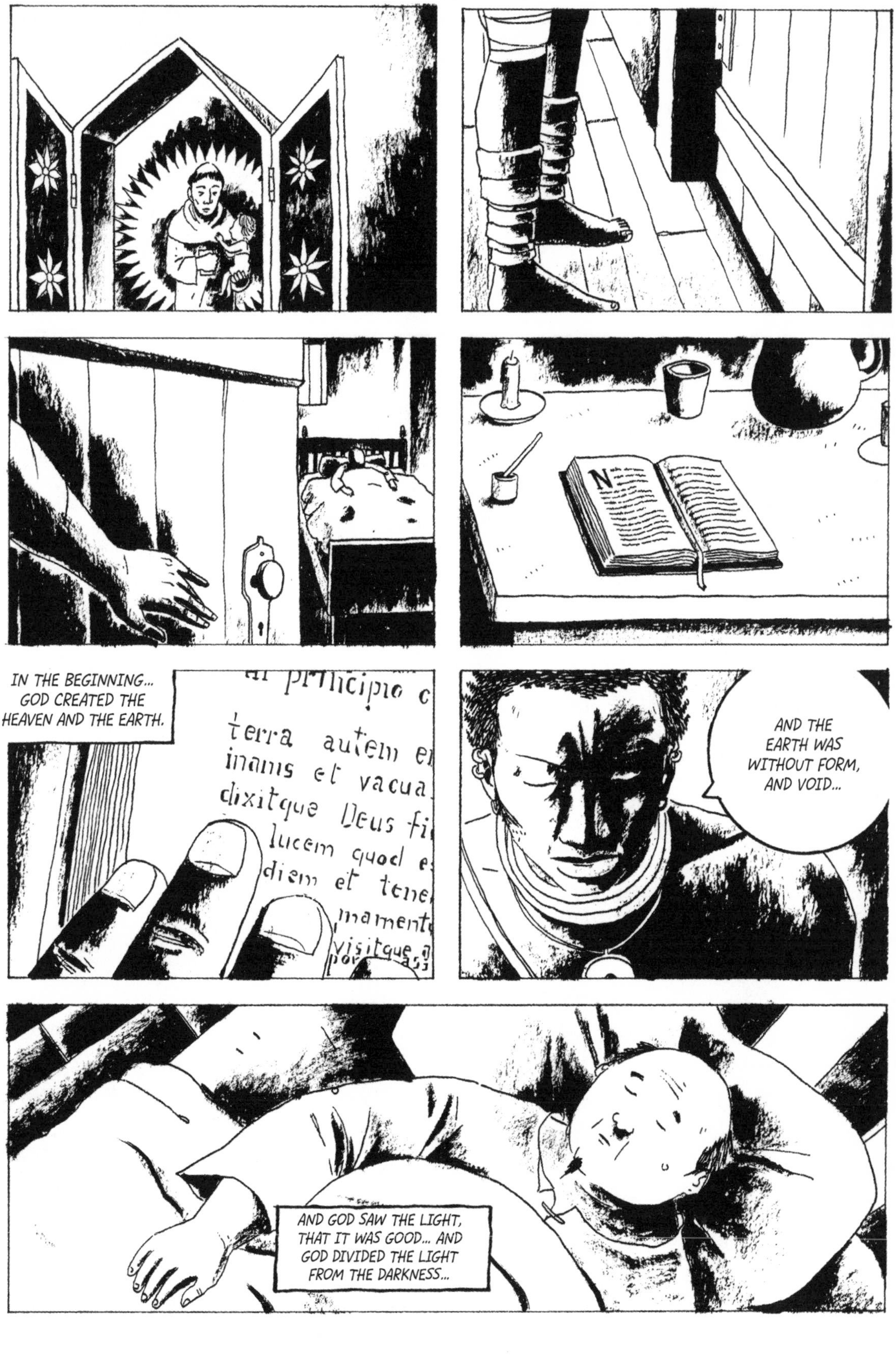
IN THE BEGINNING... GOD CREATED THE HEAVEN AND THE EARTH.
terra autem
inanis et vacua
dixitque Deus
lucem quod
diem et
AND THE EARTH WAS WITHOUT FORM, AND VOID...
AND GOD SAW THE LIGHT, THAT IT WAS GOOD... AND GOD DIVIDED THE LIGHT FROM THE DARKNESS...

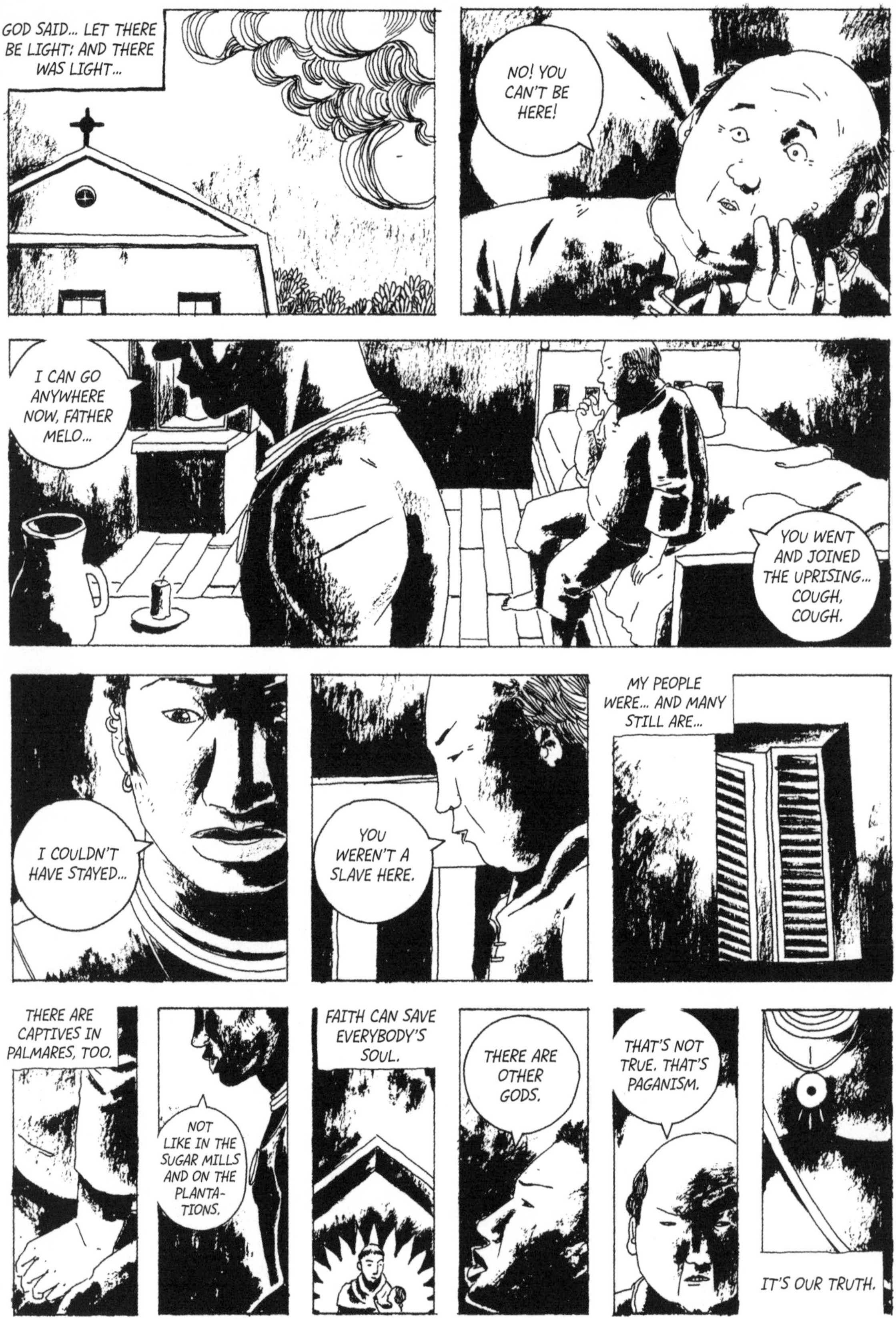
GOD SAID... LET THERE BE LIGHT; AND THERE WAS LIGHT...
NO! YOU CAN'T BE HERE!
I CAN GO ANYWHERE NOW, FATHER MELO...
YOU WENT AND JOINED THE UPRISING... COUGH, COUGH.
I COULDN'T HAVE STAYED...
YOU WEREN'T A SLAVE HERE.
MY PEOPLE WERE... AND MANY STILL ARE...
THERE ARE CAPTIVES IN PALMARES, TOO.
NOT LIKE IN THE SUGAR MILLS AND ON THE PLANTA-TIONS.
FAITH CAN SAVE EVERYBODY'S SOUL.
THERE ARE OTHER GODS.
THAT'S NOT TRUE. THAT'S PAGANISM.
IT'S OUR TRUTH.

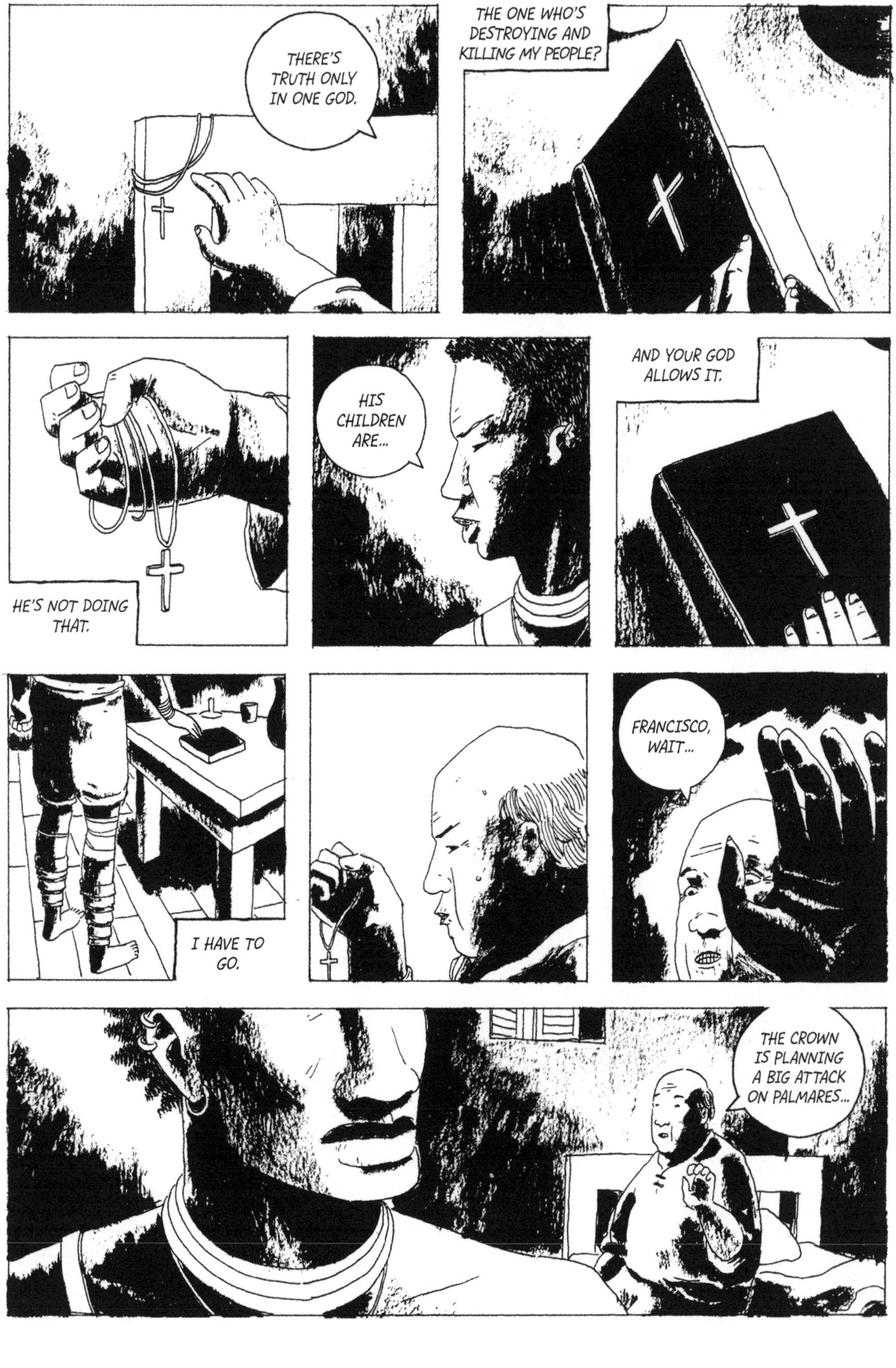
THERE'S TRUTH ONLY IN ONE GOD.
THE ONE WHO'S DESTROYING AND KILLING MY PEOPLE?
HE'S NOT DOING THAT.
HIS CHILDREN ARE...
AND YOUR GOD ALLOWS IT.
I HAVE TO GO.
FRANCISCO, WAIT...
THE CROWN IS PLANNING A BIG ATTACK ON PALMARES...

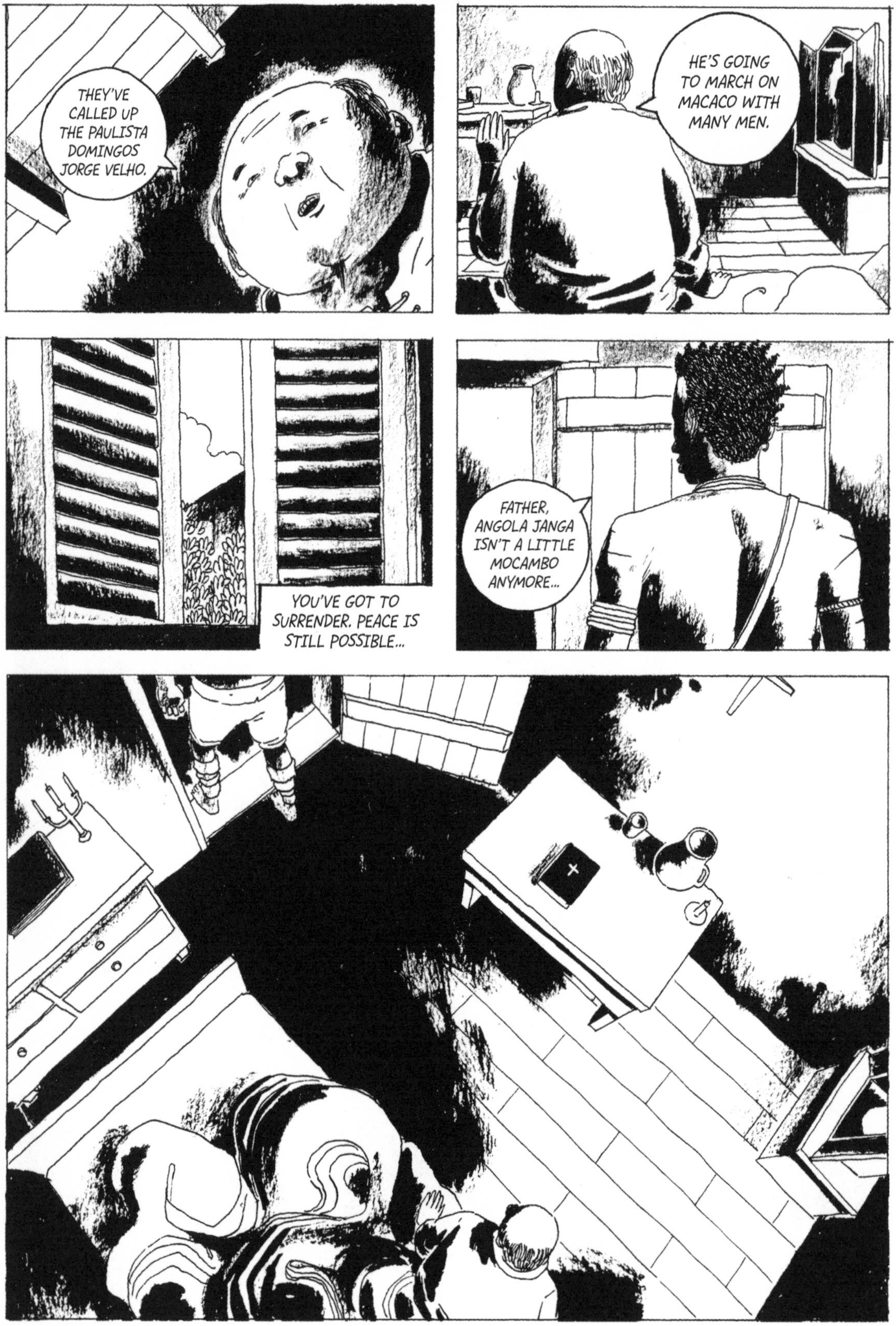
THEY'VE CALLED UP THE PAULISTA DOMINGOS JORGE VELHO.
HE'S GOING TO MARCH ON MACACO WITH MANY MEN.
YOU'VE GOT TO SURRENDER. PEACE IS STILL POSSIBLE...
FATHER, ANGOLA JANGA ISN'T A LITTLE MOCAMBO ANYMORE...

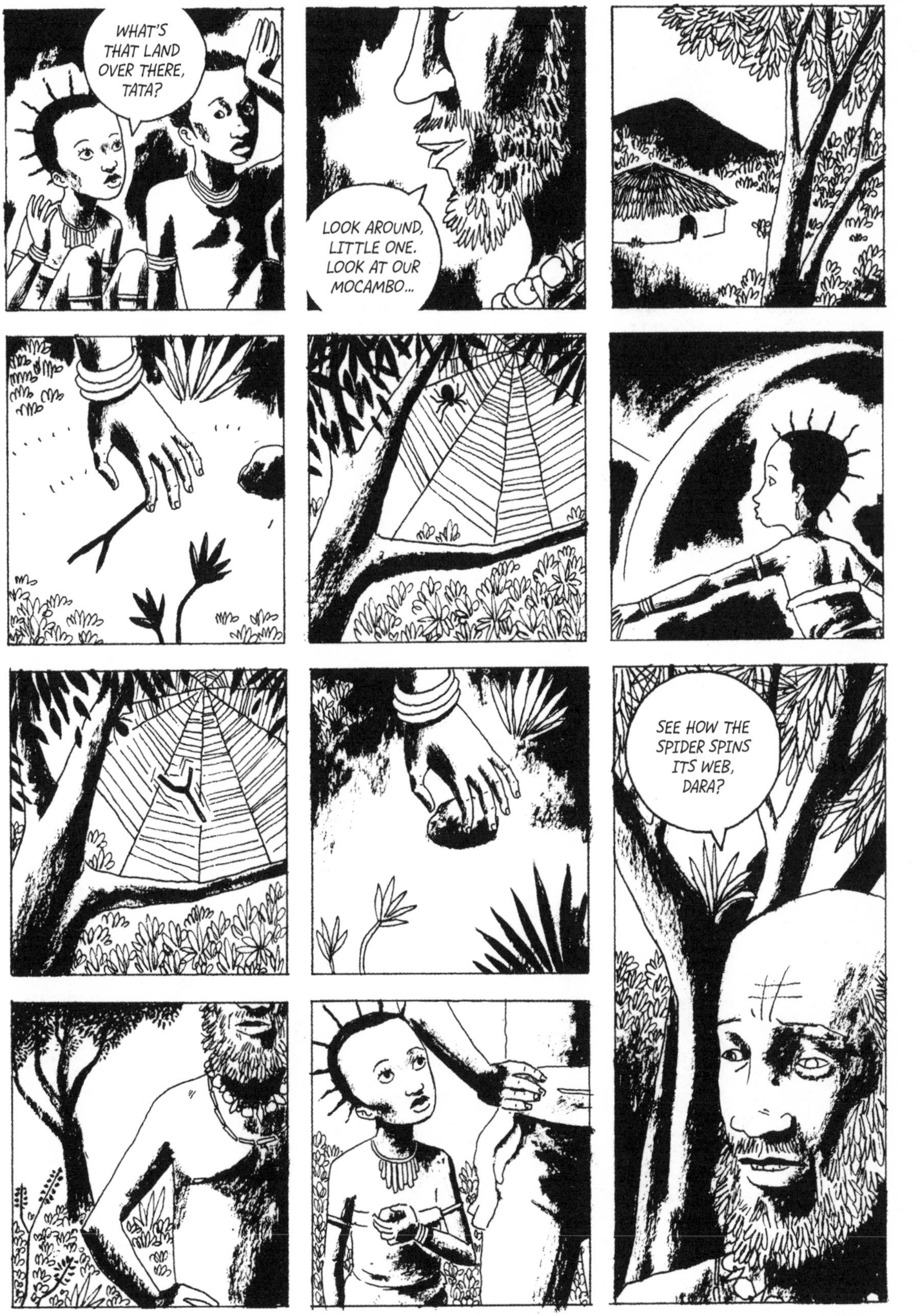
WHAT'S THAT LAND OVER THERE, TATA?
LOOK AROUND, LITTLE ONE. LOOK AT OUR MOCAMBO...
SEE HOW THE SPIDER SPINS ITS WEB, DARA?

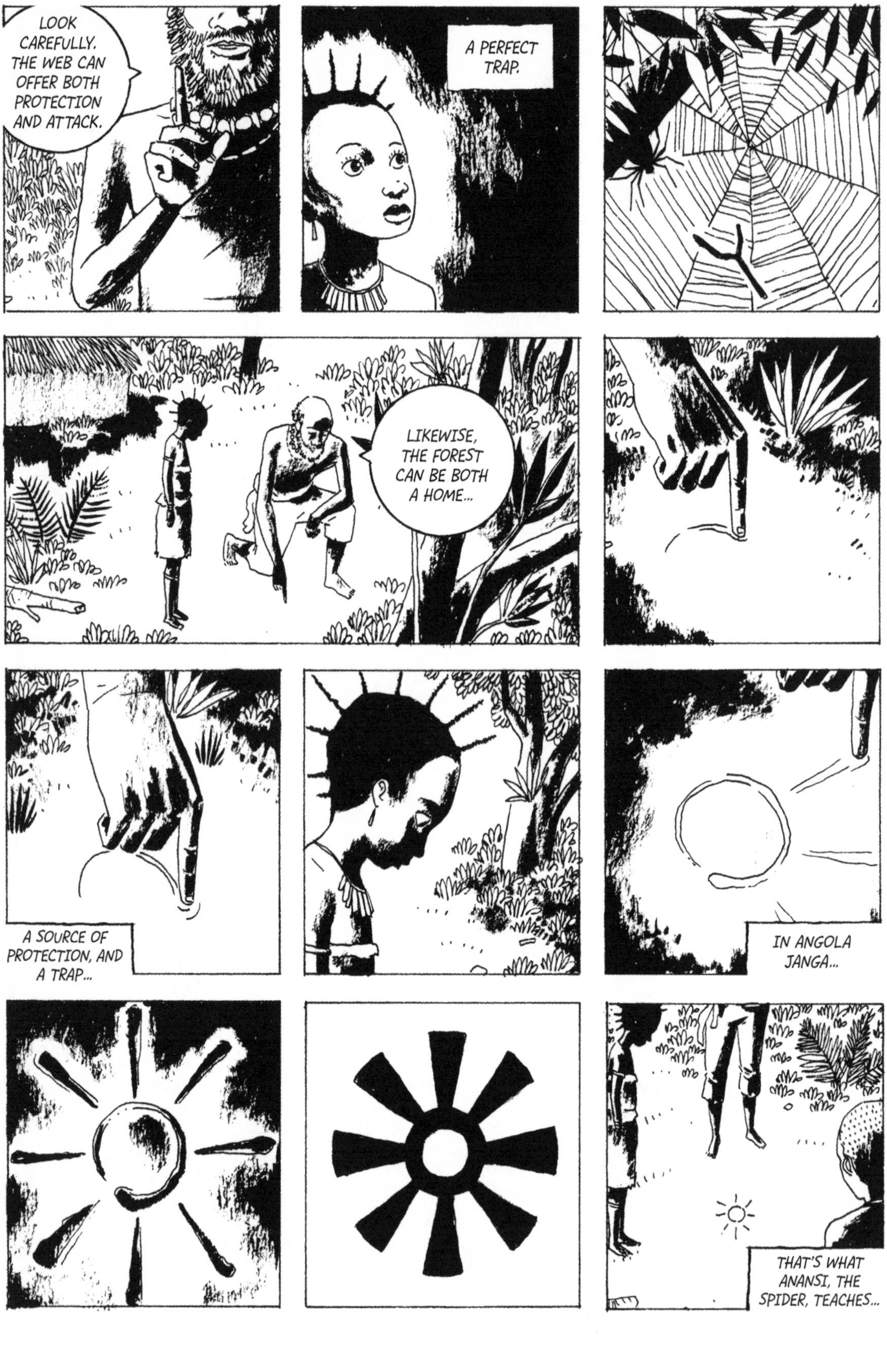

LOOK CAREFULLY. THE WEB CAN OFFER BOTH PROTECTION AND ATTACK.
A PERFECT TRAP.
LIKEWISE, THE FOREST CAN BE BOTH A HOME...
A SOURCE OF PROTECTION, AND A TRAP...
IN ANGOLA JANGA...
THAT'S WHAT ANANSI, THE SPIDER, TEACHES...

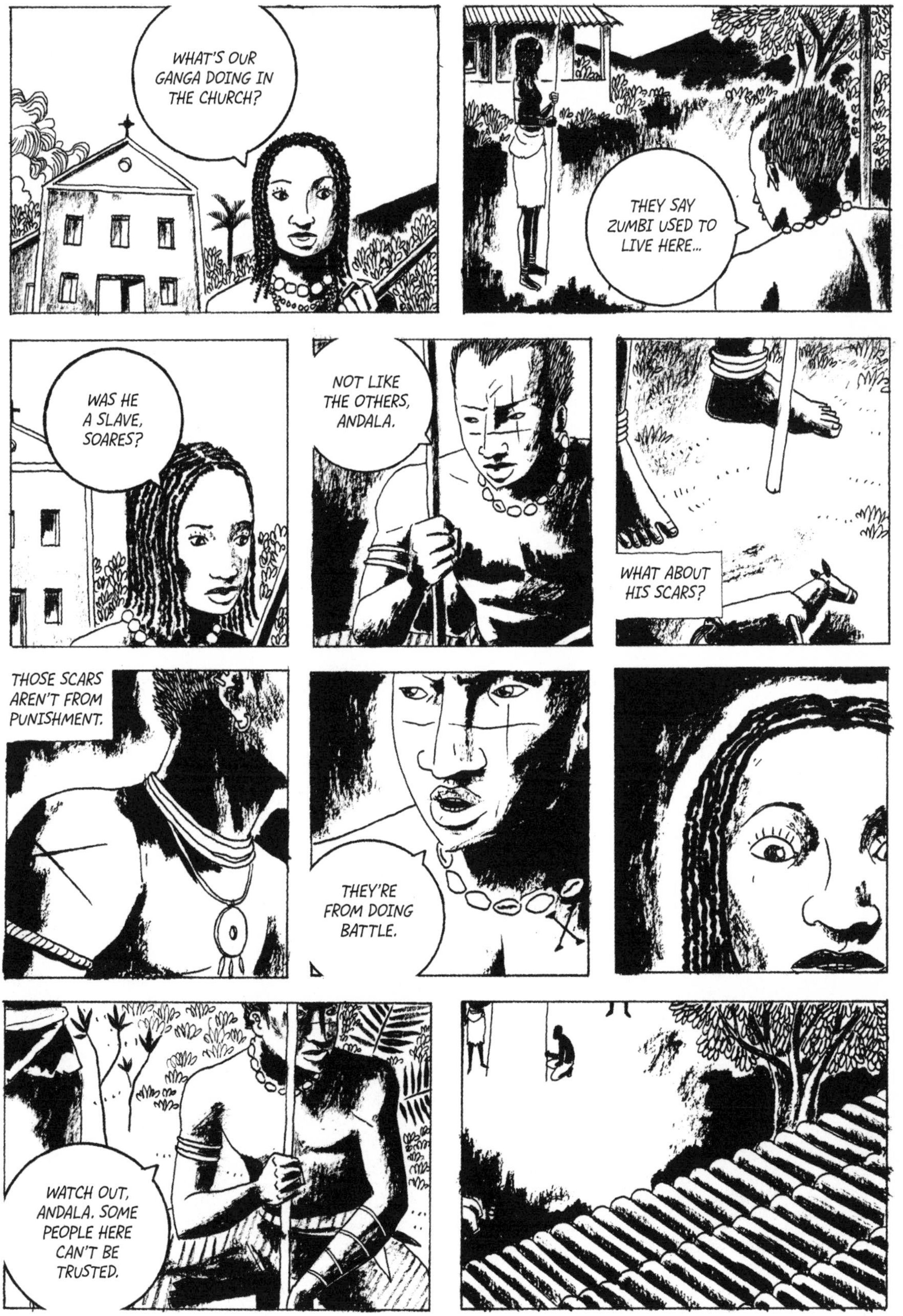
WHAT'S OUR GANGA DOING IN THE CHURCH?
THEY SAY ZUMBI USED TO LIVE HERE...
WAS HE A SLAVE, SOARES?
NOT LIKE THE OTHERS, ANDALA.
WHAT ABOUT HIS SCARS?
THOSE SCARS AREN'T FROM PUNISHMENT.
THEY'RE FROM DOING BATTLE.
WATCH OUT, ANDALA. SOME PEOPLE HERE CAN'T BE TRUSTED.

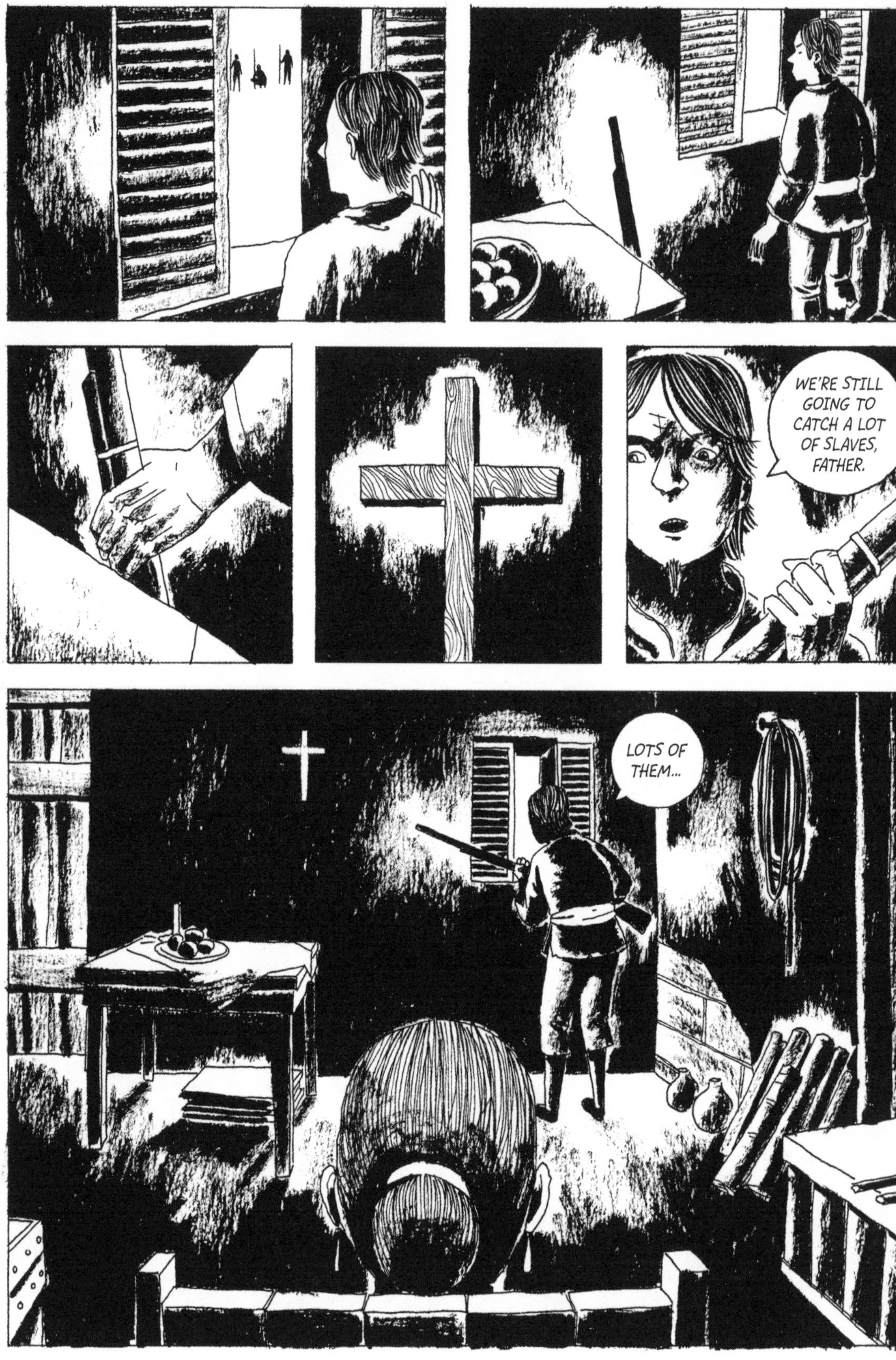
WE'RE STILL GOING TO CATCH A LOT OF SLAVES, FATHER.
LOTS OF THEM...

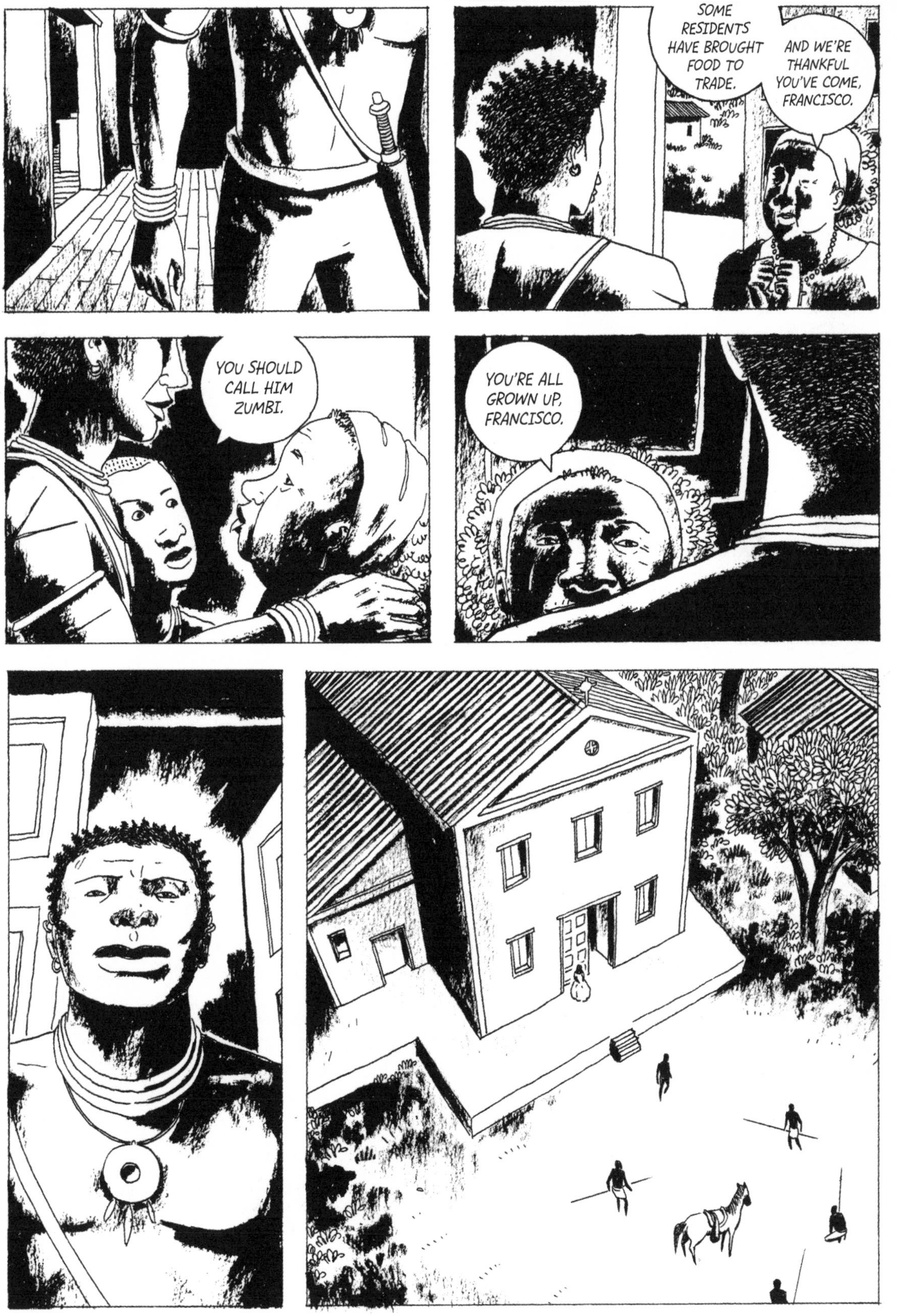
SOME RESIDENTS HAVE BROUGHT FOOD TO TRADE.
AND WE'RE THANKFUL YOU'VE COME, FRANCISCO.
YOU SHOULD CALL HIM ZUMBI.
YOU'RE ALL GROWN UP, FRANCISCO.

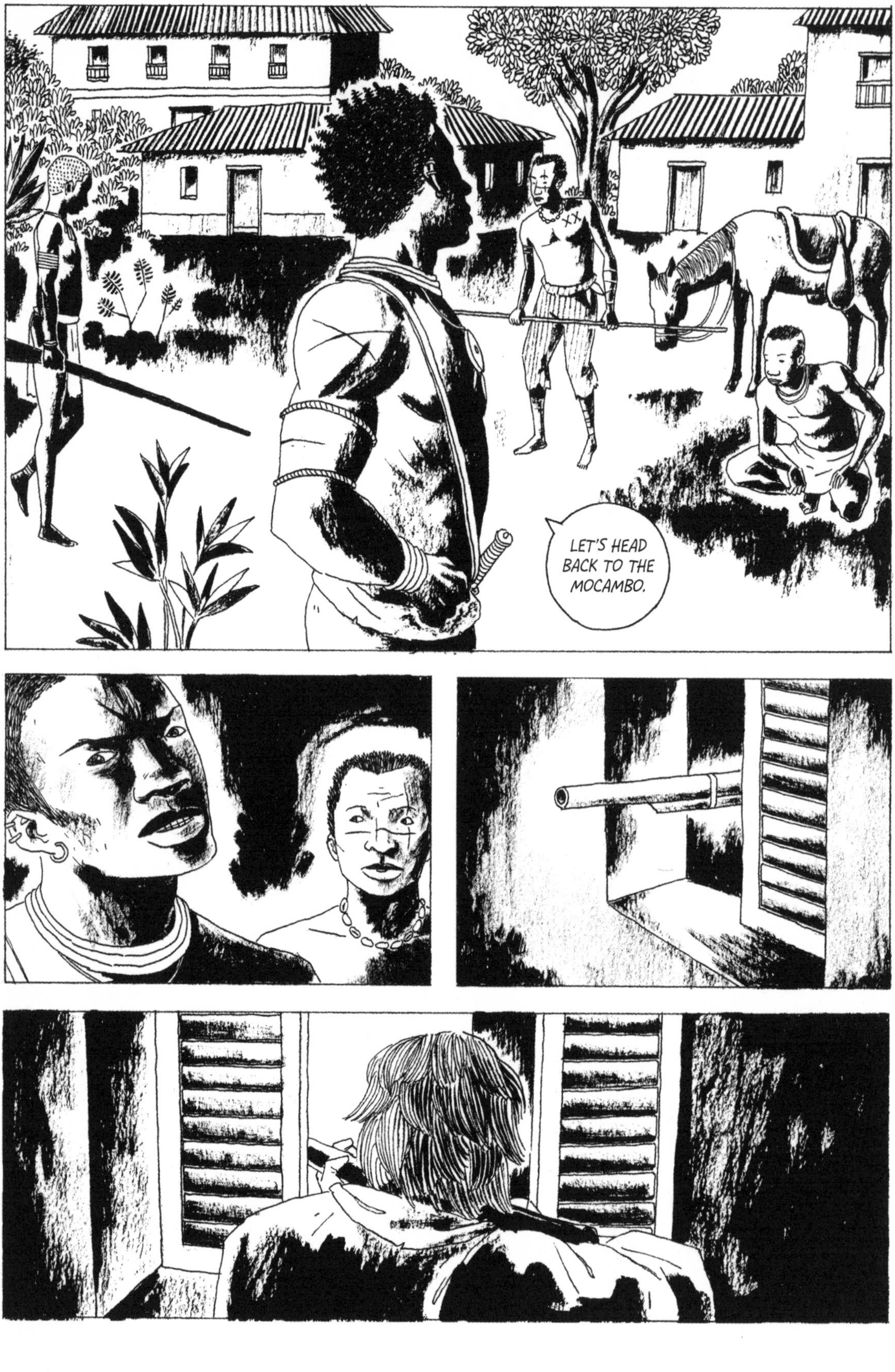
LET'S HEAD BACK TO THE MOCAMBO.

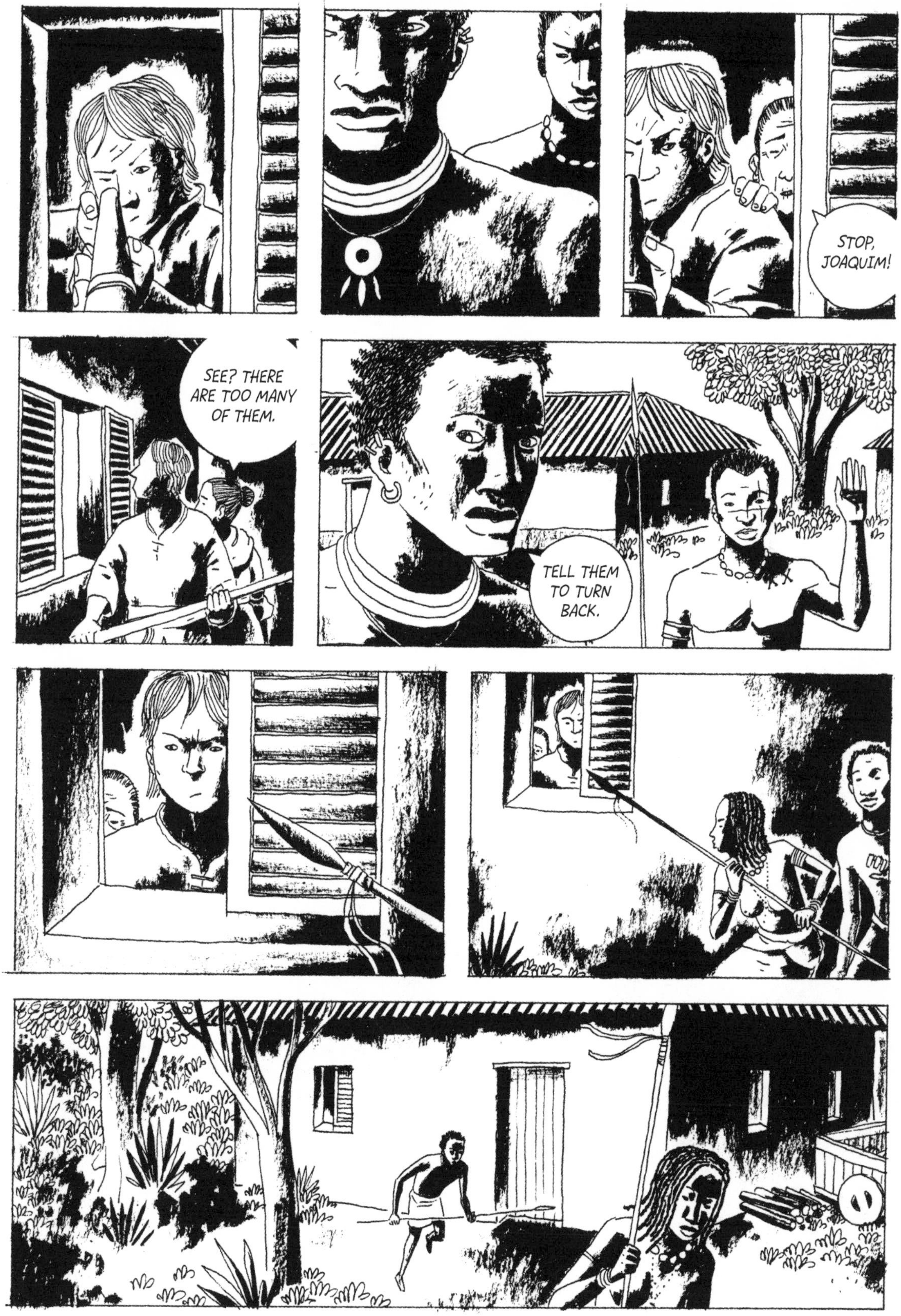
STOP, JOAQUIM!
SEE? THERE ARE TOO MANY OF THEM.
TELL THEM TO TURN BACK.

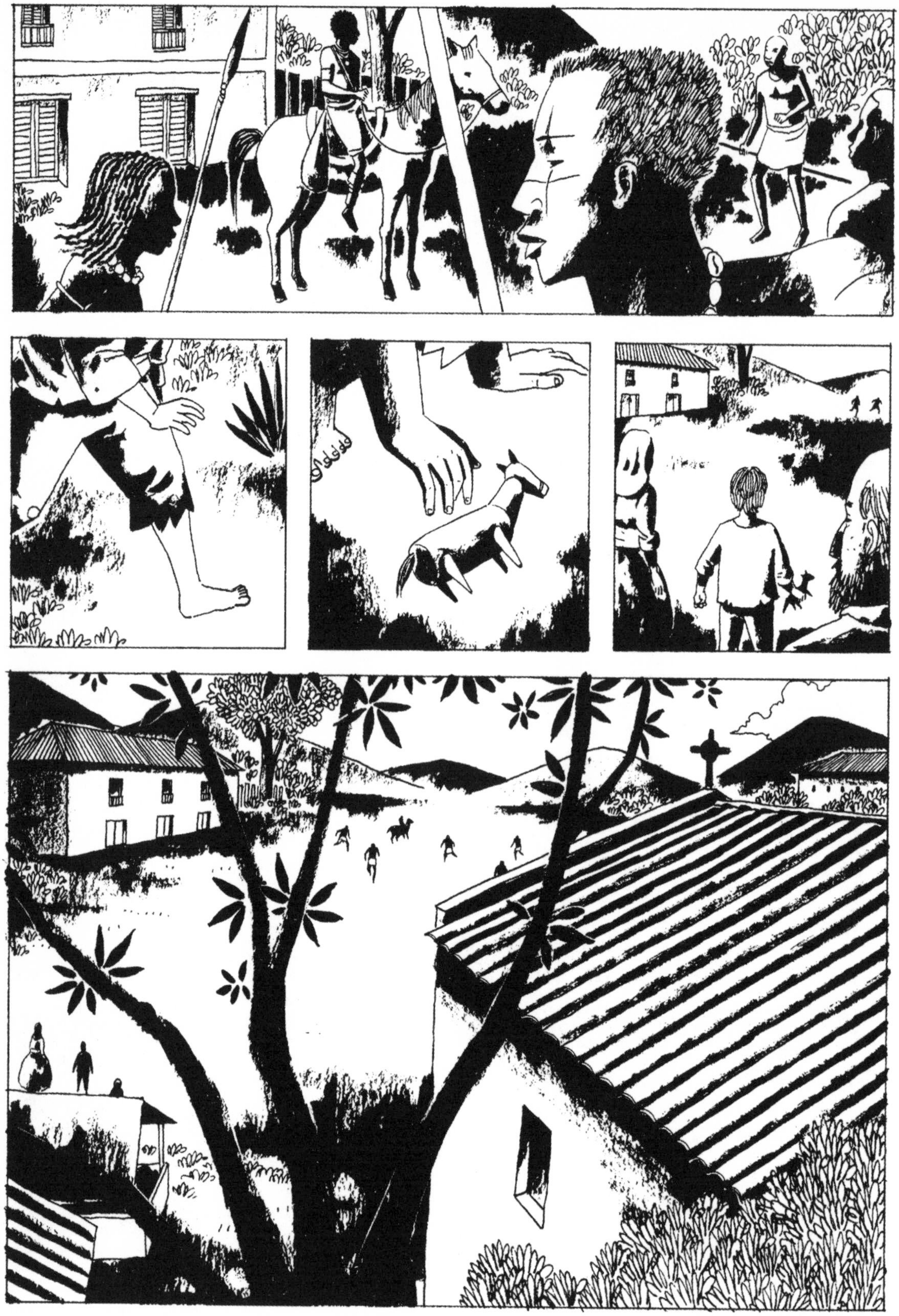

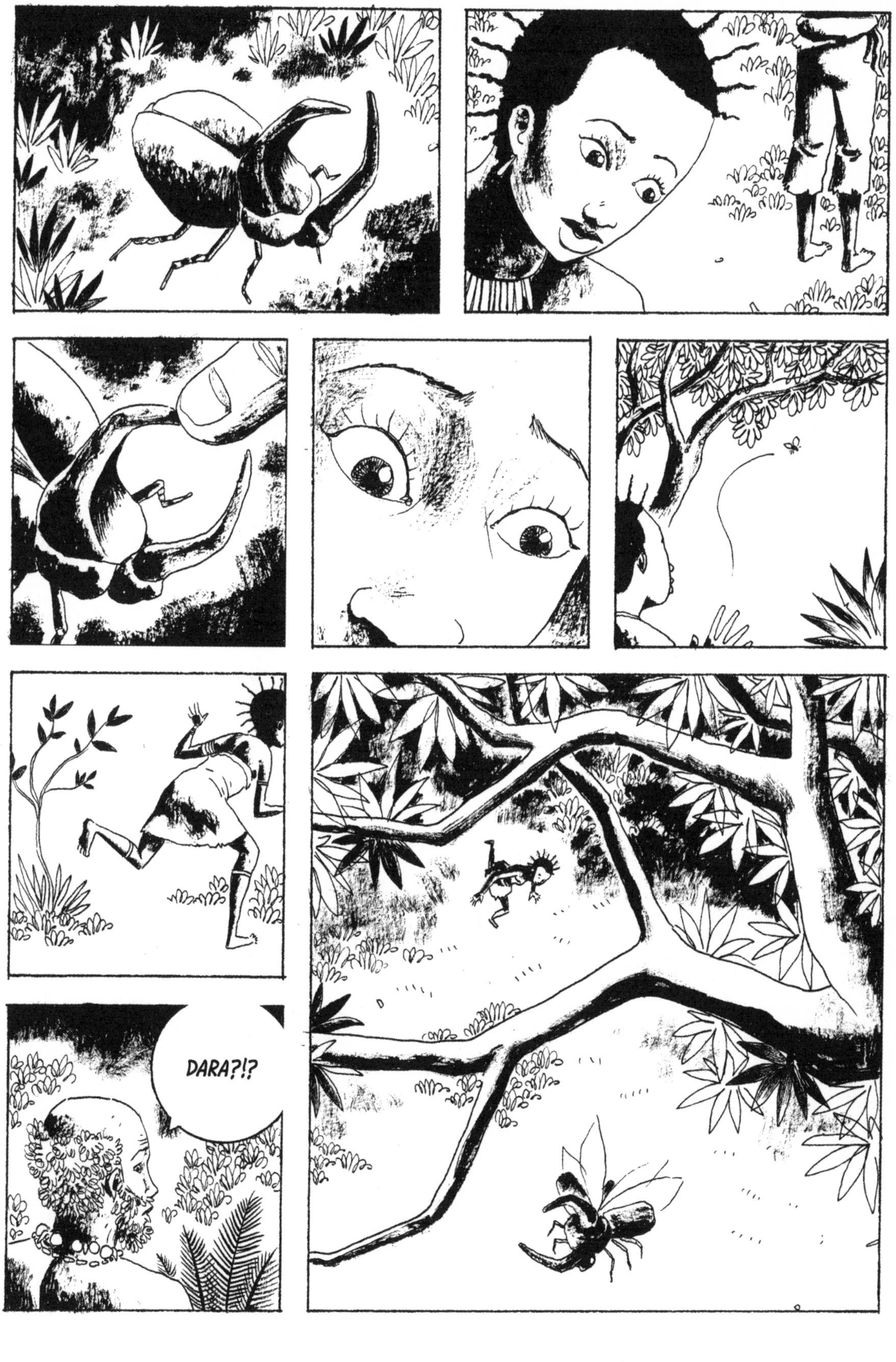
DARA?!?

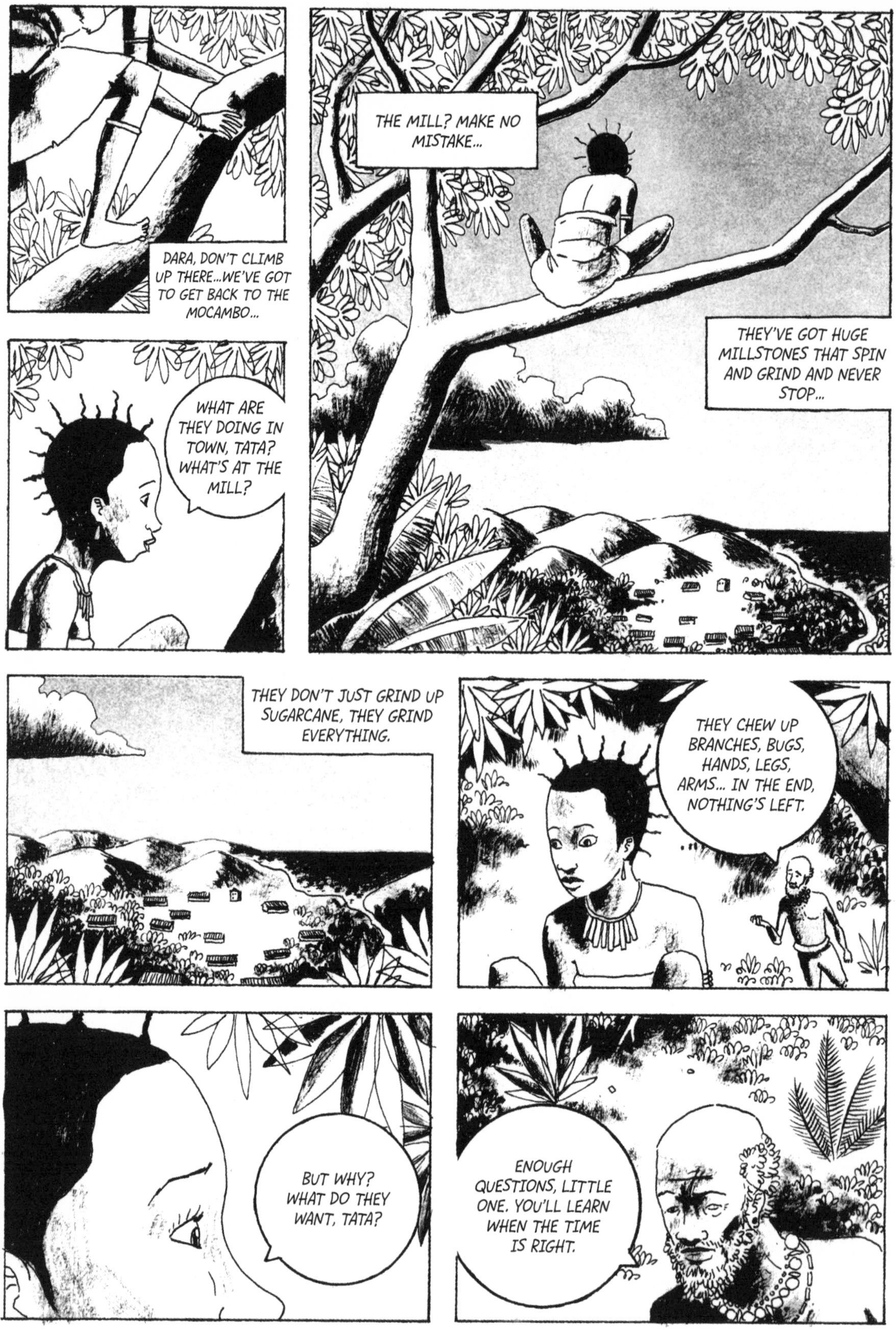
DARA, DON'T CLIMB UP THERE...WE'VE GOT TO GET BACK TO THE MOCAMBO...
WHAT ARE THEY DOING IN TOWN, TATA? WHAT'S AT THE MILL?
THE MILL? MAKE NO MISTAKE...
THEY'VE GOT HUGE MILLSTONES THAT SPIN AND GRIND AND NEVER STOP...
THEY DON'T JUST GRIND UP SUGARCANE, THEY GRIND EVERYTHING.
THEY CHEW UP BRANCHES, BUGS, HANDS, LEGS, ARMS... IN THE END, NOTHING'S LEFT.
BUT WHY? WHAT DO THEY WANT, TATA?
ENOUGH QUESTIONS, LITTLE ONE. YOU'LL LEARN WHEN THE TIME IS RIGHT.

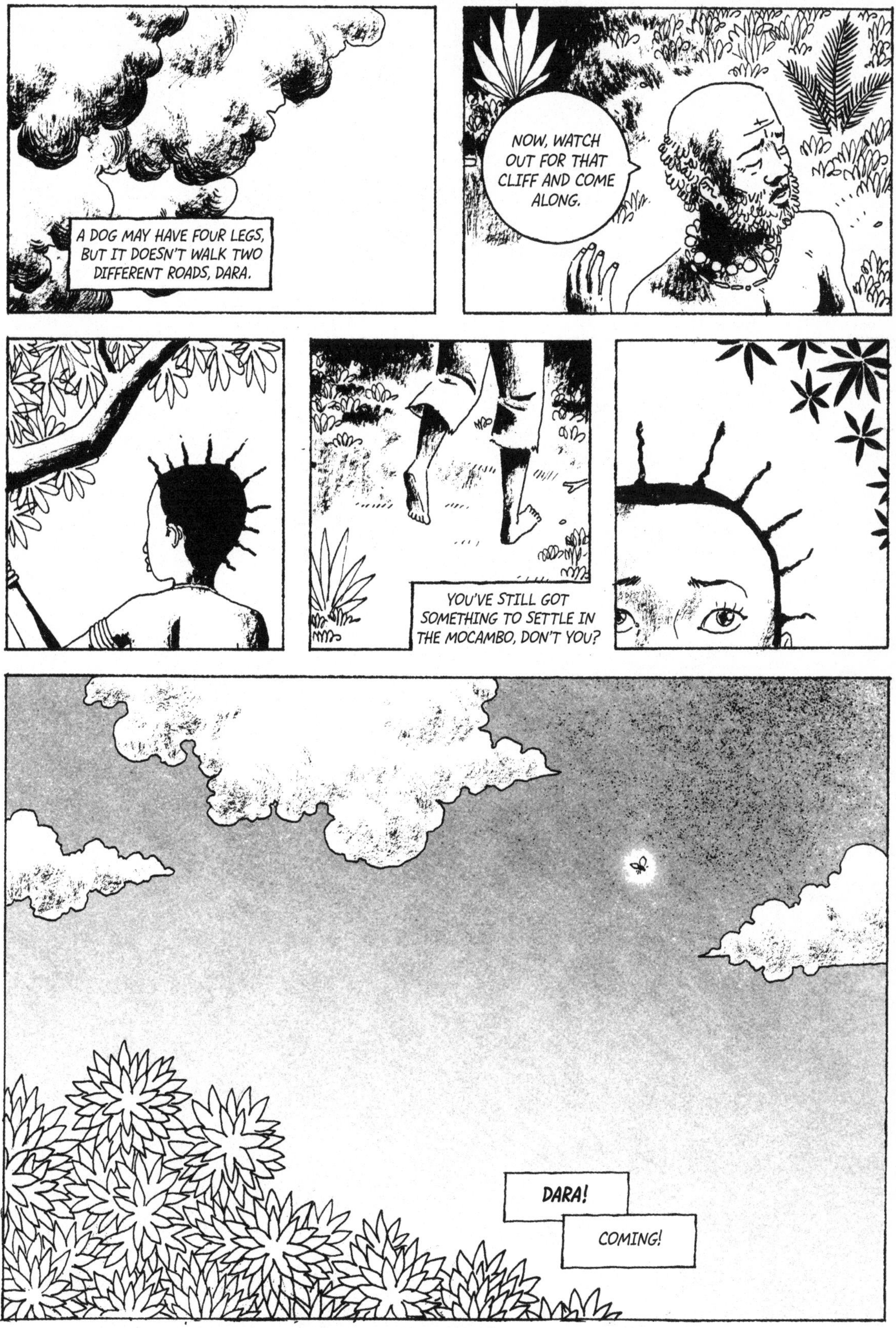
A DOG MAY HAVE FOUR LEGS, BUT IT DOESN'T WALK TWO DIFFERENT ROADS, DARA.
NOW, WATCH OUT FOR THAT CLIFF AND COME ALONG.
YOU'VE STILL GOT SOMETHING TO SETTLE IN THE MOCAMBO, DON'T YOU?
DARA!
COMING!

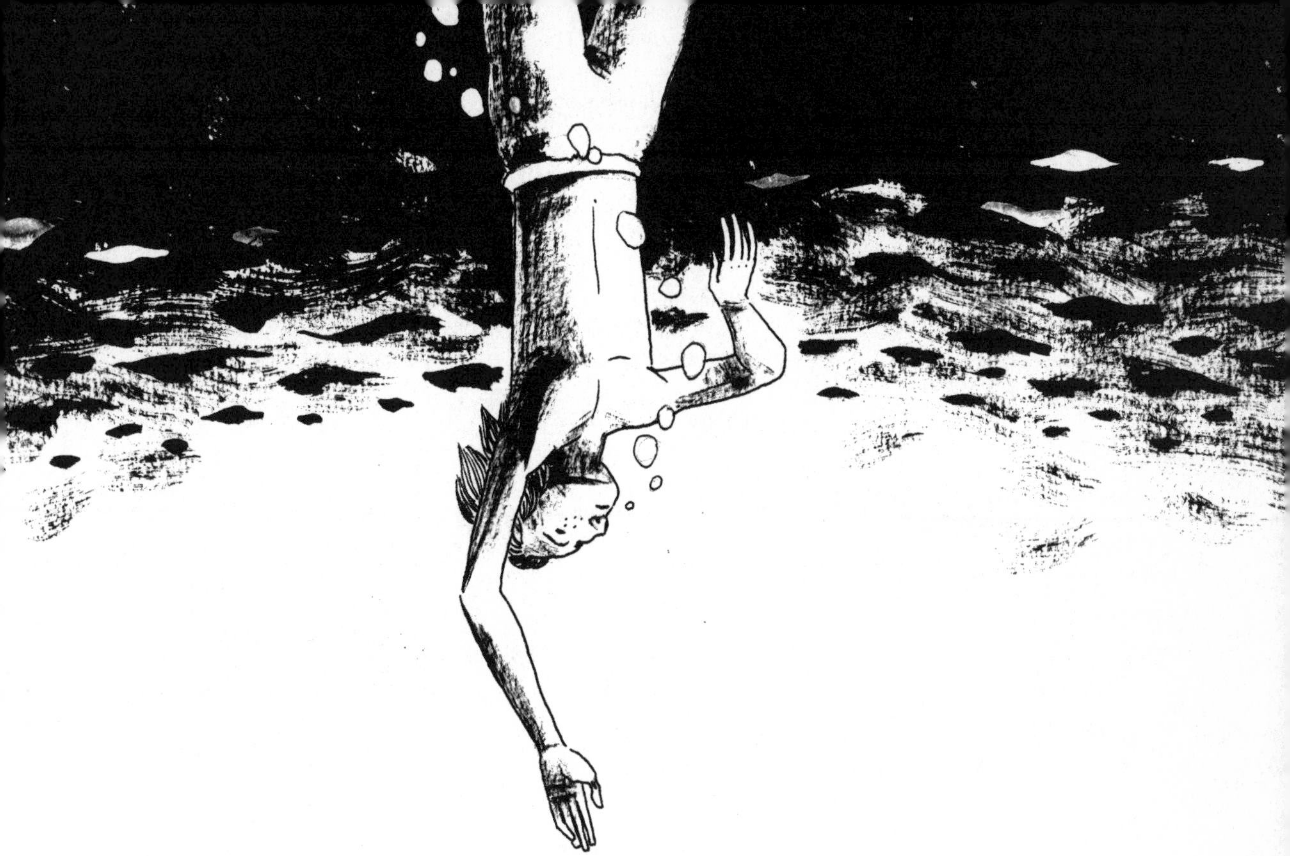

SAVAGES

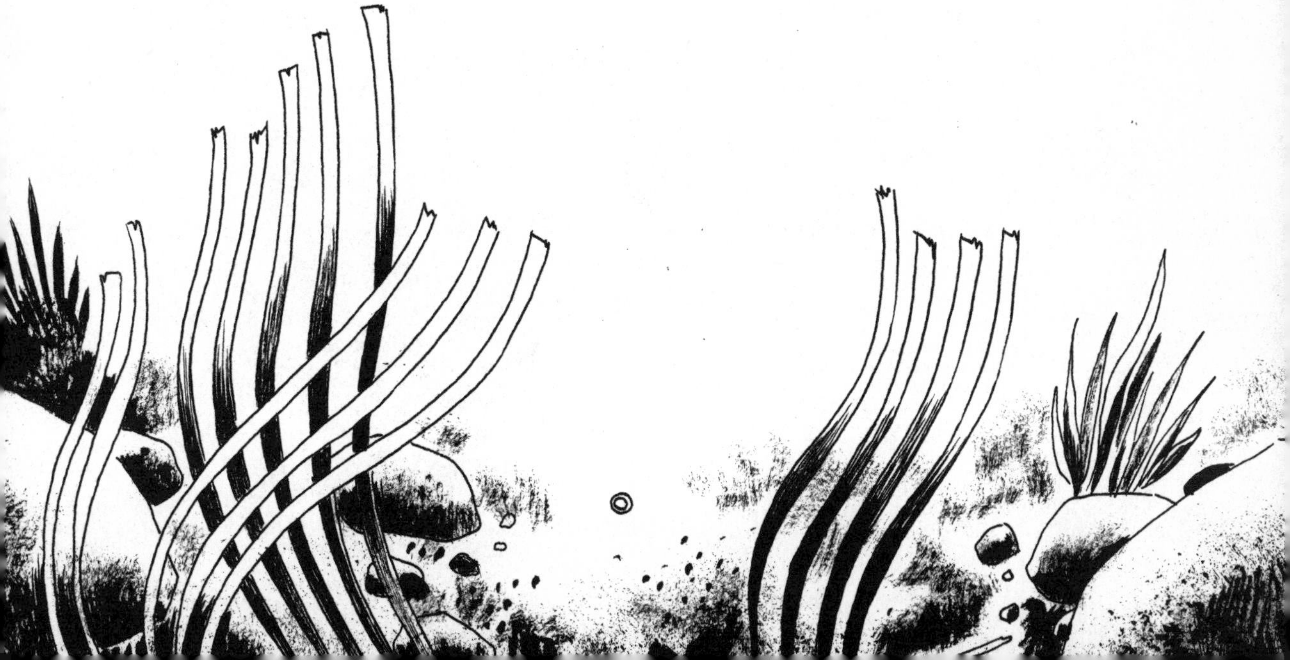

He's one of the biggest savages I've ever run across.

—*Bishop Francisco de Lima about Domingos Jorge Velho, seventeenth century*

They are barbarous people who live off what they steal.

—*Governor Caetano de Melo e Castro, seventeenth century*

The Paulistas are even worse than the Palmaristas.

—*Overseas Council, seventeenth century*

Thus, the bandeirantes served as shock troops in the service of Portuguese colonialism, and nothing else. . . . Were the Paulistas civilized or savages? Their contemporaries had trouble reaching a consensus. As one colonial chronicler noted, they lived "in the wilderness" and were "raised amid the brush like wild beasts," so that "the men living in the virgin wilderness are drawn further and further from civil society; those who were once civilized will inevitably lose the doctrine they've learned and come to resemble the heathens they've left."

—*Décio Freitas,* Palmares: The Slave War, *1982*

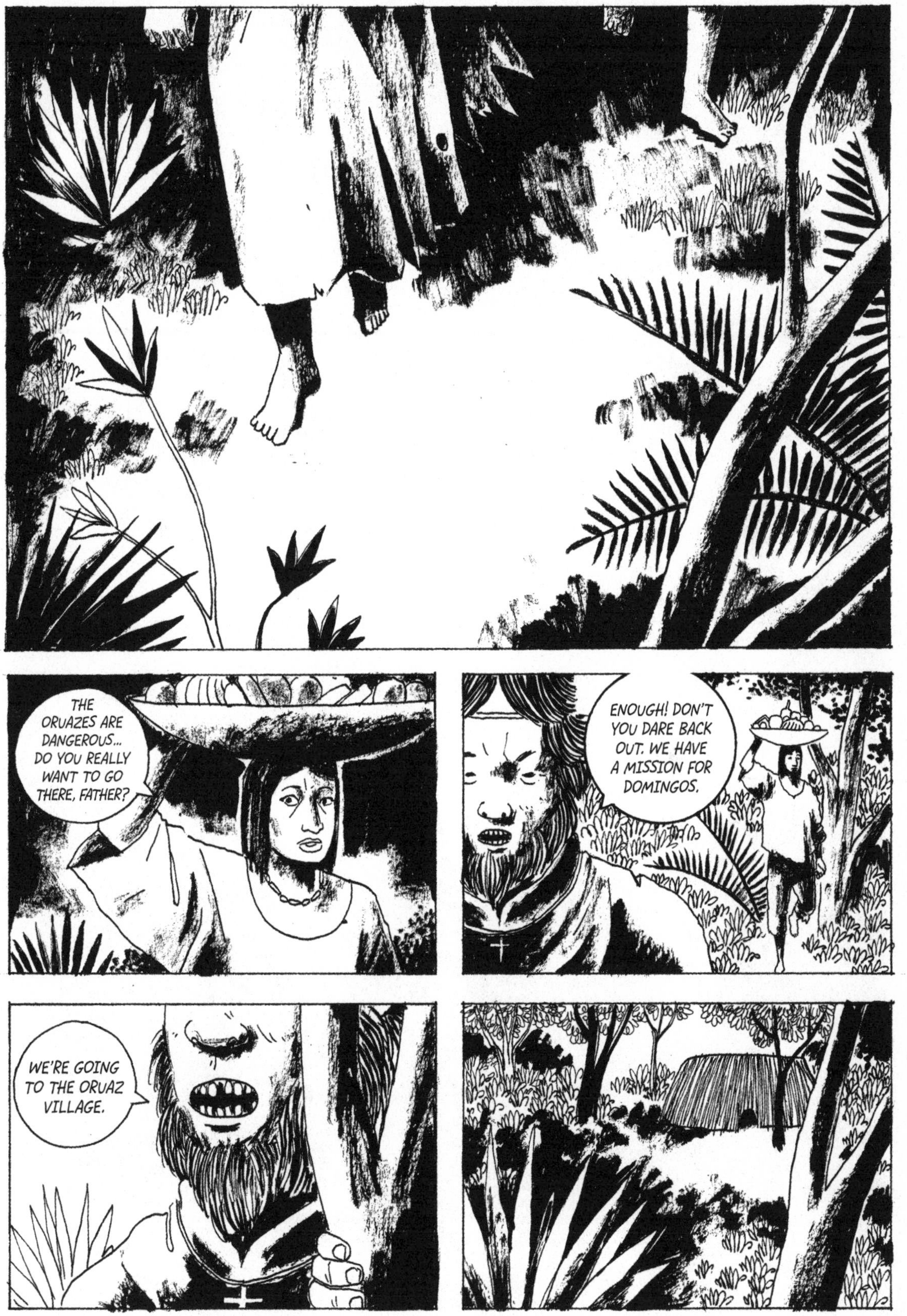
THE ORUAZES ARE DANGEROUS... DO YOU REALLY WANT TO GO THERE, FATHER?
ENOUGH! DON'T YOU DARE BACK OUT. WE HAVE A MISSION FOR DOMINGOS.
WE'RE GOING TO THE ORUAZ VILLAGE.

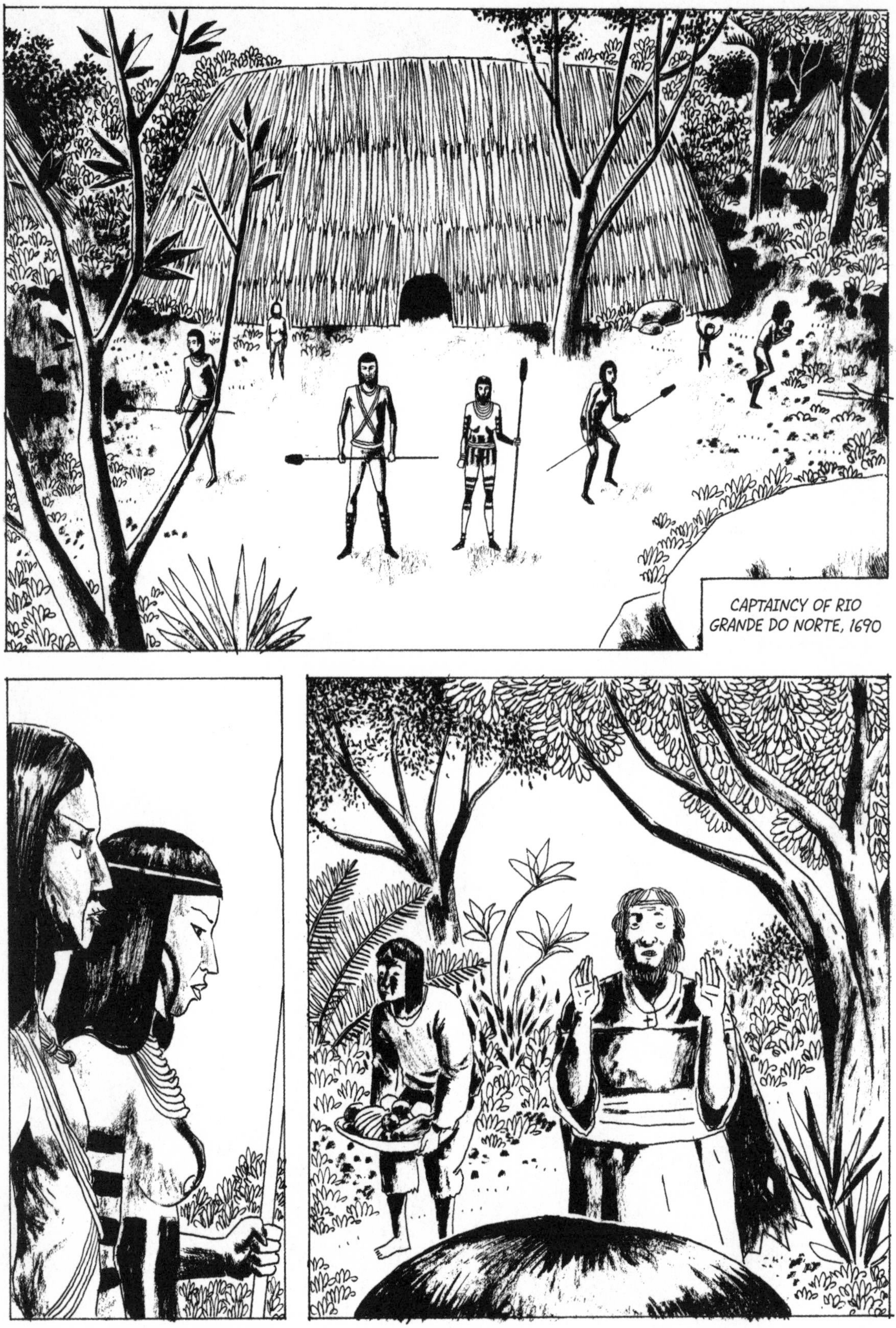
CAPTAINCY OF RIO GRANDE DO NORTE, 1690

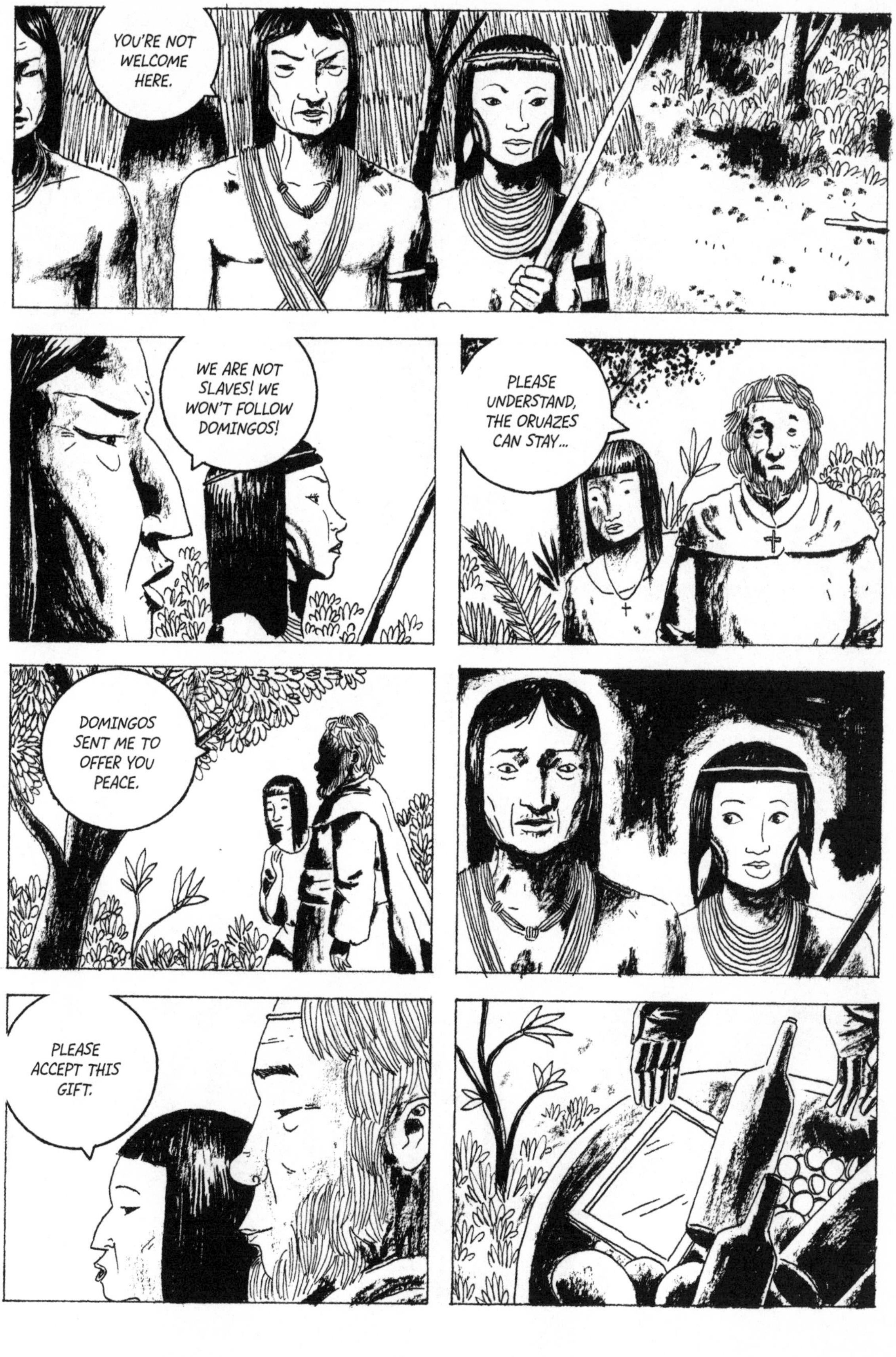
YOU'RE NOT WELCOME HERE.
WE ARE NOT SLAVES! WE WON'T FOLLOW DOMINGOS!
PLEASE UNDERSTAND, THE ORUAZES CAN STAY...
DOMINGOS SENT ME TO OFFER YOU PEACE.
PLEASE ACCEPT THIS GIFT.

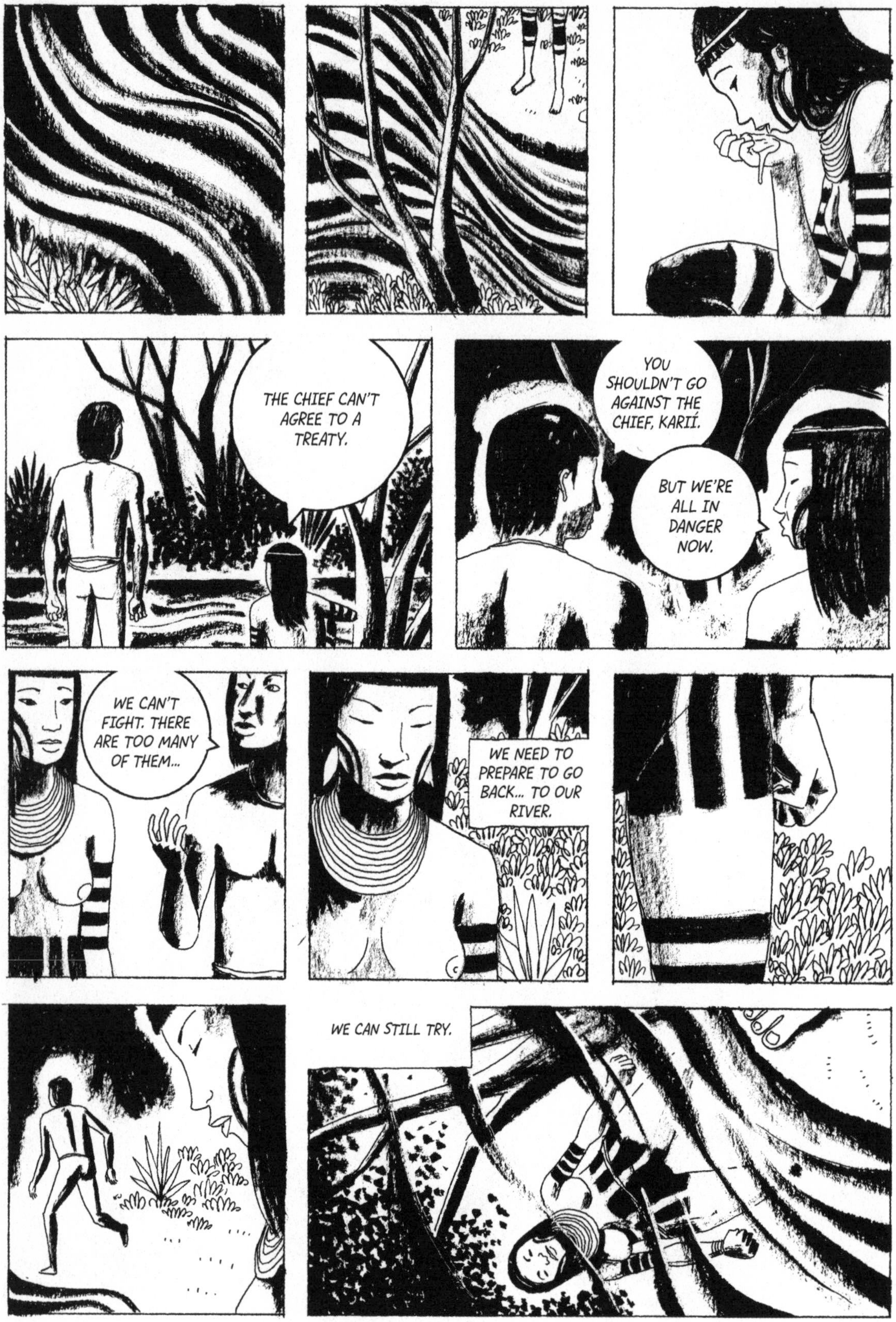

THE CHIEF CAN'T AGREE TO A TREATY.
YOU SHOULDN'T GO AGAINST THE CHIEF, KARIÍ.
BUT WE'RE ALL IN DANGER NOW.
WE CAN'T FIGHT. THERE ARE TOO MANY OF THEM...
WE NEED TO PREPARE TO GO BACK... TO OUR RIVER.
WE CAN STILL TRY.

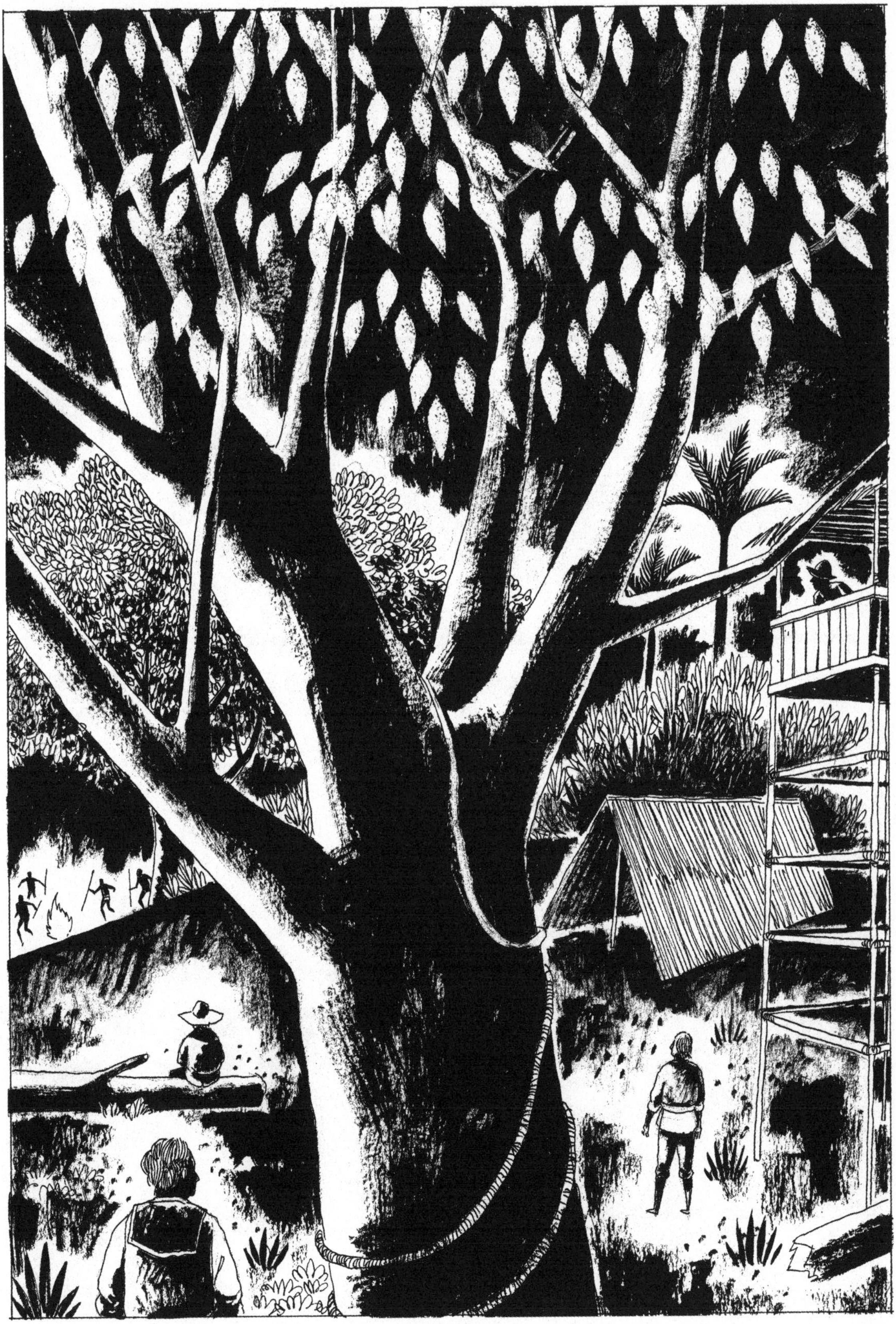

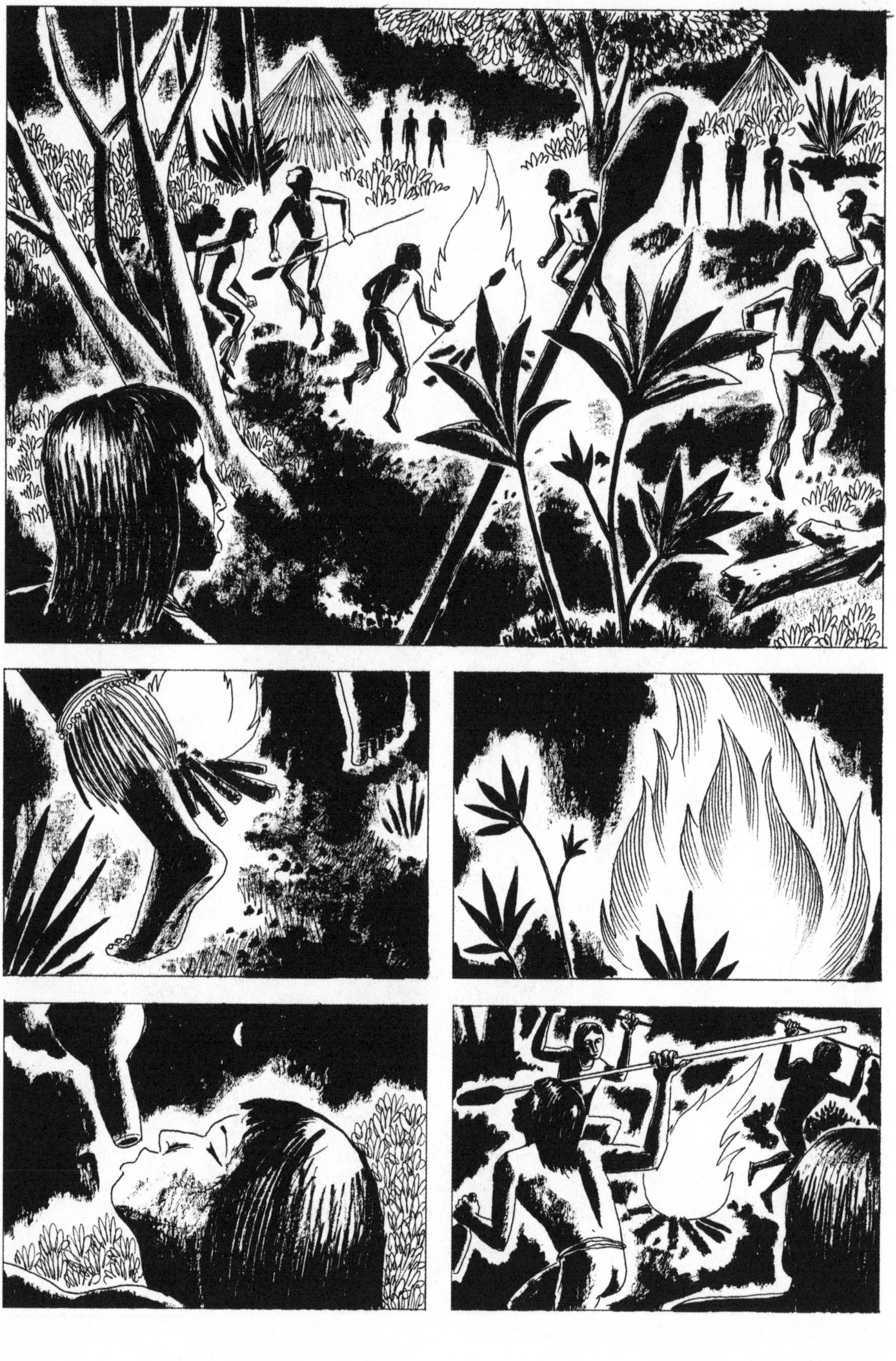

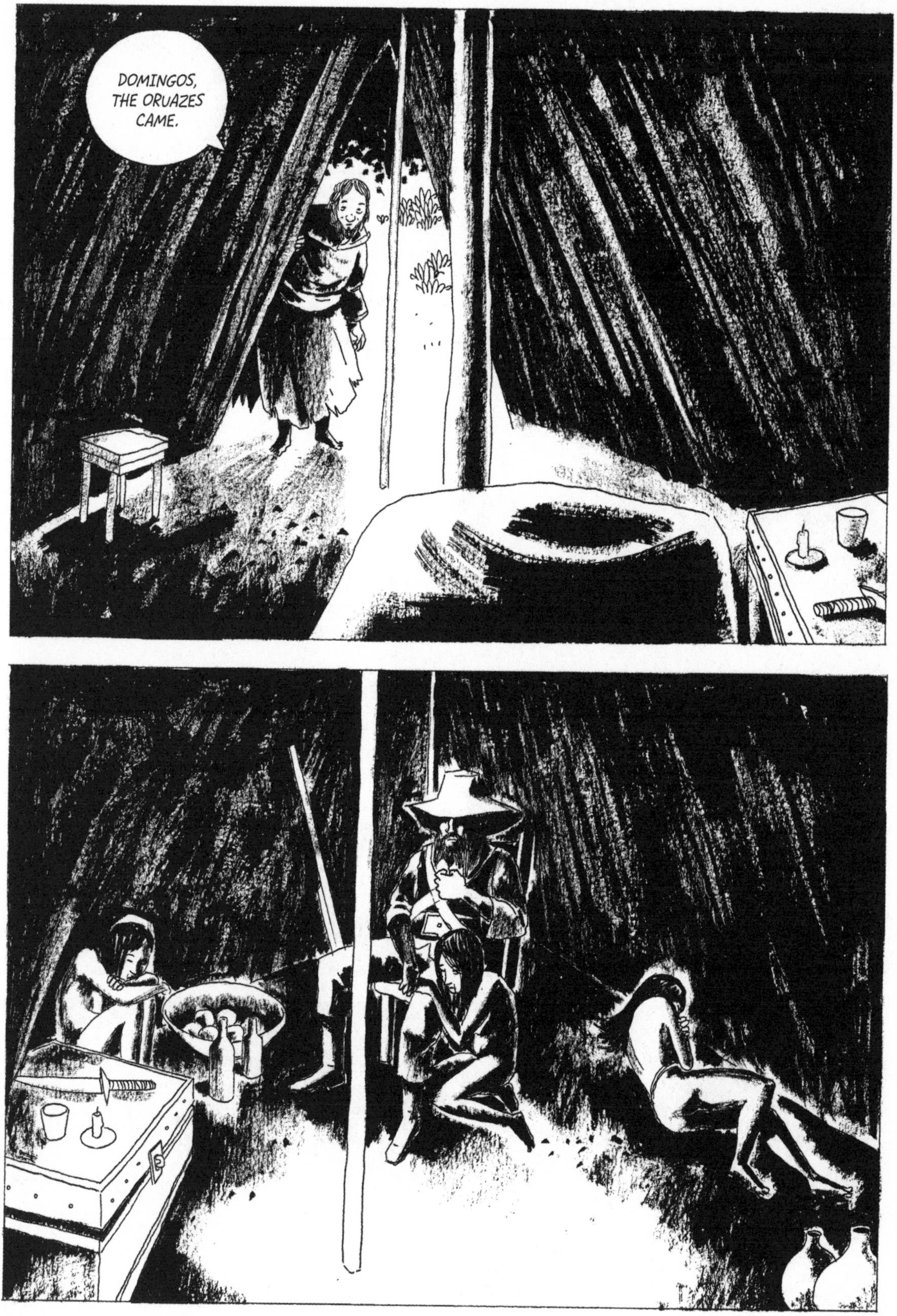
DOMINGOS, THE ORUAZES CAME.

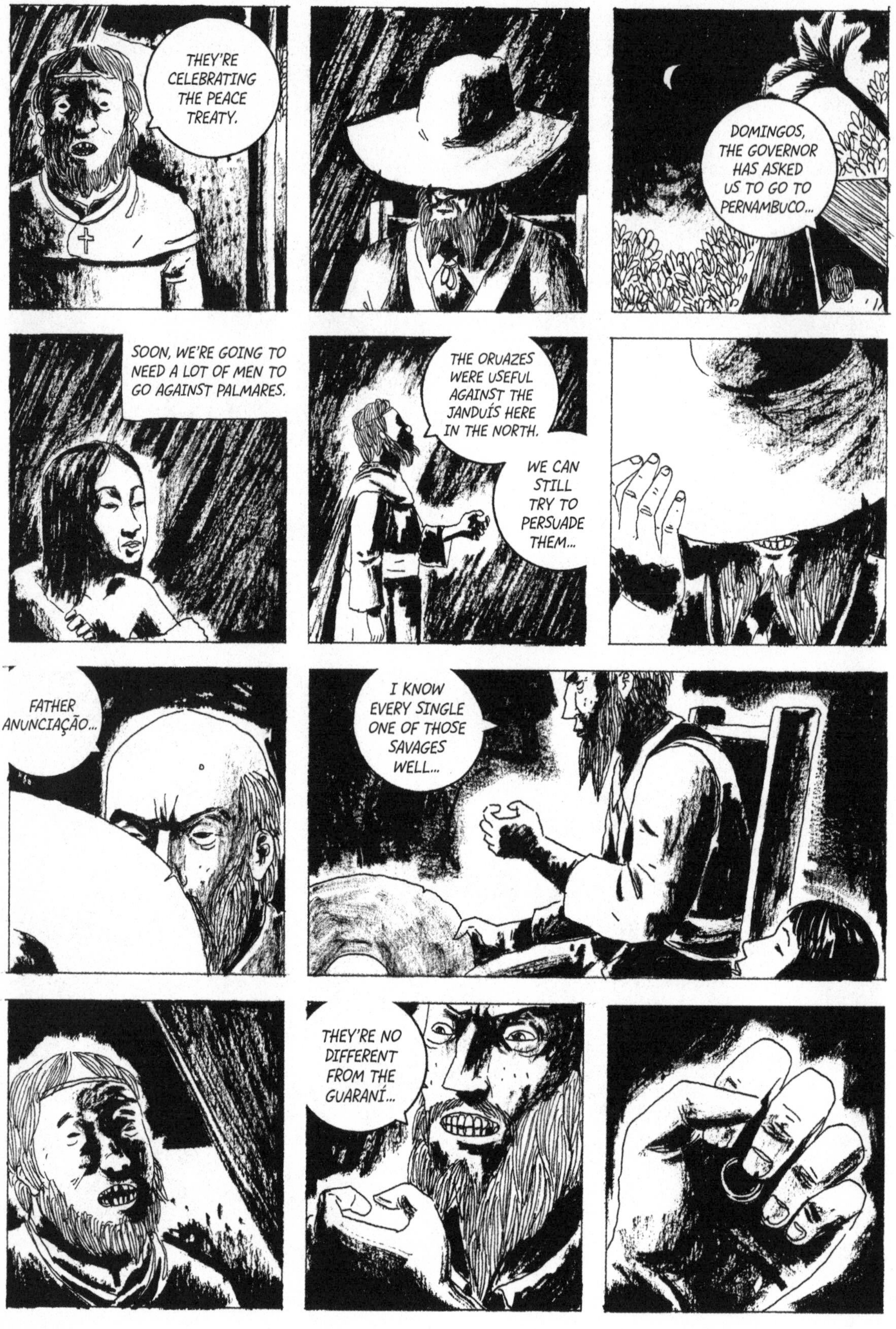
THEY'RE CELEBRATING THE PEACE TREATY.
DOMINGOS, THE GOVERNOR HAS ASKED US TO GO TO PERNAMBUCO...
SOON, WE'RE GOING TO NEED A LOT OF MEN TO GO AGAINST PALMARES.
THE ORUAZES WERE USEFUL AGAINST THE JANDUÍS HERE IN THE NORTH.
WE CAN STILL TRY TO PERSUADE THEM...
FATHER ANUNCIAÇÃO...
I KNOW EVERY SINGLE ONE OF THOSE SAVAGES WELL...
THEY'RE NO DIFFERENT FROM THE GUARANÍ...

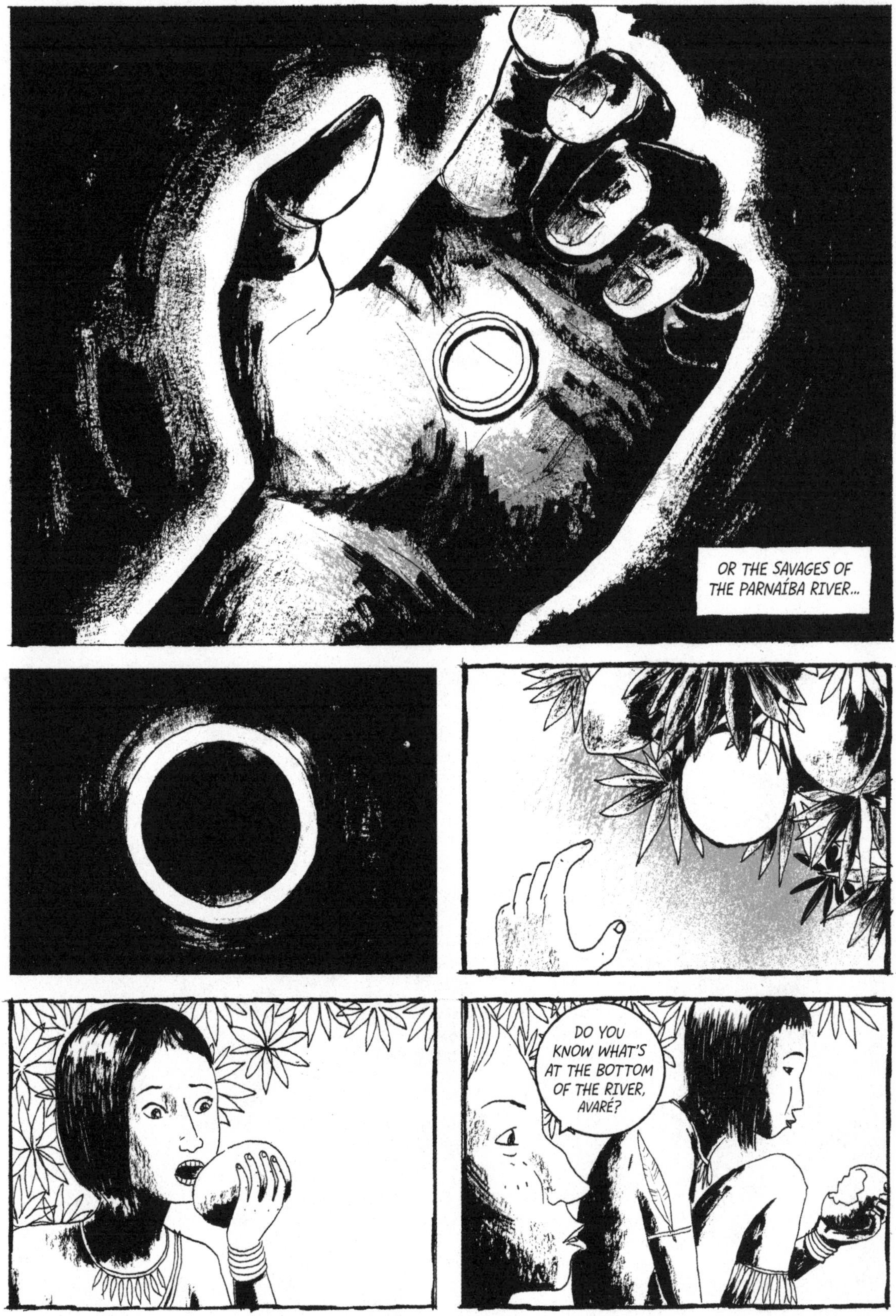
OR THE SAVAGES OF THE PARNAÍBA RIVER...
DO YOU KNOW WHAT'S AT THE BOTTOM OF THE RIVER, AVARÉ?

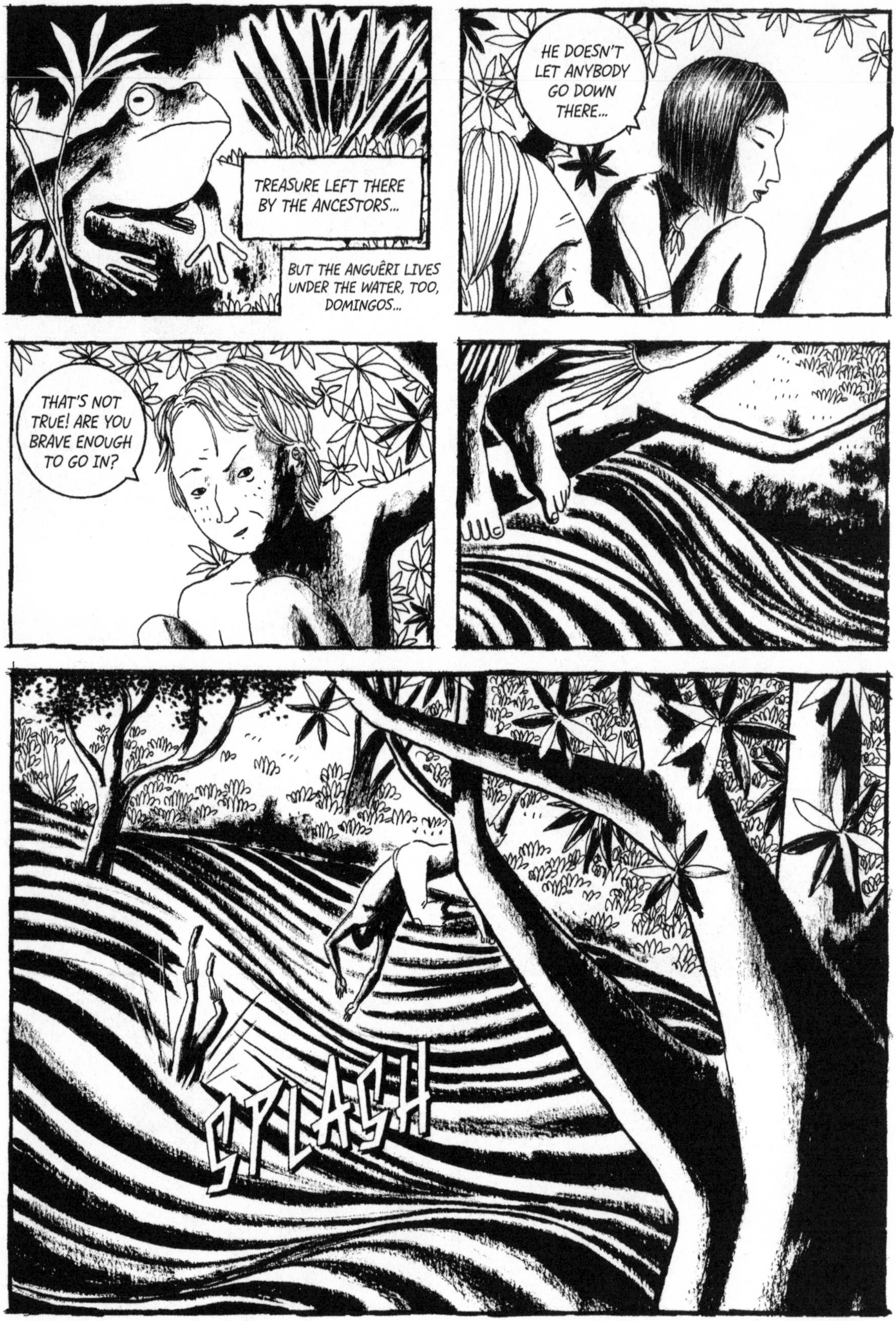

TREASURE LEFT THERE BY THE ANCESTORS...
BUT THE ANGUÊRI LIVES UNDER THE WATER, TOO, DOMINGOS...
HE DOESN'T LET ANYBODY GO DOWN THERE...
THAT'S NOT TRUE! ARE YOU BRAVE ENOUGH TO GO IN?
SPLASH

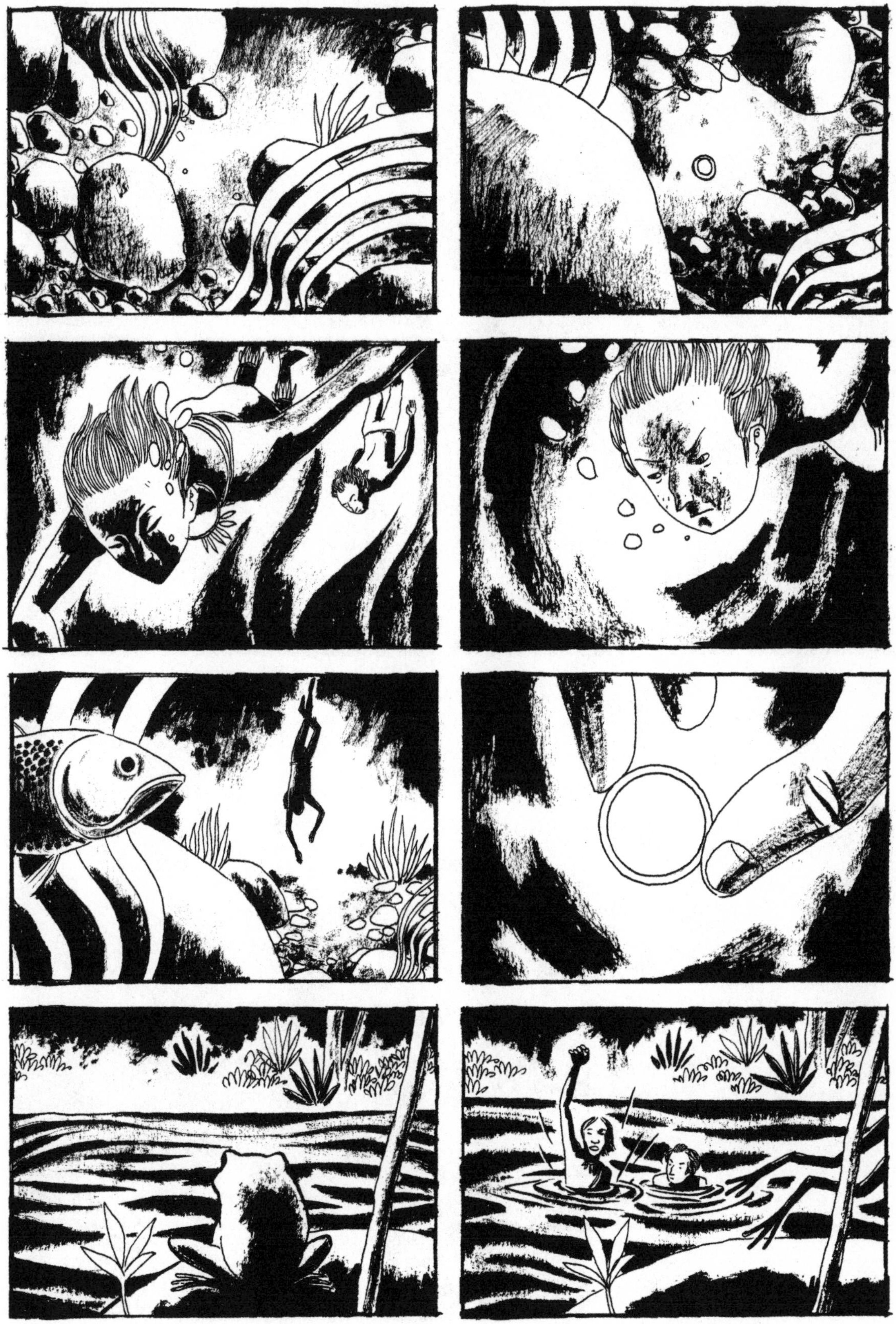

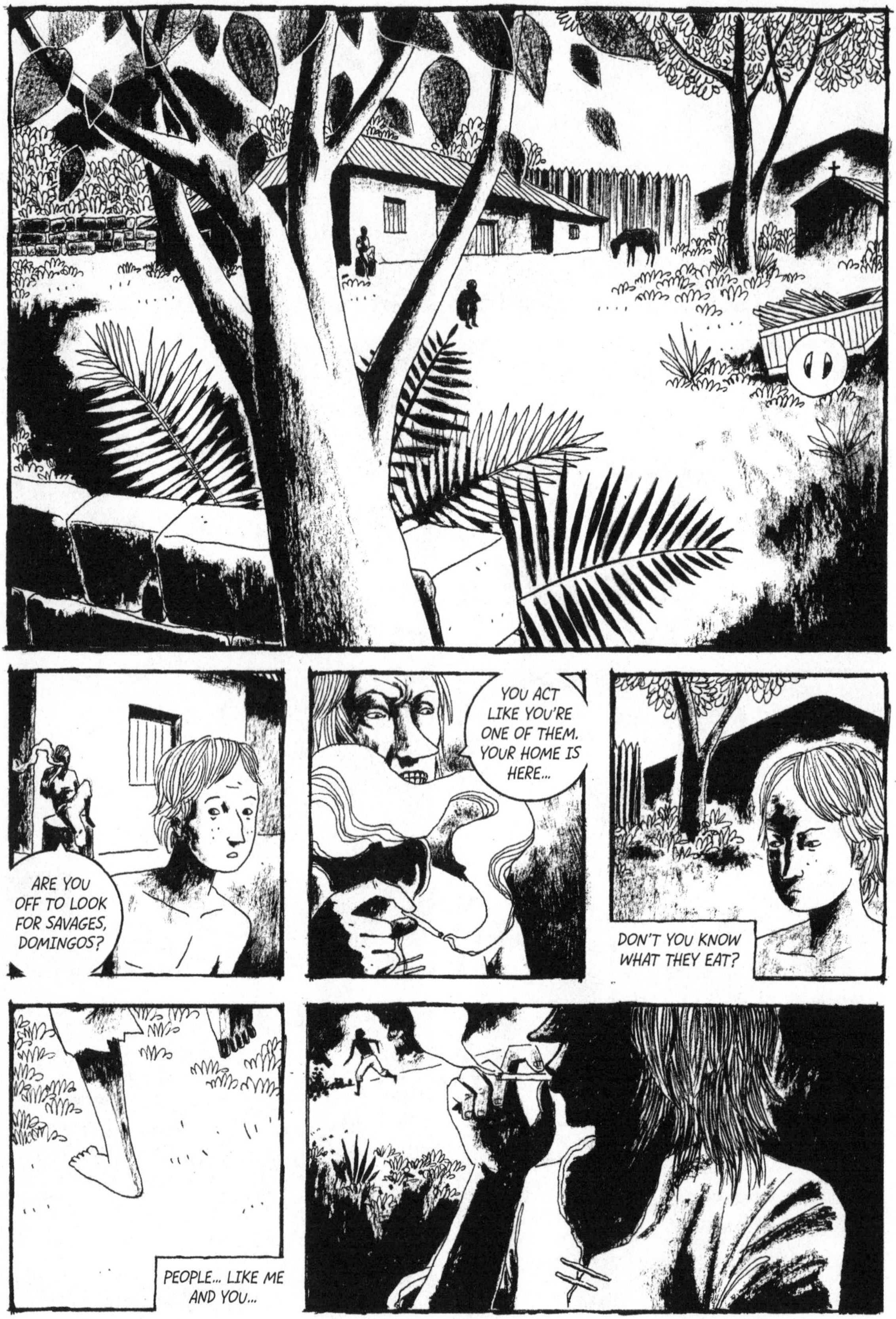
ARE YOU OFF TO LOOK FOR SAVAGES, DOMINGOS?
YOU ACT LIKE YOU'RE ONE OF THEM. YOUR HOME IS HERE...
DON'T YOU KNOW WHAT THEY EAT?
PEOPLE... LIKE ME AND YOU...

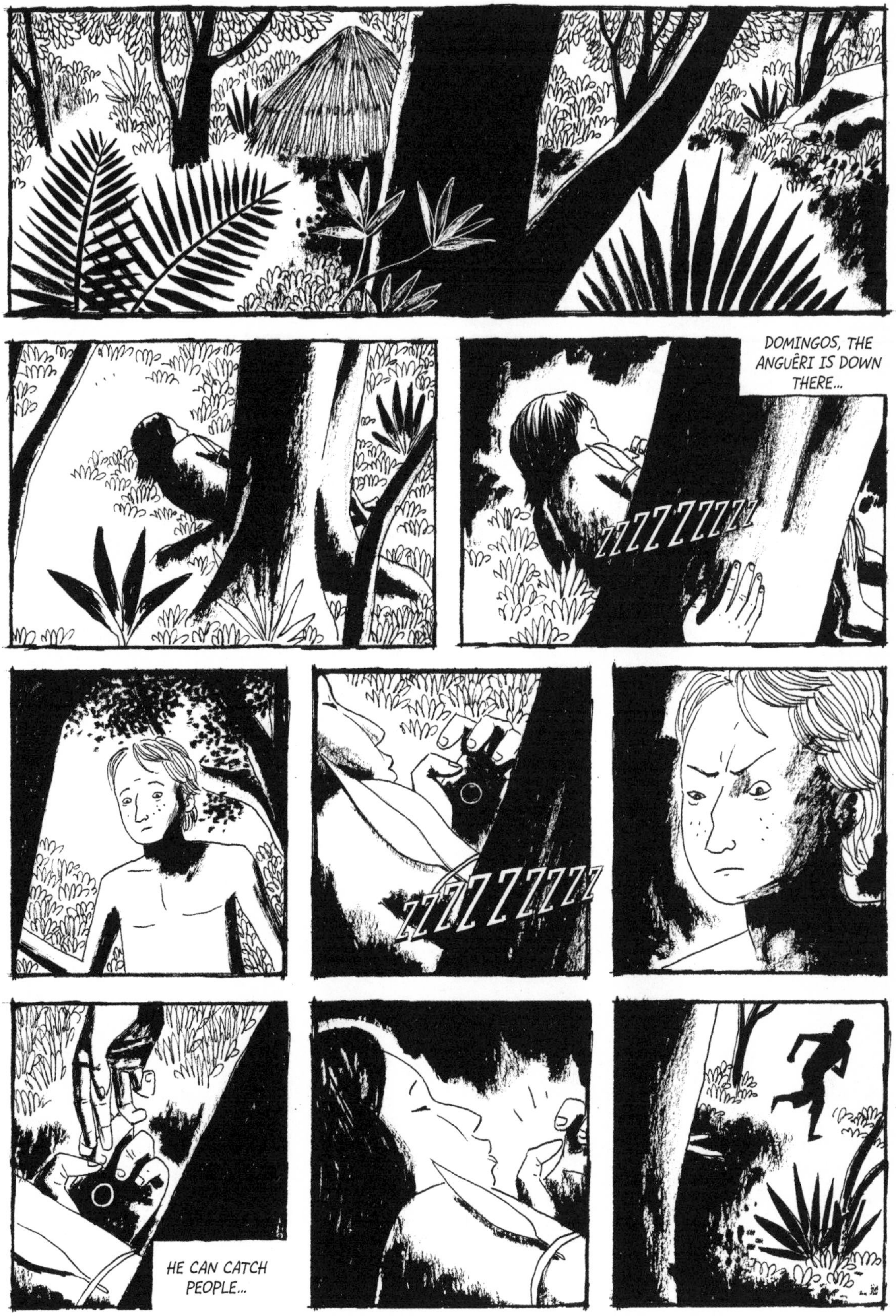
DOMINGOS, THE ANGUÊRI IS DOWN THERE...
ZZZZZZZZZ
ZZZZZZZZZ
HE CAN CATCH PEOPLE...

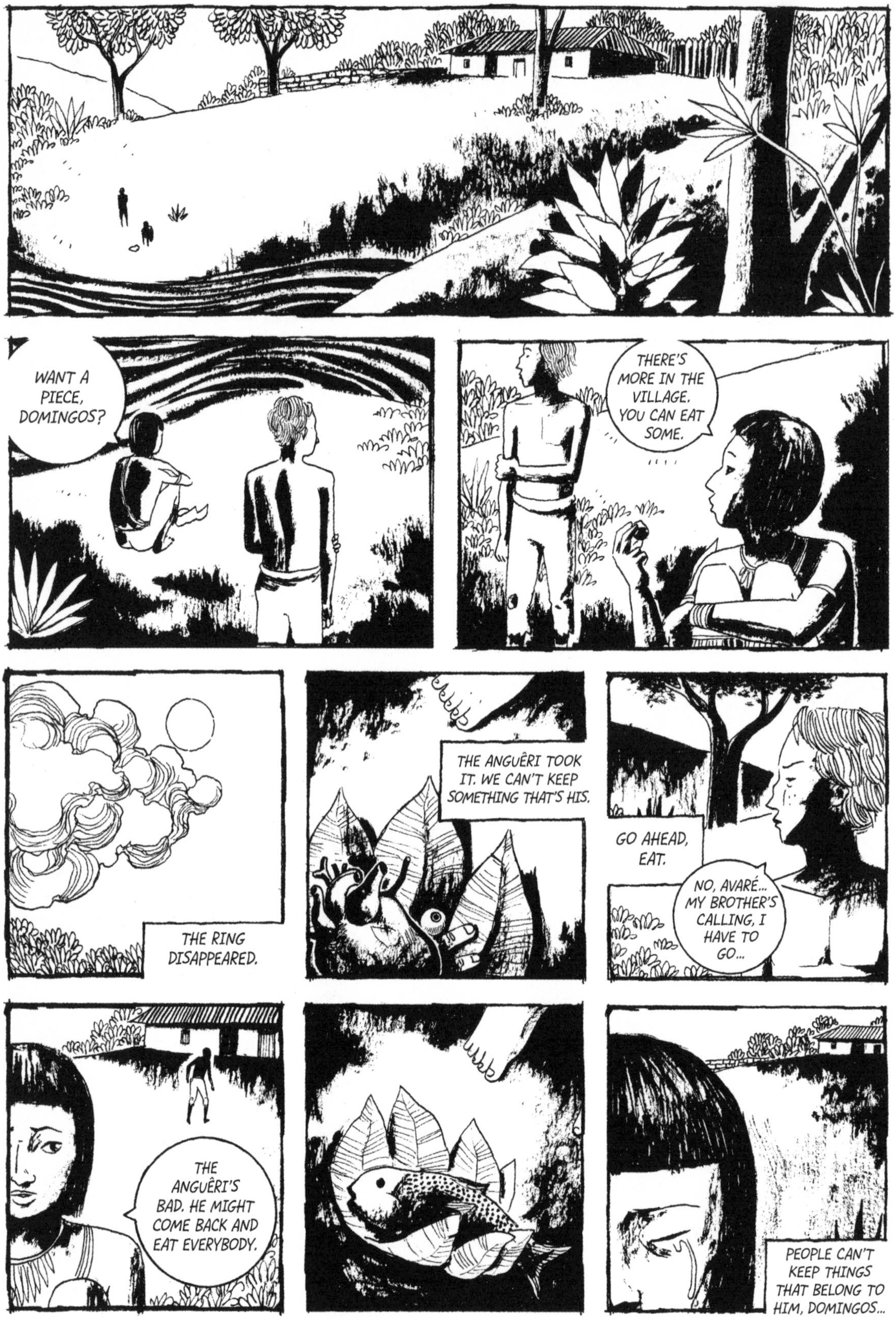
WANT A PIECE, DOMINGOS?
THERE'S MORE IN THE VILLAGE. YOU CAN EAT SOME.
THE RING DISAPPEARED.
THE ANGUÊRI TOOK IT. WE CAN'T KEEP SOMETHING THAT'S HIS.
GO AHEAD, EAT.
NO, AVARÉ... MY BROTHER'S CALLING, I HAVE TO GO...
THE ANGUÊRI'S BAD. HE MIGHT COME BACK AND EAT EVERYBODY.
PEOPLE CAN'T KEEP THINGS THAT BELONG TO HIM, DOMINGOS...

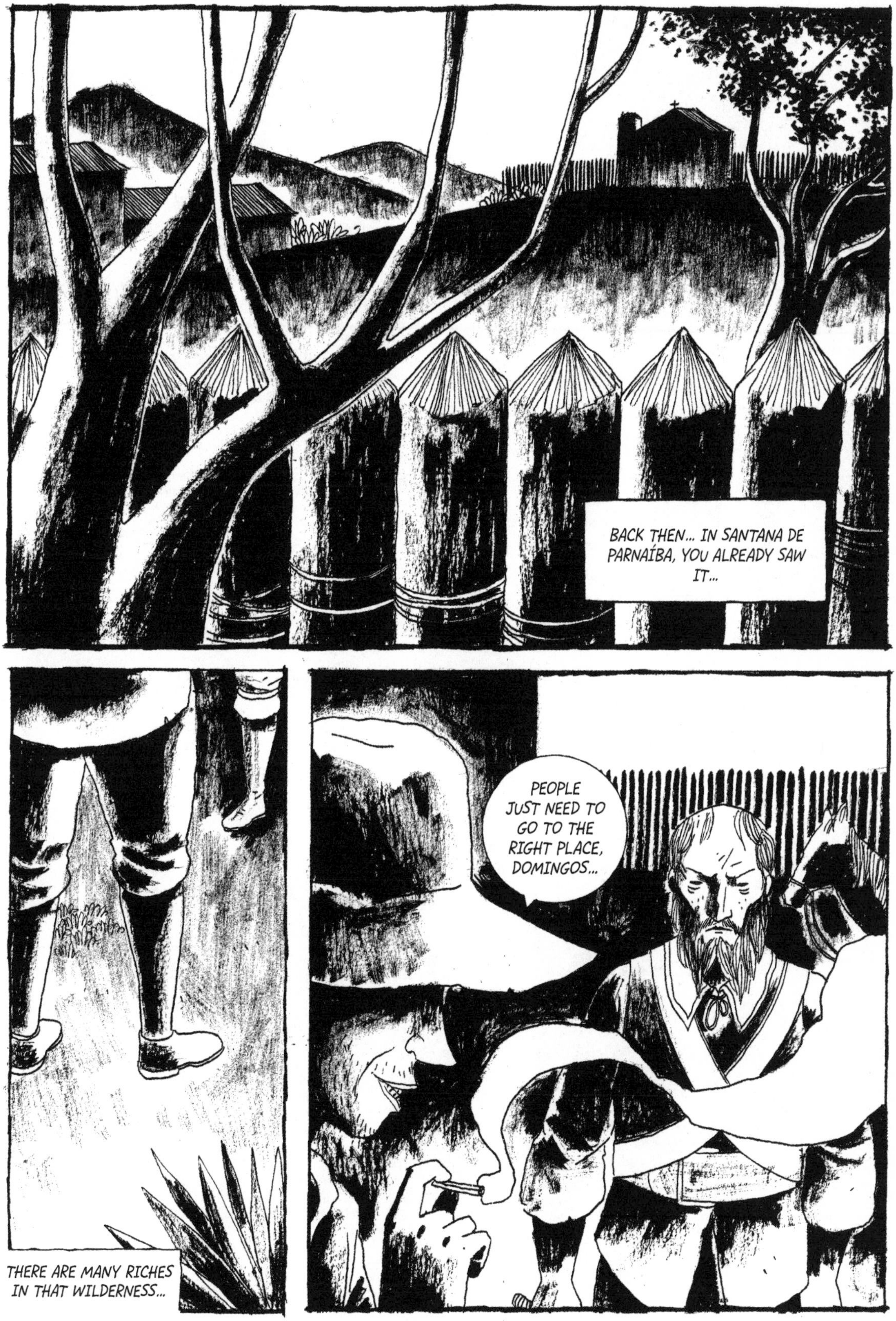
BACK THEN... IN SANTANA DE PARNAÍBA, YOU ALREADY SAW IT...
THERE ARE MANY RICHES IN THAT WILDERNESS...
PEOPLE JUST NEED TO GO TO THE RIGHT PLACE, DOMINGOS...

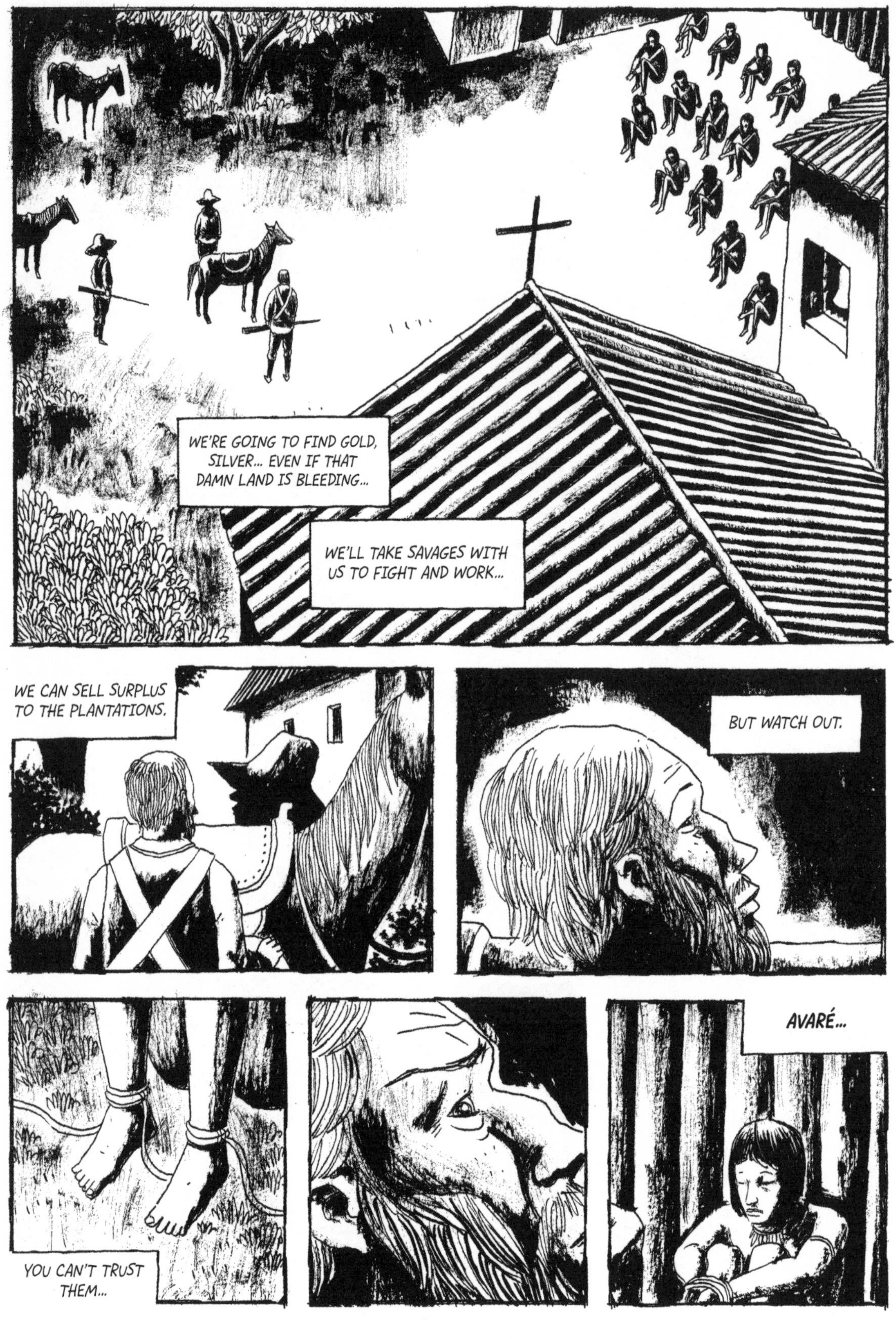
WE'RE GOING TO FIND GOLD, SILVER... EVEN IF THAT DAMN LAND IS BLEEDING...
WE'LL TAKE SAVAGES WITH US TO FIGHT AND WORK...
WE CAN SELL SURPLUS TO THE PLANTATIONS.
BUT WATCH OUT.
YOU CAN'T TRUST THEM...
AVARÉ...

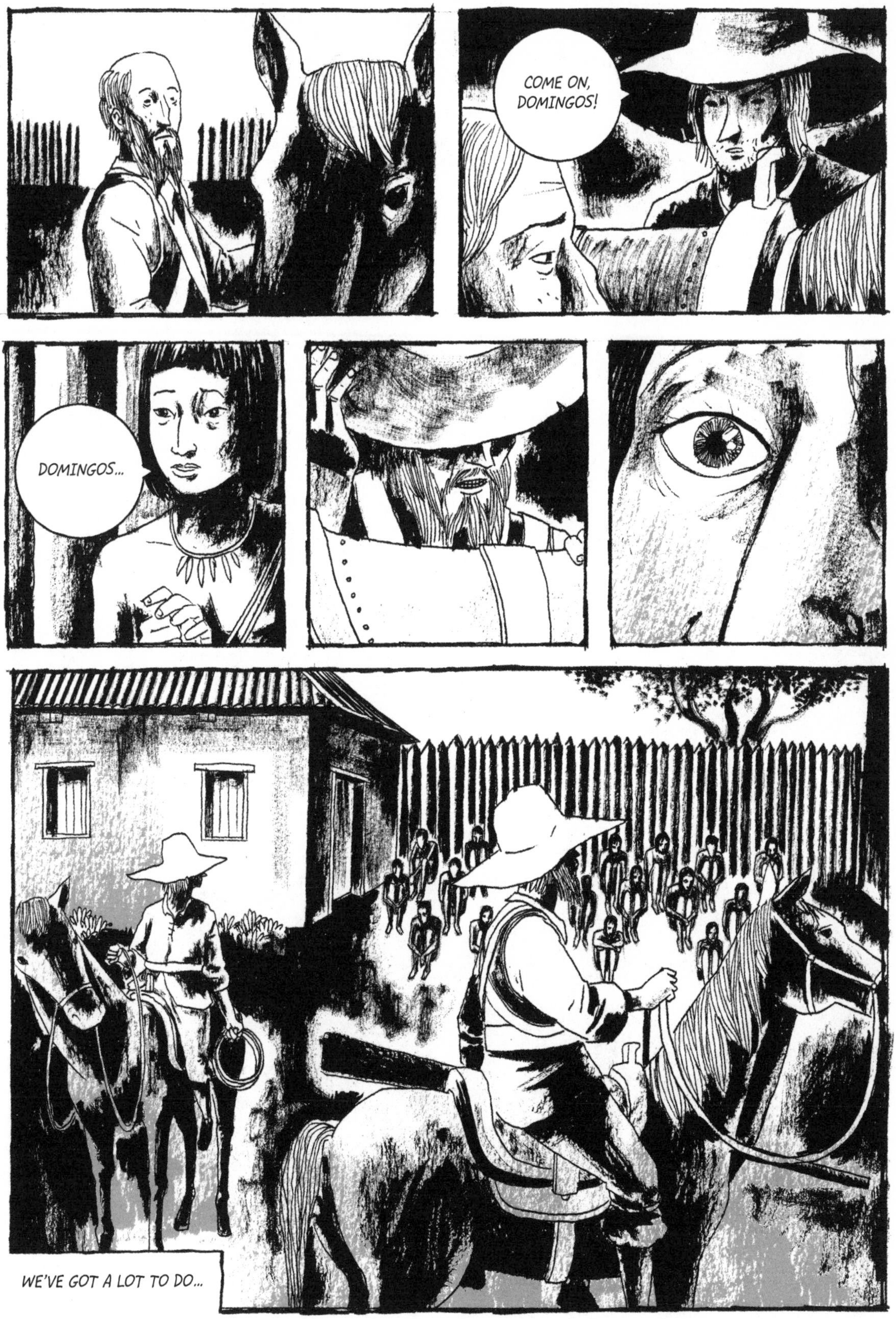
COME ON, DOMINGOS!
DOMINGOS...
WE'VE GOT A LOT TO DO...

IT'S TIME TO GO, MAN...

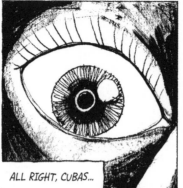

ALL RIGHT, CUBAS...

I KNOW ALL OF THEM...

FATHER ANUNCIAÇÃO, MY BROTHER DIED FIGHTING INDIANS...

I KNOW HOW TO SHOW THOSE REBELLIOUS SAVAGES THE WAY...

I UNDERSTAND, DOMINGOS...

IF THE ORUAZES DON'T WANT TO JOIN US AS WE MARCH ON PALMARES...

230

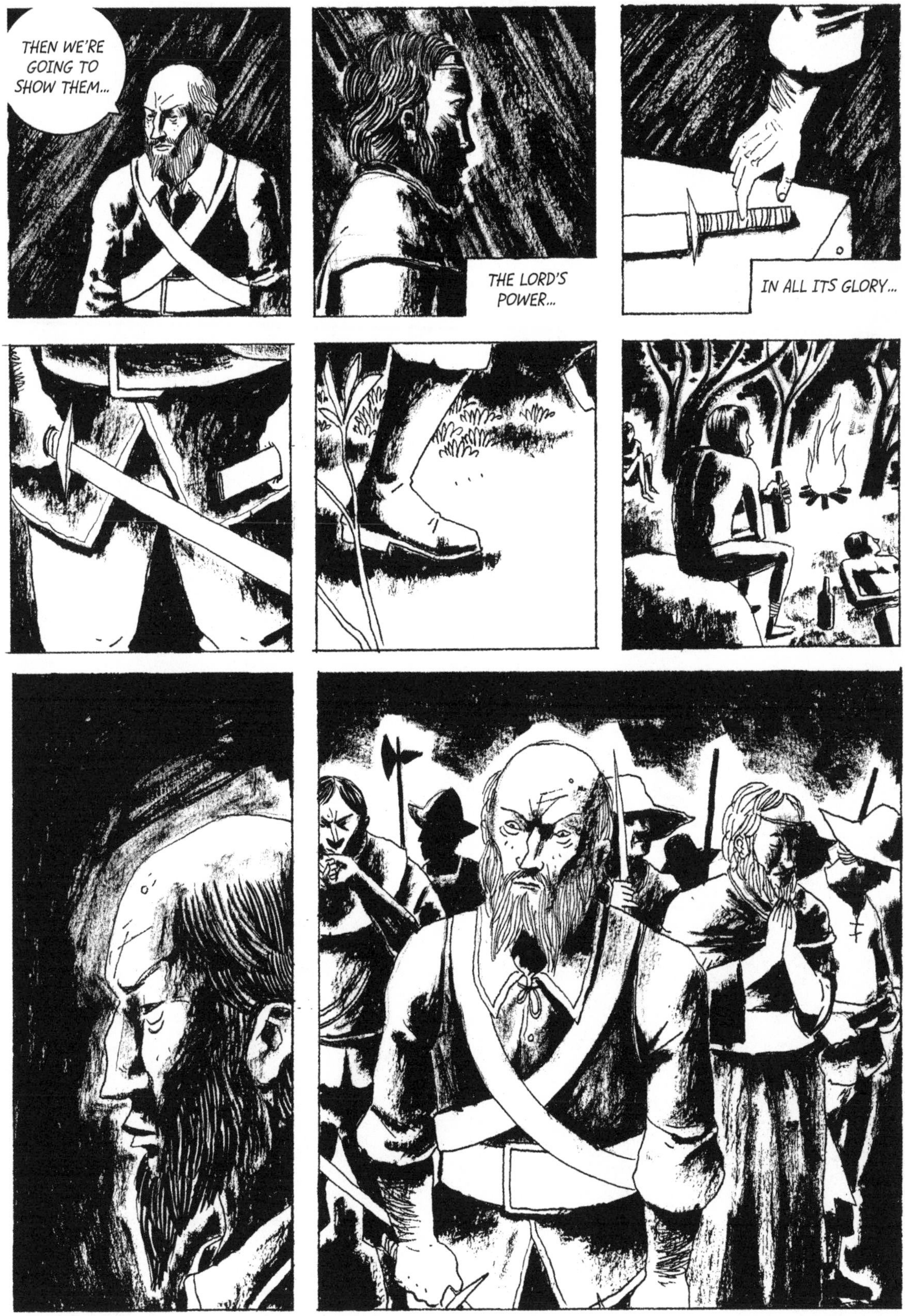
THEN WE'RE GOING TO SHOW THEM...
THE LORD'S POWER...
IN ALL ITS GLORY...

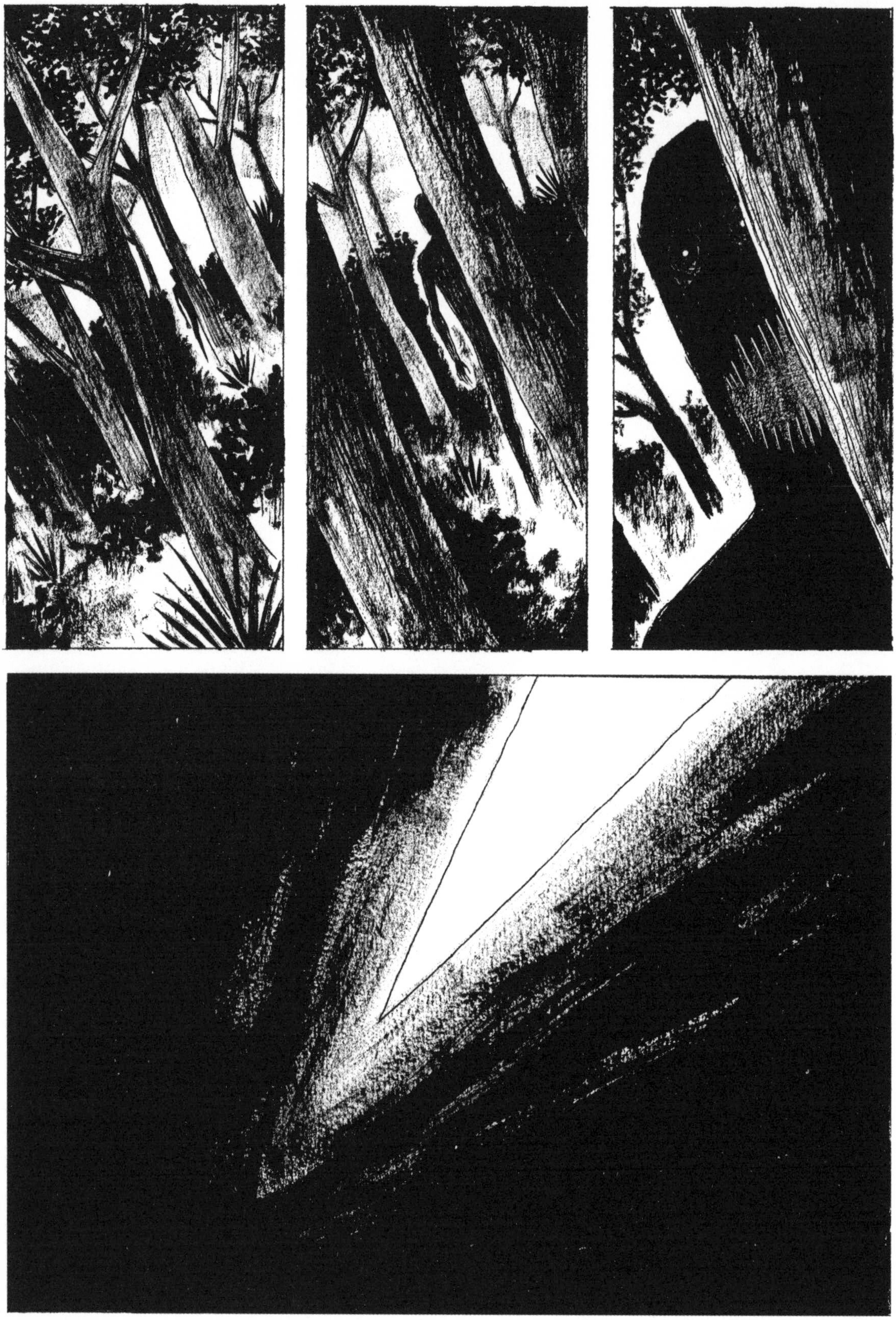

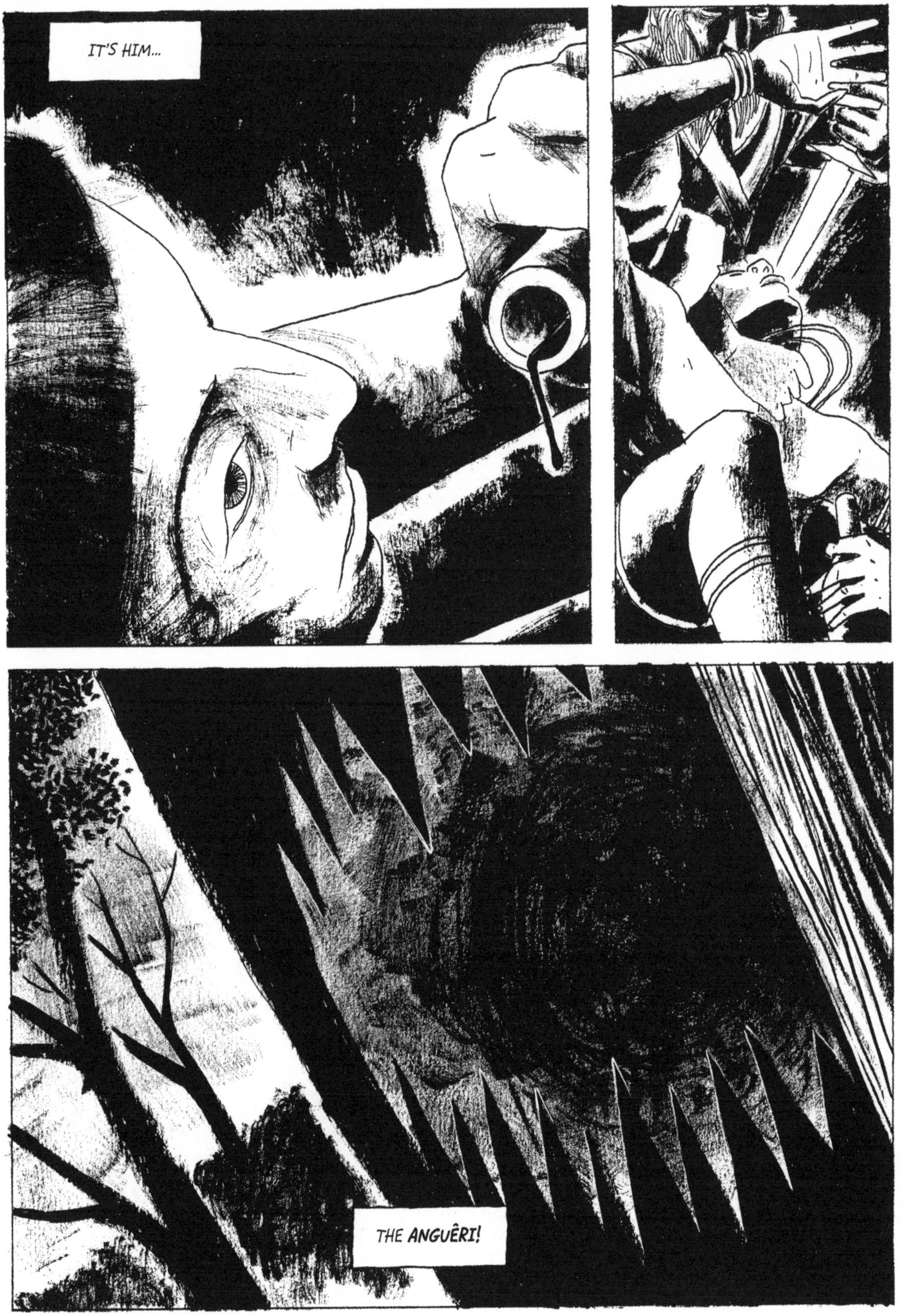
IT'S HIM...
THE ANGUÊRI!

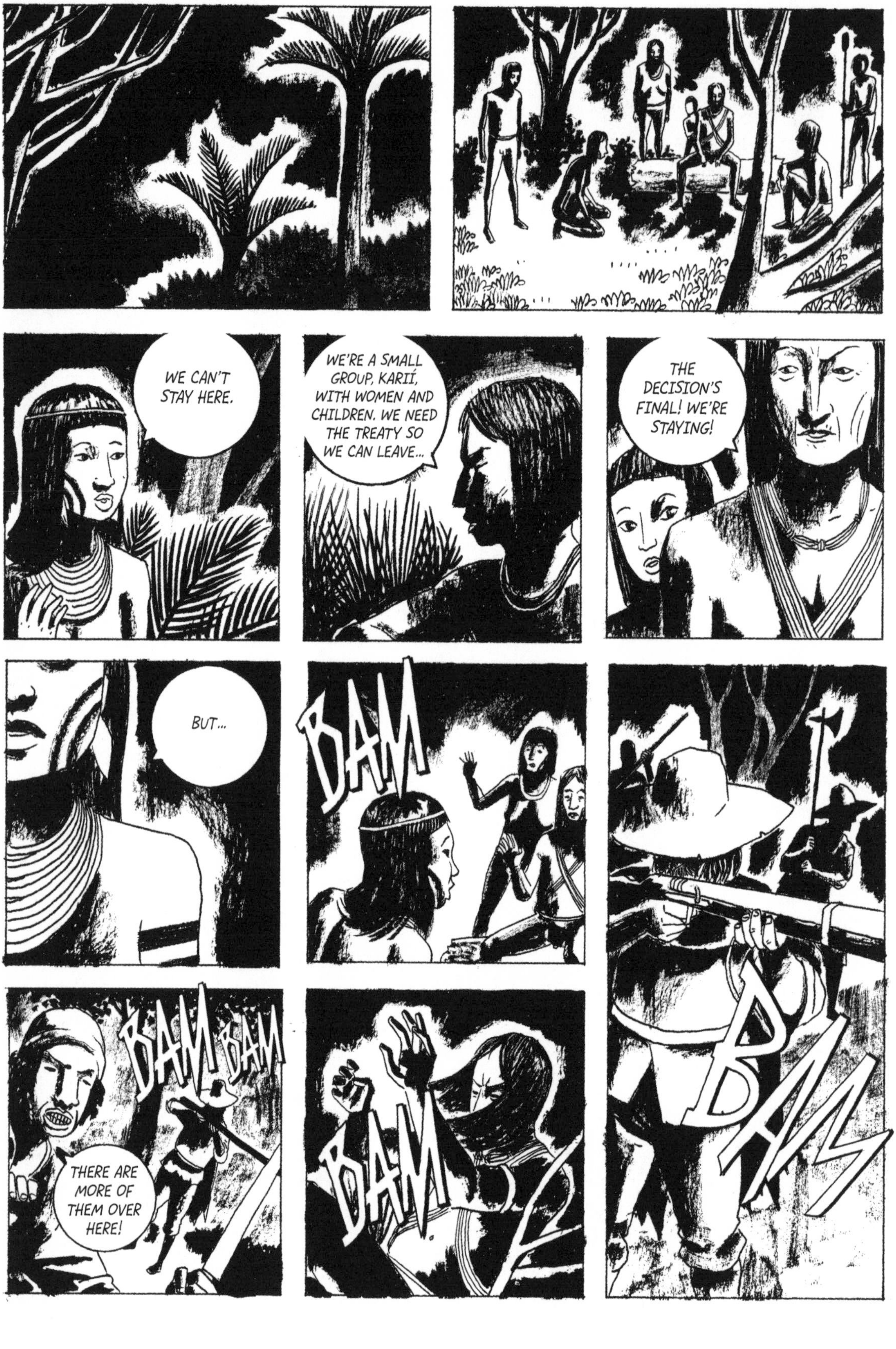
WE CAN'T STAY HERE.
WE'RE A SMALL GROUP, KARIÍ, WITH WOMEN AND CHILDREN. WE NEED THE TREATY SO WE CAN LEAVE...
THE DECISION'S FINAL! WE'RE STAYING!
BUT...
BAM
BAM
BAM BAM
THERE ARE MORE OF THEM OVER HERE!
BAM
BAM

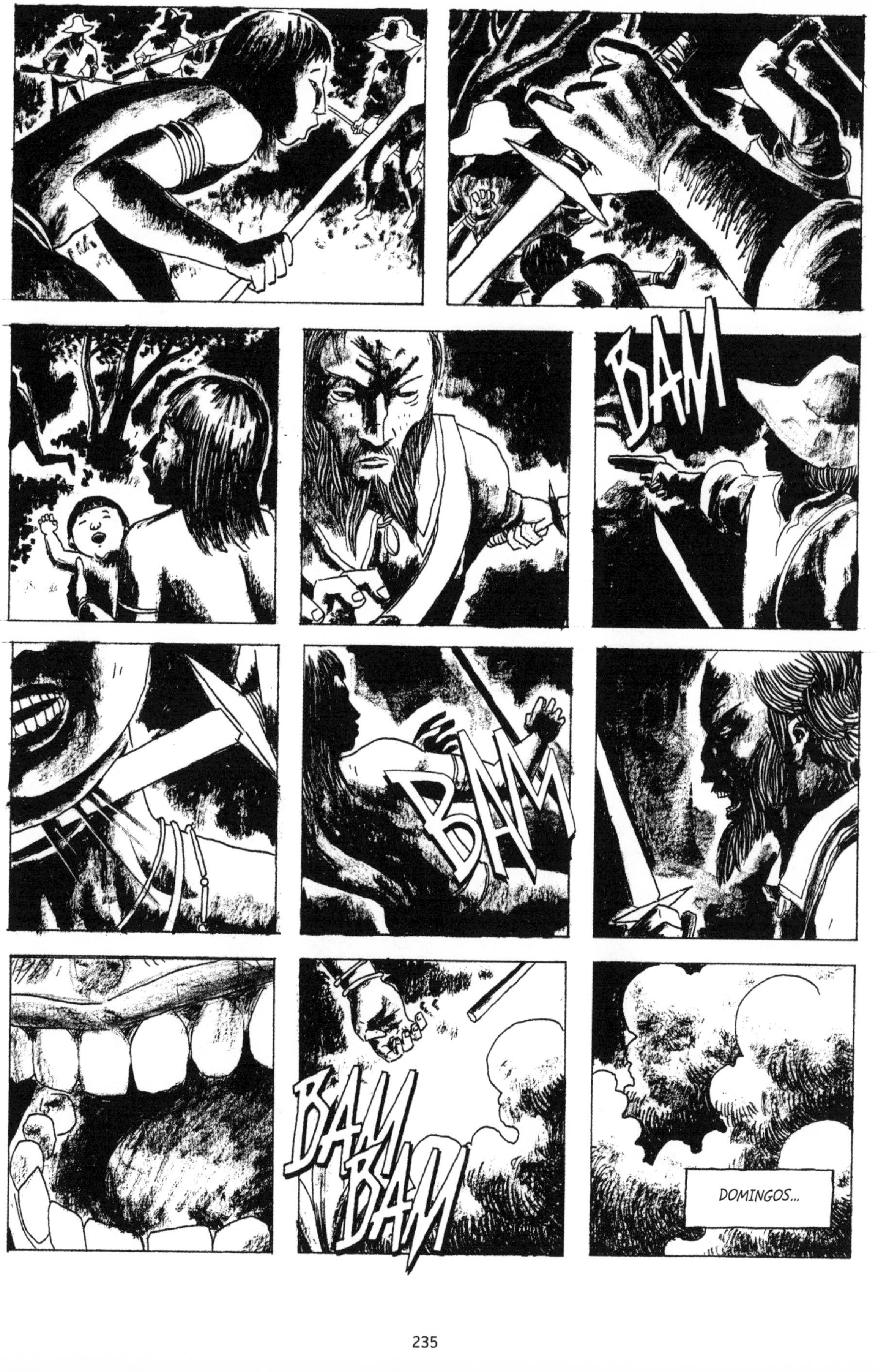
BAM
BAM
BAM
BAM
DOMINGOS...

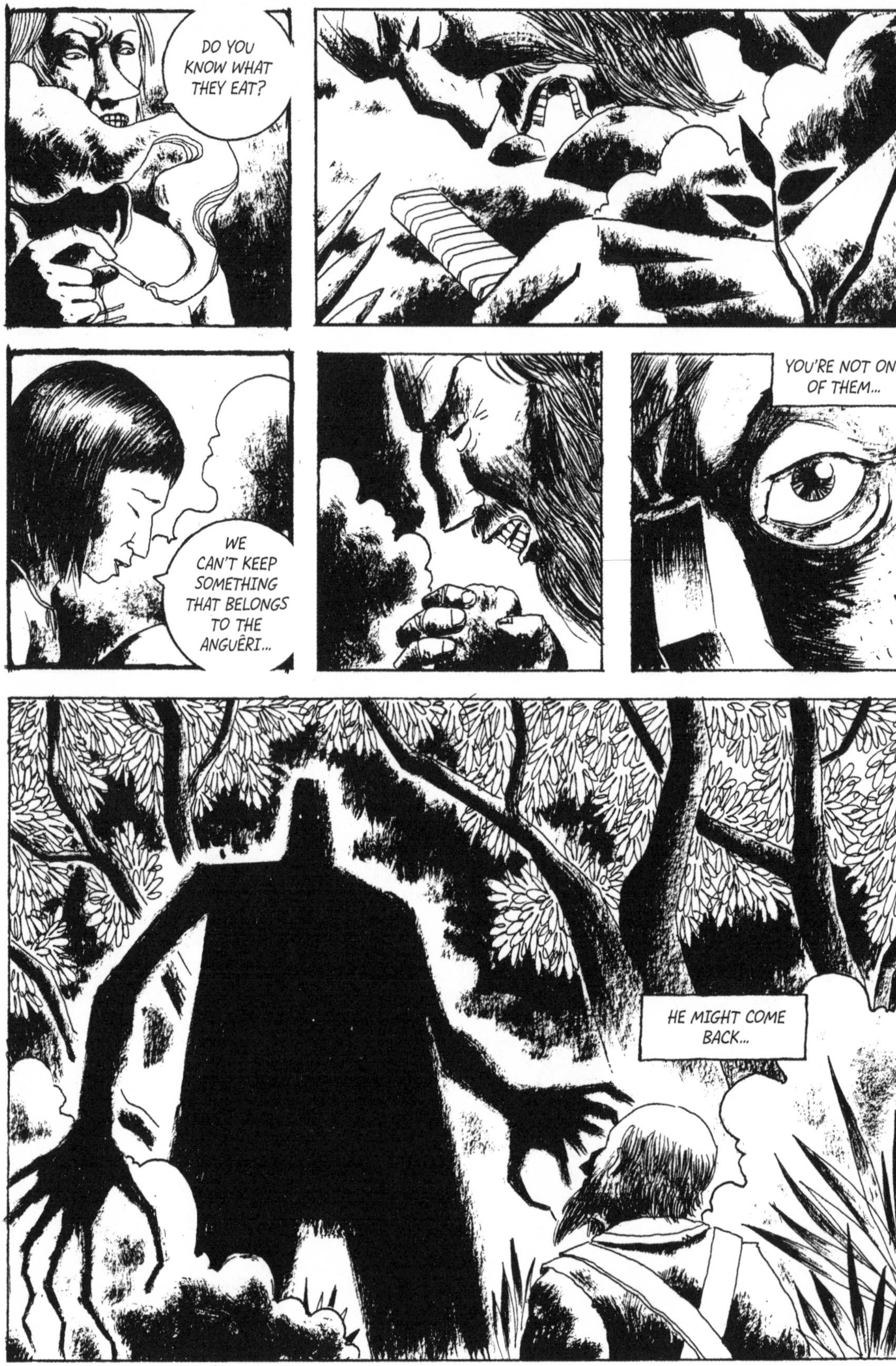
DO YOU KNOW WHAT THEY EAT?
WE CAN'T KEEP SOMETHING THAT BELONGS TO THE ANGUÊRI...
YOU'RE NOT ONE OF THEM...
HE MIGHT COME BACK...

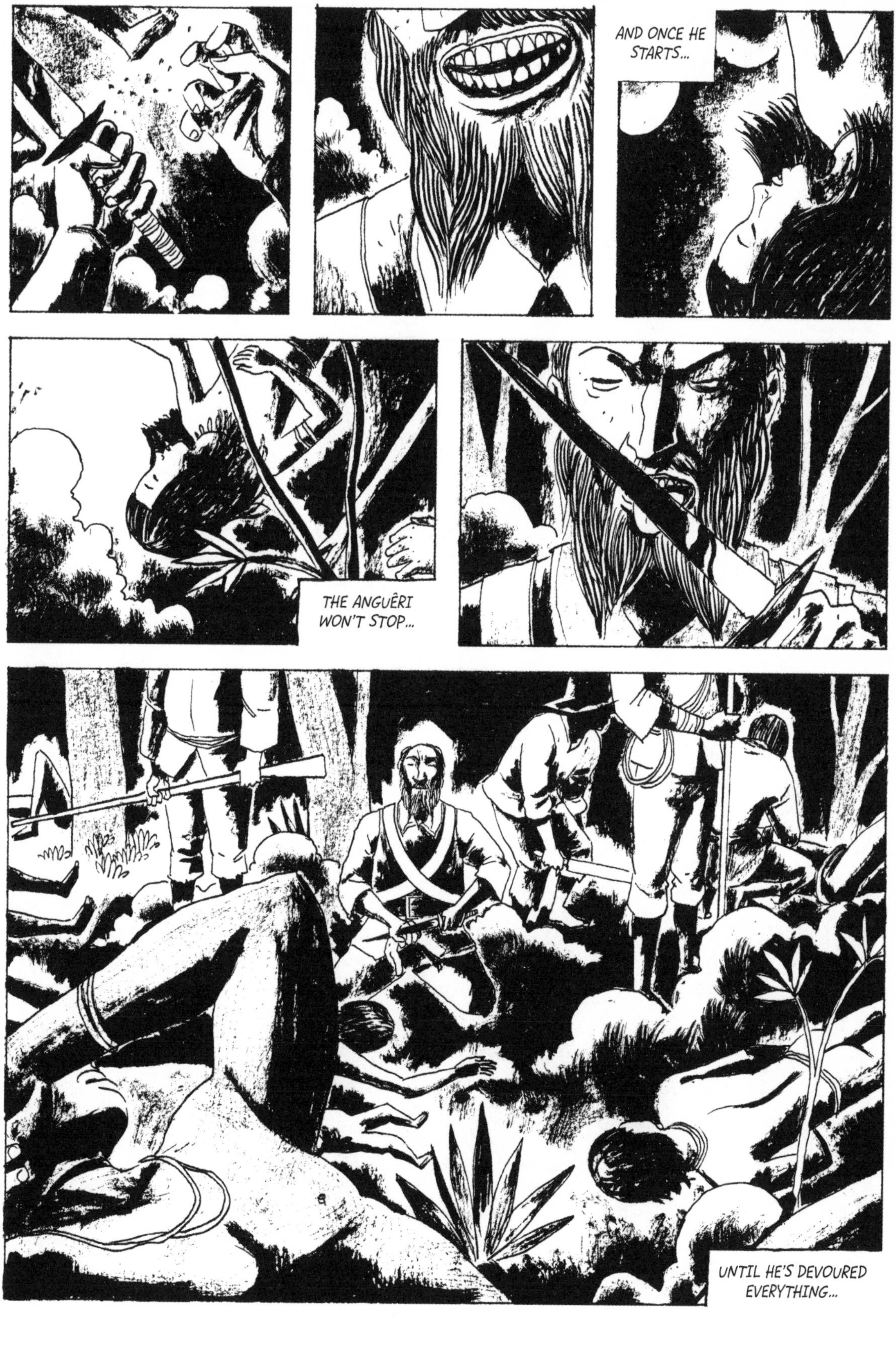
AND ONCE HE STARTS...
THE ANGUÊRI WON'T STOP...
UNTIL HE'S DEVOURED EVERYTHING...

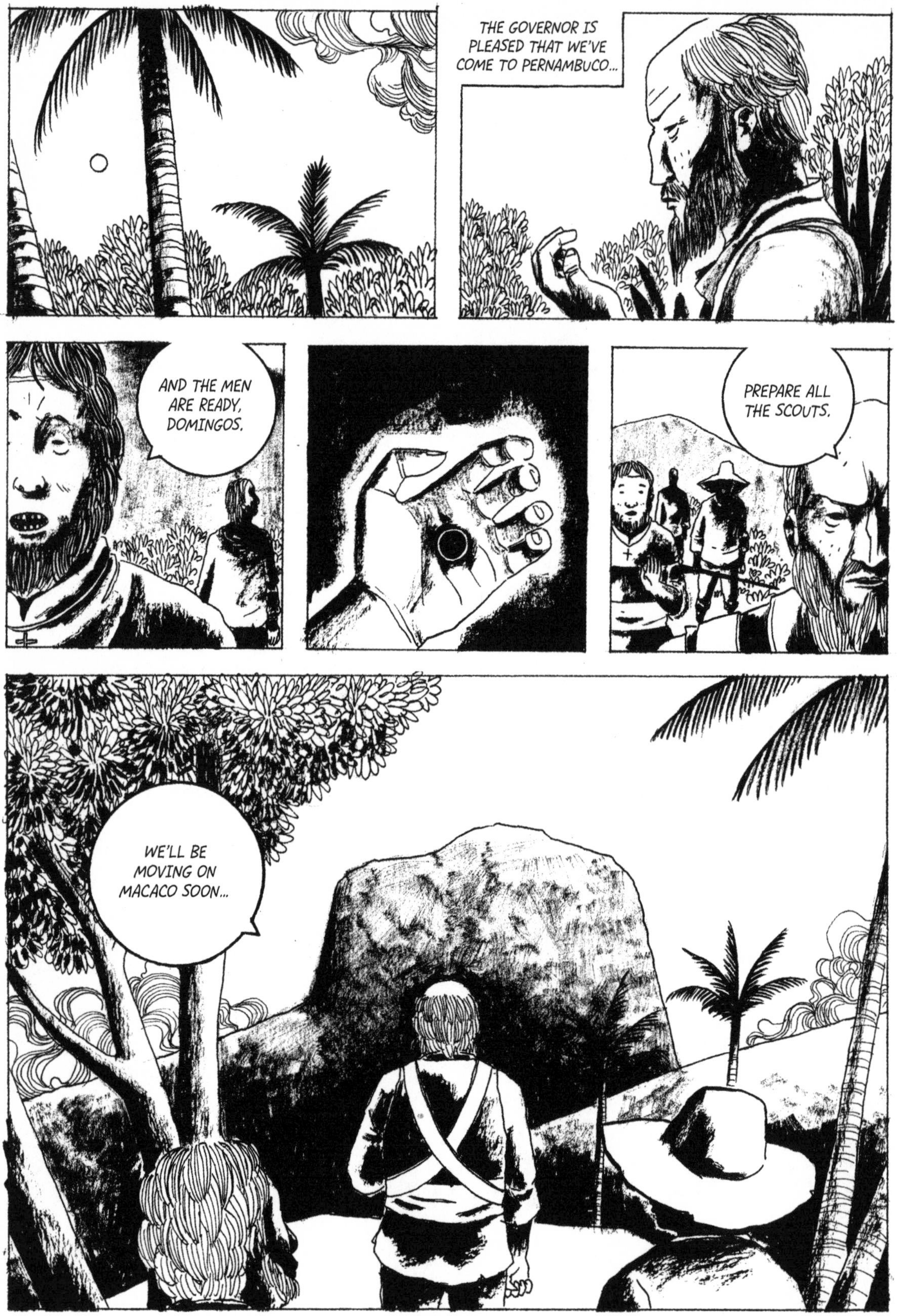
THE GOVERNOR IS PLEASED THAT WE'VE COME TO PERNAMBUCO...
AND THE MEN ARE READY, DOMINGOS.
PREPARE ALL THE SCOUTS.
WE'LL BE MOVING ON MACACO SOON...

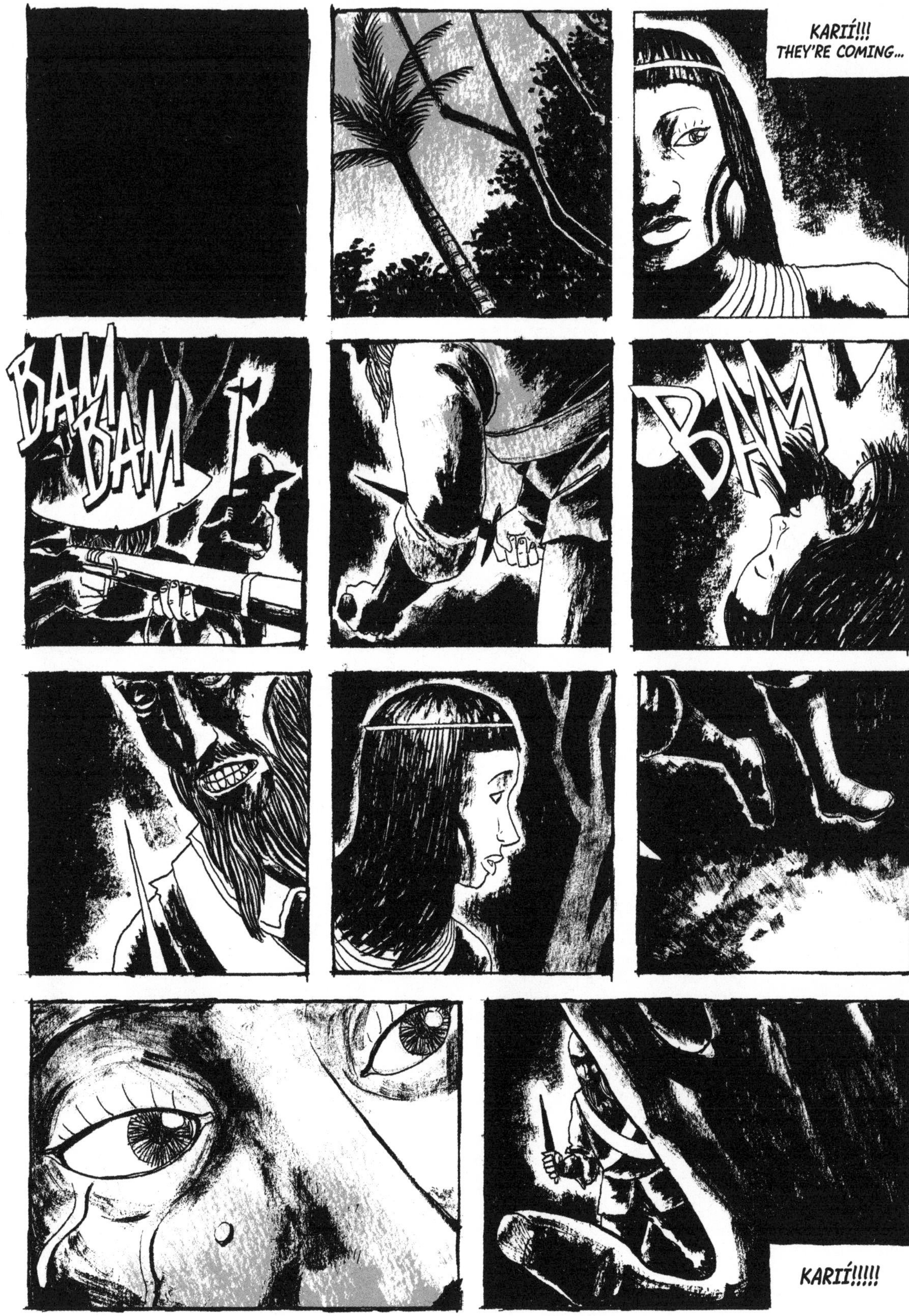
KARIÍ!!!
THEY'RE COMING...
BAM
BAM
BAM
KARIÍ!!!!!

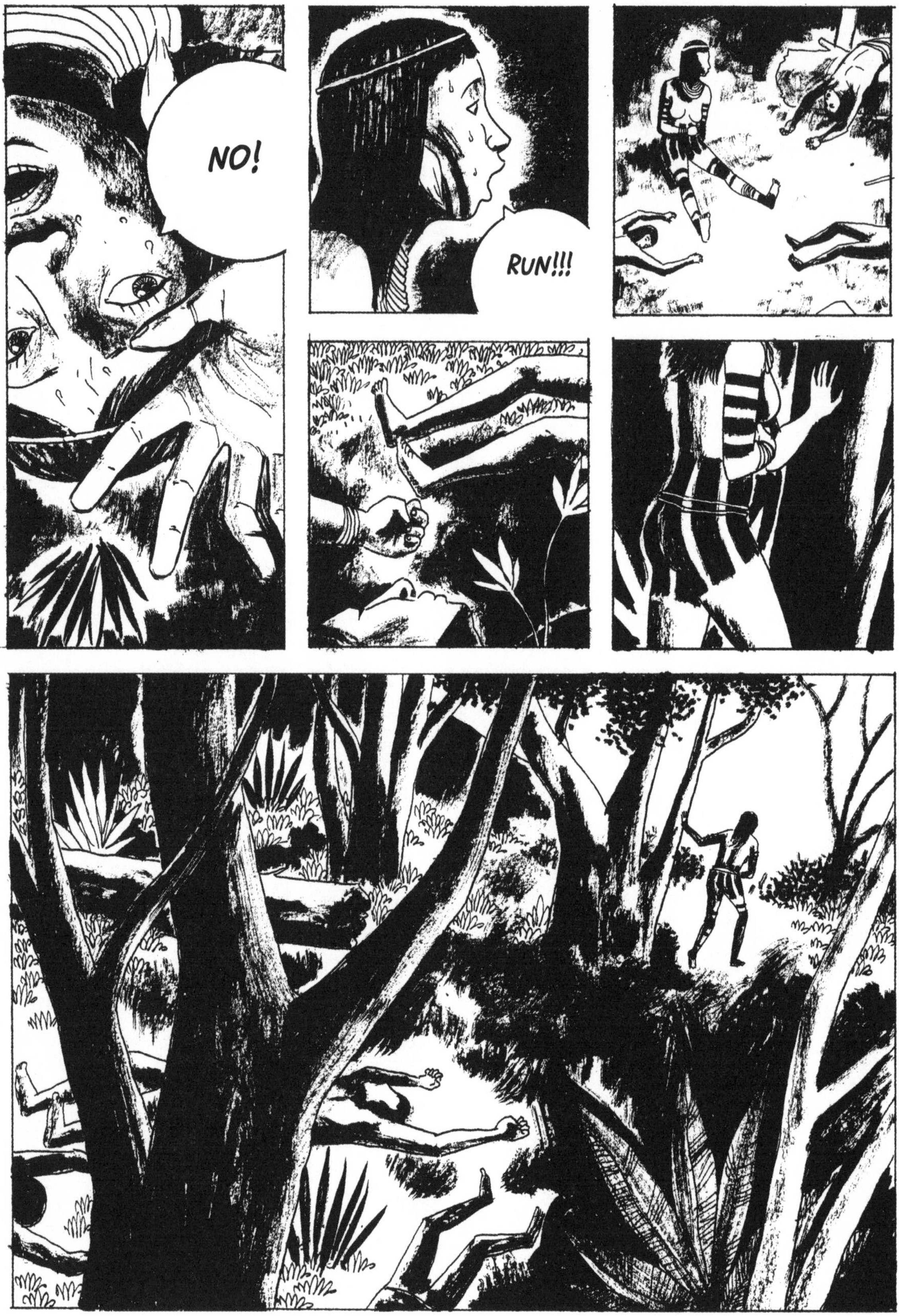
NO!
RUN!!!

WAR

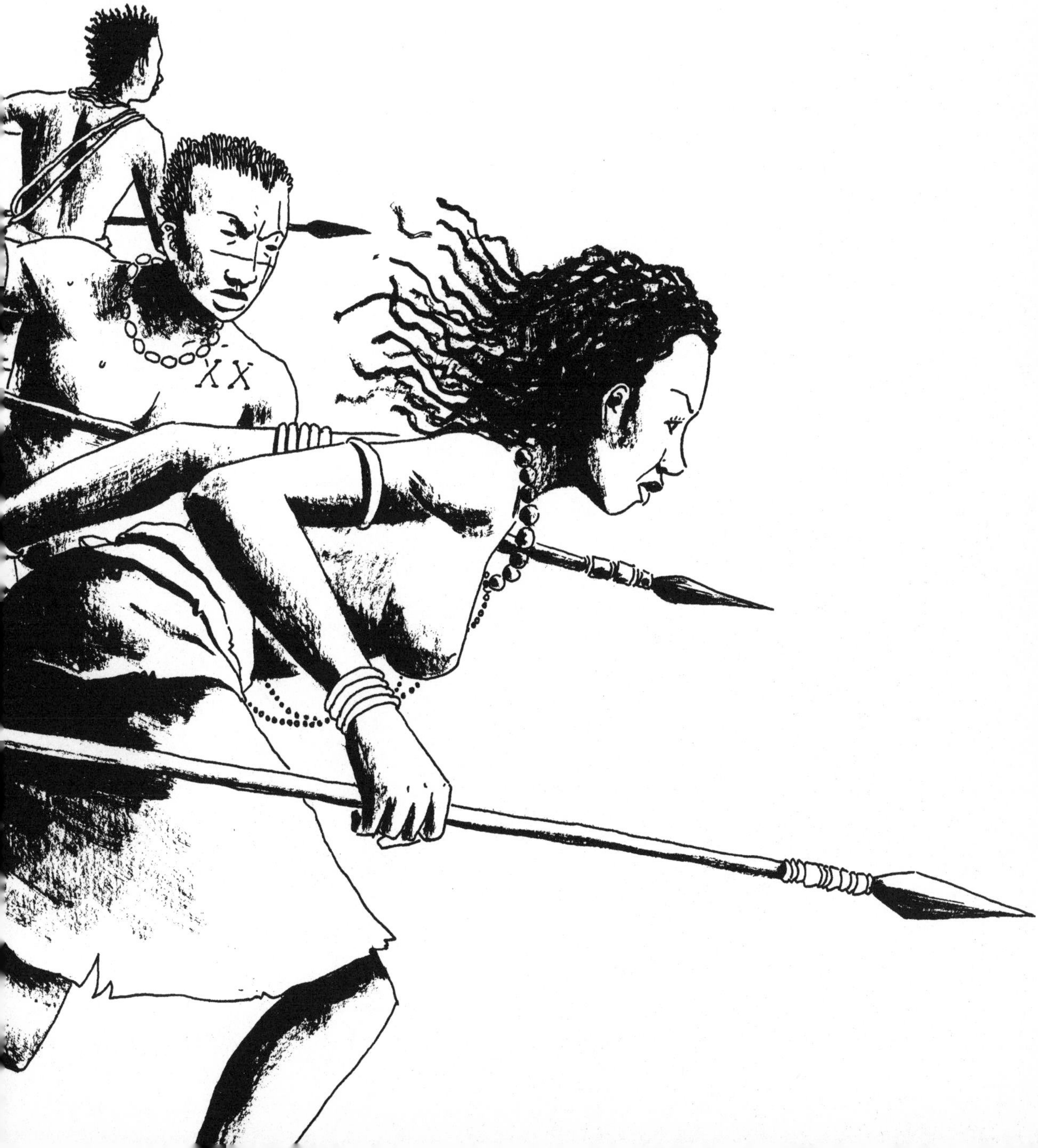

The blacks, knowing the intricate trails and hiding places, are setting traps, killing many who are on the move loaded with the sustenance they are carrying, and some even agilely flee, prolonging life but not eluding death, eventually suffering at the hands of hunger, that internal and irremediable enemy; and when our people come to the blacks' settlements, whether led there by a guide or arriving by chance, they find them to have fortified stockades and pits filled with sharp stakes for those who might fall into them; they defend themselves valiantly in that first sortie, resisting assault and warfare waged against them; when they are hard pressed, they retreat into Palmares, where they cannot be pursued because they alone know and can walk those paths and in that labyrinth of trees are alert that our weapons are seeking them. When the weary expedition withdrew, the blacks once more returned to occupy their dwelling places, work their lands, continue their plantings, and with greater violence and fury carry out their hostilities, as if in vengeance for our having disturbed them, the miserable inhabitants of these places paying in blood, farmland, and honor for the harm done to them by our soldiers.

—*Presumed to have been written by João Fernandes Vieira: letter sent to the Overseas Council, 1677*

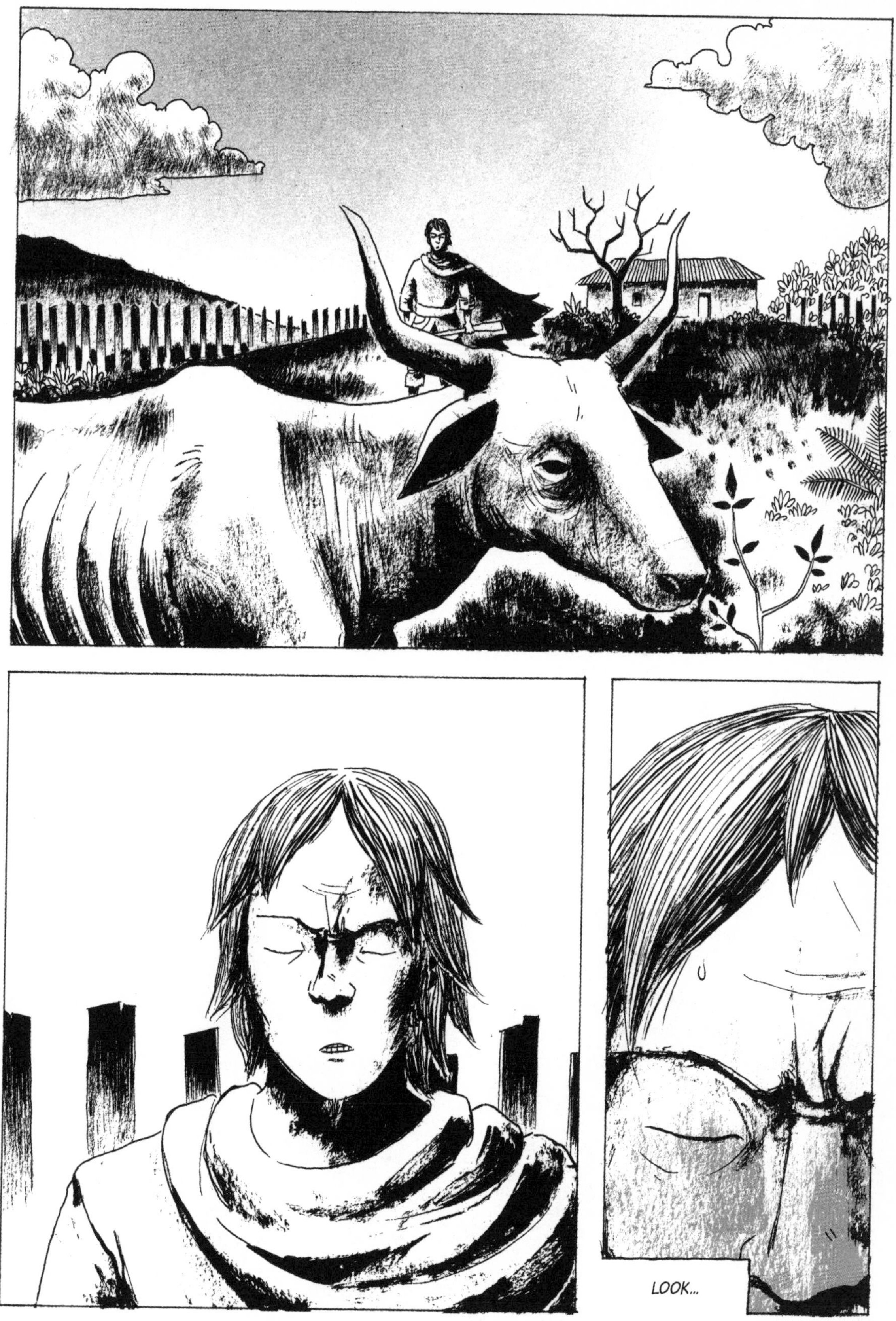
LOOK...

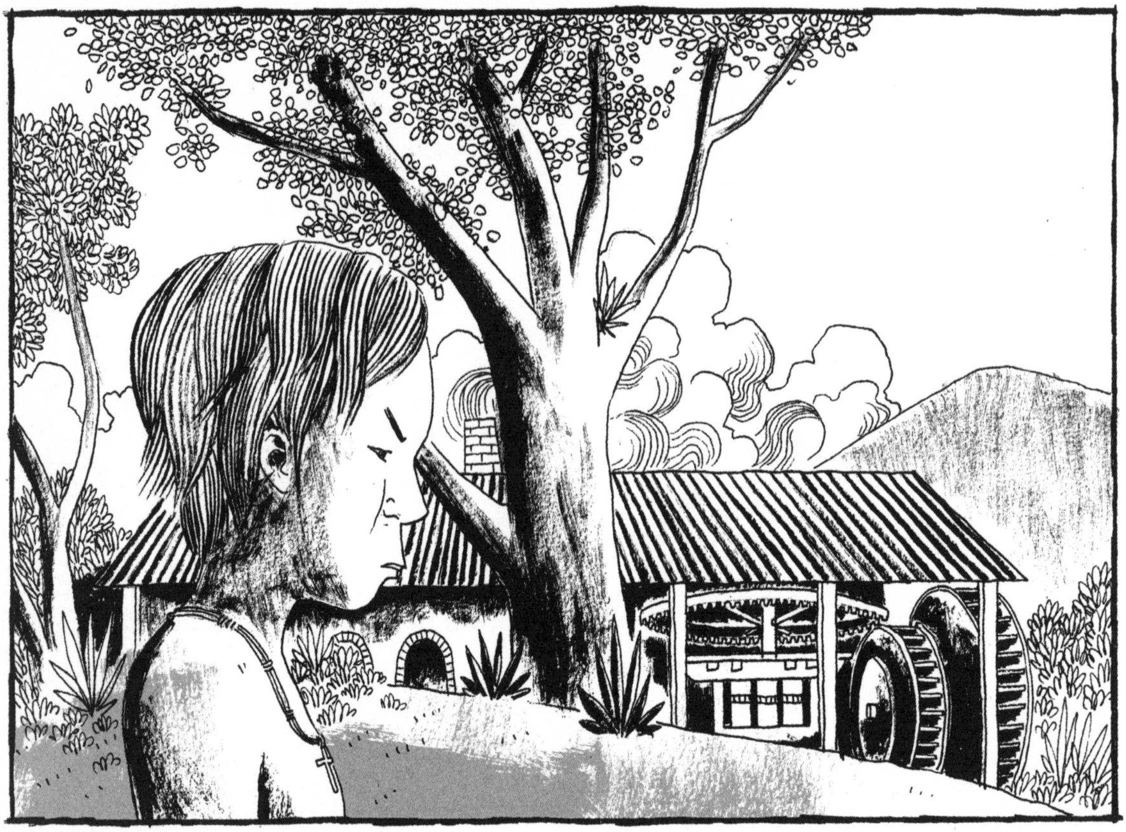

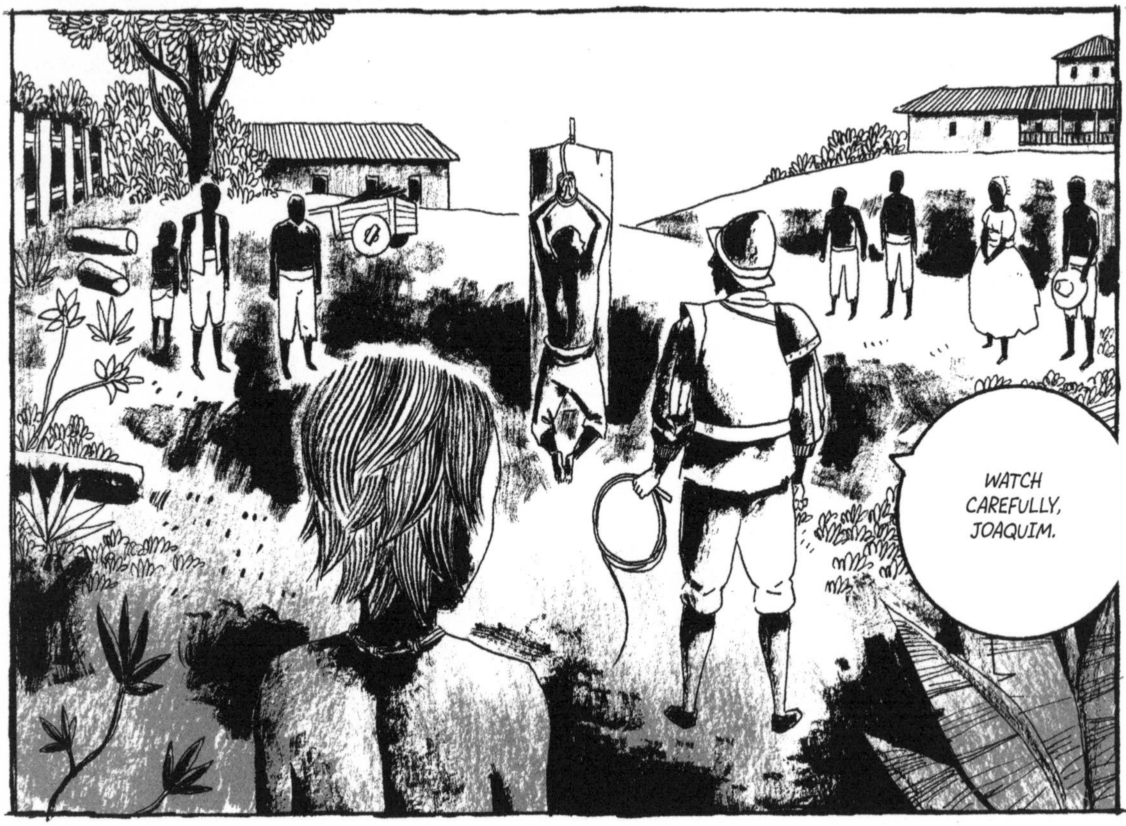
WATCH CAREFULLY, JOAQUIM.

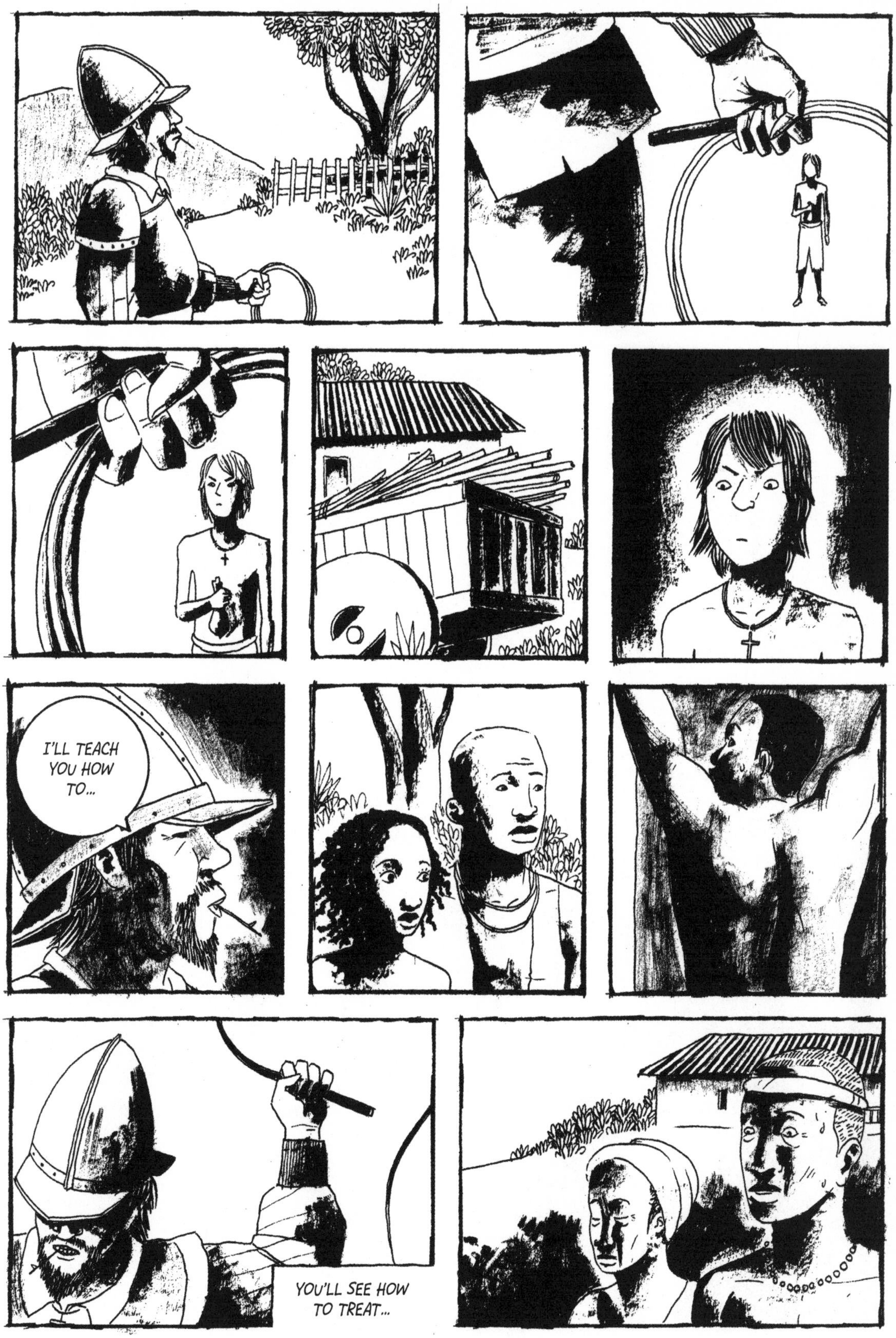
I'LL TEACH YOU HOW TO...
YOU'LL SEE HOW TO TREAT...

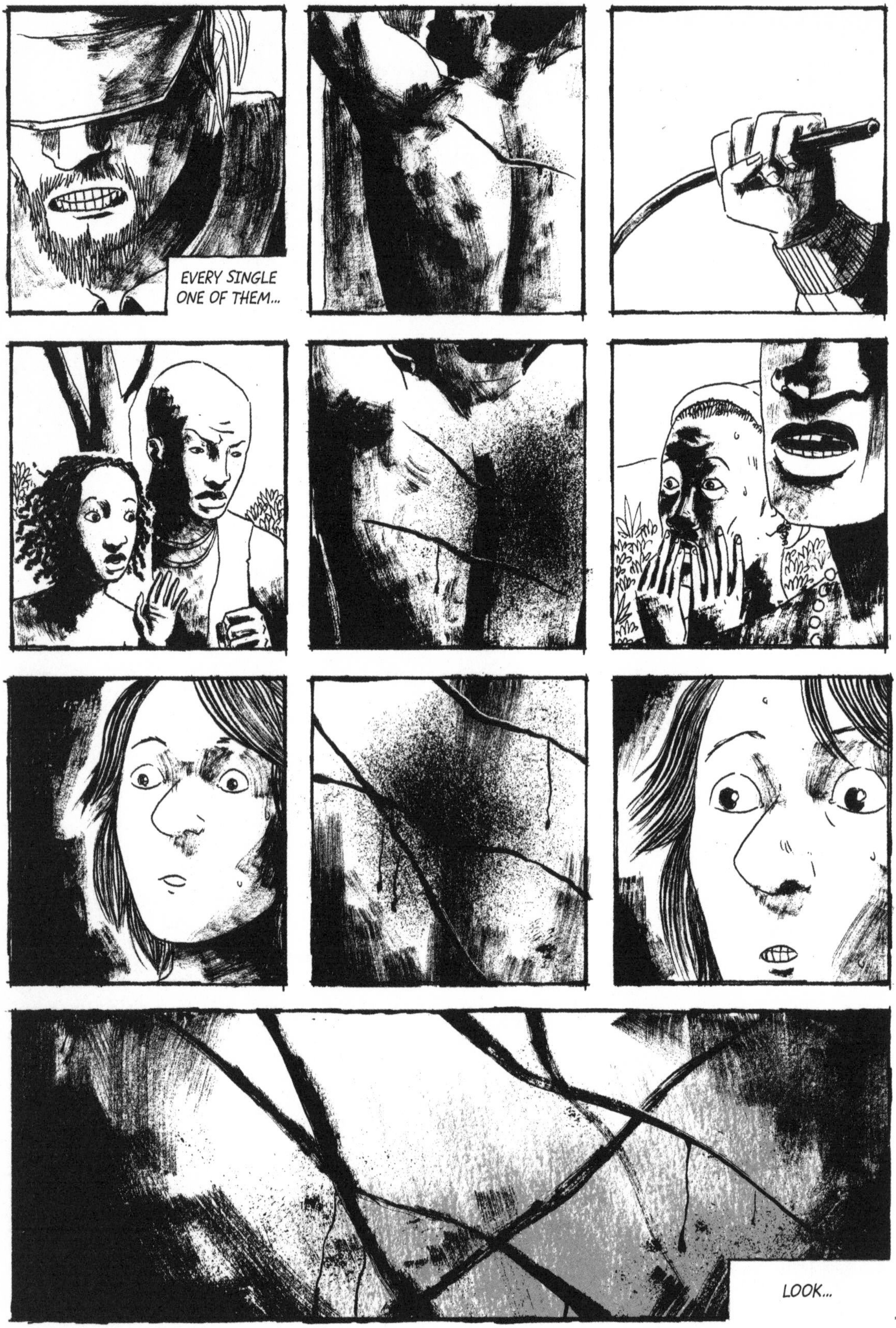
EVERY SINGLE ONE OF THEM...
LOOK...

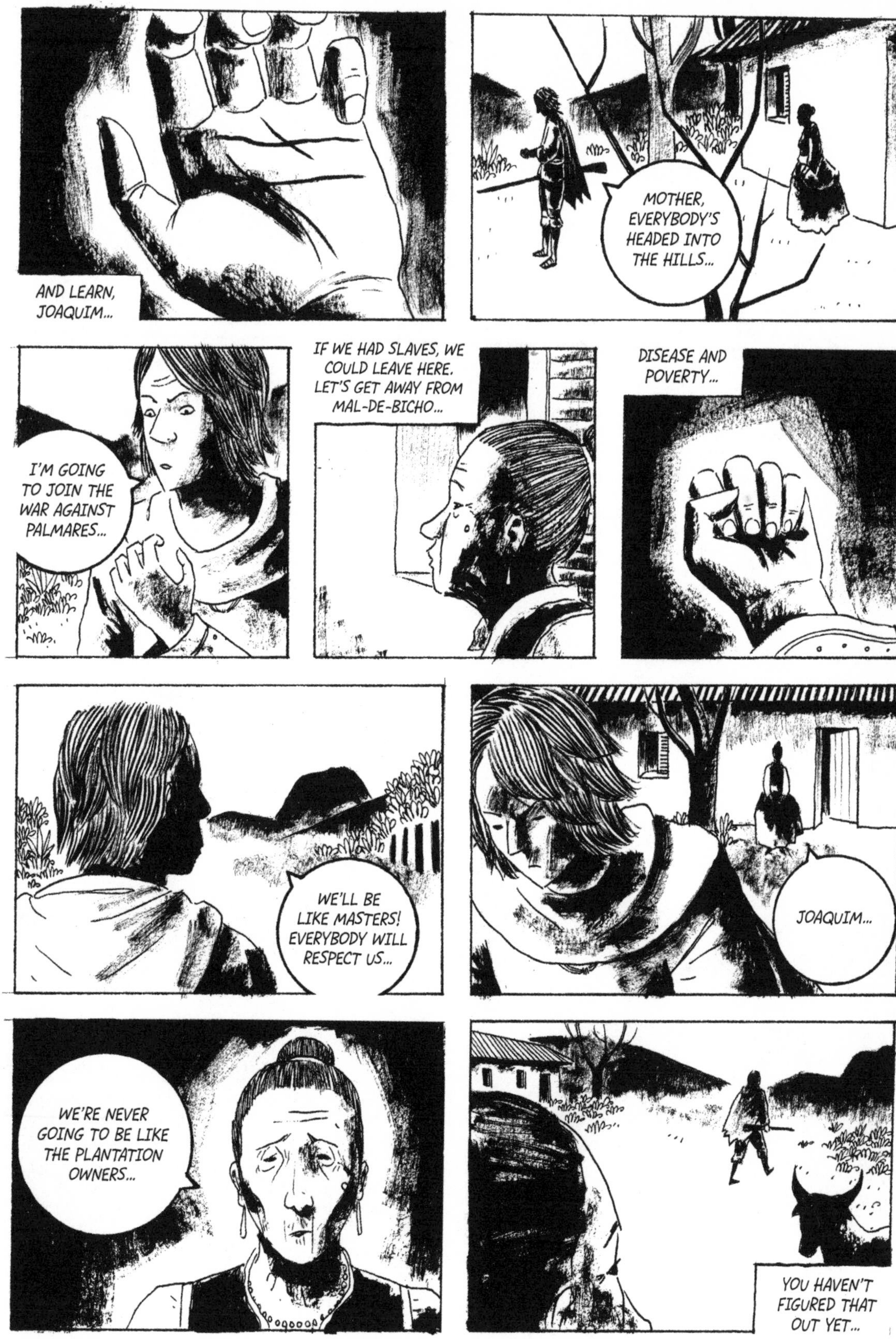

AND LEARN, JOAQUIM...
MOTHER, EVERYBODY'S HEADED INTO THE HILLS...
I'M GOING TO JOIN THE WAR AGAINST PALMARES...
IF WE HAD SLAVES, WE COULD LEAVE HERE. LET'S GET AWAY FROM MAL-DE-BICHO...
DISEASE AND POVERTY...
WE'LL BE LIKE MASTERS! EVERYBODY WILL RESPECT US...
JOAQUIM...
WE'RE NEVER GOING TO BE LIKE THE PLANTATION OWNERS...
YOU HAVEN'T FIGURED THAT OUT YET...

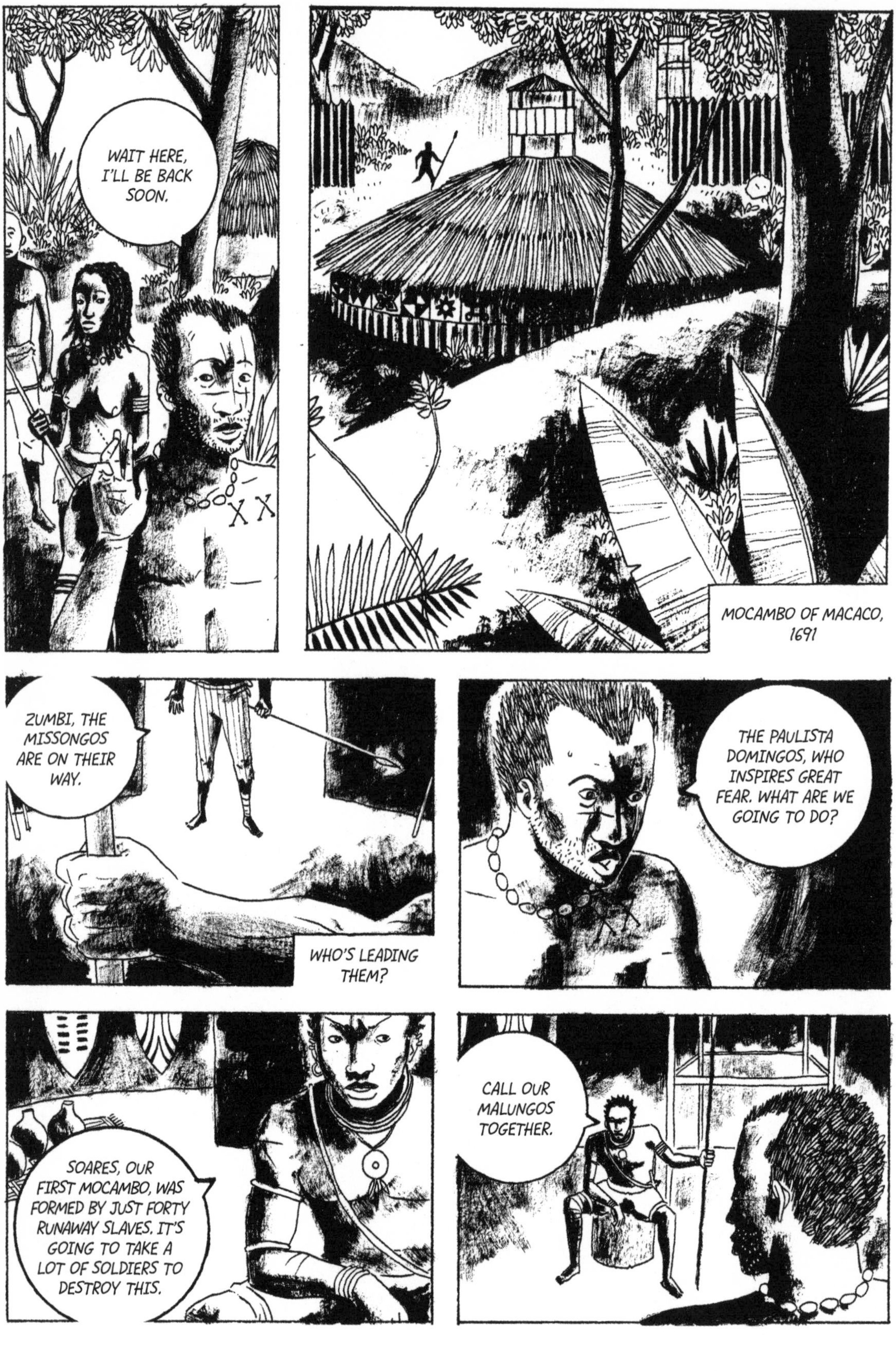

WAIT HERE, I'LL BE BACK SOON.
MOCAMBO OF MACACO, 1691
ZUMBI, THE MISSONGOS ARE ON THEIR WAY.
WHO'S LEADING THEM?
THE PAULISTA DOMINGOS, WHO INSPIRES GREAT FEAR. WHAT ARE WE GOING TO DO?
SOARES, OUR FIRST MOCAMBO, WAS FORMED BY JUST FORTY RUNAWAY SLAVES. IT'S GOING TO TAKE A LOT OF SOLDIERS TO DESTROY THIS.
CALL OUR MALUNGOS TOGETHER.

THE SLAVES IN THIS CAPTAINCY HAVE NEVER BEEN SO INSOLENT!

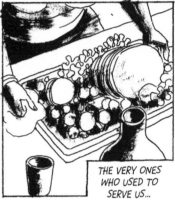

THE VERY ONES WHO USED TO SERVE US...

ARE WREAKING HAVOC TODAY! THEY'RE ATTACKING US!

WE EVEN SIGNED A TREATY WITH THOSE IDIOTS IN CUCAÚ.

WE MADE PEOPLE FREE WHO SHOULD BE SLAVES!

GENTLEMEN, IF YOU'LL ALLOW ME...

THE TOWN OF CUCAÚ HAS BEEN DESTROYED. GANGA ZUMBA WAS KILLED.

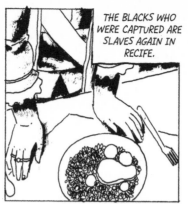

THE BLACKS WHO WERE CAPTURED ARE SLAVES AGAIN IN RECIFE.

AS WE SPEAK, SOLDIERS ARE BUILDING A CAMP UP IN THE HILLS TO DO AWAY WITH PALMARES FOR GOOD.

BUT... GOVERNOR, WHO GOES INTO THE HILLS? PAULISTAS! SAVAGES!

THEY RAID US AND STEAL OUR LIVESTOCK! THEY'RE WORSE THAN THE PALMARISTAS!

GENTLEMEN, TO FIGHT THE PALMARISTAS...

WE NEED A MAN WHO'S FEARED IN THESE PARTS.

BUT I GUARANTEE YOU, PALMARES...

SOONER OR LATER...

WILL BE OURS!

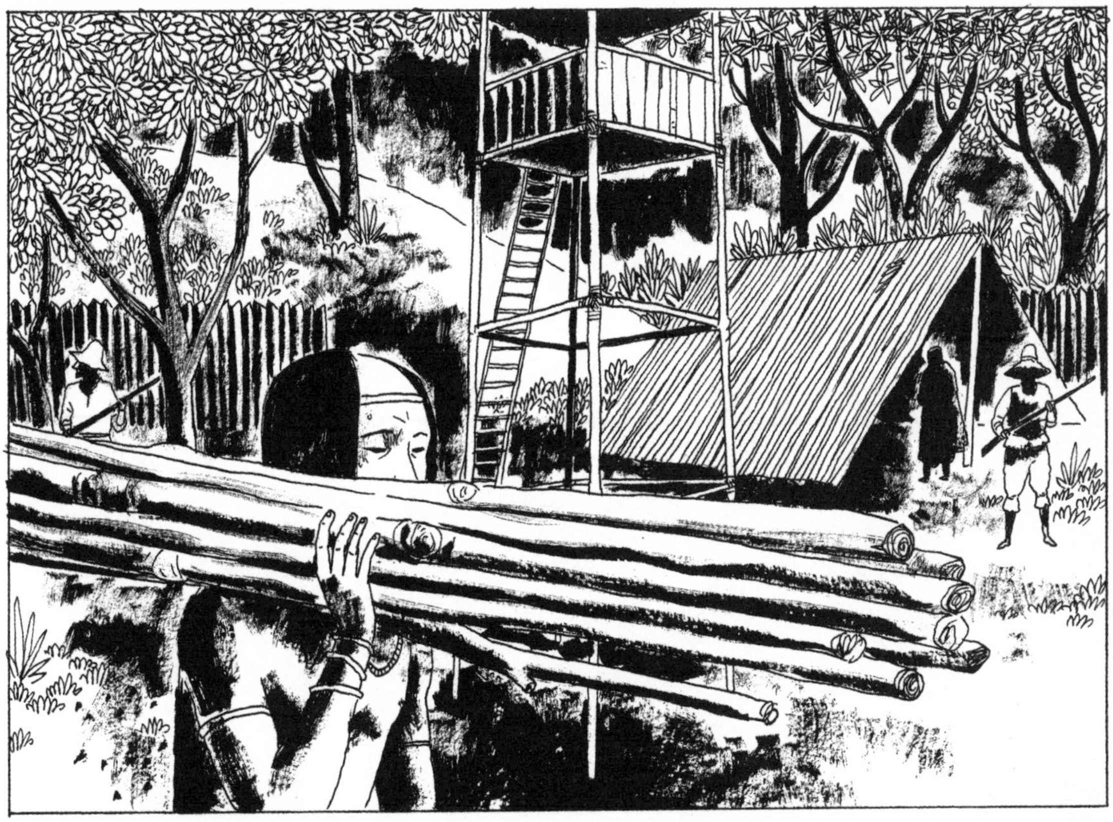

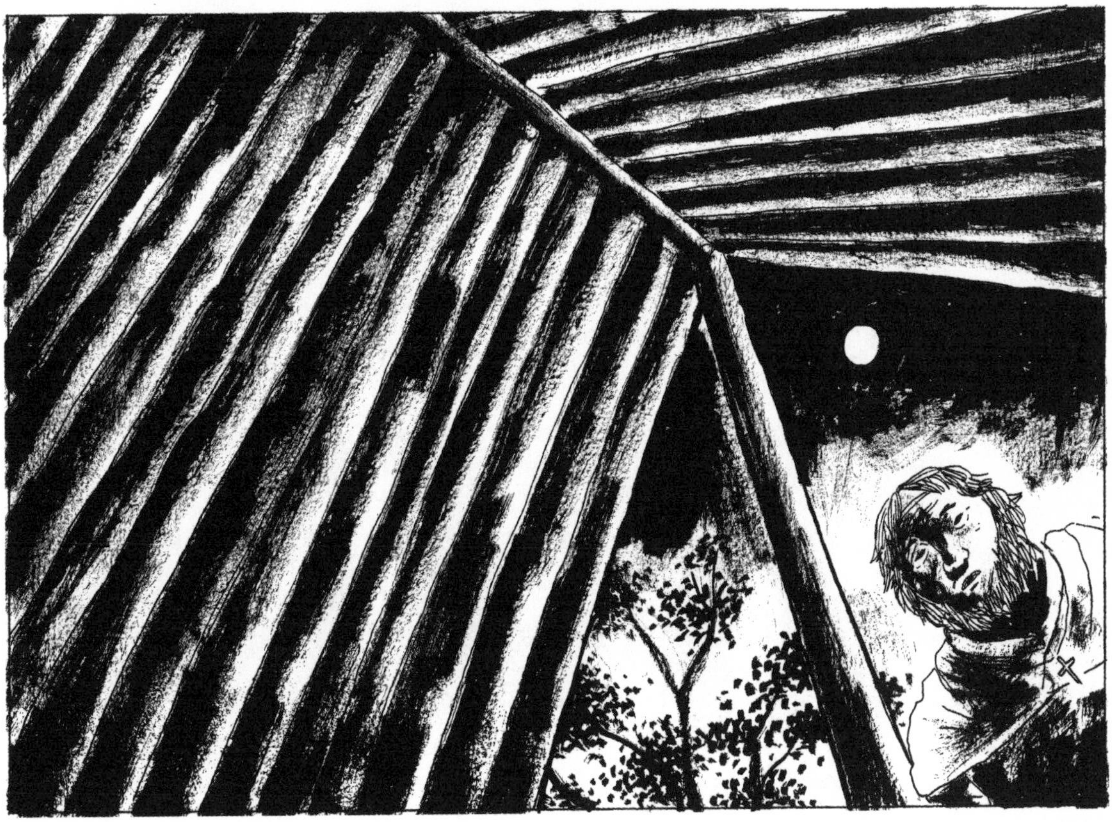

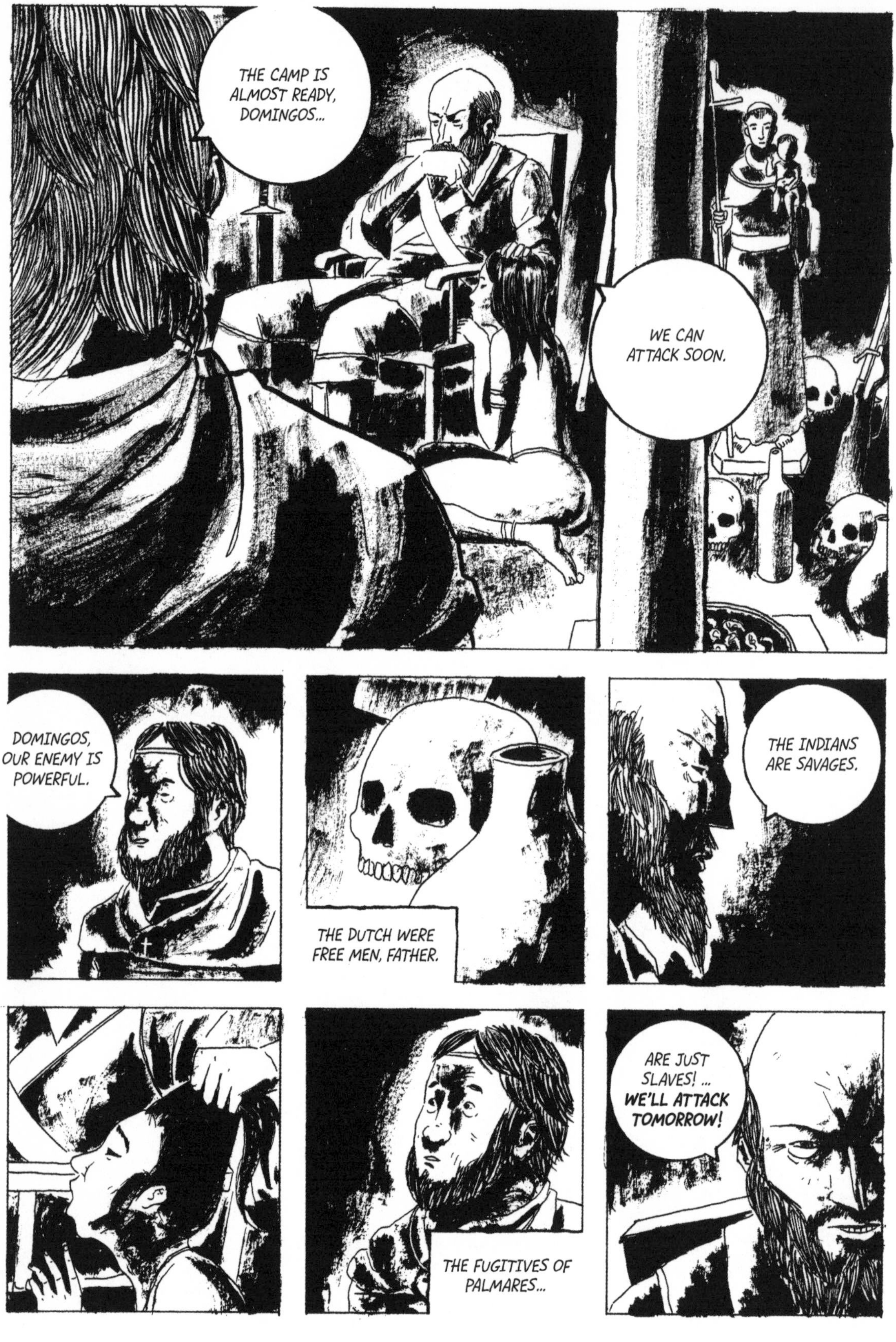
THE CAMP IS ALMOST READY, DOMINGOS...
WE CAN ATTACK SOON.
DOMINGOS, OUR ENEMY IS POWERFUL.
THE DUTCH WERE FREE MEN, FATHER.
THE INDIANS ARE SAVAGES.
THE FUGITIVES OF PALMARES...
ARE JUST SLAVES! ... **WE'LL ATTACK TOMORROW!**

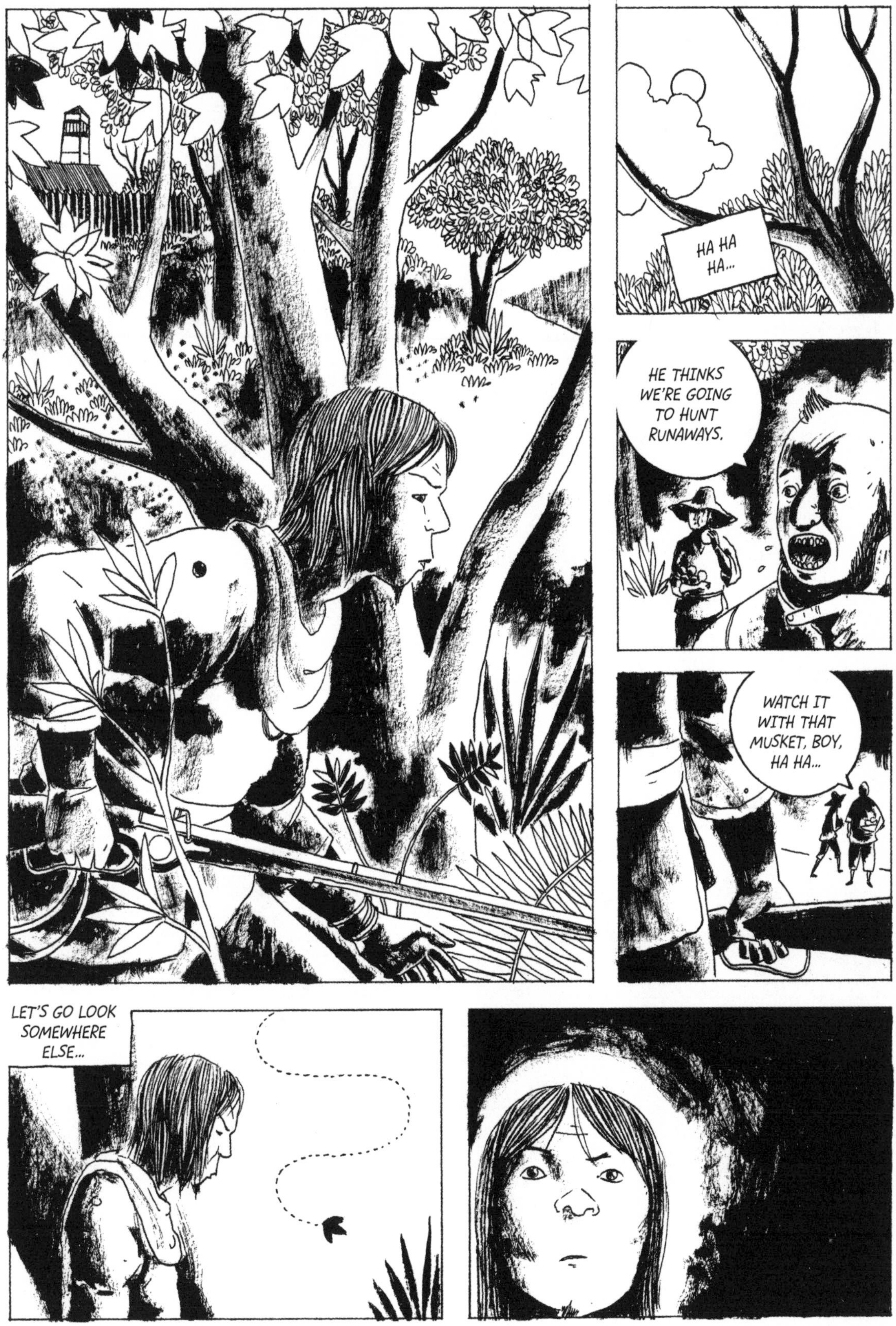
HA HA HA...
HE THINKS WE'RE GOING TO HUNT RUNAWAYS.
WATCH IT WITH THAT MUSKET, BOY, HA HA...
LET'S GO LOOK SOMEWHERE ELSE...

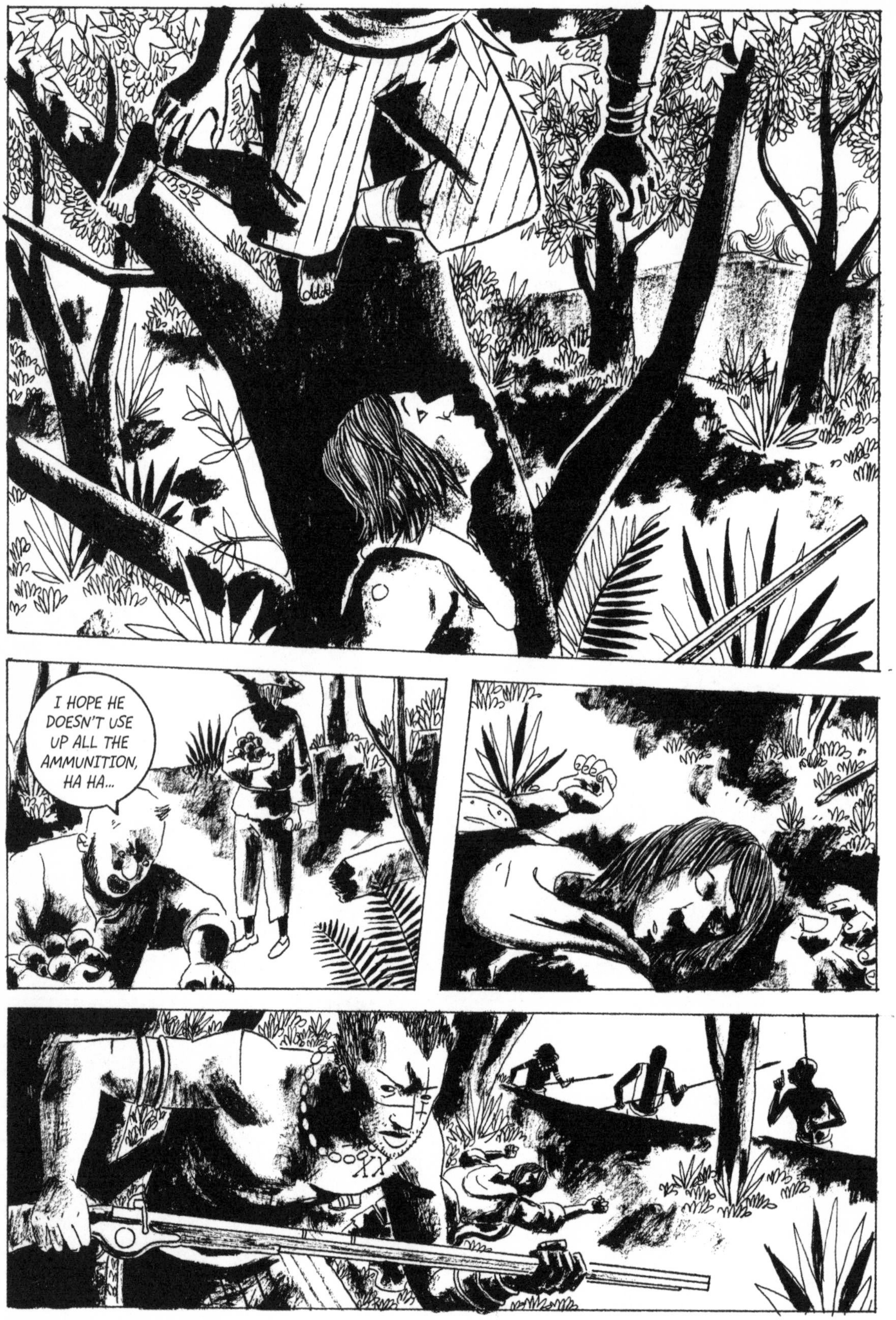
I HOPE HE DOESN'T USE UP ALL THE AMMUNITION, HA HA...

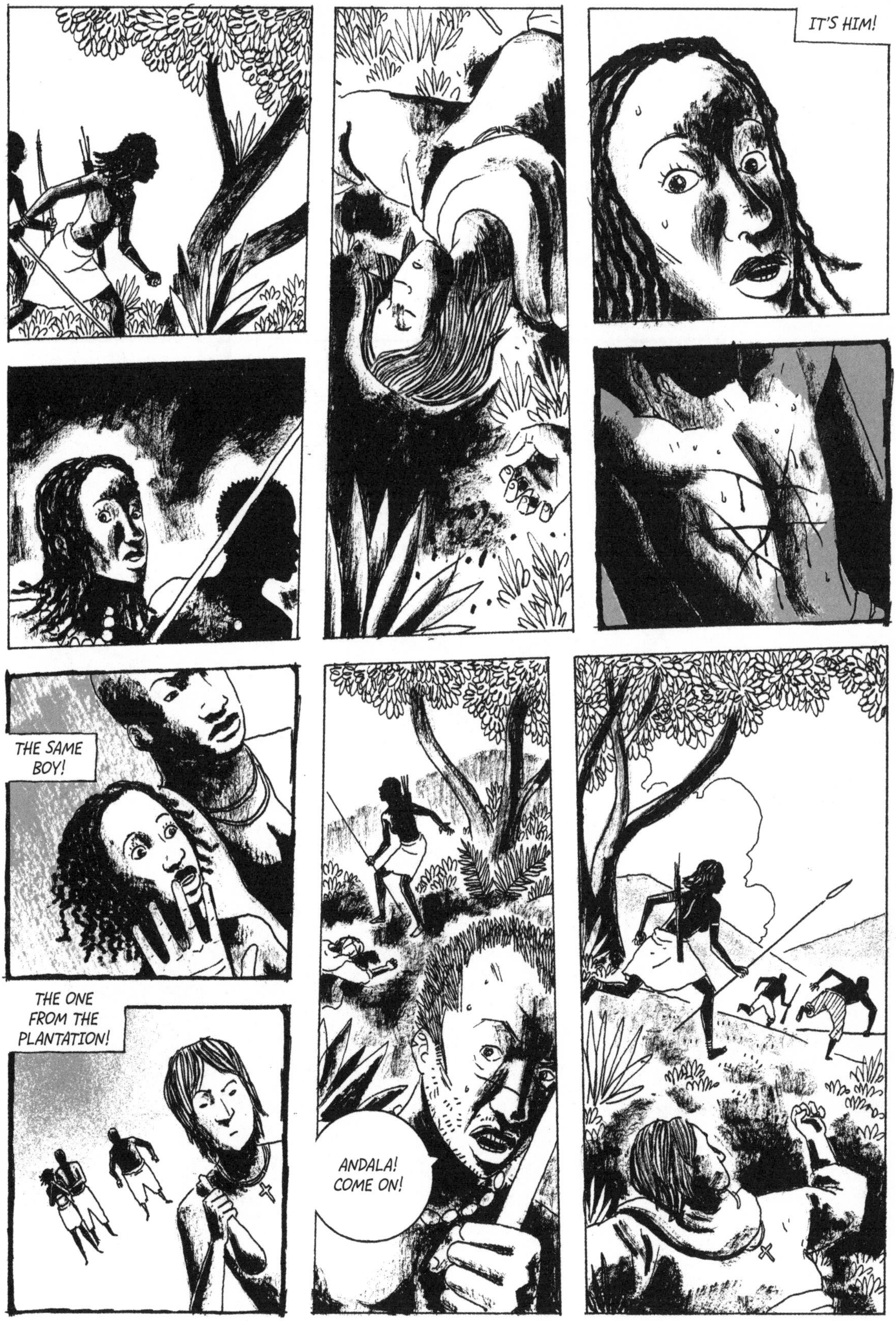
IT'S HIM!
THE SAME BOY!
THE ONE FROM THE PLANTATION!
ANDALA! COME ON!

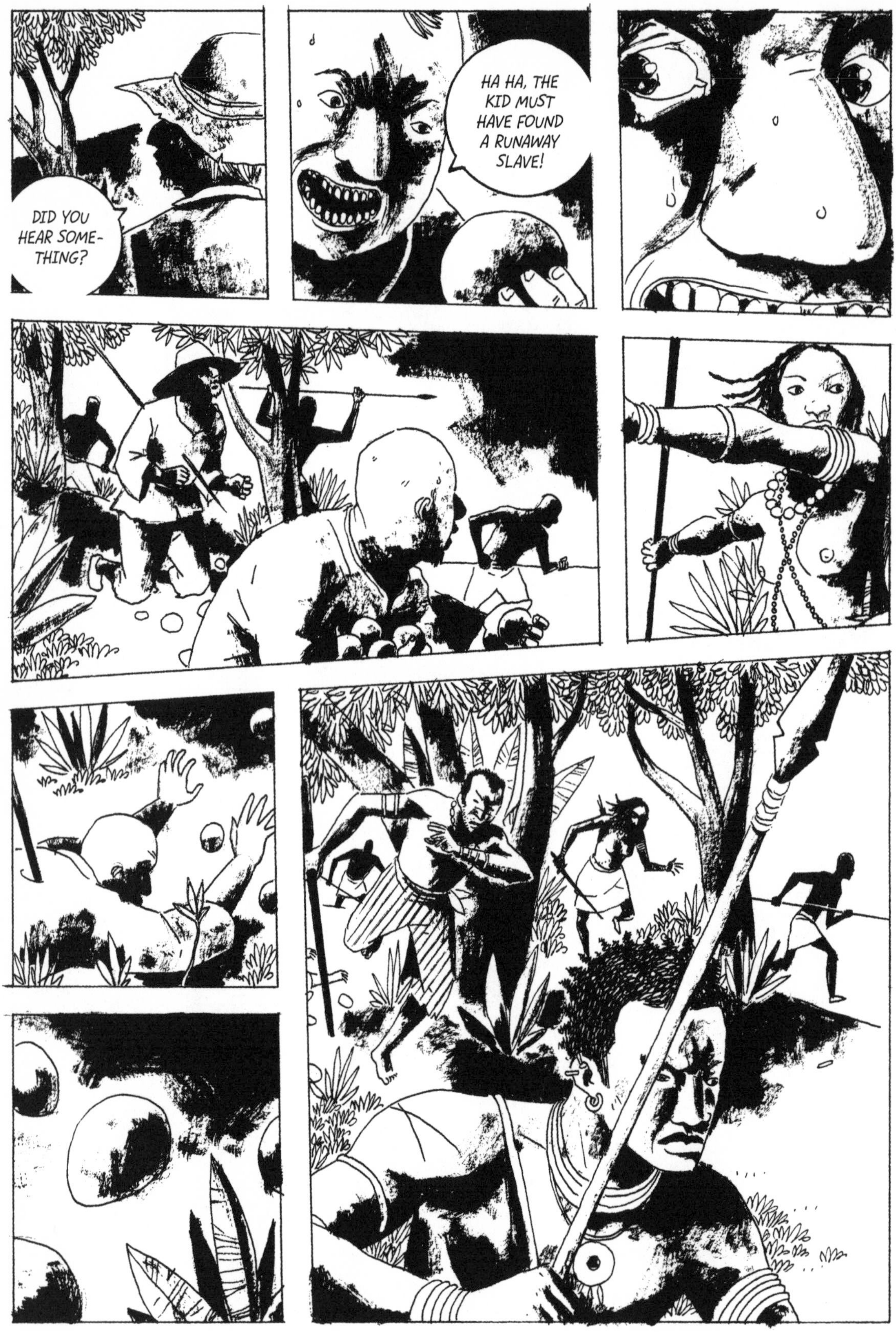
DID YOU HEAR SOME-THING?
HA HA, THE KID MUST HAVE FOUND A RUNAWAY SLAVE!

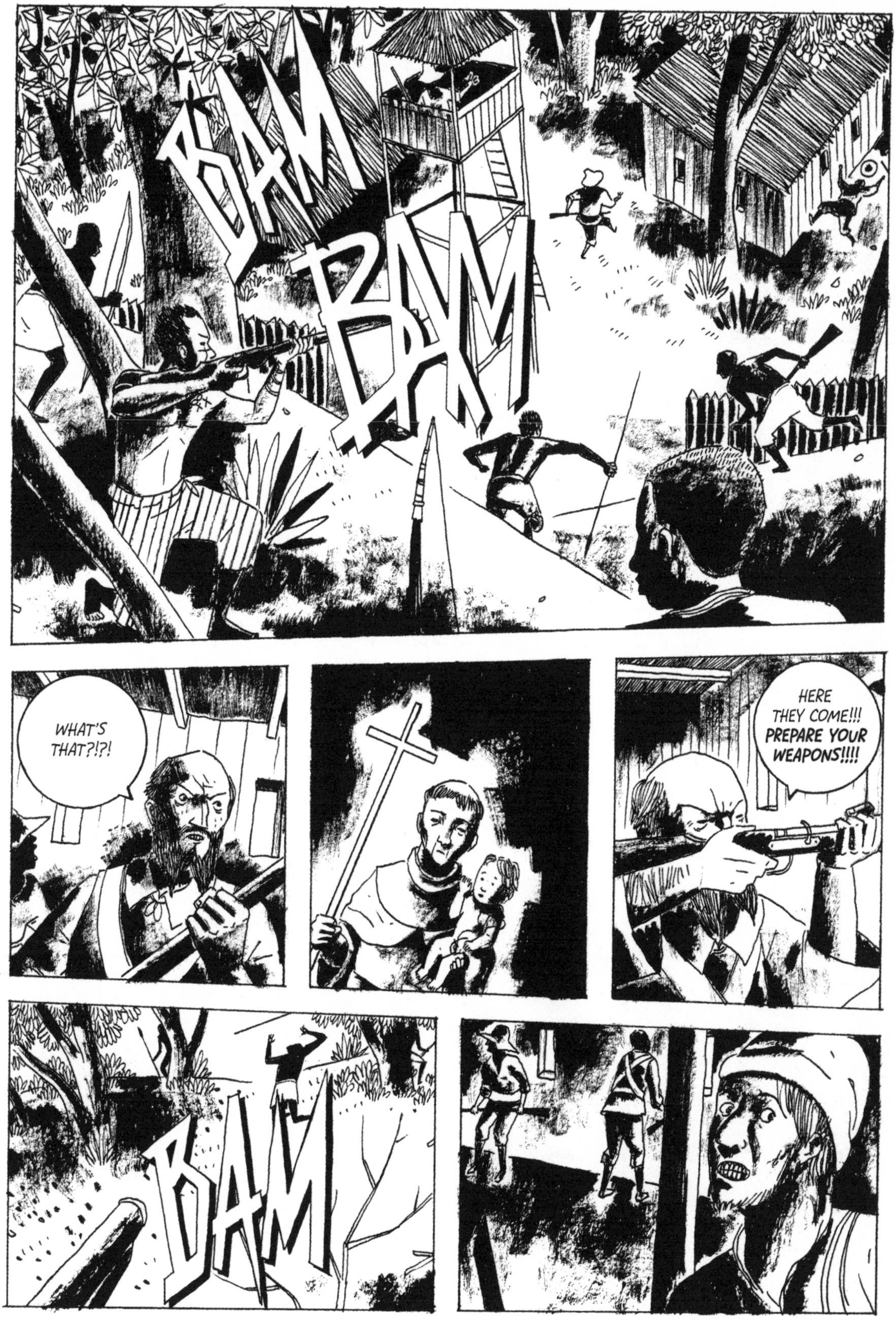
BAM
BAM
BAM
WHAT'S THAT?!?!
HERE THEY COME!!! PREPARE YOUR WEAPONS!!!!
BAM

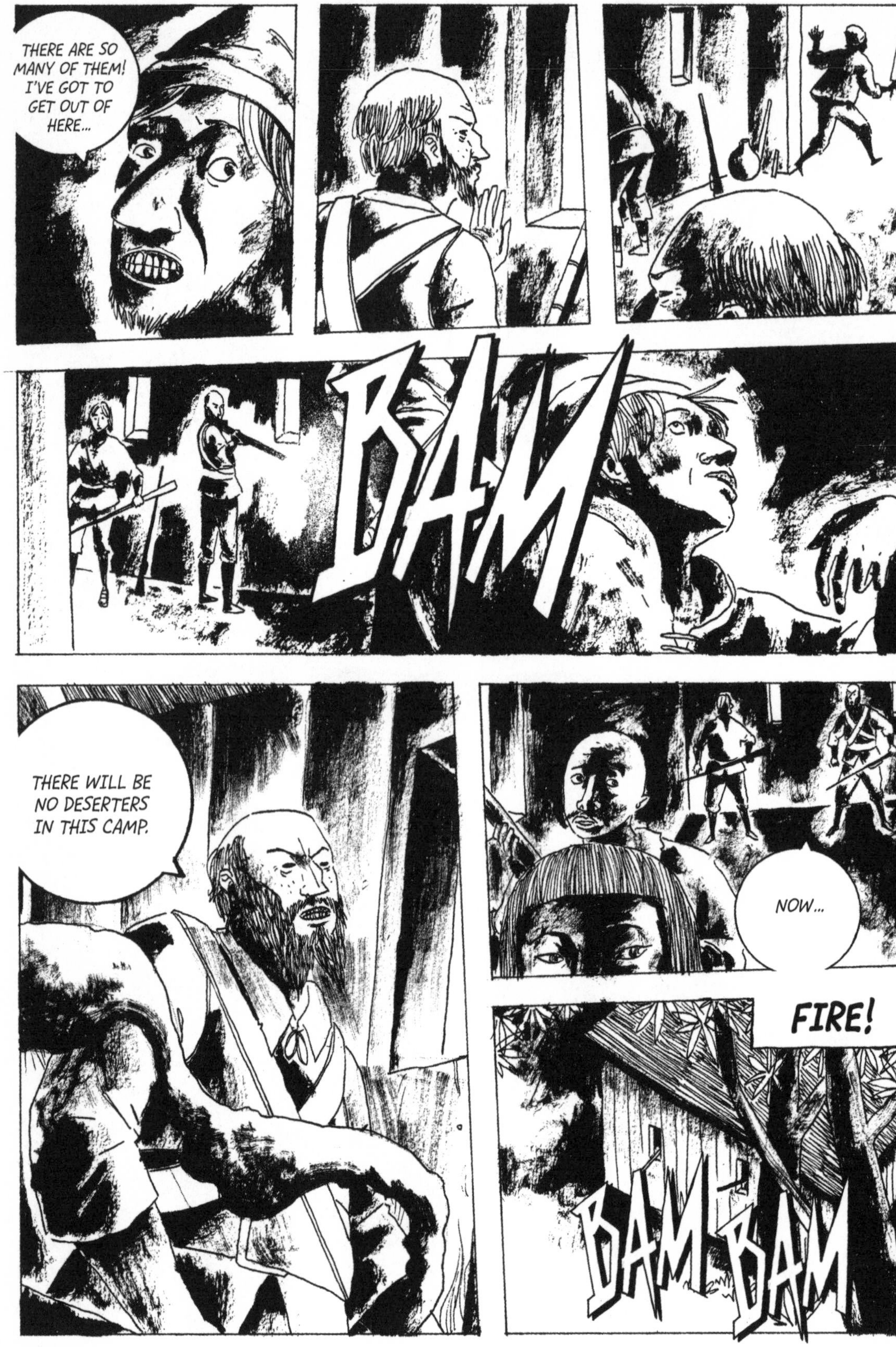
THERE ARE SO MANY OF THEM! I'VE GOT TO GET OUT OF HERE...
BAM
THERE WILL BE NO DESERTERS IN THIS CAMP.
NOW...
FIRE!
BAM BAM

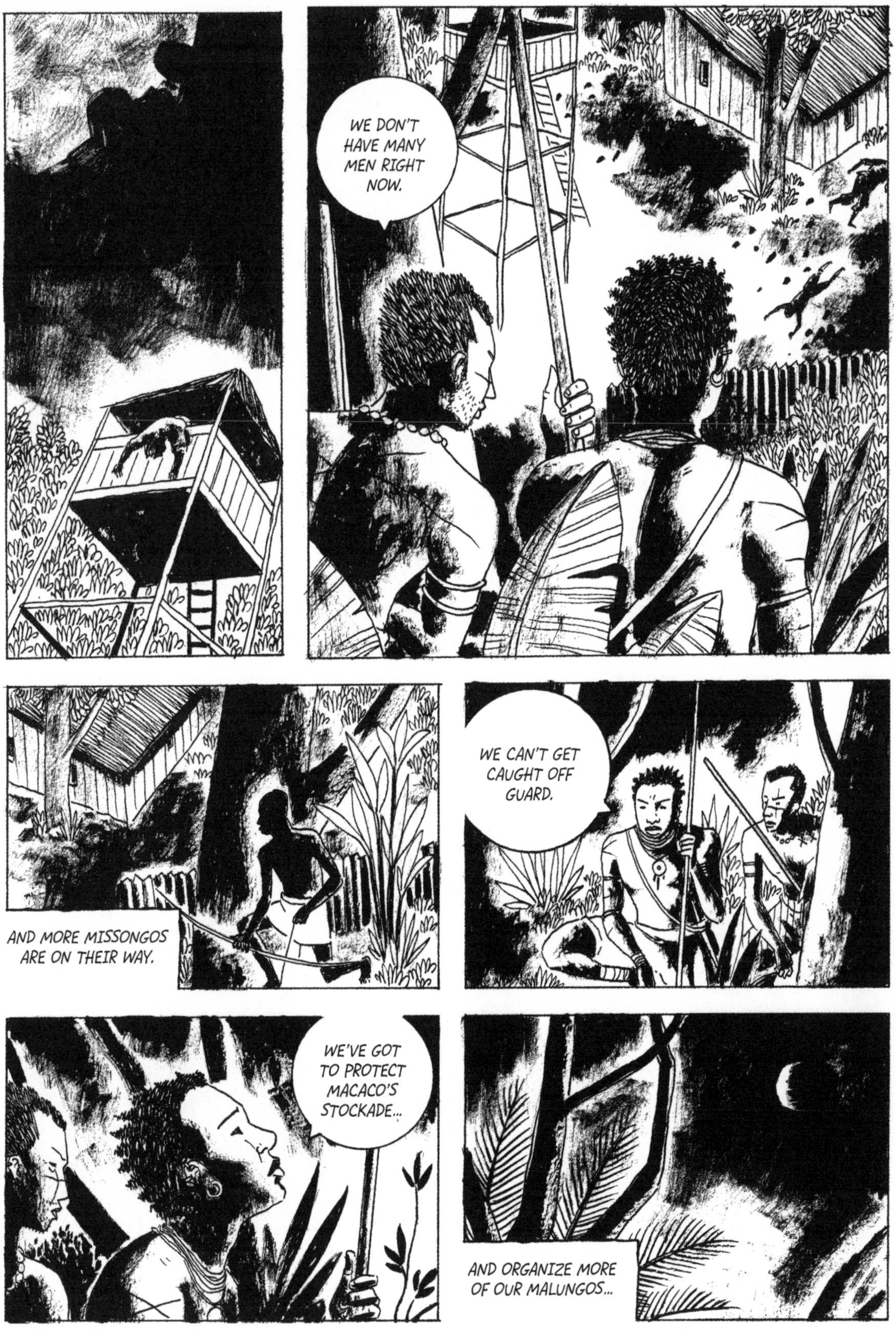
WE DON'T HAVE MANY MEN RIGHT NOW.
AND MORE MISSONGOS ARE ON THEIR WAY.
WE CAN'T GET CAUGHT OFF GUARD.
WE'VE GOT TO PROTECT MACACO'S STOCKADE...
AND ORGANIZE MORE OF OUR MALUNGOS...

THE SALT...

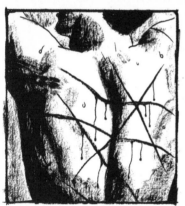

THROW THAT SALT, JOAQUIM!

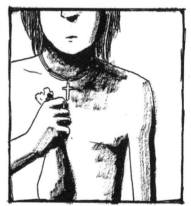

WE WON'T LET HIM **FORGET** THESE MARKS ANYTIME SOON...

COME ON, THROW THE...

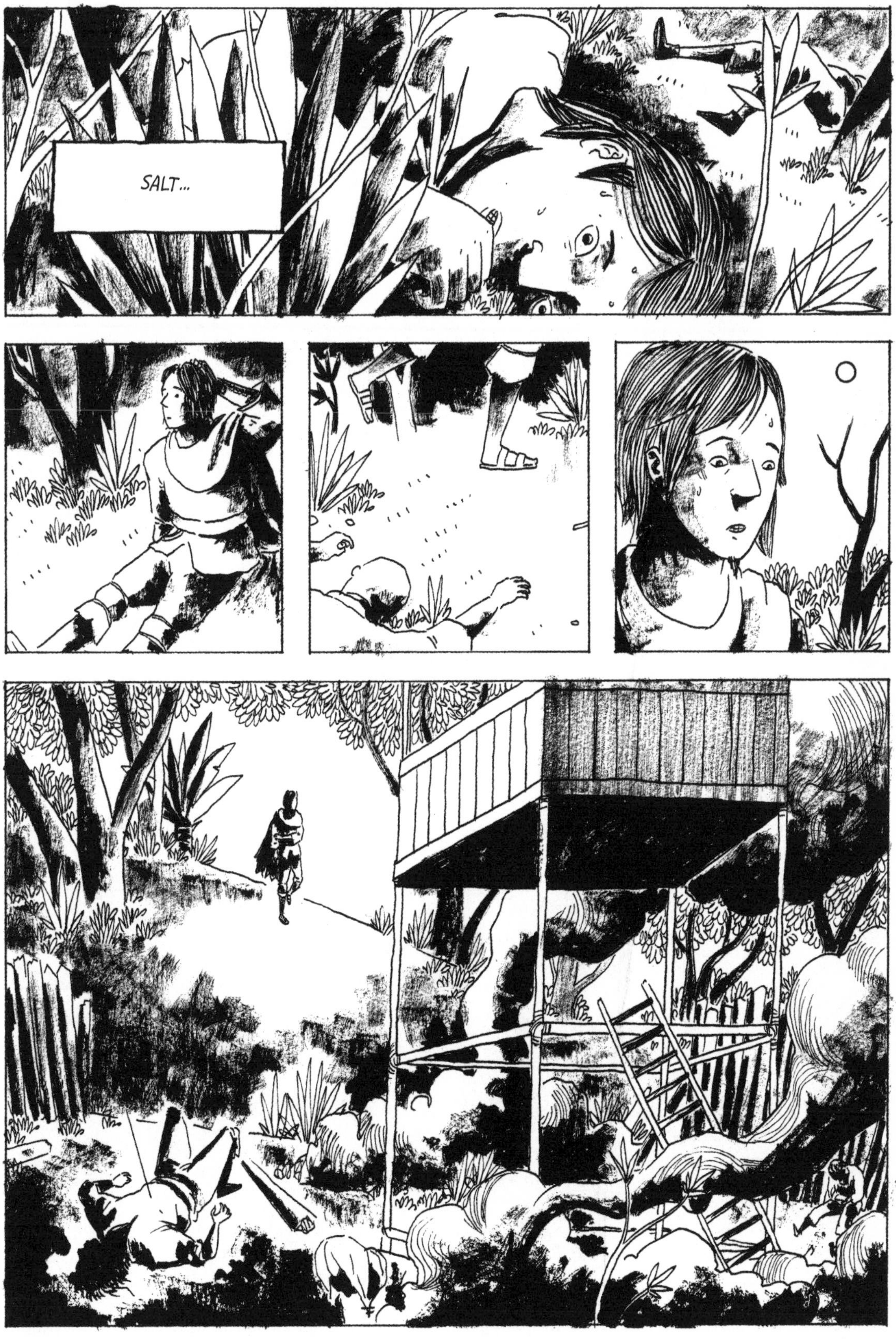
SALT...

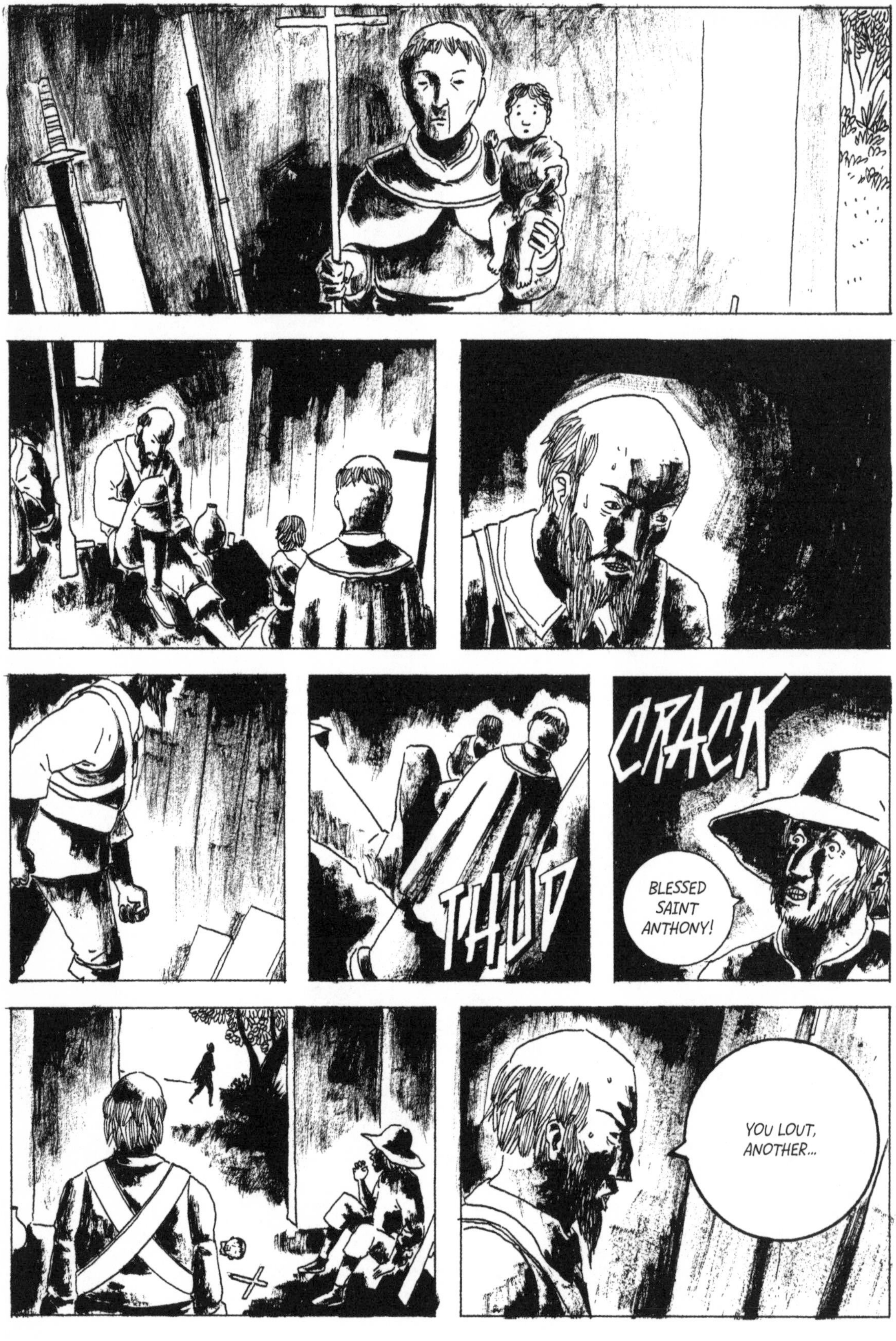
CRACK
THUD
BLESSED SAINT ANTHONY!
YOU LOUT, ANOTHER...

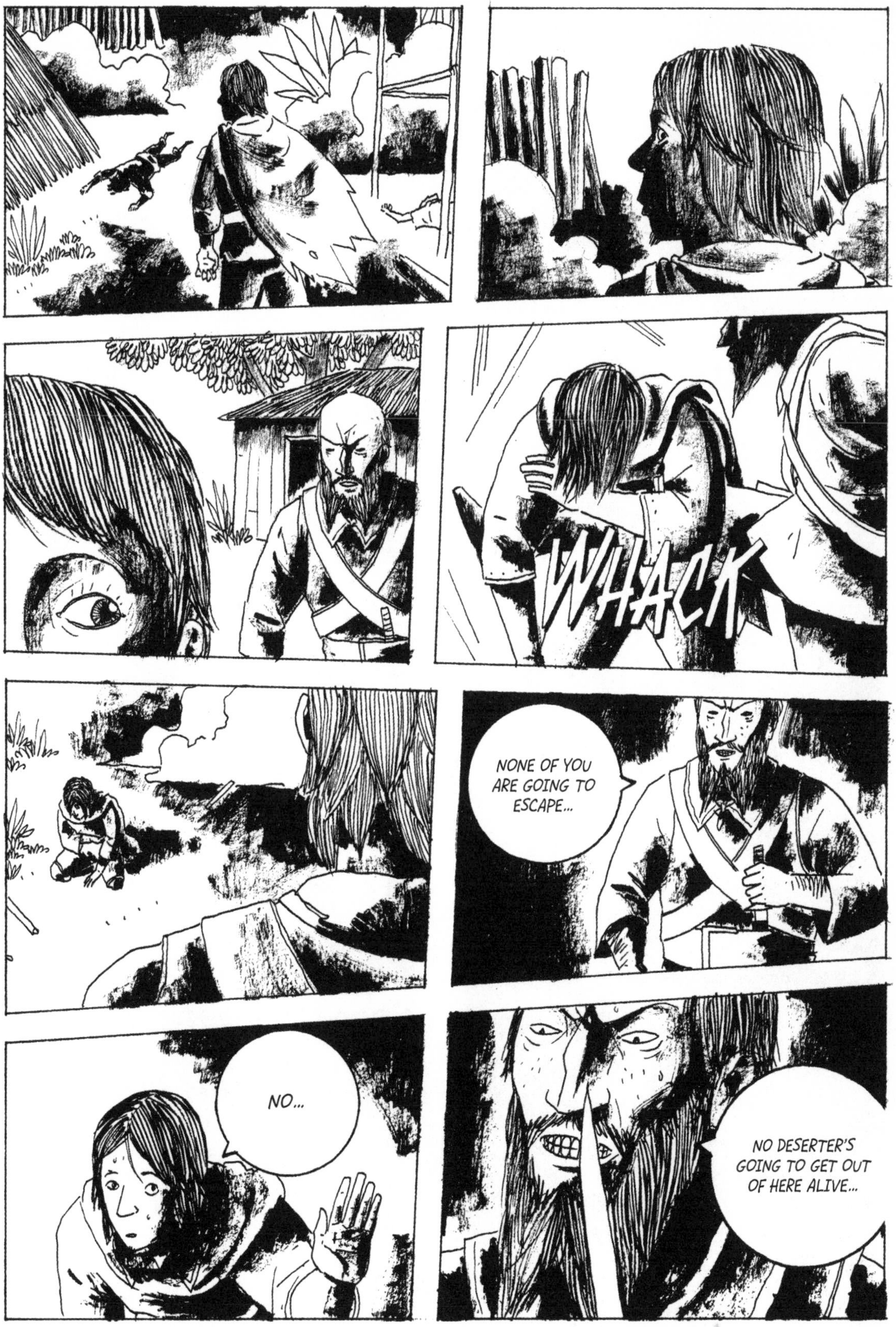
WHACK
NONE OF YOU ARE GOING TO ESCAPE...
NO...
NO DESERTER'S GOING TO GET OUT OF HERE ALIVE...

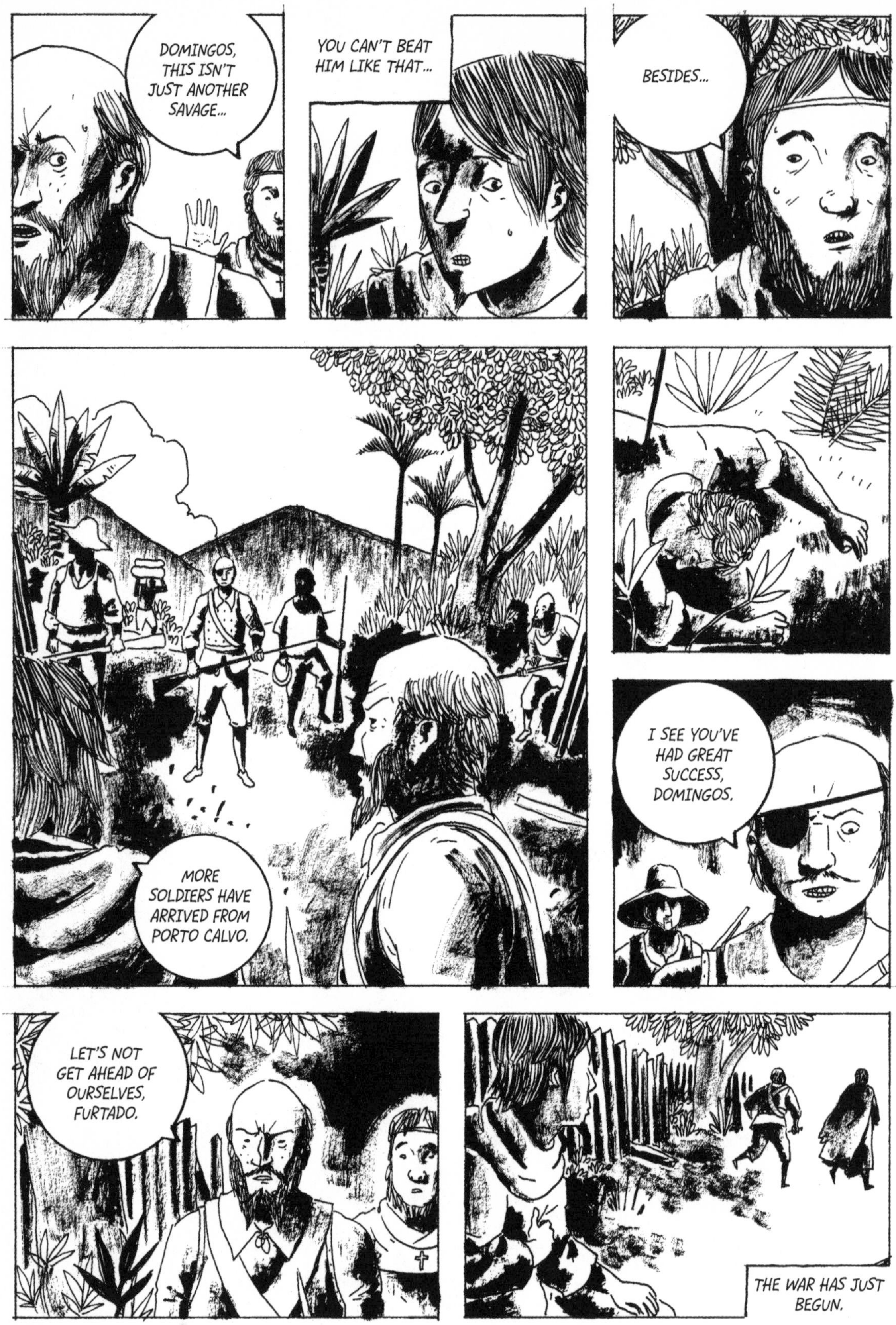
DOMINGOS, THIS ISN'T JUST ANOTHER SAVAGE...
YOU CAN'T BEAT HIM LIKE THAT...
BESIDES...
MORE SOLDIERS HAVE ARRIVED FROM PORTO CALVO.
I SEE YOU'VE HAD GREAT SUCCESS, DOMINGOS.
LET'S NOT GET AHEAD OF OURSELVES, FURTADO.
THE WAR HAS JUST BEGUN.

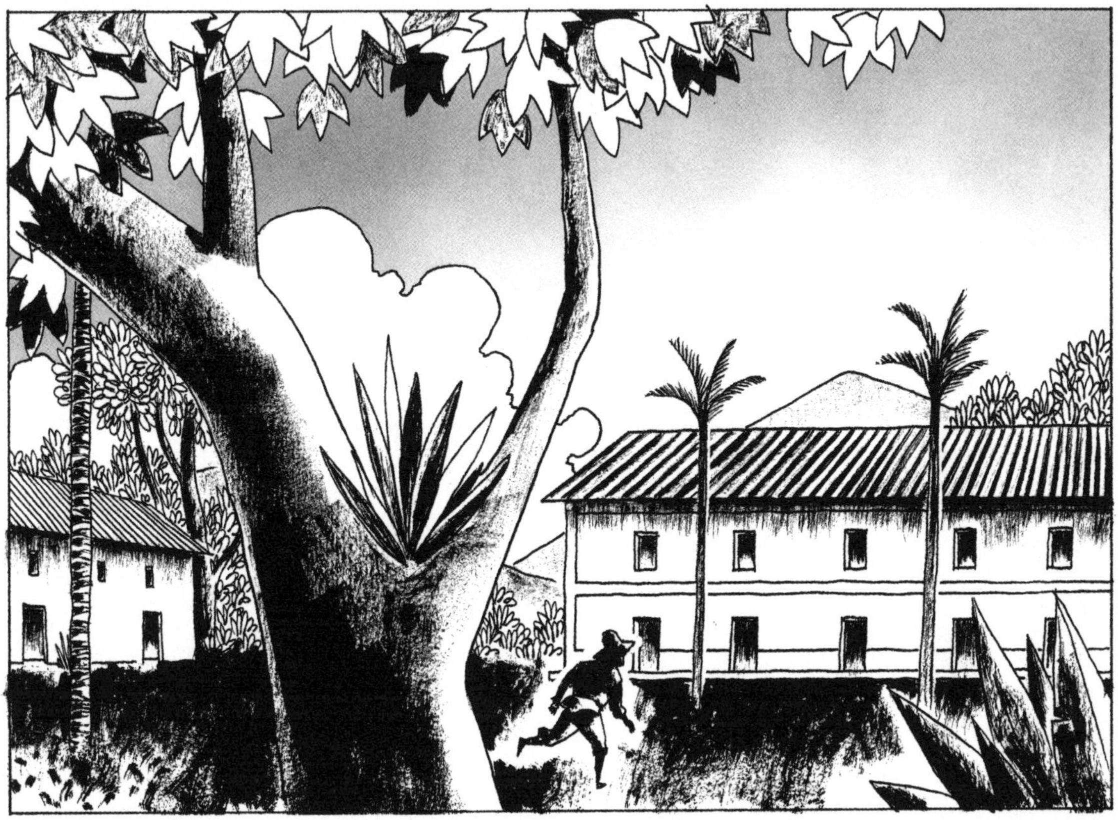

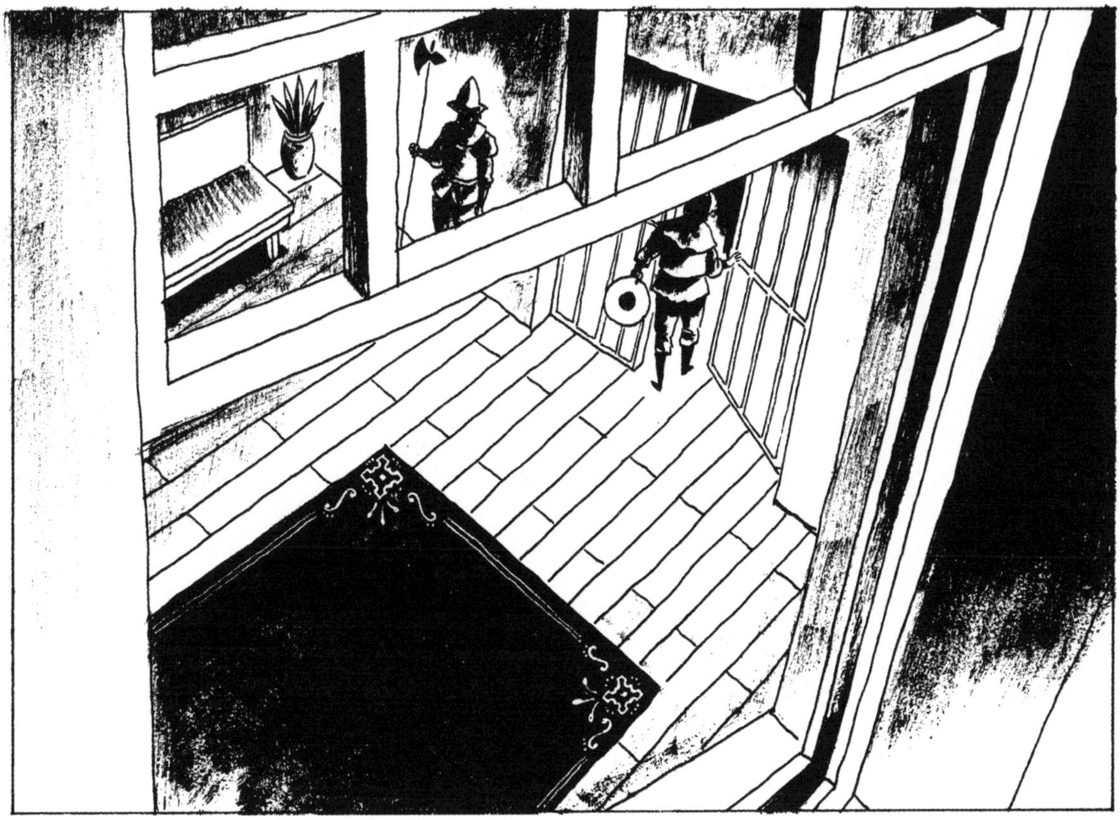

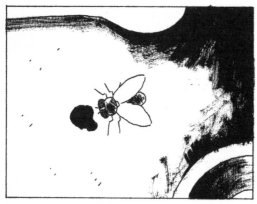

THE SOLDIERS RETREATED?!?

THAT'S NOT POSSIBLE!

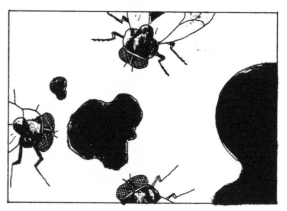

JOAQUIM...

YOU'VE GOT TO LEARN HOW THINGS WORK, BOY...

GIVE ME THAT SALT.

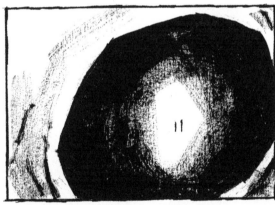

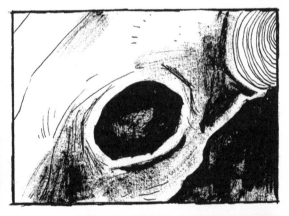

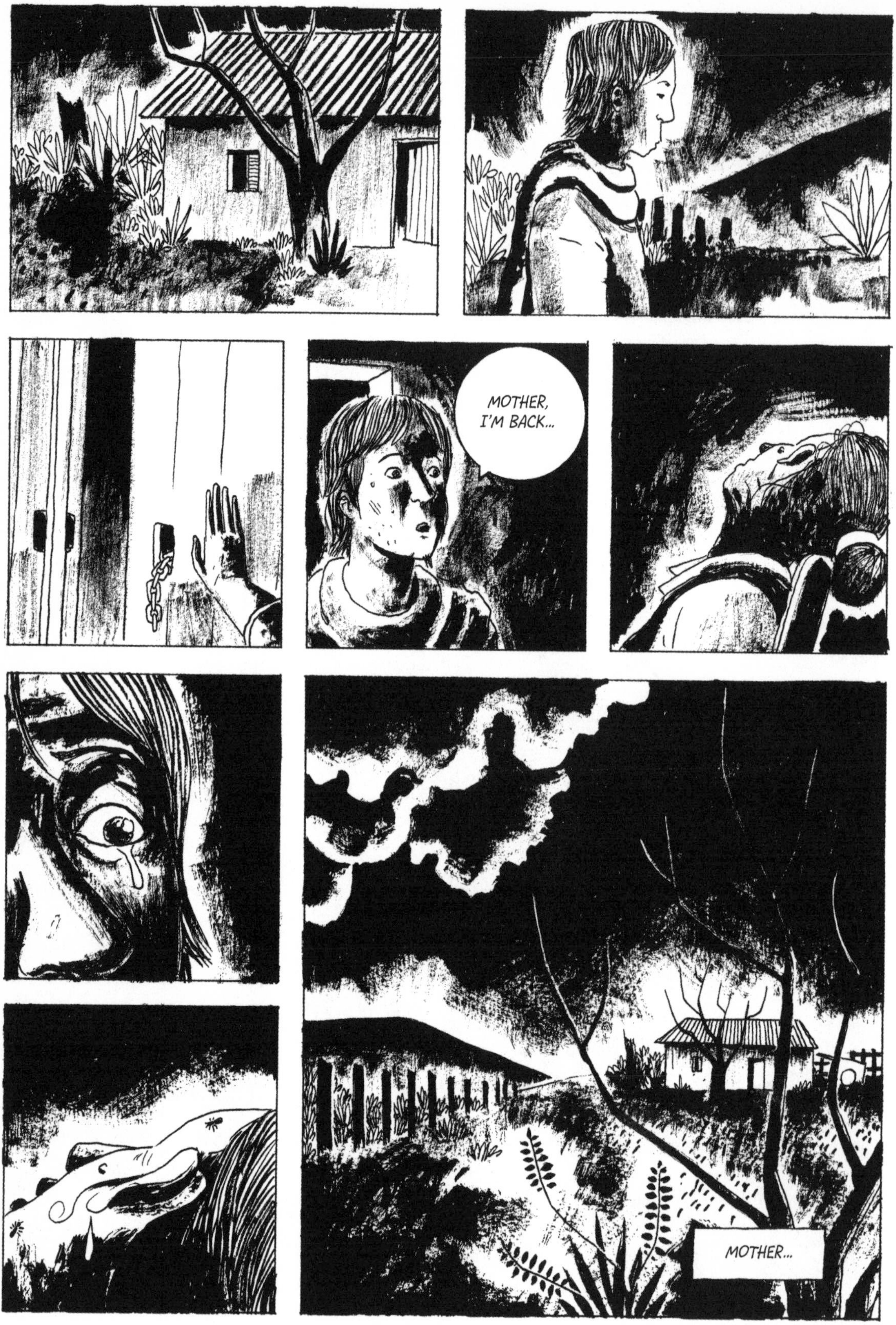
MOTHER, I'M BACK...
MOTHER...

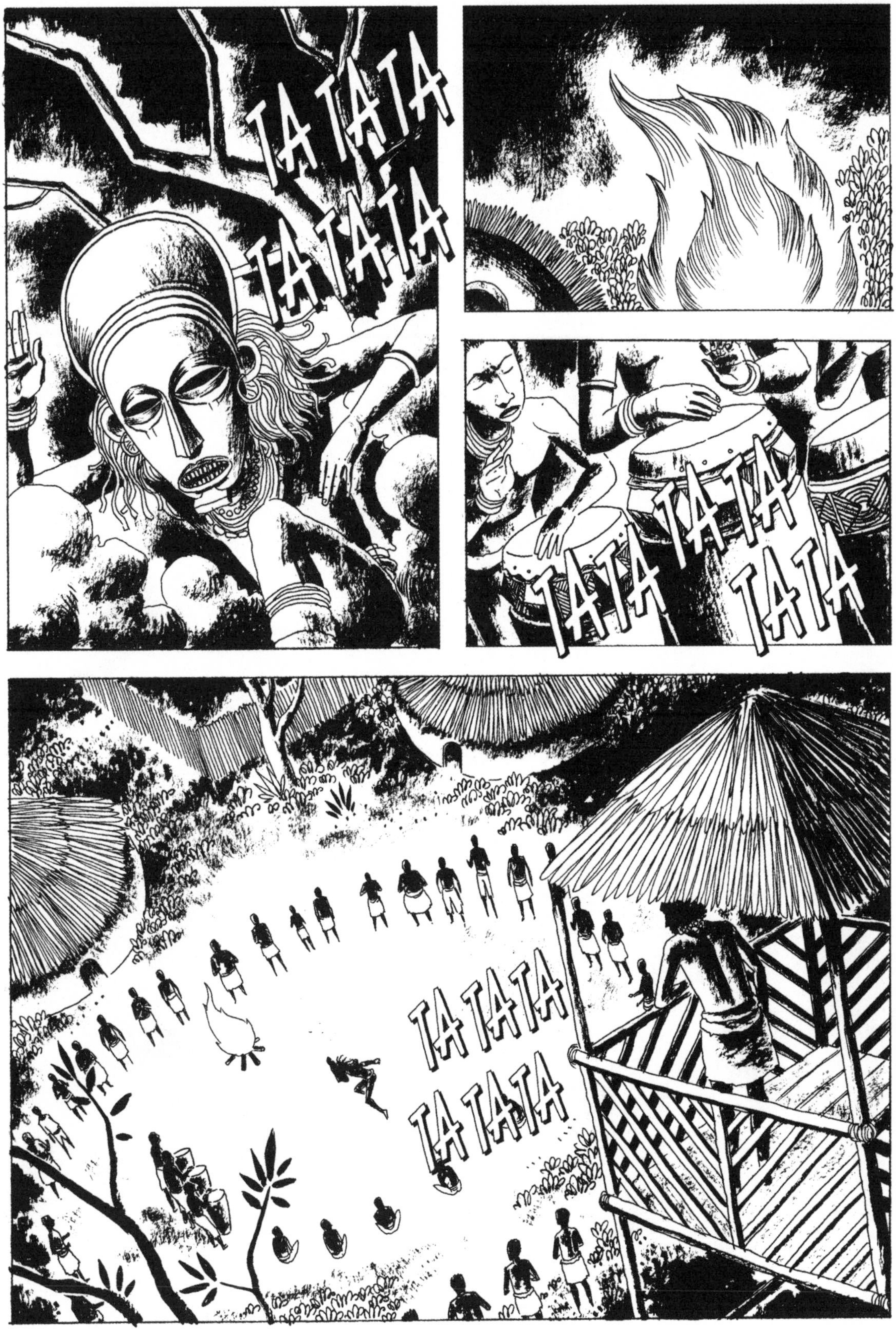
TA TATA
TA TATA
TATA TATA
TATA
TA TATA
TA TATA

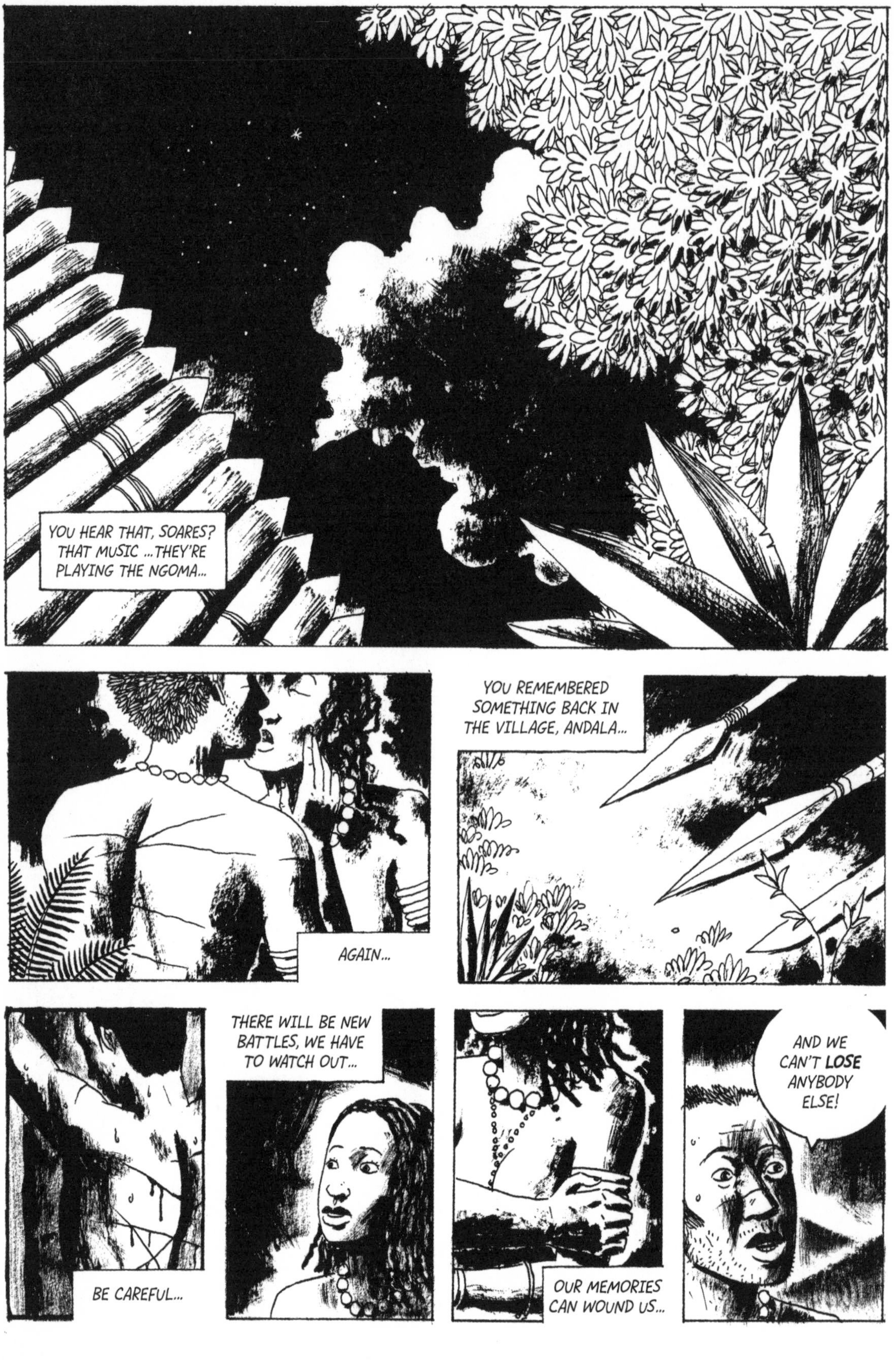
YOU HEAR THAT, SOARES? THAT MUSIC ...THEY'RE PLAYING THE NGOMA...
YOU REMEMBERED SOMETHING BACK IN THE VILLAGE, ANDALA...
AGAIN...
THERE WILL BE NEW BATTLES, WE HAVE TO WATCH OUT...
BE CAREFUL...
OUR MEMORIES CAN WOUND US...
AND WE CAN'T LOSE ANYBODY ELSE!

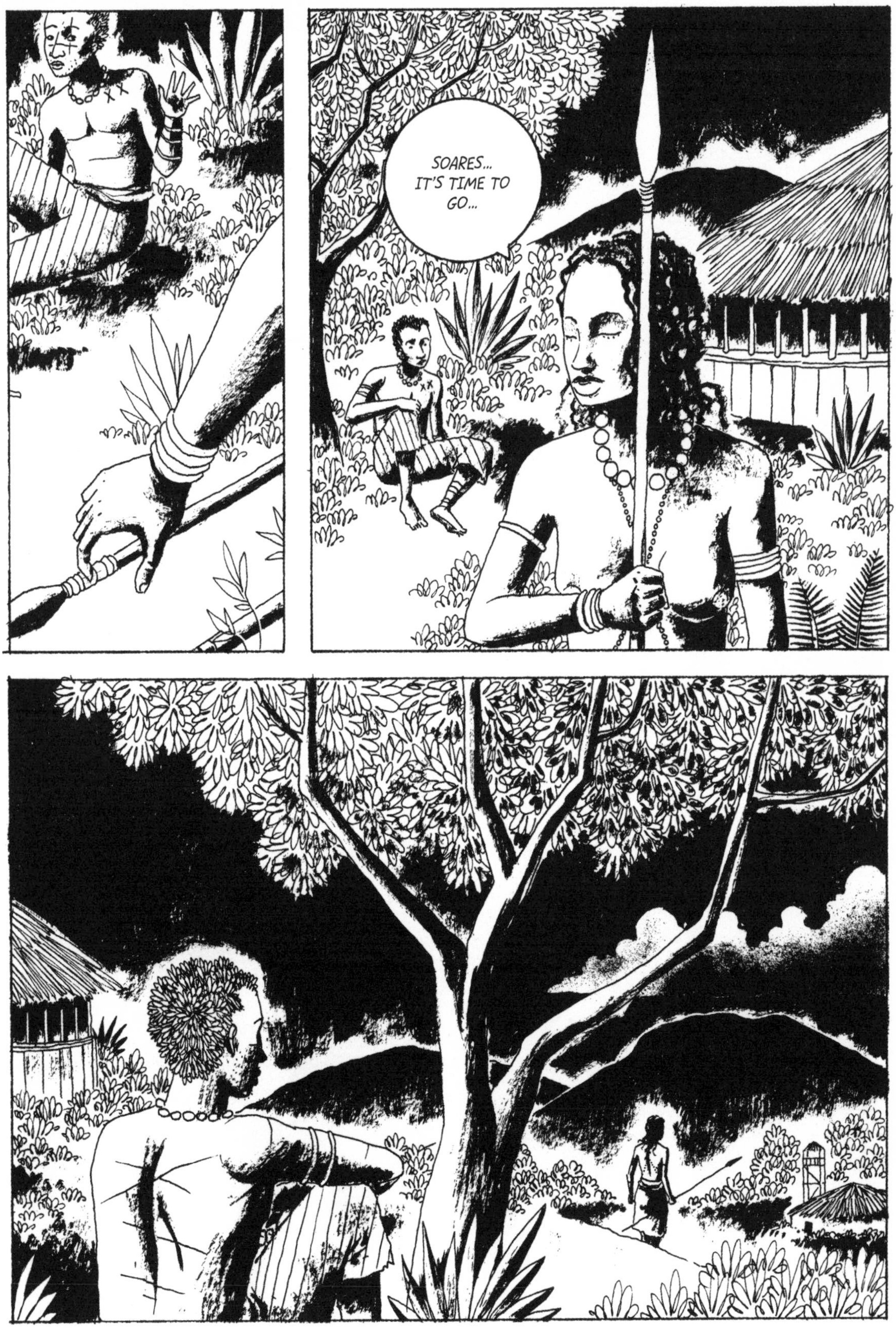
SOARES... IT'S TIME TO GO...

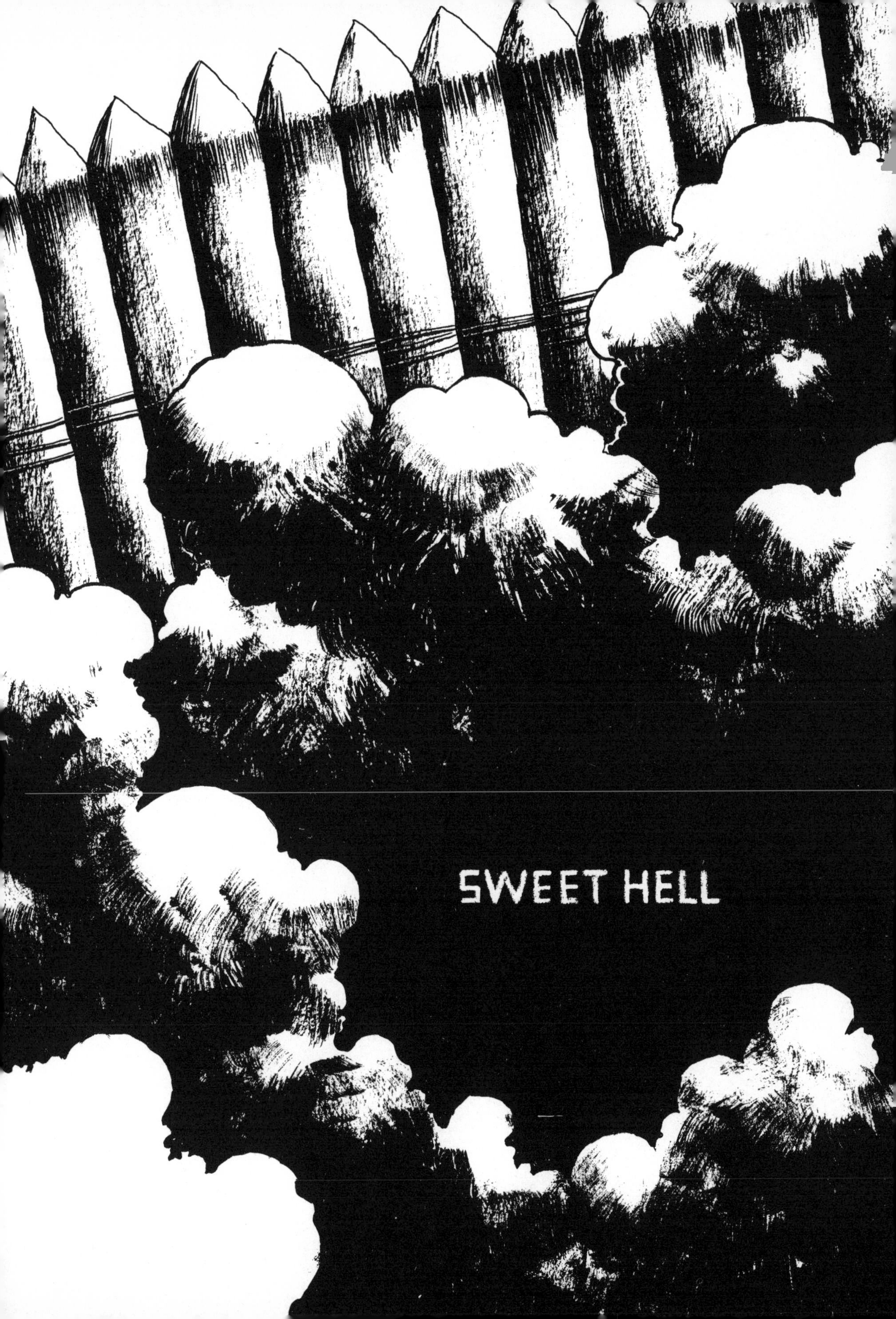
SWEET HELL

There was only one effective and efficient method by which to truly subjugate them, which was for His Majesty and all his lords to grant them immediate, complete, and guaranteed liberty, living in those places like the other Indians and free peoples, and for the priests to then be their shepherds and teach them doctrine as they do the others. But this very liberty thus considered would mean the total destruction of Brazil, because when the other blacks learned that they had managed to become free through this method, every city, every village, every place, every sugar mill would become another Palmares, running away and going into the wilderness with all their capital, which is nothing other than their own bodies.

—*Father Antonio Vieira to the King of Portugal, July 2, 1691*

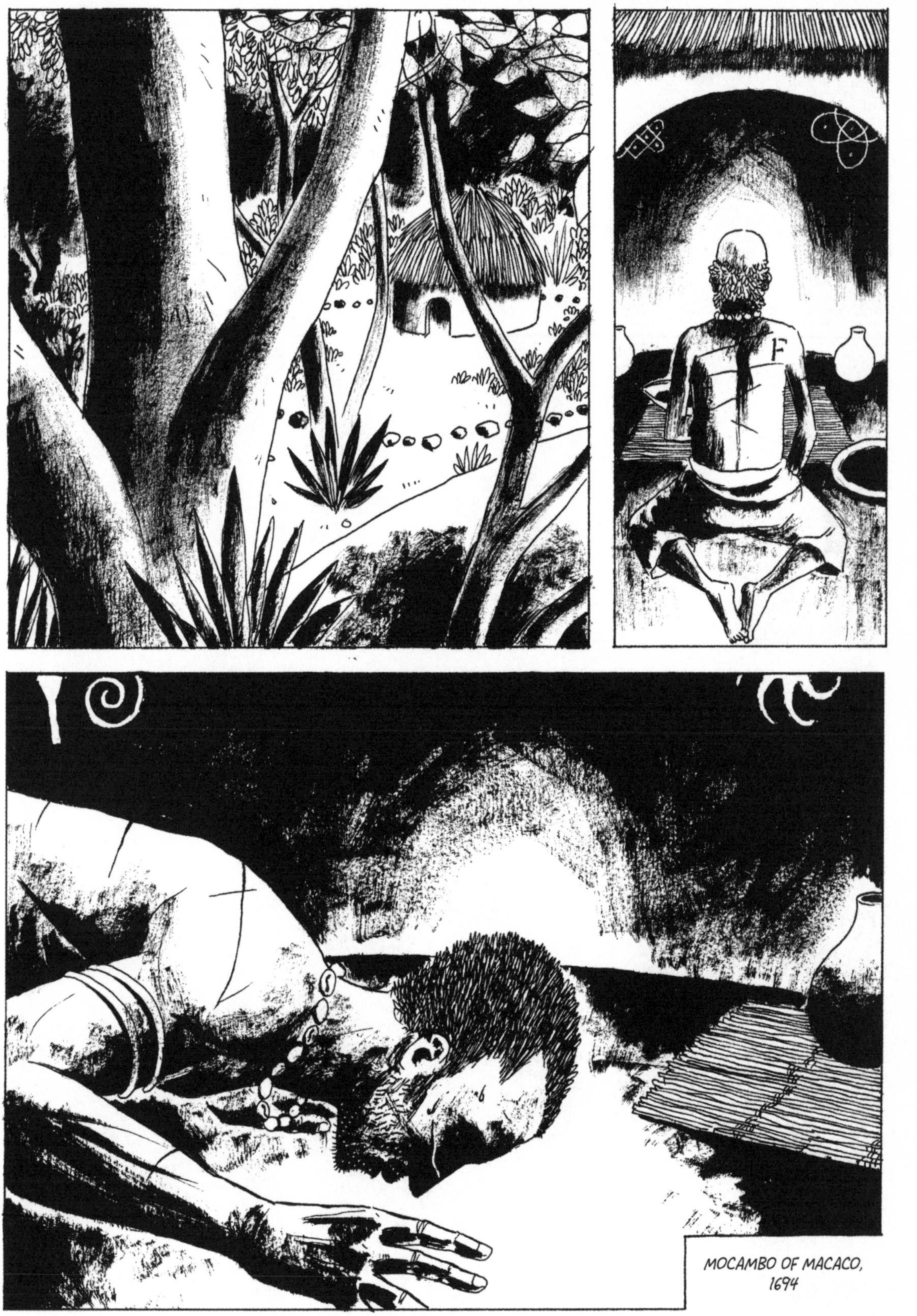
MOCAMBO OF MACACO,
1694

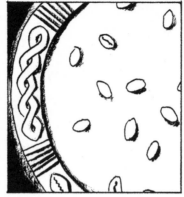

SOARES, A LINE HAS BEEN DRAWN...

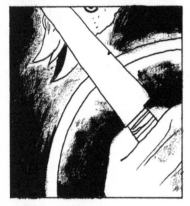

DID YOU DO THE READING, TATA? WHAT DOES MY FUTURE HOLD?

NOW YOU HAVE TO DECIDE WHETHER TO FOLLOW IT...

THAT'S A CHOICE ONLY YOU CAN MAKE...

SOARES?

WHAT DID IT SAY, SOARES?

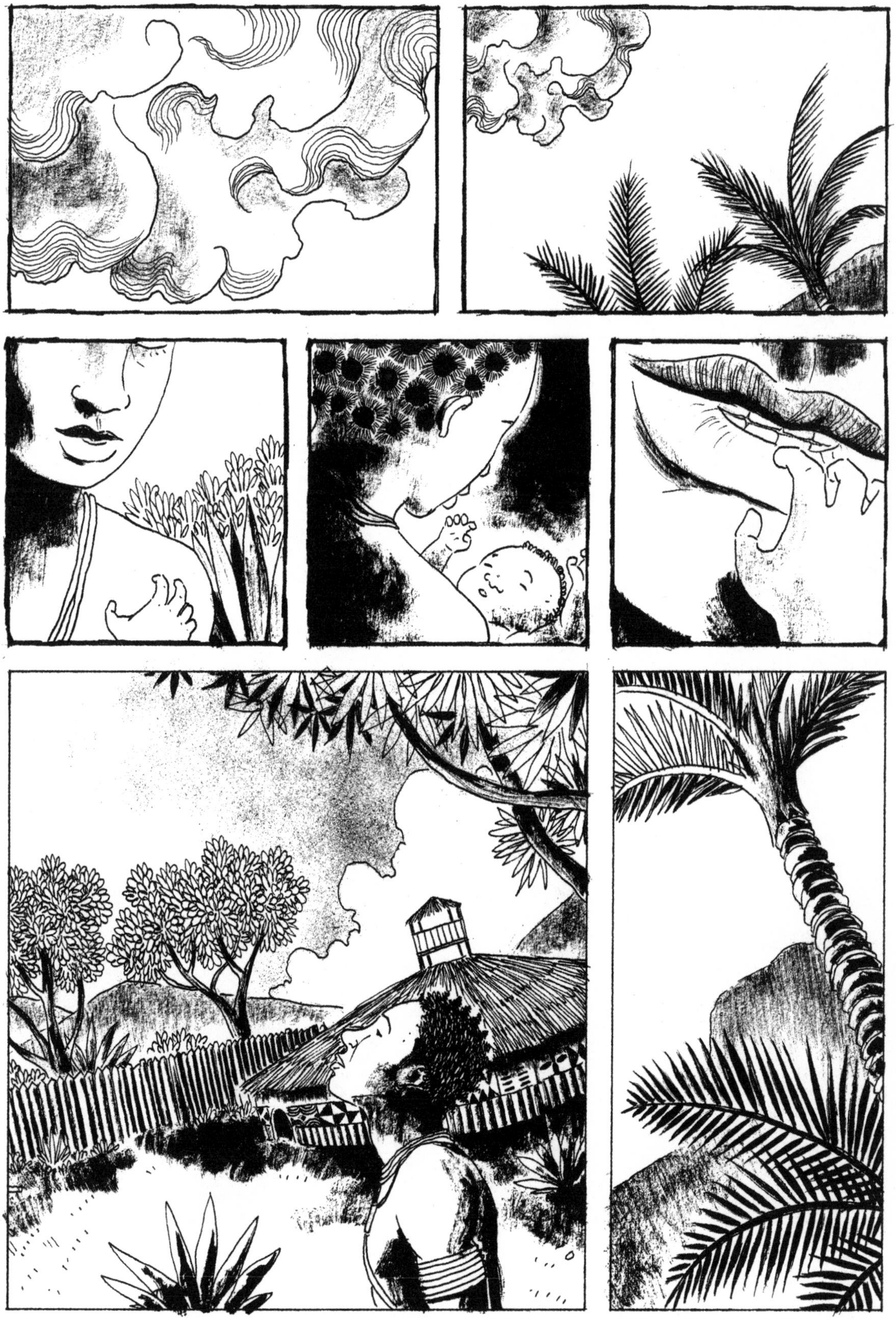

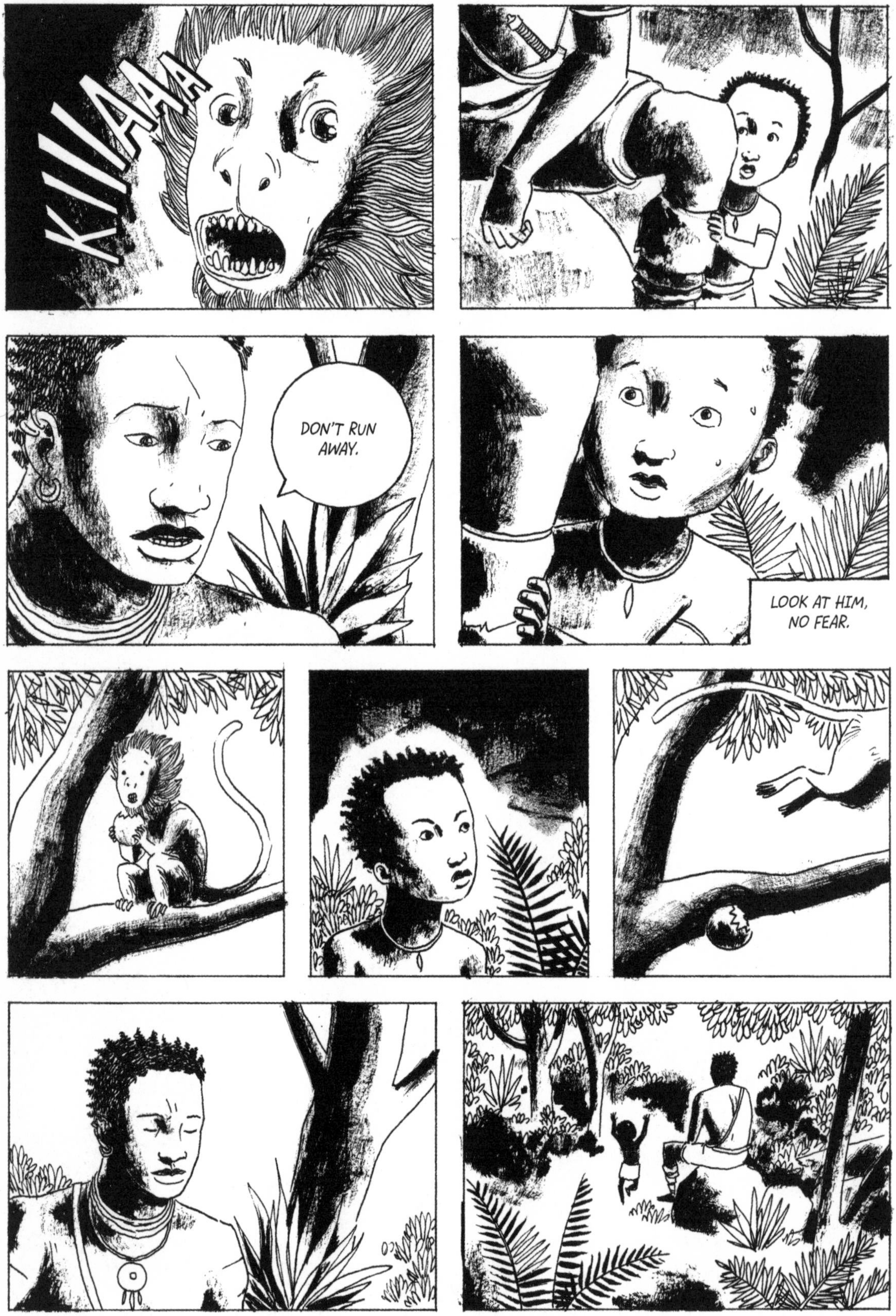
KIIIAAA
DON'T RUN AWAY.
LOOK AT HIM, NO FEAR.

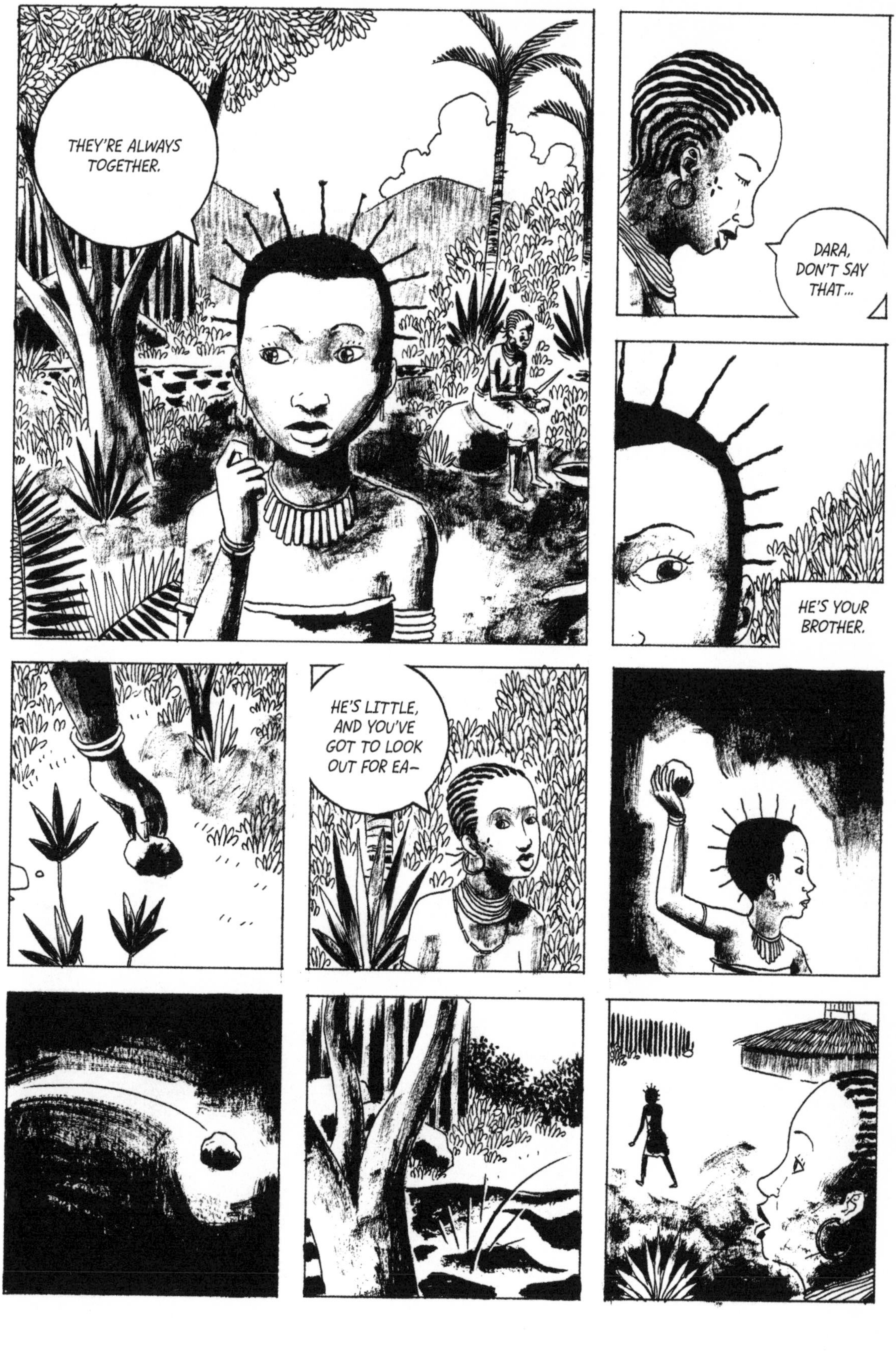
THEY'RE ALWAYS TOGETHER.
DARA, DON'T SAY THAT...
HE'S YOUR BROTHER.
HE'S LITTLE, AND YOU'VE GOT TO LOOK OUT FOR EA–

ZUMBI, THERE ARE MISSONGO FIGHTERS COMING UP INTO THE HILLS.

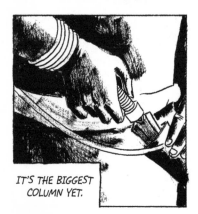

IT'S THE BIGGEST COLUMN YET.

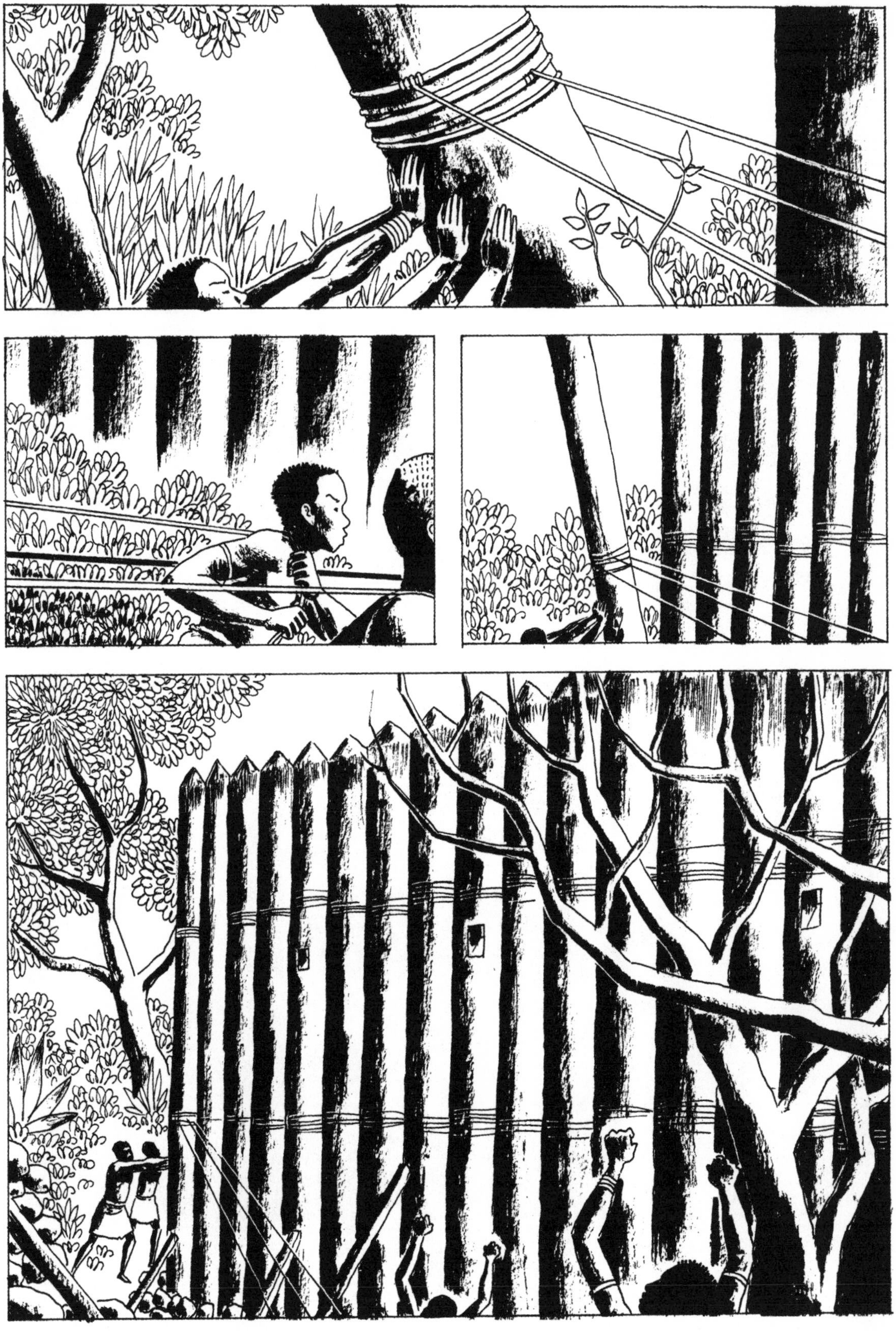

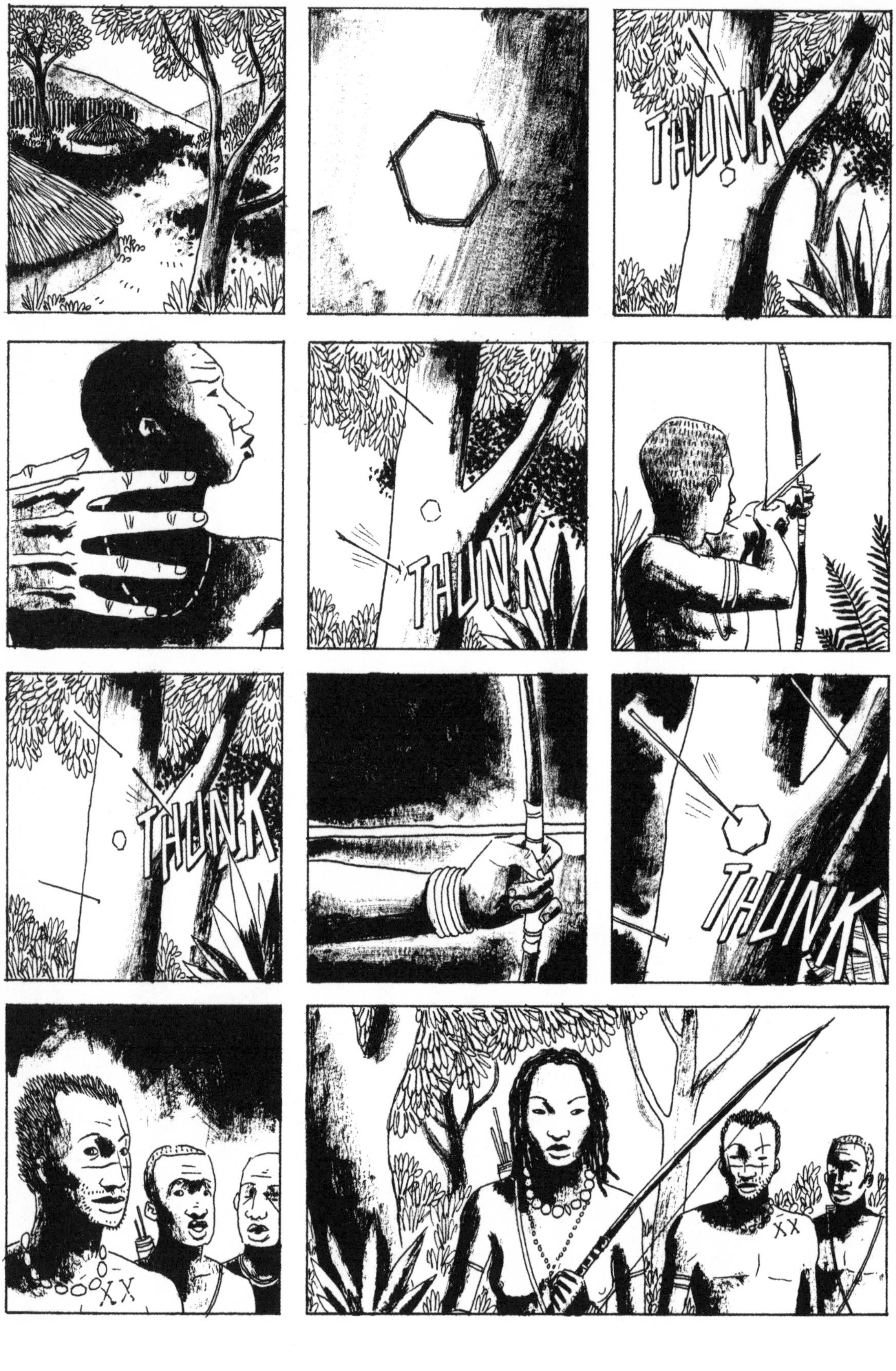
THUNK
THUNK
THUNK
THUNK

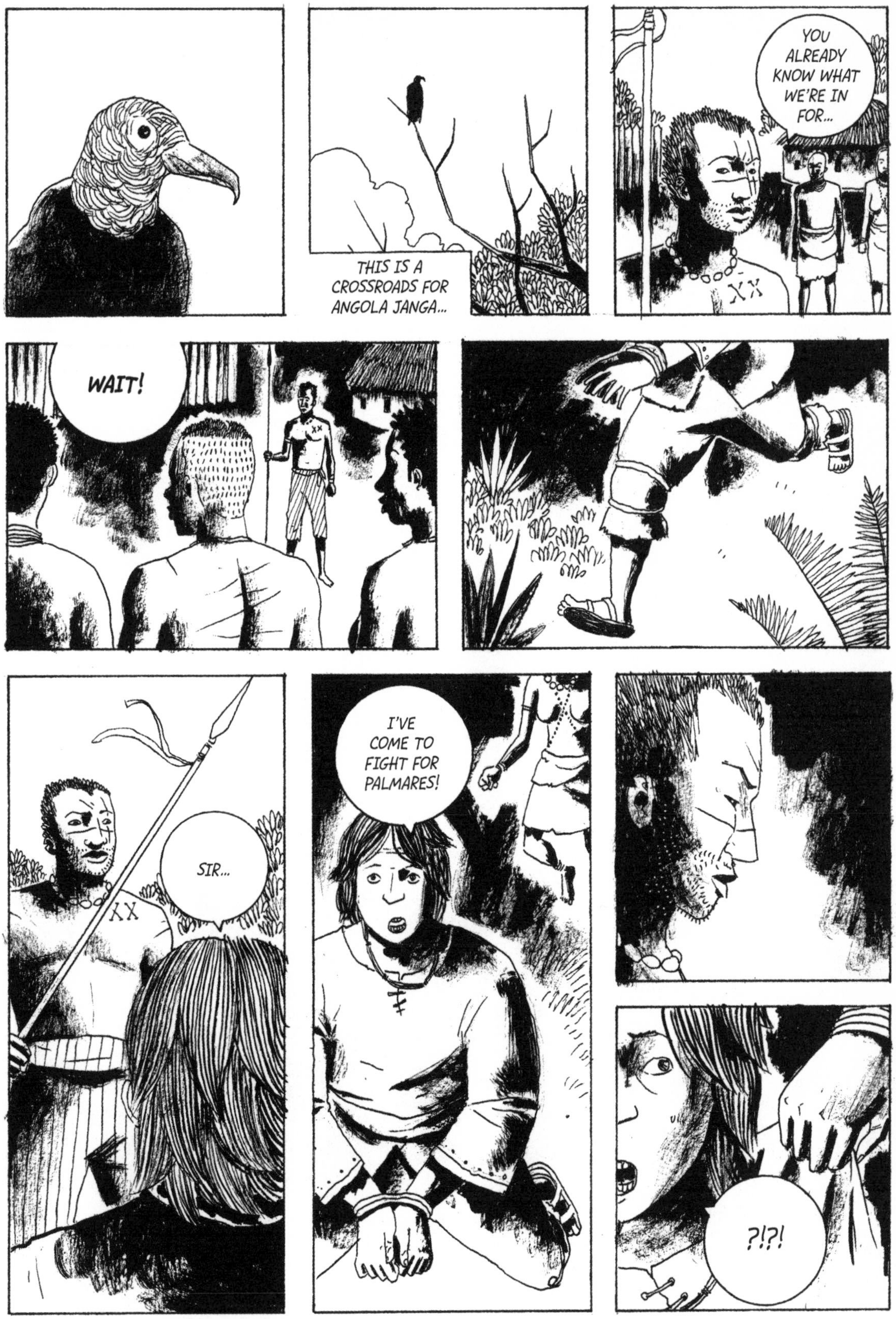
THIS IS A CROSSROADS FOR ANGOLA JANGA...
YOU ALREADY KNOW WHAT WE'RE IN FOR...
WAIT!
SIR...
I'VE COME TO FIGHT FOR PALMARES!
?!?!

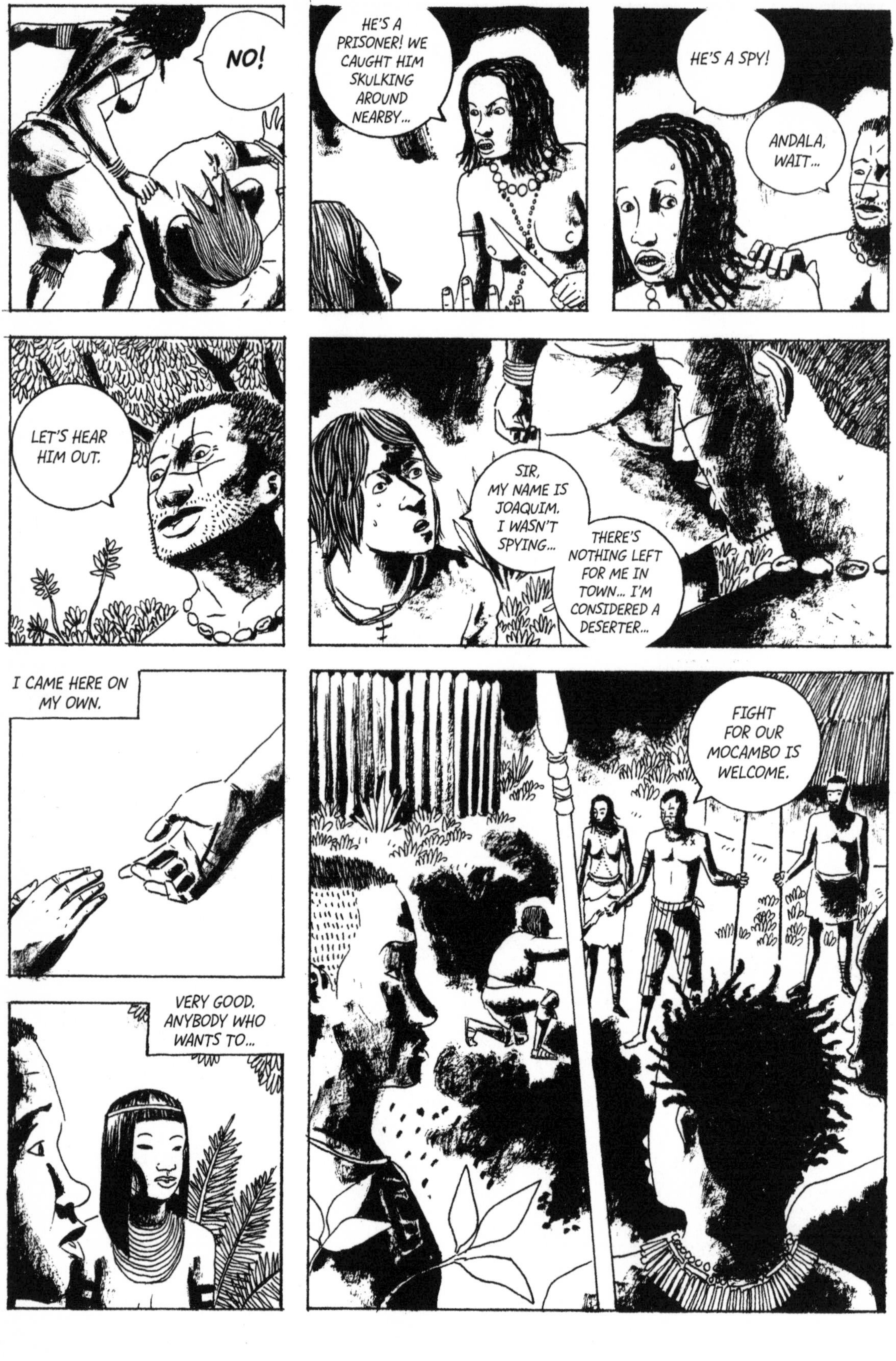
NO!
HE'S A PRISONER! WE CAUGHT HIM SKULKING AROUND NEARBY...
HE'S A SPY!
ANDALA, WAIT...
LET'S HEAR HIM OUT.
SIR, MY NAME IS JOAQUIM. I WASN'T SPYING...
THERE'S NOTHING LEFT FOR ME IN TOWN... I'M CONSIDERED A DESERTER...
I CAME HERE ON MY OWN.
VERY GOOD. ANYBODY WHO WANTS TO...
FIGHT FOR OUR MOCAMBO IS WELCOME.

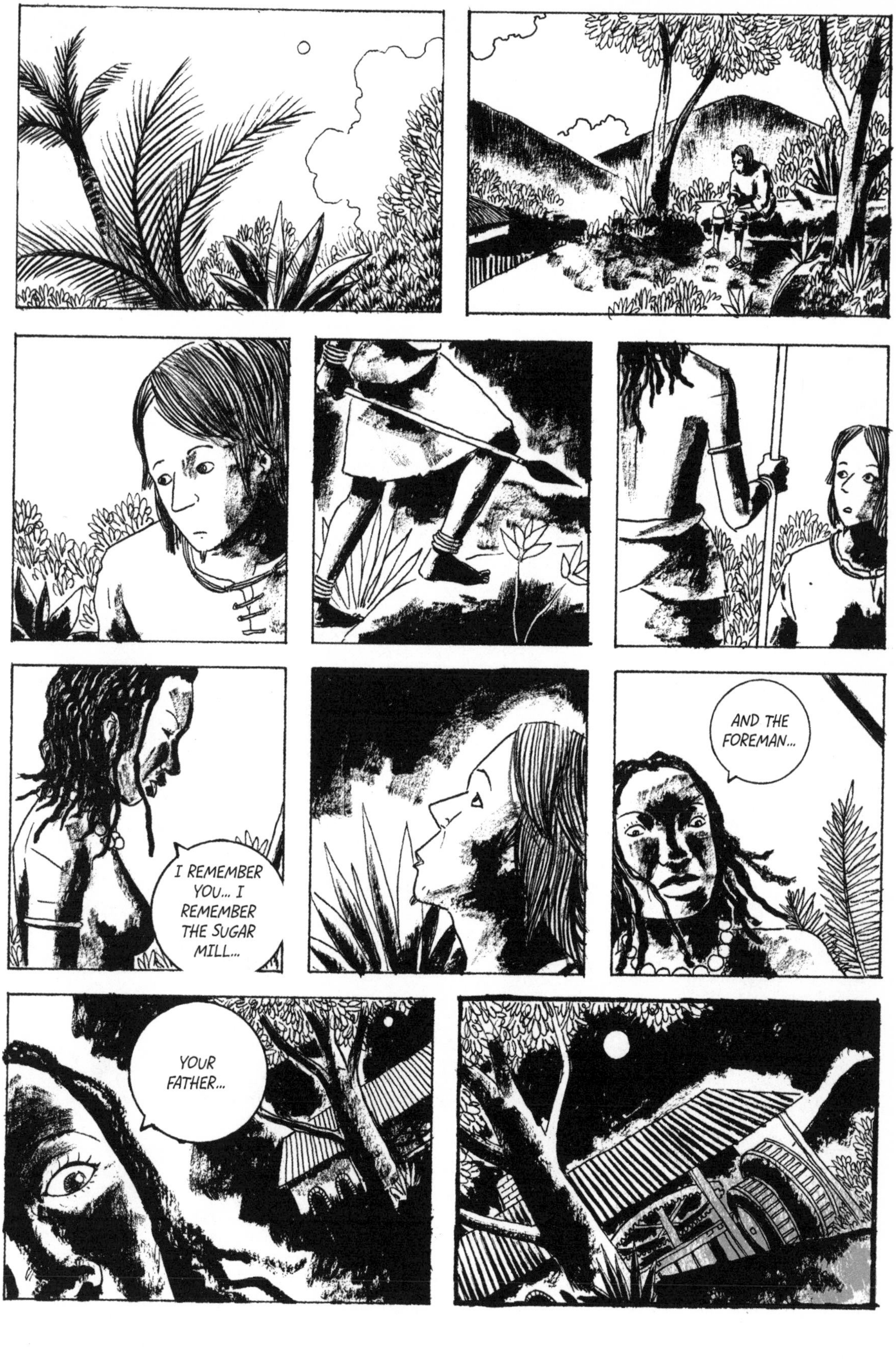
I REMEMBER YOU... I REMEMBER THE SUGAR MILL...
AND THE FOREMAN...
YOUR FATHER...

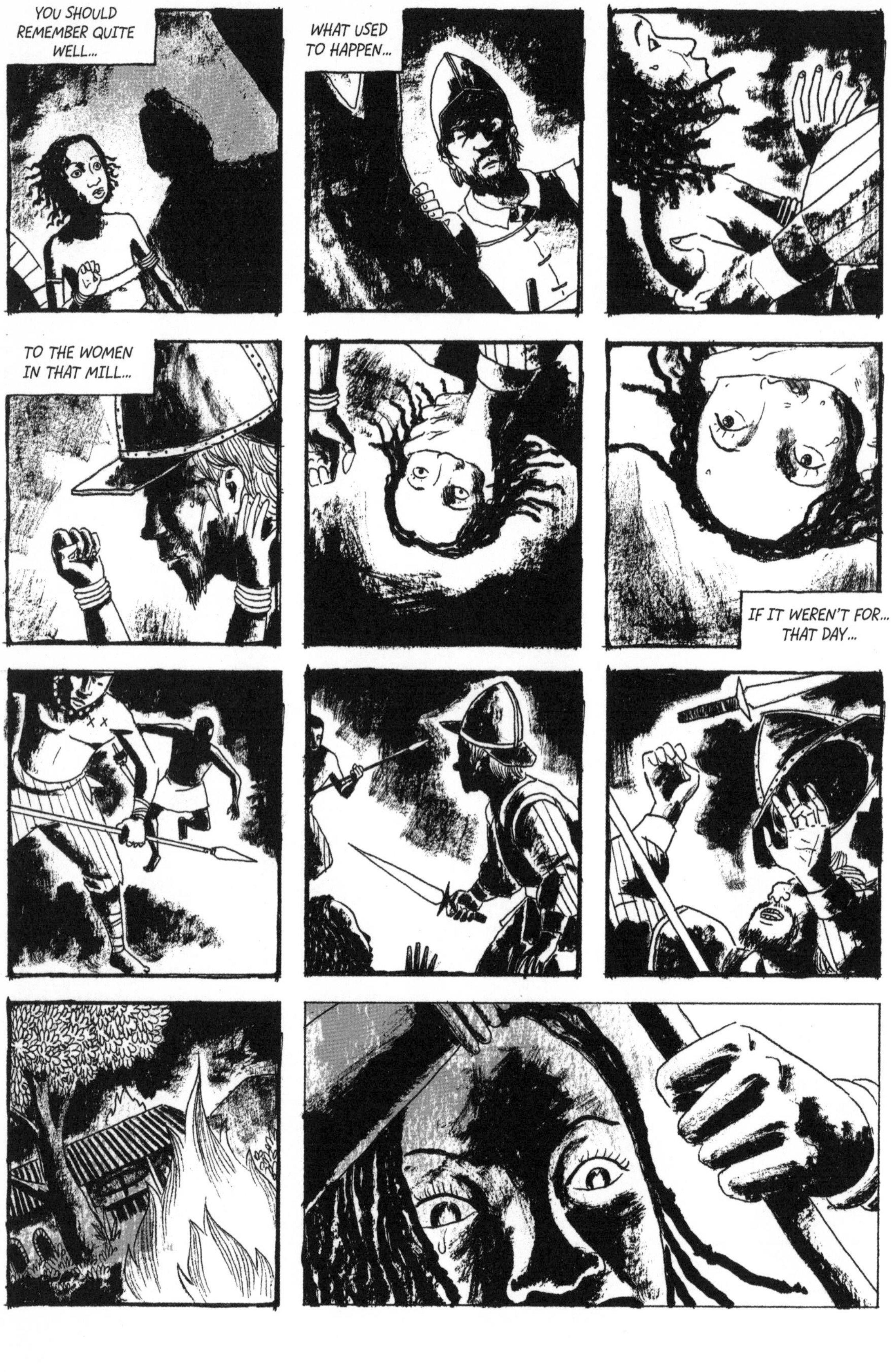
YOU SHOULD REMEMBER QUITE WELL...
WHAT USED TO HAPPEN...
TO THE WOMEN IN THAT MILL...
IF IT WEREN'T FOR... THAT DAY...

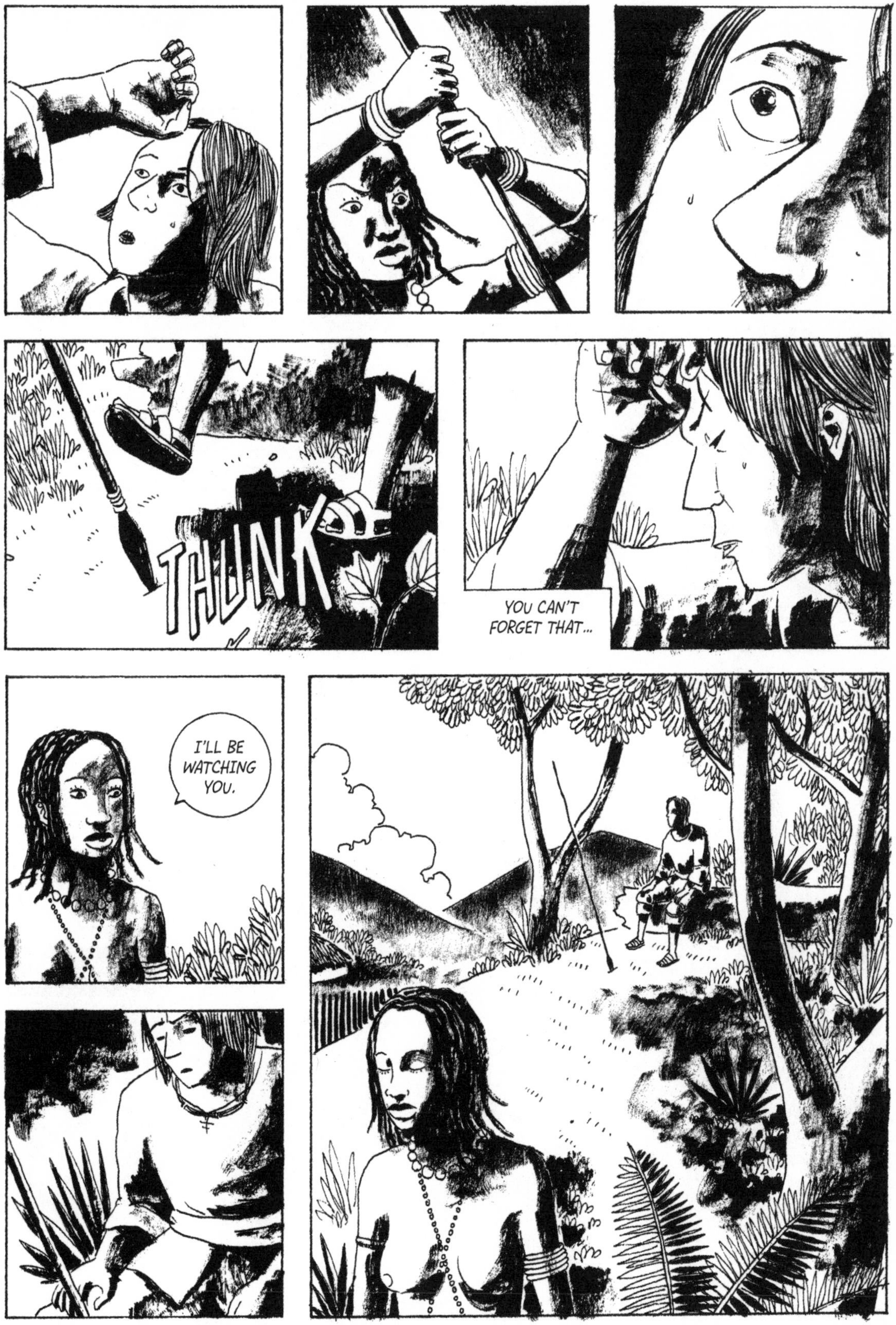
THUNK
YOU CAN'T FORGET THAT...
I'LL BE WATCHING YOU.

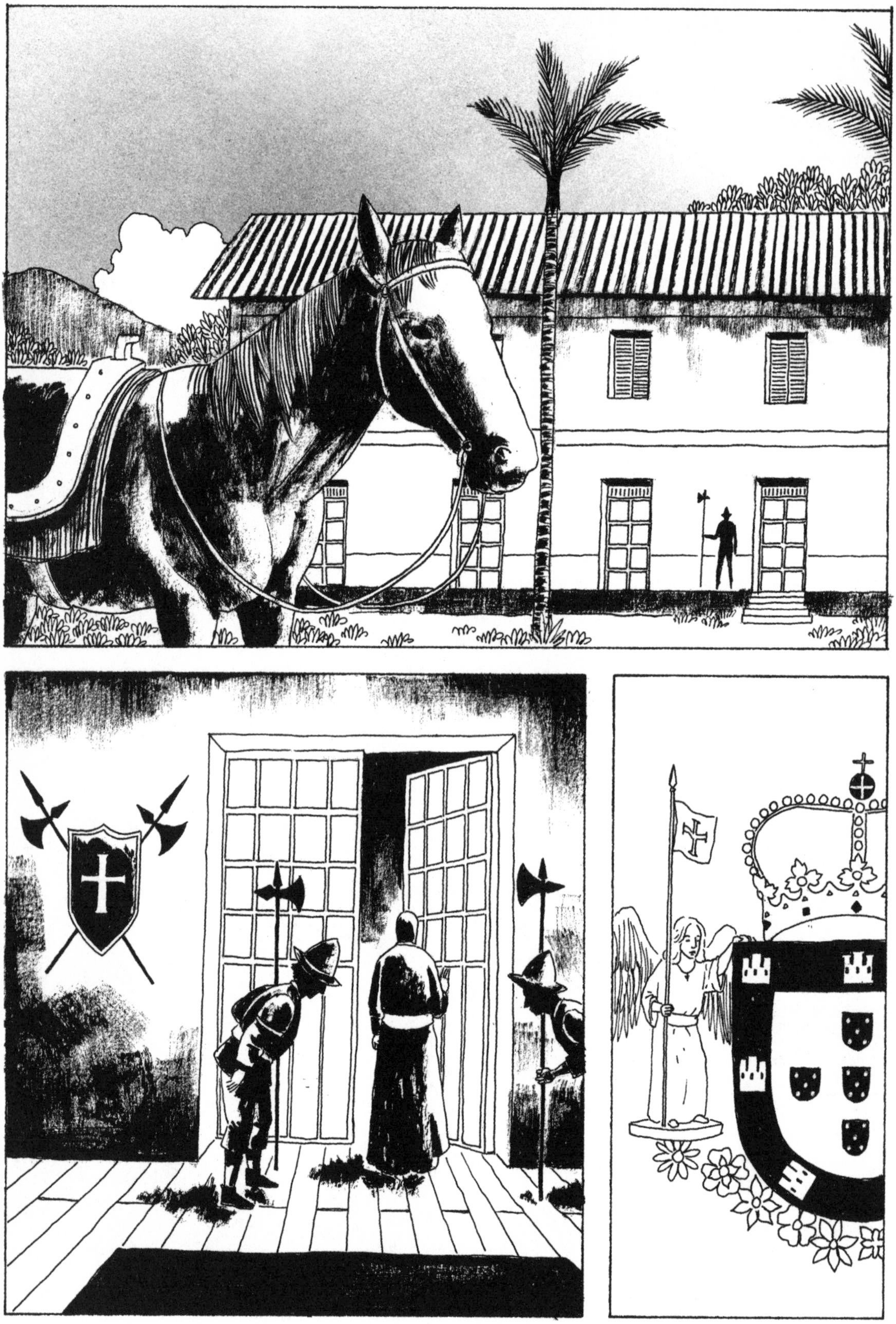

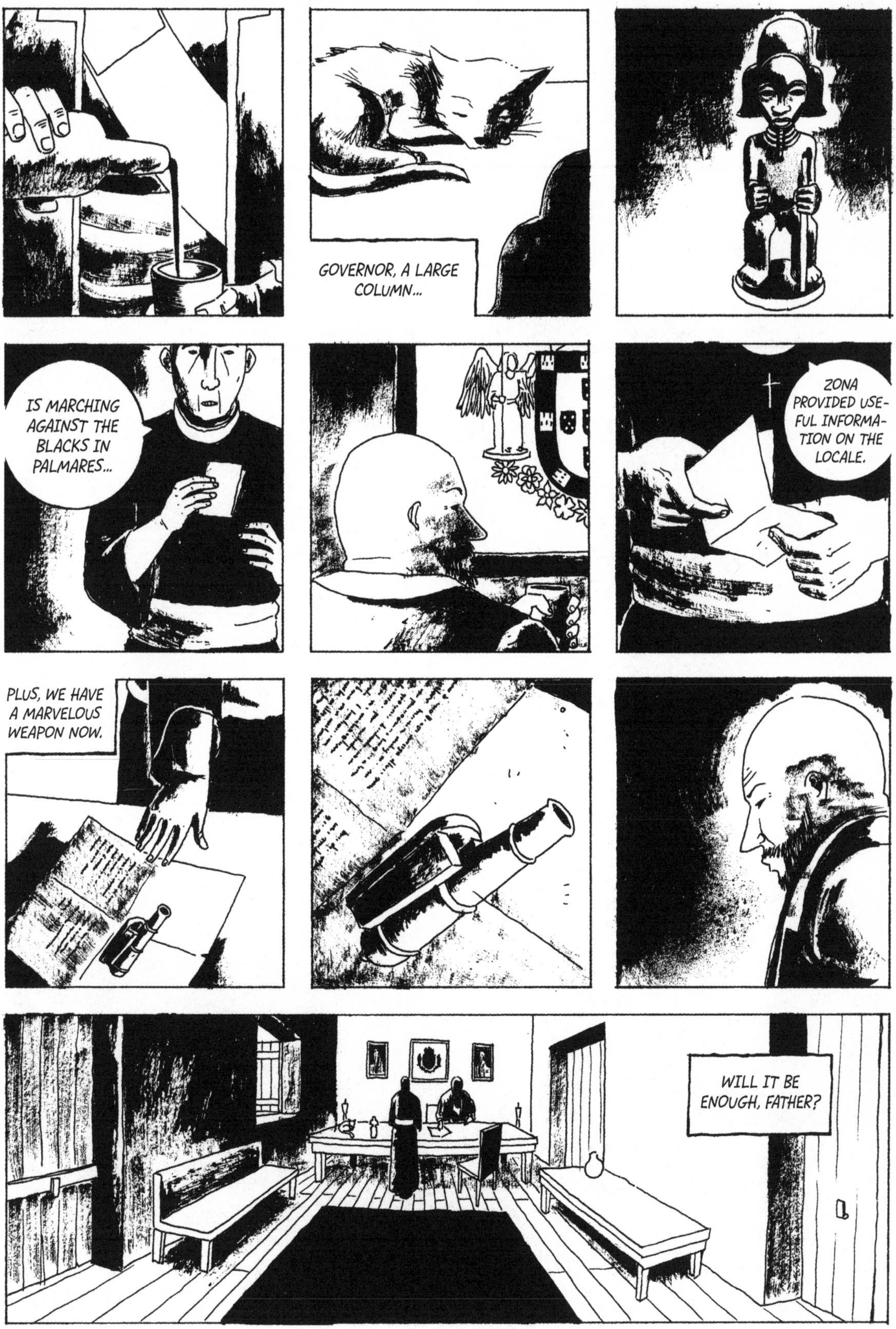
GOVERNOR, A LARGE COLUMN...
IS MARCHING AGAINST THE BLACKS IN PALMARES...
ZONA PROVIDED USEFUL INFORMATION ON THE LOCALE.
PLUS, WE HAVE A MARVELOUS WEAPON NOW.
WILL IT BE ENOUGH, FATHER?

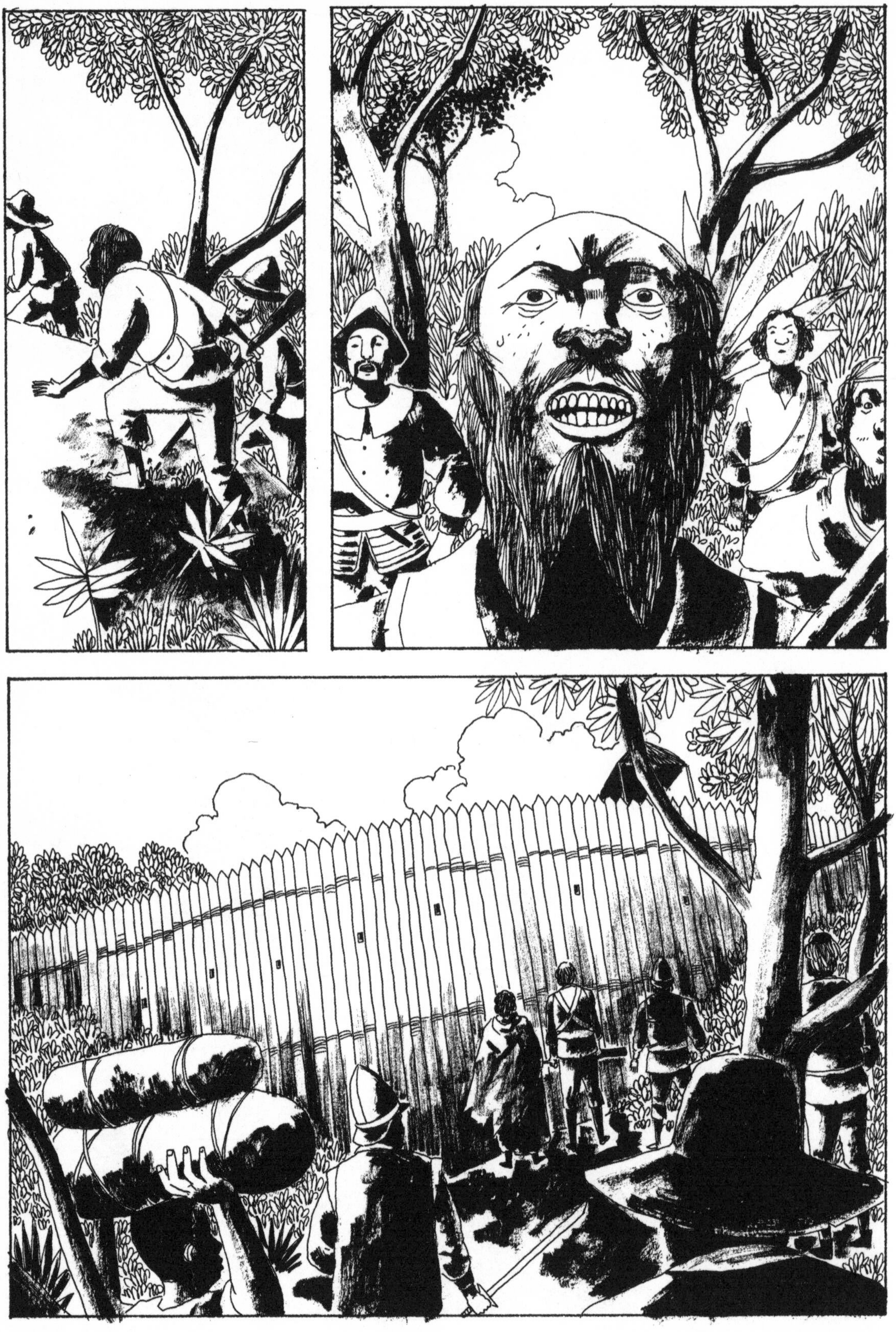

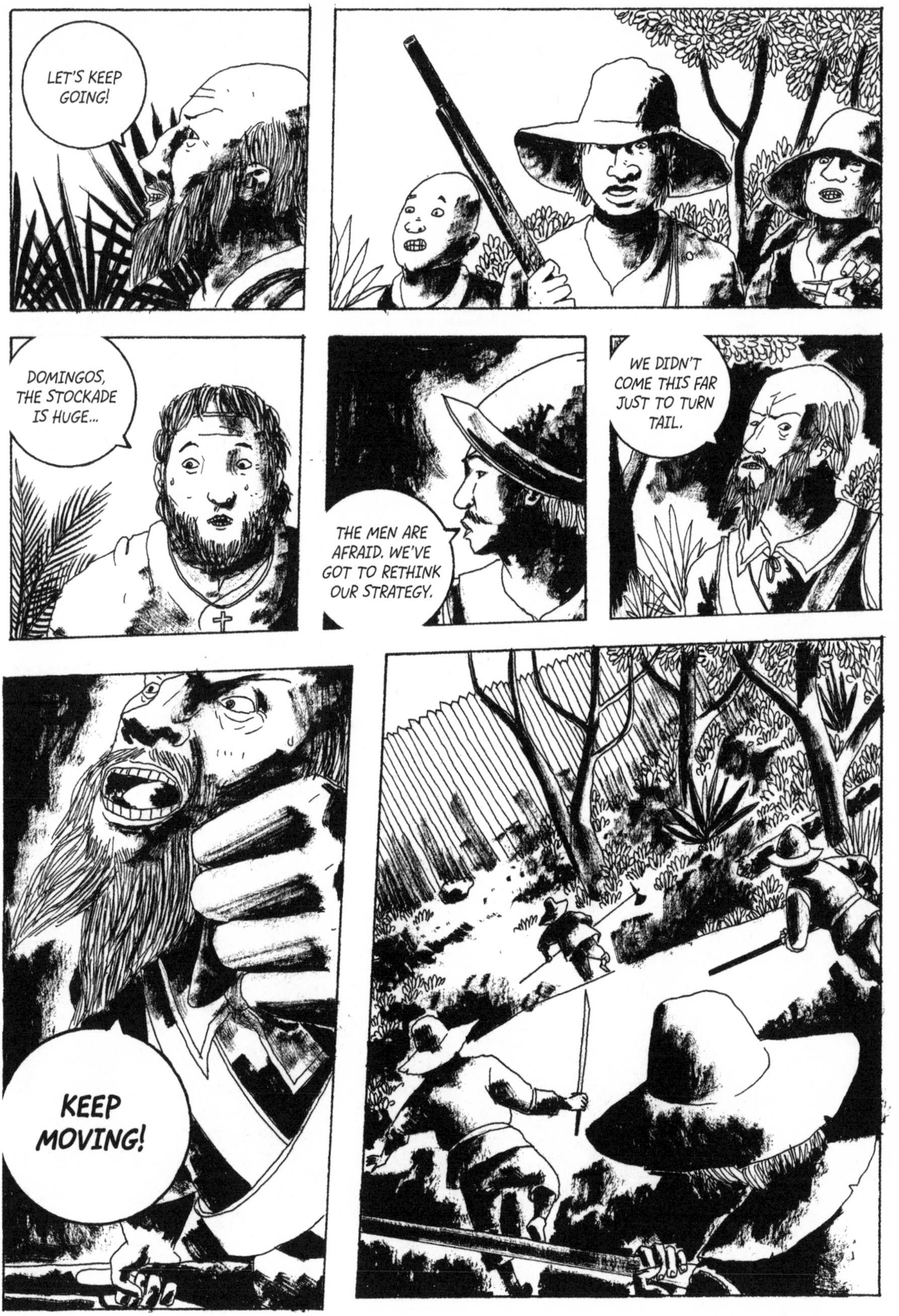
LET'S KEEP GOING!
DOMINGOS, THE STOCKADE IS HUGE...
THE MEN ARE AFRAID. WE'VE GOT TO RETHINK OUR STRATEGY.
WE DIDN'T COME THIS FAR JUST TO TURN TAIL.
KEEP MOVING!

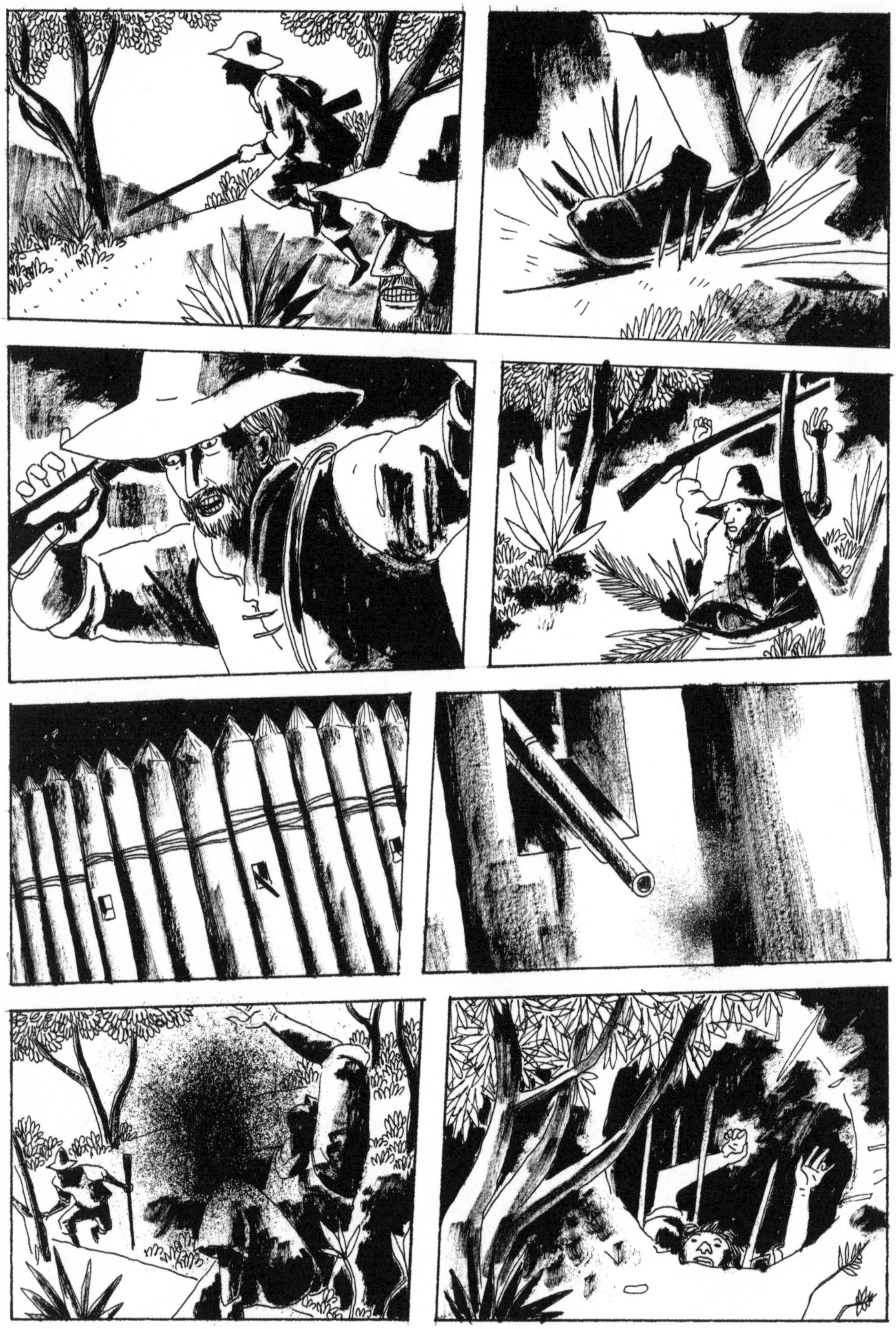

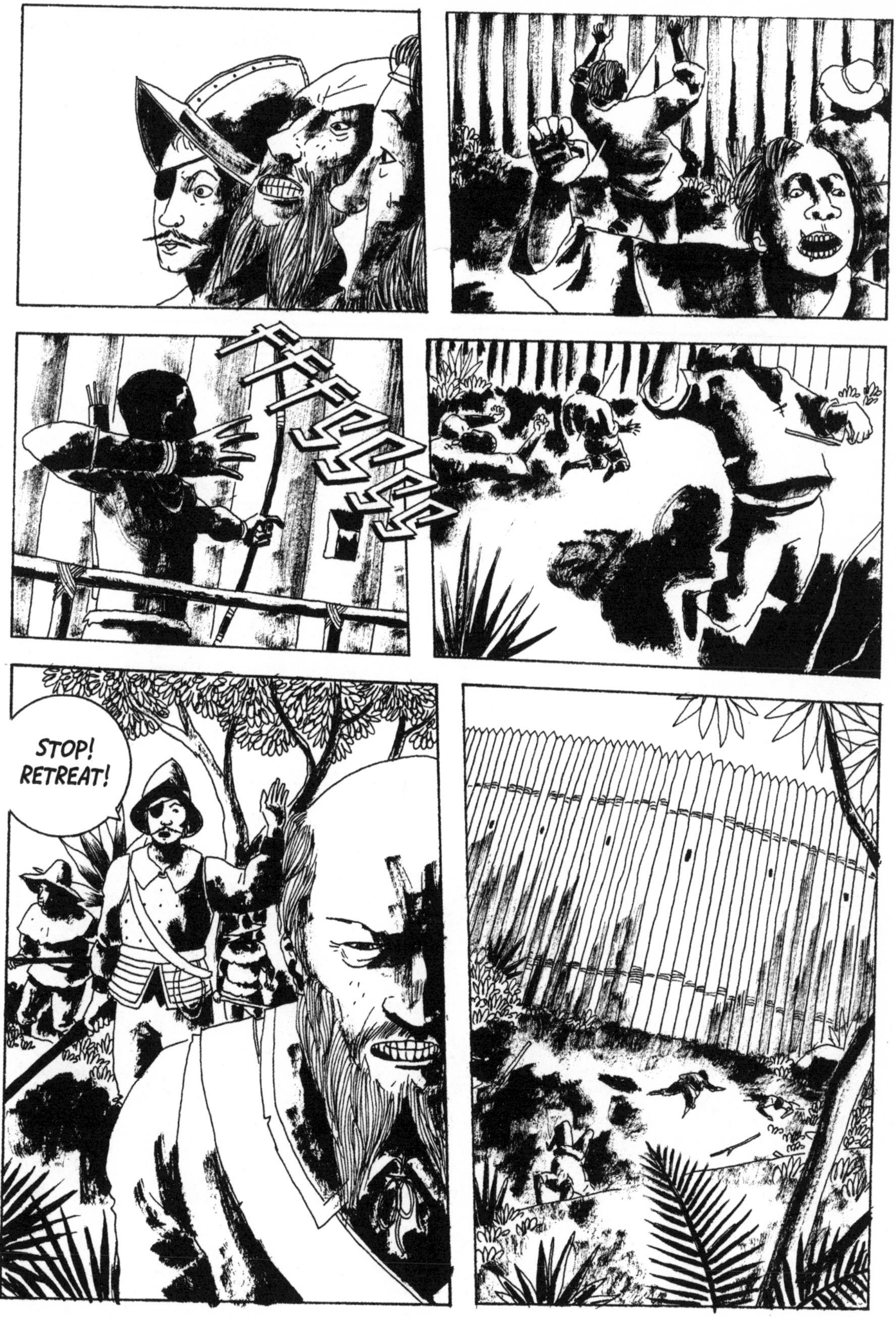
STOP! RETREAT!

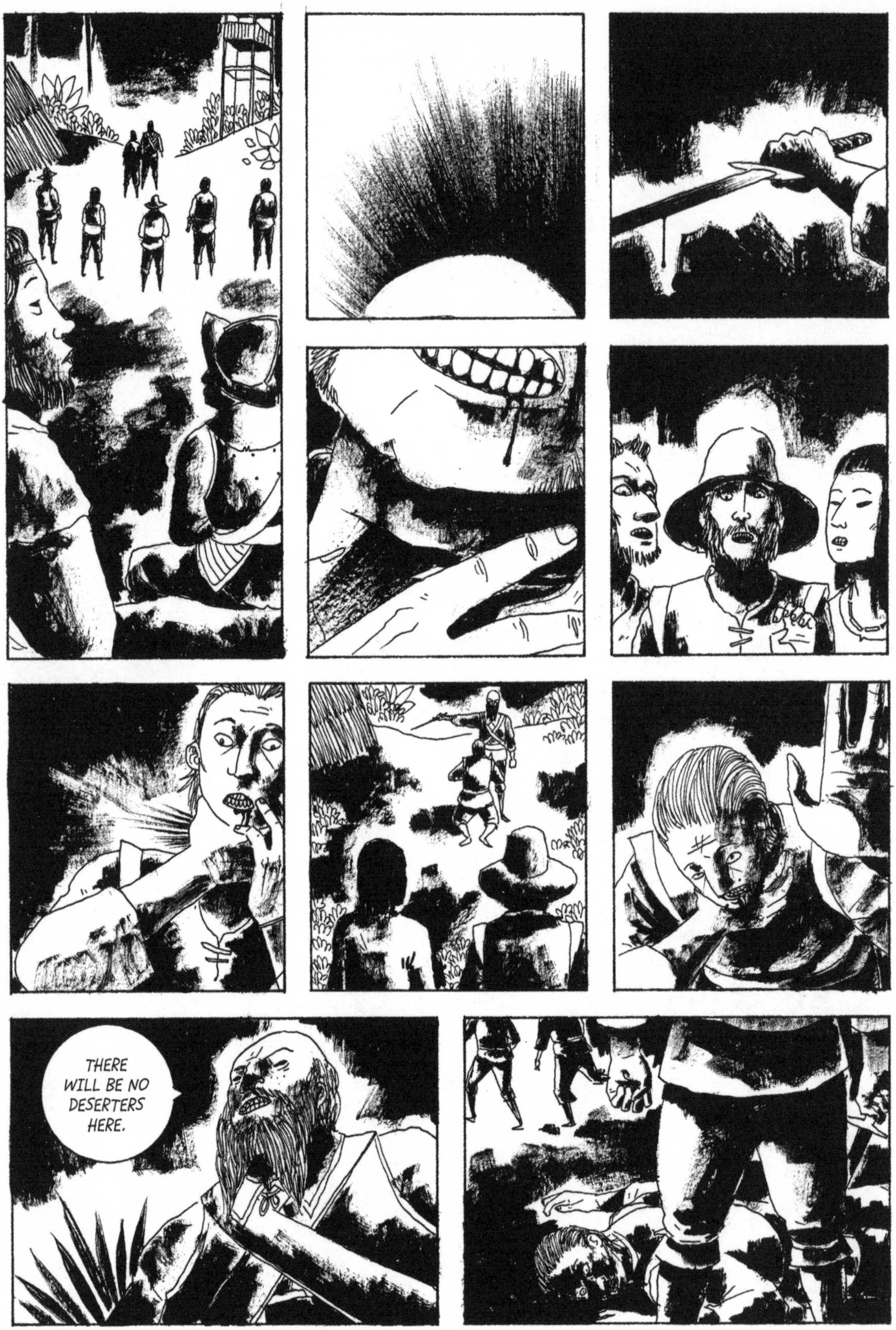
THERE WILL BE NO DESERTERS HERE.

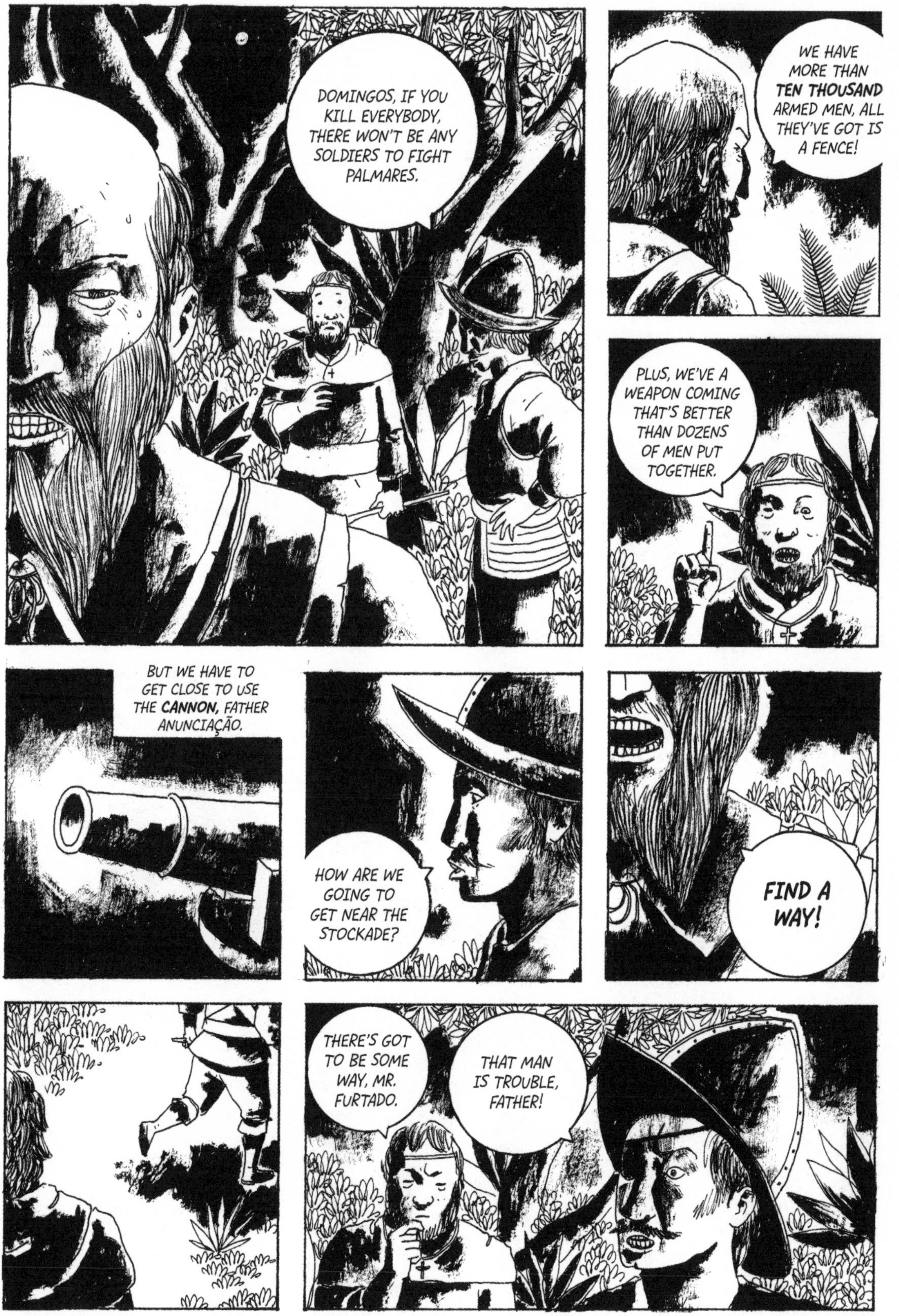
DOMINGOS, IF YOU KILL EVERYBODY, THERE WON'T BE ANY SOLDIERS TO FIGHT PALMARES.
WE HAVE MORE THAN **TEN THOUSAND** ARMED MEN, ALL THEY'VE GOT IS A FENCE!
PLUS, WE'VE A WEAPON COMING THAT'S BETTER THAN DOZENS OF MEN PUT TOGETHER.
BUT WE HAVE TO GET CLOSE TO USE THE **CANNON,** FATHER ANUNCIAÇÃO.
HOW ARE WE GOING TO GET NEAR THE STOCKADE?
FIND A WAY!
THERE'S GOT TO BE SOME WAY, MR. FURTADO.
THAT MAN IS TROUBLE, FATHER!

WE ARE HERE.

NOW'S NOT THE TIME FOR DOODLING, FATHER.

THE STOCKADE IS THERE.

WHAT'S OUR BEST COURSE OF ACTION?

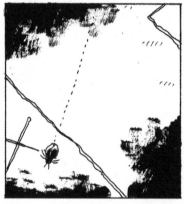

OF COURSE, THAT'S IT!

A **DIAGONAL** LINE **UP** **TO** THE STOCKADE!

IF WE BUILD A BARRIER ON THE DIAGONAL, WE CAN ADVANCE.

DIAGO... WHAT?

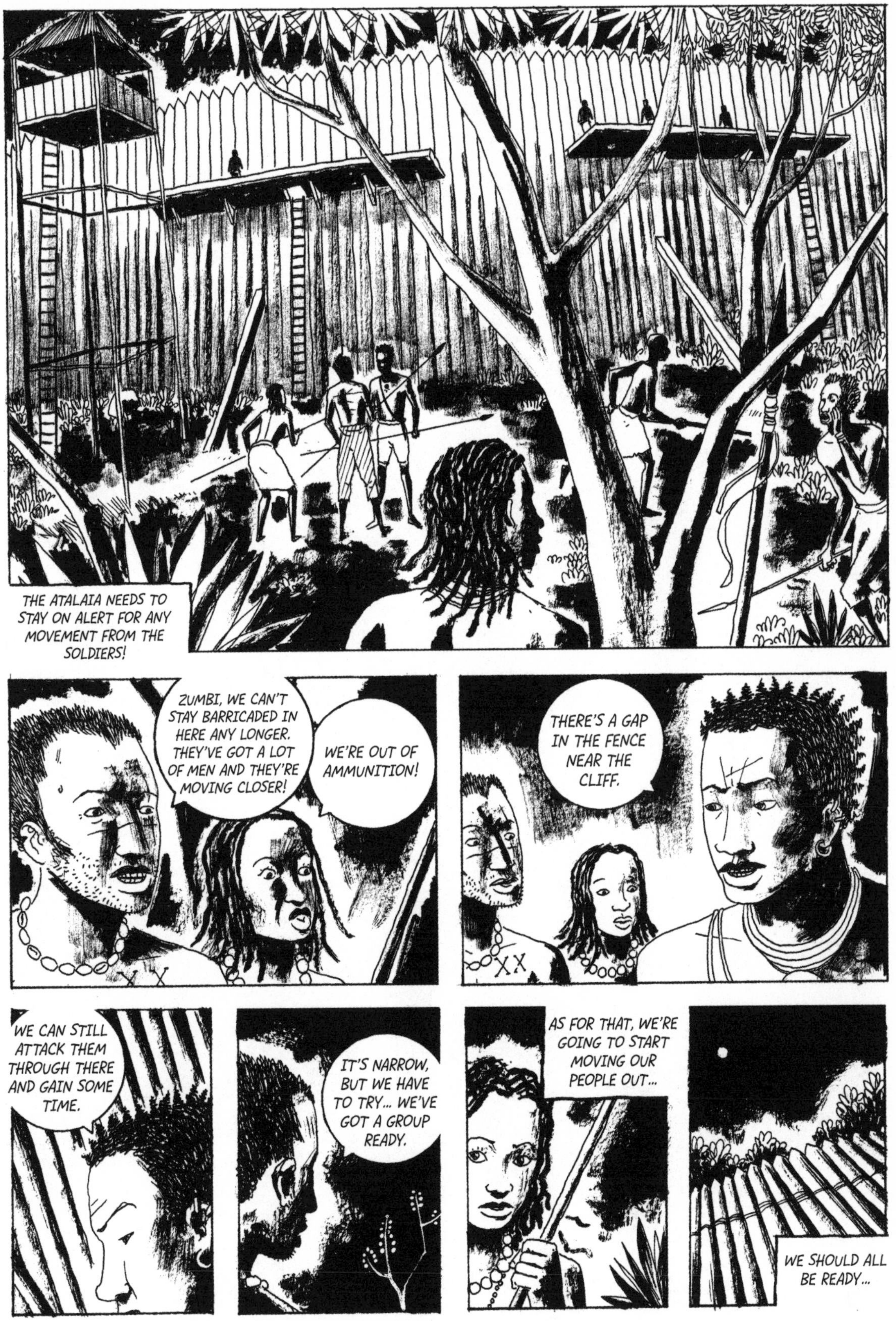
THE ATALAIA NEEDS TO STAY ON ALERT FOR ANY MOVEMENT FROM THE SOLDIERS!
ZUMBI, WE CAN'T STAY BARRICADED IN HERE ANY LONGER. THEY'VE GOT A LOT OF MEN AND THEY'RE MOVING CLOSER!
WE'RE OUT OF AMMUNITION!
THERE'S A GAP IN THE FENCE NEAR THE CLIFF.
WE CAN STILL ATTACK THEM THROUGH THERE AND GAIN SOME TIME.
IT'S NARROW, BUT WE HAVE TO TRY... WE'VE GOT A GROUP READY.
AS FOR THAT, WE'RE GOING TO START MOVING OUR PEOPLE OUT...
WE SHOULD ALL BE READY...

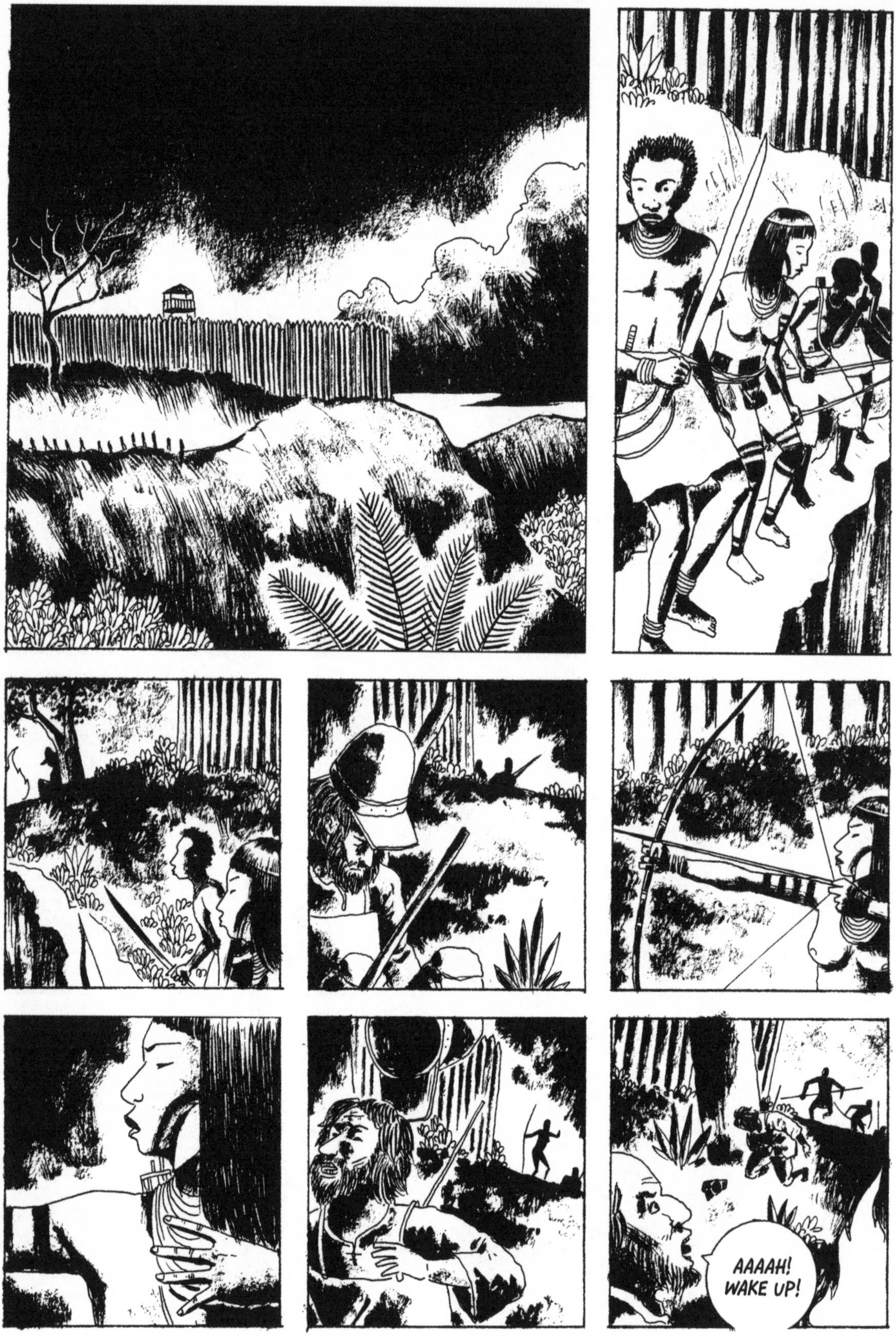
AAAAH! WAKE UP!

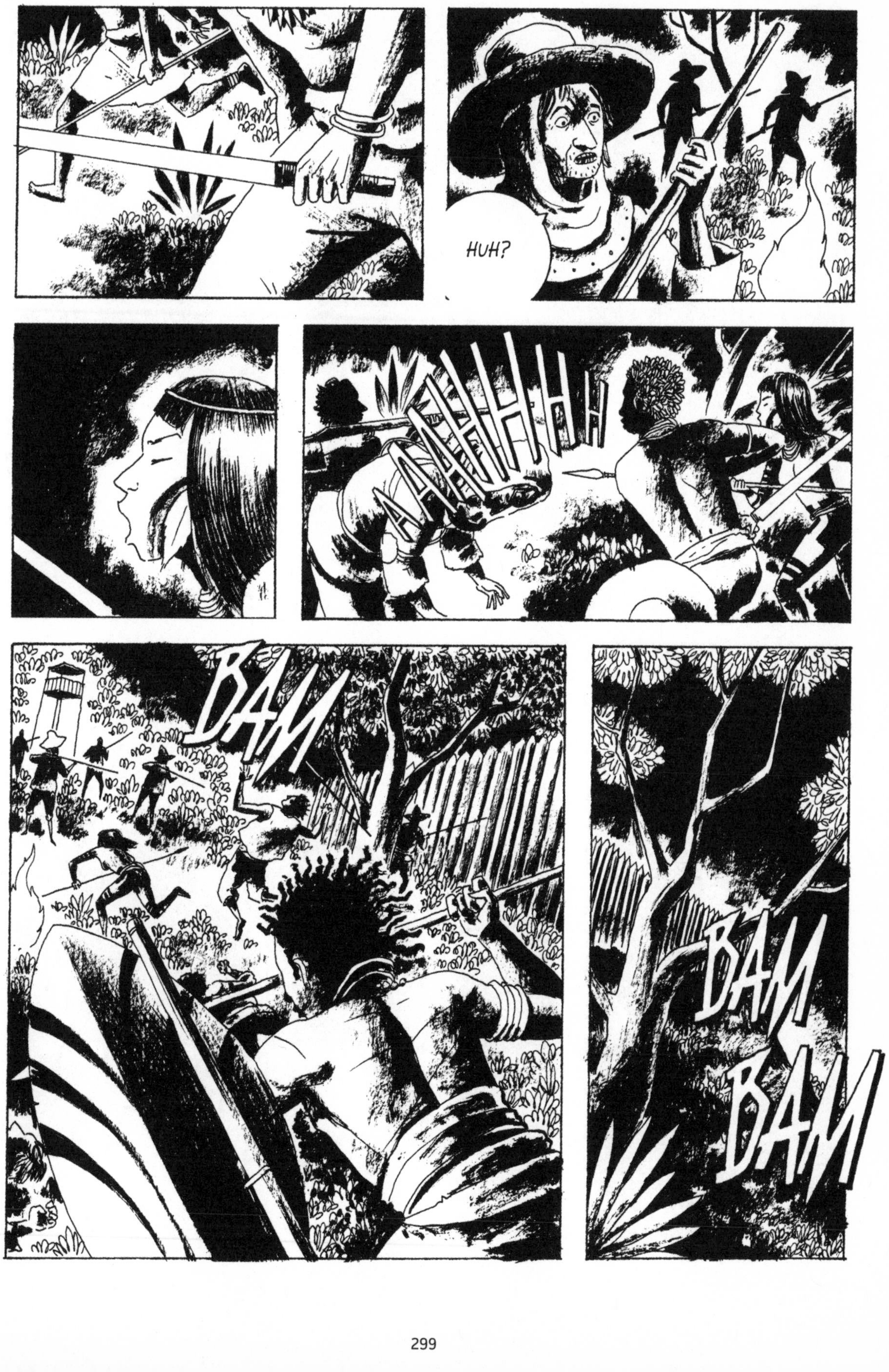
HUH?
AAAHHHHHH
BAM
BAM
BAM

SOARES, WHAT WAS IT?
ANDALA, DO YOU HEAR THAT?
BAM

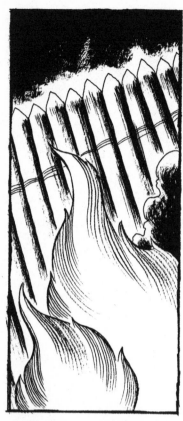

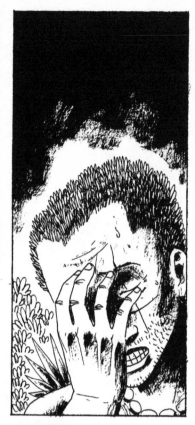

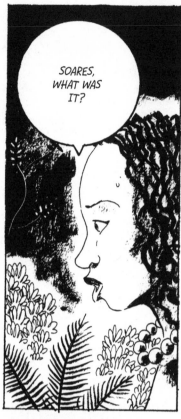

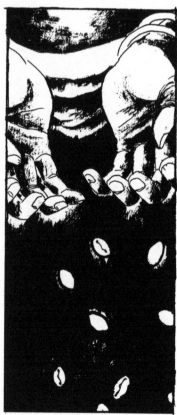

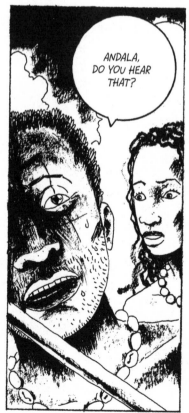

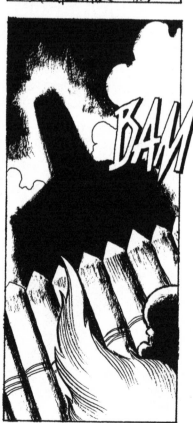

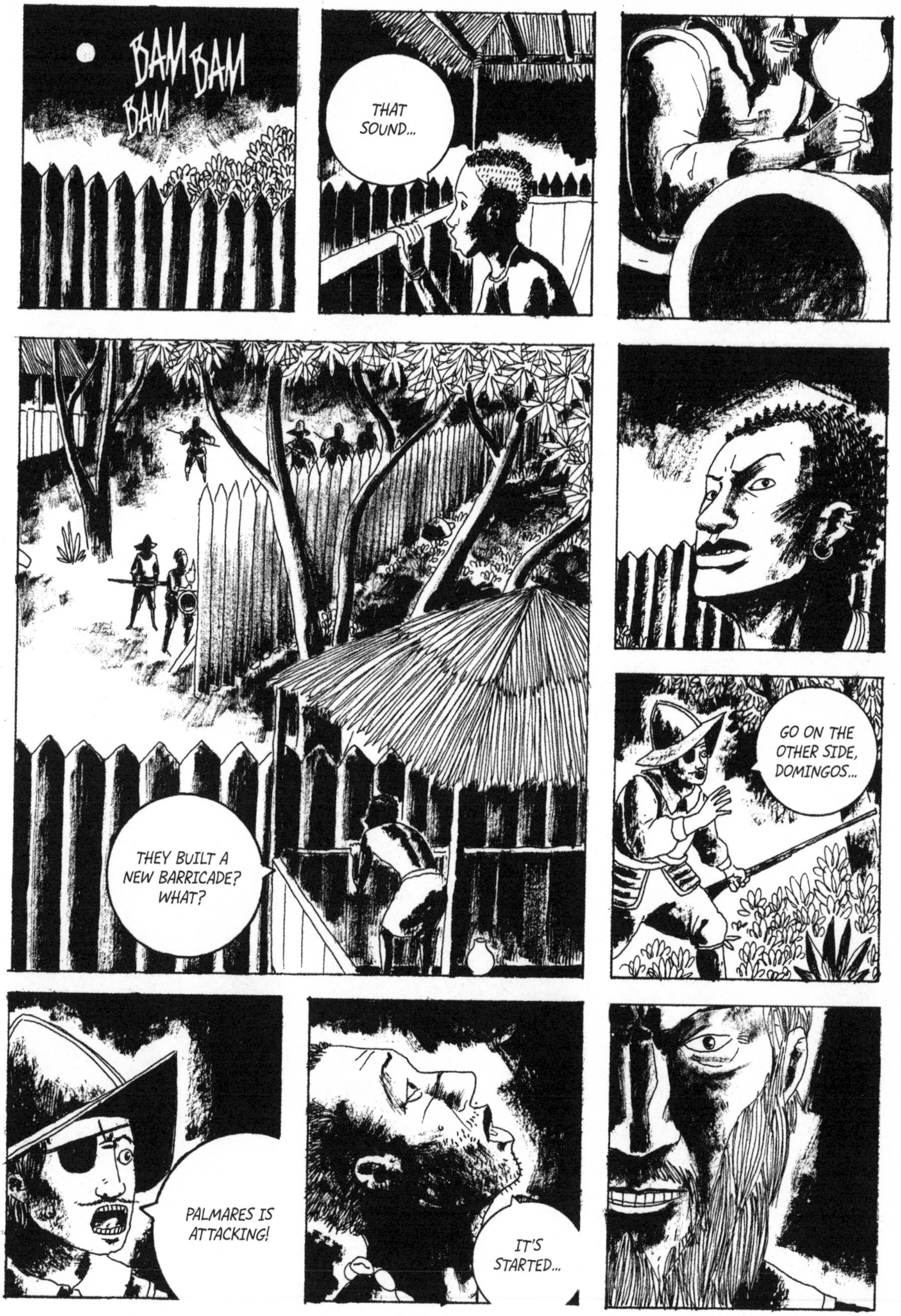
BAM BAM BAM
THAT SOUND...
THEY BUILT A NEW BARRICADE? WHAT?
GO ON THE OTHER SIDE, DOMINGOS...
PALMARES IS ATTACKING!
IT'S STARTED...

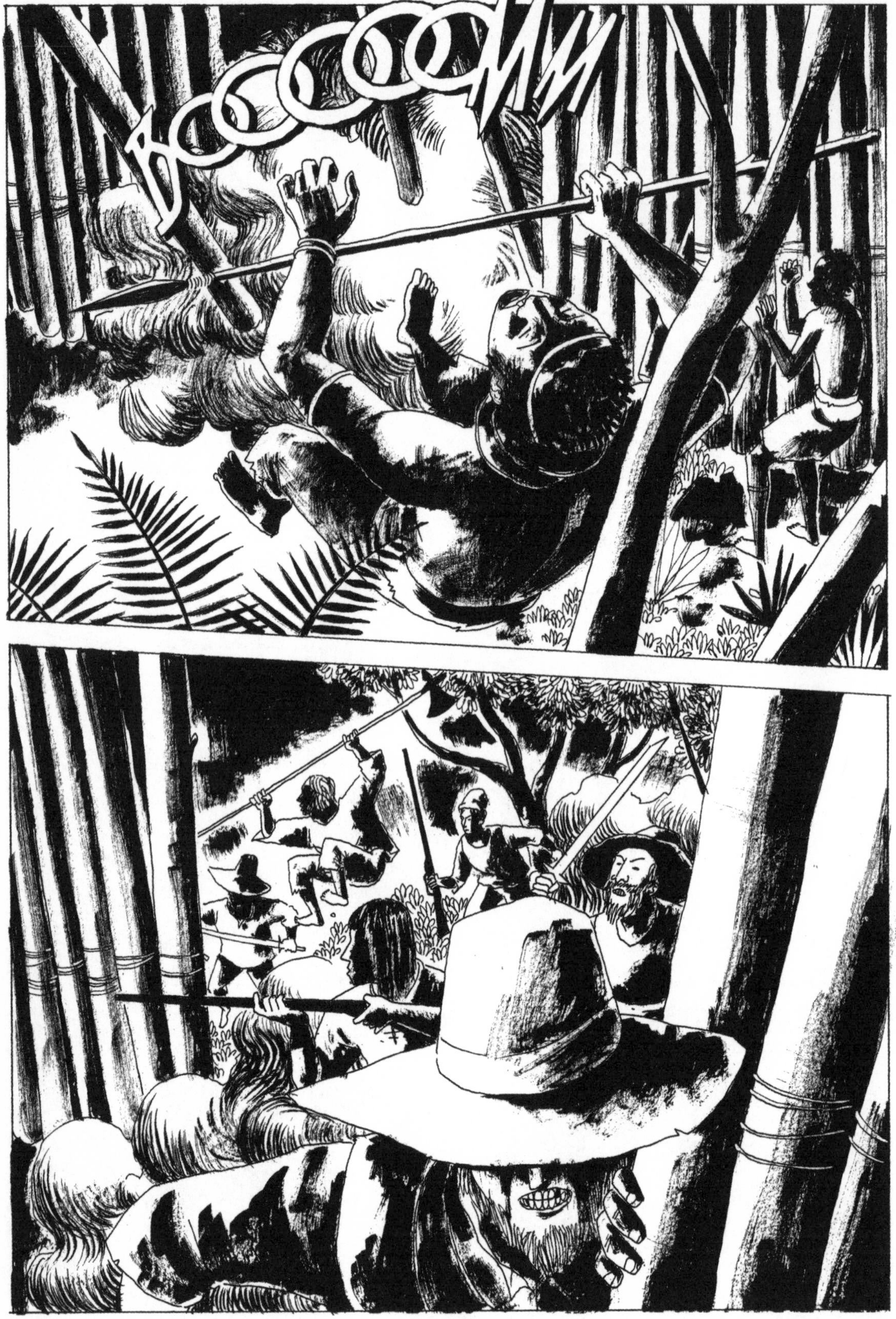
BOOOOOOMM

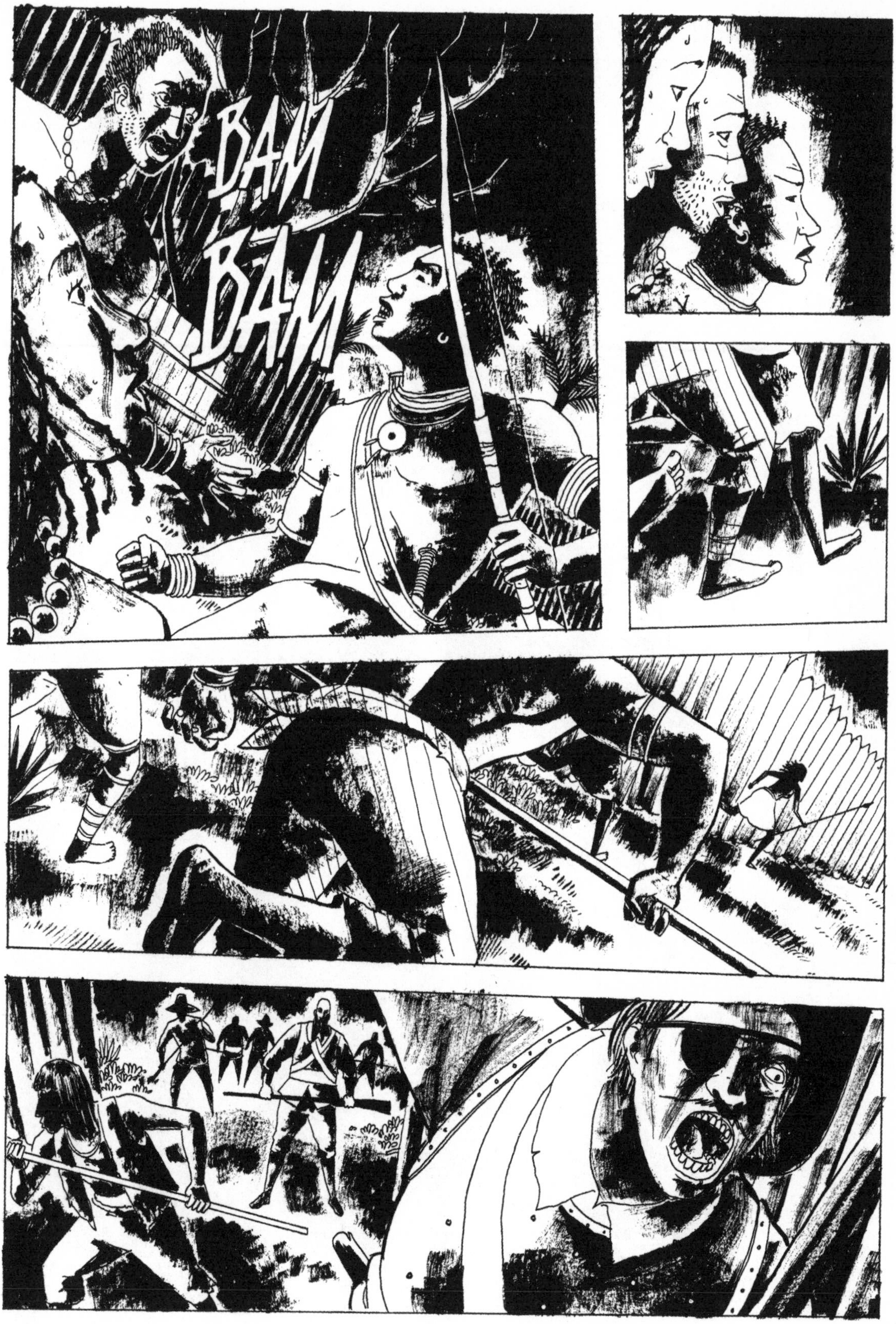
BAM
BAM

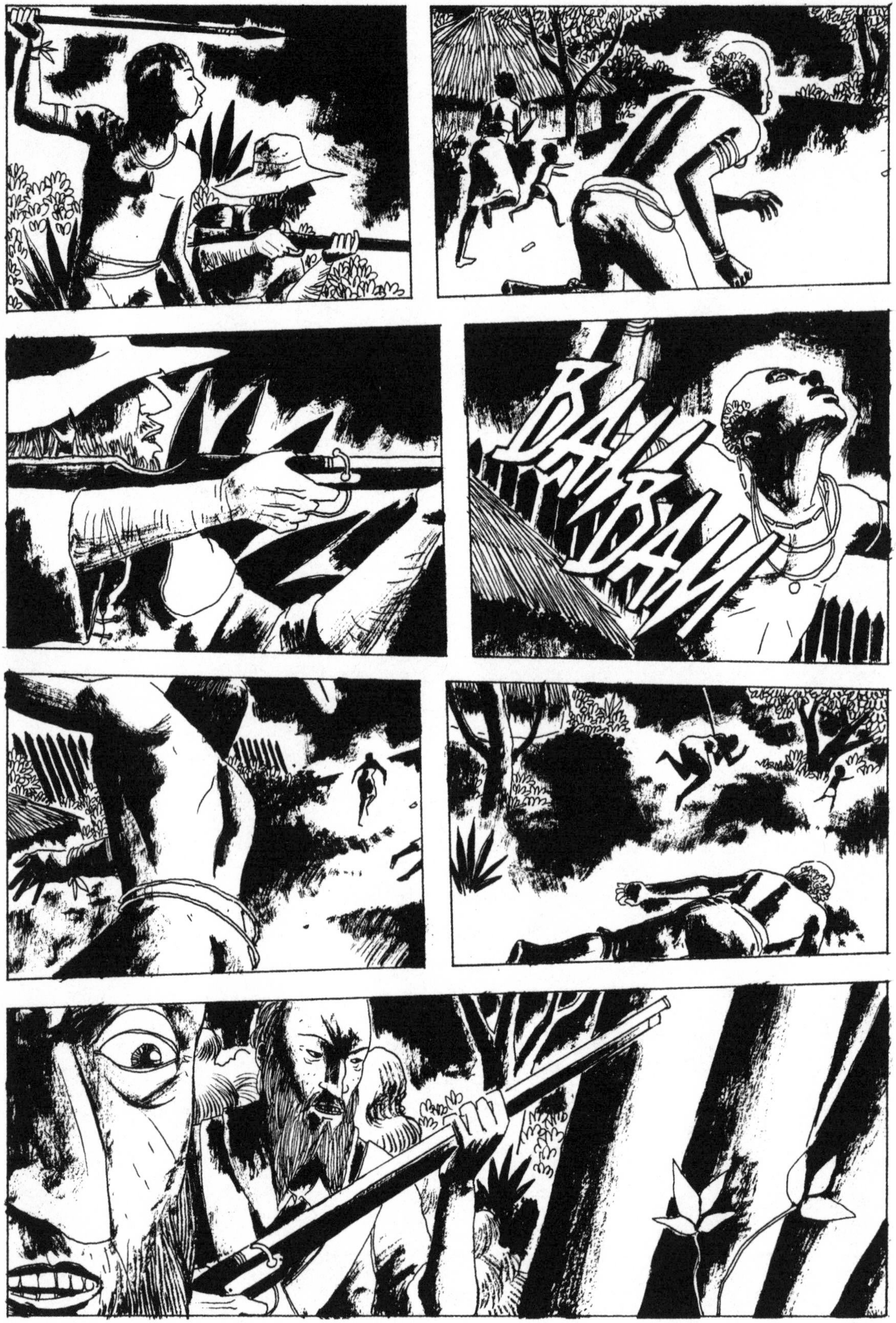
BAM BAM

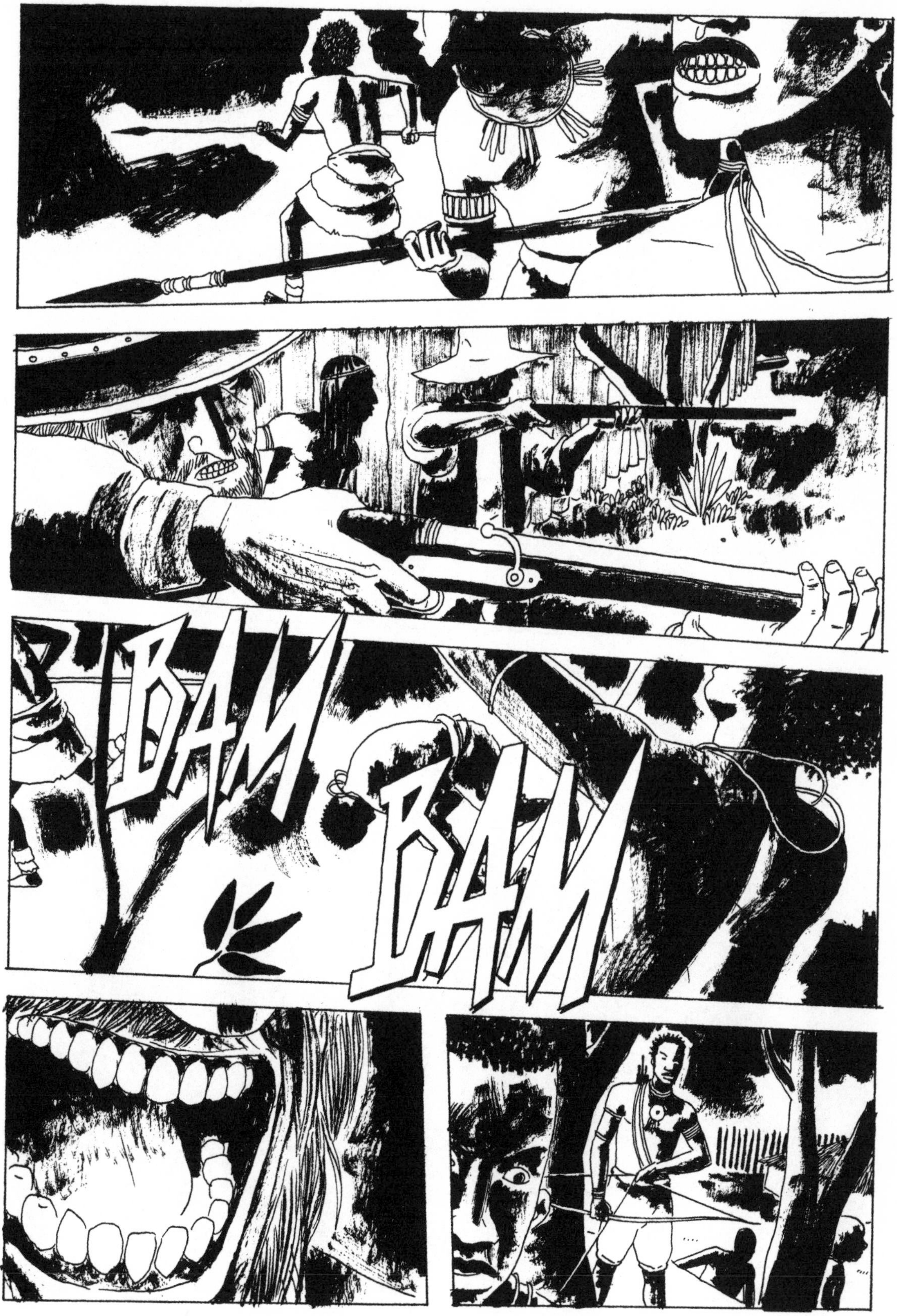
BAM
BAM
BAM

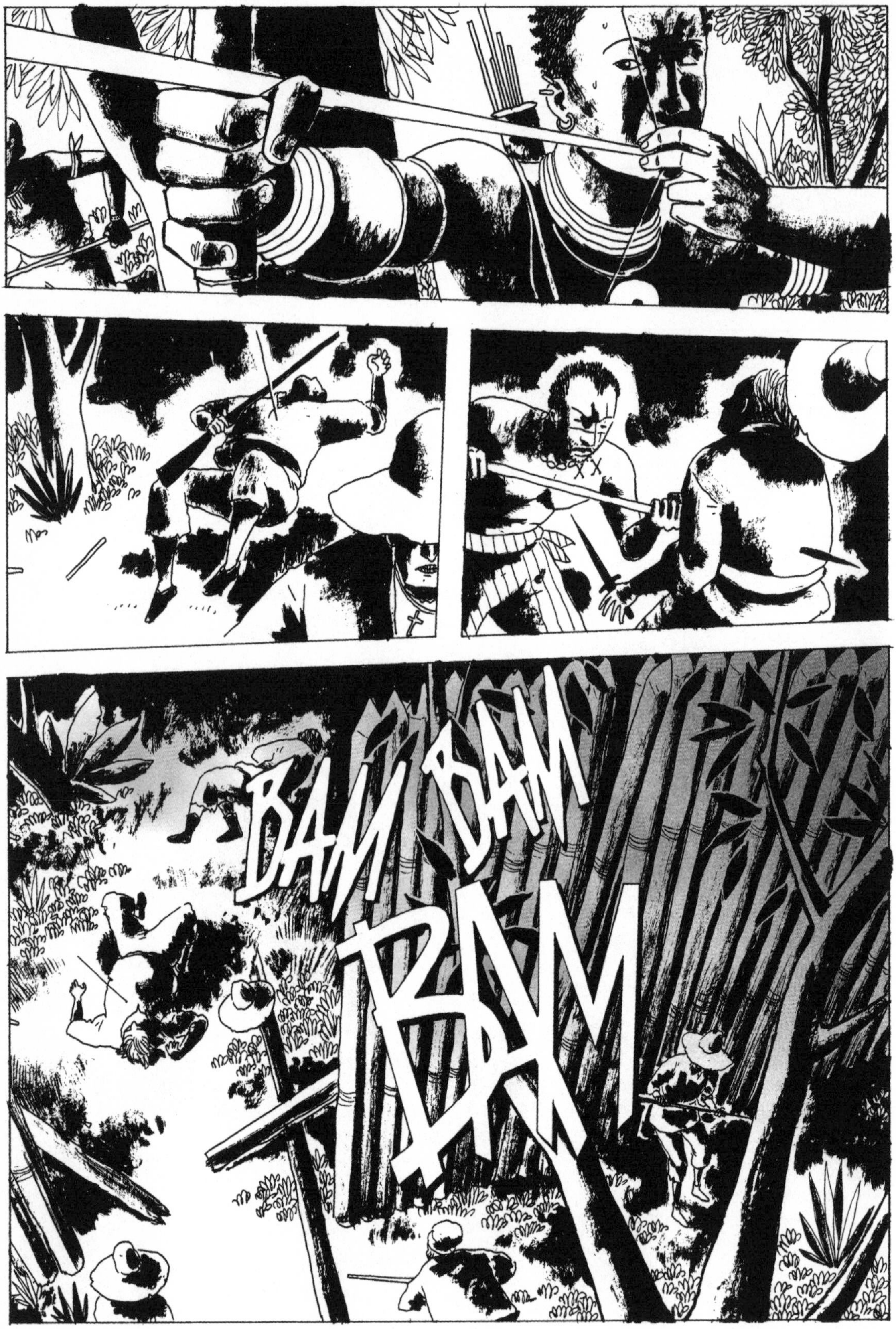
BAM BAM
BAM

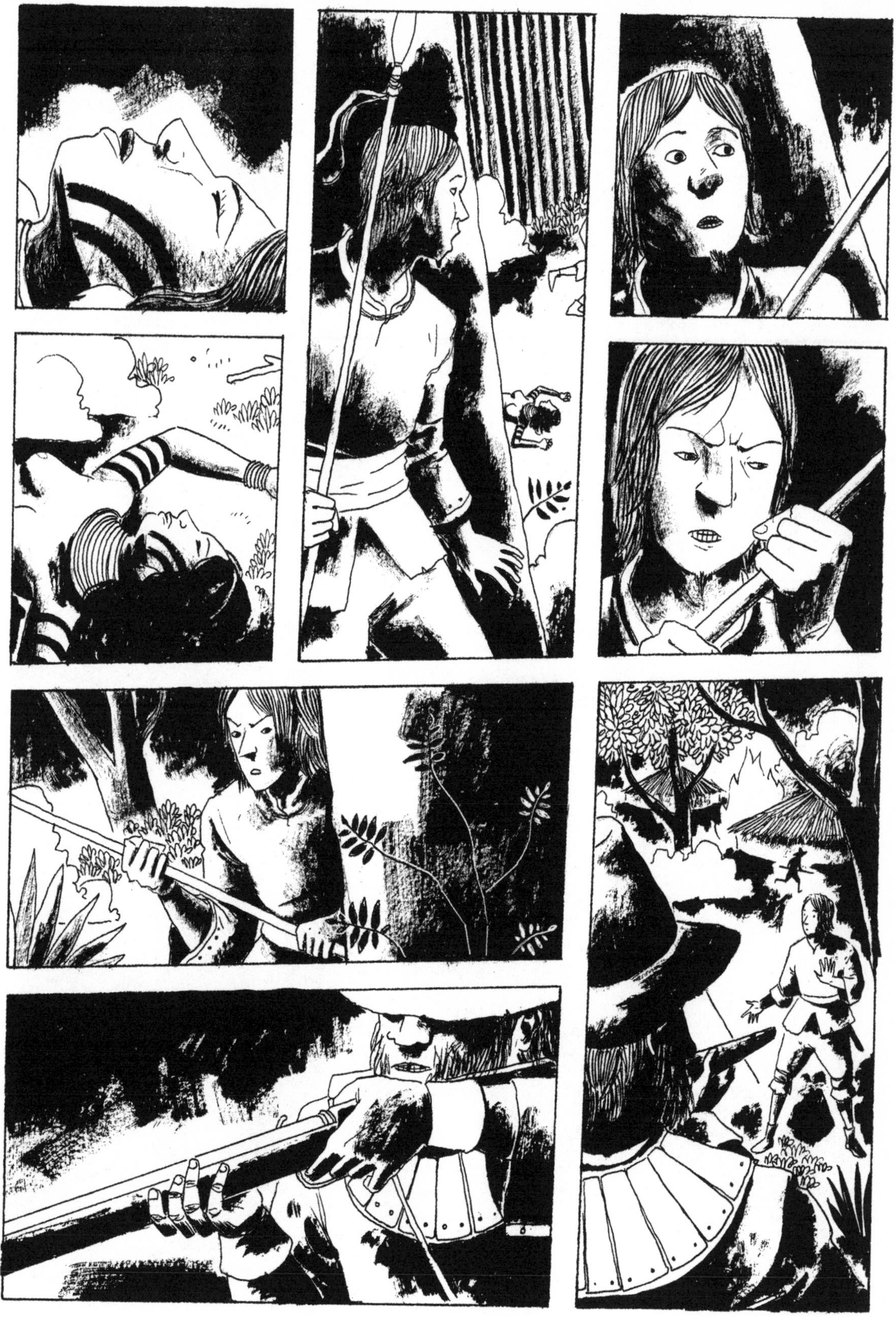

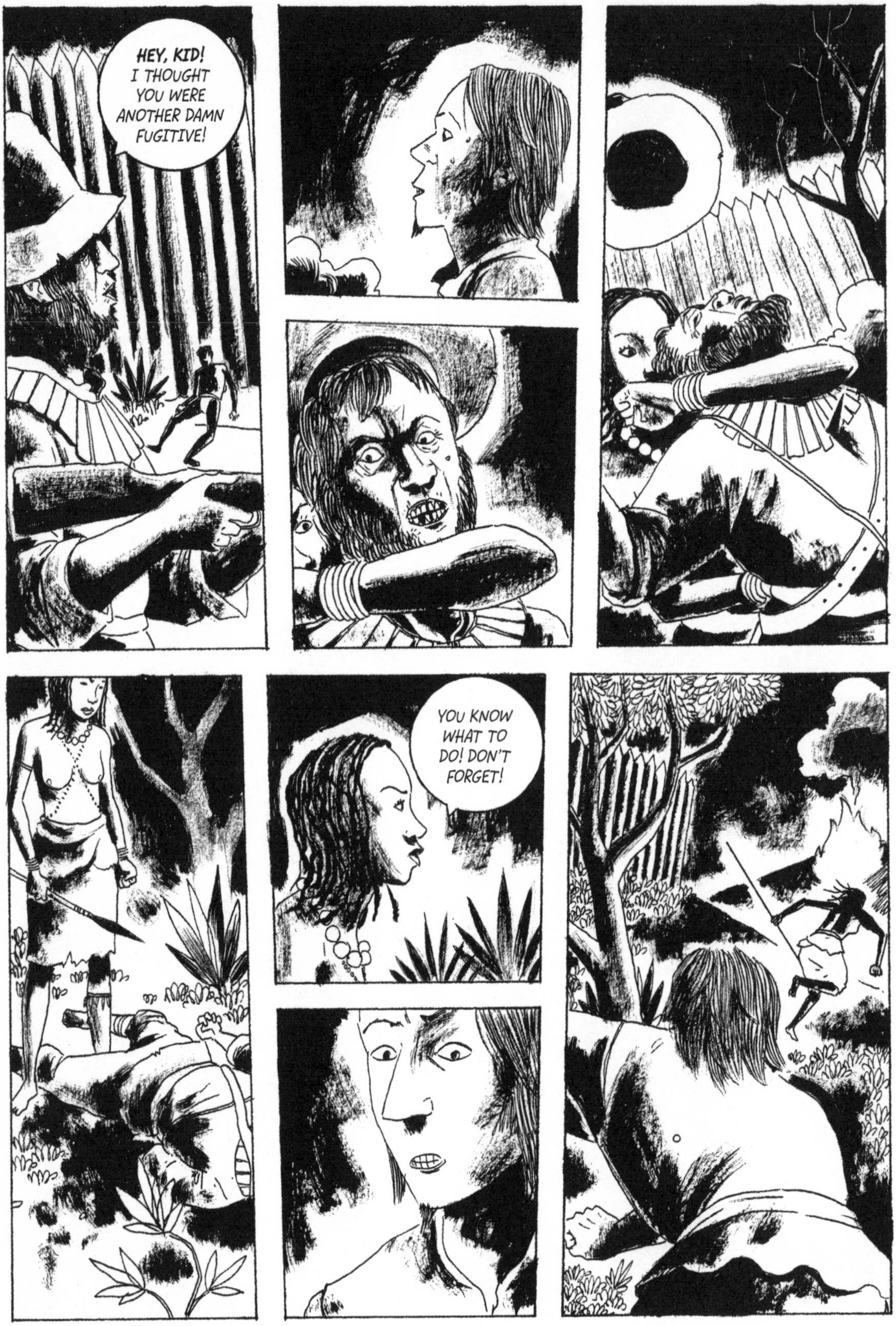
HEY, KID! I THOUGHT YOU WERE ANOTHER DAMN FUGITIVE!
YOU KNOW WHAT TO DO! DON'T FORGET!

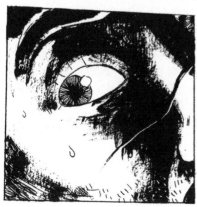

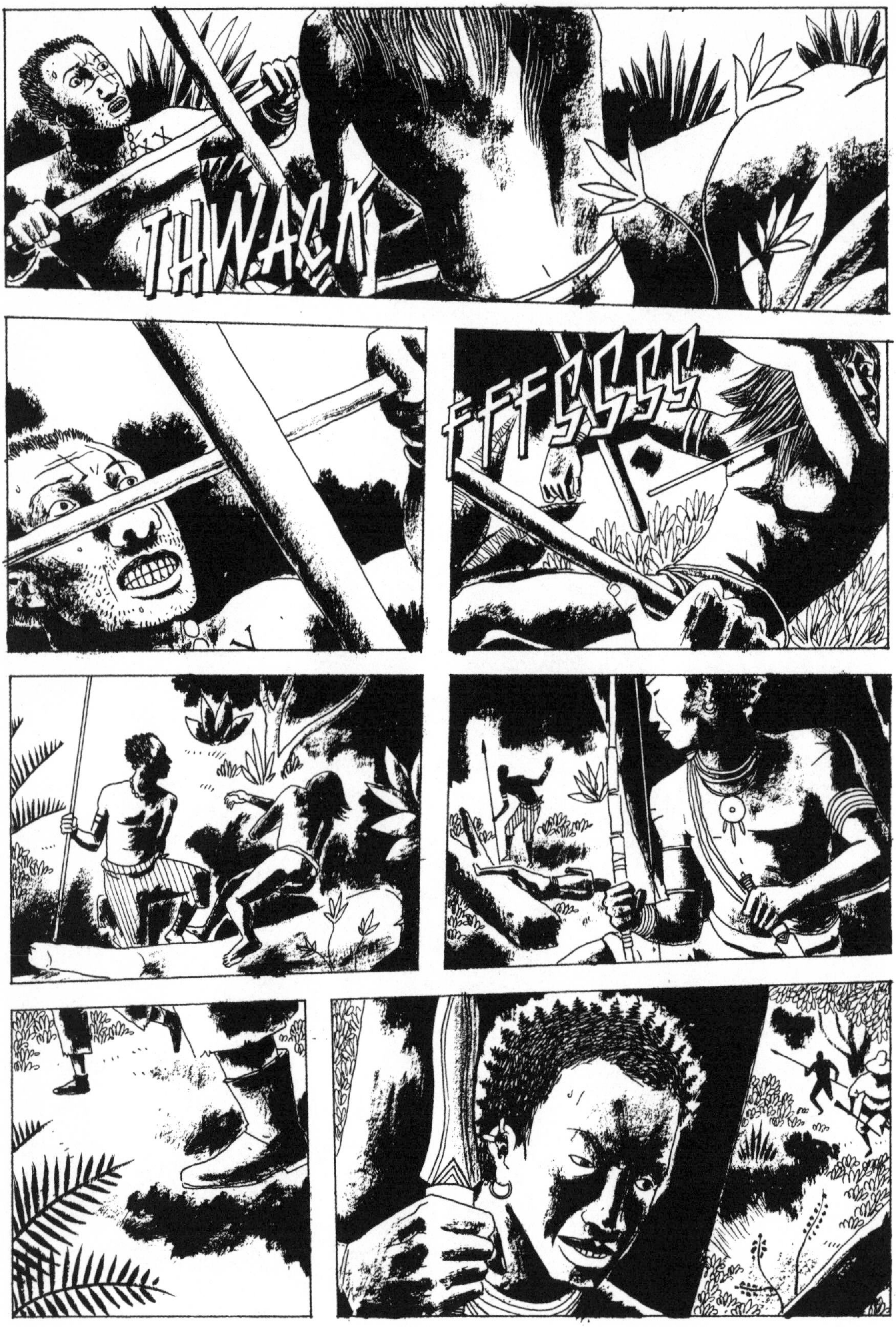
THWACK
FFFSSSS

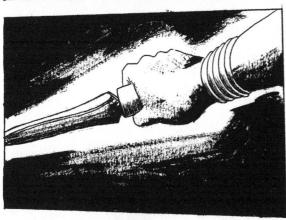

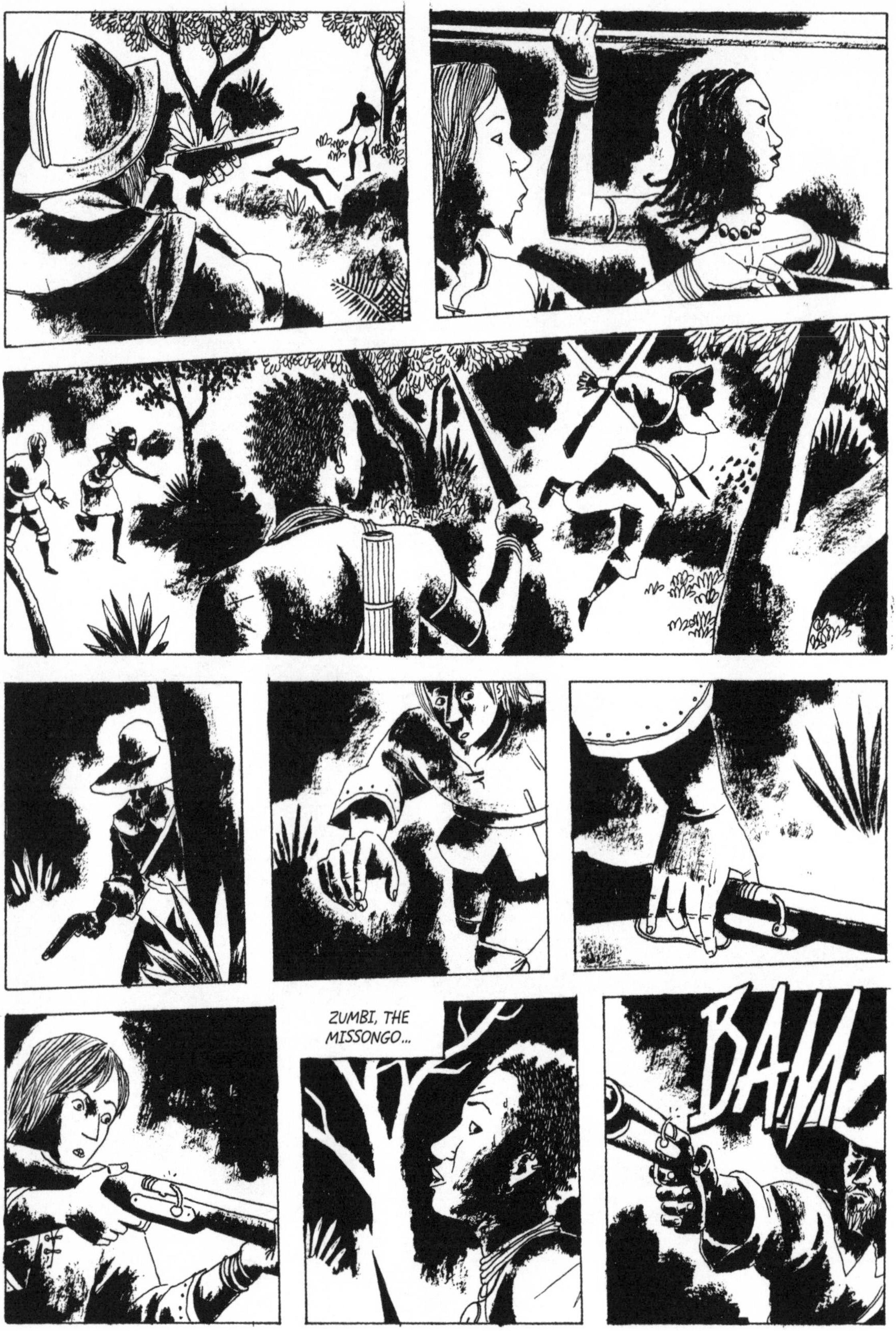
ZUMBI, THE MISSONGO...
BAM

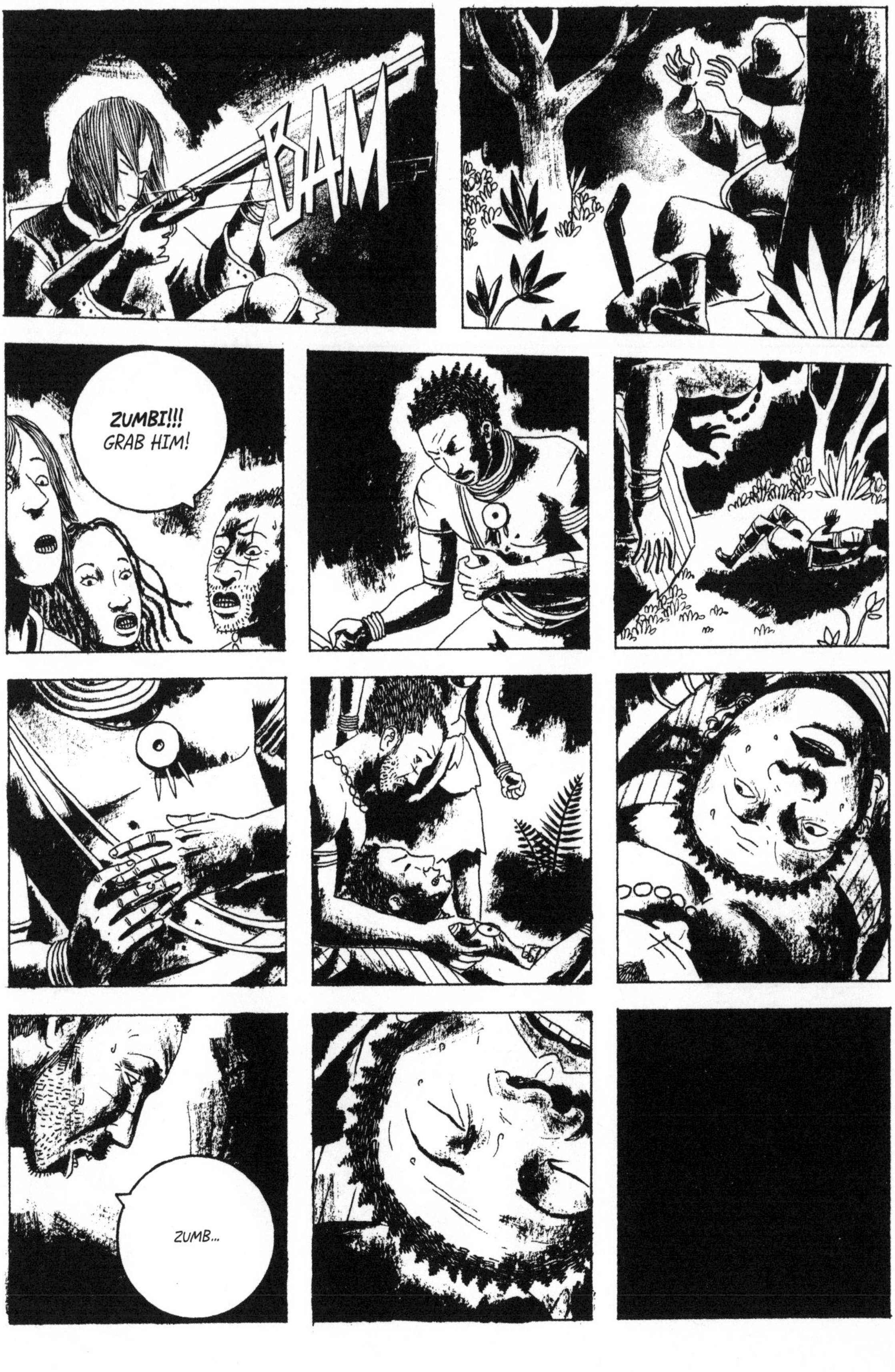
BAM
ZUMBI!!!
GRAB HIM!
ZUMB...

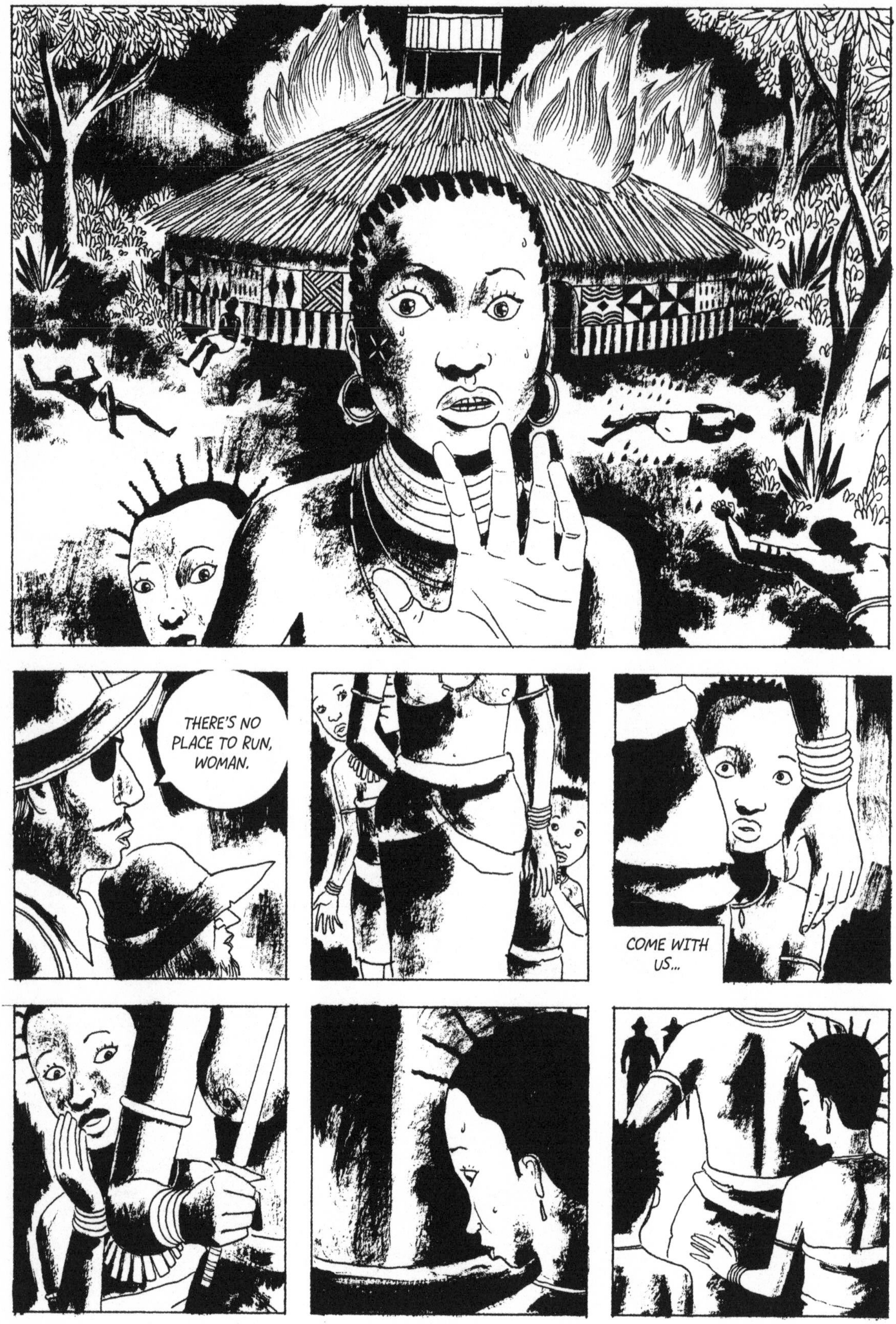
THERE'S NO PLACE TO RUN, WOMAN.
COME WITH US...

PUT DOWN YOUR WEAPON...

BAM BAM

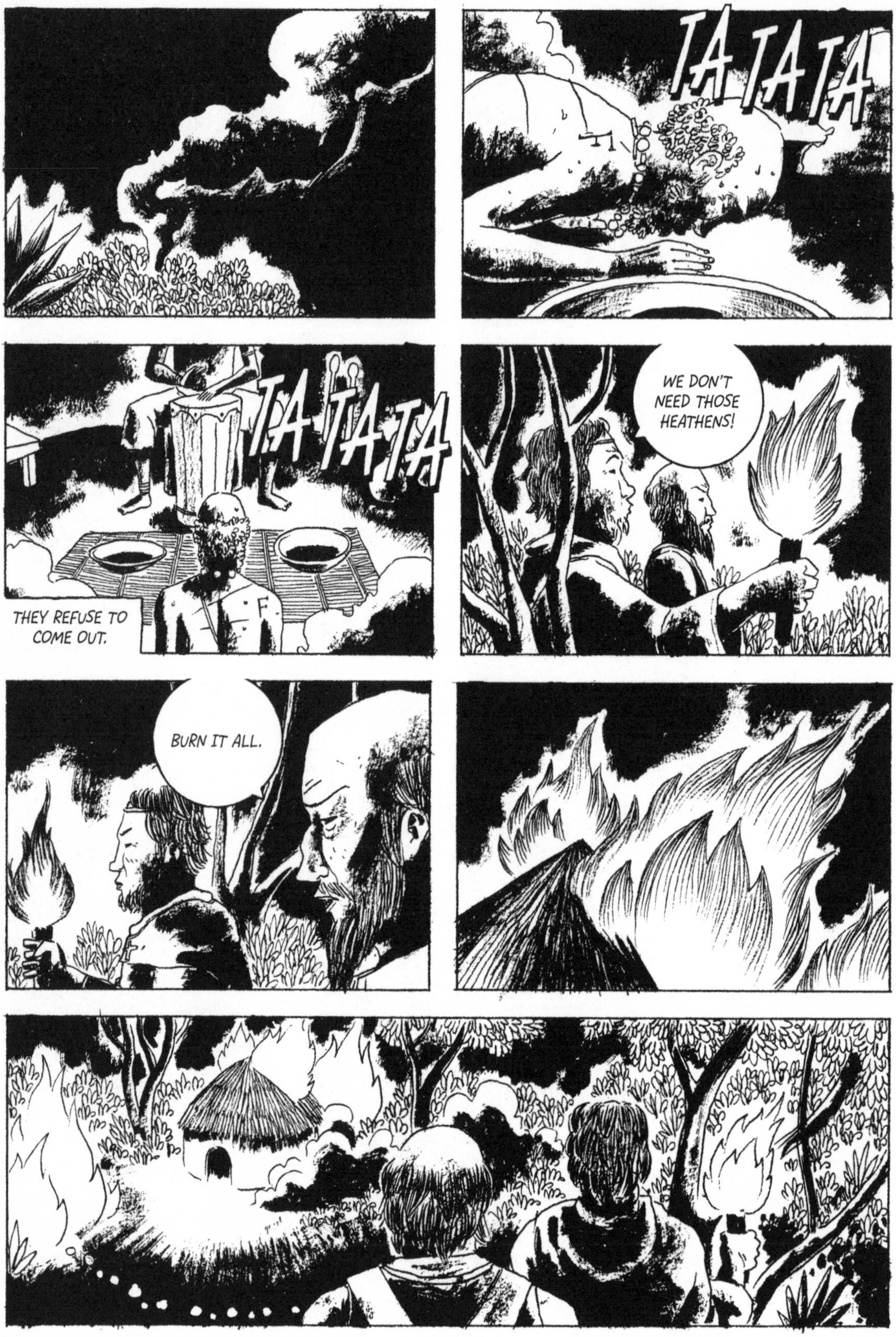
TA TA TA
TA TA TA
THEY REFUSE TO COME OUT.
WE DON'T NEED THOSE HEATHENS!
BURN IT ALL.

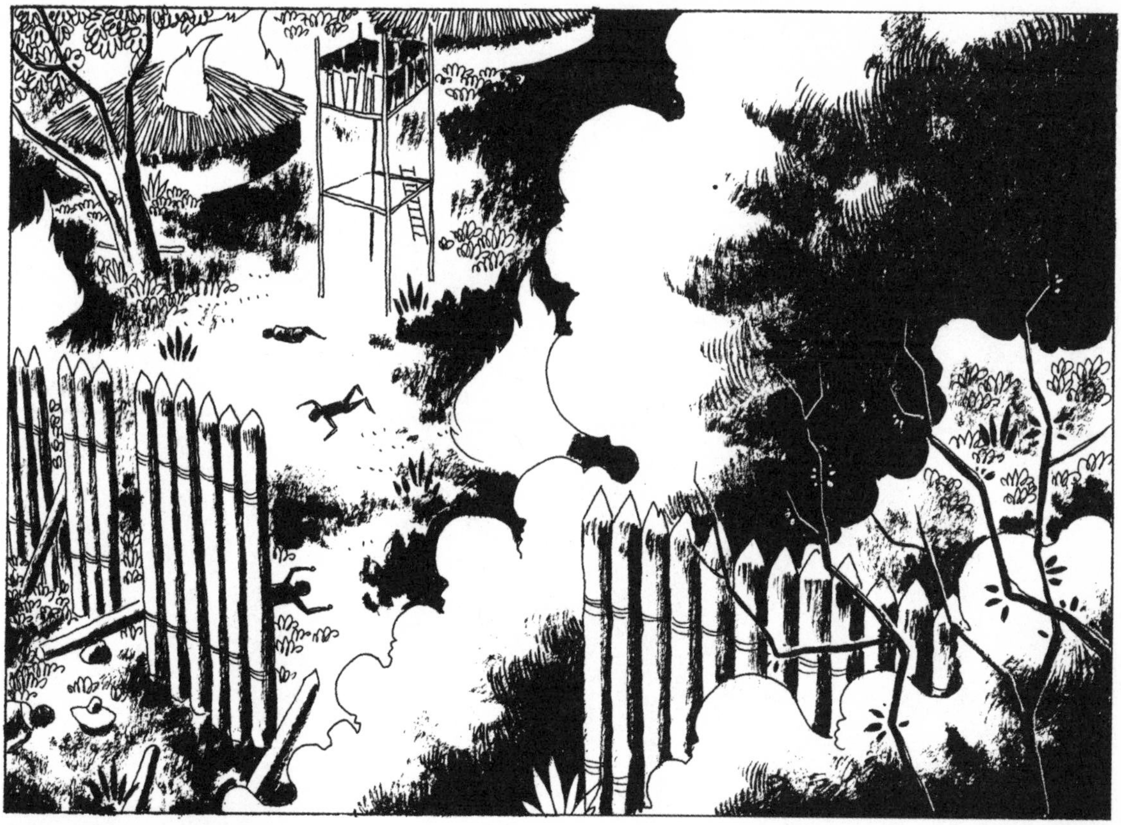

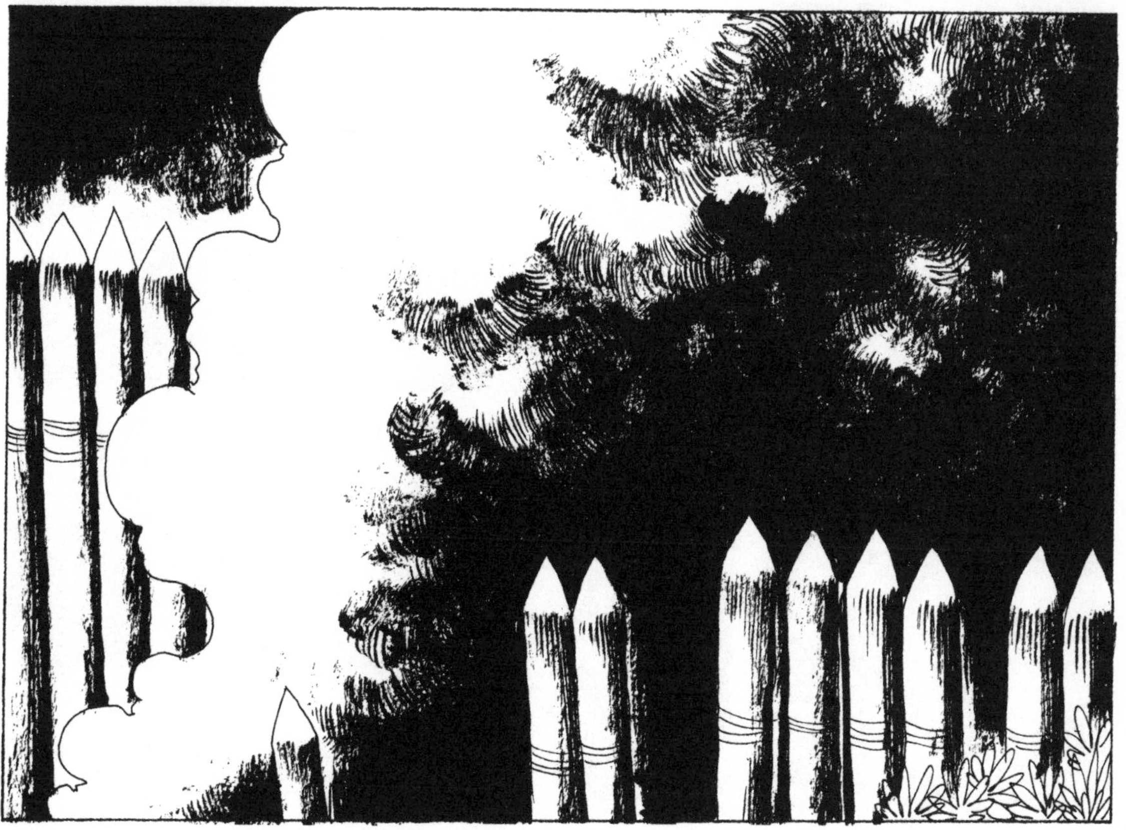

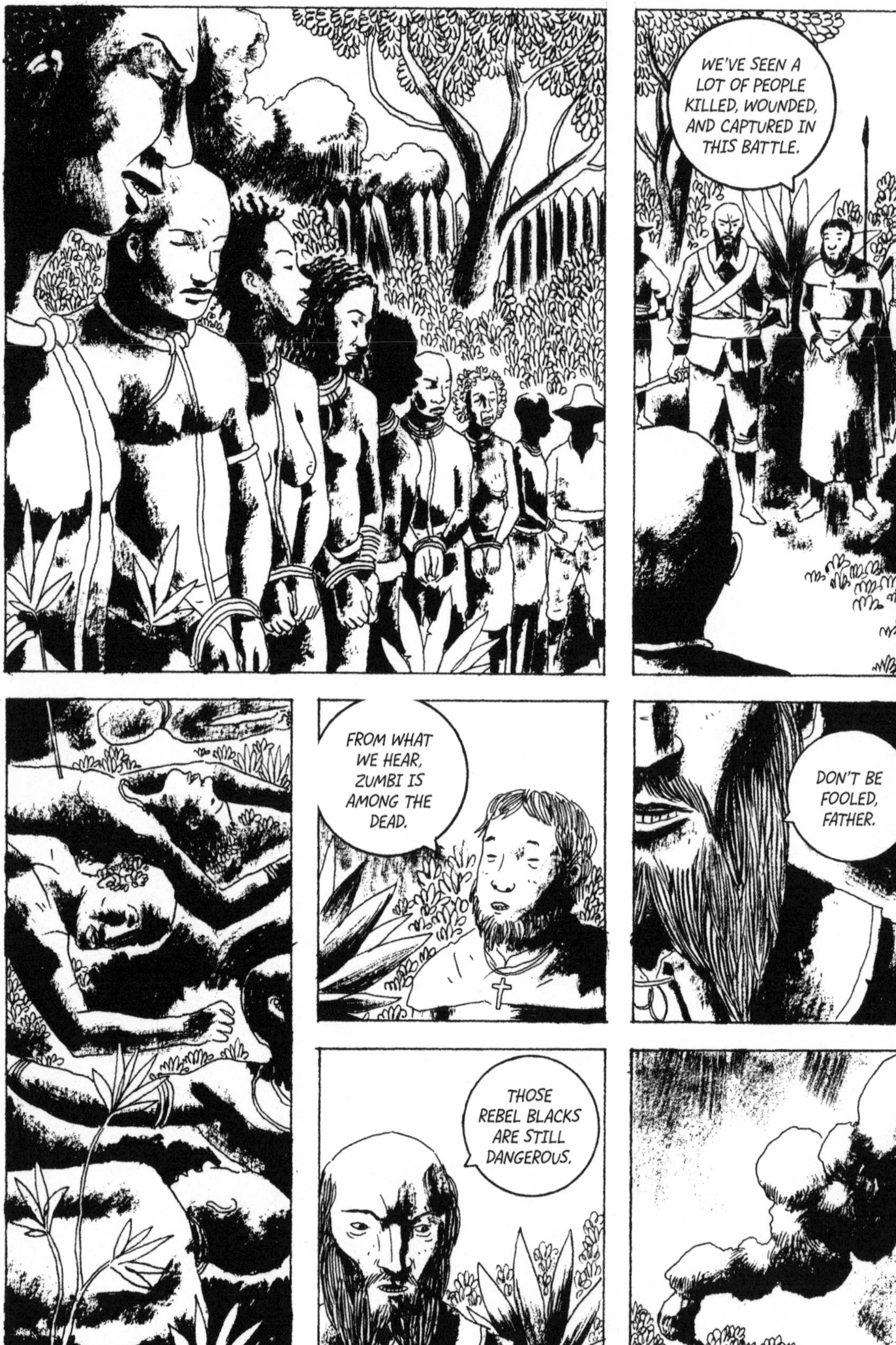

WE'VE SEEN A LOT OF PEOPLE KILLED, WOUNDED, AND CAPTURED IN THIS BATTLE.
FROM WHAT WE HEAR, ZUMBI IS AMONG THE DEAD.
DON'T BE FOOLED, FATHER.
THOSE REBEL BLACKS ARE STILL DANGEROUS.

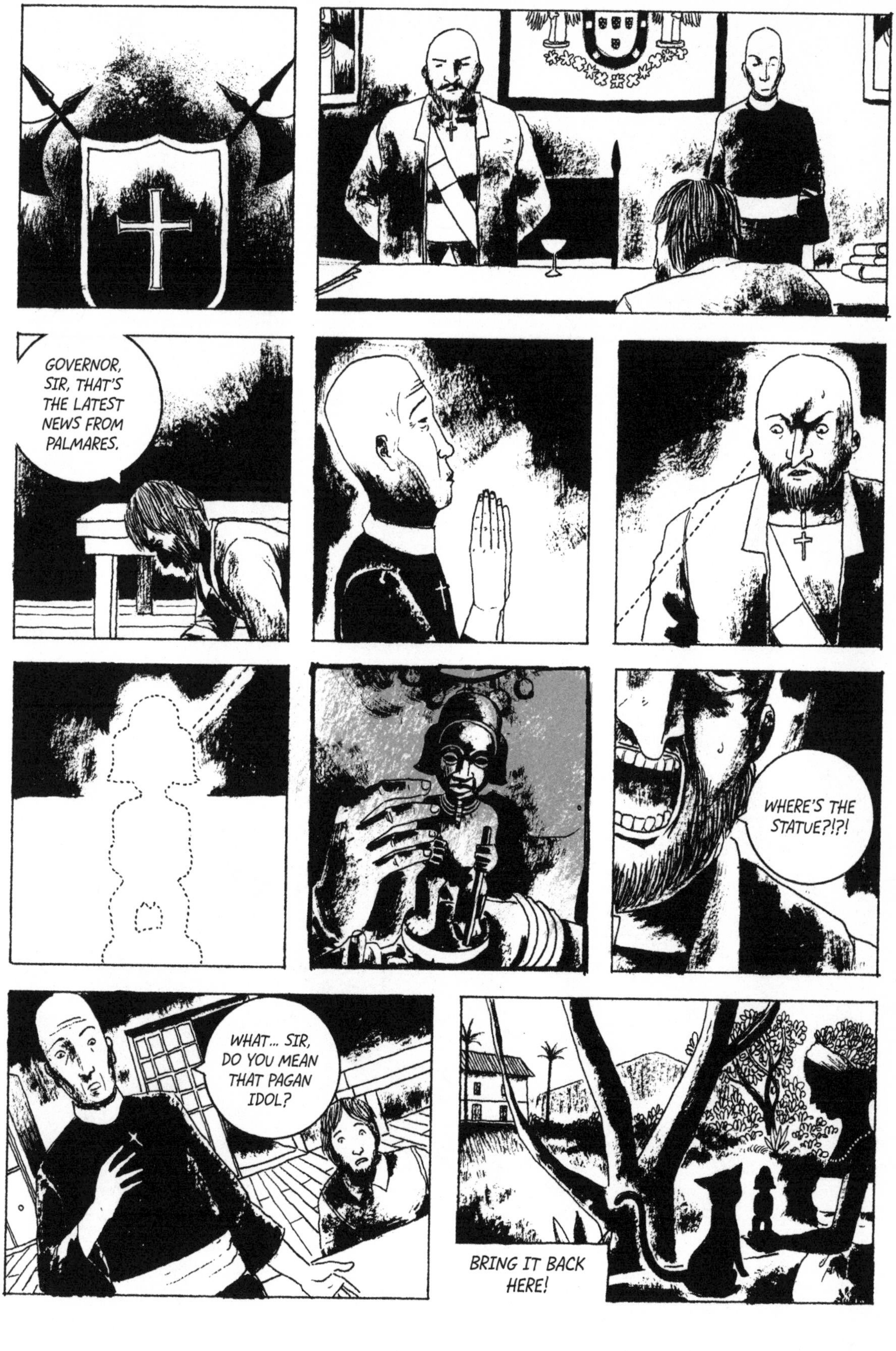
GOVERNOR, SIR, THAT'S THE LATEST NEWS FROM PALMARES.
WHERE'S THE STATUE?!?!
WHAT... SIR, DO YOU MEAN THAT PAGAN IDOL?
BRING IT BACK HERE!

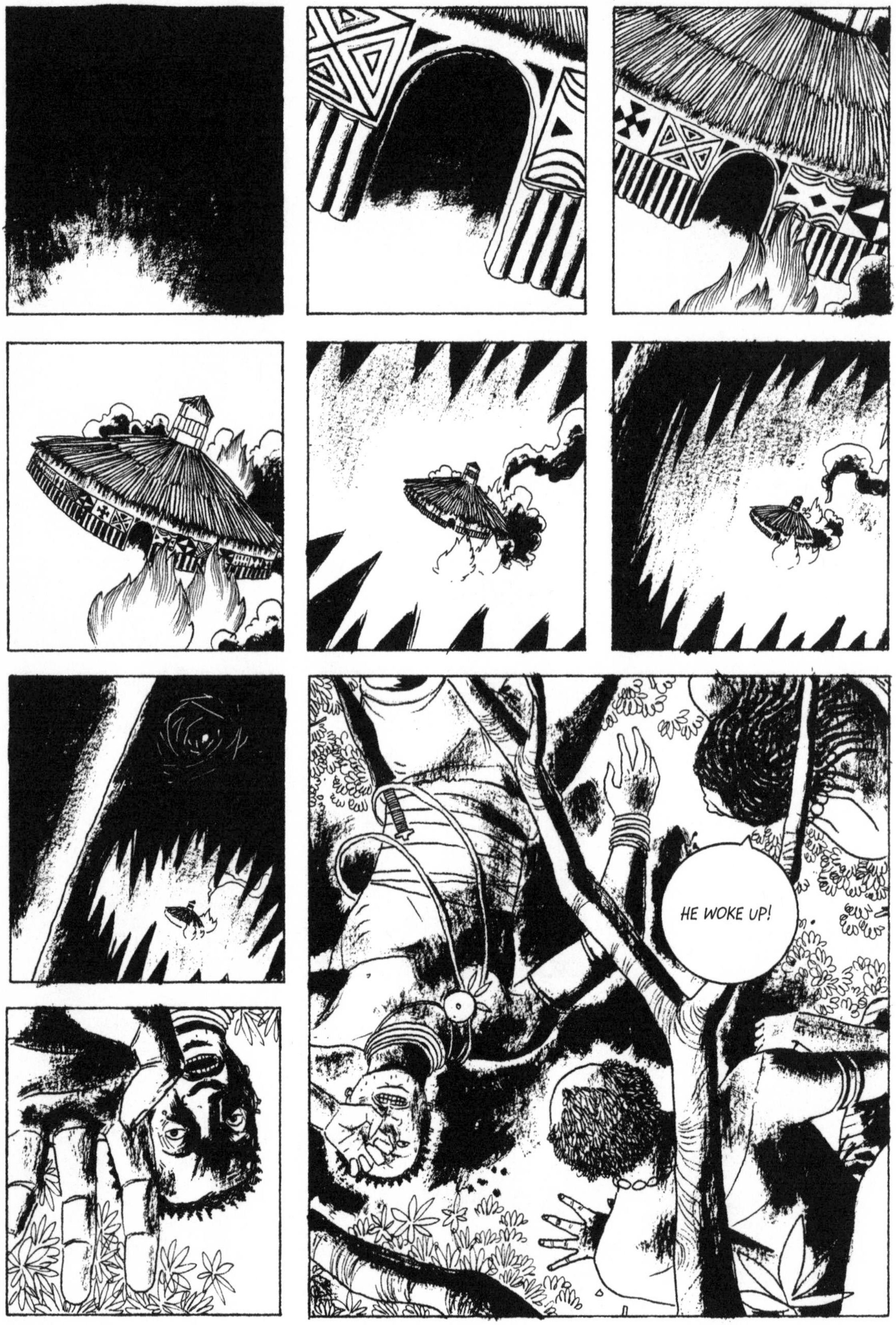
HE WOKE UP!

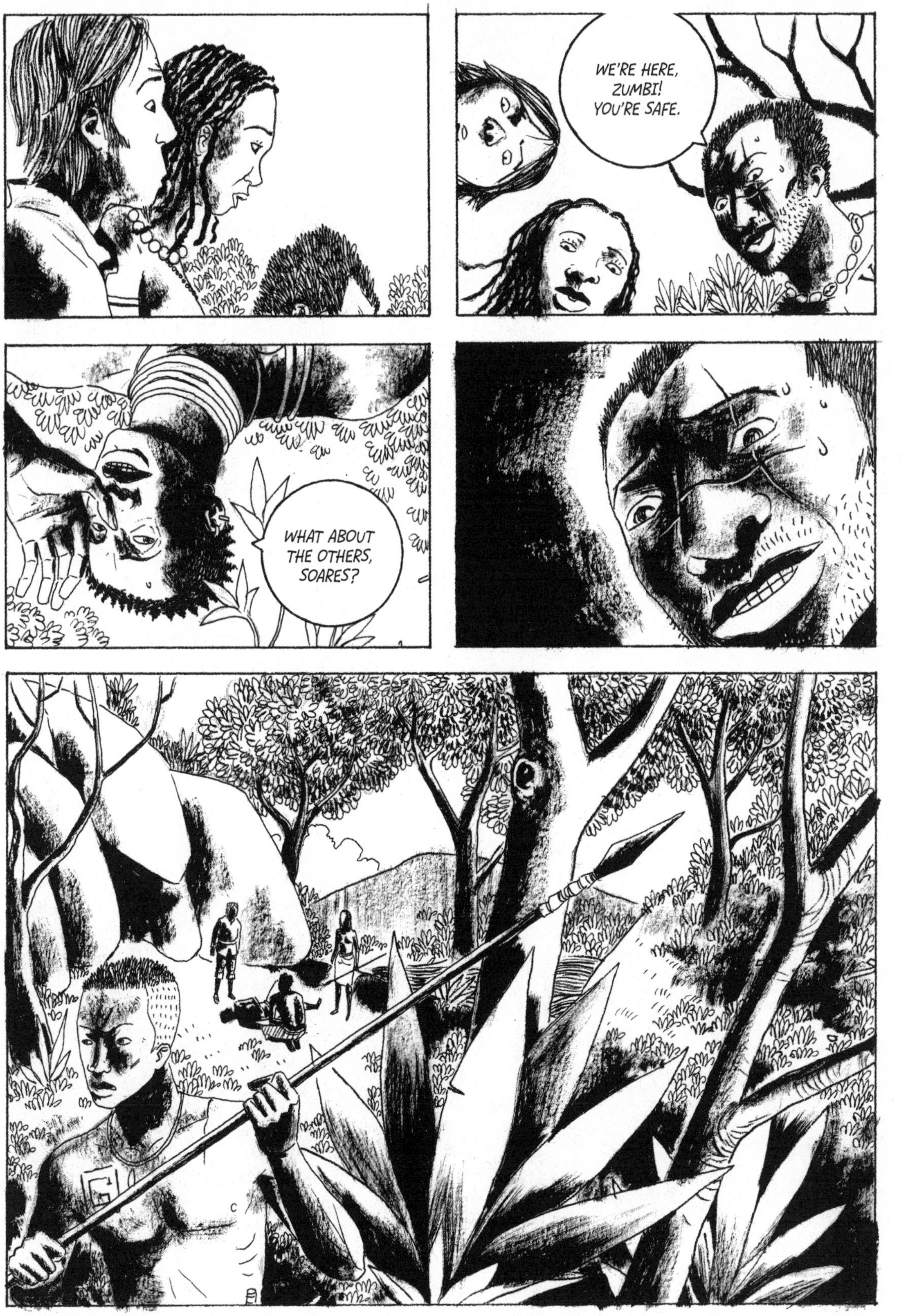
WE'RE HERE, ZUMBI! YOU'RE SAFE.
WHAT ABOUT THE OTHERS, SOARES?

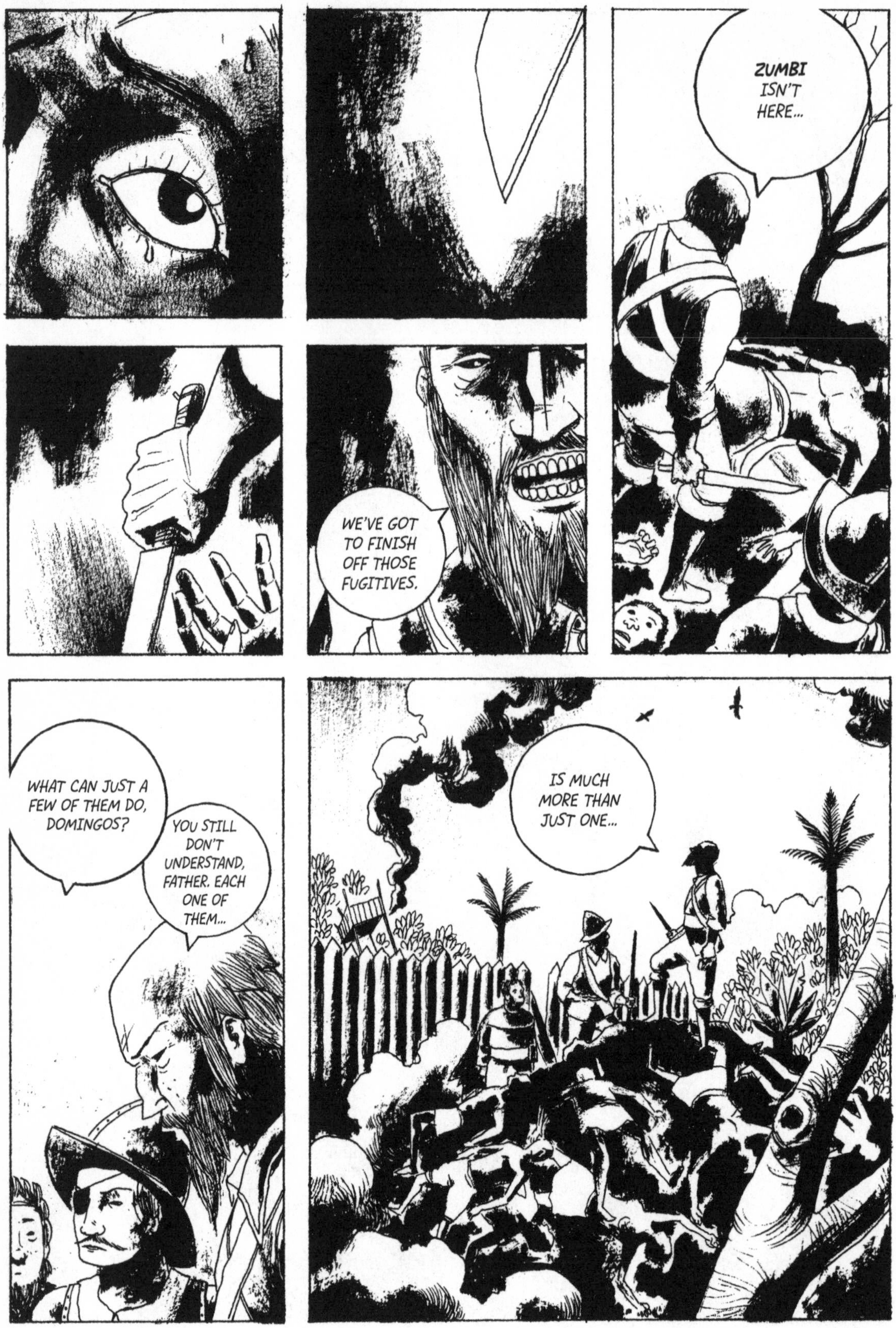
ZUMBI ISN'T HERE...
WE'VE GOT TO FINISH OFF THOSE FUGITIVES.
WHAT CAN JUST A FEW OF THEM DO, DOMINGOS?
YOU STILL DON'T UNDERSTAND, FATHER. EACH ONE OF THEM...
IS MUCH MORE THAN JUST ONE...

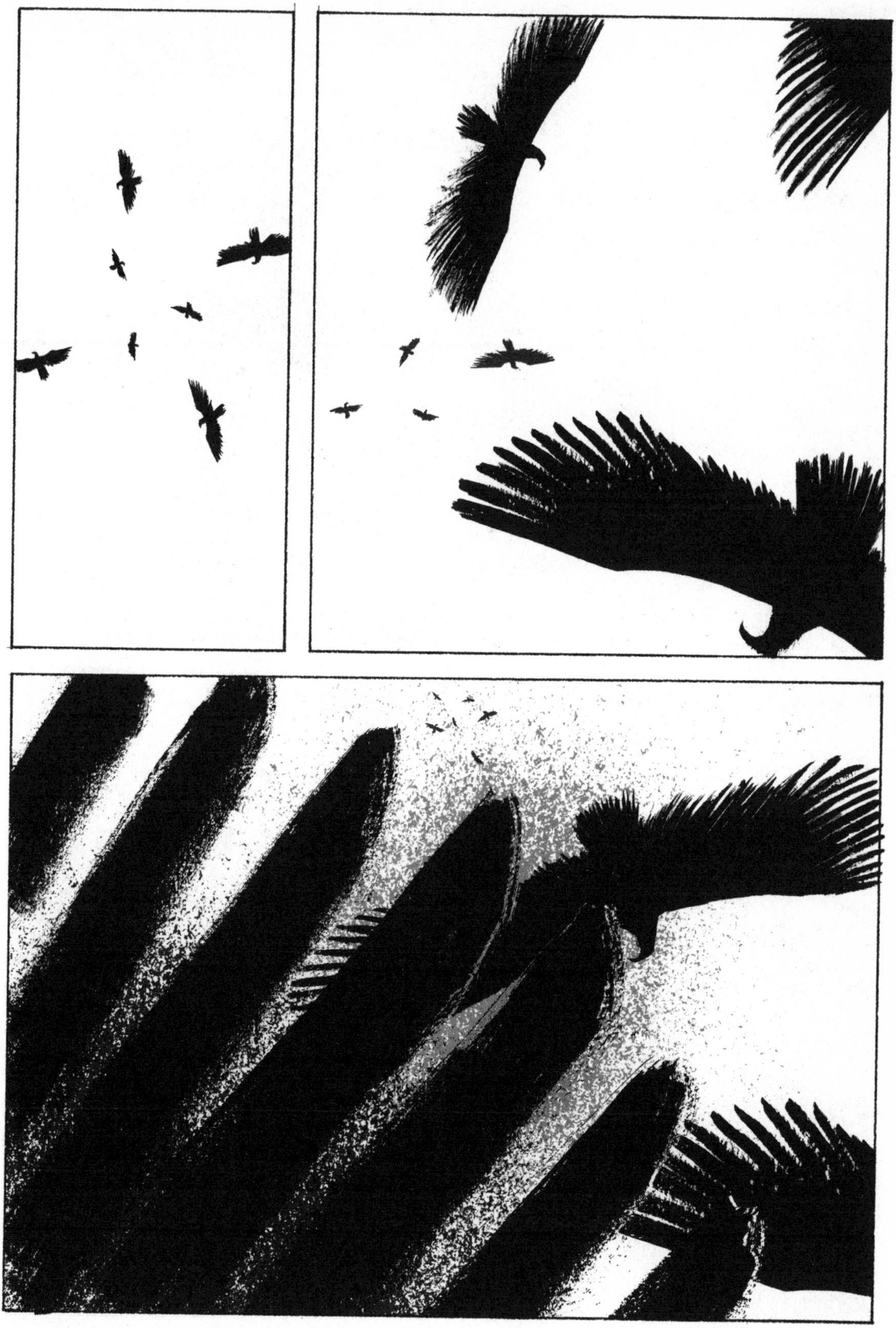

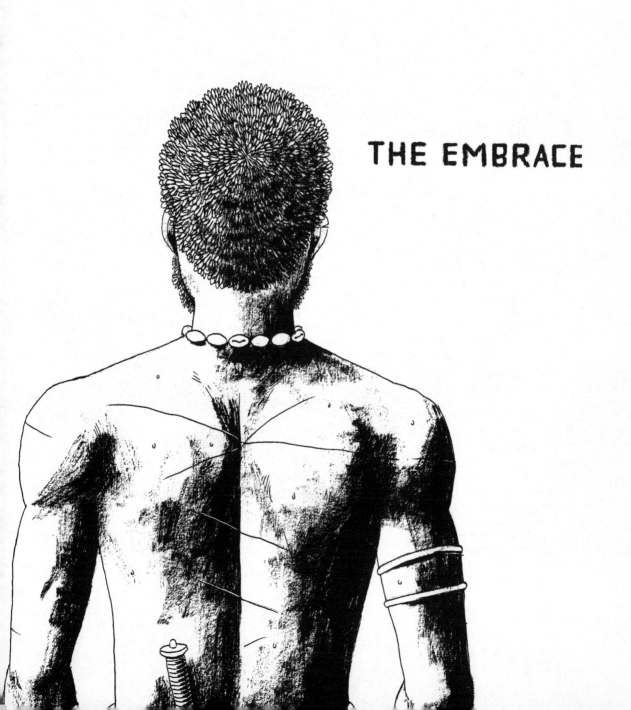

THE EMBRACE

[T]he heads of the two main conspirators who were condemned to death will be taken to the site of the crime, where they will be raised up on tall pikes in public, visible to all, and will not be taken down until time has consumed them so that this example might serve not merely to satisfy guilt but also to horrify others so that they will not dare commit similar crimes.

—*Alvará Régio, 1680s*

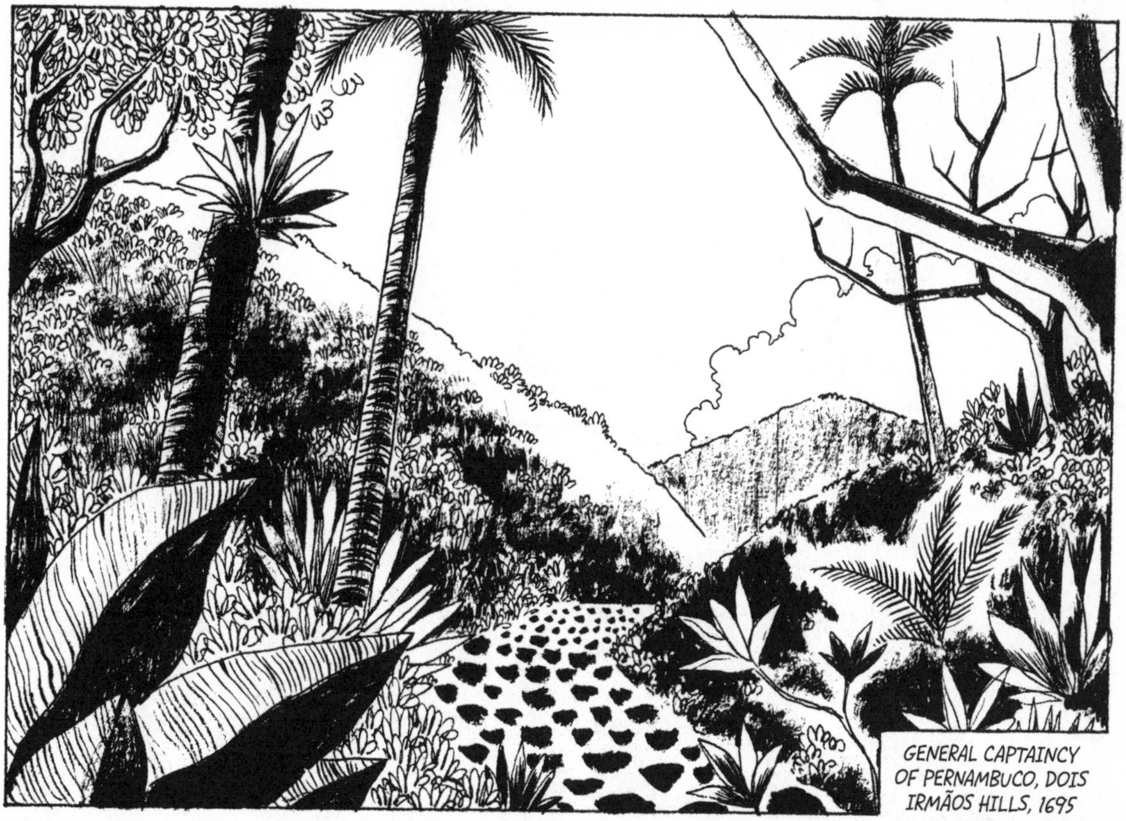

GENERAL CAPTAINCY OF PERNAMBUCO, DOIS IRMÃOS HILLS, 1695

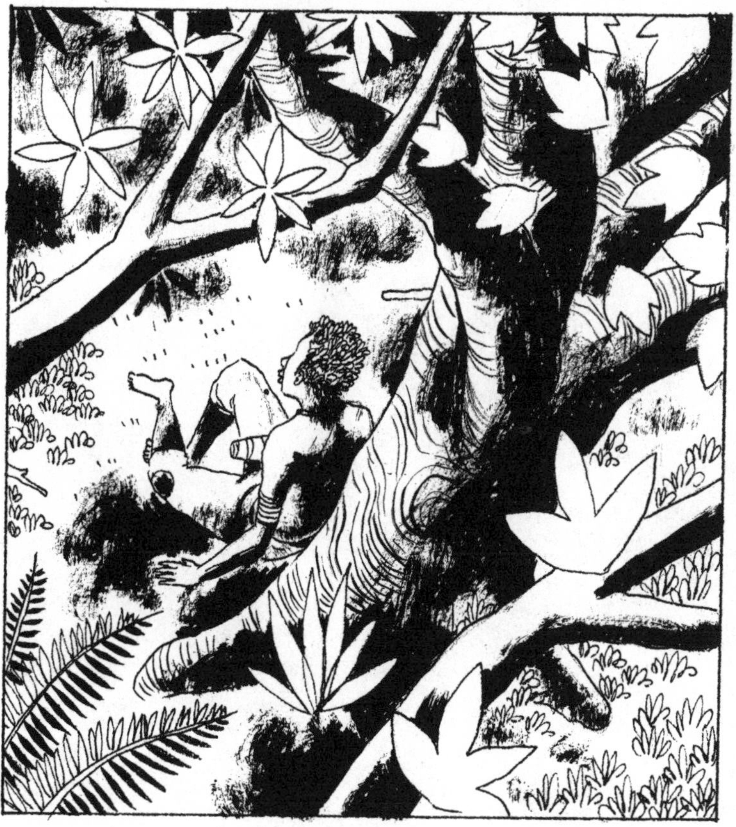

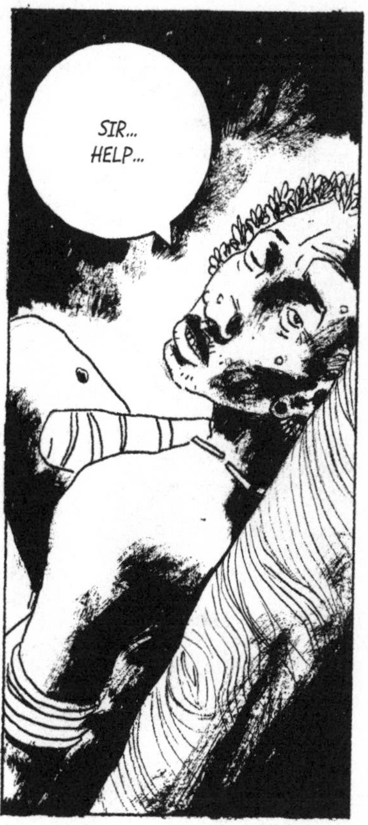
SIR... HELP...

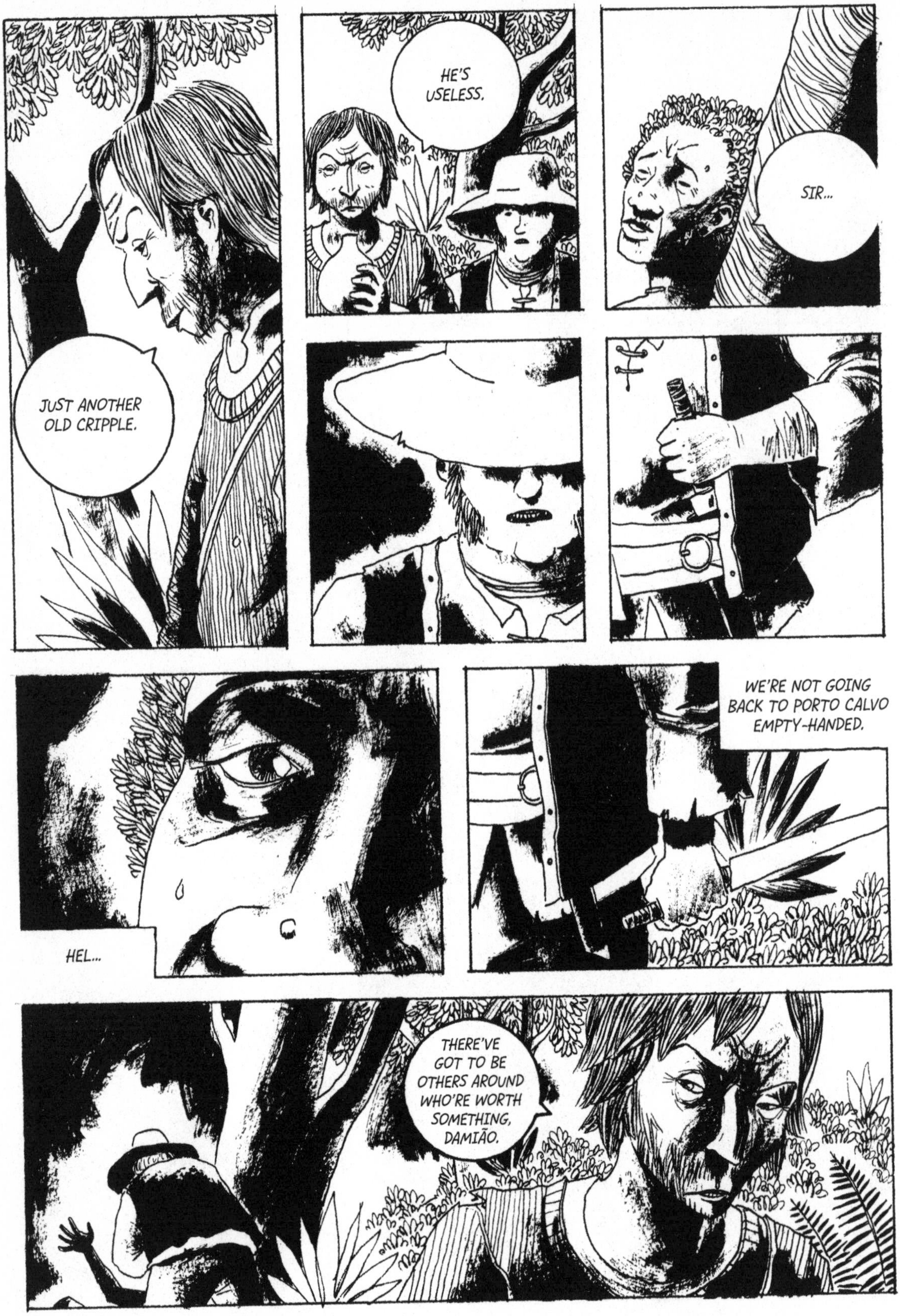
JUST ANOTHER OLD CRIPPLE.
HE'S USELESS.
SIR...
HEL...
WE'RE NOT GOING BACK TO PORTO CALVO EMPTY-HANDED.
THERE'VE GOT TO BE OTHERS AROUND WHO'RE WORTH SOMETHING, DAMIÃO.

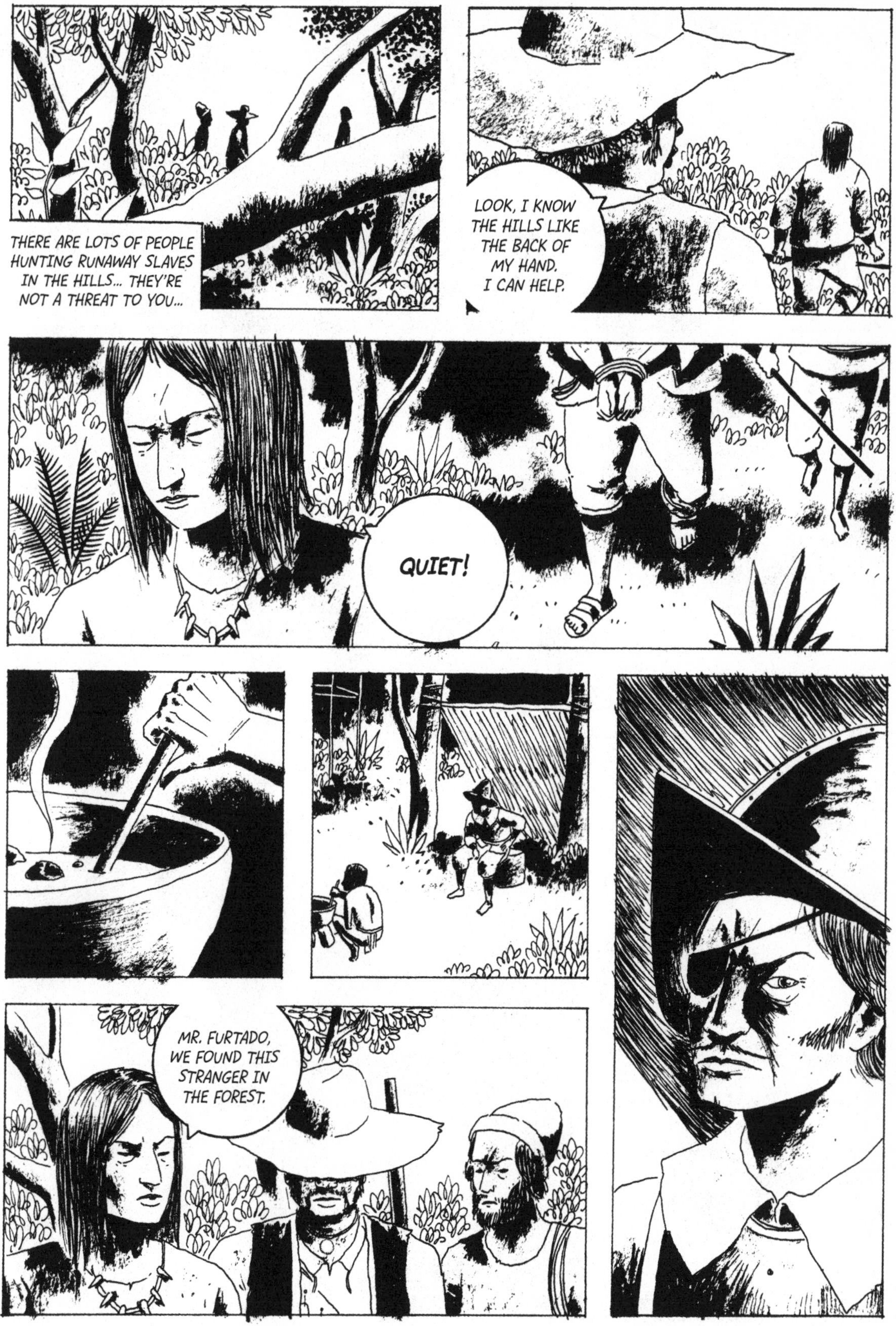
THERE ARE LOTS OF PEOPLE HUNTING RUNAWAY SLAVES IN THE HILLS... THEY'RE NOT A THREAT TO YOU...
LOOK, I KNOW THE HILLS LIKE THE BACK OF MY HAND. I CAN HELP.
QUIET!
MR. FURTADO, WE FOUND THIS STRANGER IN THE FOREST.

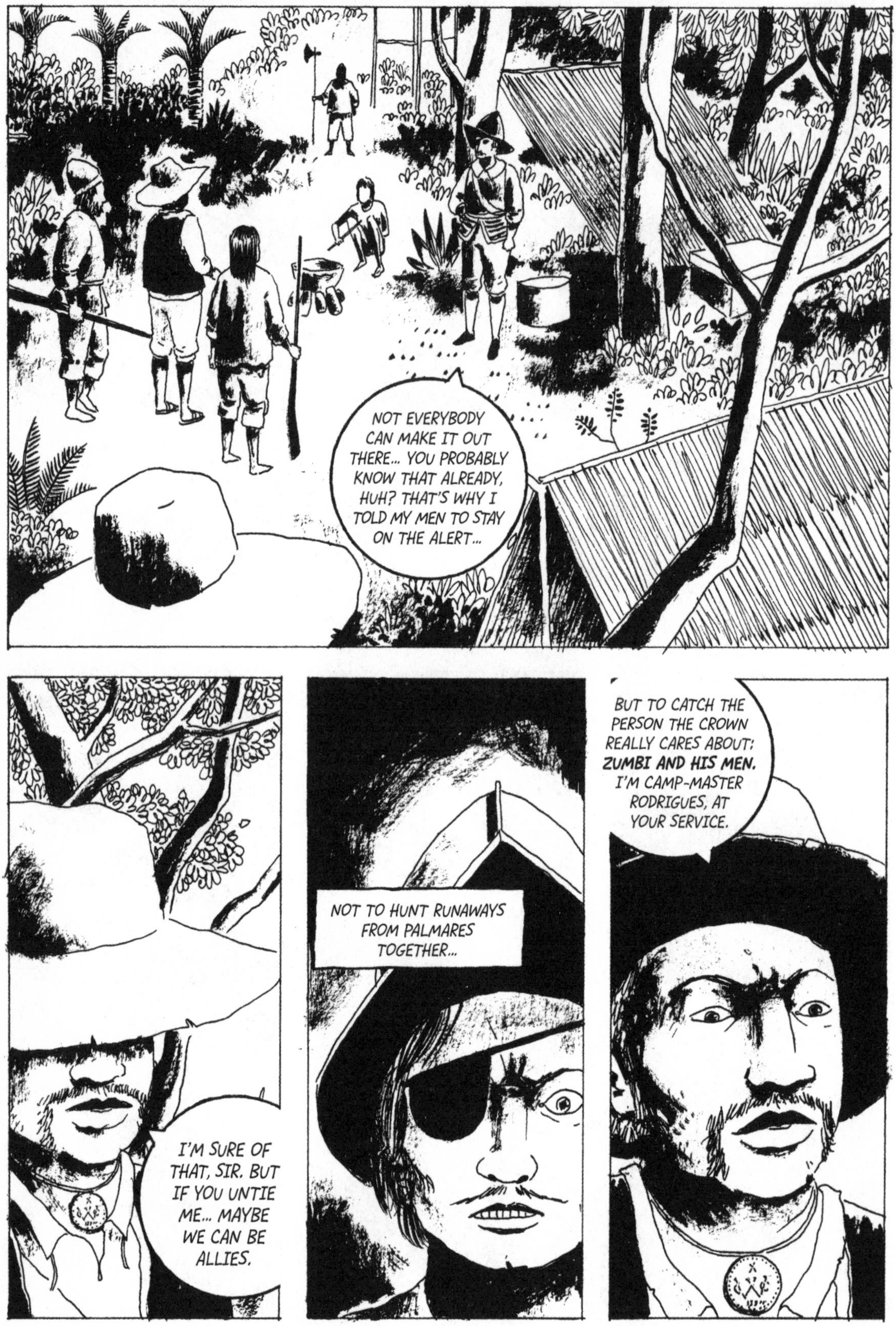
NOT EVERYBODY CAN MAKE IT OUT THERE... YOU PROBABLY KNOW THAT ALREADY, HUH? THAT'S WHY I TOLD MY MEN TO STAY ON THE ALERT...
I'M SURE OF THAT, SIR. BUT IF YOU UNTIE ME... MAYBE WE CAN BE ALLIES.
NOT TO HUNT RUNAWAYS FROM PALMARES TOGETHER...
BUT TO CATCH THE PERSON THE CROWN REALLY CARES ABOUT: **ZUMBI AND HIS MEN.** I'M CAMP-MASTER RODRIGUES, AT YOUR SERVICE.

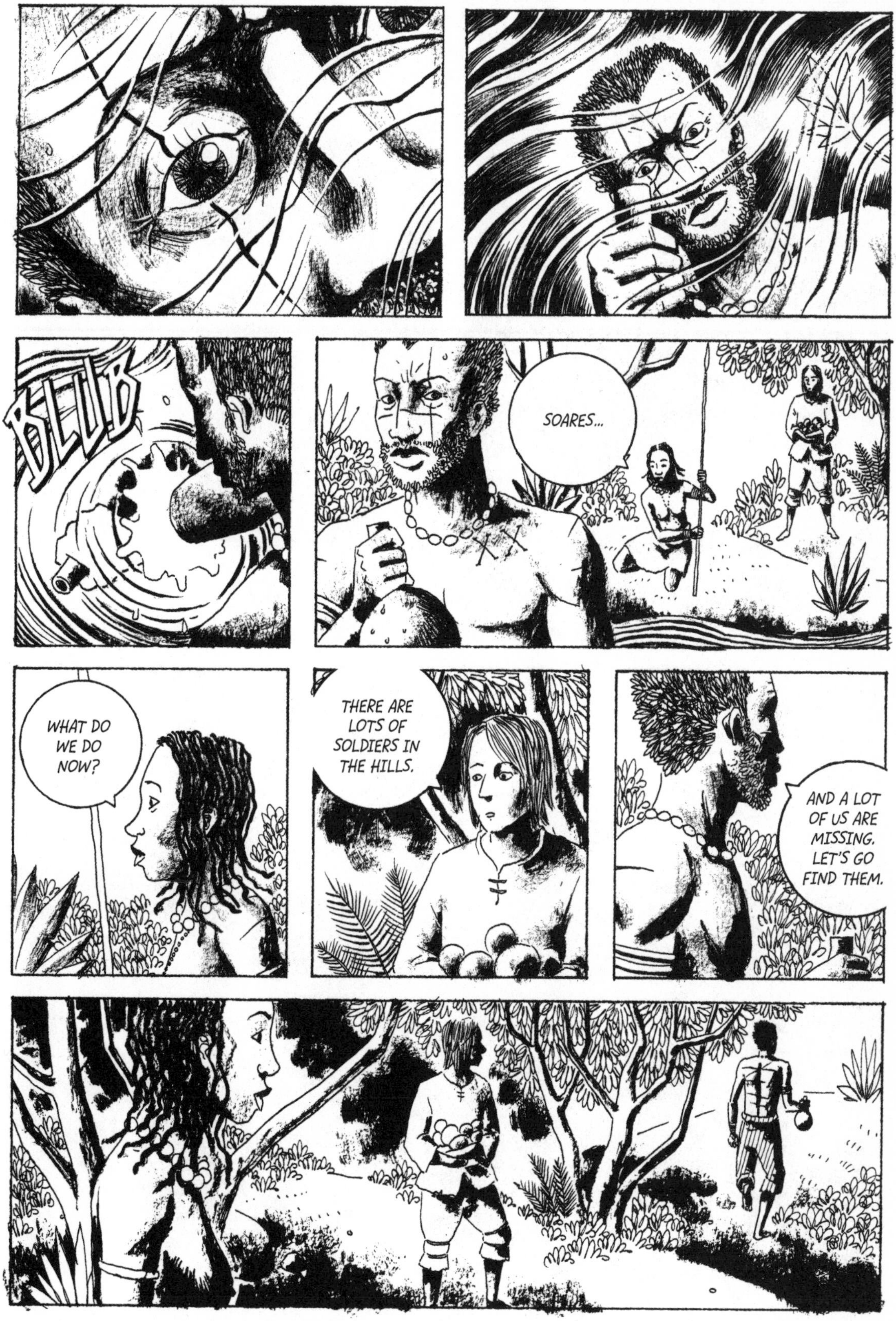
BLUB
SOARES...
WHAT DO WE DO NOW?
THERE ARE LOTS OF SOLDIERS IN THE HILLS.
AND A LOT OF US ARE MISSING. LET'S GO FIND THEM.

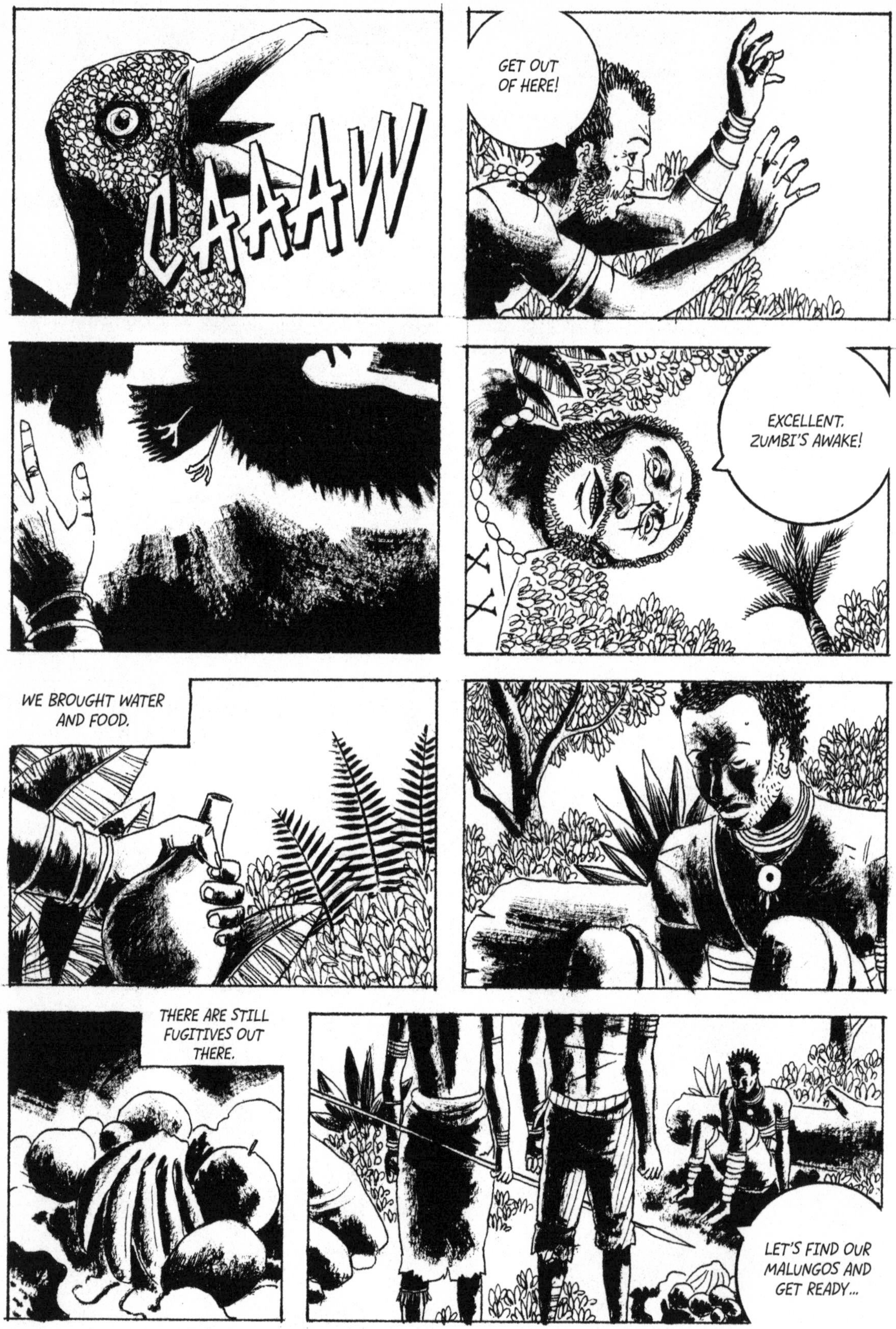
CAAAW
GET OUT OF HERE!
EXCELLENT. ZUMBI'S AWAKE!
WE BROUGHT WATER AND FOOD.
THERE ARE STILL FUGITIVES OUT THERE.
LET'S FIND OUR MALUNGOS AND GET READY...

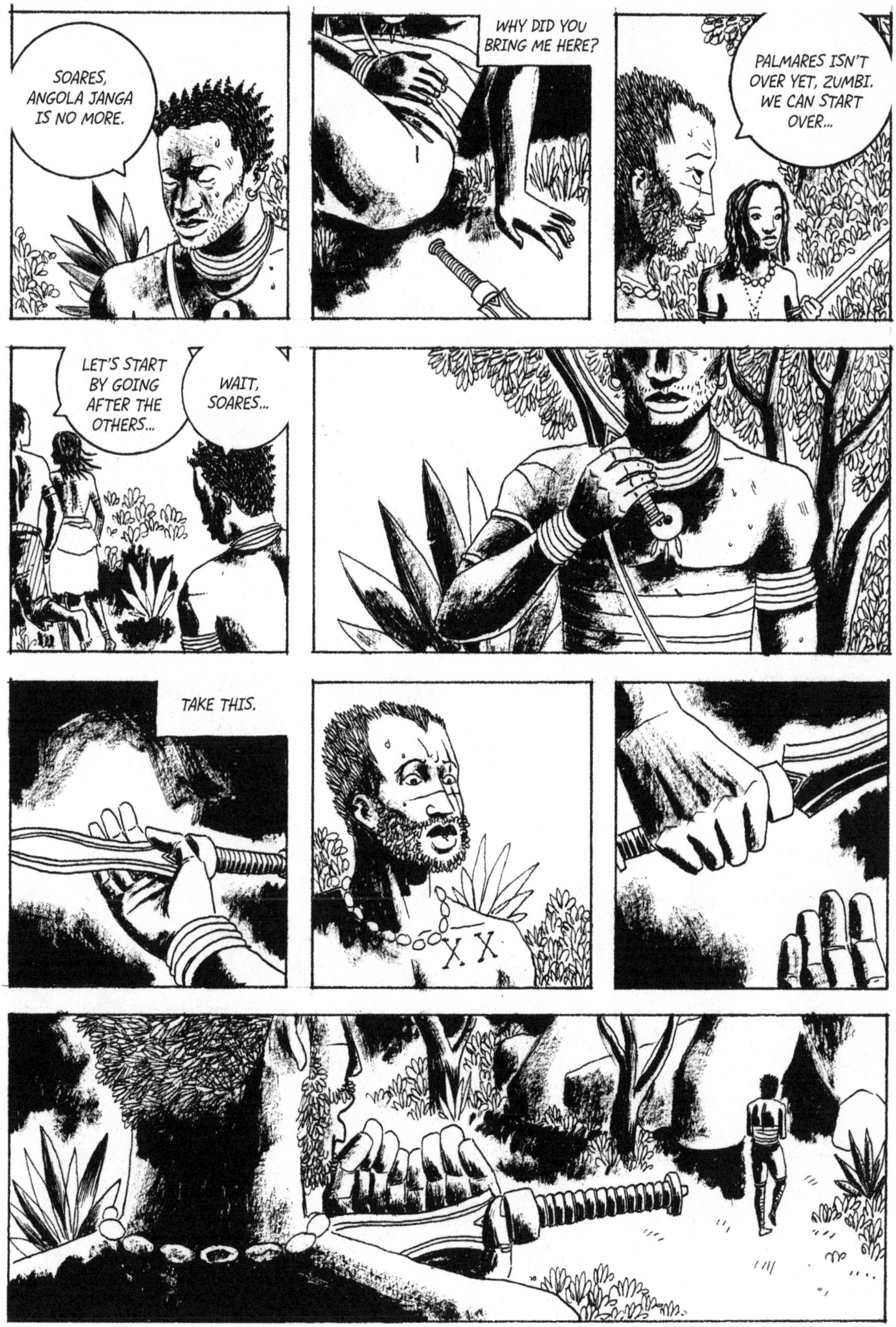
SOARES, ANGOLA JANGA IS NO MORE.
WHY DID YOU BRING ME HERE?
PALMARES ISN'T OVER YET, ZUMBI. WE CAN START OVER...
LET'S START BY GOING AFTER THE OTHERS...
WAIT, SOARES...
TAKE THIS.

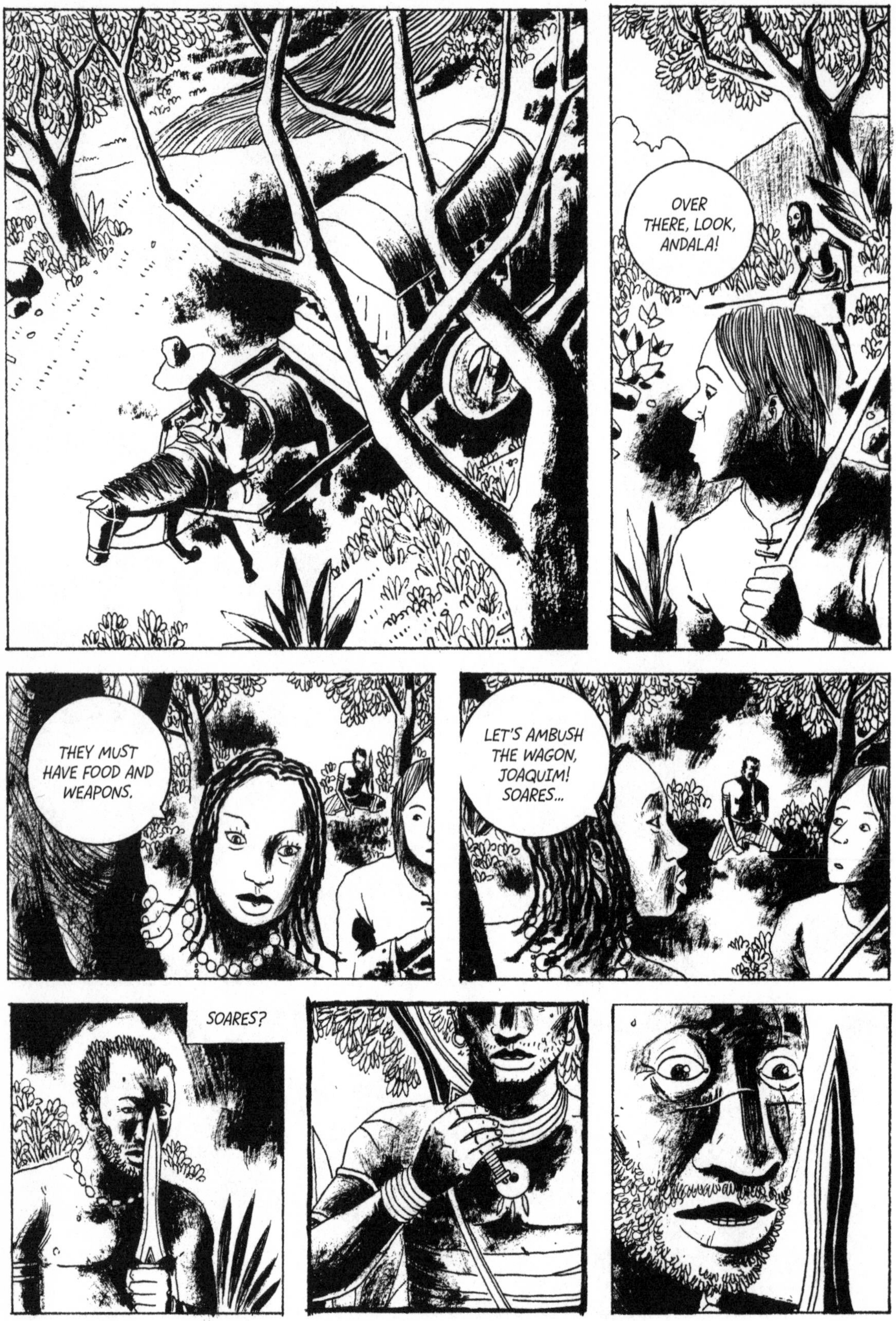
OVER THERE, LOOK, ANDALA!
THEY MUST HAVE FOOD AND WEAPONS.
LET'S AMBUSH THE WAGON, JOAQUIM! SOARES...
SOARES?

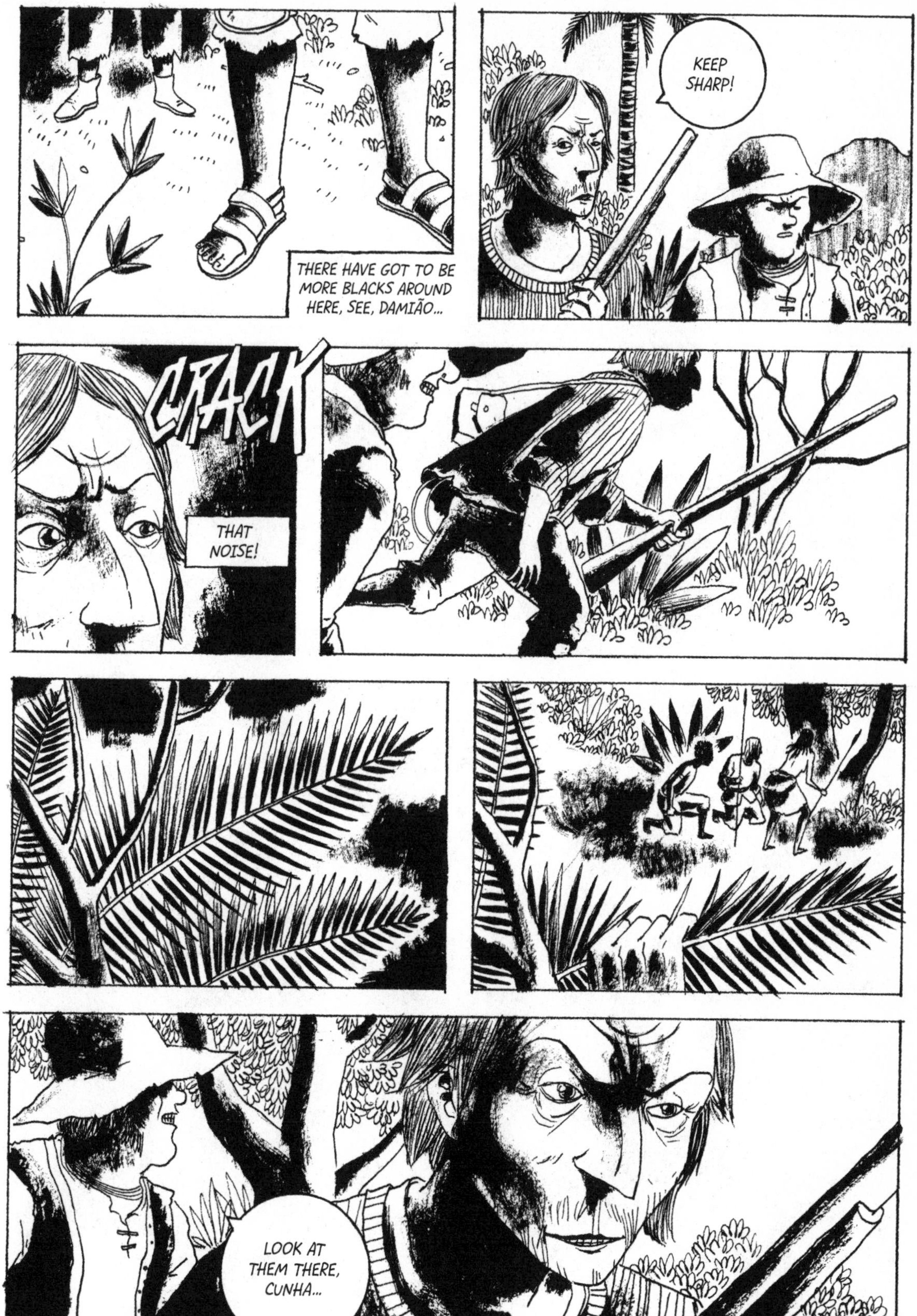
THERE HAVE GOT TO BE MORE BLACKS AROUND HERE, SEE, DAMIÃO...
KEEP SHARP!
CRACK
THAT NOISE!
LOOK AT THEM THERE, CUNHA...

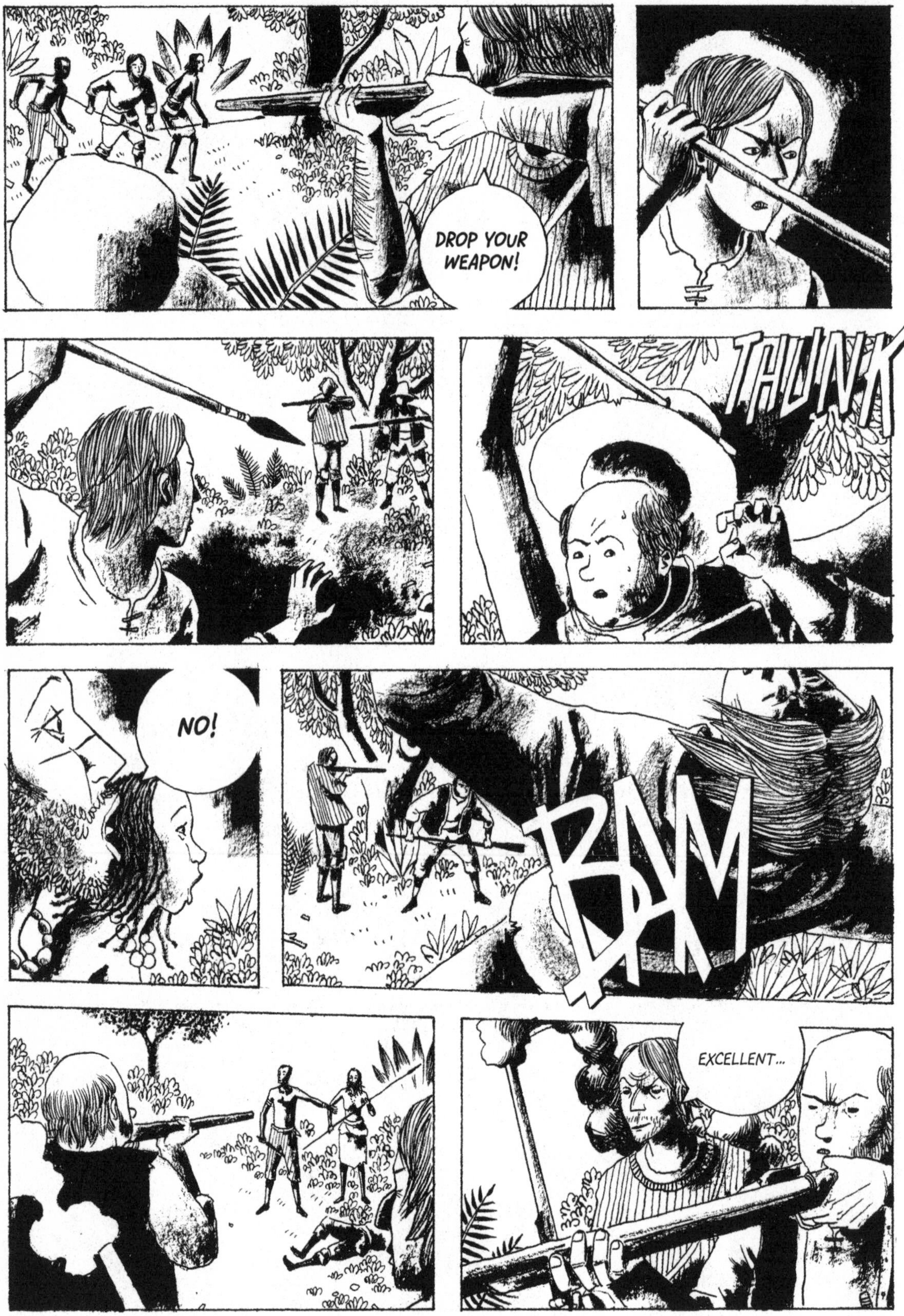
DROP YOUR WEAPON!
THUNK
NO!
BAM
EXCELLENT...

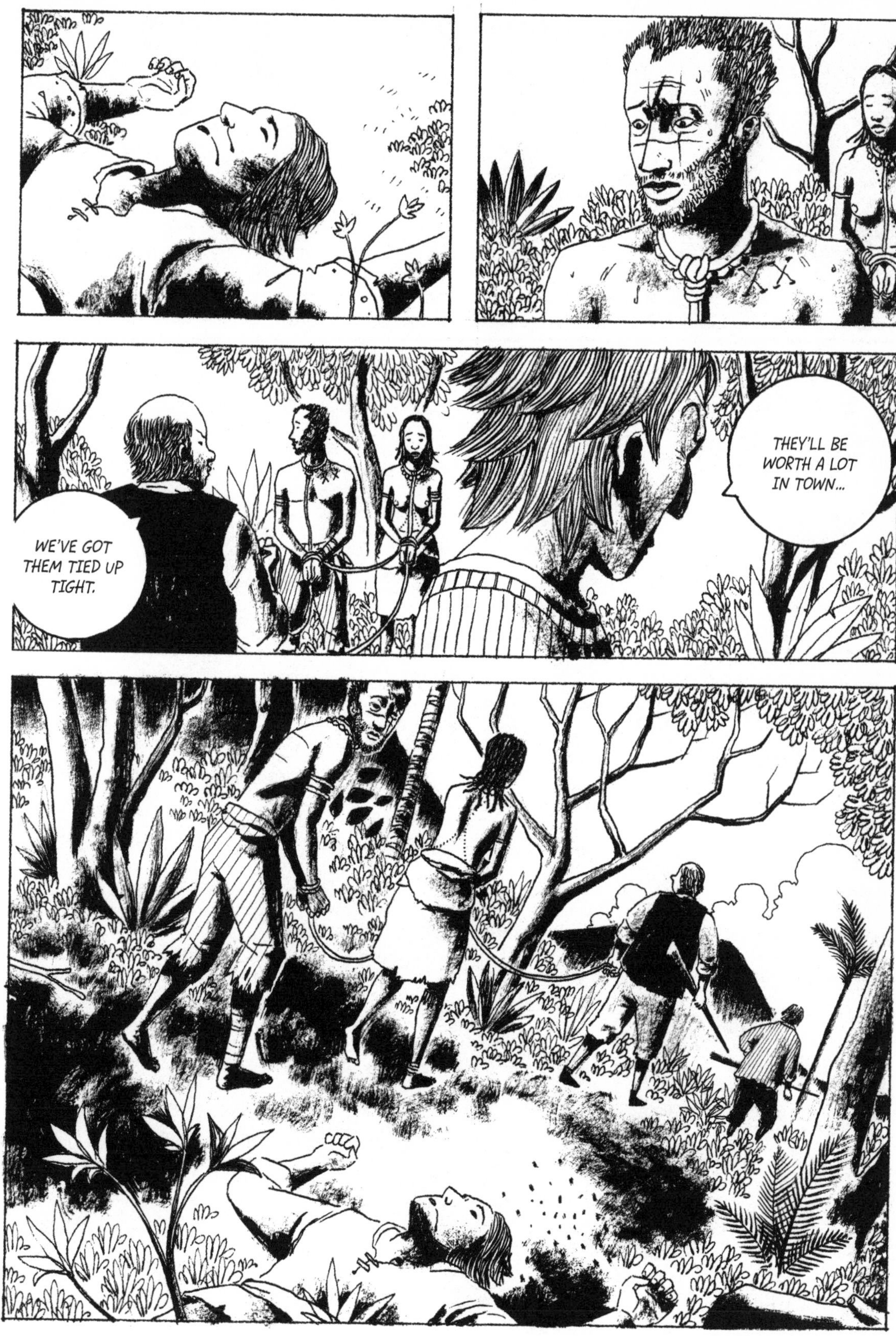
THEY'LL BE WORTH A LOT IN TOWN...
WE'VE GOT THEM TIED UP TIGHT.

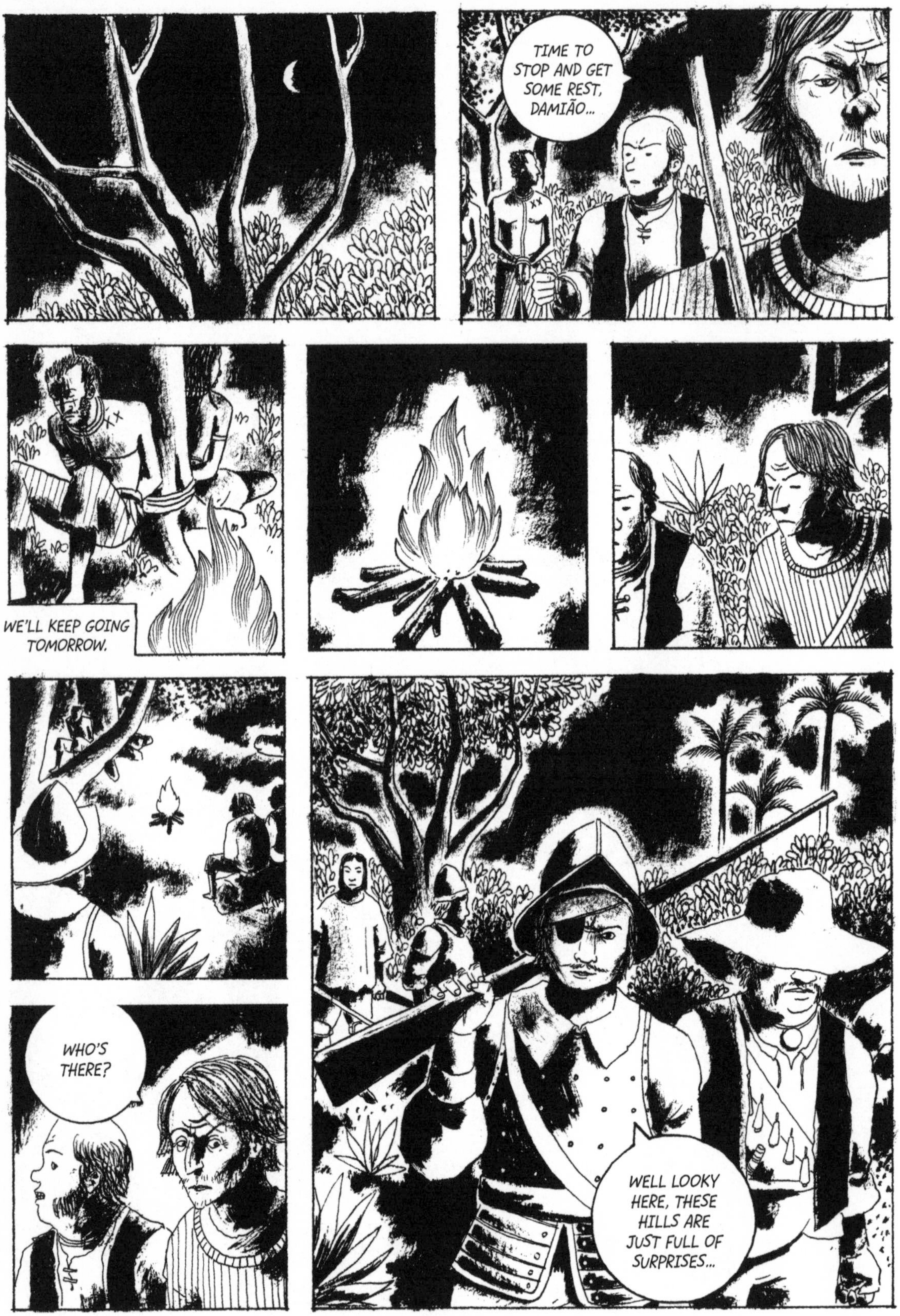
TIME TO STOP AND GET SOME REST, DAMIÃO...
WE'LL KEEP GOING TOMORROW.
WHO'S THERE?
WELL LOOKY HERE, THESE HILLS ARE JUST FULL OF SURPRISES...

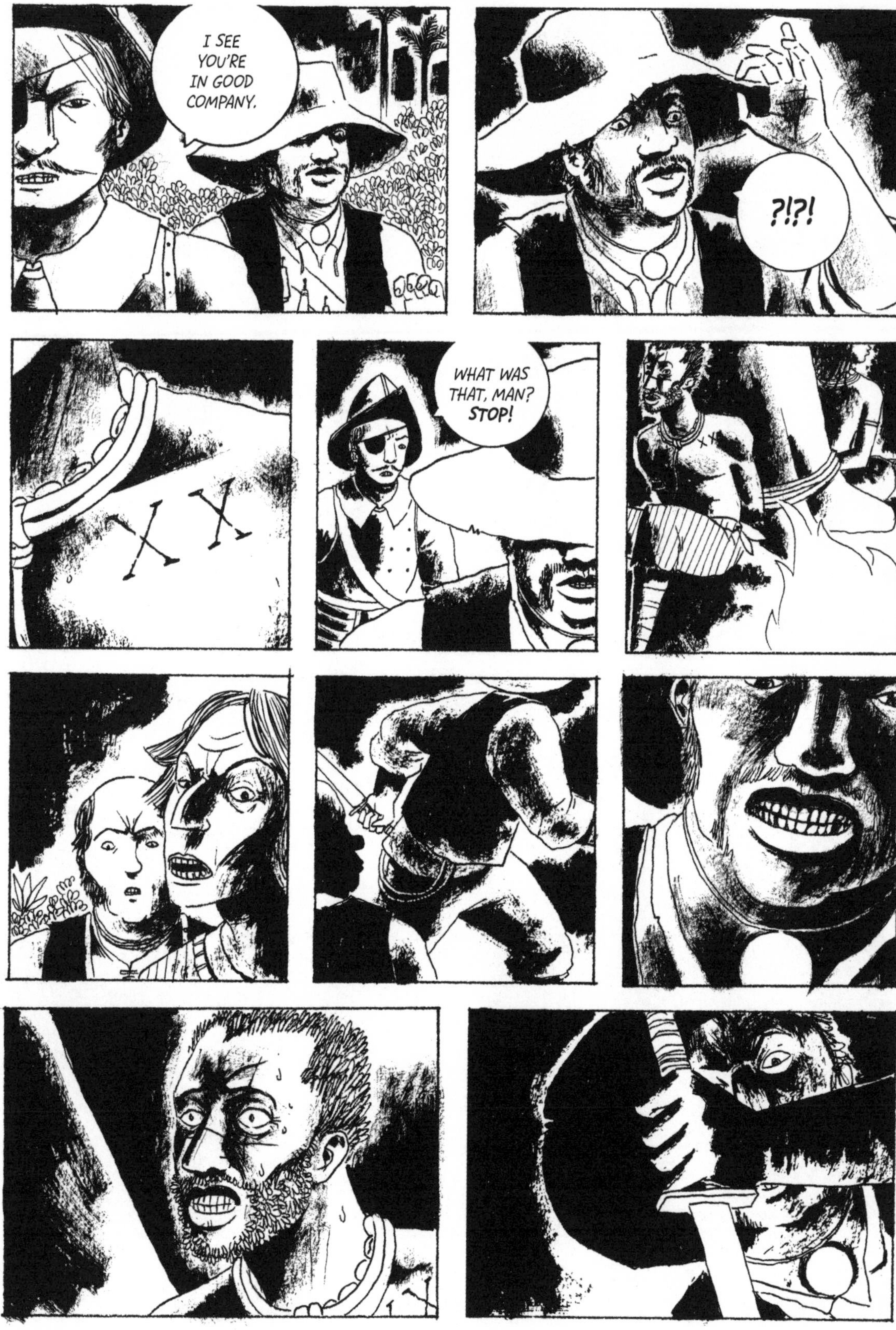
I SEE YOU'RE IN GOOD COMPANY.
?!?!
WHAT WAS THAT, MAN? STOP!

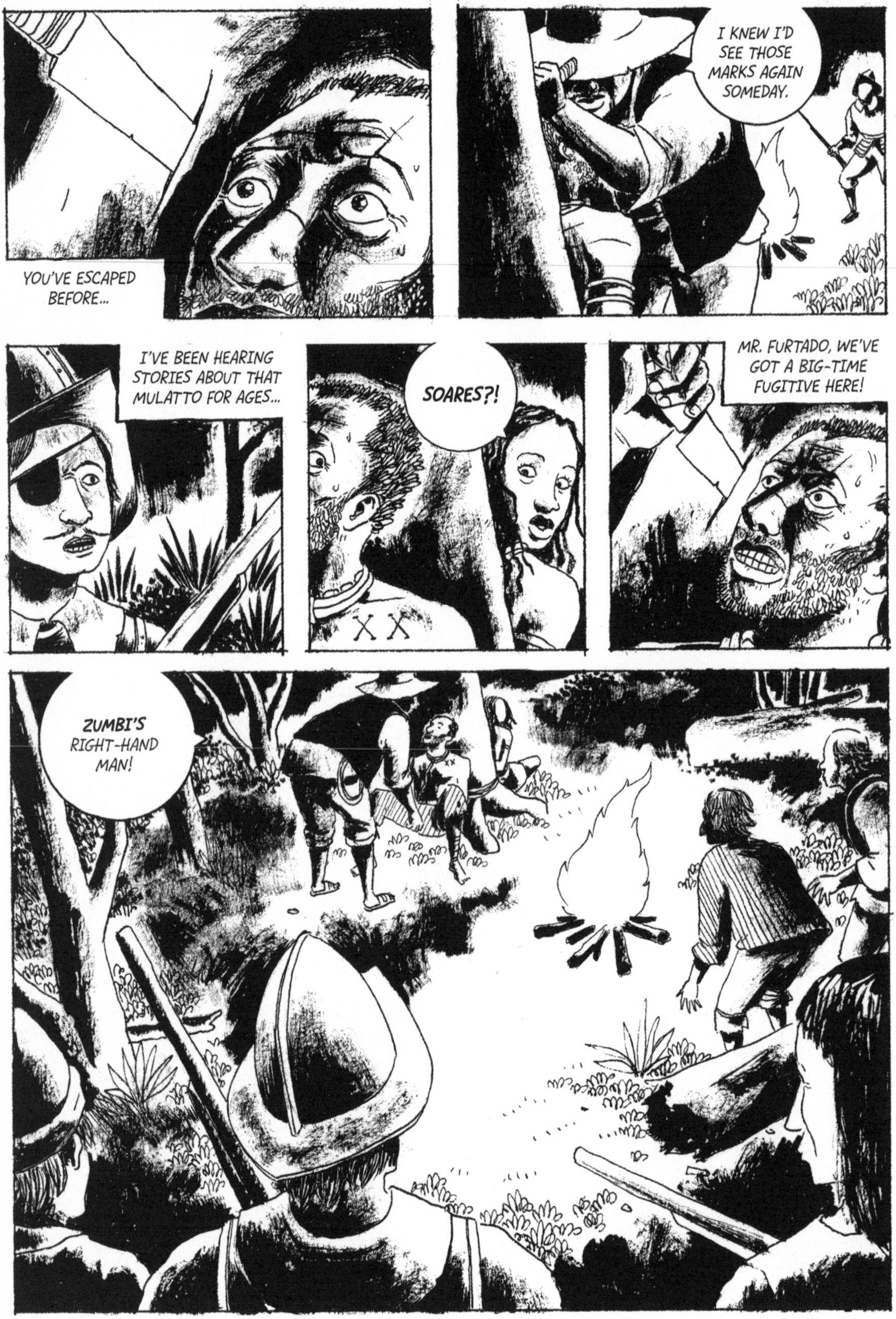
YOU'VE ESCAPED BEFORE...
I KNEW I'D SEE THOSE MARKS AGAIN SOMEDAY.
I'VE BEEN HEARING STORIES ABOUT THAT MULATTO FOR AGES...
SOARES?!
MR. FURTADO, WE'VE GOT A BIG-TIME FUGITIVE HERE!
ZUMBI'S RIGHT-HAND MAN!

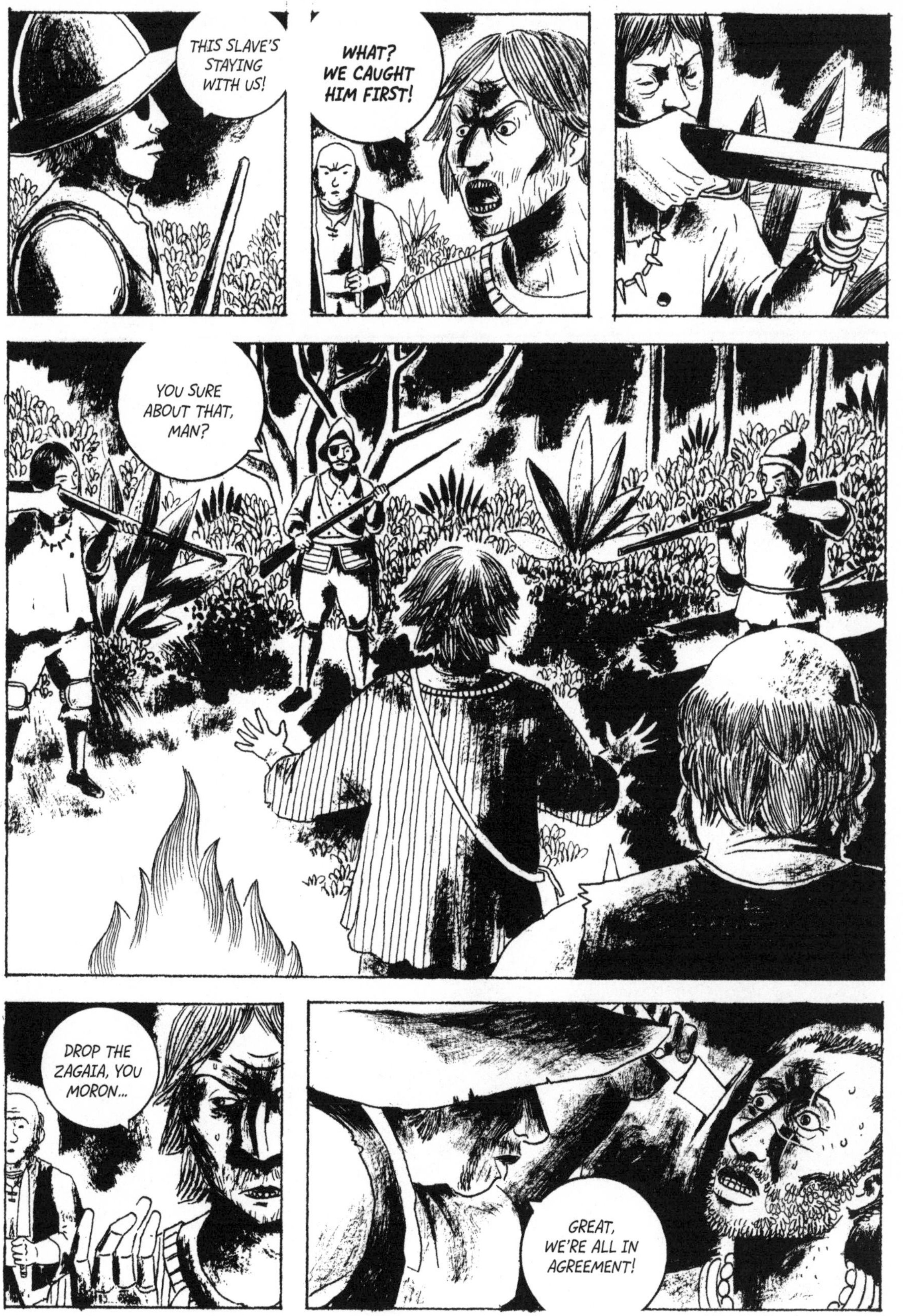
THIS SLAVE'S STAYING WITH US!
WHAT? WE CAUGHT HIM FIRST!
YOU SURE ABOUT THAT, MAN?
DROP THE ZAGAIA, YOU MORON...
GREAT, WE'RE ALL IN AGREEMENT!

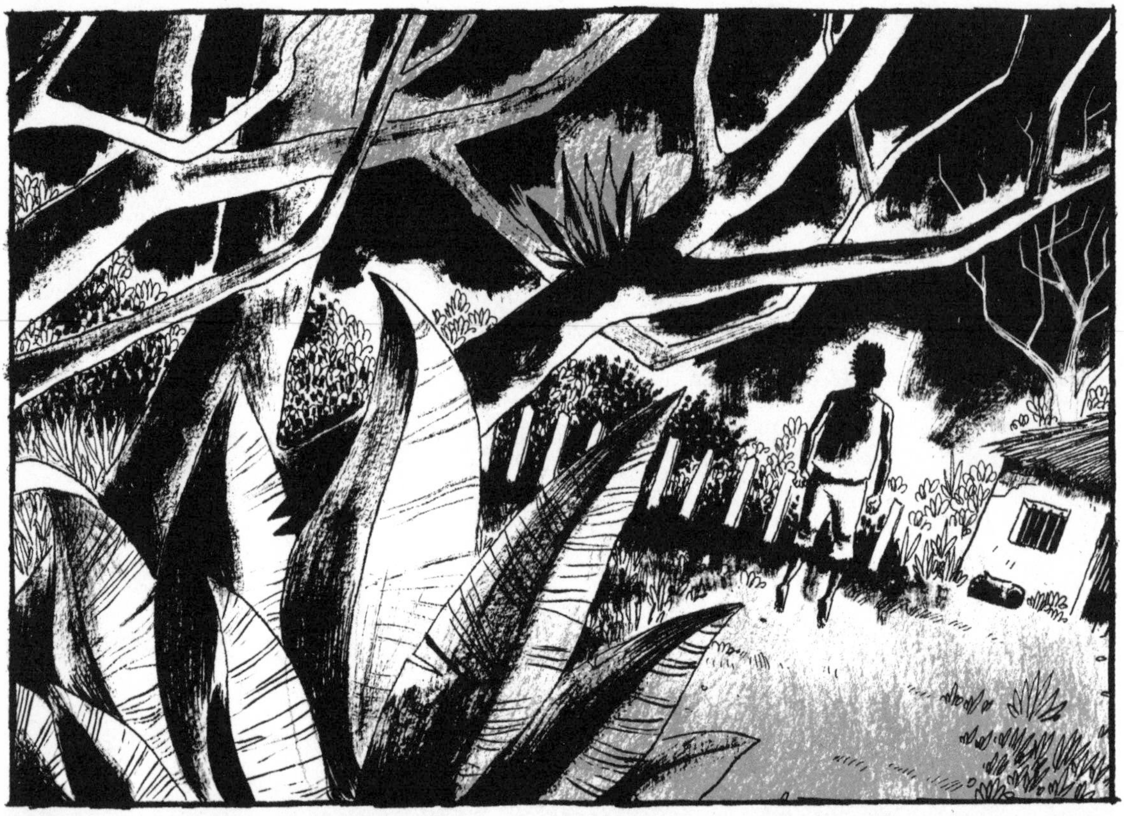

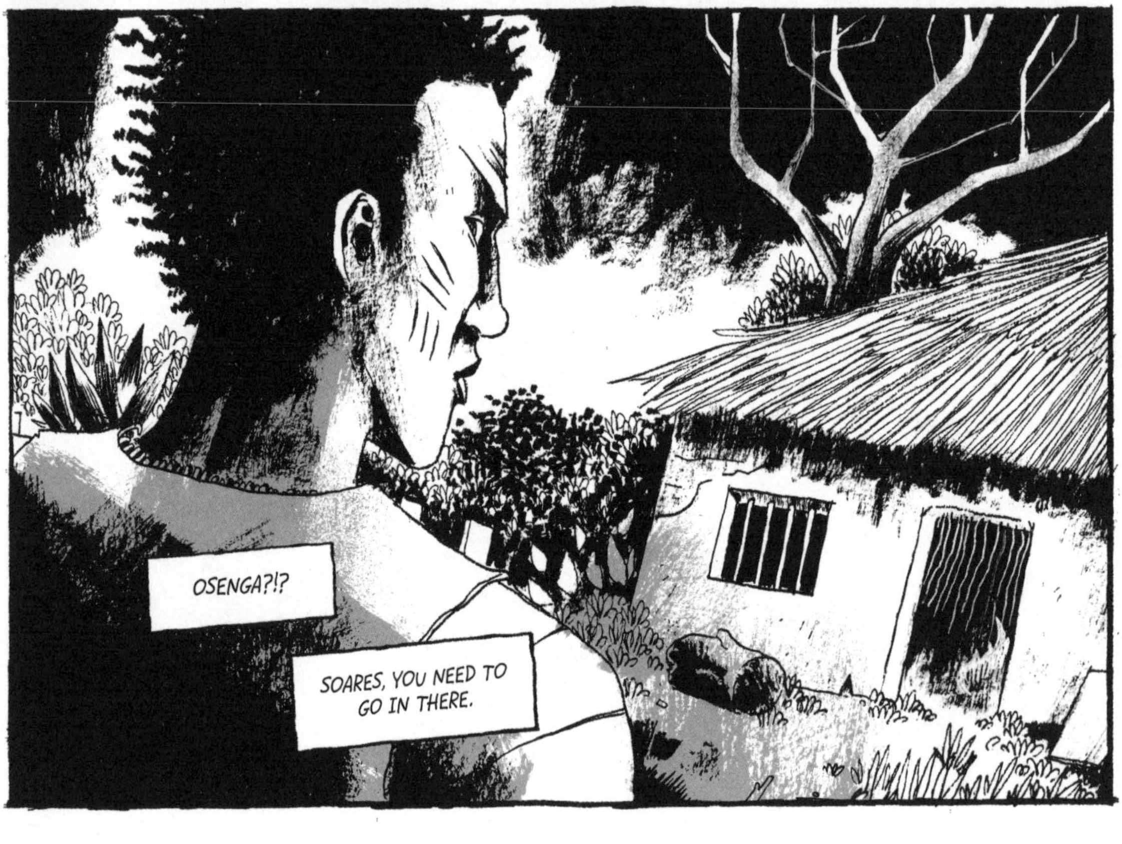
OSENGA?!?
SOARES, YOU NEED TO GO IN THERE.

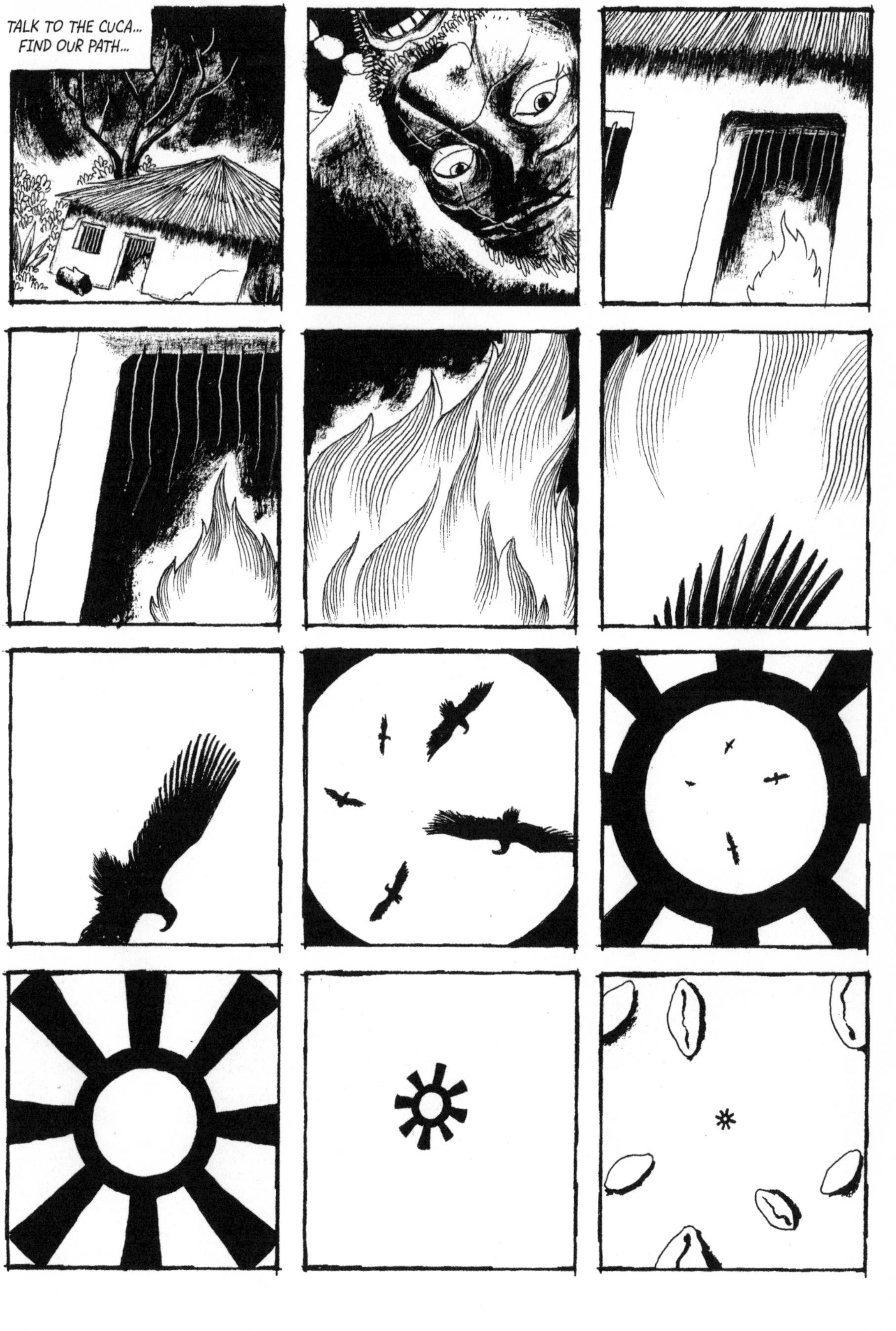
TALK TO THE CUCA... FIND OUR PATH...

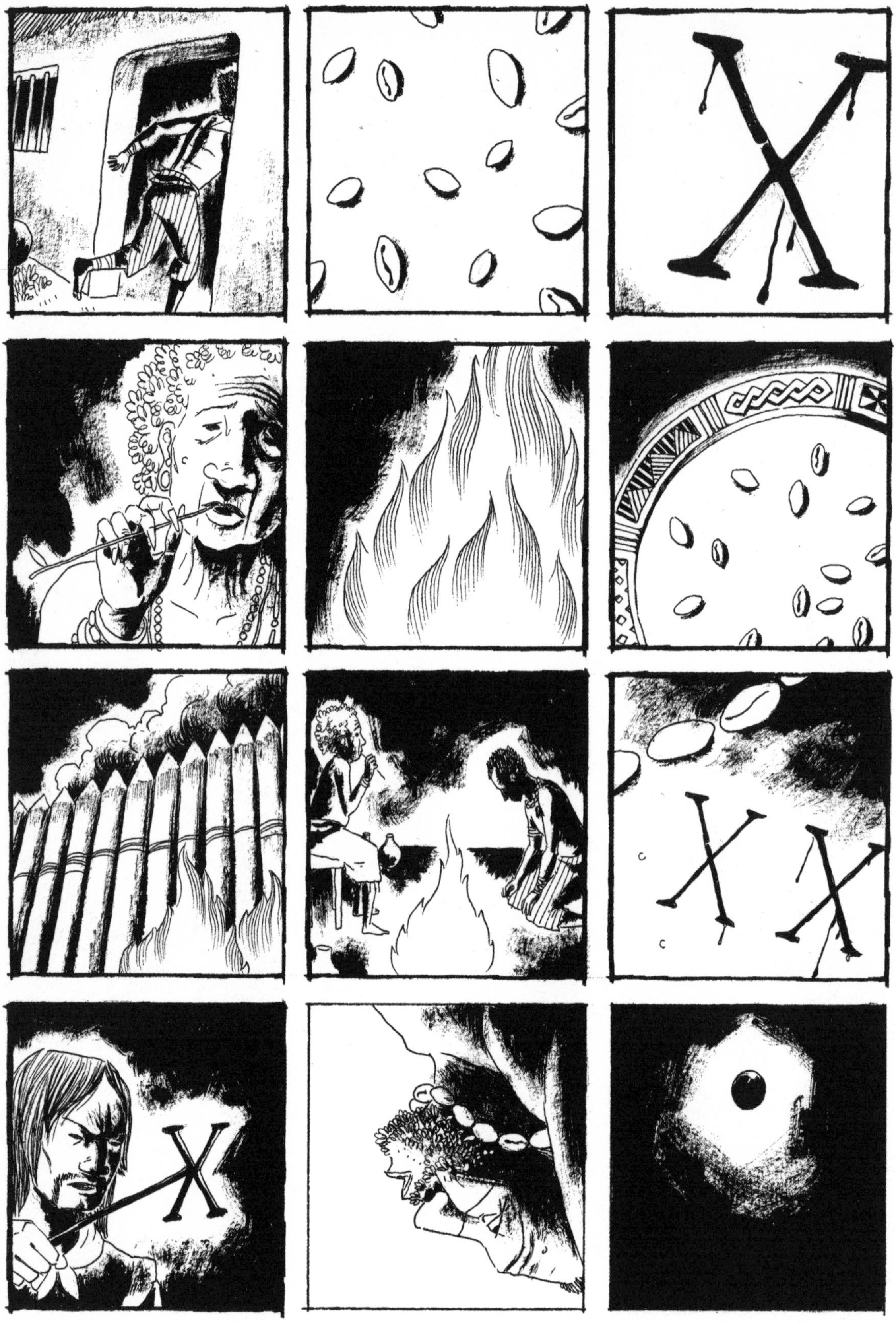
X
X X
X

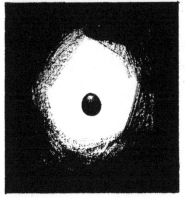

YOU'D BETTER START TALKING...

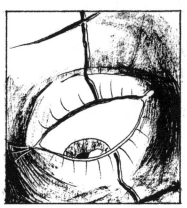

WHILE YOU'VE STILL GOT BLOOD TO SPILL.

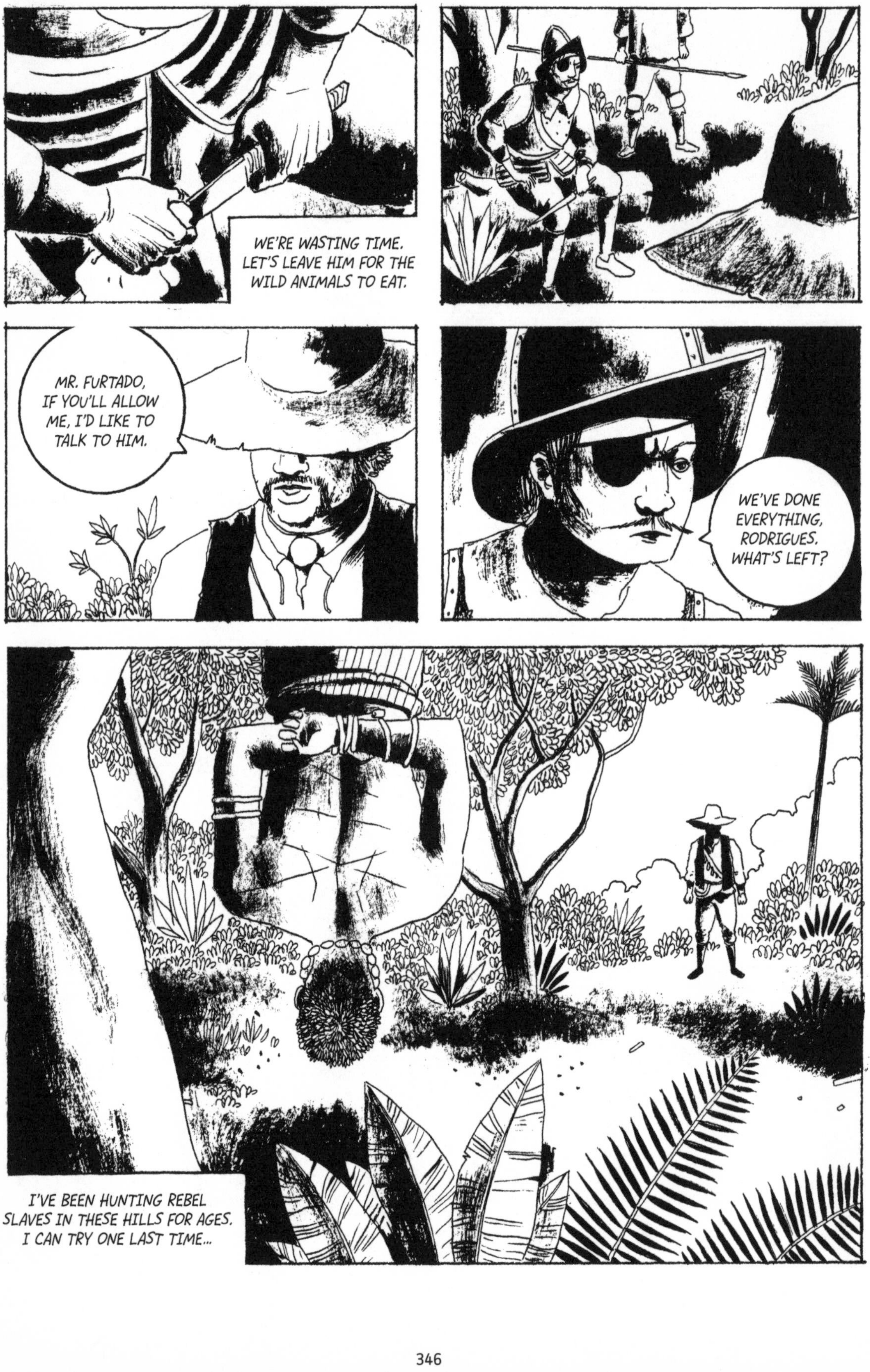
WE'RE WASTING TIME. LET'S LEAVE HIM FOR THE WILD ANIMALS TO EAT.
MR. FURTADO, IF YOU'LL ALLOW ME, I'D LIKE TO TALK TO HIM.
WE'VE DONE EVERYTHING, RODRIGUES. WHAT'S LEFT?
I'VE BEEN HUNTING REBEL SLAVES IN THESE HILLS FOR AGES. I CAN TRY ONE LAST TIME...

I'VE CAUGHT A LOT OF RUNAWAY SLAVES.

PEOPLE LIKE YOU...

I LEARNED WITH THE BEST: HENRIQUE DIAS, KNOWN AS BOCA-NEGRA.

HE LOST EVERYTHING FIGHTING DUTCHMEN, INDIANS, AND PALMARISTAS...

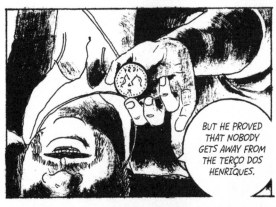

BUT HE PROVED THAT NOBODY GETS AWAY FROM THE TERÇO DOS HENRIQUES.

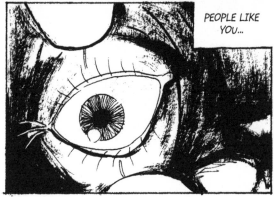

DURING THAT TIME, HE SHOWED US HOW TO MAKE A MAN BEND...

AND HE TAUGHT ME WHAT PEOPLE LIKE YOU WANT...

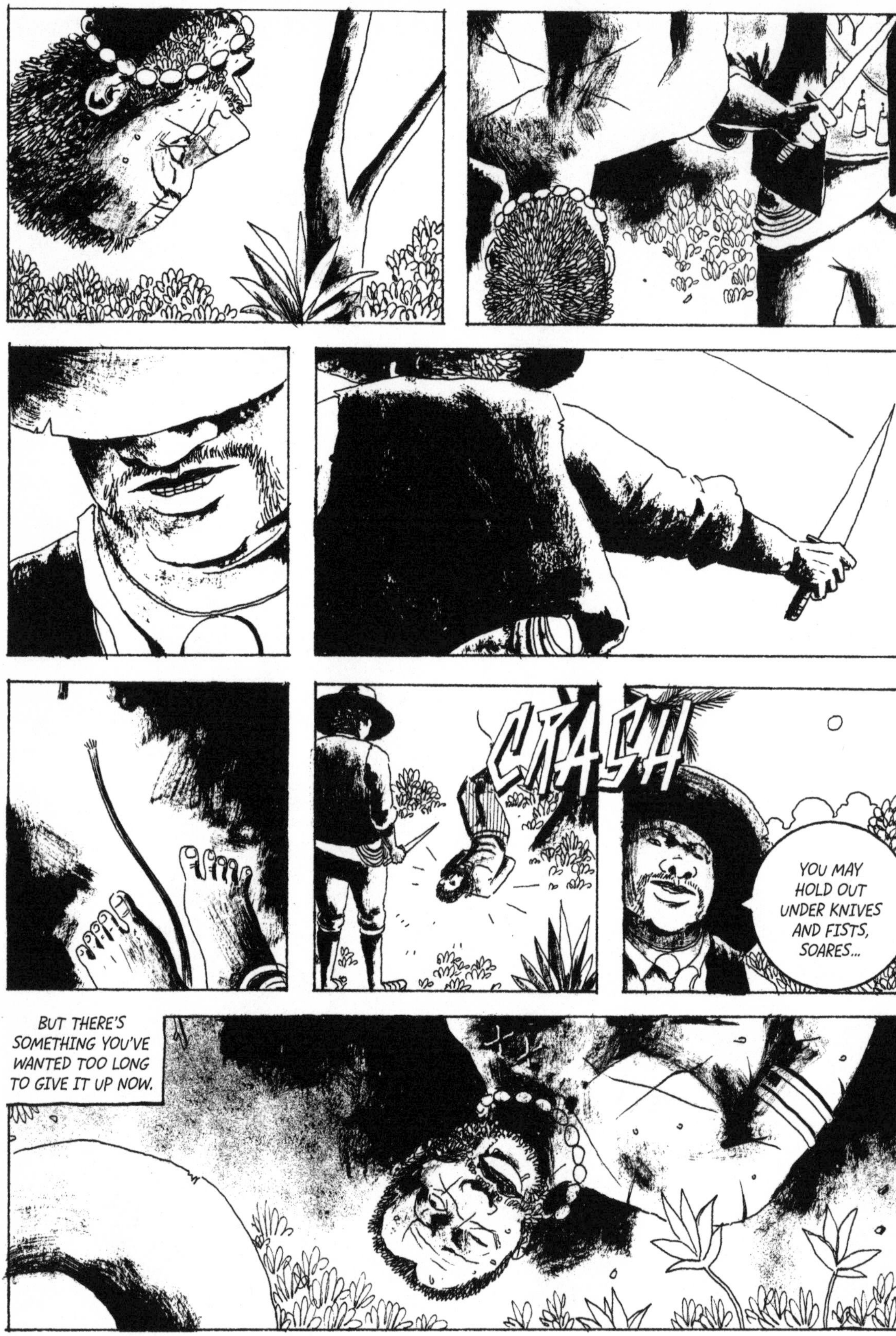
CRASH
YOU MAY HOLD OUT UNDER KNIVES AND FISTS, SOARES...
BUT THERE'S SOMETHING YOU'VE WANTED TOO LONG TO GIVE IT UP NOW.

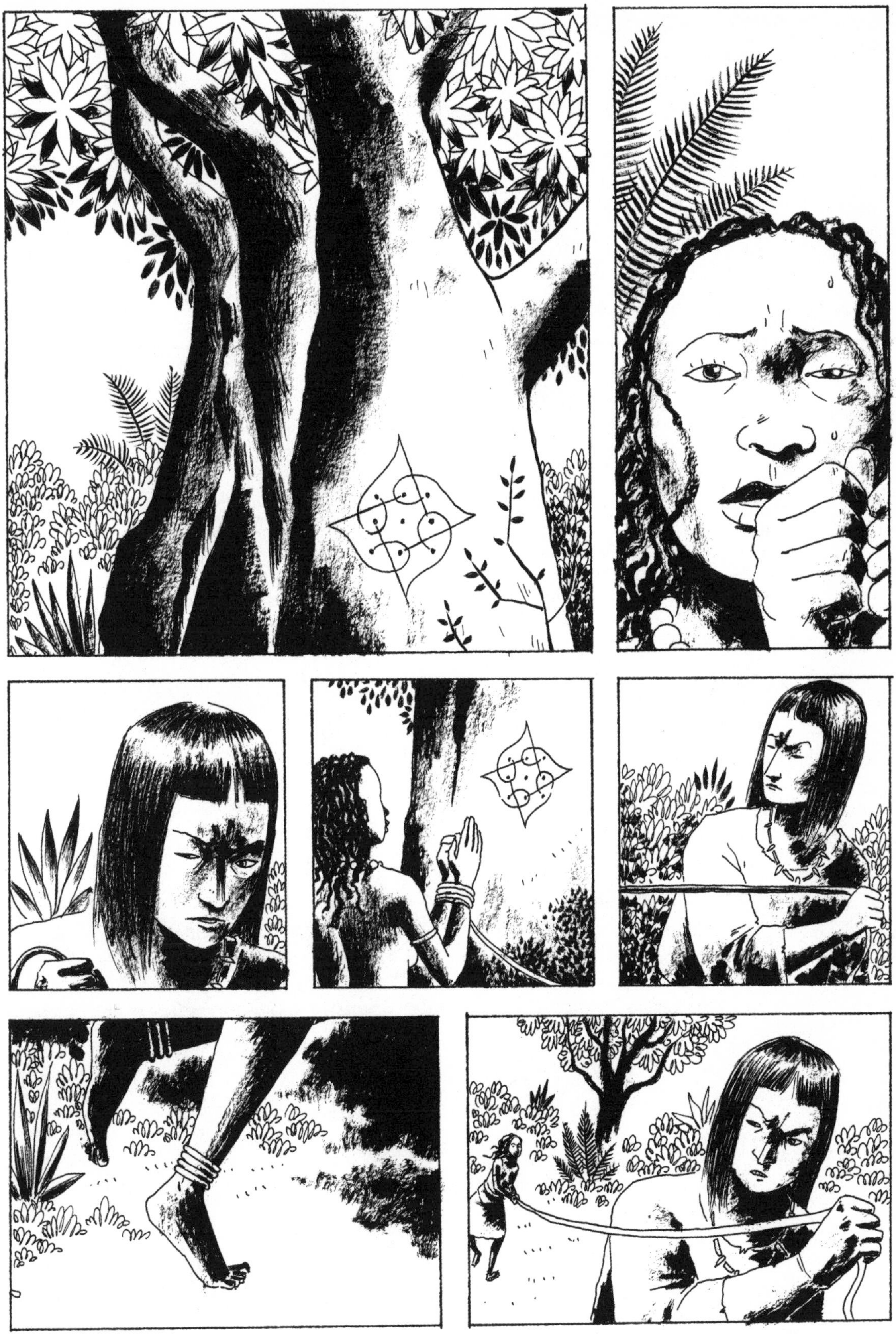

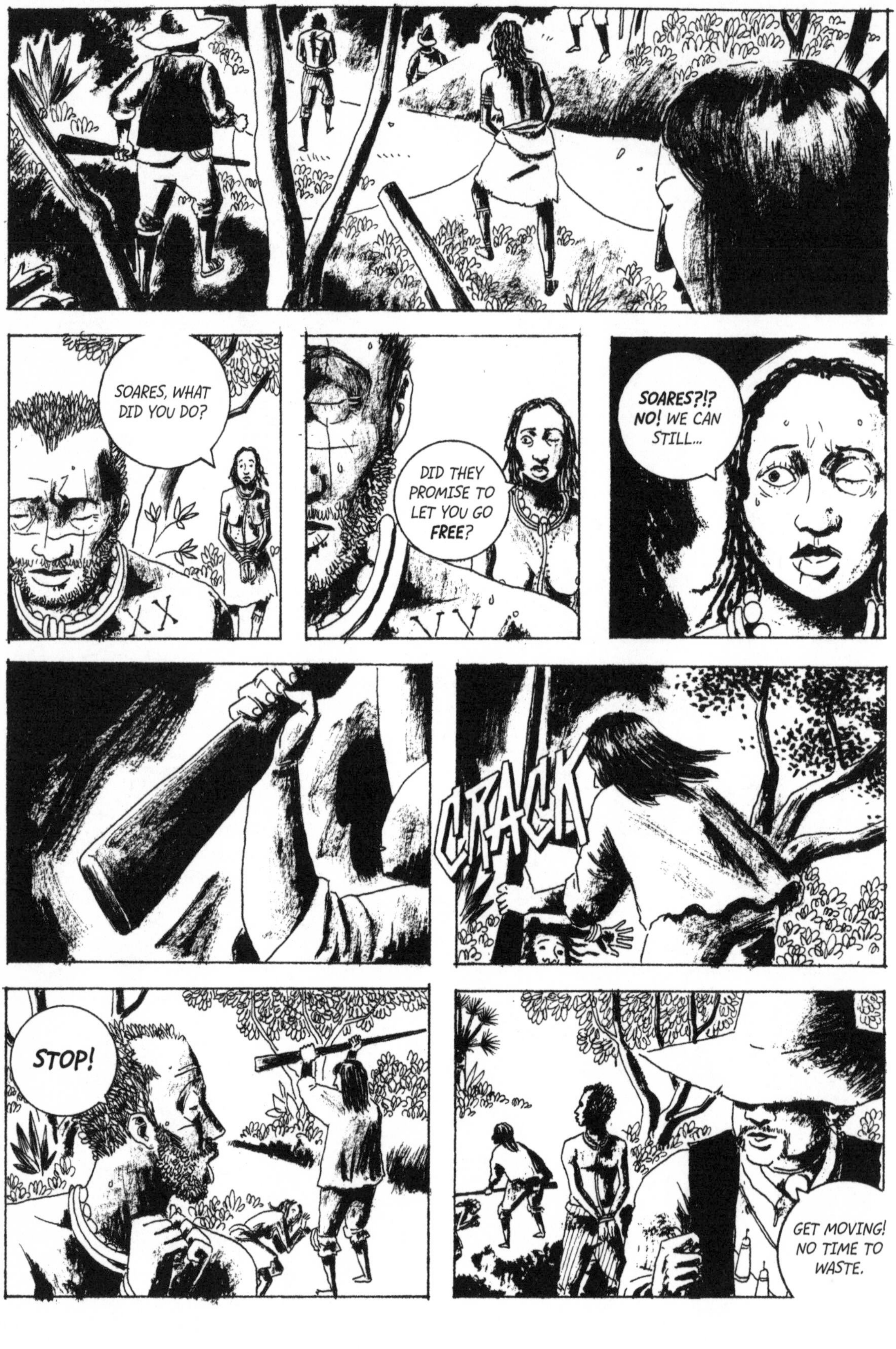
SOARES, WHAT DID YOU DO?
DID THEY PROMISE TO LET YOU GO FREE?
SOARES?!? NO! WE CAN STILL...
CRACK
STOP!
GET MOVING! NO TIME TO WASTE.

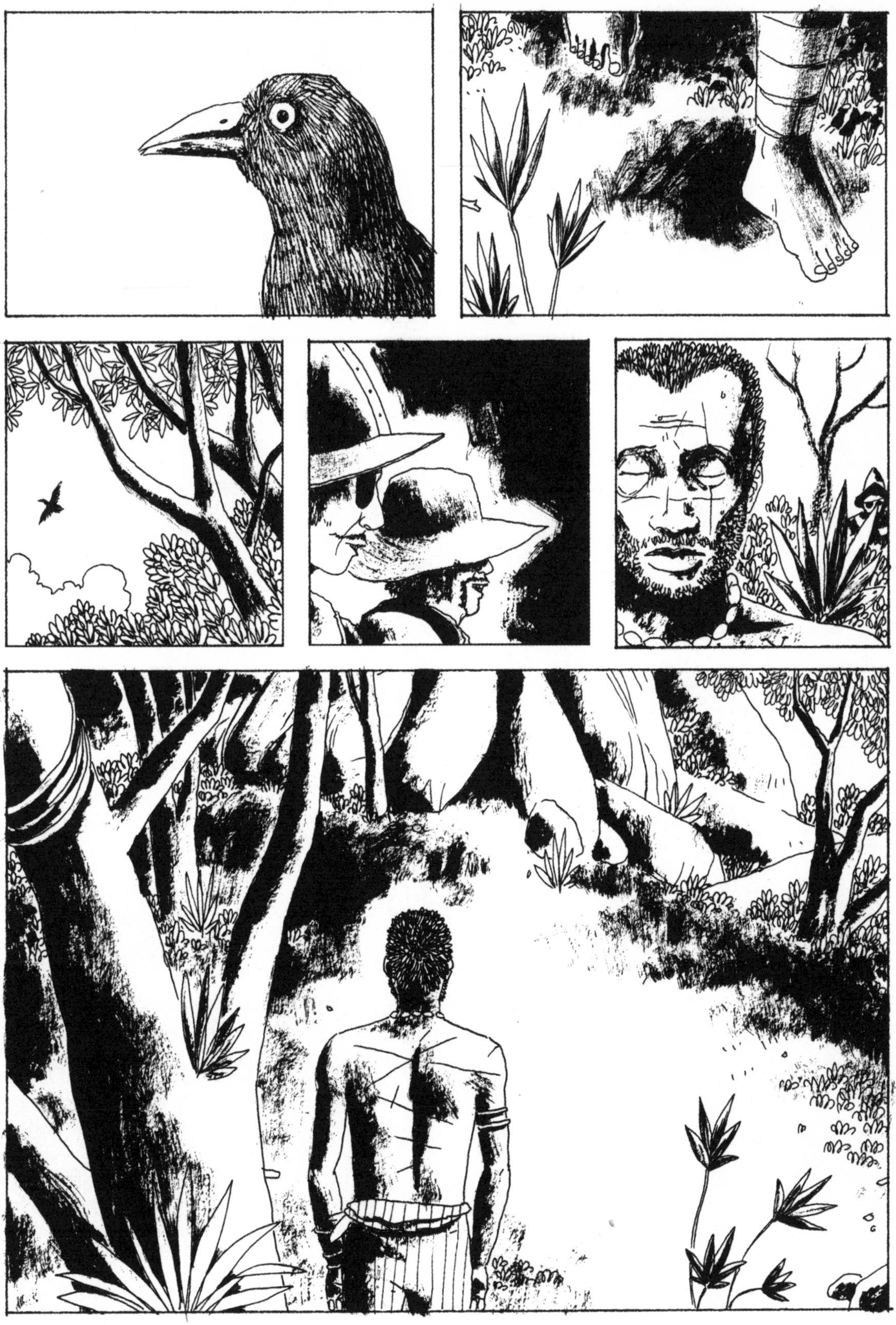

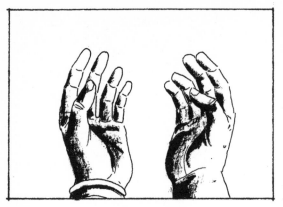

ZUMBI

WHAT ARE YOU DOING HERE ALL ALONE, SOARES?

ZUMBI

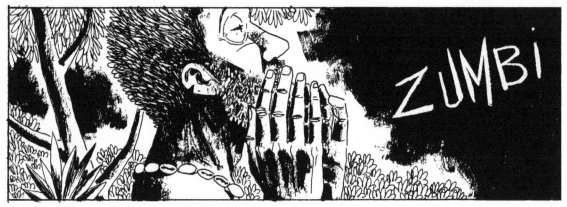

ZUMBI

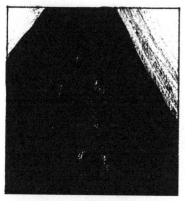

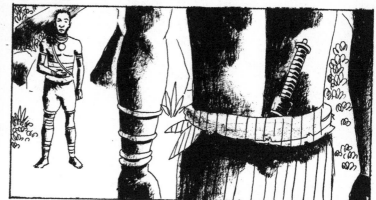

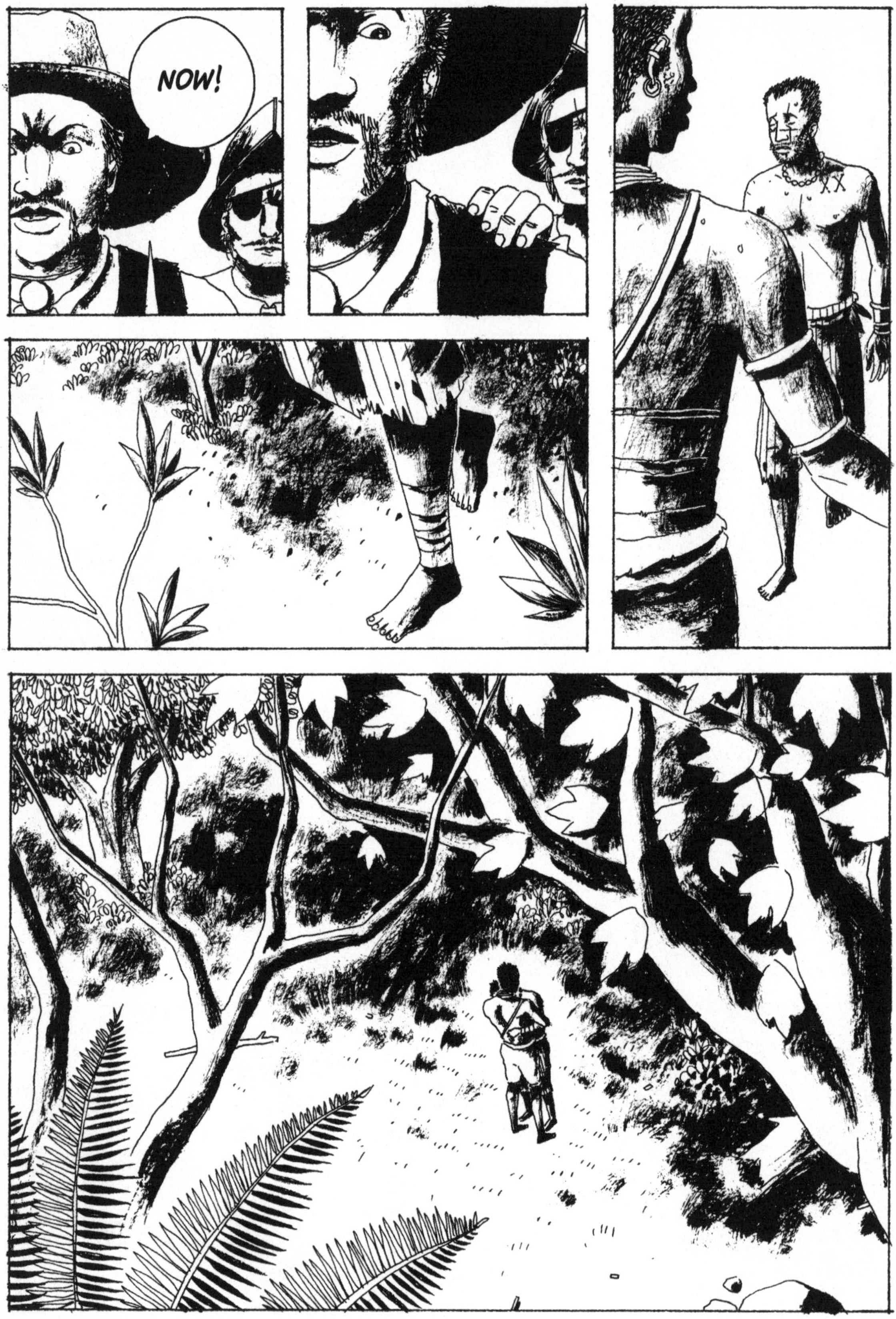
NOW!

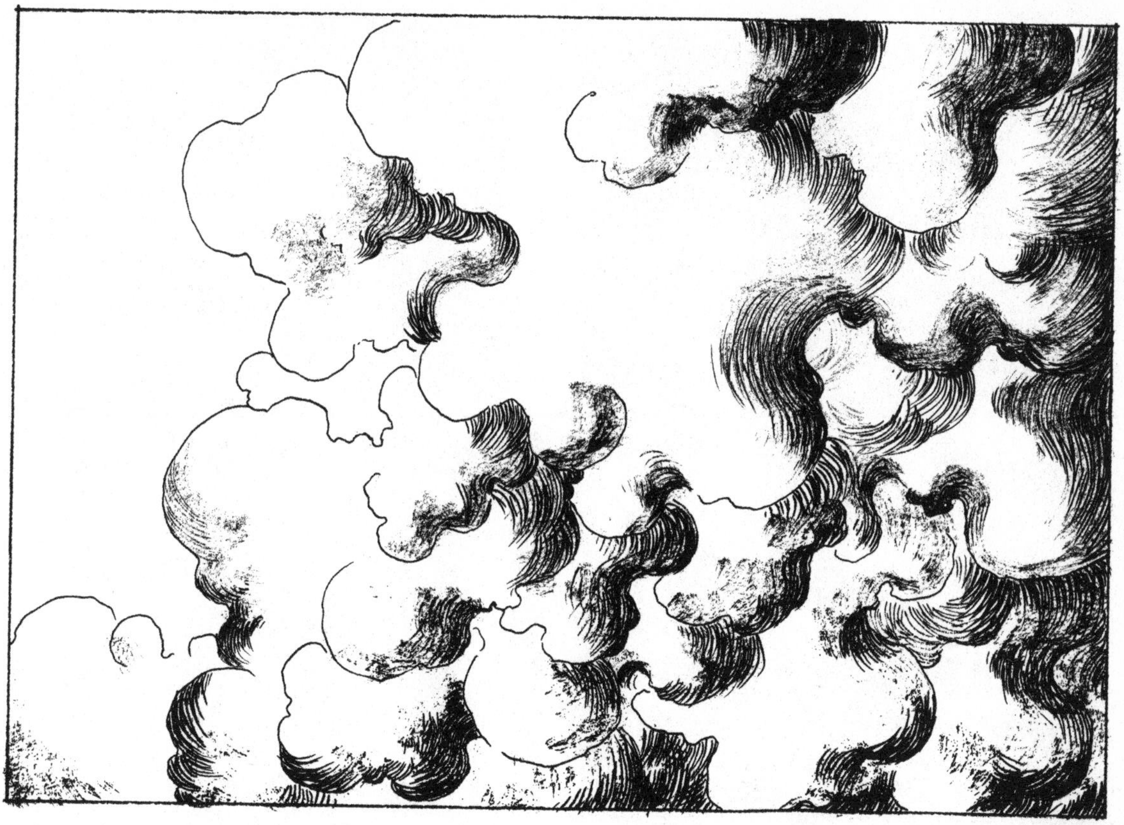

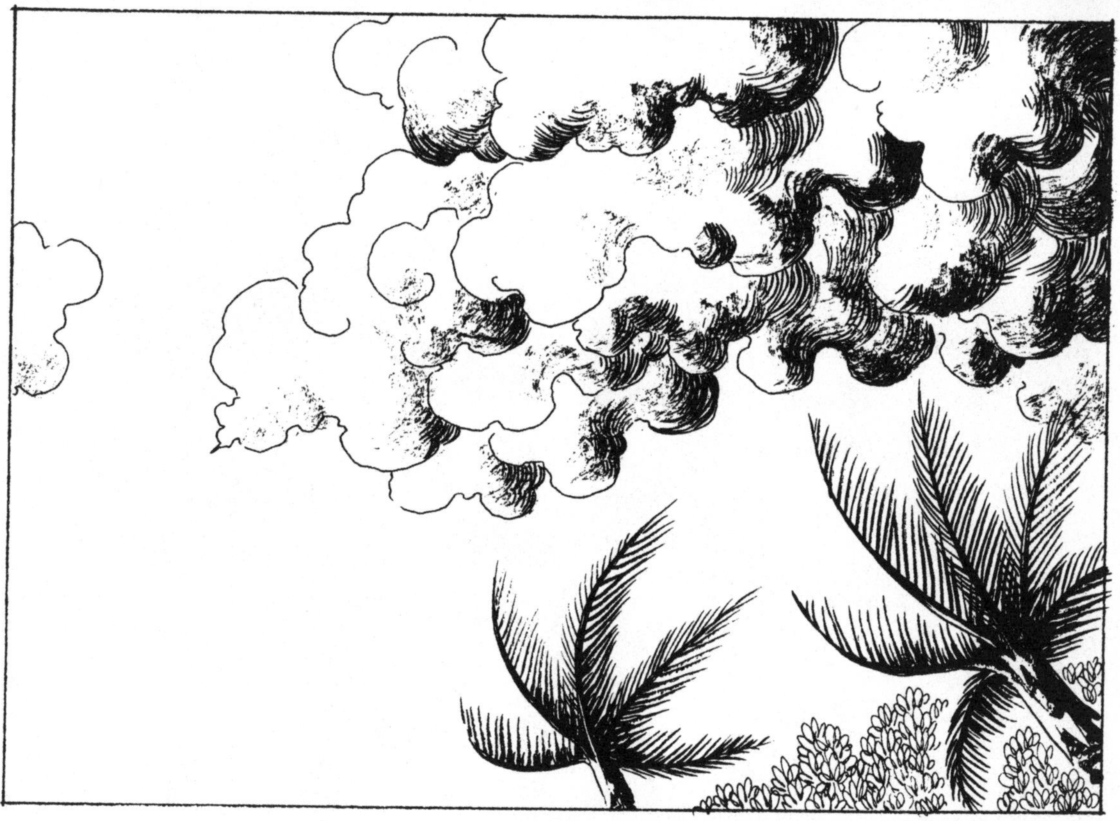

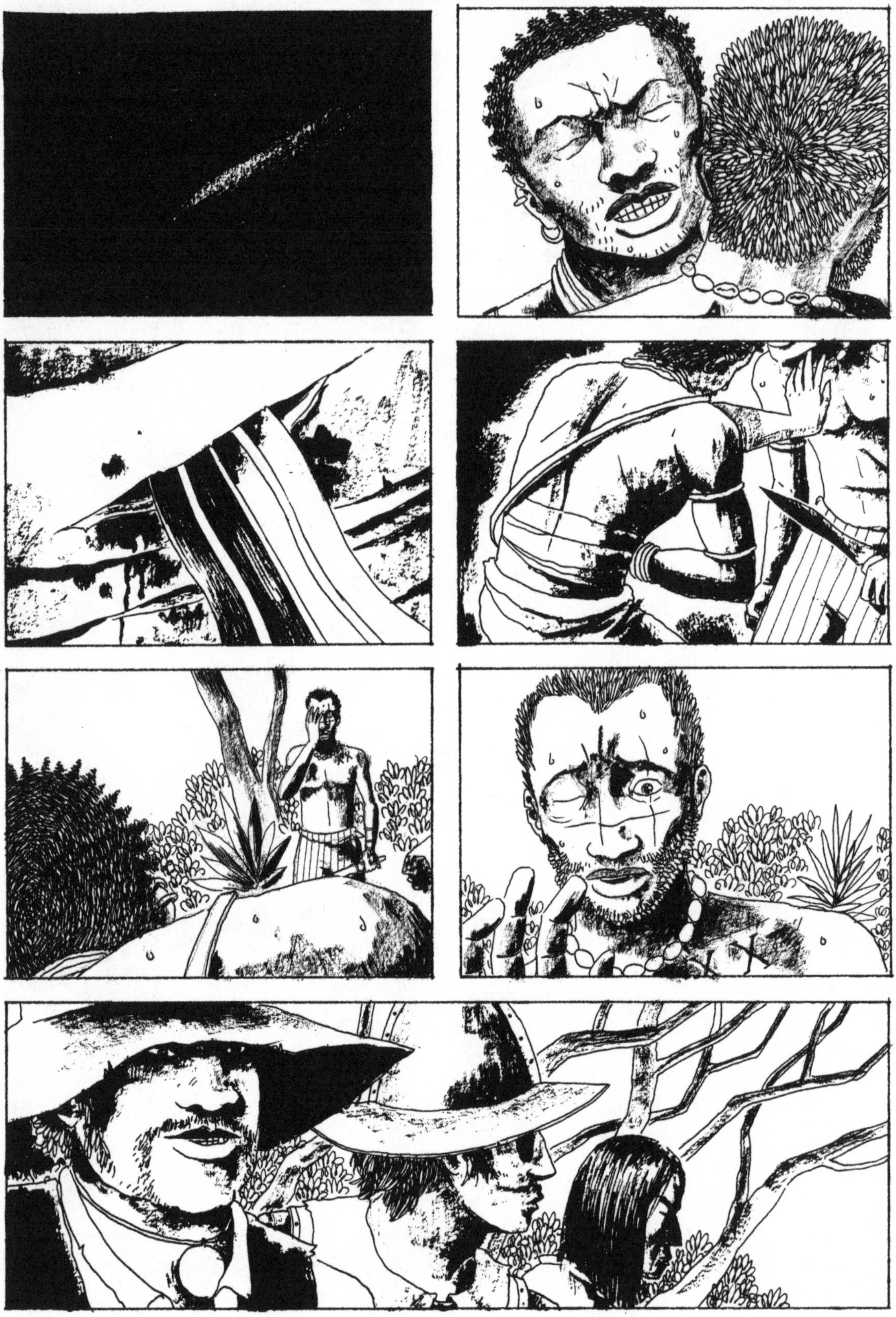

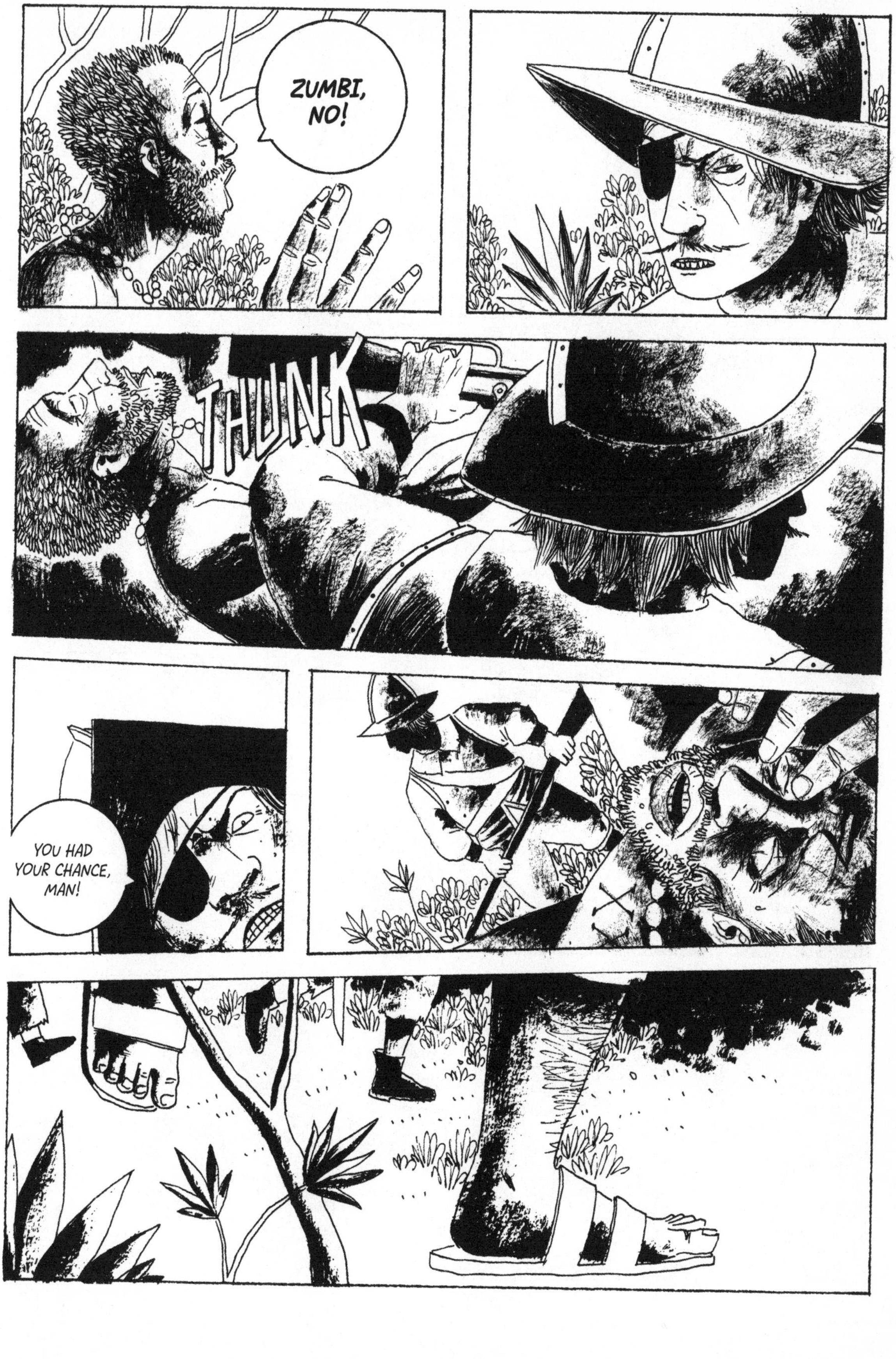
ZUMBI, NO!
THUNK
YOU HAD YOUR CHANCE, MAN!

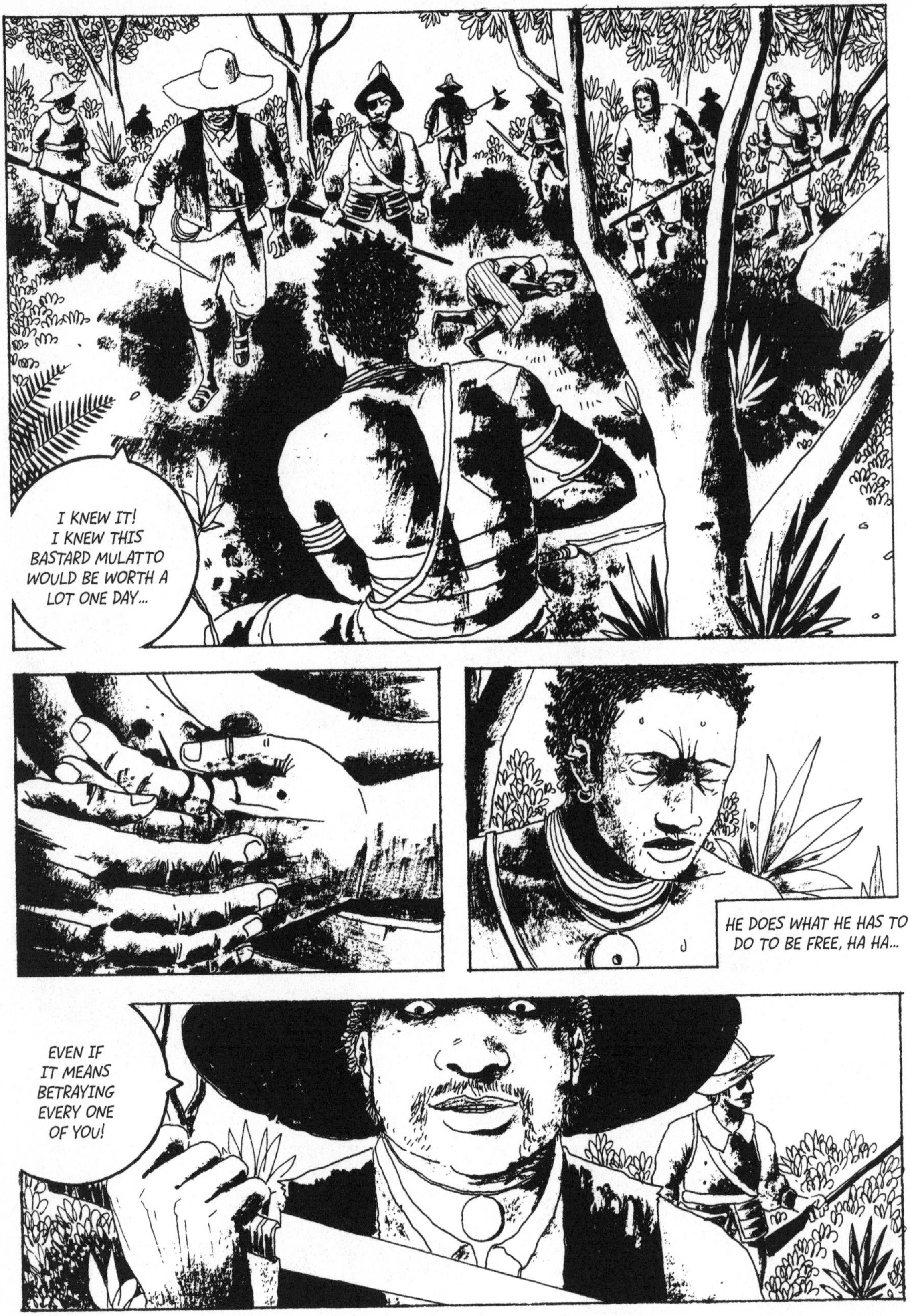
I KNEW IT! I KNEW THIS BASTARD MULATTO WOULD BE WORTH A LOT ONE DAY...
HE DOES WHAT HE HAS TO DO TO BE FREE, HA HA...
EVEN IF IT MEANS BETRAYING EVERY ONE OF YOU!

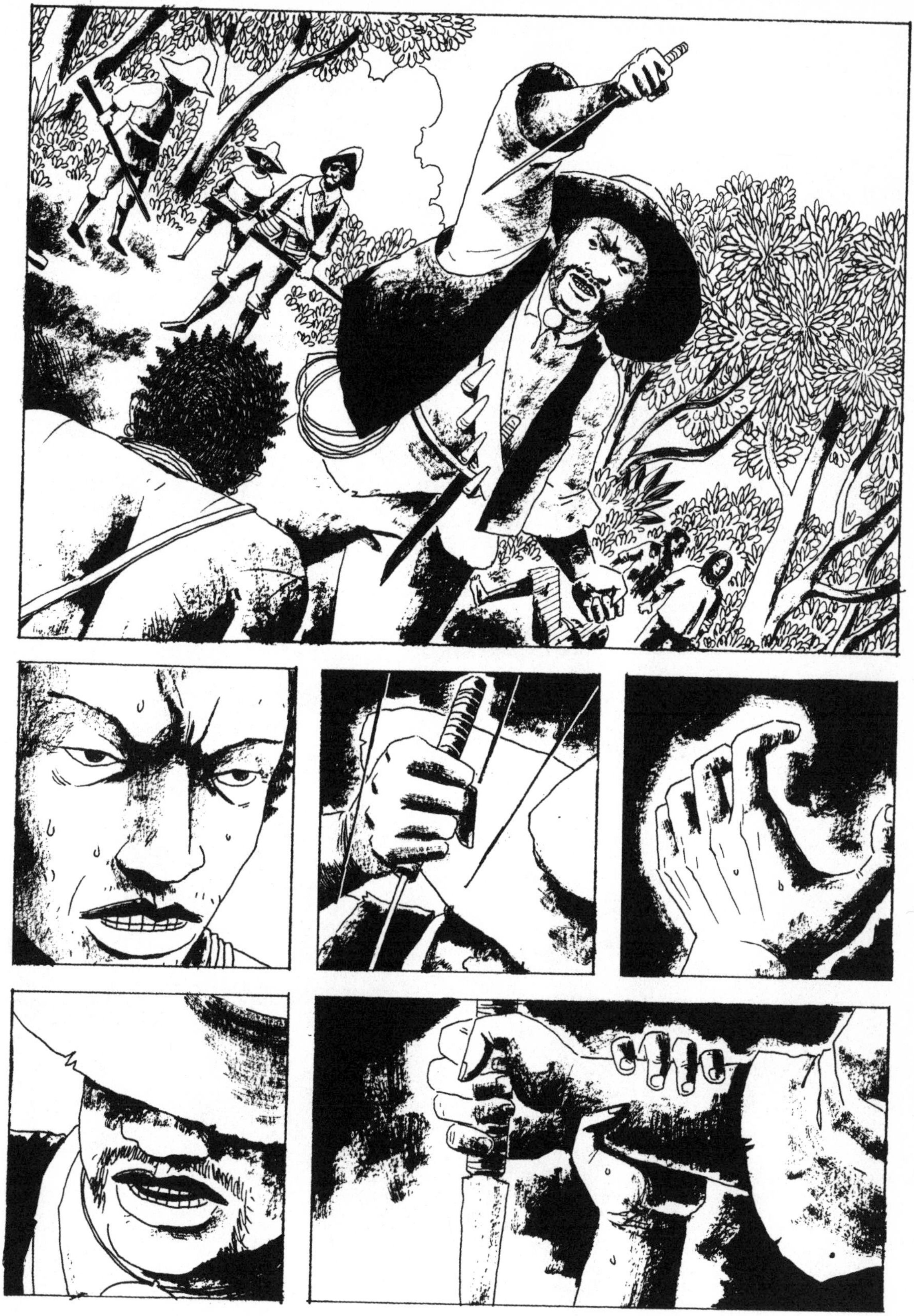

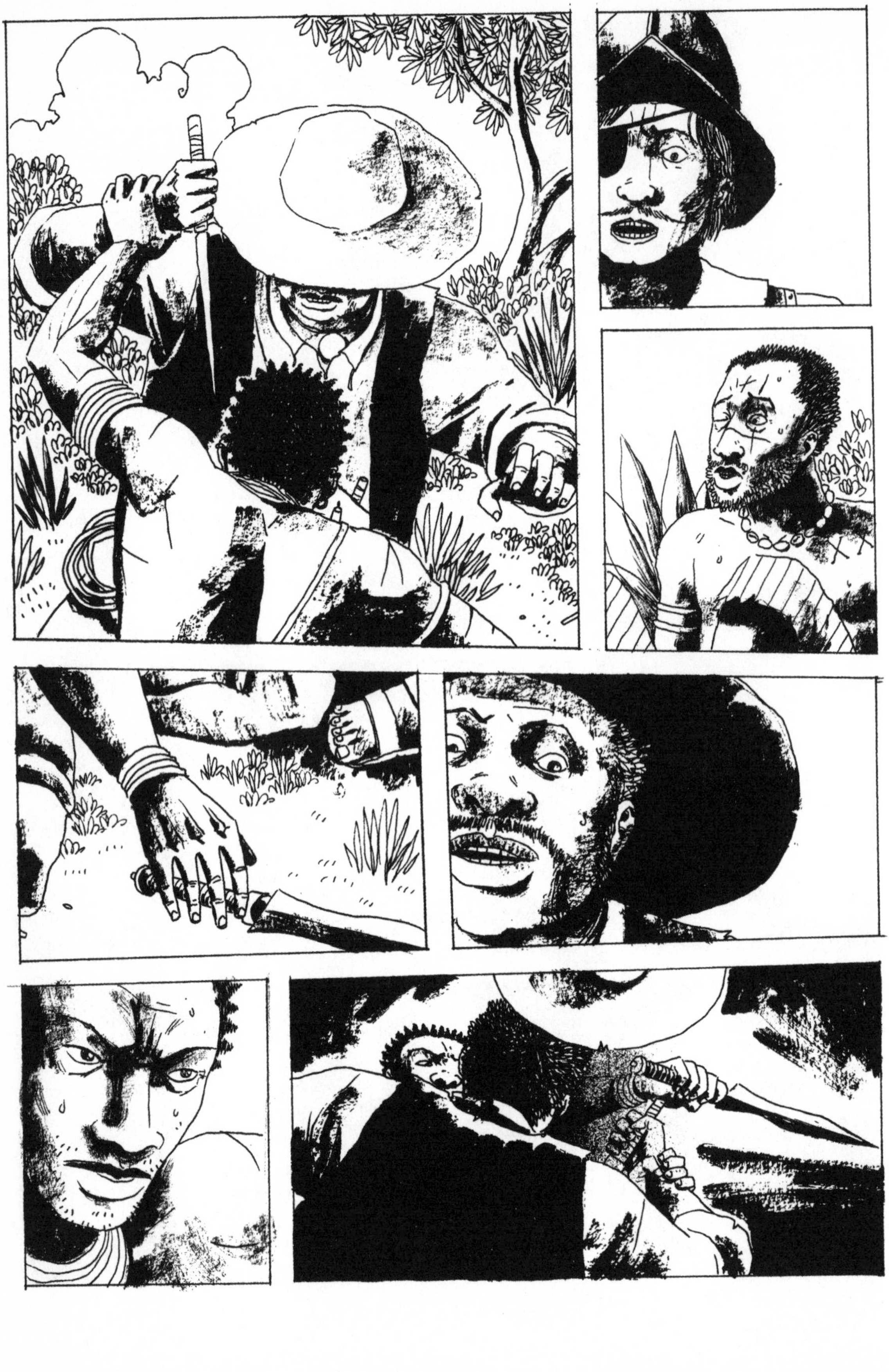

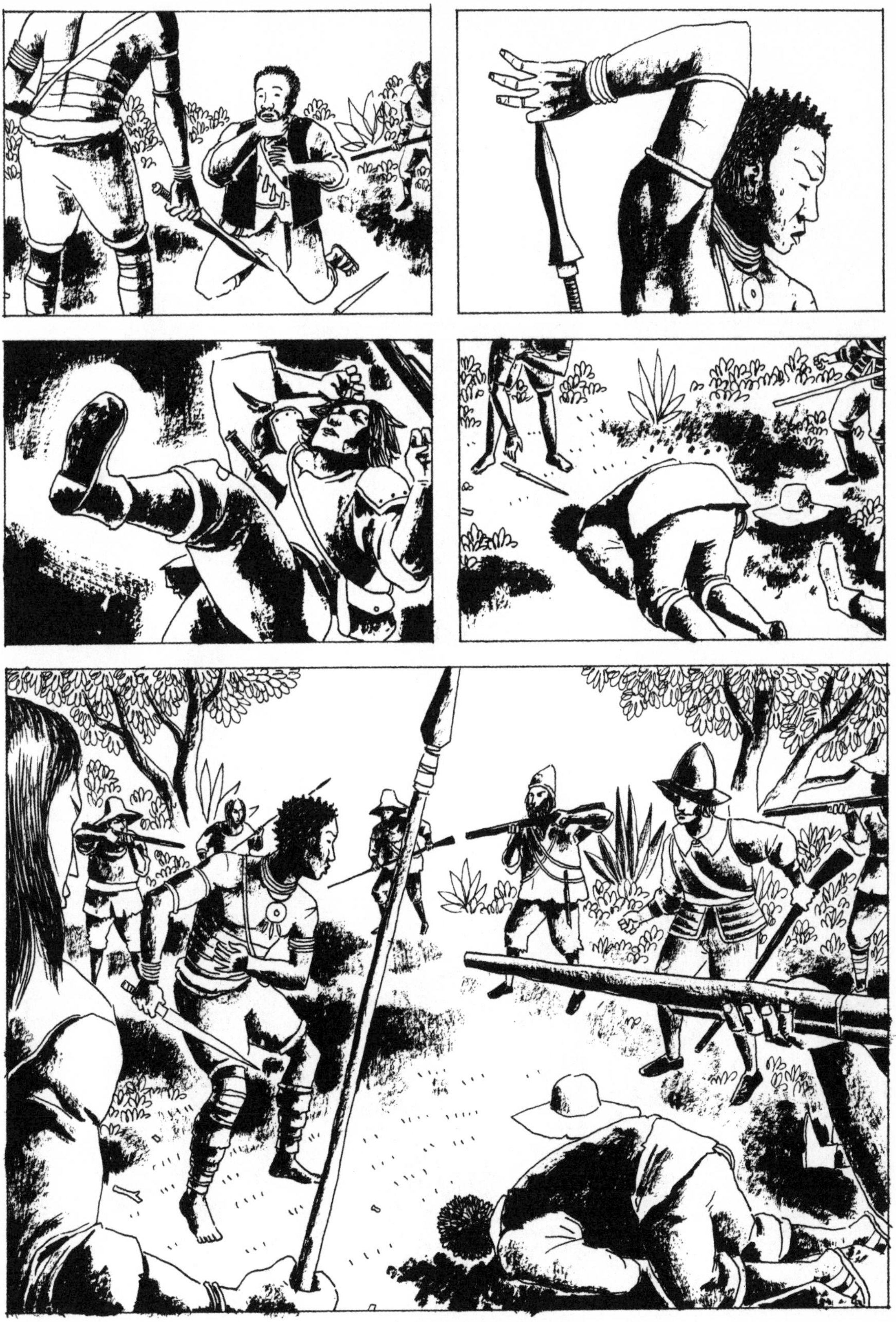

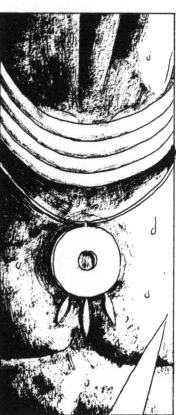

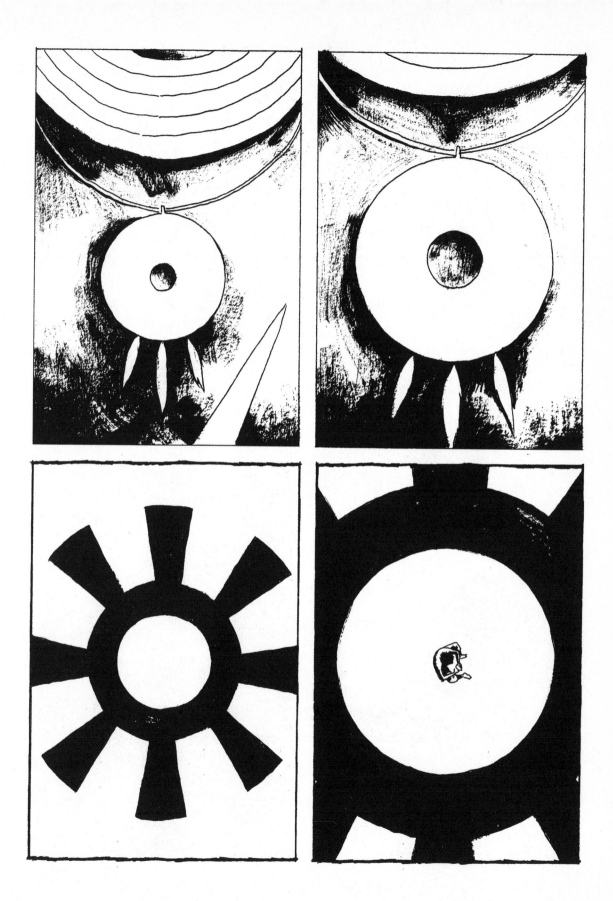

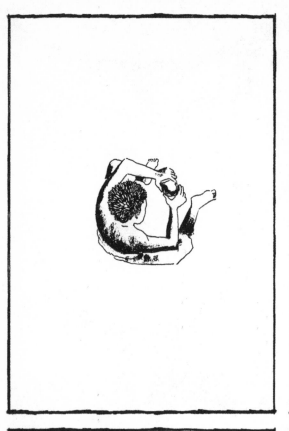

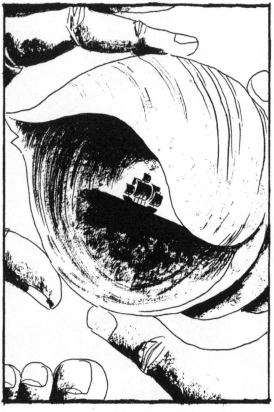

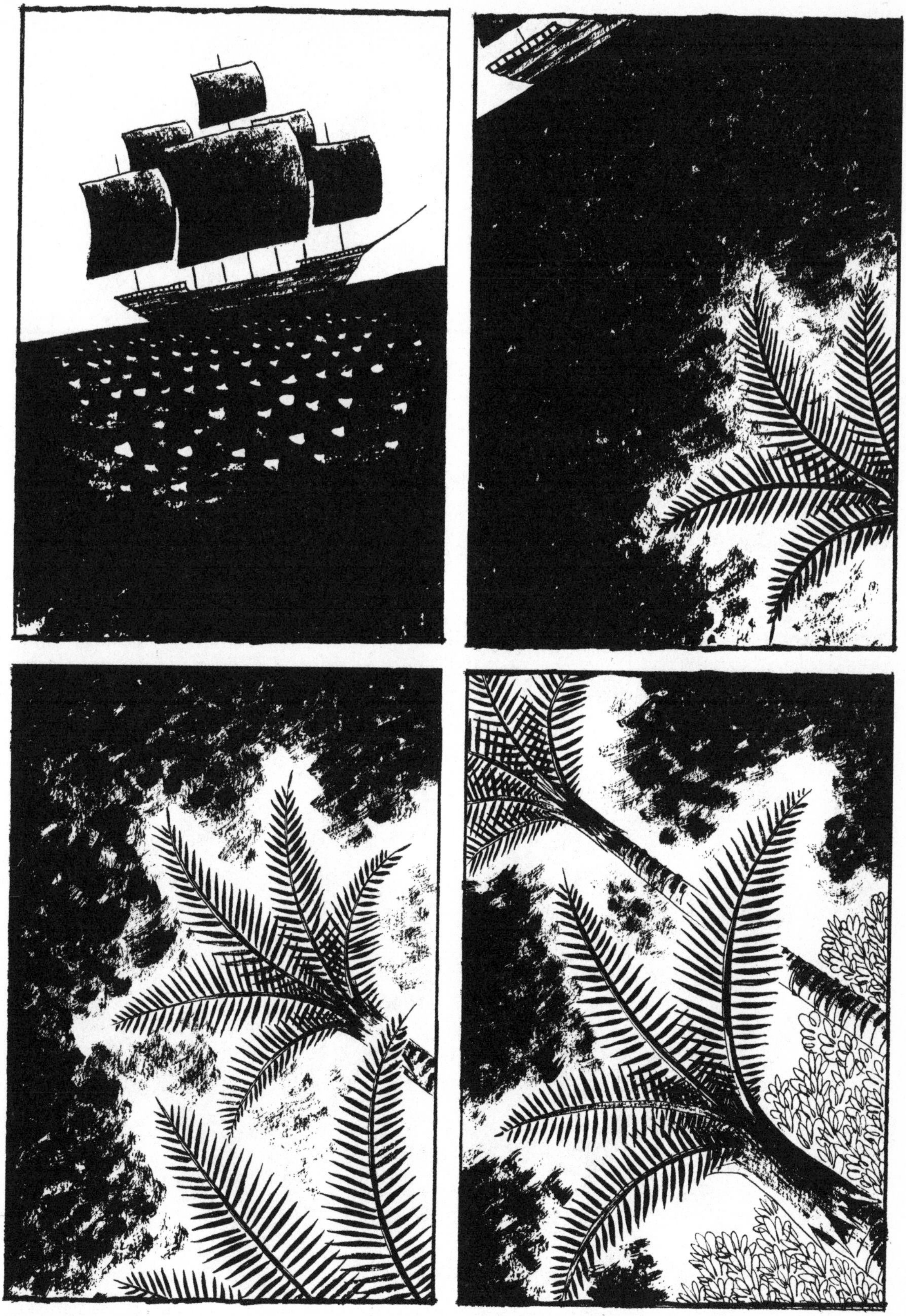

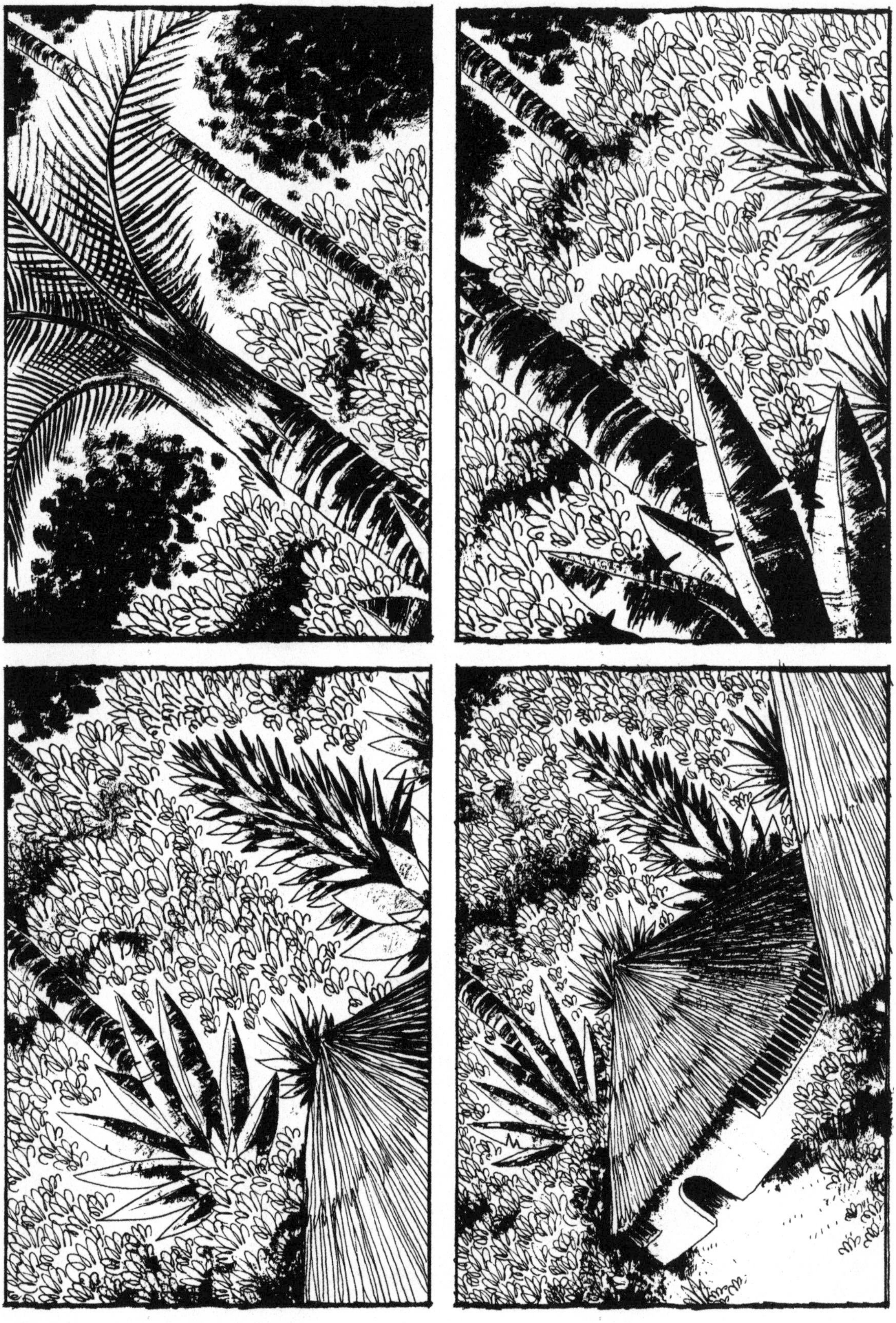

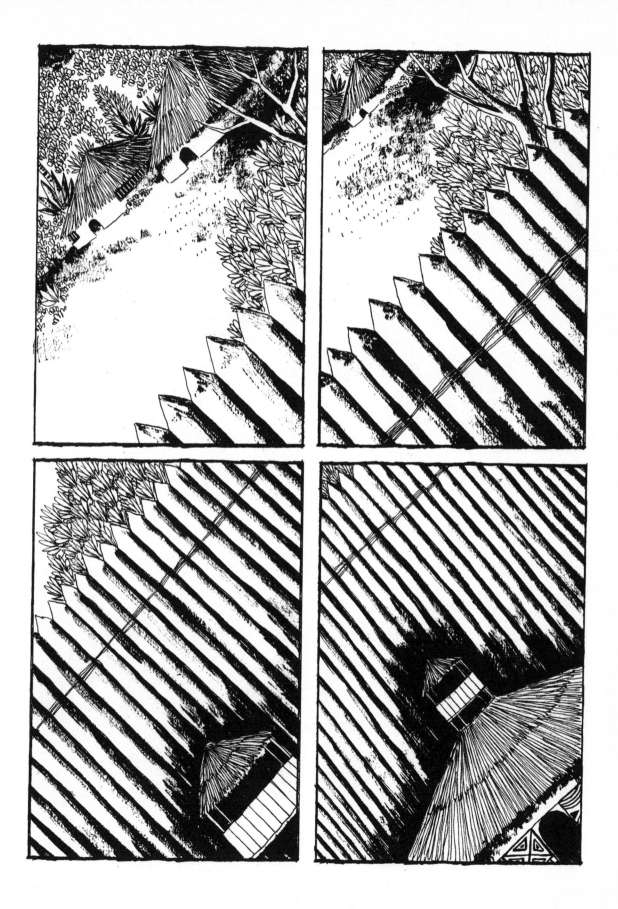

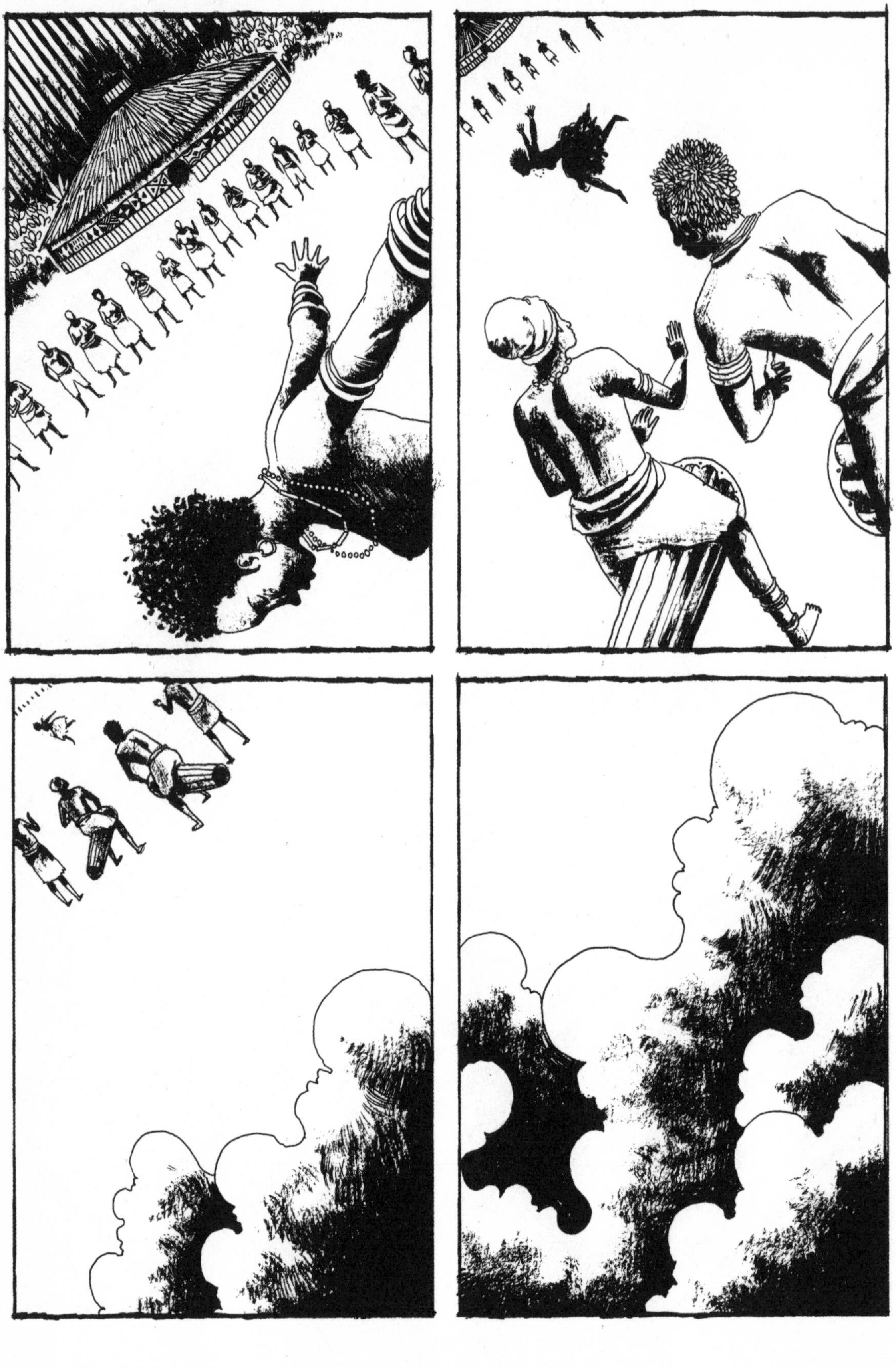

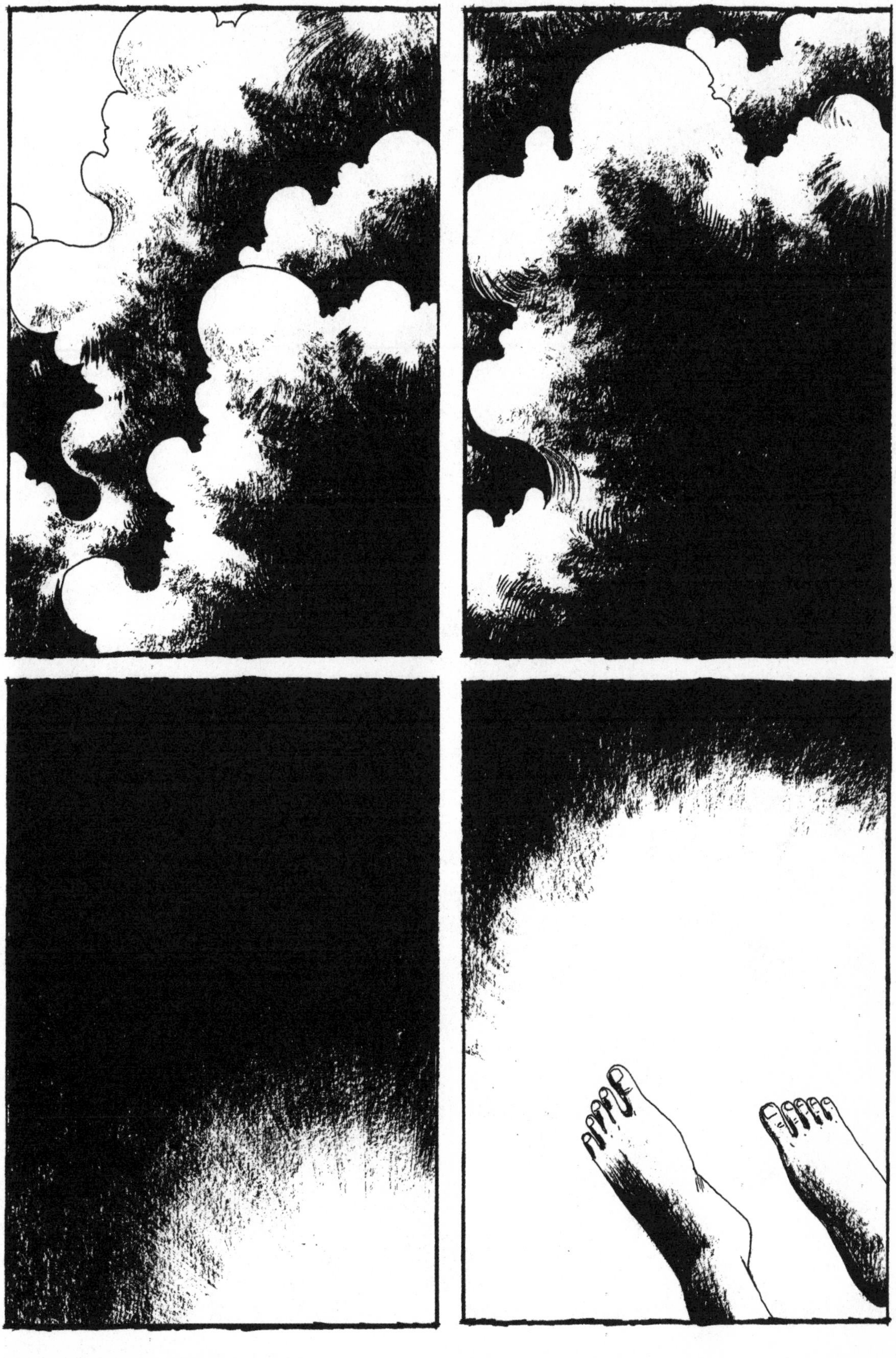

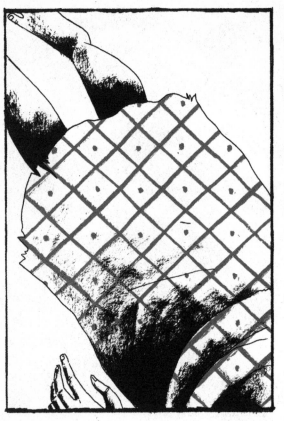

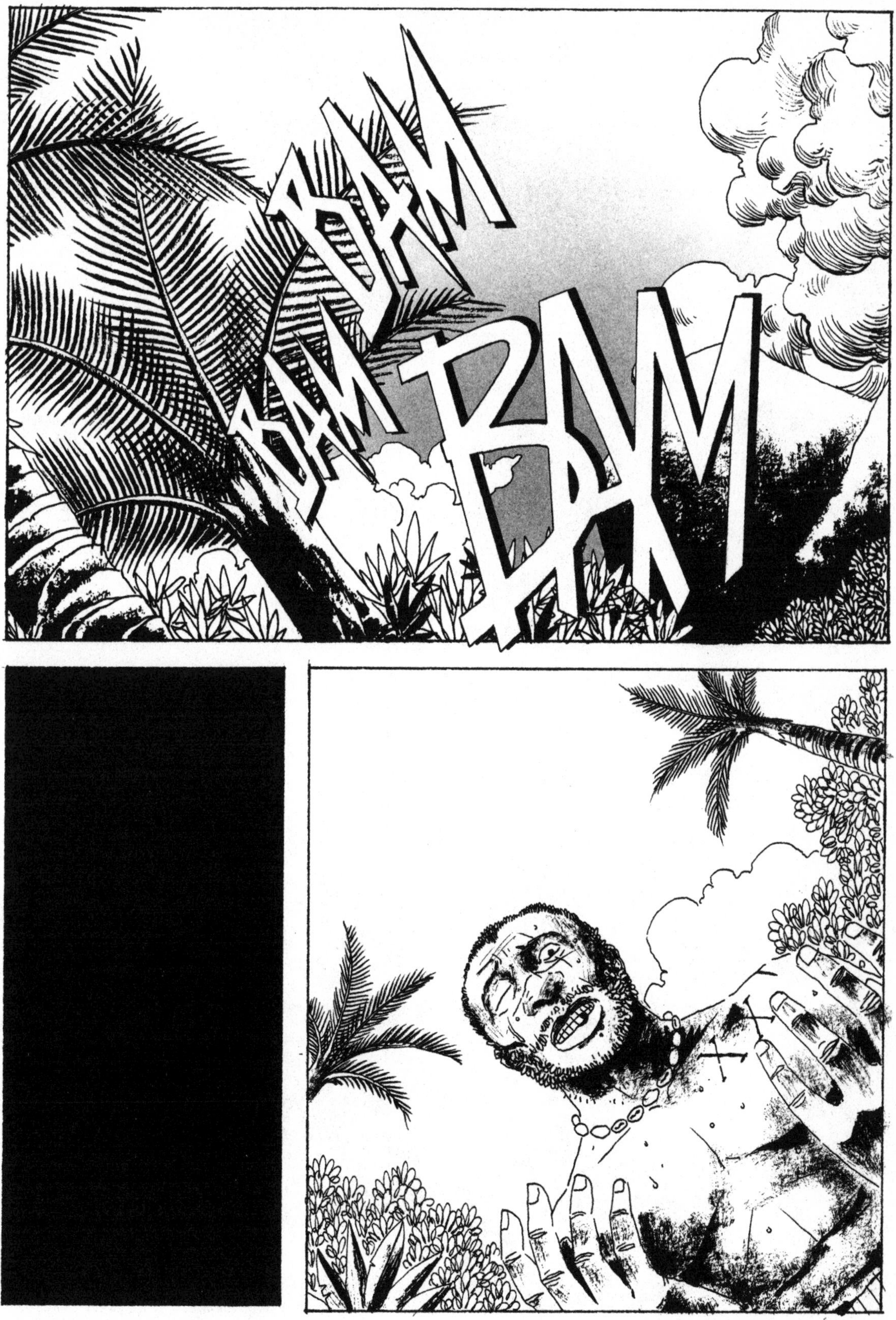
BAM
BAM
BAM
BAM

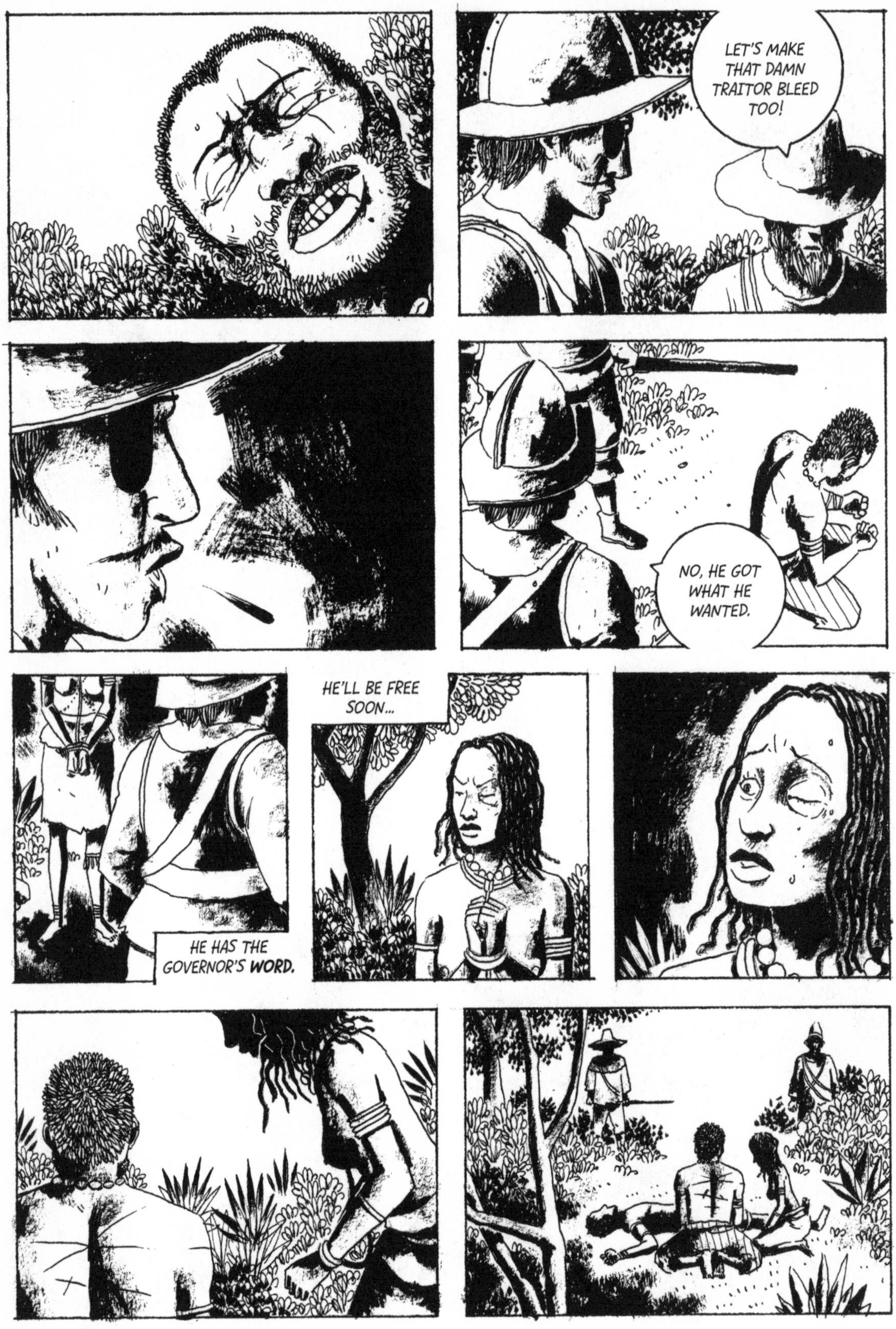
LET'S MAKE THAT DAMN TRAITOR BLEED TOO!
NO, HE GOT WHAT HE WANTED.
HE'LL BE FREE SOON...
HE HAS THE GOVERNOR'S **WORD.**

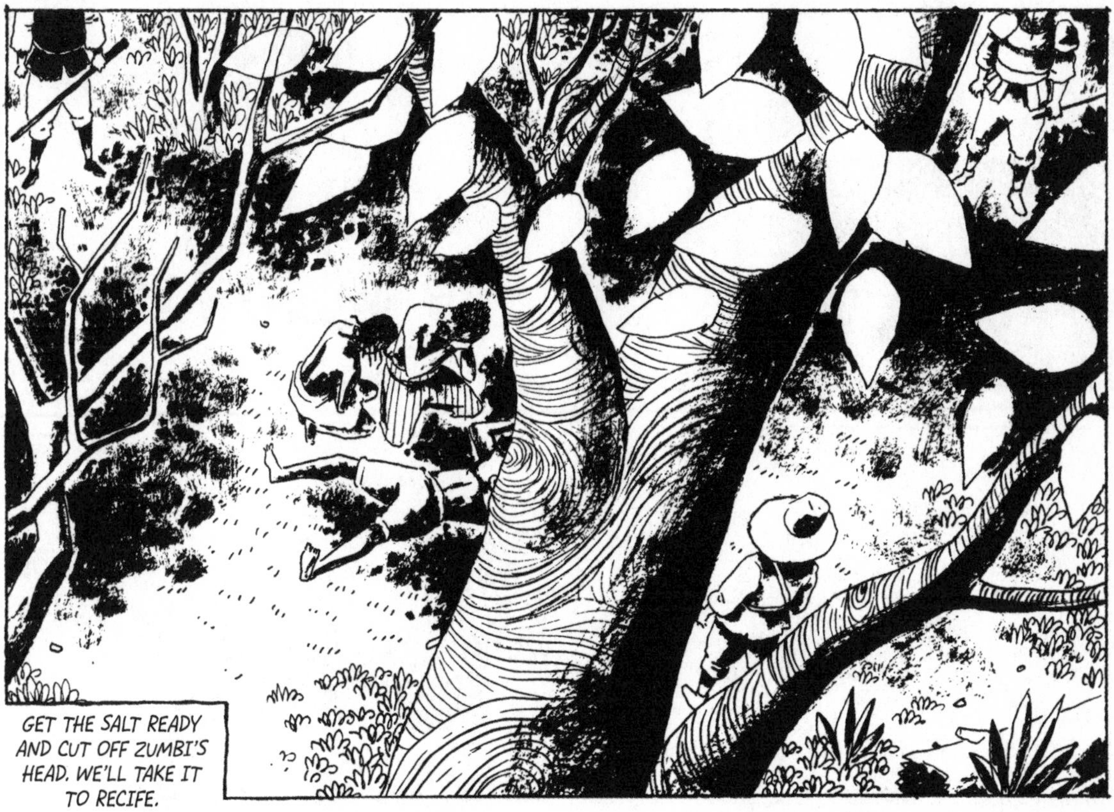
GET THE SALT READY AND CUT OFF ZUMBI'S HEAD. WE'LL TAKE IT TO RECIFE.

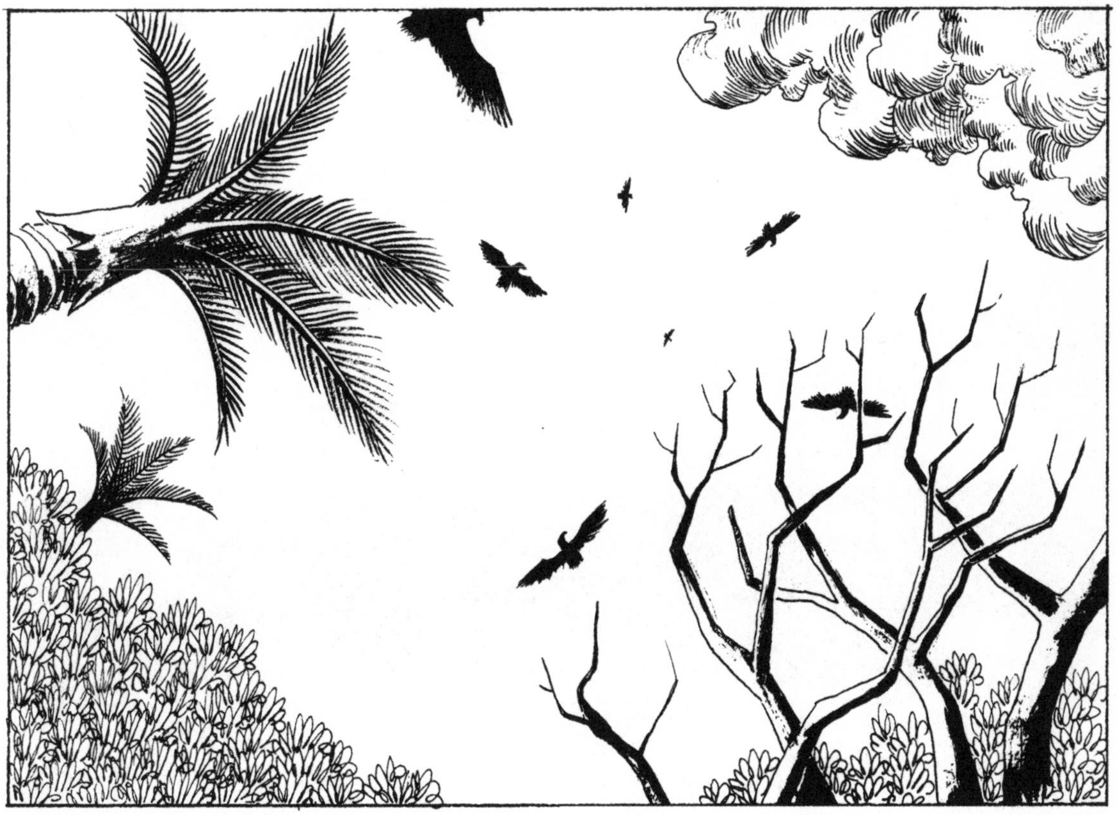

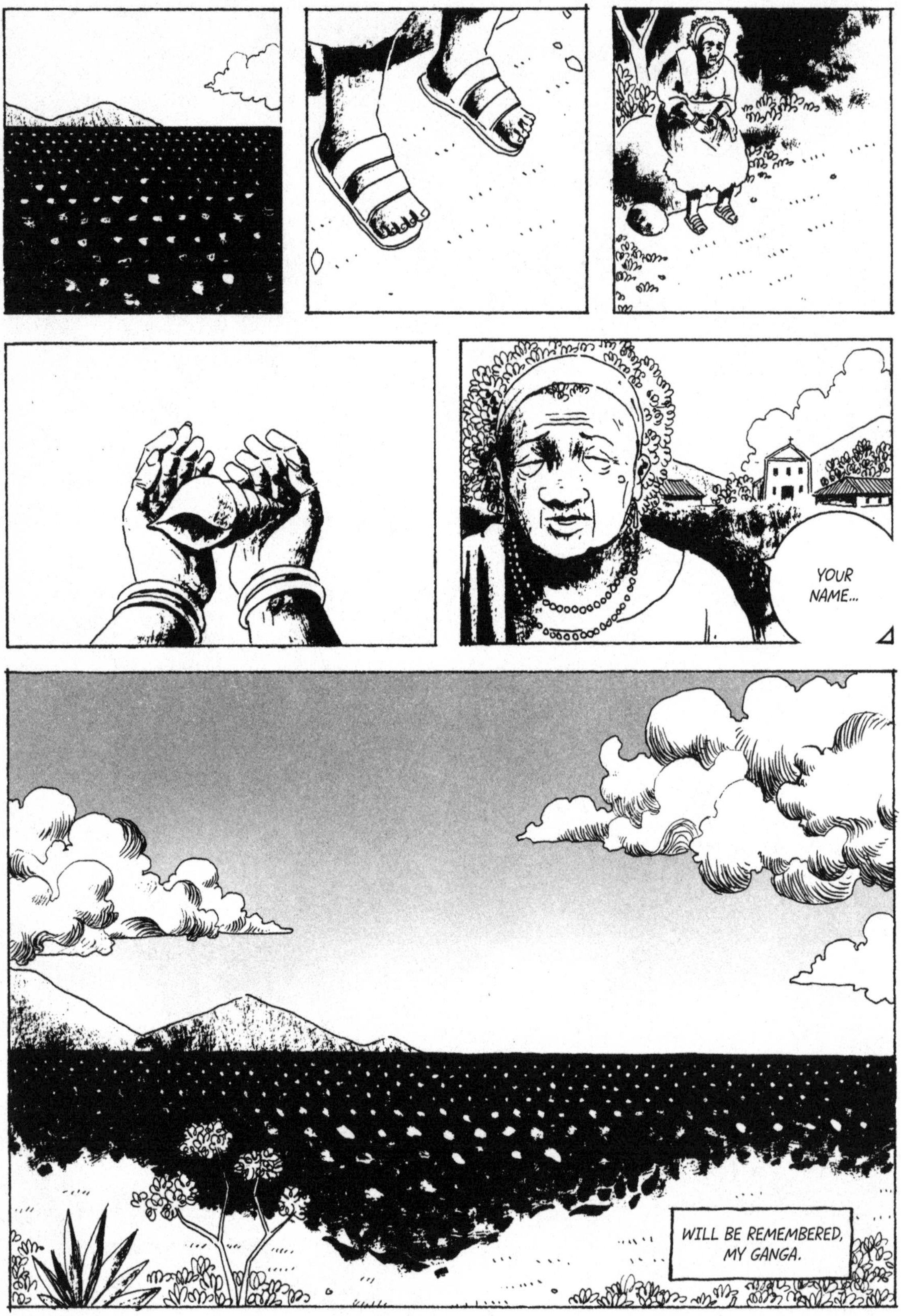
YOUR NAME...
WILL BE REMEMBERED, MY GANGA.

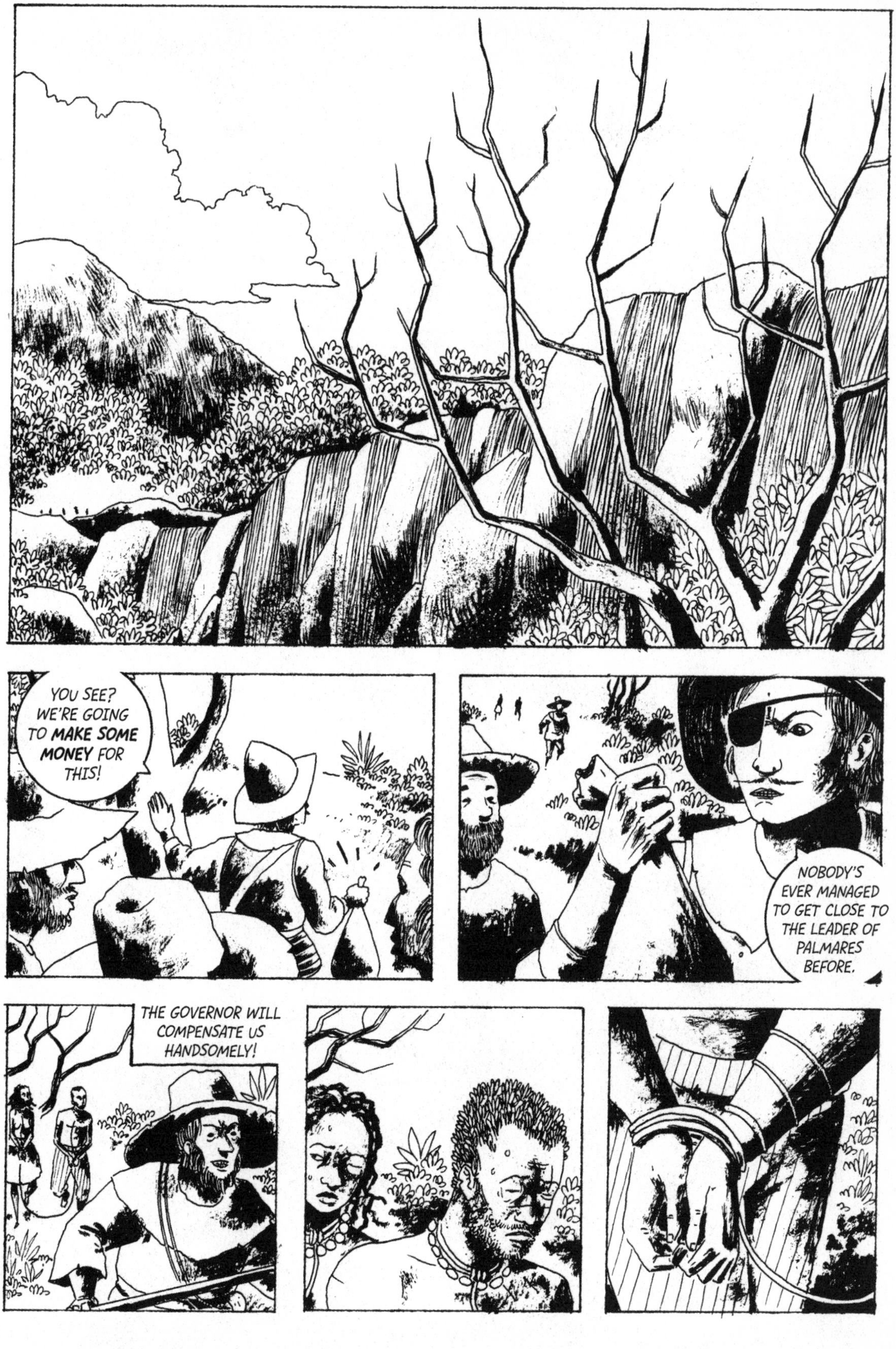
YOU SEE? WE'RE GOING TO **MAKE SOME MONEY** FOR THIS!
NOBODY'S EVER MANAGED TO GET CLOSE TO THE LEADER OF PALMARES BEFORE.
THE GOVERNOR WILL COMPENSATE US HANDSOMELY!

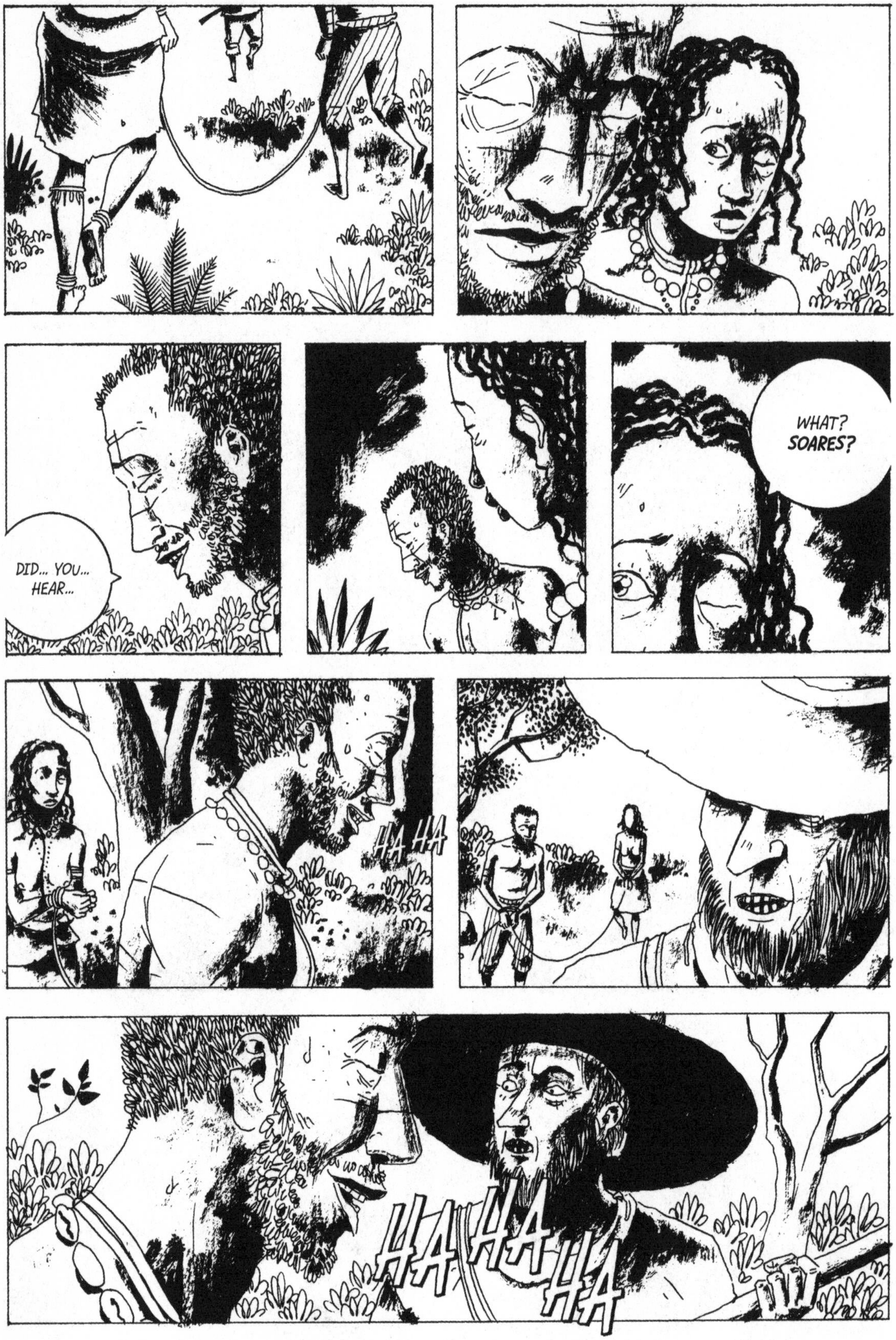
DID... YOU... HEAR...
WHAT? SOARES?
HA HA
HA HA HA HA

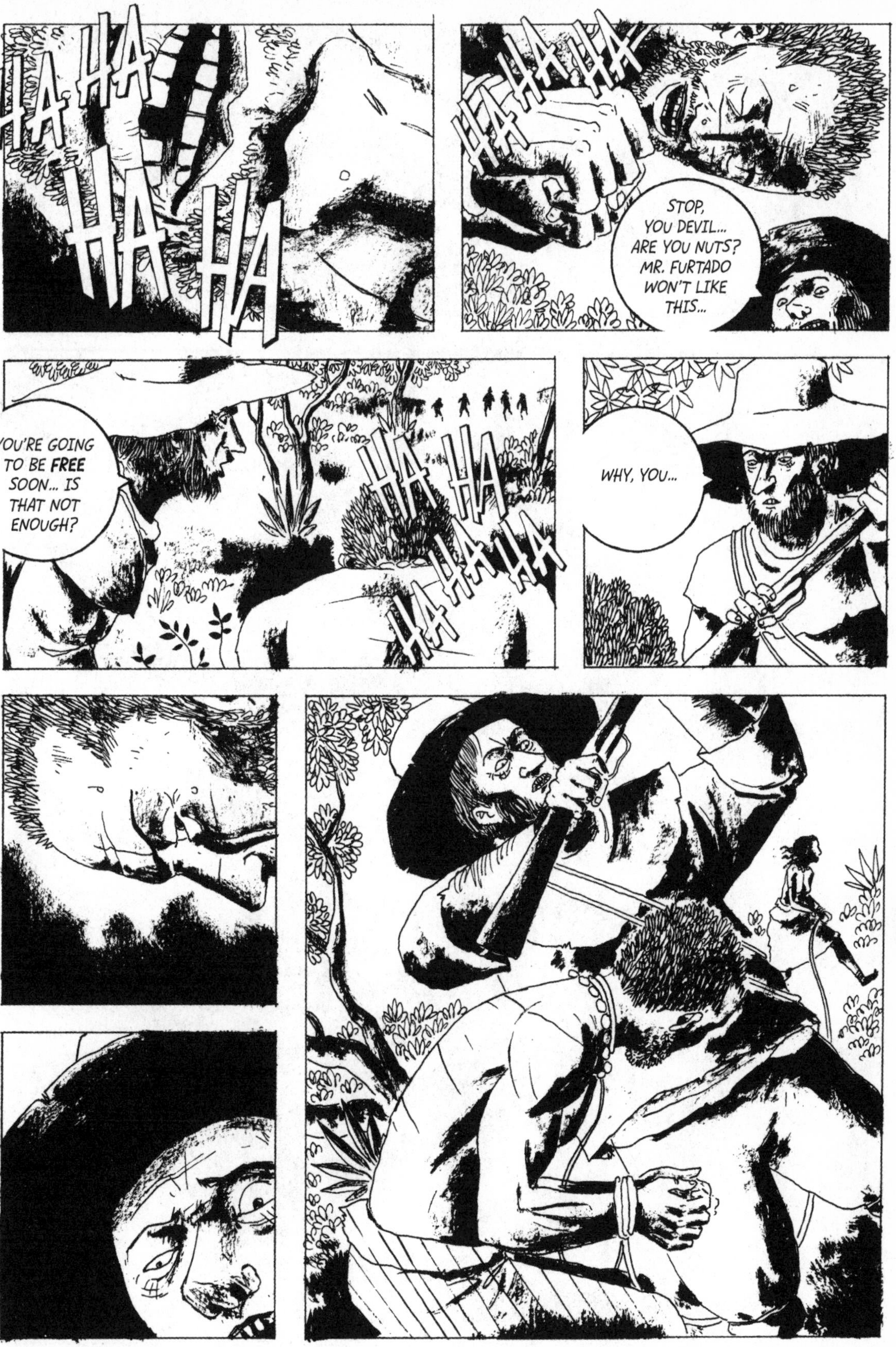
HA HA
HA HA
HA HA HA HA
STOP, YOU DEVIL... ARE YOU NUTS? MR. FURTADO WON'T LIKE THIS...
YOU'RE GOING TO BE **FREE** SOON... IS THAT NOT ENOUGH?
HA HA
HA HA HA HA
WHY, YOU...

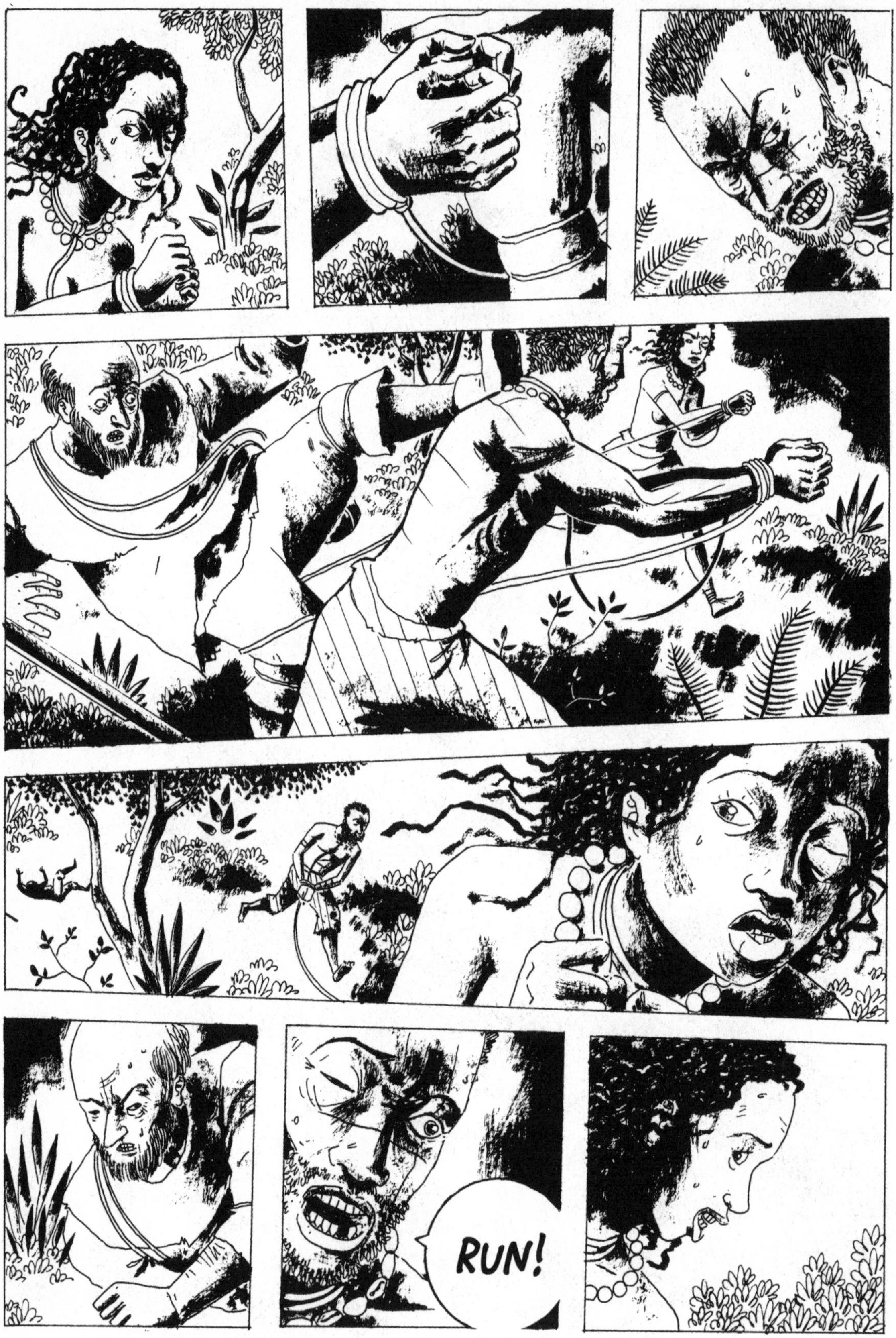
RUN!

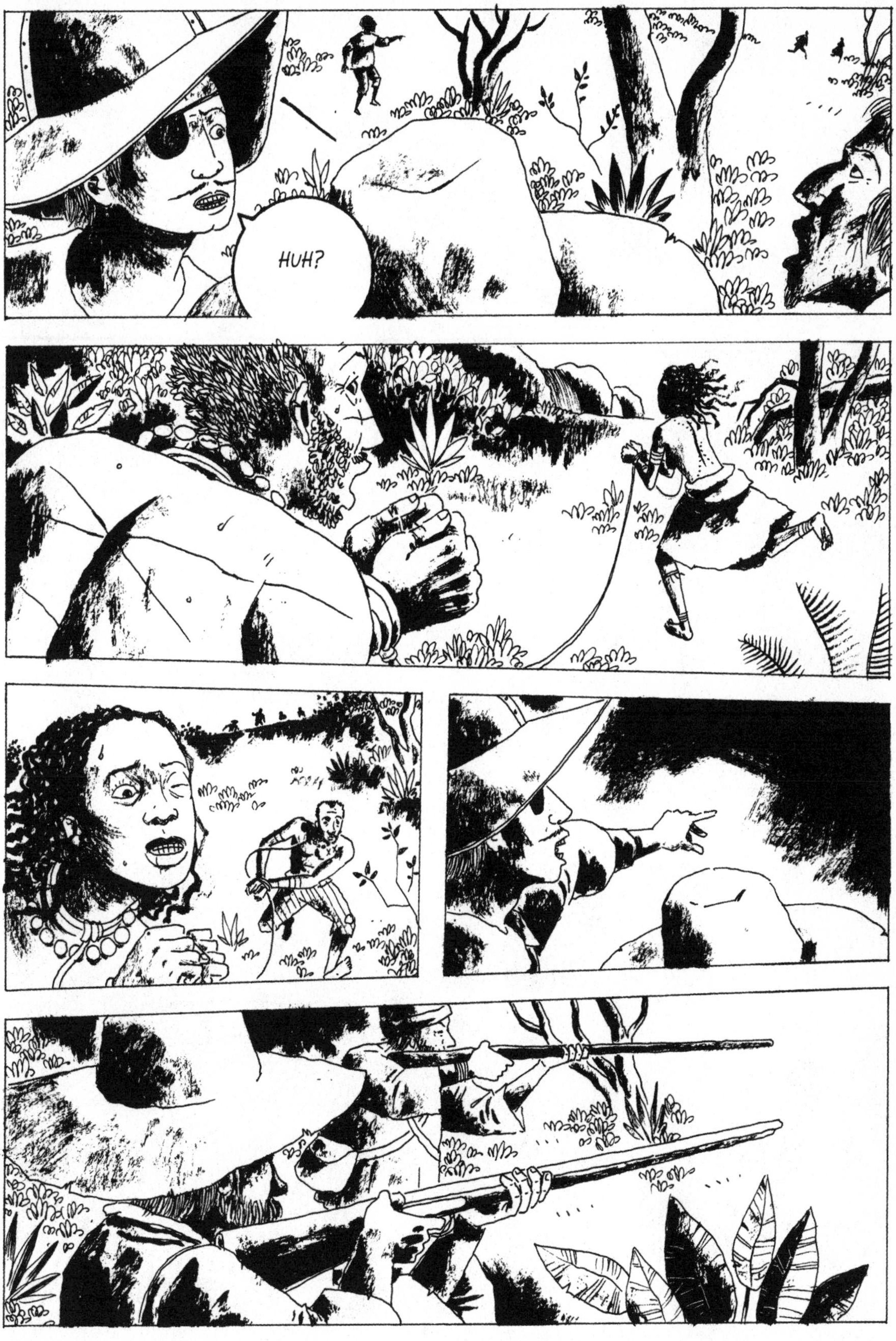
HUH?

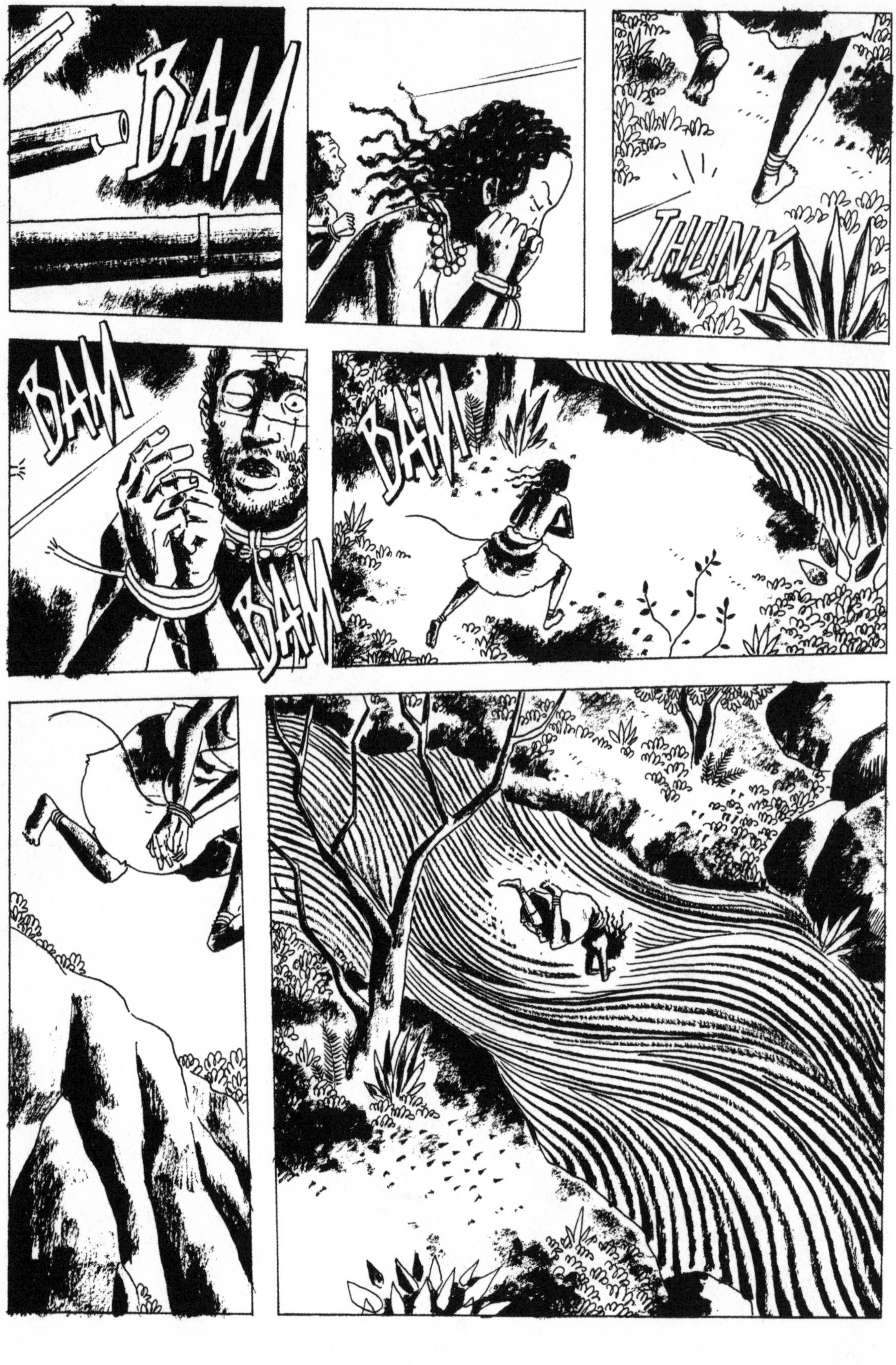
BAM
THUNK
BAM
BAM
BAM

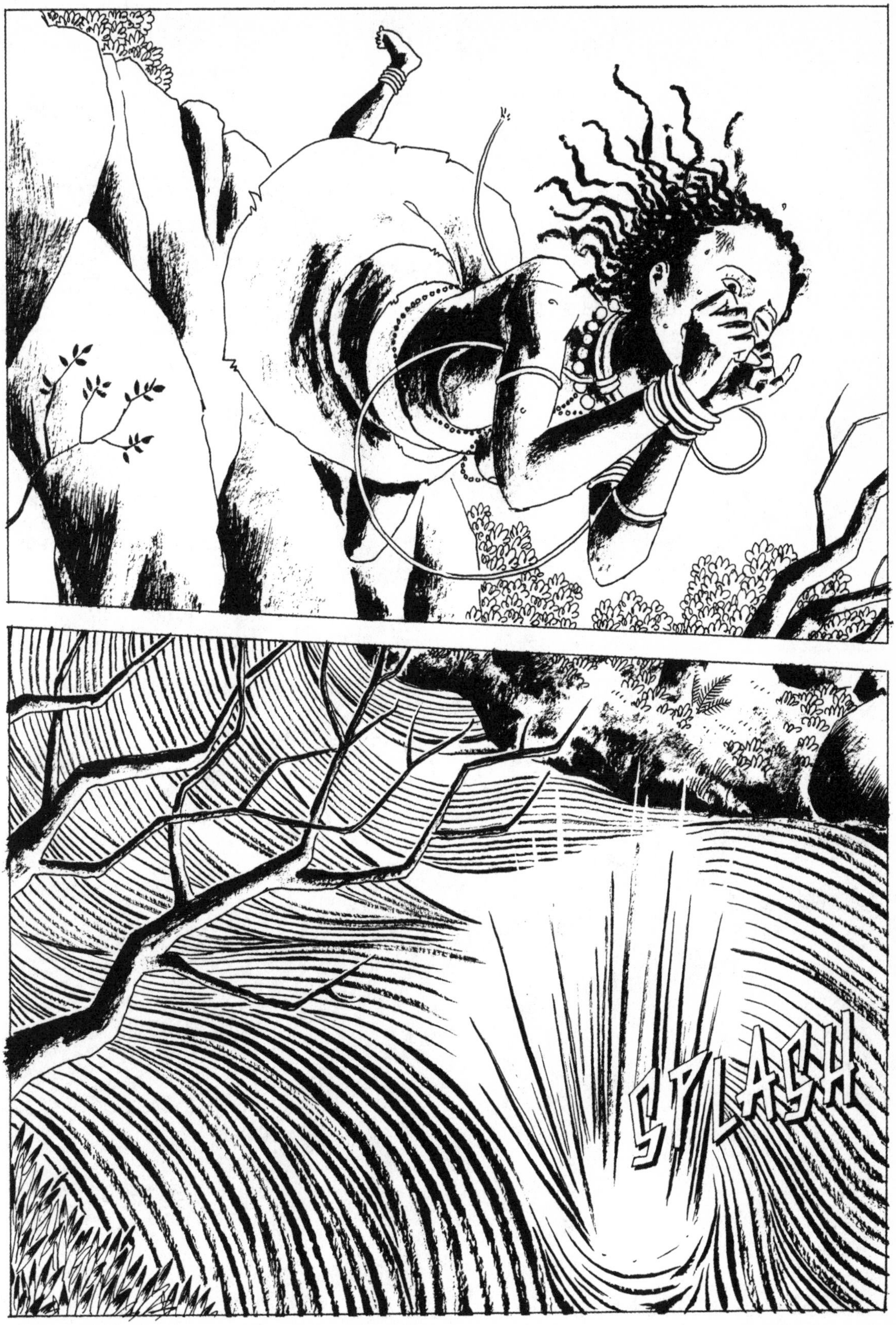
SPLASH

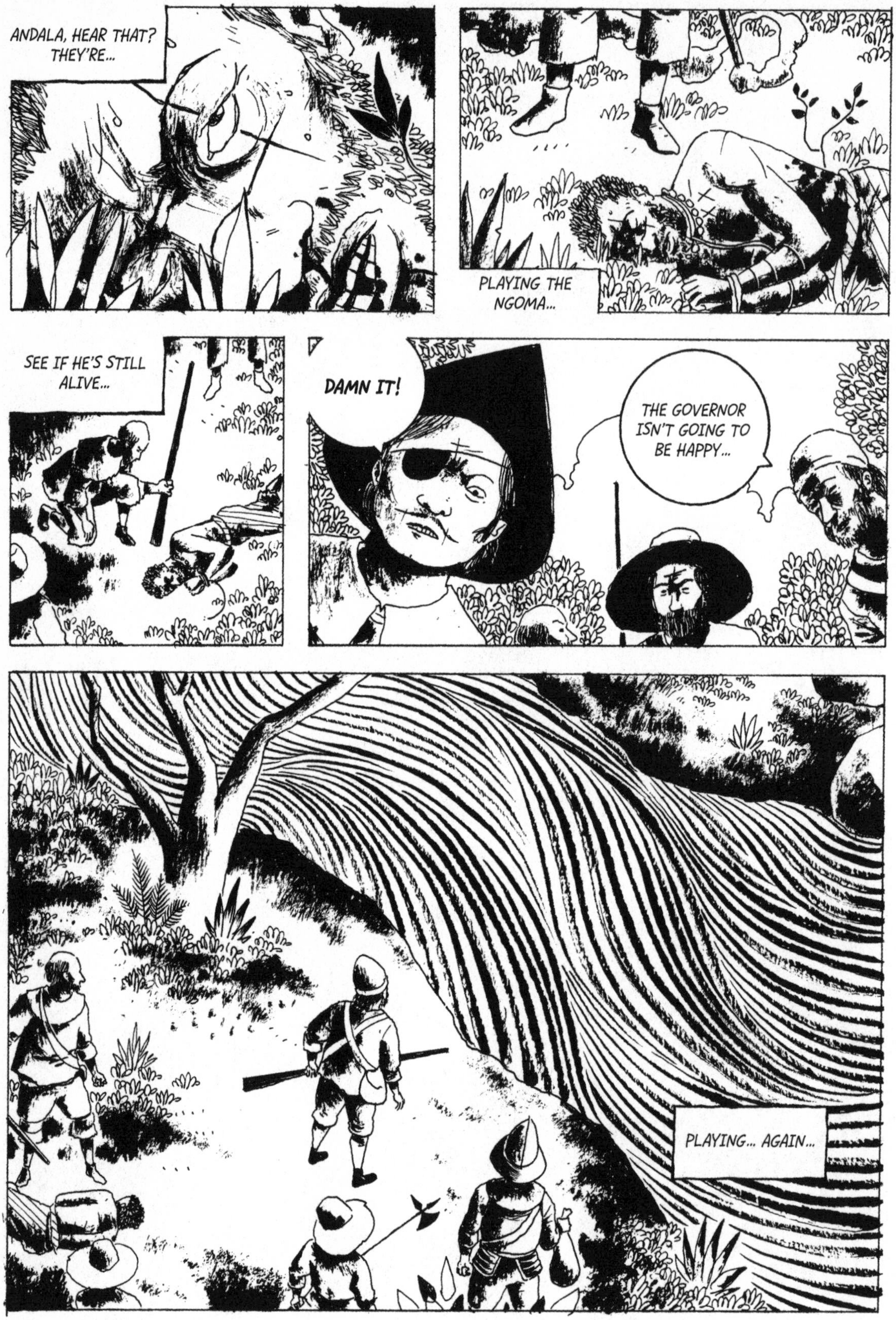
ANDALA, HEAR THAT? THEY'RE...
PLAYING THE NGOMA...
SEE IF HE'S STILL ALIVE...
DAMN IT!
THE GOVERNOR ISN'T GOING TO BE HAPPY...
PLAYING... AGAIN...

FOOTSTEPS IN THE NIGHT

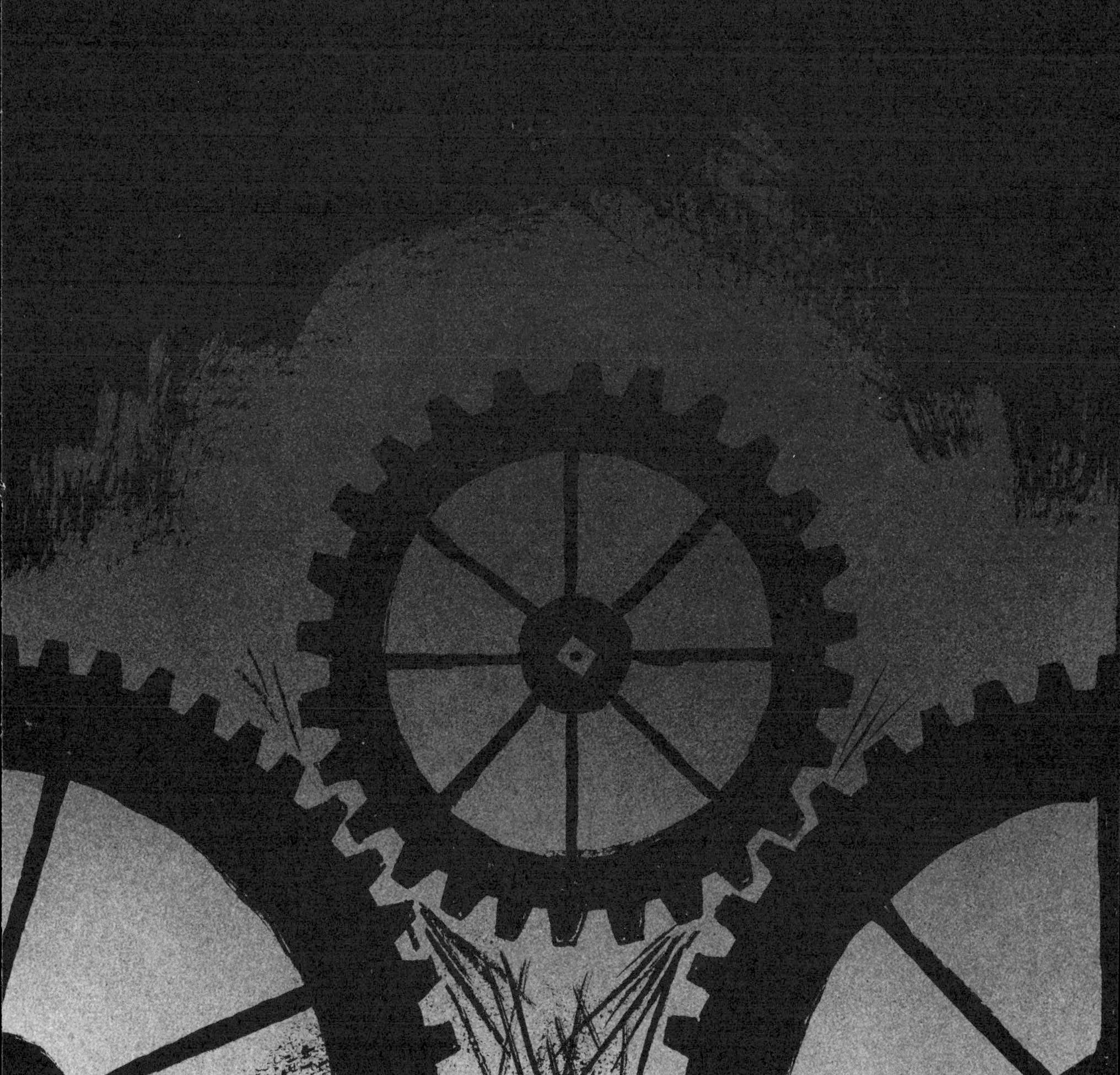

[T]he rest of said blacks are scattered among several little mocam-bos (which, however much it is claimed that such blacks do not number more than thirty, nevertheless they number thirty times that at least).

—*Domingos Jorge Velho*, Pernambuco, *1698*

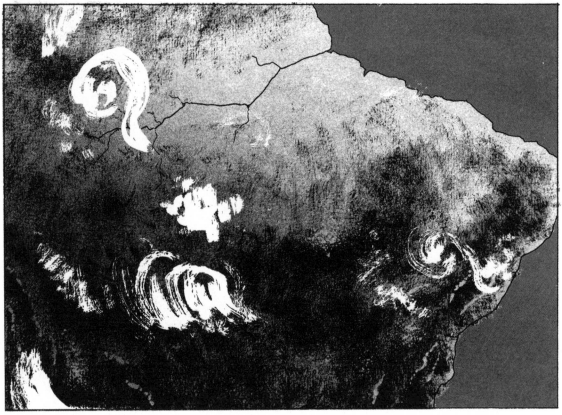

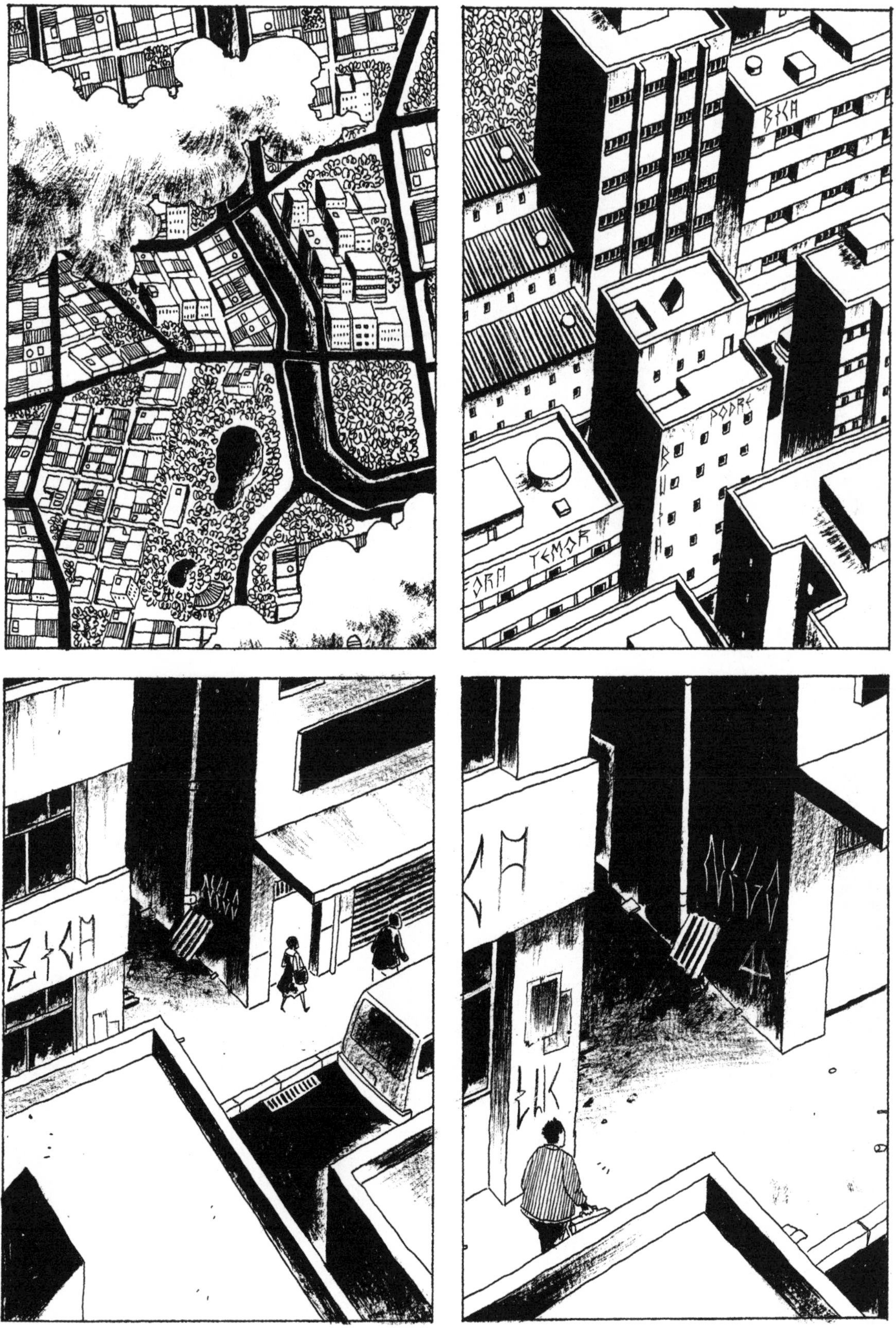
PODRE
TEMOR

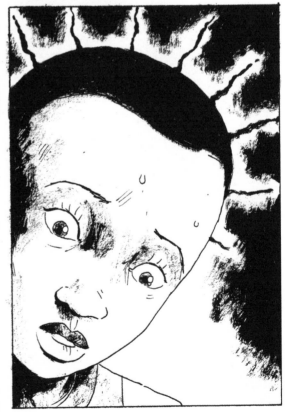

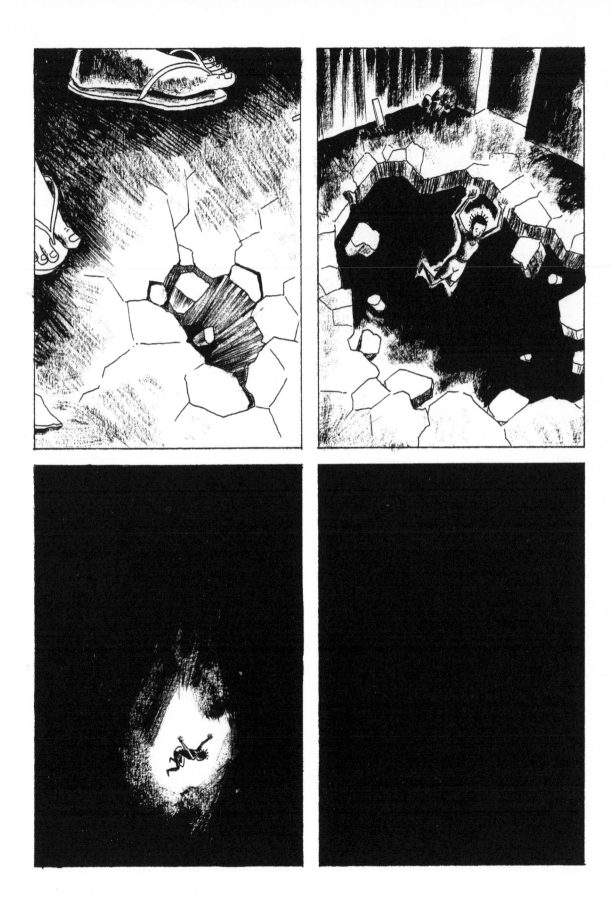

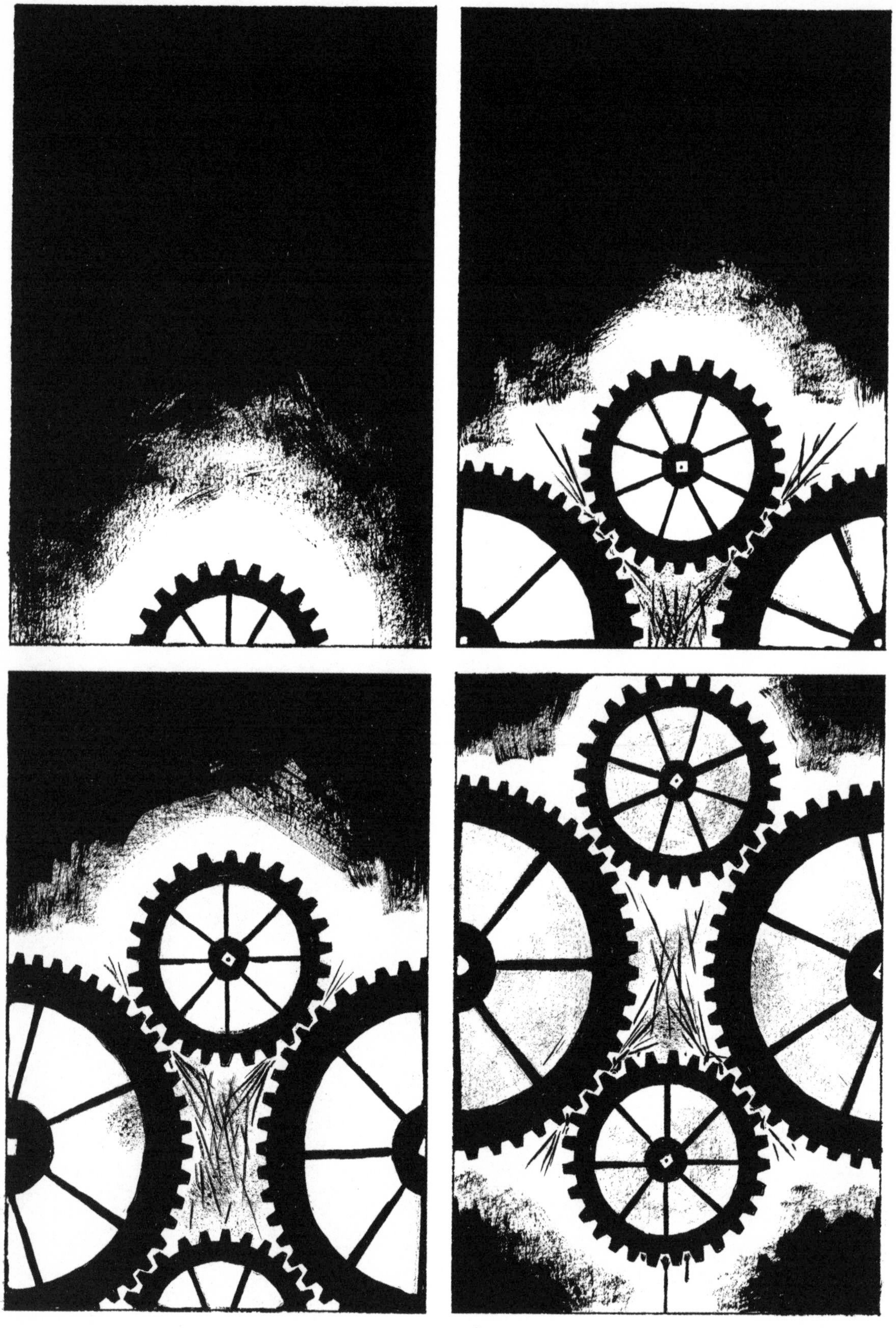

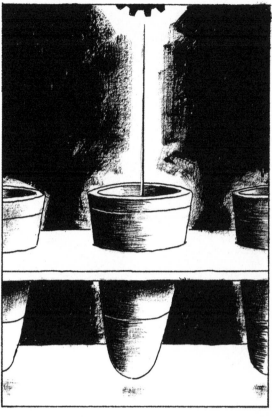

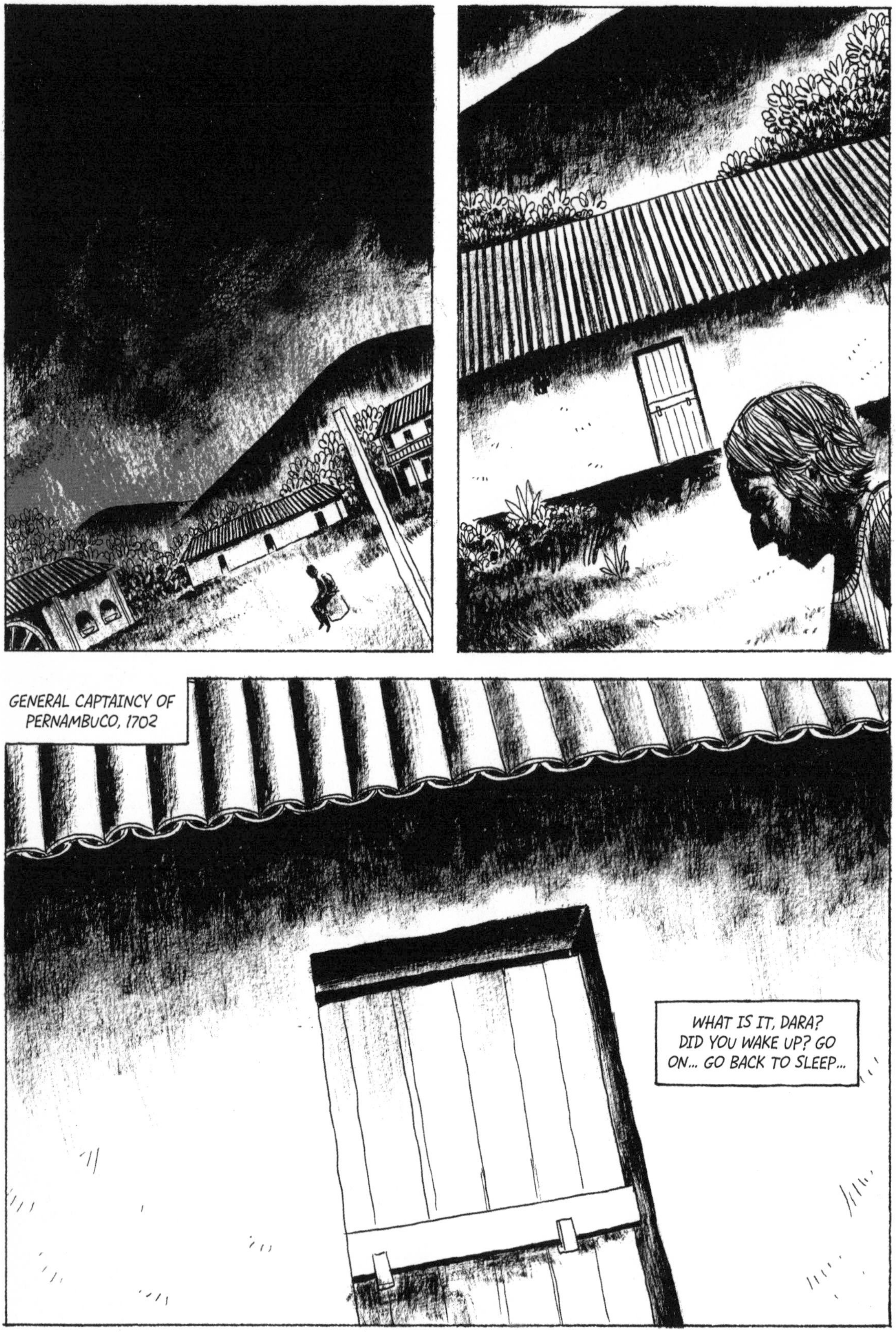
GENERAL CAPTAINCY OF PERNAMBUCO, 1702
WHAT IS IT, DARA? DID YOU WAKE UP? GO ON... GO BACK TO SLEEP...

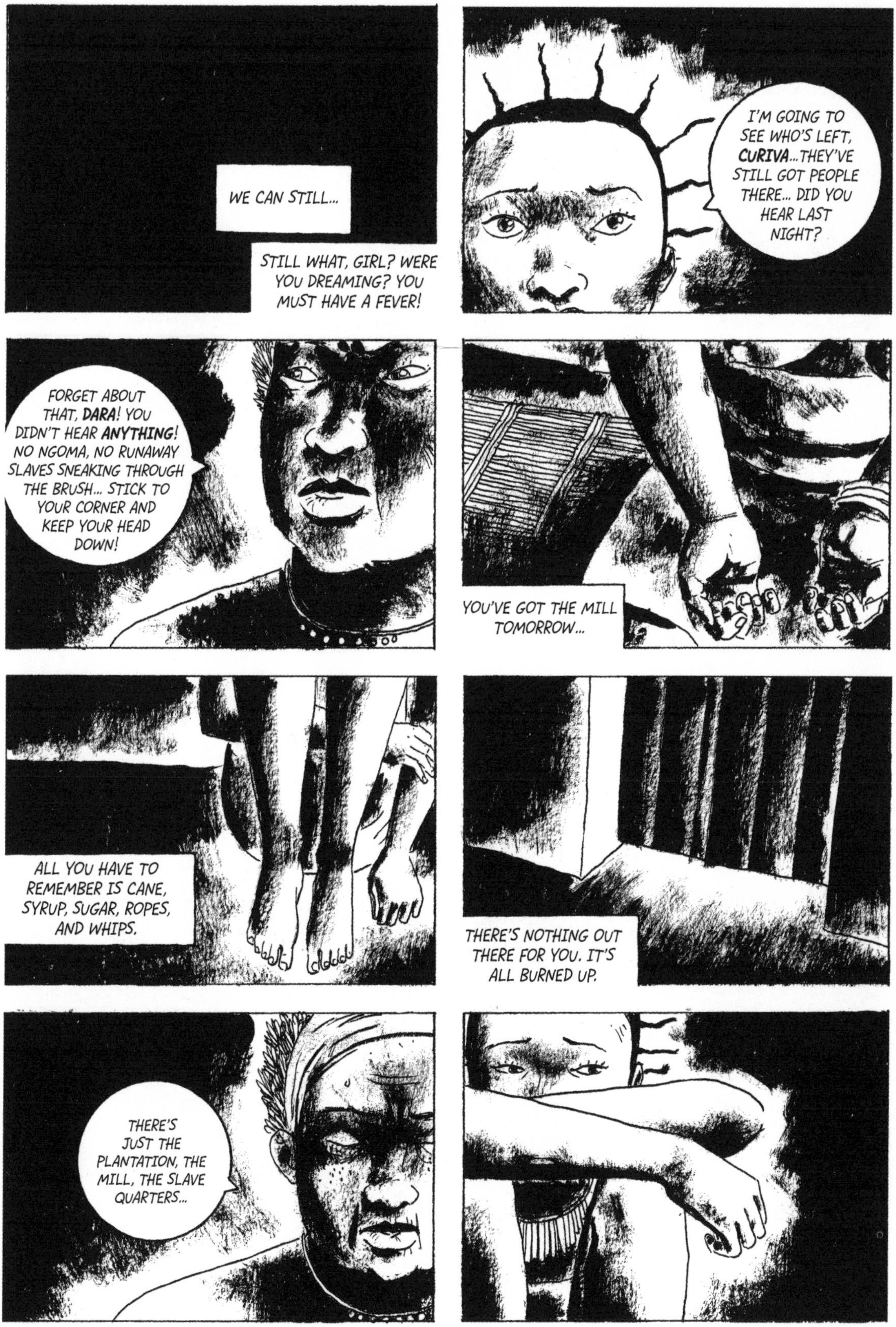

WE CAN STILL...
STILL WHAT, GIRL? WERE YOU DREAMING? YOU MUST HAVE A FEVER!
I'M GOING TO SEE WHO'S LEFT, CURIVA... THEY'VE STILL GOT PEOPLE THERE... DID YOU HEAR LAST NIGHT?
FORGET ABOUT THAT, DARA! YOU DIDN'T HEAR ANYTHING! NO NGOMA, NO RUNAWAY SLAVES SNEAKING THROUGH THE BRUSH... STICK TO YOUR CORNER AND KEEP YOUR HEAD DOWN!
YOU'VE GOT THE MILL TOMORROW...
ALL YOU HAVE TO REMEMBER IS CANE, SYRUP, SUGAR, ROPES, AND WHIPS.
THERE'S NOTHING OUT THERE FOR YOU. IT'S ALL BURNED UP.
THERE'S JUST THE PLANTATION, THE MILL, THE SLAVE QUARTERS...

LAND WHERE... SEEDS...

CAN SPROUT AND FLOURISH...

LOOK, CURIVA, ANOTHER ONE!

SHHH!

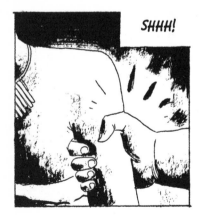

KEEP QUIET! YOU'LL WAKE UP THE OTHERS!

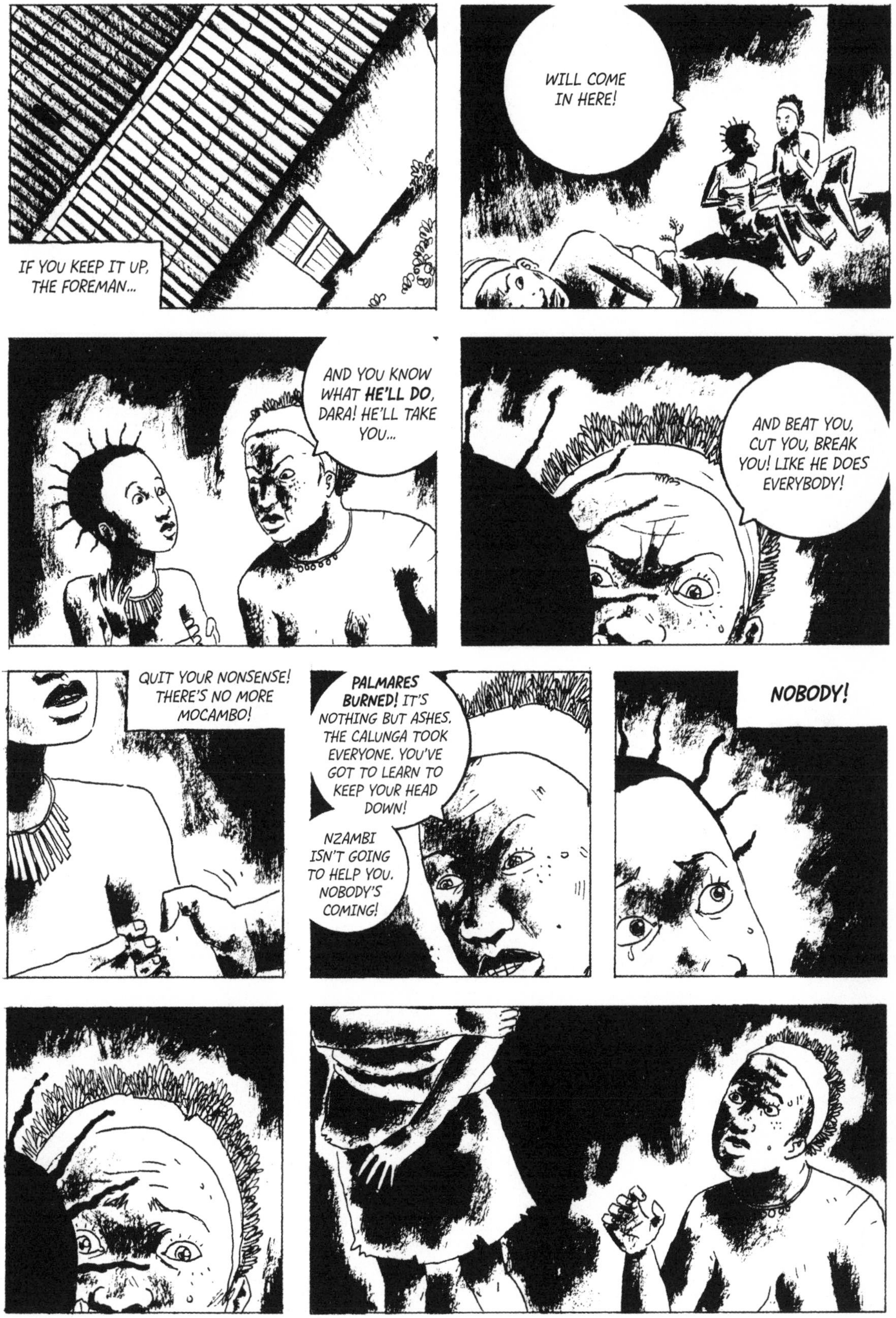
IF YOU KEEP IT UP, THE FOREMAN...
WILL COME IN HERE!
AND YOU KNOW WHAT **HE'LL DO**, DARA! HE'LL TAKE YOU...
AND BEAT YOU, CUT YOU, BREAK YOU! LIKE HE DOES EVERYBODY!
QUIT YOUR NONSENSE! THERE'S NO MORE MOCAMBO!
PALMARES BURNED! IT'S NOTHING BUT ASHES. THE CALUNGA TOOK EVERYONE. YOU'VE GOT TO LEARN TO KEEP YOUR HEAD DOWN!
NZAMBI ISN'T GOING TO HELP YOU. NOBODY'S COMING!
NOBODY!

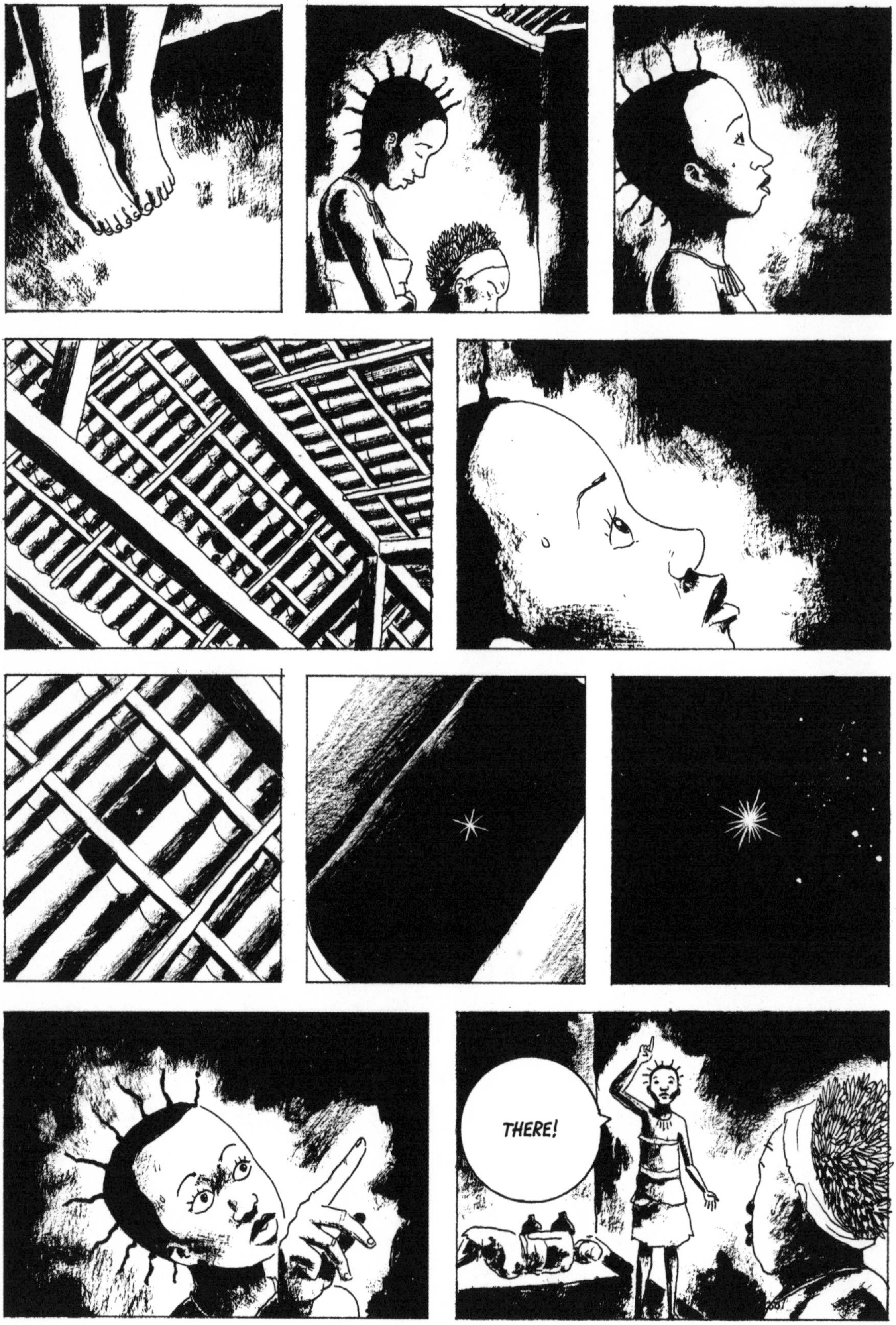
THERE!

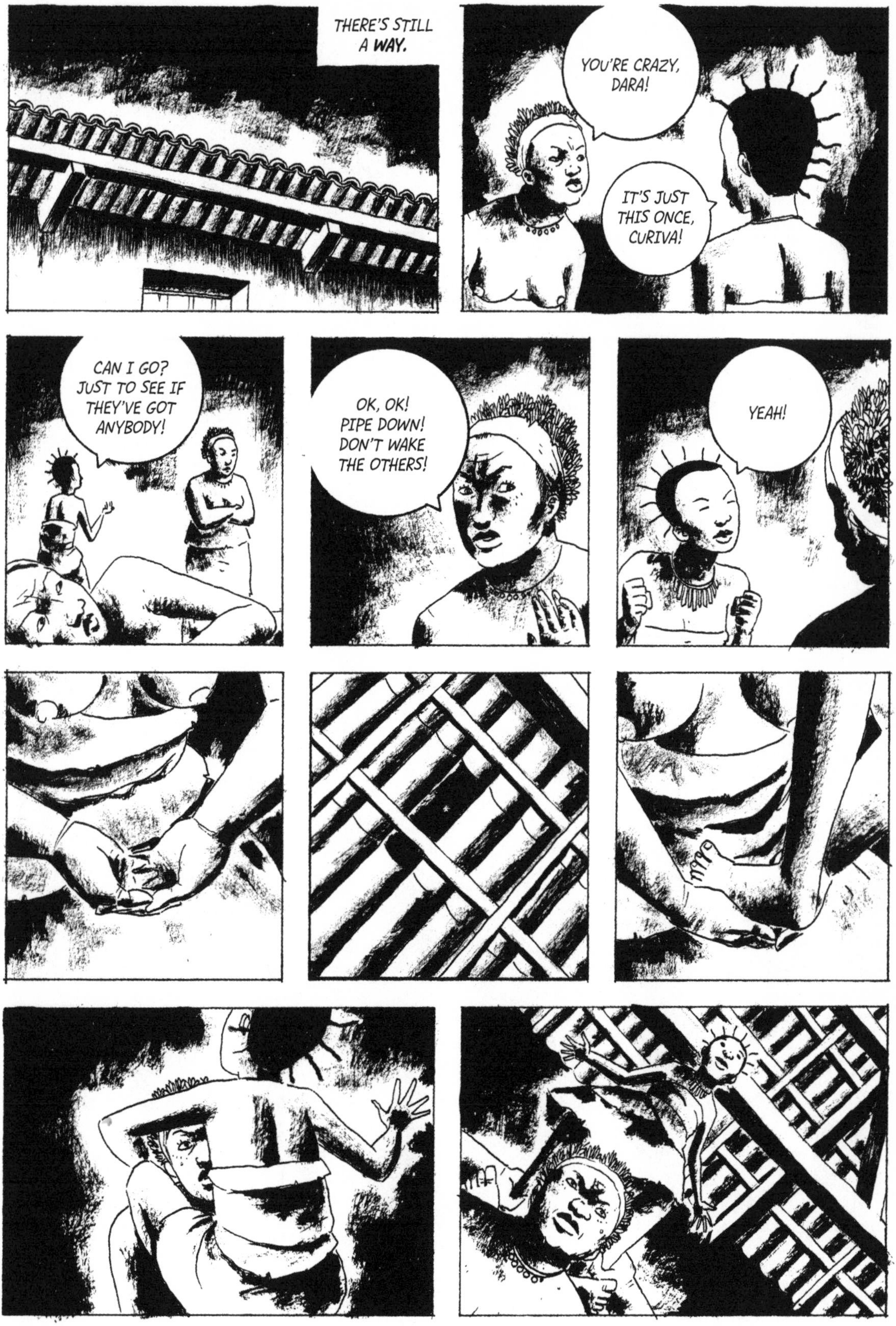
THERE'S STILL A WAY.
YOU'RE CRAZY, DARA!
IT'S JUST THIS ONCE, CURIVA!
CAN I GO? JUST TO SEE IF THEY'VE GOT ANYBODY!
OK, OK! PIPE DOWN! DON'T WAKE THE OTHERS!
YEAH!

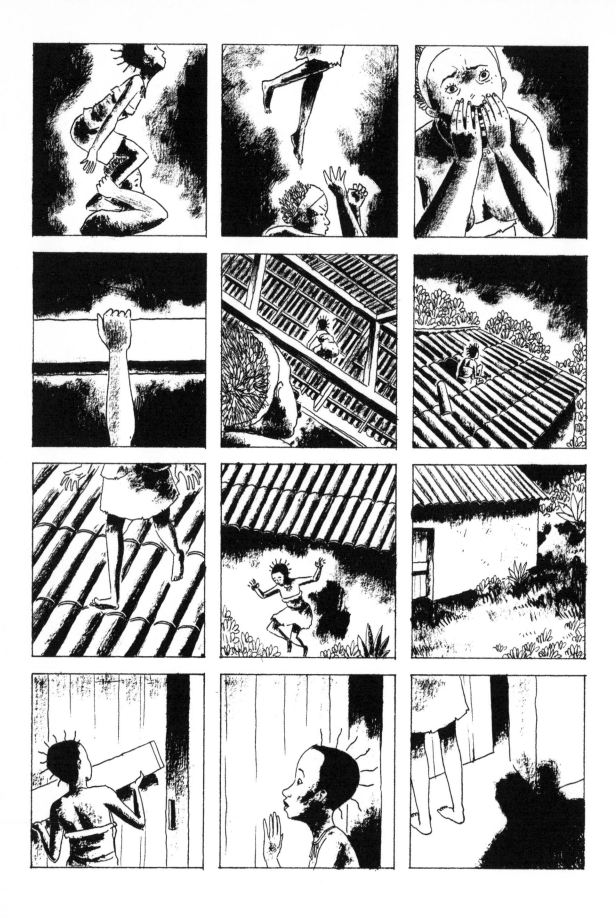

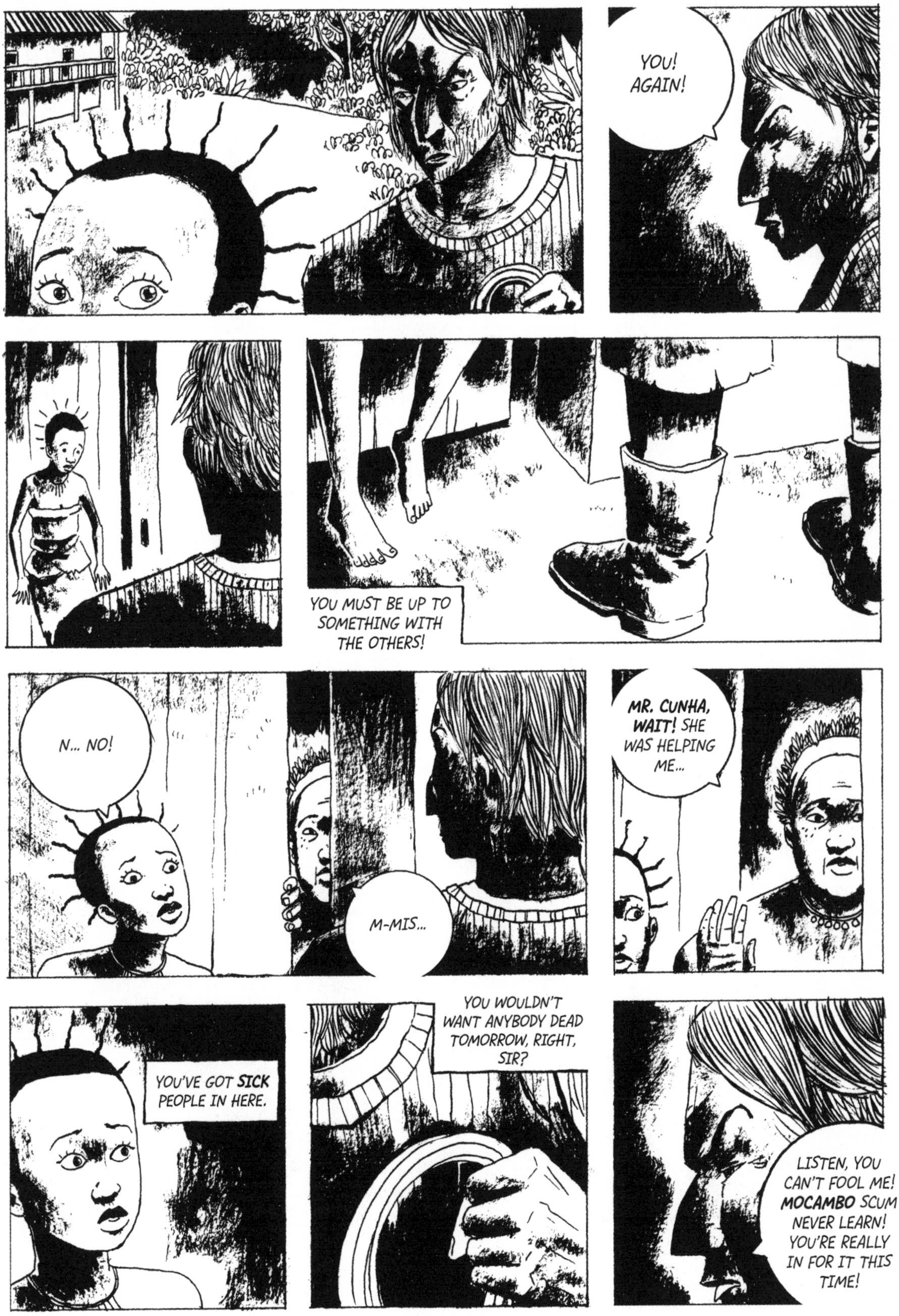
YOU! AGAIN!
YOU MUST BE UP TO SOMETHING WITH THE OTHERS!
N... NO!
M-MIS...
MR. CUNHA, WAIT! SHE WAS HELPING ME...
YOU'VE GOT SICK PEOPLE IN HERE.
YOU WOULDN'T WANT ANYBODY DEAD TOMORROW, RIGHT, SIR?
LISTEN, YOU CAN'T FOOL ME! MOCAMBO SCUM NEVER LEARN! YOU'RE REALLY IN FOR IT THIS TIME!

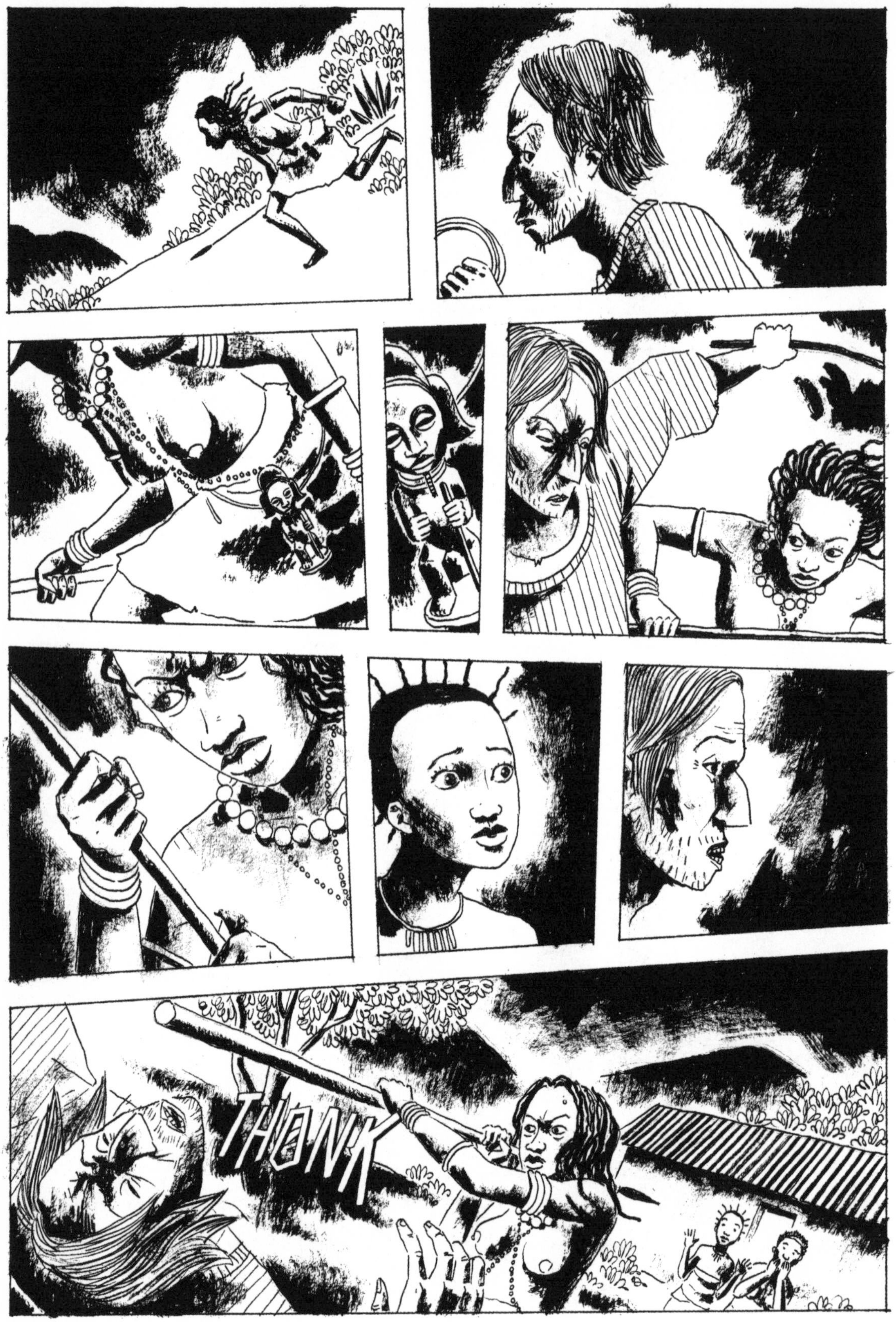
THONK

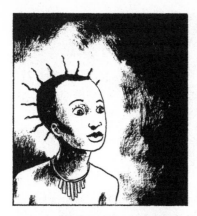

ANDALA, YOU DID IT!

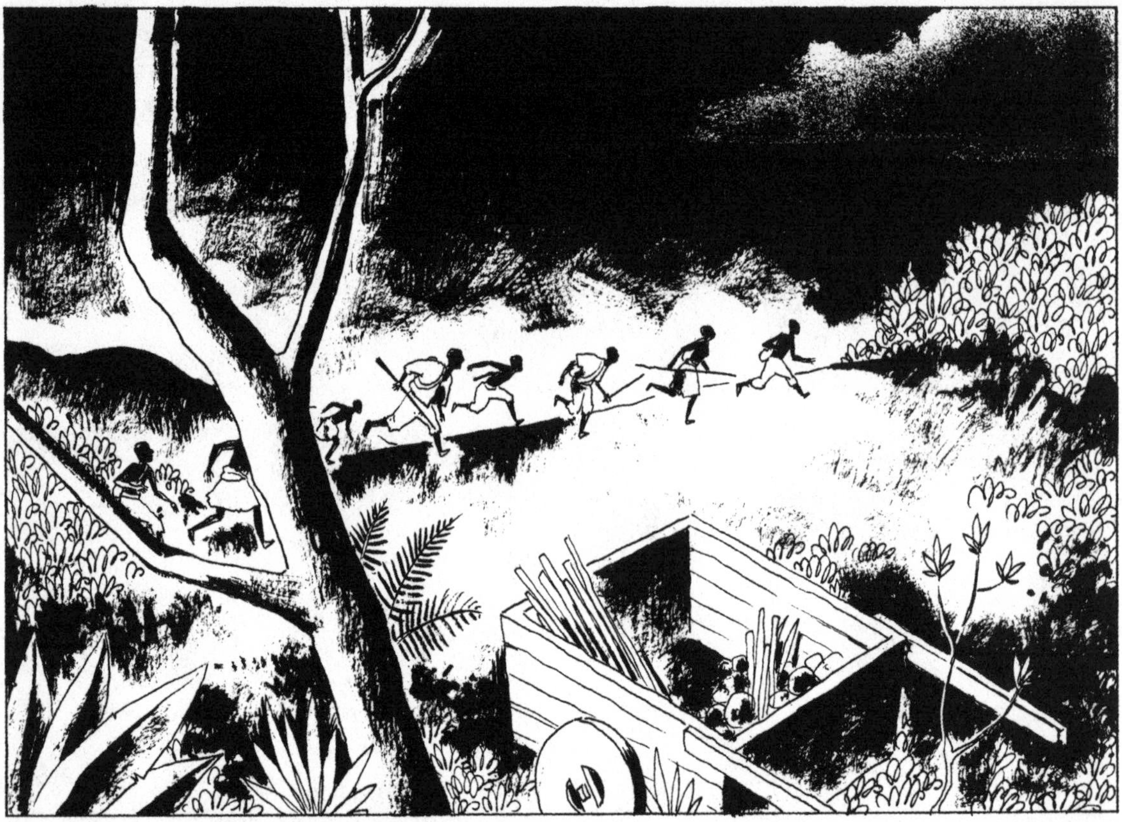

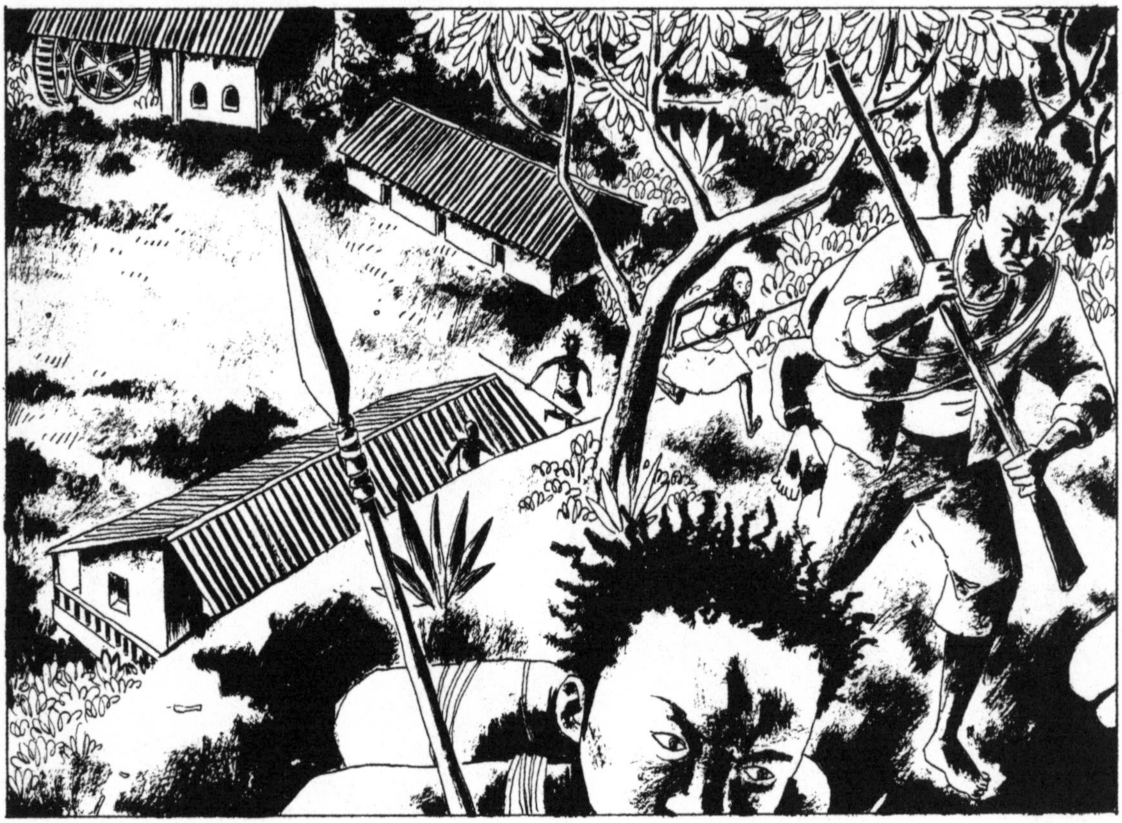

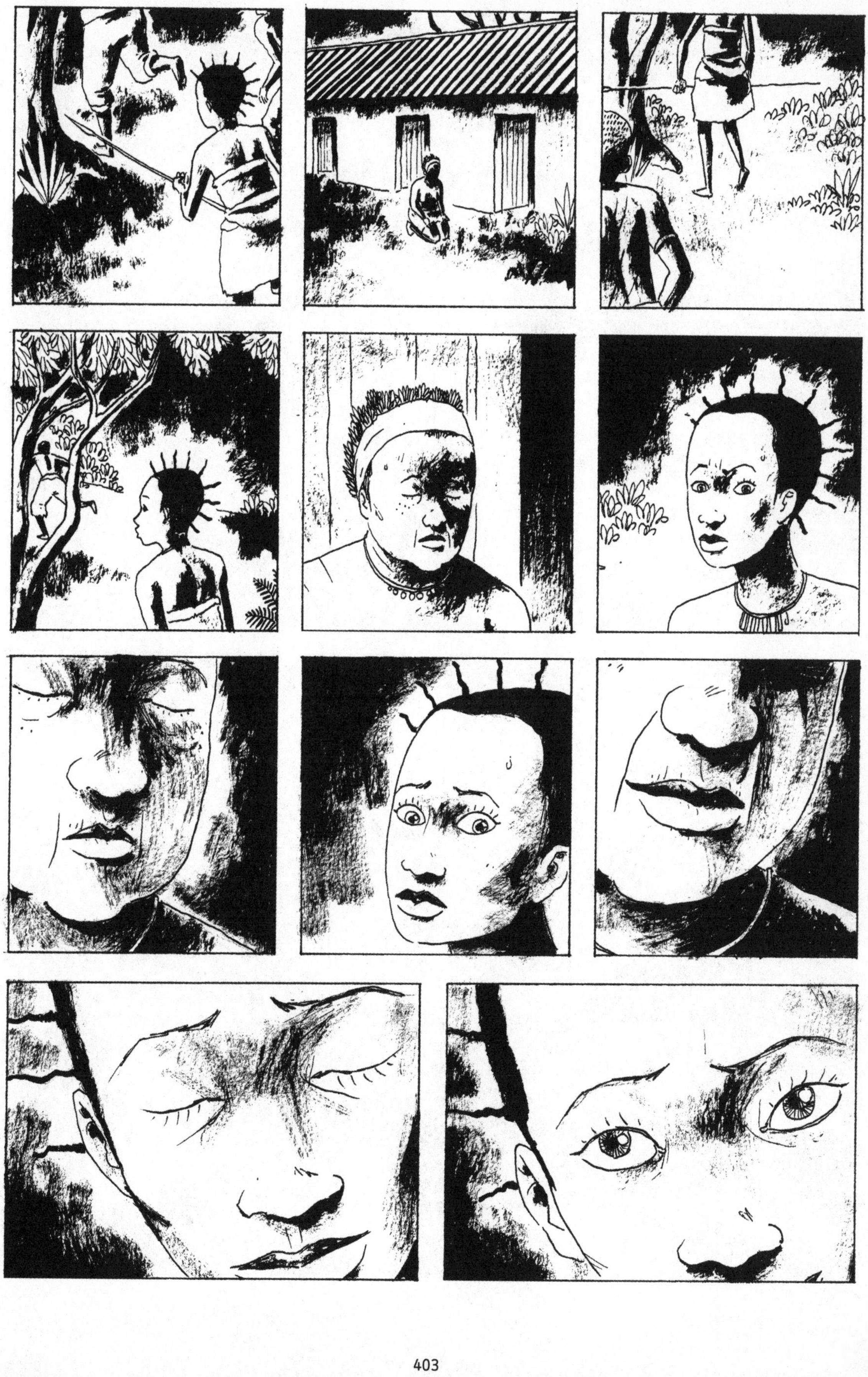

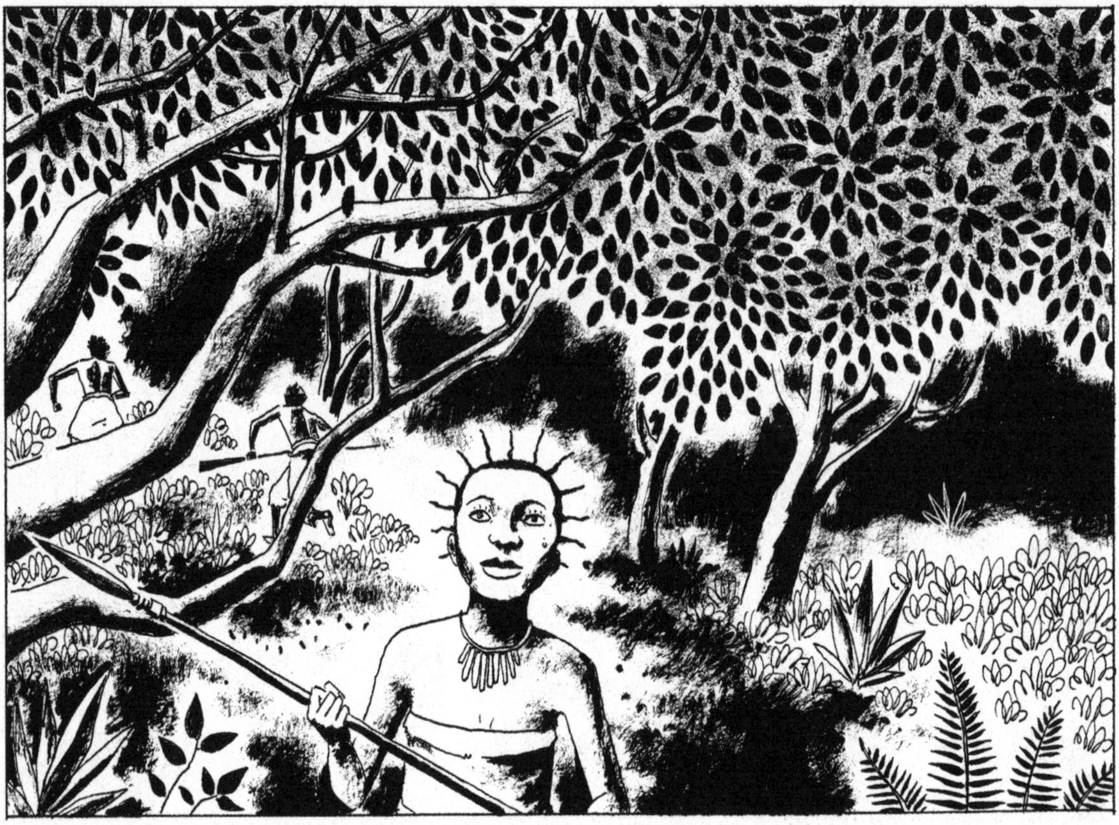

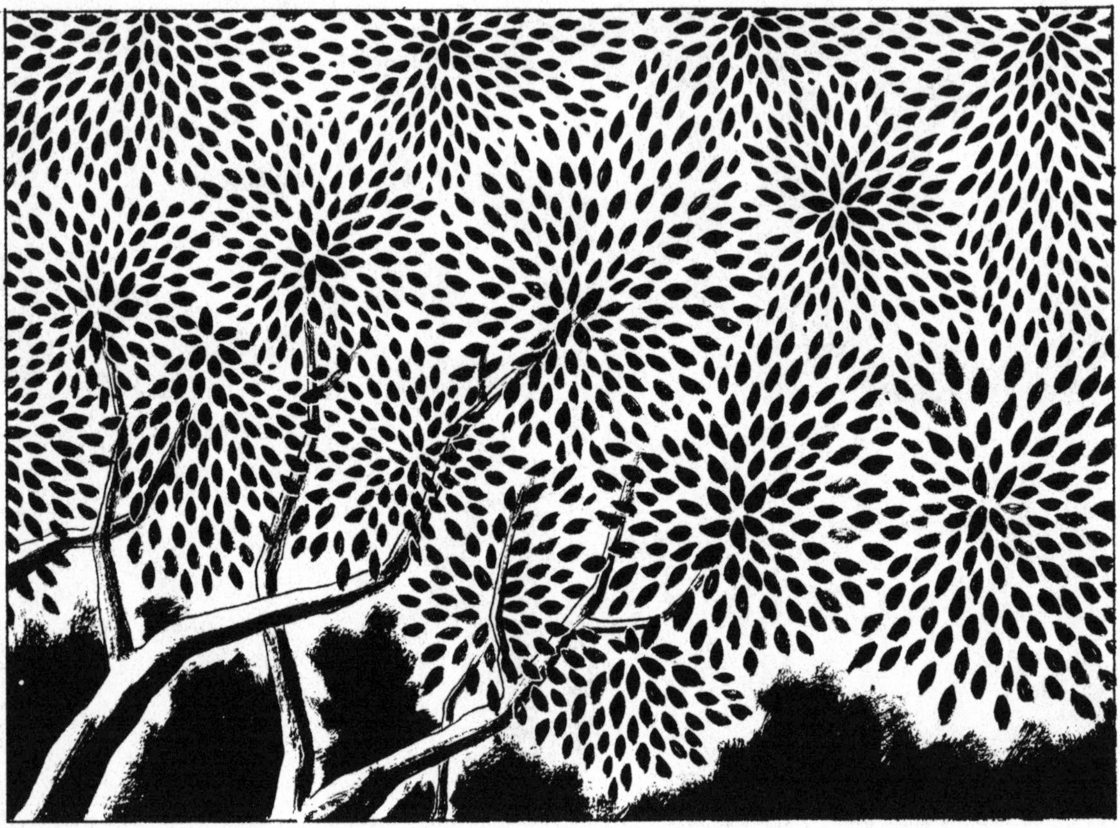

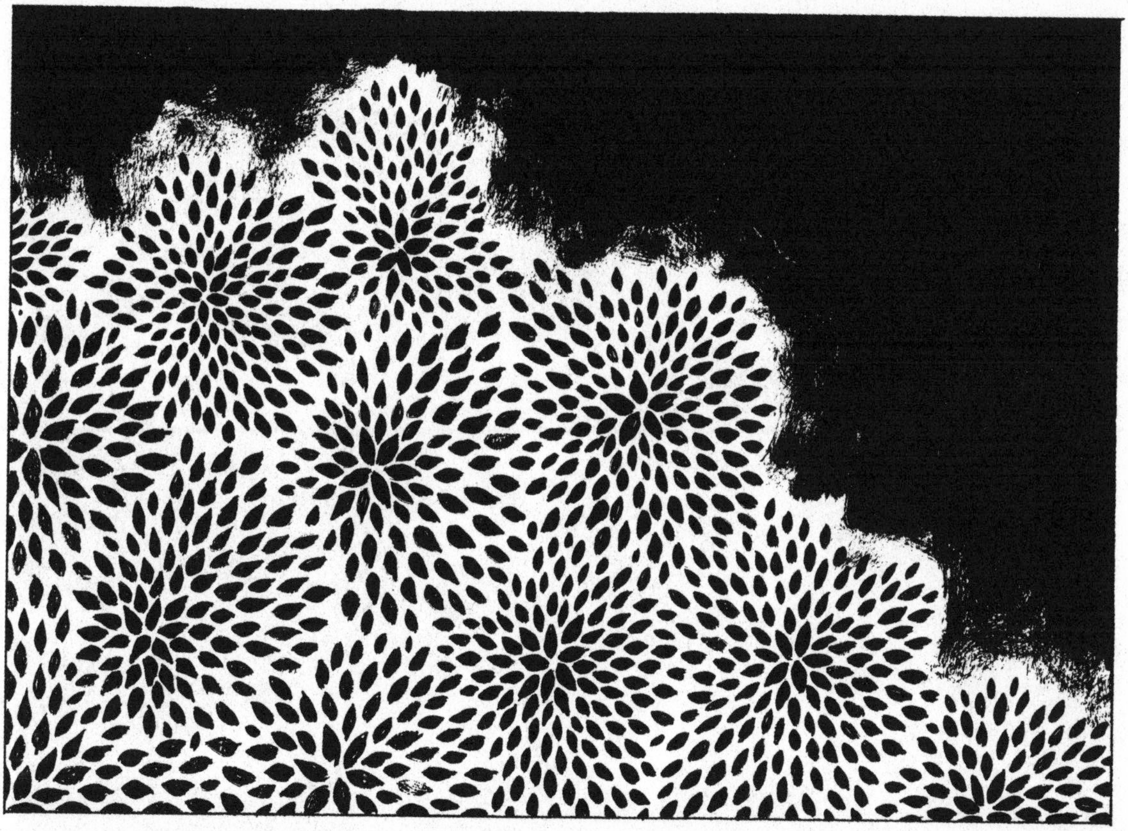

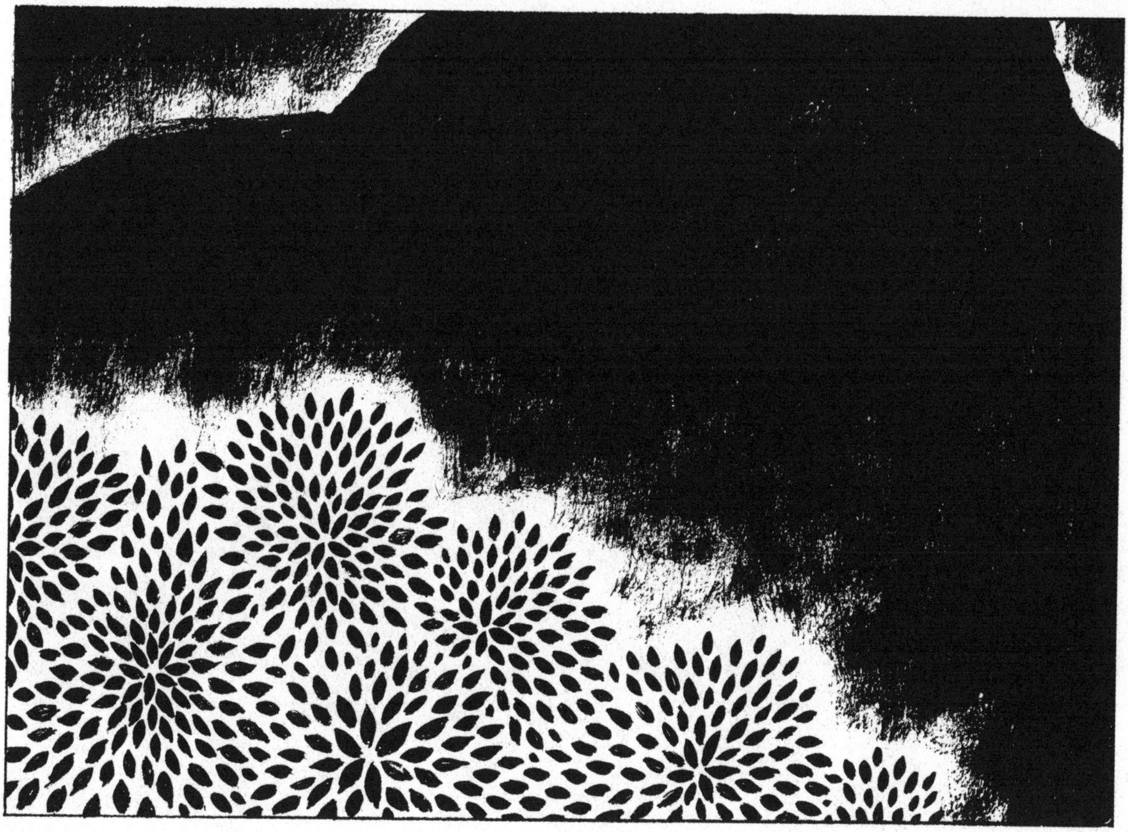

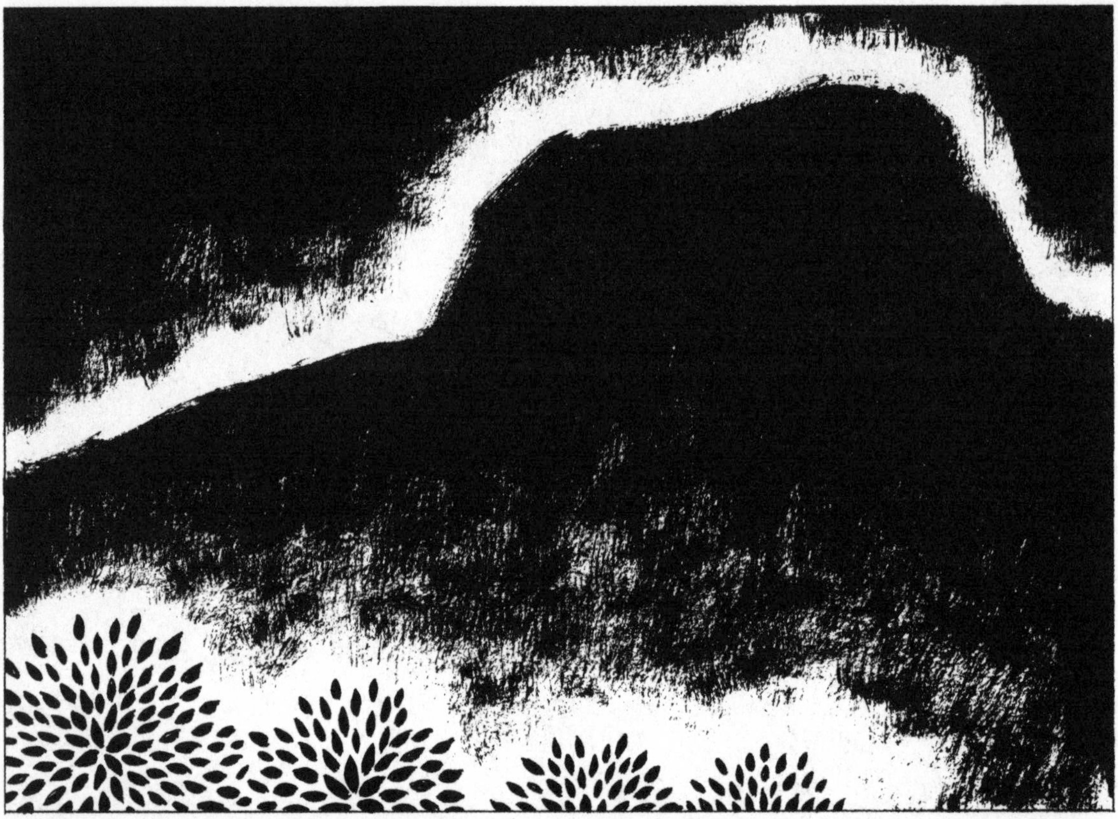

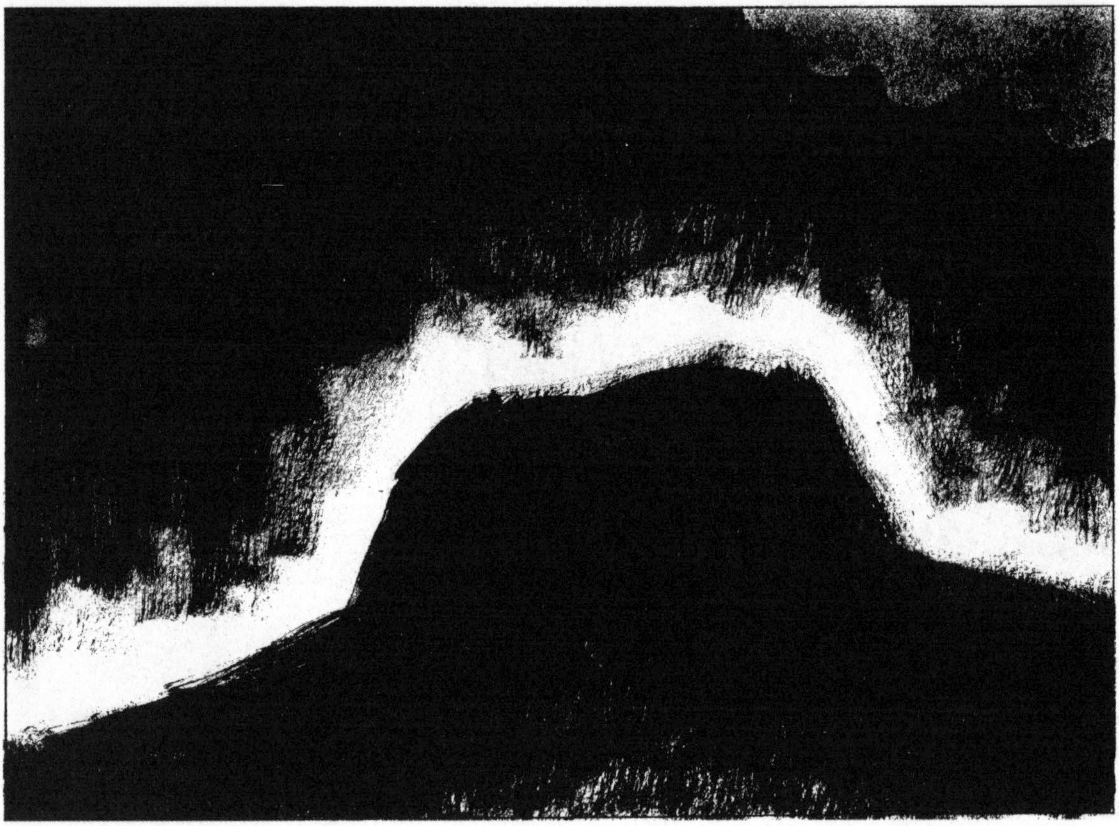

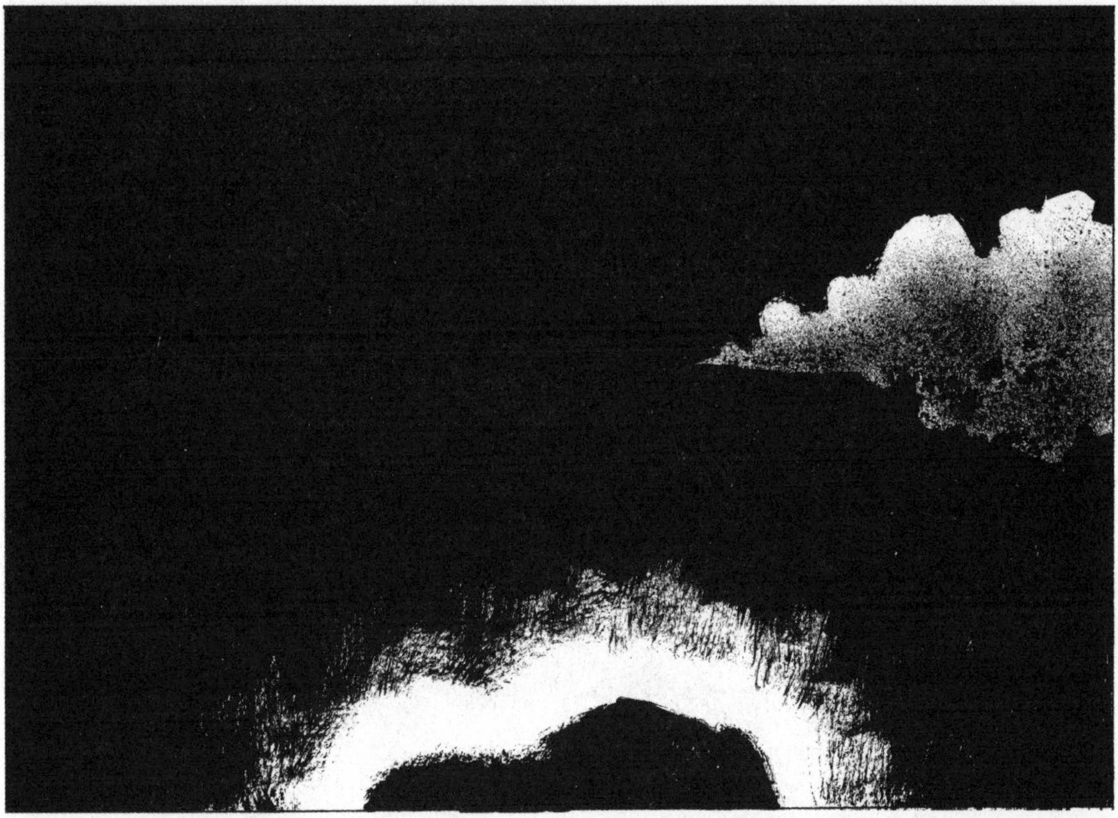
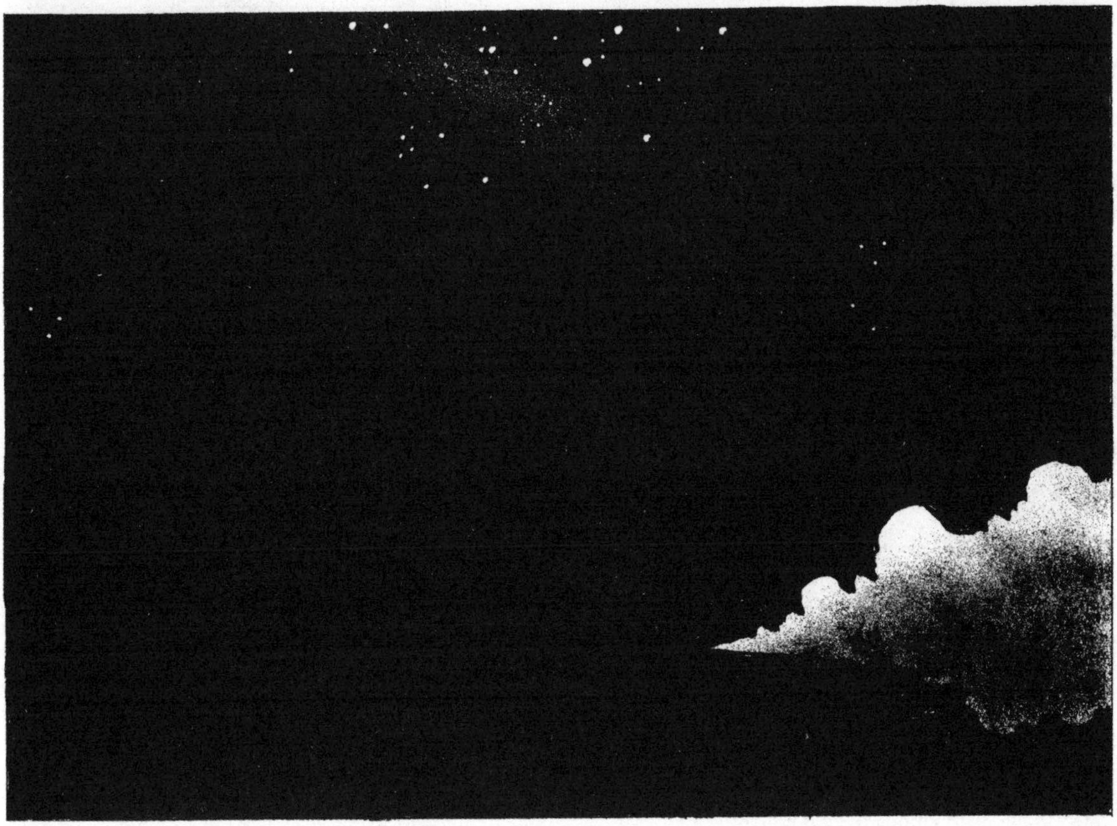

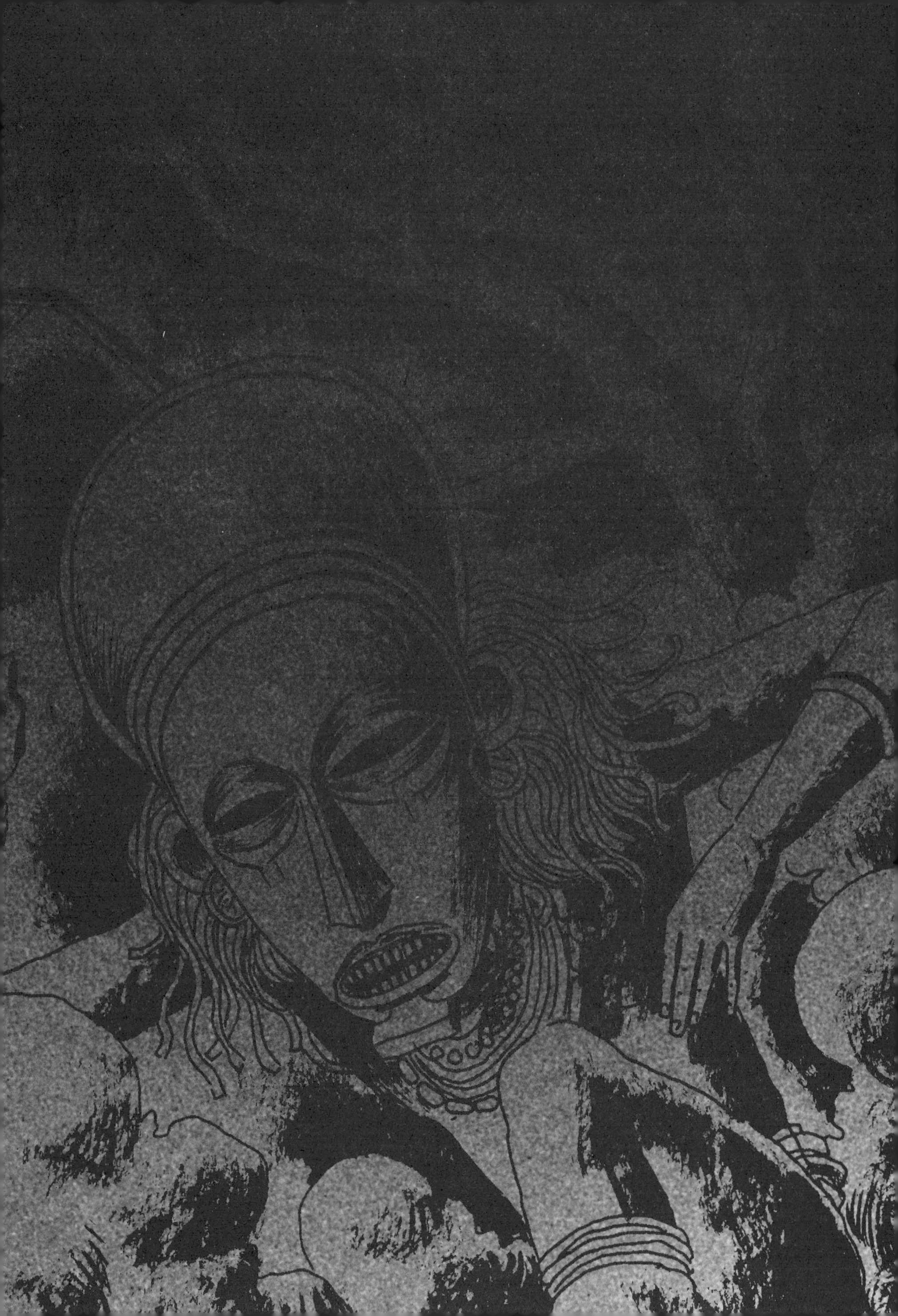

Glossary

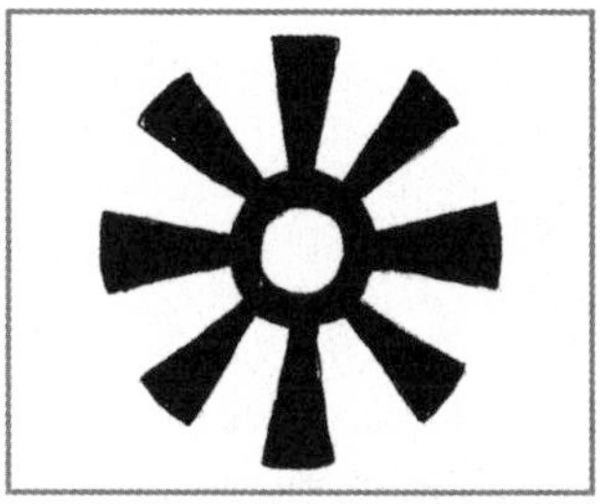

Ananse Ntontan—Spiderweb. Adinkra symbol of wisdom, expertise, creativity, and the complexity of life, according to Elisa Larkin and Luiz Carlos. Adinkra is a complex blend of ancient graphical symbols of Asante origin (Ghana). They are used on fabrics, gold weights, wooden pieces, etc. Each adinkra contains a message of wisdom transmitted down the generations.

André Furtado—A Paulista who was active in the final years of the Palmares conflict and was responsible for the death of Zumbi. He participated in Domingos Jorge Velho's attack on Macaco in 1694.

Angola Janga—Term used by the inhabitants themselves to refer to the group of mocambos of Palmares. In Kimbundu, it means "Little Angola" (Clóvis Moura, *Dicionário da escravidão* [Dictionary of Slavery]). According to Nei Lopes, in his *Dicionário Banto do Brasil* [Bantu Dictionary of Brazil], the term has its origins in other Bantu languages and means "my Angola." The area was made up of a variety of large and small mocambos; the largest had populations of more than six thousand people. The best-known Palmares mocambos were Macaco, Zumbi, Subupira, Andalaquituche, Alto Magno, Aqualtune, Acotirene, Amaro, Tabocas, Osenga, Dambraganga, and Curiva.

Anguêri—A being of Guarani origin. The anguêri is an undead being that dwells in the forest, screaming and crying at night and "walking through the places where its body walked when it was alive," according to Egon Schaden. It can have either animal or human form. It attacks at night and lives in the cemetery.

Antônio Soares—The mulatto Soares is mentioned only once in the historical record. Under torture, he revealed Zumbi's hideout in 1695.

Atalaia—Sentinel.

Bantu—According to the description by José Redinha in his *Album Etnográfico* [Ethnographic Album], "a large ethnolinguistic family to which the peoples of Angola belong, with the exception of the San, the pre-Bantu, and the Europeans." Nei Lopes says it "includes countless languages spoken today in Central, Central-Western, and Southern Africa and part of Eastern Africa."

Cafundó—A remote place that is difficult to access. From the Ambundu *ka-nfundo*.

Calunga—"The multilinguistic Bantu word *kalunga* encompasses the idea of grandness, immensity, referring to God, the sea, death," says Lopes. Maria Helena Figueiredo Lima, in her *Nação Ovambo* [Ovambo Nation], writes, "The word *kalunga* [God], from the verb *oku-lunga* [to be an expert, intelligent], is found in the Ambo dialect and other neighboring groups. The prefix *ka-* appears here without its usual diminutive function. Instead, it affirms something that is important, large, valuable."

Camp—Military post armed with Portuguese troops at strategic points in the Serra da Barriga hills. Its aim was to reduce the mobility of the inhabitants of Palmares, quashing their resistance.

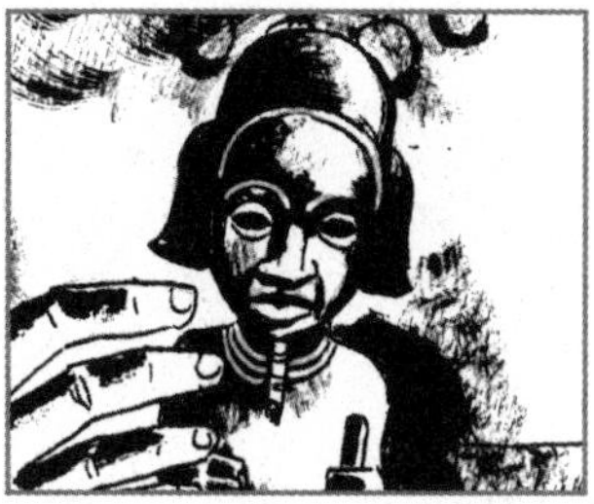

Chibinda Ilunga—The sculpture depicts Chibinda Ilunga, a mythical Chokwe (Northern Angola) king. According to one legend, Chibinda (meaning "hunter") was captured by some warriors from the kingdom of Lunda when he was hunting in their realm. Though the members of the court voted to put the intruder to death, the beautiful queen Lueji (meaning "moon") was charmed by the young man's beauty and asked that he be placed on her farm as a slave. In time, Lueji surprised the court by announcing her marriage to Ilunga, shattering the taboo that prohibited vassals from marrying nobles. This led the royal family to revolt against the queen, but it also marked the

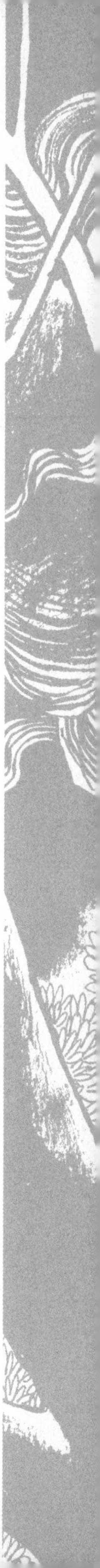

beginning of the expansion of the Lunda kingdom, which became a great empire-spanning territory that today belongs to Angola, Zambia, and Congo (see Peter Junge's *Arte da África* [African Art]).

Chusma—Crowd.

Cuca—Old medicine woman, corresponding to the Kimbundu *iakuka*.

Cuvera—Illness.

Domingos Jorge Velho—Son of Francisco Jorge Velho and Francisca Gonçalves. He participated in incursions against mocambos and rebelling Indians in places around northeastern Brazil, such as Piauí and Rio Grande do Norte. He was present at the final battles against the largest mocambo in Palmares, Macaco. In his fifties, he married Jerônima Cardim Fróis. He died in 1703 or 1704 in Piancó, in Piauí. In his family, there are other individuals with the same name.

Dutch—The Dutch invaded and controlled Pernambuco between 1630 and 1654. The enslaved Africans, taking advantage of the conflict between the Portuguese and the Dutch, escaped into the Serra da Barriga hills. Palmares grew substantially during that period.

Emancipation letter—Letter or title in which the master granted freedom to the enslaved person. The document was filed at the registry office. There were several categories of letters, and in many of them the enslaved people would still keep working for long periods after the letters were signed and could even be forced back into slavery in cases of "ingratitude," notes Clóvis Moura.

Ganga—Master, king, chief, supreme leader. According to Nei Lopes, in his *Novo dicionário banto do Brasil* [New Bantu Dictionary of Brazil], ganga can also refer to the head of a group of shrines—that is, a person who can perform religious duties.

Ganga Zona—He was considered the brother of Ganga Zumba. That designation was not a sign of blood relation but of Ganga Zona's influence and importance within the hierarchy of the mocambos of Palmares. He was an active participant in the peace negotiations for the Cucaú treaty and, later, in trying to dissuade the new leader, Zumbi.

Ganga Zumba—The first known ganga of the mocambos of Angola Janga. There are records of Ganga Zumba starting in the early 1670s. After the Palmaristas were defeated by the Portuguese several times in 1677, he was responsible for accepting the Cucaú peace treaty in 1678. He was fatally poisoned two years later, in Cucaú.

Jagas—According to Nei Lopes, the term is one used "by the Portuguese to refer to the Mbangala." It was the name of the warriors from a variety of ethnic groups who destabilized central power in seventeenth-century Angola. According to Clóvis Moura, they were "hordes of black slave hunters" who sold their captives to the Portuguese traders.

Janduís—An indigenous community. In the seventeenth century, they were also present in Rio Grande do Norte. In 1687, after the capture and deportation of a chief's children, they slaughtered more than one hundred settlers and thirty thousand head of cattle. A troop of six hundred soldiers from Pernambuco fled in the face of the uprising of the indigenous rebels. The Paulistas were called in to suppress the Janduís. "The forces of repression took no prisoners. Any Indian, man or woman, elder or child, was beheaded," notes Décio Freitas (1982). An archbishop in Bahia officially congratulated Domingos for "having beheaded 260 Tapuias."

Macaco—Large mocambo and the capital of Palmares. Accounts of the time note that Macaco had 1,500 houses and more than six thousand inhabitants. It was fortified and served as the residence of the main Palmares leaders.

Macota—Important man.

Malungo—Companion. Specifically, it was the term used by slaves to address each other during their crossings on the slave ships. The word comes from the Bantu words for boat, such as *lungo* (Kikongo) and *ulungu* (Kimbundu). Antenor Nascentes, in his *Dicionário etimológico resumido* [Abridged Etymological Dictionary], identifies its origin as being *ma'luga*, a Kimbundu word for comrade, companion. But Renato Mendonça, in his *Influência africana no português do Brasil* [African Influence in Brazilian Portuguese], suggests that the word may come from *man'ugo* [neighbor].

Mal de bicho. Epidemic that swept Pernambuco in the late seventeenth century. In the year 1686 alone, notes João Felício, mal de bicho killed more than six hundred people in Recife and Olinda, among them Governor Matias da Cunha.

Mandinga—Spell.

Matamba—Precolonial kingdom located east of Ndongo. It was from there that Nzinga a Mbande presented powerful resistance to Portuguese expansion in the seventeenth century.

Missongo—Hit man, soldier.

Mocambo—According to Nei Lopes it comes from the Kikongo *mukambu*, "rooftop, hut, in reference to the primary characteristic of this kind of dwelling: the thatched roof." The word was used to refer to the territories inhabited by blacks who had escaped from captivity until the seventeenth century, later replaced by *quilombo*.

Ndongo—Precolonial kingdom also known as Ngola, and the origin of Angola. "In the sixteenth century, Central Africa was made up of different kingdoms, which included primarily the large Kongo kingdom, but also other, smaller kingdoms to the south, such as Ndongo and Matamba, which gradually lost their spheres of influence," write Sylvia Serbin and Edouard Joubeaud. "At that time, the political and spatial organizations of those political entities were relatively similar: based on centralized power with intermediaries. In Ndongo, for example, the intermediaries were known as *sobas* (chiefs). The economic exchanges between the different kingdoms

enabled the circulation of complementary goods—namely, between the coast and the hinterlands. Of particular importance were ivory, textiles, salt, and the products of fishing, agriculture, and cattle ranching."

Ngoma—A drum made of hollowed-out wood; on one end, it is covered by a piece of stretched leather, which is played with the hand.

Nzambi—Also known as Nzambi a Mpungu, or Zâmbi. He is the creator and supreme god in Bantu cosmogony.

Nzinga—"Nzinga a Mbande (1581–1663), queen of Ndongo and Matamba, made a mark on the history of Angola in the seventeenth century. European mercantile enterprises, especially the development of the slave trade on the southern African coast, transformed the political, social, and cultural landscape of the kingdom of Ndongo and the entire region. It was in this context that Nzinga a Mbande grew up and became a remarkable example of female rule," according to Sylvia Serbin and Edouard Joubeaud.

Oruazes—This indigenous group, captured by the Paulistas, accompanied Domingos Jorge Velho on his incursions into the Brazilian interior. The Paulistas used various indigenous groups in their assaults on other

indigenous populations— and even fugitive slave communities. It appears that the Oruazes, Tabajares, and Copinharaéns accompanied Domingos at the time. Rebel groups would be systematically quashed by the Paulistas using every method available. According to Décio Freitas, "Domingos Jorge Velho was one of the bandeirantes who took off for northeastern Brazil in search of Indians and riches, establishing vast estates on land wrested from the inhabitants through horrifying massacres."

Paulistas—Also known as bandeirantes. According to Décio Freitas, in *Palmares—A Guerra dos escravos* [Palmares: The Slave War], "The bandeirantes were therefore a shock troop in the service of Portuguese colonialism, and nothing more…. [D]epopulation and depredation constituted, as Capistrano de Abreu puts it, 'the bandeirantes' essential and inseparable characteristic.'"

Palmaristas—Term used by the Portuguese to refer to the inhabitants of Angola Janga. They were also called *calhambolas*, Palmar blacks, rebel blacks, etc.

Porto Calvo—City in Alagoas that was one of the first Portuguese settlements in Brazil. It played an important role in the resistance to the Dutch invaders and later served as a base for the troops that fought in Palmares.

Razzia—Devastation, act of vandalism. Military assault, invasion with sacking and destruction.

Saint Anthony—A widely revered figure in colonial Brazil. In the seventeenth century, he was considered the saint who helped find lost items, including runaway slaves. Images of the saint were carried on military and bandeirante expeditions, and they even received salaries as if they were real soldiers.

Santana de Parnaíba—A settlement in the province of São Paulo established on the shores of the Anhembi River (known today as the Tietê River) in the sixteenth century. It was a place from which bandeirante expeditions departed for the interior of the country. Today, it is a satellite city in the greater São Paulo metropolitan area.

Scarification—Marks of initiation and belonging made on any part of the body, including the feet, face, back, and scalp. The technique is not unique to Africa, but it is especially important for marking fraternities, exile, dedication, and membership in groups or associations, which are demonstrated through the use of intentional scarring on the faces and chests of enslaved people and quilombo residents.

Sona—A group of symbols of Chokwe origin, a people that lives in northeastern Angola and the neighboring areas of the Democratic Republic of the Congo and Zambia. These designs are composed of dots and curving lines drawn in the sand and accompanied by oral narratives. They are employed in initiation rites for boys. The design below indicates a place in the forest where fruits and animals are abundant. The storyteller, while sketching the design, says, "The partridge emerges from the brush, pursued by the *mukhondo*; the antelope emerges, pursued by the lion; and the woman emerges, pursued by the man."

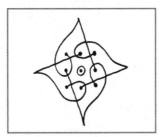

Spy—Person responsible for obtaining information on territory, weapons, routes, number of people, and military organization. There were spies acting on both sides of the conflict in the General Captaincy of Pernambuco.

Tata—In Bantu, it means "father." A term of respect, it indicates wisdom, life experience, knowledge of secrets. It is therefore used as an honorific for a father, grandfather, wise older man, or priest.

Terço Henrique Dias—Name of the troop of black and mestizo soldiers formed in the Brazilian captaincies after the Dutch war, in homage to the feats of Afro Brazilian militia leader Henrique Dias during the expulsion of the Dutch.

Uganga—Priest, medicine man.

Unit—Brazilian slaveholders used the term *peça* to refer to enslaved blacks, turning them into things. The term *peça-da-Guiné* [Guinean unit] was also in use, but it should not be understood as referring to the country of Guinea. In the seventeenth century, the word referred to any enslaved person from the region of Africa near the kingdom of Ndongo (Angola).

Zagaia—An African spear used in hunting, fishing, and war.

Zumbi—The last leader of Macaco first appeared in texts about Palmares in the mid-1670s. From there, he was mentioned frequently up until his death in 1695. The historian Décio Freitas was the first to describe his childhood with Father Antônio Melo in Porto Calvo and his later escape to the mocambos of the Serra da Barriga hills. This information should be at the Casa da Marquesa de Cadaval, in Portugal, which has endured theft, auctioning off of the archives, etc. Today, there is no evidence that these documents still exist. Nevertheless, other extant documents claim that, starting in the 1670s, Zumbi's presence and leadership in Palmares were crucial.

Author's Afterword
Trails and Dreams

I first heard of the *quilombo* (or, in the past, *mocambo*) of Palmares in my early school days. One of my classmates said excitedly, "Today's November 20, Zumbi Day!" I looked at her, curious. I didn't know much about Zumbi or any other part of black history in Brazil. That universe was revealed to me only years later, through rap, literature, and movies.

Much later, in college, I was exposed to texts about the long-ago conflict in the Serra da Barriga. I realized then that Palmares had been a major event, one of the primary conflicts of the seventeenth century and colonial Brazil. In addition, it was the largest black slave uprising in the Americas, comparable to the Haitian Revolution.

Still hesitant, I began a tentative plan for a book about Palmares. I outlined what the main events and the principal plot would be. I sketched a few drawings, but I didn't have enough information to carry out the project at that time. I spent the following years studying texts and the iconography of the period. In the meantime, I published the books *Noite Luz* (2008) and *Encruzilhada* (2011). The year 2014 saw the release of *Cumbe* (later published in English as *Run for It*), a work born directly from my research into black resistance in colonial Brazil.

I traveled to Maceió, Alagoas, to visit and obtain images of the landscape and Quilombo dos Palmares Memorial Park, in the Serra da Barriga, where Angola Janga (Little Angola, a Kimbundu term used by the Palmaristas) was located. The memorial is located where the capital, Macaco, would have been. It was established by the National Historic and Artistic Heritage Institute (IPHAN) in the early 1980s, but not completed until twenty years later, with the re-creation of houses, work sites, fences, and towers. In the seventeenth century, this territory belonged to the Captaincy of Pernambuco.

This isn't the first graphic novel about Palmares. Clóvis Moura and Álvaro de Moya (*Zumbi dos Palmares* [Zumbi of Palmares], 1955), Antônio Krisnas and Allan Alex (*Zumbi—A saga de Palmares* [Zumbi: The Saga of Palmares], 2003), and Carlos Ferreira and Moacir Martins (*A Guerra de Palmares* [The Palmares War]) have already explored these events in comic book form. In literature and film, Palmares has also been imagined by authors such as João Felício (*Ganga-Zumba*, 1961), George Landmann (*Tróia Negra* [Black Troy], 1998), and Cacá Diegues (*Ganga-Zumba*, 1963, and *Quilombo*, 1984). Nevertheless, given the significance of these events, they certainly merit new interpretations.

This is not *the* history of Palmares, only *a* history of it. Just one possibility for interpreting and reimagining the events. There are various ways of approaching the conflict. The historical data are clues, signposts that can help us forge a trail through that dense forest. There are documents, mainly from the final decades of the war. These sources are from soldiers, officials, plantation owners, governors, priests, etc.—in short, people involved in the destruction of Palmares. This work, for its part, attempts to present the narrative from the Palmaristas's point of view. Fiction has a significant role in that effort. Through it, we are able to breach walls and access, through poetry and art, the stories of those men and women.

Most of the rebels in Palmares would have come from the ancient kingdoms of Ndongo, Matamba, Kongo, and others nearby (primarily in the sixteenth and seventeenth centuries). They were Africans who spoke Kimbundu, Ovimbundu, Umbundu, etc. A smaller proportion would have come from other places. The culture of the mocambos was therefore an amalgam of traditions, mostly Bantu. The official estimates refer to more than twelve million Africans brought to the Americas, more than five million of them to Brazil. We know that the slave trade went beyond that, so the real numbers would be much larger.

In the sixteenth century, the Portuguese had access to the coast of Angola. This area's association with the Mbangala, or Jagas, increased the trading with the African interior. It's likely that news from the kingdoms of Ndongo reached Palmares. In the seventeenth century, the rise of Nzinga, for example, was contemporaneous with the saga of the Palmaristas. Many of the warriors of Nzinga, the queen of the kingdoms of Ndongo and Matamba, defeated in war, arrived in Brazil and were forced into slavery. For obvious reasons, Portuguese settlers in Brazil feared that these African warriors would make it to the hills of Pernambuco.

Portugal's colonial territories should be thought of in terms of their many contacts across the South Atlantic. Brazil and Angola were part of Portugal's unified pursuit of productive, commercial, and political interests. They depended, reciprocally, on each other, from a colonial perspective. According to historian Luiz Felipe de Alencastro, Brazil's growth in the first centuries of its existence is directly tied to the pillaging and destruction of the kingdoms of Angola.

The first news of the mocambos that had formed in Pernambuco's Serra da Barriga hills dates to 1597. Forty men and women, after destroying a sugarcane plantation, fled deep into the dense coastal forest. A few other blacks also came from neighboring regions such as Bahia. In Palmares, the first expeditions against the mocambos took place in 1602. They didn't have much of an effect. Later, the mocambos of Angola Janga resisted and expanded, primarily during the Dutch occupation of 1630 to 1654.

In the hills of Pernambuco, more than a dozen mocambos made up Angola Janga. Most of them produced corn, manioc, beans, sweet potatoes, and bananas. At its peak, Palmares comprised more than twenty thousand people. The largest mocambos, such as the capital, Macaco, had six thousand inhabitants. Subupira, for its part, was known as a military training center. Other mocambos were Zumbi, Andalaquituche, Alto Magno, Aqualtune, Acotirene, Amaro, Tabocas, Osenga, Dambraganga, Curiva, Una, etc. Owing to the continual attacks by the Portuguese colonists, the mocambos near the settlements, once discovered, couldn't last long. In the hills, the fugitives had a great ability to build new mocambos. The mobility of these mocambos in the hills, always appearing in new places, was vital to Palmares's continued existence. The mocambos' survival depended on their ability to be invisible and elude soldiers' attacks.

The mocambos of Palmares were not isolated in the Serra da Barriga. There was communication and exchange of supplies between the Palmaristas and the settlers. That contact was not insignificant. Besides exchanging strategic supplies such as gunpowder and weapons, the hilltop rebels could be alerted. In around 1690, the Paulista Domingos Jorge Velho threatened colonists who were sympathizers with the Palmaristas, fearing that they might discover his plans of attack, among other things.

The Palmaristas's tactic was to avoid making direct attacks on the enemy. The impenetrable forest, which the soldiers found threatening and exhausting, was the ideal territory for the Palmaristas. Having retreated to there, they organized their defenses and plotted skirmishes. Owing to the mocambos' remoteness and inaccessibility, after weeks of marching, any soldiers who hadn't deserted were tired, injured, famished, and on edge—easy prey for the Palmaristas's attacks.

The Cucaú treaty, drawn up in 1678 by Ganga Zumba and the governor, resulted in the concession of lands to a small group of dissident Palmaristas. Despite the governor's support, the Cucaú group, under threat from plantation owners and Zumbi loyalists, didn't last long. The venture had been an effort to dissuade and divide the Palmaristas, as occurred in other mocambos throughout Latin America. The attempts to formalize a peace treaty continued in later years; in the meantime, the strategy of total war expanded.

Though there was captivity in Palmares, it differed significantly from colonial slavery, a system in which black men and women were made the driving force behind goods production and the local economy. Captives weren't the only element of production in the Palmares mocambos, and they weren't enslaved for life or down the generations. Because the community was in a permanent state of defense and war, involving soldiers, spies, and traitors, temporary captivity may have served as a strategy for monitoring new members kidnapped from the colonial settlements.

In historians' early studies, Palmares was described as an exotic, fearsome phenomenon, a space inhabited by insurgents and corsairs. It was sometimes treated as a mortal enemy, as the colonial authorities stepped up their efforts to destroy it. The colonial elite cited the Palmares War to justify quashing, by every oppressive means available, any attempt to recreate mocambos and resistance movements.

Regarding Zumbi, one of the main leaders of Palmares, we know he existed and was a central figure from the mid-1670s to the fall of the capital, Macaco. Nevertheless, his origins remain uncertain. According to the historian Décio Freitas, he was born in Palmares, but he was kidnapped and brought up in Porto Calvo. This version, too, has its skeptics. Other researchers have found no documents to confirm it. Even so, it's important to note that the story of Palmares is bigger than its most famous leader. There were many people, with their own actions, desires, anxieties, and fears, who participated in the conflicts in the hills of the Captaincy of Pernambuco.

Women had a notable presence in Palmares. In one of the key events of the conflict, in 1677, a group of Portuguese soldiers attacked the mocambos around Porto Calvo, possibly Acotirene or Aqualtune. At one site, they seized the female rebel leader known as the "Queen of Palmares," who was possibly Ganga Zumba's mother. The surrender of Ganga Zumba in 1678 may have been provoked in part by her capture. There was, shortly thereafter, an attempt to negotiate and secure the freedom of certain Angola Janga leaders. The treaty also set aside the region of Cucaú for the use of Ganga Zumba's Palmaristas between 1678 and 1680.

Another popular female figure in the oral traditions related to the Serra da Barriga mocambos is Dandara. She is portrayed as an important leader in the fictional work of Cacá Diegues, in his movie *Quilombo* (1984). Yet this character is never mentioned by the major Serra da Barriga mocambos researchers (Edson Carneiro, Décio Freitas, Ivan Alves Filho, Flávio Gomes, etc.). According to Clóvis Moura in his *Dicionário da Escravidão Negra no Brasil* [Dictionary of Black Slavery in Brazil], the word "Dandará" appears in Brazilian history only once: attached to a priest involved in the Malê revolt in 1835, whose real name was Elesbão do Carmo.

In addition, I did make some choices in an effort to streamline the narrative and keep it engaging. Over the course of Palmares's final forty years, for example, the Captaincy of Pernambuco was led by a series of governors. I opted to condense them into a single person, known simply as the Governor. André Furtado was a major figure in the final battles against Palmares. In my version, for brevity's sake, I ended up attributing to him a number of actions that were actually carried out by Fernão Carrilho, a relevant figure in the 1670s and the later Cucaú treaty. These are choices I made in service to the narrative's dynamism, rhythm, and comprehensibility.

The capital of Palmares, Macaco, was attacked and destroyed in January 1694. The Portuguese colonists toted a new weapon up into the hills, a cannon, which was crucial in allowing them to breach the reinforced palisade. In addition, the forest was no longer unknown territory and a road had been built to provide easier access to Macaco. Zumbi was killed on November 20, 1695, by André Furtado. The conflicts over the Serra da Barriga continued for another thirty years. At that point, the remaining Palmaristas readopted a guerrilla warfare strategy. The other survivors scattered throughout the region.

No other large mocambo ever formed that brought together thousands of people like Palmares. Still, the tactic of resisting in smaller mocambos persisted during and after the colonial era. For insurgent blacks, it was a way of escaping from captivity and reclaiming autonomy in their lives. Even today, the quilombos that remain of the many that were once scattered across Brazil are fighting for the possession of their lands. Under threat, but they continue to resist.

This book was completed over the course of eleven years of research, conversation, exchange, and learning. Even today, the stories of Palmares provoke amazement and wonder.

Chronology of the Palmares War

1597   First account of mocambos established in the hills of Pernambuco.

1602–03 First expeditions against Palmares.

1630   The Dutch invade the Captaincy of Pernambuco.

1644   During the period of the Dutch occupation, many enslaved Africans flee for the Serra da Barriga hills. As a result, the Dutch send their first expedition against Palmares.

1654   After many battles and negotiations, the Dutch pull out of Pernambuco.

1655   The Portuguese Crown twice sends troops against the blacks in Palmares, capturing around two hundred of them.

1663   Troops from the Terço dos Henriques (made up of freedmen and men of color) are sent to combat the Palmaristas.

1677   Fernão Carrilho marches against Palmares with a large contingent of soldiers and wins a substantial victory.

1678   The colonial authorities propose a peace treaty to the inhabitants of Palmares.

1678   After supposed negotiations with Ganga Zumba, a committee of Palmaristas is sent to Recife, where they sign a peace accord. Ganga Zumba withdraws to the region of Cucaú with a few hundred Palmaristas.

1679   Zumbi and leaders of other mocambos in Palmares refuse to accept the peace treaty and decide to remain in the Serra da Barriga hills.

1680   In Cucaú, Ganga Zumba is killed.

1681   Zumbi is considered the Palmaristas's main leader.

1683   Captain Fernão Carrilho suffers a major defeat in Palmares. Suspected of negotiating with the Palmaristas, Carrilho is removed by the Governor.

1684   Zumbi and his fighters carry out a raid on the coast of Pernambuco, attacking a settlement called Alamo. Months later, the Palmaristas attack the fort in Garça Torta, near Lagoa do Norte. After hours of fighting, they drive out the indigenous people who are guarding the site.

1685   The King of Portugal sends a letter to Zumbi to renew the effort to draw up a peace treaty.

1687   Troops of Paulistas, commanded by Domingos Jorge Velho, are deployed to carry out punitive attacks on the Palmaristas's settlements (mocambos).

1687   Enslaved people from the Pernambuco settlements organize a rebellion to massacre the white population with the help of the Palmaristas. The plot is discovered and its leaders captured and executed.

1691	The Jesuit priest Antonio Vieira condemns the proposal to send missionaries to Palmares to convert the blacks.
1691	Domingos Jorge Velho builds a camp near Macaco. His troops are attacked by the Palmaristas; many members of the expedition flee or are killed. Domingos survives.
1692–93	The Paulista troops and the Palmaristas engage in intense combat in the Serra da Barriga.
1693	Pernambuco is in dire economic straits thanks to low sugar prices, famine, and the mal-de-bicho epidemic. The anti-Palmares discourse gains steam.
1694	Using cannons and palisades, Paulista troops invade Macaco, the main mocambo in Palmares.
1694	Zumbi is wounded in combat and seeks refuge in the Serra Dois Irmãos hills.
1695	Intense attacks against Zumbi and various mocambos continue in the Serra da Barriga.
1695	On November 20, Zumbi is killed after Antônio Soares's betrayal.
1696	Zumbi's severed head is displayed in Recife.
1701	Camoanga assumes the leadership of Palmares.
1703	Camoanga is killed.
1704	Mouza, a black man, becomes the new leader of Palmares.
1711	Mouza is captured, sent to Recife, and eventually deported.
1725–36	Paulista troops occupy the region in an attempt to prevent the Palmaristas from regrouping.

Summary of the Palmares War

First phase (1596–1630)	2 colonial expeditions; more than 6 attacks by Palmaristas	The aim of the colonial attacks was to reach four or five quilombos located in the Serra da Barriga
Second phase (1631–1654)	4 colonial expeditions; 4 attacks by Palmaristas	Phase of the Dutch occupation
Third phase (1655–1694)	31 colonial expeditions; 13 attacks by Palmaristas	Most intense point of the war. In addition to these numbers, there were private expeditions organized by plantation owners.

Pernambuco, Palmares, towns, mocambos (seventeenth century)

CAPTAINCY OF PARAÍBA
N
0 20
Km
Olinda
Recife
Amaro
Acotirene
Tabocas
Una River
Cucaú
Serinhaém
Dambrabanga
Zumbi
Aqualtune
ATLANTIC OCEAN
Subupira
Alto Magno
Curiva
Osenga
Macaco
Porto Calvo
Approximate territory of Palmares
Mocambos
Towns
União dos Palmares (1831)
Camaragibe River
São Miguel
Andalaquituche
Paraíba River
Rio Mundaú
Viçosa
Atalaia
CAPTAINCY OF PERNAMBUCO
Alagoas
São Francisco River
Penedo
CAPTAINCY OF SERGIPE
Capitania do Maranhão
Capitania de S. José do Rio Negro
Capitania do Pará
Capitania do Ceará
Capitania do RGN
C. do Piauí
Capitania da Paraíba
Capitania de Pernambuco
Capitania Geral da Bahia
Capitania de Sergipe
Capitania de Goiás
Capitania de Mato Grosso
Capitania de Minas Gerais
Capitania de São Paulo
Capitania de Santa Catarina
Capitania do Rio Grande

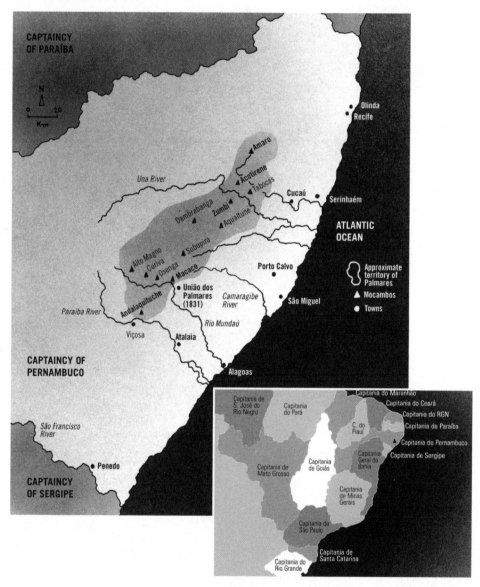

The map above shows the major mocambos of Palmares during the seventeenth century. The towns and sugarcane plantations of the Portuguese colonists were situated along the coast. Along with the mocambos marked here, there were other transitory mocambos that cropped up during the final decades of the conflict. Worth mentioning are the mocambo of Macaco, the former capital of Palmares, and the short-lived town of Cucaú, given to Ganga Zumba and his sympathizers. The present-day town of União dos Palmares, in Alagoas, was founded in 1831. In the seventeenth century, this area was known as the General Captaincy of Pernambuco. Today, what was once the territory of Palmares straddles the states of Pernambuco and Alagoas. The inset map shows Brazil's administrative divisions around 1700.

Map of the principal quilombos and quilombola regions in Brazilian territory (seventeenth to nineteenth centuries)

TROMBETAS (19th c.)
PRETO COSME (19th c.)
TURIAÇU (19th c.)
PALMARES (17th c.)
CALUNGA (18th c.)
CARLOTA OU PIOLHO (18th c.)
OITIZEIRO (19th c.)
CAMPO GRANDE (18th c.)
AMBRÓSIO (18th c.)
JABAQUARA (19th c.)
20,000–30,000 inhabitants
More than 10,000 inhabitants
More than 3,000 inhabitants
Region with significant concentration of quilombos
0 255 KM

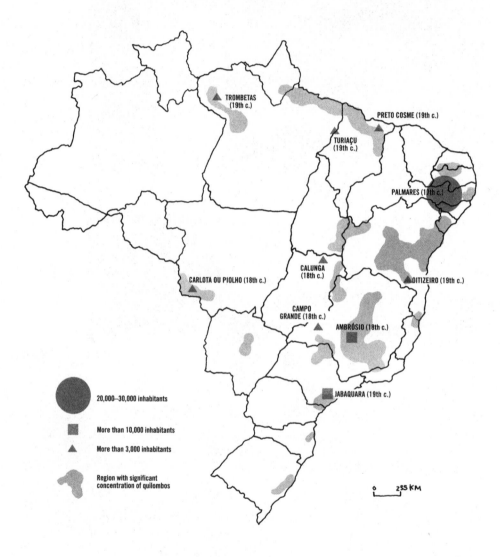

Note: Map created based on the work of Rafael Sanzio A. Anjos in *Coleção África-Brasil/Cartografia para o Ensino-Aprendizagem* [Africa-Brazil Collection: Cartography for Teaching and Learning], 2005.

Estimates of embarkation and disembarkation of enslaved Africans

North America
Europe
Caribbean and Central America
Senegambia
Sierra Leone
Gold Coast
Bight of Benin
Windward Coast
Bight of Biafra
Maranhão
Pernambuco
Bahia
West Central Africa and St. Helena
Rio de Janeiro
Southeast Africa and Indian Ocea islands
River Plate

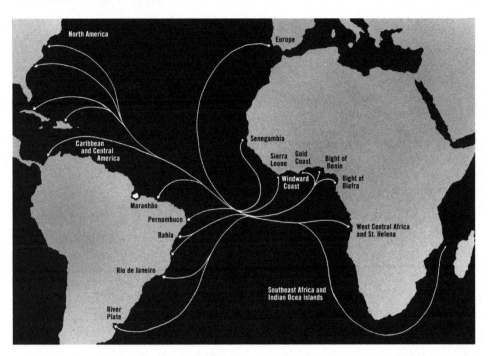

Estimates from 1501 to 1900

Locations and Estimates of Embarkations in Africa		Locations and Estimates of Disembarkations	
Senegambia	755,000	Europe	10,000
Sierra Leone	388,000	North America	472,000
Windward Coast	336,000	British Caribbean	2,763,000
Gold Coast	1,209,000	French Caribbean	1,328,000
Bay of Benin	1,999,000	Dutch Americas	514,000
Bight of Biafra	1,594,000	Danish West Indies	129,000
West Central Africa	5,694,000	Spanish America	1,591,000
Southeast Africa and Indian Ocean islands	542,000	Brazil	5,532,000
		Africa	178,000
Estimated Total: 12,521,000,000		**Estimated Total:** 12,521,000,000	

Note: These are the official statistics of embarkations and disembarkations of enslaved Africans. The real numbers for the slave trade, including illegal commerce and deaths, may be much higher. Source: http://www.slavevoyages.org/

Map of the region of Angola, one of the largest sources of Africans sent to Brazil

BAKONGO
Luanda
Cuanza River
AMBUNDU
CHOKWE
Kasai River
OVIMBUNDU
GANGUELA
GANGUELA
HERERO
Cunene River
HANECA-HUMBE

Luanda

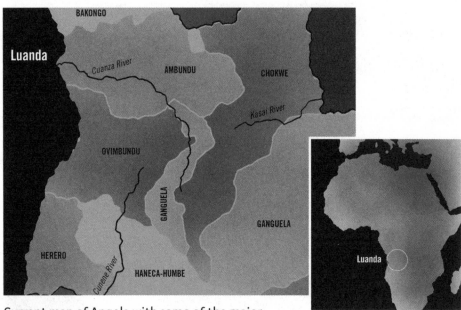

Current map of Angola with some of the major ethnic groups.

Loge River
Kwango River
Matamba
Dande River
Ilha de Luanda
Bengo River
Lucala
1590
MATAMBA
Luanda
NDONGO
1583
Lucamba
Ambaca
Andala Kisua
1605
1616
Massangano
1671
Pungo Andongo
Cambembe
Cuanza River
Kingdom of Nzinga (1625–1663)
Area under Portuguese control
Portuguese attacks
Longa River

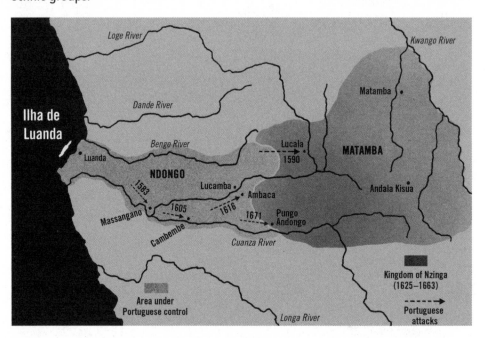

Enlarged map showing the major battles involving the Portuguese, both along the coast and in the Ambundu kingdoms of Ndongo and Matamba, in the sixteenth and seventeenth centuries.

References

Alencastro, Luiz Felipe de. *O trato dos viventes*. São Paulo: Companhia das Letras, 2015.

Altuna, Pe. Raul Ruiz de Asúa. *Cultura tradicional bantu*. Angola: Paulinas, 2006.

Alves Filho, Ivan. *Memorial dos Palmares*. Brasília: Fundação Astrogildo Pereira; Editorial Abaré, 2008.

Anjos, Rafael Sanzio Araújo dos. *Coleção África-Brasil/Cartografia para o ensino-aprendizagem*. Brasília: Mapas Editora & Consultoria, 2005.

Araújo, Emanoel (curador). *Para nunca esquecer* (catálogo de exposição). Museu Histórico Nacional, 2002.

Assis Junior, Antônio de. *Dicionário kimbundu-português*. Luanda: Argente Santos.

A destruição de Angola Janga (Documentos Palmares, 1671 a 1700). Salvador: P555 Edições, 2006.

Bourdoukan, Georges. *Capitão Mouro*. Casa Amarela, 2001.

Branco, Renato Castelo. *Domingos Jorge Velho e a presença paulista no Nordeste*. São Paulo: Editora T. A. Queiroz, 1990.

Carneiro, Edson. *O quilombo dos Palmares*. Rio de Janeiro: Civilização Brasileira, 1966.

França, J. M. C., and R. A. Ferreira. *Três vezes Zumbi—A construção de um herói brasileiro*. São Paulo: Três Estrelas, 2012.

Freitas, Décio. *Palmares—A guerra dos escravos*. Rio de Janeiro: Edições Graal, 1982.

Felício, João. *Ganga Zumba*. São Paulo: Círculo do Livro, 1964.

Folha de São Paulo. *Especial história do Brasil—Zumbi*, 2000. Available at http://www1.folha.uol.com.br/fol/brasil500/hist_6.htm#zumb13. Accessed August 8, 2017.

Glasgow, Roy. *Nzinga*. São Paulo: Editora Perspectiva, 1982.

Gomes, Flávio dos Santos. *Mocambos e quilombos—Uma história do campesinato negro no Brasil*. São Paulo: Claro Enigma, 2015.

___. *Palmares*. São Paulo: Editora Contexto, 2005.

___. *Zumbi dos Palmares—histórias, símbolos e memória social*. São Paulo: Claro Ennigma, 2001.

Junge, Peter (curator). *Arte da África—obras-primas do Museu Etnológico de Berlim* (exhibition catalog). São Paulo: Centro Cultural Banco do Brasil, 2003.

Landmann, Jorge. *Tróia negra: A saga dos Palmares*. São Paulo: Mandarim, 1998.

Lopes, Nei. *Bantos, malês e identidade negra*. São Paulo: Forense Universitária, 1988.

___. *Enciclopédia brasileira da diáspora africana*. São Paulo: Selo Negro, 2004.

___. *Novo dicionário banto do Brasil*. São Paulo: Pallas, 2006.

Mello, José Antônio Gonsalves de. *Henrique Dias—Governador dos crioulos, negros e mulatos do Brasil*. Recife: FUNDAJ; Editora Massangana, 1988.

Montecúccolo, João Antonio Cavazzi. *Descrição histórica dos três reinos do Congo, Matamba e Angola*. Junta de Investigações do Ultramar, 1965.

Moura, Carlos Eugênio Marcondes. *A travessia da Calunga Grande*. São Paulo: EDUSP, 2000.

Moura, Clóvis. *Dicionário da escravidão negra no Brasil*. São Paulo: EDUSP, 2004.

___. *Rebeliões da Senzala*. Livraria Editora Ciências Humanas, 1981.

Museu Nacional de Etnologia. *Escultura Angolana* (catalog). Lisbon: Museu Nacional de Etnologia, 1994.

Nascimento, Elisa Larkin, and Luiz Carlos Gà. *Adinkra—Sabedoria em símbolos africanos*. São Paulo: Pallas, 2009.

Nascimento, Rômulo Luiz Xavier Nascimento. *Palmares—Os escravos contra o poder colonial*. São Paulo: Terceiro Nome, 2014.

Oliveira, Ana Maria de. *Angola e a expressão da sua cultura material*. Rio de Janeiro: Odebrecht, 1991.

Péret, Benjamin. *O quilombo dos Palmares*. Porto Alegre: Universidade Federal do Rio Grande do Sul, 2002.

Rede Angola. *A arte de contar histórias em desenhos*, 2015. Available at http://www.redeangola.info/multimedia/arte-de-contar-historias-em-desenhos/. Accessed August 9, 2017.

Redinha, José. *Etnias e culturas de Angola*. Luanda: Instituto de Investigação Científica de Angola, 1974.

___. *Album etnográfico*. Luanda: CITA, 1966.

Reis, João José. *Liberdade por um Fio*. São Paulo: Companhia das Letras, 1996.

Rufino, Joel. *Zumbi*. São Paulo: Editora Moderna, 1985.

Schaden, Egon. *Aspectos fundamentais da cultura Guarani*. São Paulo: EDUSP, 1974.

Slenes, Robert. "*Malungu, ngoma vem!*": *África coberta e descoberta do Brasil*. *Revista USP* 12 (December 1991).

___. *Na senzala uma flor: Esperanças e recordações da família escrava*. Rio de Janeiro: Nova Fronteira, 1999.

Toral, André. *Holandeses*. São Paulo: Veneta, 2017.

UNESCO. *História Geral da África*, vol. 5. Paris: UNESCO Publications, 1998.

___. *Njinga a Mbande—Rainha do Ndongo e Matamba*. Ed. Edouard Joubeaud, Sylvia Serbin, and Pat Masioni. Paris: UNESCO Publications, 2014.

PHOTO: RAFAEL RONCATO

Marcelo D'Salete is a comic book author, illustrator, and teacher. He studied graphic design at the Colégio Carlos de Campos and has a bachelor's degree in visual arts and a master's in art history from the Universidade de São Paulo.

He created the graphic novels *Noite Luz* (2008), *Encruzilhada* (2011), and *Cumbe* (2014). *Cumbe* has also been published in Portugal (Polvo), France (Çà et Là), Italy (Becco Giallo), Austria (Bahoe Books), Germany, and the United States (Fantagraphics; *Run for It*, 2016). It was nominated for the 2015 Troféu HQ Mix, selected by Plano Ler + to be read in Portuguese schools, and nominated for the 2017 Rudolph Dirks Award in Germany.

He has participated in the magazines *Front*, *Graffiti*, *Ragu*, *Stripburger* (Slovenia), and *Suda Mery k!* (Argentina) as well as in exhibitions including his works both in Brazil (FIQ, Rio Comicon) and abroad (Amadora, Luanda, etc.).

As an illustrator, he worked on the books *Ai de ti, Tietê* by Rogério Andrade Barbosa, *Duas Casas* by Claudia Dragonetti, *E Assim Surgiu o Maracanã* by Sandra Pina, *Zagaia* by Allan da Rosa, *A Rainha da Bateria* by Martinho da Vila, and many others.

Learn more about D'Salete at www.dsalete.art.br

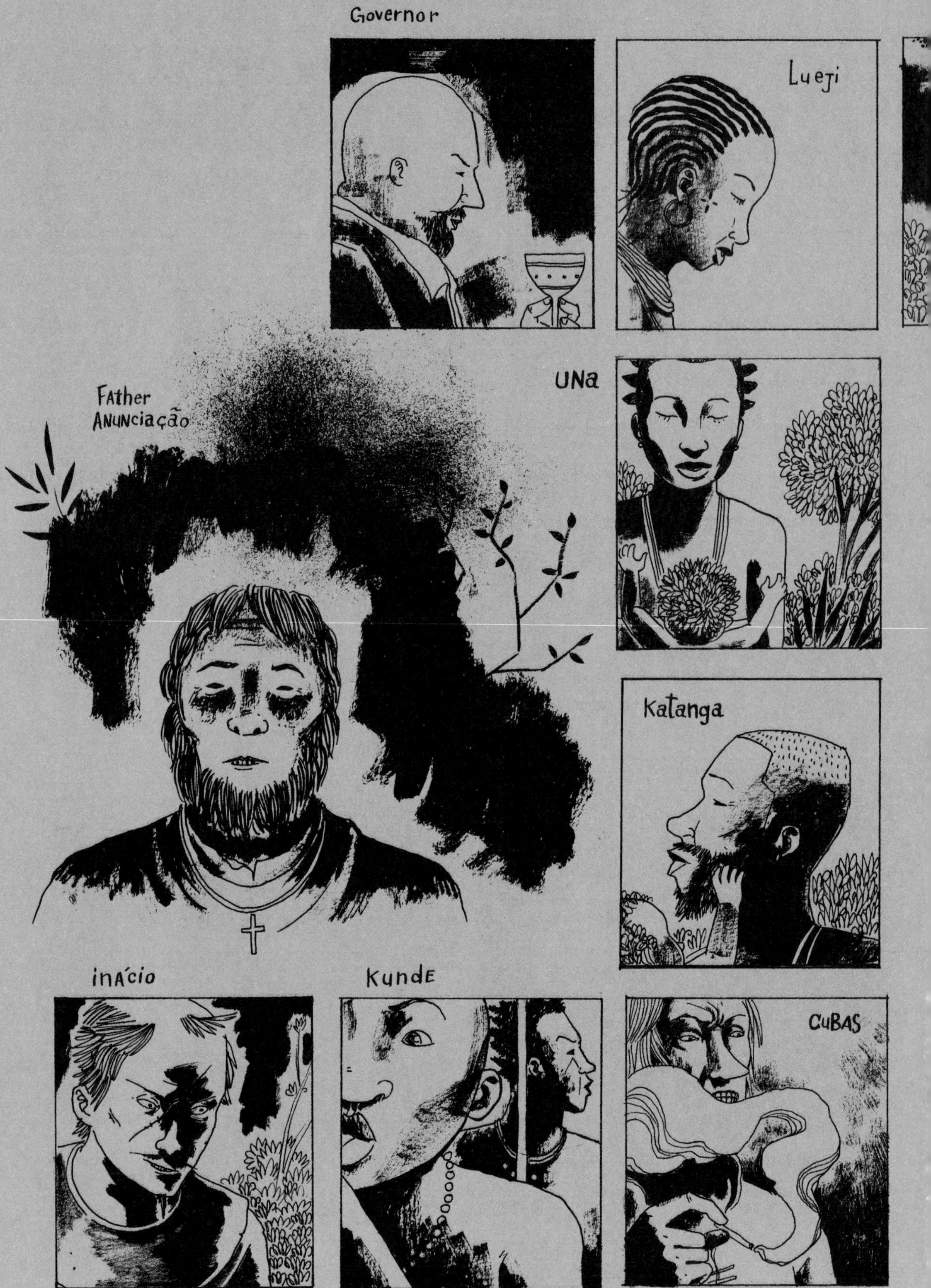
Governor
Lueji
Una
Father Anunciação
Katanga
Inácio
Kunde
CUBAS